THE PRACTICAL
GARDENER'S
ENCYCLOPEDIA

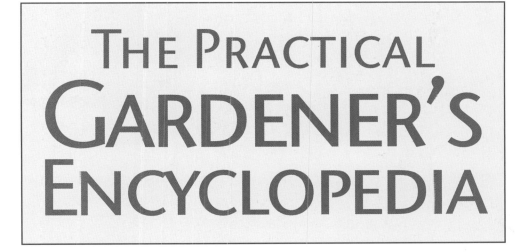

THE PRACTICAL
GARDENER'S
ENCYCLOPEDIA

RED
LEMON
PRESS

Published by Red Lemon Press
(an imprint of Weldon Owen)
Deepdene Lodge
Deepdene Avenue
Dorking, Surrey
RH5 4AT

Copyright © 2000 Weldon Owen Pty Ltd
This edition 2015

Chief Executive Officer: John Owen
President: Terry Newell
Publisher: Lynn Humphries
Managing Editor: Janine Flew
Design Manager: Helen Perks
Editorial Coordinator: Jennifer Losco
Production Manager: Caroline Webber
Production Coordinator: Monique Layt
Sales Manager: Emily Jahn
Vice President International Sales: Stuart Laurence

Project Editor: Susan Tomnay
Designer: Melanie Feddersen, i2i design
Consultant: Geoffrey Burnie
Contributors: Bonnie Lee Appleton, C. Colston Burrell, Linda A.Gilkeson,
Lewis and Nancy Hill, Erin Hynes, judywhite, Cheryl Long, Susan McClure,
Kris Medic, Patricia S. Michalak, Nancy J. Ondra, Rob Proctor, Lee Reich,
Sally Roth, Alfred F. Scheider, Elizabeth Stell
Cover images: Shutterstock

ISBN: 978-1-78342-099-5

Printed in Latvia
A Weldon Owen Production

Contents

How to Use This Book

The Practical Gardener's Encyclopedia is designed to help, encourage and inspire gardeners, both novice and experienced. It is packed with information about buying plants, planting, propagation, soil conditions and cultivation. The book is easy to read and each page has colourful photographs showing how beautiful your garden can be. Section Five of the book is an encyclopedia of plants to help you choose and identify them.

Each section is colour-coded for easy reference.

General information about planting, propagating and caring for your plants to get the optimum results.

The beginning of a new chapter within one of the five major sections in the book. The line above is the section heading.

Illustrations show various planting designs. There are many other helpful illustrations in the book.

Clear and simple step-by-step photographs, in this case to show you how to pot up seedlings.

Colourful photographs give you guidance and inspiration in planning and planting your garden.

The following text appears within the reproduced sample pages shown on this page.

56 CREATING YOUR GARDEN

distribute tiny seeds more evenly, mix them with a spoonful of dry sand, and scatter the mixture over the surface of the mix with a saltshaker. Label each row of seed as you sow.

If the seeds should be buried (as indicated on the seed packet), sprinkle the needed amount of dry mix over the seed. Fine seeds are usually not covered; just press them lightly into the surface of the mix with your fingers. Mist the surface lightly to moisten it. Seeds will rot if they are submerged in water.

Set the containers in a well-lit spot where you can check them daily for signs of the first sprouts. Keep the planting medium moist but not soggy. Cover the container with clear plastic wrap to keep the soil evenly moist until the seeds germinate, but make sure the plastic doesn't touch the soil. Remove the covering as soon as the seedlings appear. Ventilation is important as poor ventilation encourages the development of seedling diseases.

Temperature and light
Most annual seeds will sprout and grow well at average indoor temperatures between 60° and 75°F (16° and 24°C). Vegetable seeds germinate best at higher temperatures between 75° and 90°F

Get a head start on spring plants by starting your seeds indoors under lights. In the heat of summer, start seeds of cool-season crops indoors, perhaps under lights in a basement or garage.

(24° and 32°C). On top of a water heater or refrigerator are good positions for these. You can buy horticultural heating mats to keep warm. Place the mats on a flat surface and set flats on top. As the seedlings are up and growing, require less warmth and good light; 60° to 70°F (16° to 21°C)...

Once your seedlings are up, important that you provide them sunny window or set them under lights. Garden centers and catalog sell lights...

STEP-BY-STEP POTTING UP
1. Place moist growing medium into new containers. Make a hole large enough to accommodate the root system of the seedling.

2. Remove...

---

142 THE PRODUCTIVE GARDEN

The Herb Garden

There are so many wonderful herbs that it can be hard to decide which ones to grow. Some herbs, like oregano and peppermint, are used in cooking or for tea; others, like lavender and sage, are ideal for potpourris and other fragrant crafts. Some herbs, like bee balm, thyme,

and yarrow, are attractive in their own right as ornamentals, even if you never plan to harvest them for any purpose. Many herbs fall into more than one of these categories.

How you plan to use your herbs will affect how you'll grow them and how much attention they'll need from you. If you're just growing herbs to use fresh in cooking, you don't need much space for an herb garden, since one or two plants of each kind you like should be enough. You'll be most likely to use your culinary herbs if you plant them close to the house. If you're only growing one or two types, try growing them in large pots on the deck or patio. You'll need more space to grow quantities of herbs if you plan to harvest them for drying and crafting.

Grown in the right conditions, herbs such as chives will reward you with flowers as well as edible leaves.

Growing Your Herbs
Most herbs prefer full sun, although some (like sweet woodruff, chervil, lemon balm, and many mints) will grow in partial shade. Many herbs tolerate rocky, thin soils, but they will be more productive in average, well-drained soil. You may choose to plant your herbs in a separate garden, but they also look great mixed into flower beds and vegetable gardens.

You can grow many herbs—including such favorites as dill, sage, marjoram, and basil—from seed sown directly in the garden. Other herbs are easier to grow from transplants than seeds; these include rosemary, lavender, peppermint, and tarragon, among others.

When planning your herb garden, don't forget to take into consideration your climate, topography, and soil conditions. Ask your neighbors what grows well in their garden—and what doesn't.

Herb Garden Style
Regardless of the size, shape, or location of your garden, its style is a reflection of your own tastes. At one extreme are the formal herb gardens with their angular knots and pruned hedges, and at the other are random groupings of whatever suits the season. The number of possible herb-garden styles is limited only by your imagination and creativity. You can plan one or more theme gardens to concentrate on a particular aspect.

These diagrams show four practical approaches to designing an herb garden. Avoid circles and curves if space is limited.

them to accent the shape of a building. If you want to be especially creative, garden within unusual boundaries like circles or ovals. You can make a garden in the shape of a spiral with one continuous bed beginning in the center and spiraling out in circles. A book or magazine on garden landscaping will offer you examples to follow in shaping your garden beds.

If you choose to garden in several small patches, position plants that need daily attention or frequent picking close to the

As you choose herb plants, consider how they are going to look when grouped together.

Garden Shape
The simplest gardens to set out and manage are square or rectangular. If you must take advantage of every square inch of space, it makes sense that you will follow the general outline of your property, and land is most often sold in boxlike shapes. Laying out your herb garden with square or rectangular beds may be not only the most practical way, but can give the garden a formal look that appeals to many gardeners.

Of course, squares and rectangles aren't the only shapes. You may choose to lay your garden beds following the curve of a hill, stream, fence, or stone wall, or design

house. If space is limited, take advantage of borders along paths and fences. At the least, you can dress your windows close at hand.

Garden Design
Whatever design you choose, try it out on paper first. If you're planting in beds, keep them under 5 feet (1.5 m) wide, not more than twice the distance you are able to reach from the side. You'll want to avoid walking on beds as you work. Make garden paths 4 to 5 feet (1.2 to 1.5 m) wide. Once you've located your paths, beds, or rows, begin selecting and

Working with the natural landscape, simple terracing is used to create a level herb garden on a slope.

THE HERB

BASIC PLANTING TECHNIQUES 57

set the container of seedlings in a tray of water so the growing medium can soak up moisture without disrupting the seedlings. If you water from overhead, you may wash the seedlings away. Place pots away from direct light and wind for a day until the shock of transplanting is over. Feed the young plants lightly with compost tea or liquid seaweed.

Thinning and Transplanting
The first leaves to appear on the plant are actually specialized food-storage organs. These drop away quickly, and the leaves that follow are the first "true leaves."
When seedlings develop their first set of true leaves, they need special attention.
If seedlings are in separate pots or cells, thin off the extra seedlings by clipping them off at soil level with sharp scissors. One healthy specimen should remain in each pot or cell. If your seedlings are crowded together in a flat, you'll need to transfer them to their own containers. Fill pots or cells with a humus-rich medium. Scoop one or more seedlings from the flat (a teaspoon works well), separating their root systems as gently as possible with your fingers. Poke a hole in the potting soil deep enough to accommodate the new seedling and its root system, then transfer it and firm the soil. Water as often as necessary to keep the soil moist and to prevent wilting. When you water,

Hardening Off
Hardening off allows young plants to adjust slowly to the extremes of wind, temperature, and light. At least two weeks before transplanting time, begin watering less frequently and withhold fertilizer. One week before you transplant, move the plants outdoors to a spot protected from strong light and wind. Starting with one or several hours, gradually increase their time spent outdoors. Within a week, they should be outdoors permanently. They'll need more water at this time, since sun and wind quickly dry the soil. Be prepared to bring them back indoors if a cold snap or storm threatens.

Sowing Seed in the Garden
Some plants like morning glories (Ipomoea spp.), beans, peas, and root crops, grow better from direct-sown seed because they prefer cool outdoor temperatures or because they don't respond well to transplanting. Planting seeds outdoors is also a good idea for seeds that are hard to germinate, or for plants that need a long, warm growing season.
Before the season begins, check your seed package or catalog for the best time to plant outdoors. You'll need to know the expected date of the last frost for your area; ask local gardeners, or contact your local Cooperative Extension Service.
Get the soil ready for planting (see page 50) and if you're planting in rows, as with vegetables, mark them before planting with wooden stakes at both ends. Stretch a section of lightweight string down the row, and use it as a guide to keep your rows straight while you plant.

Dealing with Damping-Off

Damping-off is a disease that can strike young seedlings, killing them just before or after they emerge. Affected seedlings tend to topple over, since their stems are damaged at the soil level. Once a few seedlings are affected, the disease can quickly spread to other seedlings in the same pot or tray.
Since there's no real cure, the best way to handle damping-off is prevention. Here are some tips that might help.
• Always use fresh, "sterile" seed-starting mix.
• If you're reusing old pots or trays, knock out the old soil, dip the containers in a 10 percent bleach solution (1 part household bleach to 9 parts water), and let the containers dry before using them.
• Sprinkle a thin layer of milled sphagnum moss on top of newly planted seeds.
• Improve air circulation in a small fan set to blow lightly just over the tops of the seedlings.
• If damping-off strikes outdoor sown seeds, discard them, wait until the weather warms up (maybe two to three weeks), then try sowing again.

Lupine seed, like others of the pea and bean family, can be sown directly into the soil in fall.

If you're planting annuals or perennials, sow medium-sized and large seeds individually, or scatter them evenly over the surface. Try to space them ½ to 1 inch (12 to 25 mm) apart. If you have very small seeds, mix them with a handful of dry sand and scatter over the surface.
Cover most seeds with a thin layer of fine soil or sand. After sowing, make sure the seedbed stays moist until the seedlings are visible. If rainfall is lacking, water gently with a watering can, sprinkler, or fine hose spray. Covering the seedbed

with a layer of floating row cover helps to keep the soil moist and protects the seed from drying winds, heavy rain, and birds. (Remove the cover once the seedlings start to emerge.)
If seedlings are crowded, you'll need to thin them out for good growth. Dig up and carefully transplant extra seedlings, or use scissors to cut off the stems of unwanted seedlings at ground level.

Planting Container-Grown Plants
If you are planting a potted plant, you can easily see how deeply to plant it. Dig deeply enough so the surface of the container soil will be at the top of the hole (adjusting accordingly for new beds).

---

3. Holding the seedling by its leaves, place it into its new container and gently firm the soil around it. Thin seedlings by clipping them off at soil level with a pair of scissors.

---

190 ENCYCLOPEDIA OF POPULAR GARDEN PLANTS

ANNUALS 191

Centaurea cyanus
COMPOSITAE
CORNFLOWER

Stick brushy prunings into the ground around young cornflower plants to support the stems as they grow; pinching off spent blooms can prolong the flowering season.

Other common names Bachelor's buttons.
Description This is a dependable, easy-care, hardy annual. The bushy plants have narrow, lance-shaped, silvery green leaves and thin stems topped with fluffy flower heads. The 1–2-inch (2.5–5-cm) flowers bloom through the summer in white or shades of blue, purple, pink, or red.
Height and spread Height 12–30 inches (30–75 cm); spread to 12 inches (30 cm).
Best site Full sun, but tolerates partial shade; average, well-drained soil.
Growing guidelines Grows easily from seed sown directly into the garden in early fall (in mild-winter areas) or early spring. Plant seed ⅛ inch (3 mm) deep. To extend the flowering season from an early-spring planting, sow again every two to four weeks until midsummer. Other ways to establish cornflowers include buying transplants in spring or starting the seed indoors about eight weeks before your last frost date. Set plants outdoors about two weeks before the last frost date. Cornflowers will self-sow if you leave a few flowers to set seed.
Landscape uses Cornflowers are charming in meadow gardens and flower beds. They are also excellent cut flowers.

Cheiranthus cheiri
CRUCIFERAE
WALLFLOWER

The fragrant blooms of wallflowers are normally orange or yellow, but they also bloom in shades of red, pink, or creamy white. The flowers are ideal for spring arrangements.

Description This perennial is commonly grown as a half-hardy annual or biennial. The bushy clumps of slender green leaves are topped with clusters of 1-inch (2.5-cm) wide four-petaled flowers from midspring to early summer.
Height and spread Height 12–24 inches (30–60 cm); spread to 12 inches (30 cm).
Best site Full sun to partial shade; average to moist, well-drained soil, ideally with a neutral to slightly alkaline pH.
Growing guidelines Sow outdoors in early spring or indoors about eight weeks before your last frost date. Plant seed ¼ inch (6 mm) deep. Set plants out 8–12 inches (20–30 cm) apart around the last frost date. In frost-free areas, grow wallflowers as biennials. Sow seed in pots or in a nursery bed in early summer; move plants to their flowering position in early fall. Water during dry spells to keep the soil evenly moist. Pull out and compost plants when they have finished blooming.
Landscape uses Grow in masses or in flower beds for spots of early color. One classic combination is orange wallflowers underplanted with blue forget-me-nots (Myosotis sylvatica). Wallflowers also combine beautifully with tulips.

Cleome hasslerana
CAPPARACEAE
CLEOME

Cleome is a must for butterfly-attracting gardens; it's also popular with bees. Plant it in large groupings to show off the spidery white, pink, or rosy lavender flowers.

Other common names Spider flower.
Description Cleome is a fast-growing half-hardy annual. Its tall, sturdy stems and palmlike leaves are slightly sticky and have a musky (some say skunk-like) odor. Small spines form on the stems and on the undersides of the leaves. From midsummer until midfall, the stems are topped with globes of four-petaled flowers. Long stamens protrude from the flowers, giving them a spidery look. The blooms are followed by long, narrow seedpods.
Height and spread Height 3–4 feet (90–120 cm); spread 18 inches (45 cm).
Best site Full sun to light shade; average, well-drained soil with added compost.
Growing guidelines Easy to grow from seed sown directly in the garden in mid- to late-spring. For earlier bloom, buy seed indoors about four weeks before your last frost date. Lightly press the seed into the surface, then enclose the pot in a plastic bag until seedlings appear. Set plants out around the last frost date.
Landscape uses Try cleome in the back of flower beds and borders. Its pretty, delicate blooms look particularly nice in cottage gardens.

Coleus x hybridus
LABIATAE
COLEUS

Keep favorite coleus plants from year to year by taking cuttings in summer; they'll root quickly in water. Pot up the cuttings for winter; then put them outdoors in spring.

Description These tender perennials are grown as bushy, tender annuals. Their sturdy, square stems carry showy, patterned leaves with scalloped or ruffled edges. Each leaf can have several different colors, with zones, edges, or splashes in shades of red, pink, orange, yellow, and cream.
Height and spread Height 6–24 inches (15–60 cm); spread 8–12 inches (20–30 cm).
Best site Partial shade; average to moist, well-drained soil with added well-rotted organic matter.
Growing guidelines Buy transplants in spring, or start your own by sowing seed indoors eight to ten weeks before your last frost date. Don't cover the seed; just press it lightly into the soil and enclose the pot in a plastic bag until seedlings appear. Set plants out 8–12 inches (20–30 cm) apart after the last frost date. Water during dry spells. Pinch off the spikes of the pale blue flowers to promote more leafy growth.
Landscape uses Coleus are great for adding all-season color to beds, borders, and container plantings. Groups of mixed leaf patterns can look too busy when combined with flowering plants, so grow them alone in masses.

Coreopsis tinctoria
COMPOSITAE
CALLIOPSIS

Calliopsis grows easily from direct-sown seed and needs little fussing. Shearing the plants back by one-third in mid- to late-summer can prolong the bloom season.

Description Calliopsis is a colorful, fast-growing, hardy annual. Its wiry stems carry narrow, green leaves and 1–2-inch (2.5–5-cm)-wide, single or double, daisy-like flowers. The flowers are usually golden yellow with maroon centers but may also be all yellow or all orange. Plants can bloom from midsummer until frost.
Height and spread Height 24–36 inches (30–90 cm), depending on the cultivar; spread to 12 inches (30 cm).
Best site Full sun; average, well-drained soil. Adapts well to poor soil.
Growing guidelines Grows quickly from seed sown directly into the garden in early spring. You can also sow seed ⅛ inch (3 mm) deep indoors about six weeks before your last frost date. Set plants out around the last frost date. Space transplants or thin seedlings to stand about 8 inches (20 cm) apart. Push twiggy brush into the soil around young plants of tall-growing cultivars to support the stems as they grow.
Landscape uses Depend on calliopsis for adding fast, easy-care color to beds and borders. It also looks wonderful in meadow gardens. Grow some in the cutting garden for fresh arrangements.

Cosmos bipinnatus
COMPOSITAE
COSMOS

Use fast-growing cosmos to fill spaces left by early-blooming annuals and perennials. Pinch off spent flowers to encourage more bloom; leave a few to self-sow.

Description These popular half-hardy annuals are grown for their colorful blooms. The bushy plants bear many finely cut, green leaves. In late summer and fall, the stems are topped with white, pink, or daisy-like blooms can grow up to 4 inches (10 cm) across.
Height and spread Height 3–4 feet (90–120 cm); spread to 18 inches (45 cm).
Best site Full sun is best, although plants can take partial shade; average to moist, well-drained soil.
Growing guidelines For earliest blooms, buy transplants in spring or start seed indoors three to four weeks before your last frost date. Plant seed ¼ inch (6 mm) deep. You can also sow seed directly into the garden around the last frost date. Pinch off stem tips in early summer to promote branching and more flowers. Stake individual stems as needed, or just let the plants sprawl; they'll send up more flowering stems.
Landscape uses Cosmos adds height and color to flower beds, borders, and meadows. They look great in cottage gardens. Grow a few in the cutting garden for arrangements.

Chapter heading indicates the subject being discussed within a main section.

Detailed information about problems with plants and how they can be dealt with.

Photograph of individual plants, showing what they look like when grown in the right conditions.

Botanical name

Family name

Common name

Information about plant

Gardening Basics

*You need the right growing conditions, the right tools,
the right plants and, most important of all,
energy and enthusiasm. These are
the basics of good gardening.*

Understanding Your Garden

You may have some idea of what you want from your garden but do you know what kind of growing conditions you have to give the plants? A new garden will get off to a successful start if you take stock of your growing conditions, including your climate and your garden's soil, topography and exposure. These factors will have a great effect in determining which plants will grow well in your garden, as well as how and where you plant them.

Basic Botany

What's in a Name?
One of the tricks to growing plants successfully is to learn their names. Members of your neighbourhood plant society may understand common names, like bee balm for instance. But if you go to an out-of-town nursery and ask for bee balm, you may only get puzzled stares. Perhaps they call the plant Oswego tea, based on the fact that American pioneers used it as herbal tea. Or if you are looking for bee balm in a catalogue, you may only find it listed under its botanical name, *Monarda didyma*.

You can see from this example that one plant can have several common names. Likewise, one common name can apply to several different plants. For instance, the common name loosestrife can refer to a creeping perennial with golden flowers known by the botanical name *Lysimachia nummularia*; to a tall perennial with white flowers in a swan-necked spike, *Lysimachia clethroides*; to its less invasive counterpart, *L. ephemerum*; or to a spreading, long-blooming purple-flowered plant, *Lythrum salicaria*. If you order 'loosestrife' by post without using a botanical name, you have a good chance of receiving the wrong plant.

Get to know botanical names so you know exactly which plant you are talking about, planting or ordering. Most botanical names are based on Latin, so they can be a mouthful. However, they will be the same in America, Japan and Europe, despite differences in the native language. Botanical names change rarely, usually only when scientists update the name to better reflect what they have discovered about the plant's heritage. If you have learned an older name, you will usually find it listed beside the newer names in nursery catalogues. For instance, hollyhock has changed from *Althaea rosea* to *Alcea rosea*. Both may be listed for the same plant.

As you've probably noticed by now, botanical names are usually given as two words. The first word, the name of the . genus, refers to a group of closely related plants. The second word indicates the species, a particular kind of plant in that genus. You may end up growing several different species from the same genus. *Achillea millefolium* and *Achillea tomentosa*, for example, both belong to the genus *Achillea*, commonly known as yarrow.

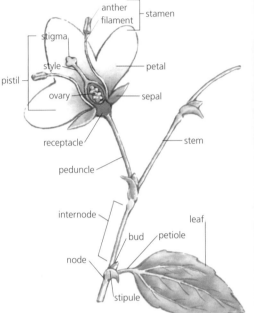

This diagram identifies some of the most common plant parts. Knowing a bit of botanical jargon will help you understand the plant descriptions you read in books and catalogues.

But *Achillea millefolium* refers to a species with finely cut leaves, while *Achillea tomentosa* refers to one with particularly fuzzy leaves.

Botanical names can be easier to remember if you determine what they tell about the plant. Some refer to the person who discovered the plant or to what part

LEFT: Bearded irises are among the most lovely of the *Iris* spp. They flower in early summer.
RIGHT: As its name suggests, sweet violet (*Viola odorata*) bears charming spring flowers that are delightfully fragrant.

of the world it was discovered in. For instance, *Sanguisorba canadensis* is Canadian burnet, native to Canada and the Eastern United States. Other botanical names are descriptive. *Viola odorata* is sweet violet, which bears an especially fragrant flower.

Horticulturists and botanists recognise two other classifications of plants that you will often encounter: varieties and cultivars. Although the names are sometimes used interchangeably, plants that develop a natural variation in the wild are called varieties, and the varietal name is included as part of the botanical name after the abbreviation 'var.'. This is the case, for example, with the white-flowered, peach-leaved bellflower (*Campanula persicifolia* var. *alba*). In this case the species, which normally has blue flowers, produced plants with white ones. Cultivars, whose names are set in single quotes after the botanical name, are plants that gardeners or horticulturists have selected and propagated as part of a breeding programme or from a chance mutation in a garden. For example, Aster *novi-belgii* 'Professor Kippenburg' is a dwarf type of lavender-blue Michaelmas daisy.

You may also come across hybrids, blends of two species or, more rarely, two genera. One example is *Anemone* x *hybrida* – the 'x' indicates that this plant is a hybrid. A few hybrids come from two different but related genera, such as x *Heucherella tiarelloides*.

In this book, you will find plants listed by the most widely used common name. But to avoid confusion, we will also include the botanical name. When we use 'spp.' we are discussing several related species in the same genus. For *Iris* spp., this could include bearded, Siberian and Japanese irises. Take note of both common and botanical names for your garden planning.

Parts of Plants

You can choose plants for your garden for their attractive leaves, useful fruits, fragrant flowers or perhaps deep taproots

The Logic of Botanical Names

Learning botanical names may seem intimidating at first, but you'll be surprised at how easily you pick them up as you read. Besides being a tool for accurately communicating about plants, a botanical name can often tell you something about the plant it identifies, such as its flower colour or growth habit. Listed below are some words that commonly appear in botanical names, along with their definitions.

Albus: white
Argenteus: silver
Aureus: golden yellow
Caeruleus: blue
Luteus: yellow
Nanus: dwarf
Niger: black
Palustris: swampy, marshy
Perennis: perennial
Prostratus: trailing
Punctatus: dotted
Purpureus: purple
Reptans: creeping
Roseus: rosy
Ruber: red
Sempervirens: evergreen
Speciosus: showy
Spinosus: spiny
Stoloniferus: with stolons
Tomentosus: with thick, short hair
Variegatus: variegated
Viridis: green
Vulgaris: common

that cope better with poor water supply. Knowing about the functions and characteristics of the various plant parts will help you identify, select and maintain your plants most effectively.

Foliage Leaves come in a tremendous variety of shapes and colours. It's true that most leaves are green, but there are many shades of green! Leaves that are striped, edged or blotched with different colours, like those of some types of geranium, are called variegated.

Plant Stems The stems of plants not only support the leaves, but also serve as pathways for movement of nutrients and water between roots and leaves. Like roots, stems are storage organs, too. Bulbs, like garlic, are actually specialised storage stems. Some plants have stems that are specially adapted for vegetative reproduction. Stolons (also called rhizomes) are stems that travel horizontally along the soil surface. At certain intervals along the stolon, new shoots and roots will form, giving rise to new plants. Sweet woodruff and sweet violets are examples of plants that produce stolons.

Plants like mint form new plants from underground stems, called rhizomes. The creeping stems of mint spread quickly, travelling just below the surface of the soil

fibrous root

rhizome

bulb

corm

tuberous root

Although they grow in the ground, bulbs, corms and rhizomes are not true roots, they are underground stems.

and rooting as they go. For this reason you may want to grow them in containers, preferably large bottomless tubs or plastic pots. Otherwise build a wooden barrier about 30 to 35 cm (12 to 14 inches) deep around the mint patch to keep the plants under control.

Many plants can be easily propagated by taking stem cuttings. Swollen buds, or nodes, located along the stems are the sites for new growth. When you take stem cuttings to make new plants, the new root systems form underground at active nodes on the cutting.

Root Systems Roots help to hold the plant firm in the soil and provide it with a system for absorbing water and nutrients. They may also act as storage organs, as in the carrot family, holding nutrients to be used later, during times of vigorous growth or flowering.

Many plants have a fibrous root system, made up of many fine and branching roots. Annual herbs, for example, have fibrous roots that do not penetrate particularly deeply, so you'll need to pay special attention to the water requirements of such plants when rain is scarce.

Some plants have strong central roots, called taproots, that travel straight down in search of water and nutrients. The taproot is a single, thick and tapering organ (a carrot is actually an enlarged taproot) with thin side branch

Grasses and annual plants tend to form spreading, branching root systems. Biennials (like carrots) and many perennials produce deeper taproot systems.

roots. Taprooted plants can more easily withstand fluctuating soil moisture conditions, but many, like parsley, are more difficult to transplant because their roots are so sensitive.

About Plant Growth

Throughout the life of your plants, the soil provides many of the things they need to germinate, grow and thrive. Understanding how your plants interact with the soil will help you manage your garden to provide the best possible growing conditions.

Start with the Seed

The first two things a seed needs are warmth and water. If the soil is too cold or too dry, the seed remains dormant. This makes sense; it would do a seed little good to germinate if it's still winter or if there isn't enough water around to support growth.

TOP: Orange coneflowers (*Rudbeckia* spp.) may reseed prolifically if you don't cut off the spent flowers in the autumn.
BOTTOM: Annual roots don't grow very deep, but they do spread wide to get the nutrients the plants need for fast growth.

Warmth is usually more reliable than water. Soil temperatures don't change as rapidly as air temperatures, so once the soil is warm enough for growth to begin – and that temperature varies, depending on the plant species – it usually stays warm enough for growth to continue. If you want to warm the soil more quickly in spring, there are a few things you can do: remove heavy mulches, cover the soil with black plastic or plant in raised beds.

Water is less dependable than warmth. If the soil dries out after germination begins, the young seedling soon dies. Soils with good structure increase the odds that the seed will germinate; the soil particles in rich, loamy soil are fine enough to closely surround the seed, holding moisture against it. Clayey soils hold too much moisture, while loose, sandy soils may dry out too quickly. Improving your soil by digging and adding organic matter can help keep moisture at the ideal level for seedling growth.

Shoots and Roots

When the seed germinates, it puts out a temporary root, called the primary root or radicle. The radicle stores some of the food that provides the energy that the first above-ground shoot needs to push up through the soil (the rest is in the seed leaves, which are the leaf-like parts attached to the shoot). The radicle also anchors the plant, so the shoot won't blow or wash away.

About the time the first shoot reaches the soil surface, lateral roots begin to grow from the radicle. Like the radicle, the lateral roots anchor the plant in the soil. Throughout most of the plant's life, the roots expand to counterbalance the above-ground parts of the plant. In many cases, the root mass is larger than that of the stems and leaves.

As roots grow, they produce chemical compounds that help make nutrients more soluble and therefore more available to the plant. Throughout their life, roots absorb water and dissolved nutrients from the soil. When they die, the roots add organic matter to the soil.

The chemicals roots produce and the dead cells they shed create an environment that soil microorganisms find attractive. They multiply more rapidly in the root zone than they do in the surrounding soil. As a result, organic matter breaks down faster, making nutrients more available in the soil the roots touch.

All the things you do to encourage soil organisms – providing air, moisture and ample amounts of organic matter – will help ensure a steady supply of nutrients when and where plants need them. Plus, the moist, well-aerated, fertile conditions that promote a healthy soil community also provide ideal conditions for root growth. More roots encourage more organisms, which release more nutrients that promote more roots – a productive natural cycle.

Growth and Flowering

As plants grow, the water and nutrients the roots absorb flow up through the plant to the leaves and stems. During photosynthesis, the leaves and stems convert the water and nutrients to sugars; the sugars then flow down to the roots to be stored as carbohydrates – food energy.

Before it flowers and sets seed, the plant uses that energy for growth. While the stems and leaves are growing, the roots rapidly expand both out and down through the soil to reach water and nutrients. Root growth slows once the plant flowers and the seed ripens.

If the plant is an annual, it grows old and dies after the seed ripens. Its decaying roots, leaves and stems return nutrients

Hardiness Zones

It's important that you know what hardiness zone you live in so you can choose appropriate plants. The most commonly used hardiness zone reference is the United States Department of Agriculture Plant Hardiness Zone Map (see page 310). It divides the continental United States and Canada into several numbered zones, from 10 in the South to 1 in the North. Many common plants grow well in the middle range of hardiness zones. If you live in the very warm and cold climates at either end of the zone scales, it is still possible to have a lovely garden, but you'll need to take a bit more care in selecting plants that can tolerate your extreme conditions. If you want to know if a plant may be hardy in your zone, look in the Encyclopedia of Popular Garden Plants, starting on page 170. Nursery catalogues also often list hardiness zones for their plants.

to the soil. If the plant is a perennial, it stores carbohydrates in its roots to use to start growing in the spring. Its leaves and stems die back, adding nutrients to the soil to start the cycle over.

What Are Annuals, Biennials and Perennials?

Annuals

True annuals germinate, grow, flower, set seed and die all in one season. Their single goal is to reproduce themselves. This is good news for the gardener, since it means that most annual plants will flower like mad to achieve this goal. Some of the best-known annuals – including petunias and marigolds – have achieved their popularity because of their free-flowering nature. If you use tricks such as

deadheading (removing spent flowers) to prevent seed formation, many annuals will step up flower production and bloom well over an extended period until cold weather arrives. The first hard frost usually kills the plants and signals the end of the bloom season for that year. Although you'll need to replant most annuals the following spring to get another show, some will sprout from seed dropped by last year's plants. Besides these true annuals, there are a number of perennial plants that are often thought of as annuals. These include tropical perennials, such as zonal geraniums, or perennials that will flower the first season from seed, such as four o'clocks (*Mirabilis jalapa*). These plants can live for years in frost-free climates and flower season after season, but, like true

TOP: Shirley poppies (*Papaver rhoeas*) are hardy annuals. You can sow them in early spring, or even in autumn in mild areas.
BOTTOM: Evergreen perennials, such as bergenias, offer winter interest in climates that don't have heavy snow cover.

annuals, they meet their death at the hands of freezing temperatures in cold-winter climates.

Kinds of Annuals

Annuals are sometimes further separated into three groups – hardy, half-hardy and tender – based on their cold tolerance. It's useful to know which kind of annuals you're growing so you'll know how soon you can get away with planting the annuals in the spring. The catalogue, seed packet or plant tag should tell you whether your plant is hardy, half-hardy or tender.

Hardy Annuals Hardy annuals include forget-me-nots (*Myosotis* spp.), pansies, snapdragons and other plants that withstand several degrees of freezing temperatures. Most of these plants perform best during cool weather. They are often planted in early spring by gardeners in cold-winter areas or in winter by gardeners in milder areas. Some hardy annuals, such as ornamental kale, are also associated with cool autumn weather.

Half-Hardy Annuals Half-hardy annuals fit somewhere in the middle of hardy and tender. They will often withstand a touch of frost near the beginning or end of the gardening season. Many of the most commonly grown annuals fit in this middle category.

Tender Annuals Tender annuals, originally from tropical or subtropical climates, can't stand a degree of frost. More than that, they often grow poorly during cold weather and may be stunted by prolonged exposure to temperatures below 10°C (50°F). For best results, wait until late spring to plant tender annuals, such as celosia (*Celosia* spp.) and Joseph's coat (*Amaranthus tricolor*).

Biennials

Biennials have much in common with annuals, but they differ in one major respect: they take two years to complete their life cycle. The first year after sowing, they produce a leaf structure, building energy for the next year. The second year they flower, set seed and die. Common garden biennials include honesty (*Lunaria annua*), foxglove (*Digitalis purpurea*) and sweet William (*Dianthus barbatus*).

Perennials

Perennial plants live and bloom for more than two growing seasons. Many will survive a decade or longer if planted in the right location. But even the shorter-lived plants are worth growing. For instance, blanket flowers (*Gaillardia* x *grandiflora*) bloom vigorously for a long portion of the summer, although they seldom return more than two years. Other perennials, such as columbines (*Aquilegia* spp.) and hollyhocks (*Alcea rosea*), have a short natural lifespan but set seed that replaces the parent plant. Occasionally, a biennial plant like foxglove (*Digitalis grandiflora*) or sweet William (*Dianthus barbatus*), which normally grows foliage the first year and flowers the second, will live on for the third year. Despite their differences in life span, you can call all of these perennials. In most cases, the foliage of perennials dies back to the underground roots each dormant season. A few perennials, like coral bells (*Heuchera* spp.) and rock cresses (*Arabis* spp.), have evergreen foliage that persists through the winter.

How to Create a Healthy Garden

Creating and maintaining a naturally . healthy garden isn't a simple one- or two-step process. Every decision you make (or don't make) plays a part in the results you get throughout the season. And every year you're faced with new conditions, new questions and different results. That's what makes gardening such a challenging but rewarding hobby.

Fortunately, there are some simple but effective steps you can follow each year to help promote the health of your garden.

The basic thing to remember is this: vigorous plants grown in fertile soil attract fewer pests and are less susceptible to infection by plant pathogens than plants grown in poor soil. Start with a variety of healthy plants suitable for your climate, give them the right growing conditions and keep an eye out for potential problems. These simple stepswill go a long way towards producing a successful garden.

TOP: Mixing annuals, bulbs and grasses with your perennial plantings adds height, colour and season-long interest.
BOTTOM: Including a diversity of flowering plants helps attract beneficial insects and makes your garden beautiful as well.

Create Diversity

Diversity is a key part of growing a healthy garden. Nature creates diversity by mixing many kinds of plants together. Think of a forest, with a mixture of trees, shrubs, climbers and wildflowers, or maybe a meadow, with a variety of flowers and grasses. These ecosystems provide habitats for a wide range of insects and animals. Predators and parasites help to keep pest populations at a relatively constant level.

In your garden, you can promote this natural system of checks and balances by growing lots of different kinds and cultivars of vegetables, flowering plants and fruits. Diverse plantings attract beneficial insects and may deter some garden pests. You can take this diversity a step further by practising crop rotation and changing the location of annual plants each year. This will help to discourage the build-up of some soil-borne pest insects like beetle grubs, and diseases like potato scab.

Provide Good Growing Conditions

Many good garden plants are adaptable to a wide range of growing conditions. But if you want your plants to thrive, not just survive, it's worth your time to investigate their particular needs. Vegetables, for example, generally grow best on a site that has lots of air circulation and good water drainage, with 8 to 12 hours of full sunlight each day and at least 2.5 cm (1 inch) of water each week. Fruits also tend to need lots of sun and fertile soil, while ornamental plants vary widely in their sun and soil needs. Before buying new plants, make sure you can supply the conditions they prefer. If you already have a plant that is struggling to survive in less than ideal conditions, consider moving or replacing it before problems strike.

Build Soil Fertility

Healthy soil produces healthy plants. Adding lots of organic matter will improve the physical characteristics of your soil and encourage the beneficial soil microorganisms that help make nutrients available to your plants.

Check for Problems

Giving all of your plants a close look at least once a week can help you spot potential problems before they get out of hand. Become familiar with both pests and beneficials so you'll know which to control and which to leave alone. If you do spot pests, don't immediately grab a bottle of insecticide. Check again each day over the next few days to see if the beneficial insects step in to help. If the pests are multiplying rapidly, then consider taking control measures. With a little experience, you'll learn how much damage your plants can tolerate before you have to take action.

Before spraying for pests, look around for beneficial insects, like ladybirds.

You'll also want to keep an eye out for signs and symptoms of plant diseases. Snipping off the infected part is often enough to stop a disease before it spreads. If you're growing disease-susceptible plants like fruit trees, you should also keep track of the environmental conditions that favour disease development – like wet, warm spells – and be prepared to apply preventive measures like sulphur or copper sprays.

Know Your Options

Become familiar with the types of controls available to you before you need them so you will know when and how to use them. The best pest control strategies usually include a combination of control methods.

Monitoring soil fertility will help ensure strong, healthy stems and leaves, vigorous roots and beautiful flowers.

Keep Good Records

Good garden records can be one of your most valuable control tools. As you check for and deal with problems, keep track of when and where they occurred and what you did to control them. Write down what worked and what didn't work. If you tried new cultivars for their insect or disease resistance, jot down a few sentences on how they performed during the season. In future years, you can review your notes and be prepared for problems before they happen.

Ask About Organics

If you want your garden to be completely organic, don't forget to ask your plant suppliers how they raise their stock. Many conventional growers use synthetic fertilisers and pesticides. Organic growers use starting and growing mediums that are high in organic matter and free of pesticides or synthetic nutrients. If you can't find a supplier of organically grown plants, you may decide to grow them yourself.

Petunias

Companion Planting

In the simplest terms, companion planting is the technique of combining two plants for a particular purpose (usually pest control). In practice, though, you'll find that there are many different factors that influence how plants work together as companions. For instance, if your plants are regularly attacked by insects, you can use companions to hide, repel or trap pests. Other companions provide food and shelter to attract and protect beneficial insects. And some plants grow well together just because they don't compete for light or rooting space.

Cabbage, lobelia and yellow calendulas make colourful companions. Calendulas also attract beneficial insects, like hoverflies.

Repelling with Smells

One way to use companion planting to protect your plants is to mask their odours with other powerful smells. Plants like garlic, for instance, release deterrent aromas into the air that may chase away insects such as bean beetles and potato bugs. Try pungent plants as an edging around garden beds or mix them in among your other plants. Or, try spreading clippings of the scented plants over garden beds for the same effect.

Luring Pests from Your Garden

Some plants have an almost irresistible appeal for certain pests. Nasturtiums, for instance, are an excellent attractant plant because they're a favourite of aphids. Attractant plants can protect your plants in two ways. First, they act as decoys to lure pests away from your desirable plants. Second, they make it easier to control the pests since the insects are concentrated on a few plants. Once pests are 'trapped', you can either pull out the attractant plants and destroy them along with the pests, or apply some other type of control measure to the infested plants.

The aroma of garlic is a powerful deterrent to many pests.

Sheltering Beneficial Insects

Not all insects are garden enemies. Many actually help your garden grow by eating or parasitising plant pests. You can encourage these beneficial creatures to make a home in your garden by planting their favourite flowering plants. Growing dill, for example, can attract pest-eating spiders, lacewings and parasitic wasps, which will help control caterpillars on cabbage, beetles on cucumbers and aphids on lettuce.

Combining Complementary Plants

Some plants make ideal garden companions simply because they don't compete, even when planted close together in small spaces. Plants like deep-rooted squash and shallow-rooted onions occupy different soil zones, so their roots can draw on different nutrient

Nasturtiums entice aphids away from the vegetables and deter whiteflies.

Lettuce and sunflowers can be good garden companions. The low-growing lettuce acts as a living mulch to keep the soil moist, while tall sunflowers to the south or west provide light shade for this heat-sensitive salad crop.

LEFT: Besides producing pretty (and edible) flowers, nasturtiums may lure aphids from your crops.

RIGHT: A fence can reduce the force of winds, so your plants are less likely to be blown over.

sources. Plants that need lots of nutrients (heavy feeders, like cabbage, sweetcorn, aubergine and squash) combine well with light feeders, like garlic and beans. Taller plants like sweetcorn, trellised beans and sunflowers can provide welcome light shade for ground-hugging cucumbers and lettuce. Besides making more efficient use of space, mixing plants with compatible growth habits also increases the diversity in your garden. This, in turn, makes it harder for some pests to find and move between your plants.

Climate

Climate – the seasonal cycles of rainfall, temperatures, humidity and other factors – has a major influence on which plants will thrive in your landscape. Some tough plants, like day lilies (*Hemerocallis* spp.) and hostas (*Hosta* spp.), can grow in a wide range of temperature and moisture conditions. Other plants can take varying temperatures but absolutely must have a certain amount of rainfall (or irrigation if the rains don't come).

All plants have a certain range of temperatures and moisture levels that they will grow best in. If you know what your garden has to offer, you can look for plants that are naturally adapted to those conditions and be fairly confident that they will grow well with a minimum of fuss on your part.

Think About Temperature

If you want to grow plants that will live for more than one year – including trees, shrubs, grasses and perennials – you have to consider your area's average low and high temperatures. Plants that are naturally adapted to this temperature range will tend to survive and thrive in your landscape.

Most plant recommendations are based on an area's low temperatures. Refer to the plant hardiness zone maps on pages 310–11 to find the zone you live in, and limit your selections to plants that are reliably cold-hardy for your area. Marginally hardy plants may survive for several years, but it's likely that they won't thrive, and an unusually cold spell can kill them off.

Summer high temperatures also limit which woody plants, flowers and lawn grasses you can grow. Even if a plant can

eucalyptus

cotton lavender

rosemary

yarrow

thyme

Plants with small or silvery leaves are often well adapted to low-water conditions.

tolerate the heat, it may demand frequent watering in return, and it probably won't look great. Many delphiniums, for instance, will limp along in hot-climate summers and die out after one or two years, while the same plants grown in cooler areas will probably bloom and thrive for several years.

Plants that can't take the heat are a bad choice if you want a good-looking, easy-care garden. Unfortunately, it's difficult to put a number on a plant's heat tolerance. Plant descriptions in books and catalogues often suggest both lower and upper hardiness zone ranges (as in 'Zones 5 to 8'). Use these recommendations as guidelines, but also check around local neighbourhoods and botanical gardens to see how the plant actually performs in your area before you decide to include it in your landscape.

Rainfall

Rainfall, like temperature, has a great impact on determining which plants will grow in an area without supplemental water. If you don't mind lugging hoses around for frequent watering or if you plan to have an automatic irrigation system, you may choose to grow plants that need extra water. If you want to grow just a few moisture-loving plants, site them close to the house where you can give them special attention more easily. But if

The Effect of Water

Large bodies of water like oceans and lakes influence the climate of the land nearby. The larger the body of water, the greater its effect. Since water temperatures rise and fall more slowly than land temperatures, they modify the air temperatures of the surrounding land. Coastal gardens, for example, do not experience the same extreme temperatures as inland gardens. Similarly, a garden near a lake will experience less extreme air temperatures than one farther away. The effect of the water on temperatures may be enough to hold late and early frosts at bay, giving you a longer growing season, and temper the summer heat, making it possible for you to grow a wider range of plants.

Columbines provide colourful late-spring flowers for shady gardens.

adapted to low-water conditions. One of the best ways to get ideas on other plants that grow well in your region without extra water is to investigate what's growing in local natural areas that have similar conditions to your garden.

Microclimates

Microclimates are small areas where the growing conditions differ from the norm. For example, an L-shaped corner next to your house might be sheltered enough from the winter wind and hold sufficient heat radiating from the house to let you grow a marginally hardy plant that would struggle in an open area. In the northern hemisphere, tomatoes planted in the warm soil on the south side of your house can get a head start on more exposed plants in the middle of the garden.

Topography

Topography means the lie of the land. As hills and valleys dip and rise, small changes in altitude and slope and wind shelter create microclimates in particular areas. If your garden is on a hill or in a valley, you'll probably be faced with slightly different conditions from the average climate of your region.

Gardening on a Flat Area

If you live in a relatively flat, exposed area, you may need to deal with soil erosion – not by water, but by wind, which blows strongly across level open areas. You may also find you have drainage problems after heavy rains, when the level land fails to channel away excess water. If you're near a body of water, the land may flood.

Gardening in a Valley

Valleys tend to be cooler than the higher land around them. This happens because cool air is heavier than warm air. Cool air tends to drain towards lower ground. For this reason, gardens located at the bottoms of valleys suffer the latest frosts in the spring, the earliest frosts in autumn and the severest frosts in winter. The absence of wind in valleys increases susceptibility to frost.

Soil tends to be wetter in a valley, and where drainage is poor, water will puddle, creating spongy, wet areas so fungal diseases of plants are more likely to occur.

your goal is to save time, money and natural resources, you'll definitely want to include naturally adapted plants in your landscape. Small, fuzzy or silvery leaves – such as those on many herbs – are fairly reliable clues that a particular plant is

Moisture-loving plants like primulas and astilbes thrive in cool, humid climates with high rainfall.

Cool-loving primroses will thrive and spread in a shady microclimate.

Sunny walls can provide a warm, protected microclimate that is ideal for heat-loving plants.

On poorly drained flat sites, a raised bed can provide ideal conditions for a wide range of colourful plants.

One of the great advantages of gardening in a valley is that you are likely to find the best topsoil there. As water flows downhill, it washes away the slopes above and carries topsoil and organic matter away, depositing it lower down.

Gardening on a Hilltop

Air temperatures on hills tend to be lower than on flat land. You'll have greater protection from frost and plant disease on a hill, compared with a valley, since air movement is greater. Excessive winds, however, can damage plants, increase soil erosion and speed the loss of moisture from the soil. The soil will generally be thinner and more easily lose its nutrients.

Gardening on a Slope

Slopes are often cooled by breezes in the afternoon or evening, while warm air rising over them in the morning keeps away frost. In cool northern hemisphere climates, a slope with a southern exposure warms more quickly in the spring, and remains warm for a longer period at the end of the growing season.

Slopes, however, are subject to erosion from water drainage and wind.

Exposure

Exposure refers to the amount of sun and shade your garden receives throughout the day. The exposure of different places on your property can vary widely, depending on where each garden is in relation to the house and to other shade-casting features such as trees and fences.

South-Facing Sites

Locating a garden on the south side of your house (or a wall or fence) provides the maximum amount of light in the northern hemisphere.

Eastern Exposures

Many plants thrive with an eastern exposure. Plants on these sites receive up to a half day of direct light, and they're sheltered from the hot afternoon sun, prolonging bloom time in hot summers.

The amount of sun your garden receives can vary through the day. Consider this factor as you plan your plantings.

West-Facing Sites

Western exposures are a challenge for plants. The site is generally cool and shady in the morning, but the temperature can change dramatically when strong sun hits it during the warmest part of the day.

Northern Exposures

A north-facing garden receives much less light and remains cool throughout the day. If the site is open (without large trees or buildings to the east or west), it will probably still be bright. A bright, evenly cool spot is ideal for most shade-loving plants; even those preferring full shade should grow well here.

Many colourful plants, including irises and primroses, thrive in shade.

Reduce maintenance on tough-to-mow slopes by replacing turf with a mixture of wildflowers.

Sunny sites can provide ideal conditions for lush borders packed with light-loving, flowering plants.

All About Soil

Study Your Soil

Before you start planning and planting, invest a little time in learning about your soil. Once you know what soil conditions your garden has to offer, you can choose plants that will grow and thrive there for years to come. Your hands, a trowel to dig up a little soil and a simple soil test kit are all you need to get a basic picture of what's going on in the earth beneath your feet.

Clay soil is nutrient-rich but drains poorly.

Sandy soil drains quickly and is usually dry and infertile.

Loamy soil tends to be moist and fertile.

Structure below the Surface

While it's relatively easy to develop good soil structure at the surface, you have much less influence over the subsoil. There, the parent material plays a greater role in determining how the particles group themselves.

Next time you dig a deep hole, take a look at the structure of the deepest soil. you can see. Observe the soil in place on the side of the hole, break off a hand-sized piece. Loose, structureless subsoil may allow water and nutrients to drain away from roots too quickly, leading to droughty conditions at the surface. A tight, massive subsoil will interfere with the drainage of excess water, usually leading to waterlogged conditions.

While granules are fairly uncommon in the subsoil, you may see other kinds of structures there. In uncultivated soils, or those laid down by water or ice (along rivers and streams or in glacial areas), particles often arrange themselves in flat sheets, called plates. In dry regions, you're likely to see vertical columns that may be 15 cm (6 inches) or more in diameter and of varying lengths.

In humid regions the subsoil is usually made up of angular or slightly rounded cubes that range in size from less than 2.5 cm (1 inch) wide to 5 cm (2 inches) wide or more.

Tight, platy soil can discourage growth.

Roots grow easily in granular soil.

Soil Structure Helpers

You have allies in your battle for good soil structure – the small creatures that crawl through your soil. Earthworms are perhaps the most famous soil builders. Their tunnelling loosens and aerates tight soil, and the organic matter they drag down encourages stable soil granules. Rodents churn the soil as they dig and mix organic matter into the subsoil. Plant roots also improve soil structure by adding organic matter below the surface as they break down. Plus, the tiny passages left by the decayed roots allow water and air easier access to lower soil layers, in turn encouraging even better micoorganism and plant growth.

RIGHT: Healthy soil builds healthy plants. Your role in the cycle is keeping the soil stocked with organic matter to provide ideal conditions for beneficial soil organisms and good root growth.

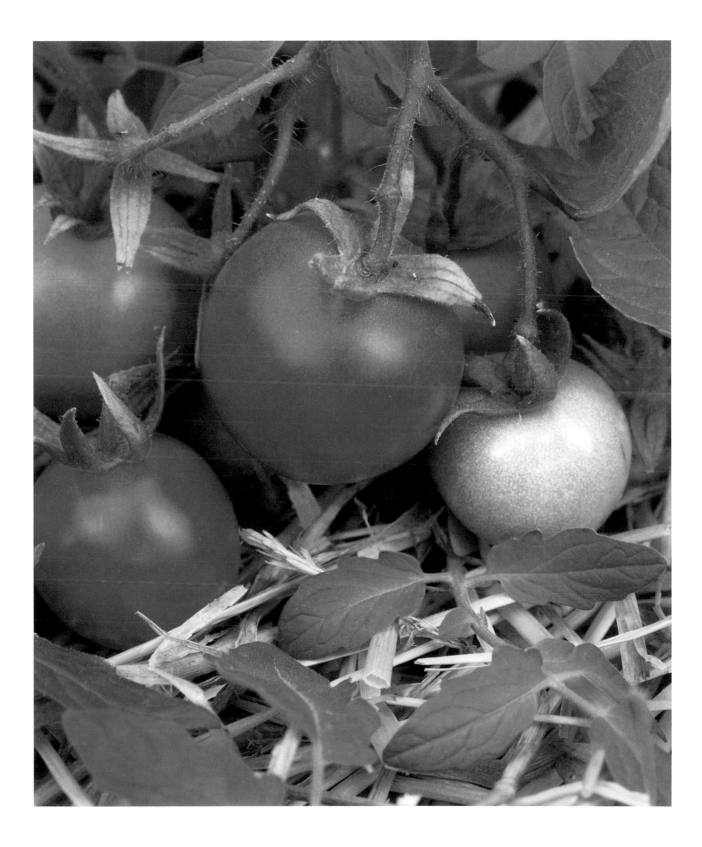

Soil Texture

Almost all soils are made up of three basic mineral components: sand grains, somewhat smaller silt particles and extremely fine clay particles. The relative amounts of these three mineral particles determine the texture of your soil.

You can get a very basic idea of your soil's texture by doing a simple test: just take a handful of moist soil, squeeze it and match the results you get with one of the points below.

- If the soil won't stay in a clump in your open hand, it's on the sandy side.
- If the soil forms a loose clump that breaks apart when you tap it lightly with your finger, it's a loam – a balanced mixture of sand, silt and clay that's ideal for many garden plants.
- If the soil forms a sticky lump that you can mould into various shapes, it's high in clay.

Soils that have lots of sand are said to be light or sandy. Light soils lose water and dissolved nutrients quickly, so they tend to be dry and infertile. Loamy soils usually drain well but hold enough water and nutrients for good plant growth. Heavy (clayey) soils tend to hold a lot of water and nutrients, but they can be waterlogged when wet and hard when dry.

There isn't any practical way to change the texture of your soil. You can, however, improve the soil's structure to make it more suitable for the plants you want to grow in your garden.

Puzzling Out pH

Plant nutrients tend to be most available to roots when the soil pH is near neutral (around 6.5 to 7.0). When the soil is either very acid (with a lower pH) or alkaline (with a higher pH), some nutrients form chemical compounds that make them unavailable to your plants. A home test kit (which you can buy at a garden centre) or a professional soil test can tell you what pH your soil has. Balance acid soils by adding lime and alkaline soils by adding sulphur. Your test kit or results sheet should tell you how much to apply.

To have your soil analysed by a professional soil laboratory, contact your local Cooperative Extension agent, land-grant university, or professional soil-analysis laboratory for information or directions.

Plants for Acid Soil

Here are just a few plants that appreciate or tolerate soil with a pH below 6.5.

Shrubs

Camellias (*Camellia* spp.)
Heaths (*Erica* spp.)
Bayberries (*Myrica* spp.)
Pieris (*Pieris* spp.)
Yews (*Taxus* spp.)
Mountain laurel (*Kalmia latifolia*)
Azaleas and rhododendrons (*Rhododendron* spp.)
Blueberries (*Vaccinium* spp.)

Flowers

Chrysanthemums (*Chrysanthemum* spp.)
Lily-of-the-valley (*Convallaria majalis*)
Lilies (*Lilium* spp.)
Marigolds (*Tagetes* spp.)

Trees

Firs (*Abies* spp.)
Cedars (*Cedrus* spp.)
Spruces (*Picea* spp.)
Pines (*Pinus* spp.)
Oaks (*Quercus* spp.)

Soil Structure

Structure refers to how the sand, silt and clay particles in your soil stick together. Many small, crumb-like clumps create ample space for the air and water that roots need to grow well. Tight, compacted soils have little or no structure, making them hard for you to dig and hard for the roots of your plants to grow through. Loose, sandy soils with little structure lose water and nutrients quickly.

Organic matter provides the basic materials that help to clump the soil particles together. To improve and maintain good soil structure, work in generous amounts of decomposed garden compost before planting, and use organic mulches like chopped leaves and grass clippings, or, for the vegetable garden, hay and straw, to keep the soil well stocked with organic matter.

Understanding Organic Matter

Organic matter and humus are essential parts of healthy soil. Organic matter is the 'fresh' dead material that gets added to the soil, such as fallen leaves and grass clippings. As soil organisms feed on the organic matter, they break it down into nutrients, which your plants can use, and humus. Humus forms loose connections between soil particles and gives the soil a good crumbly structure. It acts like a sponge to hold water and nutrients where roots can absorb them. Adding ample quantities of organic matter – in the form of aged compost, chopped leaves, grass clippings, mushroom compost or similar materials – will help to improve just about any kind of soil.

Knowing about Nutrients

Soil with lots of organic matter is called 'rich' because it holds ample reservoirs of nutrients. The big three plant nutrients are nitrogen (N), phosphorus (P) and potassium (K). (The 5-10-5 or 5-10-10 listed on bags of fertiliser is the percentage of these three elements [N-P-K].)

Plants need nitrogen to grow healthy green leaves and to regulate the use of other nutrients. Phosphorus helps form healthy roots and flowers; it also strengthens resistance to pests. Potassium also promotes strong roots and general resistance, but it's important in photosynthesis as well.

Plants need several other nutrients, such as iron and calcium, in smaller quantities. Soils with ample amounts of organic matter usually contain enough nutrients to keep many kinds of plants thriving. But you'll also need to make sure your soil is at the right pH so those nutrients will be available to your plants. A soil test can tell you whether your soil is acid or alkaline and if the supply of different nutrients is adequate for your needs.

While most plants grow best when the soil contains an ample supply of balanced nutrients, some actually grow better if soil nutrients are low. Nitrogen-rich soils, for instance, will cause plants like yarrow and coreopsis to form lush, floppy growth that requires staking. In less fertile soil the same plants will grow stronger. Knowing the nutrient content of your soil will help you select the most appropriate plants for your conditions.

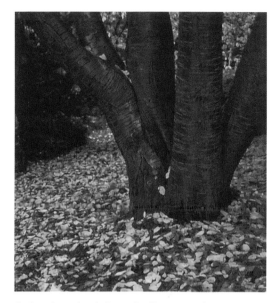

As these leaves break down, they'll return nutrients to the soil; the tree's roots will take in the nutrients to help boost next year's growth.

Plants for Alkaline Soil

If you soil's pH is on the high side (7.0 or higher), consider some of these plants; they're naturally adapted to alkaline soil.

Trees

Catalpas (*Catalpa* spp.)
Redbuds (*Cercis* spp.)
Green ash (*Fraxinus pennsylvanica*)
Bur oak (*Quercus macrocarpa*)
Lilacs (*Syringa* spp.)

Shrubs

Barberries (*Berbis* spp.)
Box (*Buxus* spp.)
Cotoneasters (*Cotoneaster* spp.)
Forsythias (*Forsythia* spp.)

Flowers

Ageratum (*Ageratum houstonianum*)
Japanese anemone (*Anemone x hybrida*)
Snapdragon (*Antirrhinum majus*)
Cosmos (*Cosmos* spp.)
Pinks (*Dianthus* spp.)
Baby's-breath (*Gypsophila paniculata*)
Peonies (*Paeonia* spp.)
Zinnias (*Zinnia* spp.)

Climbers

Clematis (*Clematis* spp.)
Virginia creeper (*Parthenocissus quinquefolia*)
Boston ivy (*Parthenocissus tricuspidata*)

Snapdragon

Taking Care of Your Soil

- Keep the soil covered. Use organic mulches like compost, shredded leaves and grass clippings around plants to help prevent soil erosion, retain soil moisture, keep the soil cool, add organic matter and nutrients, and provide safe hiding places for beneficial insects like ground beetles. Mulches also serve as a barrier between plants and pathogens.

- Grow a flowering, living mulch. Sow cover crops like buckwheat or clover in any vacant garden spot. The living mulch will protect the soil as it provides nectar and shelter for beneficial insects.

- Keep tillage to a minimum, especially when soil is wet or dusty dry. Soil is too wet to work if it sticks to your shoes or easily holds its shape when formed into a ball. Working wet soil can ruin the soil's structure. Tillage destroys some insect pests, but kills beneficial insects and animals as well.

Tools and Equipment

Choosing the Right Tool

Using the right tool really does make any job easier, as you know if you've ever used a butter knife when you couldn't find the screwdriver or the heel of a shoe as a substitute for a hammer. But a shopping trip for garden tools can be so baffling that you may well decide to stick with the butter knife and shoe. When faced with a wall-long display of shovels, spades, forks, rakes, trowels and cultivators, it can be hard to decide what tools, and what version of them, you need.

A Basic Tool Collection

Fortunately, most gardeners can get away with half-a-dozen basic tools. You'll need a spade to turn the soil and a shovel for digging holes and for moving soil, sand and compost around. A spading fork is useful for turning the soil, working in dressings and green manures, turning compost and dividing perennials. You'll also need a metal rake for smoothing the soil, a hoe for weeding and a trowel for planting and transplanting. If you have a huge vegetable garden, you may want to get a rotary tiller, wheel hoe or even a garden tractor to which you can attach various implements. If you garden in containers, a trowel and hand cultivator will suffice.

Buying Good Tools

There's nothing quite like the feel of working your soil with a good-quality, well-constructed tool. Here are some things to consider as you shop for garden equipment, so you'll get the best tools for your money.

Cost How much you spend on your tools depends on how long you want them to last. If you want to keep the tools for decades, get the best you can afford. If you're on a tight budget, if you plan to move in a few years and don't want the extra baggage or if you leave your tools outside all the time, buy the bargain-basement kind. Be warned, though, that cost-cutting materials and designs make cheap tools more difficult to use than their more expensive counterparts. And cheap tools might not even make it through a season without bending or breaking.

Construction When you go tool shopping, read the label to see whether the metal part of the tool is stamped steel or forged steel. Forged steel is much stronger, but makes the tool cost 20 to 30 per cent more than a tubular steel tool. If you want the item to last, go for a forged steel product; if budget is a limitation, consider stamped steel.

Whether you have a whole collection of garden tools or just a few basic ones, you need to know when and how to use them properly.

Also investigate how the handle attaches to the metal part. Don't buy the tool if the metal wraps only part-way round the handle; this construction, called open socket, leaves the wood exposed to water and mud, which can lead to rot. Also avoid tools where the handle is poked onto a spike at the top of the metal portion of the tool, then surrounded with a metal collar to keep the handle from splitting. Neither this type of construction, called tang and ferrule, nor open socket is durable and may only last a season or two.

Instead, choose tools with metal that wraps all the way round the handle (called solid-socket construction) or has strips of metal bolted to the handle (known as solid-strap construction).

Handles If you want a wooden handle, look for one made of white ash. Handles of spades and forks are sometimes made from hickory, but it's heavier and less flexible. The grain should run the length of the handle, without knots. Painted handles often hide low-quality wood;

don't buy them. Alternatives to wood are fibreglass or solid-core fibreglass. Both are stronger than wood; solid-core fibreglass is nearly unbreakable. They cost more than wood, but it's worth it if you want a tool that will last for many years.

Grips If the end of the handle has a grip for you to hang on to, check how the grip is designed. Make sure it is fastened to the handle and not just slipped over it. Beyond that, the style you choose is a matter of preference (and availability). Try out a few to see which feels best.

Size If you have a choice, pick the handle length that feels most comfortable. Shovels should be at least shoulder height; rakes can be even longer to give you a better reach. A hoe's handle should be

YD-grip   T-grip   D-grip

Tool handles come with several types of grips; choose the one that feels most comfortable to you.

long enough to let you stand upright when the blade is about 60 cm (2 feet) from your feet and just about flat on the ground. Short-handled tools, such as spades and spading forks, usually have 70-cm (28-inch) handles, but tall gardeners should look for ones with 80-cm (32-inch) handles. For hand tools such as trowels, choose the length that feels comfortable

Neater Weeders

Ordinary hoes are traditional favourites for weeding vegetable gardens, but they aren't the last word in weeding tools. If you need a special tool for weeding in tight spots or if you just enjoy trying out handy garden gadgets, give some of the implements discussed below a try.

Paving weeders are short-handled, with an angled, pointed blade used to scrape weeds growing between bricks or sections of paving or in driveway cracks.

Dandelion weeders, also called asparagus knives or fishtail weeders, have a blade that resembles a forked, tongue; the handle may be long or short. Use this tool to dig out grasses, small tree seedlings or weeds with long taproots (such as curly dock [*Rumex crispus*]).

Cape Cod weeders and hot-bed weeders are short-handled, angled blades for cutting small weeds in tight places.

Hand cultivators have three clawlike tines for raking weeds from the soil; they may have short or long handles.

String trimmers can be powered by gas or electricity; high-powered models may have a blade attachment that can handle tough-stemmed weeds. Power trimmers are useful for quickly cutting weeds along fences and walls and for mowing small meadow areas. The drawbacks are their noise and the safety hazards they present.

Secateurs, shears and loppers are handy for cutting back climbers and clump-forming weeds.

Mattocks and pickaxes give the 'umph' you need to dig out the roots of woody-stemmed weeds, such as shrubs and some climbers.

Good-quality tools can be expensive, but they are a pleasure to use and can last for many years with good care.

in your hand. When buying a mattock or pickaxe, choose a weight that you can lift and swing without strain.

Caring for Tools

Once you've gone to the trouble of buying good tools, it's worth a little extra effort to keep them in shape. Without proper care, even the best built and most expensive tool can get corroded and dull after a season or two, making it as unpleasant to use as the cheapest department-store tool. When you are ready to dig, you'll be glad of the few minutes you put in to keeping your tools clean and sharp.

Keep Them Clean

It's pretty easy at the end of a hot and grimy day in the garden to justify putting the tools away dirty. And you can even get away with it a few times. But eventually the moist soil clinging to your tools will make them rust. And once you finally do get around to cleaning them, the dry soil is harder to get off than the moist soil would have been.

For that reason, it's a virtue to force yourself into the habit of cleaning your tools when you're done with them. This doesn't mean just scraping the shovel off with the trowel. For one thing, then you have to scrape the trowel off with the shovel, then the shovel off with the trowel again, and so on. Also, all that scraping of metal against metal damages tools.

Better alternatives include using a stick, wooden spoon or paint stirrer to scrape off the clinging soil. Or use a long-handled scrub brush that you keep in a convenient spot. Another trick is to keep a tub of sharp sand around and dip the tool up and down in it until the soil comes off.

It's especially worthwhile to clean tools before you store them for the winter. Clean off the soil, then use steel wool or a wire brush to remove any rust. Coat the metal with a light oil and hang the tools somewhere you can see and admire them all winter long.

Since your skin touches the handle the most, you may want to keep wooden

Spare Your Back

If Monday mornings often find you aching from a weekend of digging, don't give up on the garden; learn how to dig the right way! Here are some tips that can help save your muscles next time you turn the soil.

First, insert the tool into the soil so the blade is straight up and down. Now follow these steps:

1. Keeping your back straight and your foot on the upper edge of the spade, use your weight to push the spade into the soil.
2. Bend both your waist and knees as you slide the spade under the soil, then straighten both to lift the load.
3. Turn your whole body before depositing the earth – don't just twist your torso as you fling the soil off to the side.

It's easy, in your rush to finish up, to ignore pain. But pain has a purpose, and that purpose is to tell you to knock it off and go in the house for something to drink. You'll get more done and feel better if you take regular breaks, preferably before you start to feel pain!

handles smooth by sanding any rough spots. If you wish, apply varnish or another sealer (like tung oil) to protect the wood. If a handle breaks, pick up a replacement during your next trip to the hardware store; don't just try to tape the old one.

Keep Them Sharp

Your spade and hoe will do a better job for you if you keep them sharpened. You'll get the best results if you sharpen them briefly and often rather than making it a big job for the end of the year. For most gardeners, a metal file is an adequate

sharpening tool. Use a file that matches the contour of the tool's surface – a flat file for a flat-bladed hoe or spade and a half-round file for a curved shovel blade. If you have many tools, a whetstone or grindstone will take care of them more quickly. If you don't want to sharpen them yourself, you can take your tools to someone who does it professionally (some hardware stores offer this service). The best time to do this is in late autumn, as you are preparing your tools for storage. Professional sharpeners are often swamped with work in spring, and they may not have time to do your tools as soon as you need them if you wait until the last minute.

To Sharpen a Hoe
Hold the hoe where the metal and handle meet, with the cutting edge face down and the handle pointing away from you. Holding the metal file flat against the bevelled edge, stroke downwards towards the edge of the blade, at a 30 to 40 degree angle to the length of the blade. Use medium pressure and make quick strokes. Go in one direction only – don't saw the file back and forth across the blade.

Maintaining a Tiller
If you own a rotary tiller, it's important to clean off the soil after each use. Wash both the tines and the body with a soft cloth. If you keep the painted parts waxed, you'll find the soil will dislodge much more easily.

Look for any loose or missing screws, nuts or bolts; replace as necessary. Once a year, or every 25 hours of use (whichever comes first), clean the air cleaner by tapping it against something; if it's really filthy, wash it. You'll need to clean it more often if your soils are powdery. Use the same timetable for changing the oil. Change the spark plug every year, too, or every 50 hours of use.

Before storing the machine for winter, clean out the fuel line by draining out all the petrol and then running the machine until it stops. Remove, clean and replace the spark plug, leaving the spark plug wire disconnected. If the machine has a four-stroke engine, change the oil. Check the blades or tines, and sharpen them if needed. Check with your owner's manual for other suggested maintenance tips.

The Trouble with Tillers
Their speed and power make rotary tillers very useful, but they do have several drawbacks. For one thing, they're a big investment. Unless you have a huge garden, you may not want to spend the money for a machine that you'll only use for a few hours each season. (Of course, if you can't afford to buy your own tiller, you can usually rent one for a day or weekend for a reasonable fee.) Tillers also use petrol, which bothers gardeners trying to cut back on the use of fossil fuels. And some people just don't like the noise.

But perhaps the biggest drawback is that they are tempting to use, and their overuse can damage the soil. The spinning metal blades can break crumbly granular soil into fine powder, ruining soil structure. If you repeatedly till to the same depth, you can create a layer of hardpan right below the blade depth. Finally, tillers work in large quantities of air, which can cause a population boom of soil microorganisms. While this is good to some extent, the stimulated microorganisms can rapidly deplete your soil's supply of organic matter unless you add enough material to make up for it.

Scrape any clinging soil off the blade of spades, shovels, forks and hoes to prevent rusting.

Brush your tools off after each use, and give them a thorough cleaning and oiling before storage.

Planning Your Garden

Starting from Scratch

If you've just moved into a new development, built a new house or inherited a particularly uninspired all-lawn landscape, you may be staring at bare soil or an expanse of grass where you want a garden to be located.

Live with It

The best way to start a new landscape may be not to start it – at least for a year or so. If you can stand it, live with the landscape through one year. See where water puddles after storms or where it runs off quickly, taking valuable topsoil with it. Note where structures and trees cast shadows on your property throughout the seasons. See how traffic patterns develop: where do you always walk to reach the car? Where do visitors and utility people tend to tread on their way to the door? Take note of these patterns and problems, and incorporate them into your landscape plan.

Look at Your Landscape

Before you start digging, walk round your garden and look at it from all angles – from the street, from the back door, from the side of the house. Think about where a garden would look good and enhance your plot. You might decide on a

perennial planting in front of a shrub border, and a herb and vegetable garden just outside the back door. In short, you want to give the garden a reason for being wherever it is.

Garden Styles

You'll also need to decide whether it is to be a formal or informal garden, or a mixture of both.

Formal Gardens

Formal landscaping uses straight lines, sharp angles and symmetrical plantings with a limited number of different plants. They are usually laid out in squares or rectangles with low hedges of clipped box, hollies or other evergreens to define different spaces in the garden. Often the beds on either side of a straight central path are planted with the same sequence of plants, forming a mirror image of each other. Formal designs tend to have a restful feel. But they may not be as restful for the gardener since you'll need to clip, stake and weed on a regular basis to keep the plants looking perfect.

For a formal look, include elements like straight paths, symmetrical plantings and tightly-clipped, closely planted low edgings.

Informal designs include mixed plantings, curved edges and winding paths.

Informal Gardens

Informal landscapes use curving lines to create a more natural feeling. They tend to have few permanent features such as walls, although elements such as rustic split-rail fences and wood-chip paths add greatly to the informal feel. These kinds of gardens generally include many different kinds of plants – trees, shrubs, annuals, herbs, climbers and perennials. Informal designs are relaxed and lively. Since the plants are free to spread, sprawl and lean on each other, they tend to need less regular maintenance to still look well tended. You won't need to keep sharp edges on the beds, and the few weeds that pop up won't be immediately obvious and ruin the look of the garden.

Beautiful gardens such as this don't happen by accident – they start with careful planning.

For a formal look, try a classic single border. A hedge or fence provides a good background; a solid edging strip makes for easy maintenance.

Mixed Gardens

It's difficult to mix informal and formal areas effectively, but sometimes the classic formal garden seems too rigid. The modern approach is to plant sections of a formal garden with a touch of informality by maintaining the basic geometric shapes but softening the angles with creeping and trailing edgers.

Put Your Ideas on Paper

Once you've chosen a site and style for your garden, you can start putting your plans down on paper. Measure the length and width of the area you have targeted for your garden. Determine an appropriate outline and draw it to scale on a piece of graph paper. Draw in the major existing features, such as buildings, trees, shrubs and paths. This is also a good place to jot down notes about the soil conditions in

Design Rules for Your Garden

While designing a garden is a very personal and creative activity, following some basic design rules will give your finished garden a very polished or natural look. The key rules are to create balance and rhythm and to add a dominant feature to tie the garden together.

First, keep the garden in balance. Include plants with a mix of heights and sizes throughout your planting. Don't plant all of the tall or massive flowers on one side, with a group of low, delicate plants at the other end. In formal gardens, you may balance one side of the garden by planting the same design on the other, making a mirror image. For an informal garden, you can vary the planting, perhaps matching a large blue-flowered perennial on one side with a lower-growing plant that has bright red flowers. In this case, you are balancing brighter colour with larger size.

Second, create a rhythm, or a sense of continuity, throughout the entire garden. You can repeat groupings of the same plant or use other plants with identical colours or similar flower shapes. Let a middle-of-the-border plant drift from the foreground to the background, giving a sense of movement and uniting the different layers of the garden.

Third, establish a dominant feature. This focal point can be a path, sculpture, birdbath or tree with the garden built round it.

the various planting areas (is it frequently wet, often dry or evenly moist?), as well as the amount and type of sunshine available (does it get full sun, just a few

This charming cottage garden combines perennials with annuals, shrubs and trees for season-long interest.

hours of morning or afternoon sun, or no direct sun at all?).

Make a couple of photocopies of your base plan, or lay sheets of tracing paper over the original sketch. On one copy or overlay, circle or otherwise mark the problem areas you identified on your stroll round the garden. On the other copies, try sketching in possible solutions. Maybe you could plant groundcover on that grassy slope to eliminate mowing, or link that group of shrubs with mulch and groundcover, so you don't have to mow around the individual plants. Experiment with different arrangements until you're happy with the results on paper. Then go out into the garden and try to visualise how the landscape will look with the solutions you've come up with. Make sure you've planned for access by equipment (like mowers and wheelbarrows).

For a charmingly informal look, interplant your vegetables with other flowering plants and herbs to add colour, and also to save space.

Pick Your Plants

Now you can start identifying the plants you want to grow. A fun way to do this is to keep a wish list of plants that you've admired in catalogues, read about in books or seen in neighbours' gardens. For each species or cultivar, write down growth rates and mature sizes, flower colour, shape, height, season of bloom, foliage appearance and cultural requirements. Then you can start matching up the plants you want with the growing conditions you have available.

Putting Plants into Your Plan

As you finalise your plant list, start thinking about how to organise the different plants in the garden. To visualise possible colour combinations, cut circles representing each group of flowers out of coloured paper, matching the paper colour to the flower colour. Juggle these around until you find combinations you like.

It is worth the effort to work out an initial plan for your garden. Factors to take into consideration include light, moisture, soil and topography.

Set Priorities

As you install your new landscape, it's wise to start on the 'hard' elements – like walls, fences and paths – first. This is also a good time to plan and install an automatic irrigation system if you need one. Once the permanent elements are in place, then you can start planting. Whenever possible, begin with slow growers like trees and shrubs, then the groundcover. You may choose to plant a few beds of annuals for quick colour during the first few seasons or to just wait for the perennial garden to develop. Don't forget that annuals are also great for filling in gaps in young perennial gardens.

Regrading

Sometimes terracing or regrading is necessary to make land usable. Consult professionals such as landscape architects, engineers or surveyors if extensive grading is necessary. If you do have regrading done on your property, make sure you keep the topsoil separate from

the subsoil. When you're ready to finish the job, use the reserved topsoil as the top layer – it's much better and richer soil for your plants.

Protecting Trees During Regrading

If you plan to have regrading done on your property, keep in mind that changing the soil level around a tree can severely damage it. If you add soil over its roots, they may die due to reduced soil oxygen or due to excess water held against them. If you remove soil, you'll actually remove much of your tree's roots, because most of the small feeder roots are within the top 30 cm (1 foot) of soil. Removing roots prevents your tree from absorbing enough water and nurients for growth and may hinder its ability to hold itself upright. One strong windstorm can easily topple a tree with damaged roots.

If you must grade around trees, build 'wells' around your trees large enough to protect their roots. Use brightly coloured construction tape to mark off a protected

area round your trees, at least as far away from the trunks as the drip line, farther if it is possible, to keep heavy equipment from compacting or damaging the roots and soil.

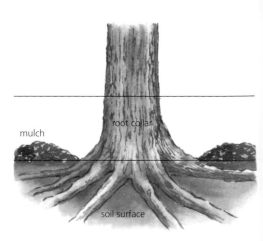

During regrading, avoid piling soil round the root collar of your tree. Keep mulch a few inches away, too.

Liven up mass plantings with a focal point. A birdbath, for example, adds interest to this bed of mums.

A flagstone path admits visitors to the heart of a cottage garden. Low-growing plants between the paving soften the edges.

Adapting an Existing Landscape

In some ways, adapting an existing landscape is more challenging than starting from scratch. Although your garden may have nice features like large trees or an established lawn to work with, you also have someone else's mistakes to undo (or maybe your own, which are even harder to face).

If you've lived with the garden for at least a year, you are probably acutely aware of its troublesome or high-maintenance points. Don't try to change the whole garden at once, but identify the elements you want to change, and choose a few (or one major one) to work on each year.

Trees and Shrubs

Whenever possible, try to keep existing trees and shrubs. If the shrubs are overgrown, you might be able to give them a facelift with drastic pruning. If you do decide to remove a tree or shrub, make sure you dig out the stump, too – it's a lot of work, but it will make replanting much easier, and you won't have to deal with suckers sprouting from the roots. If you are tired of pruning hedges, consider replacing these high-maintenance elements with informal shrub borders.

Flowers

If your existing perennial plants are overgrown, dig them out, divide them and replant the vigorous outer parts into enriched soil. If they are in the wrong spot, dig and move them in the spring.

If you don't mind replanting them each year, annuals are great for season-long colour. For lots of colour without the hassle of digging flower beds, consider a few container plantings (if you're willing to do some extra watering).

Lawns

Reduce mowing chores by replacing some of the lawn with shrubs, trees or groundcover. Install mowing strips to cut down on edging chores. Make maintenance easier by eliminating grass growing under or along fences and walls, on steep slopes and under any trees with low branches or shallow roots, or anywhere where the grass is not green, lush and thriving.

Paths and Walkways

If your existing paths are in the wrong spot, or made from the wrong material, it's simplest in the long run to rip them up and start again. The paving material you choose should match or complement the style or colour of your existing landscape or home. For example, a brick path looks good with a brick home. A stone walk complements a country cottage. The paving material should also be easy to maintain. Although they are expensive to buy, paving blocks, stone and brick require little additional maintenance after they are installed.

Make sure your path is wide enough so that it is easy to use. A walk to your door should be 1.2 m (4 feet) wide, spacious enough to accommodate two people walking side by side. It's important, too, that the path is well drained so you can use it during wet weather and so it won't shift as the soil freezes and thaws.

Designing Your Garden

Creating a Colour-Themed Garden

You can design beautiful gardens around a theme as simple as a single colour. This may sound plain, but it's anything but that – colour-themed gardens are attractive and dramatic additions to any landscape. Even gardens that are based on green leaves contain varying tints and shades, as well as textures and patterns, from the frosty blue-greens of some hostas to the deep glossy green of European wild ginger (*Asarum europaeum*). When you start including flower colours against the greens, you add an extra level of interest. Even if the flowers you choose are all in the same colour group, the many different shades and tints create a mosaic of changing colours throughout the season.

Planning a colour-themed garden starts by picking the colour you want to work with. Try a monochrome (based on one flower colour) border if you have a favourite colour or love collecting flowers of a particular colour. Or make a small monochromatic section part of a long mixed-colour border, perhaps using silver foliage to separate it from flowers of other colours.

If you have a couple of unconnected small beds, you might want to try a different colour in each. Or choose a single colour for the whole garden in each season: perhaps pink for spring, white for summer and yellow for autumn, or whatever colours appeal to you.

Another option to consider is a two-colour border. Blue and white make a classic combination. Or perhaps pinks and yellows are more to your liking. Yellow or chartreuse with maroon or burgundy is another popular colour combination.

The key to creating a beautiful and effective colour-themed garden is to pick the colours that you like and those that blend well with your house. White flowers, for instance, can look

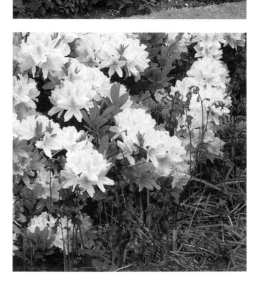

dirty against cream-coloured cladding or walls, while bright pinks can clash unmercifully with rusty orange brick. Try growing the plants there in a container for a year. If the colours look good to you, go ahead and plan a full-scale garden; if they don't fit the bill, move the pot elsewhere, and try a different combination in that spot next year. If you're not sure exactly which colour to choose, think about the time of day you'll usually view the garden and what kind of weather prevails in your area. If your climate tends to be cloudy and misty, whites, yellows and pastels can be useful for adding a bright touch to your garden. White flowers also tend to glow luminously in twilight or moonlit gardens. If sun shines down on your garden for most of the season, consider bright colours for your theme.

Themes to Try

Hot-Colour Borders If knock-your-socks-off colour is what you want, consider planning a garden around the hot colours: reds, oranges and yellows. These colours are ideal for accenting outlying areas of your garden, since they tend to catch your eye from a distance.

Hot-colour borders are exciting and vibrant. Yellow gardens have a sunny, cheerful look and are fairly easy to arrange without fear of clashing colours. Reds and oranges make the loudest statements of the various colour themes, but red flowers also have the greatest potential to clash with each other. Before planting a whole border of these bright colours, consider trying a small bed or part of a border first to see if you like the effect.

TOP LEFT: Add sparkle to beds and borders by pairing spring bulbs with early annuals.
MIDDLE LEFT: Red flowers look marvellous against green leaves. The contrast of these colours is dynamic and exciting.
BOTTOM LEFT: Bluebells (*Hyacinthoides* spp.) and other early bulbs blend beautifully with spring-flowering shrubs.

Cool-Colour Borders If you're not especially adventurous in your colour choices, a planting of cool colours may be more to your liking. Blue-themed gardens have a cool, restrained look, but they're tricky to pull off successfully. Blue and green are such similar colours that blue flowers tend to blend into the background sea of green leaves. Blues, violets and greens are best planted where you can see them up close – perhaps along a path or near a deck.

Annuals for an All-Blue Garden

Varying the different kinds of blue – from soft lavender blue to bright sky blue and deep cobalt blue – is one way to add extra interest to a cool-colour planting. Companion plants with silver or chartreuse leaves, such as dusty miller or golden feverfew (*Chrysanthemum parthenium* 'Aureum'), are also excellent additions for contrast.

The following list contains a few blue flowered annuals you might want to include in your cool-colour garden.
Ageratum houstonianum (ageratum)
Brachycome iberidifolia (Swan River daisy)
Browallia speciosa (browallia)
Centaurea cyanus (cornflower)
Consolida ambigua (rocket larkspur)
Convolvulus tricolor (dwarf morning glory)
Ipomoea tricolor (morning glory)
Lobelia erinus (edging lobelia)
Myosotis sylvatica (forget-me-not)
Nemophila menziesii (baby blue eyes)
Nigella damascena (love-in-a-mist)
Salvia farinacea (mealy cup sage)

Perennials for an All-Blue Garden

Blue is also a popular colour theme for perennial plantings. Many beloved summer-flowering perennials have blue flowers, including delphiniums, Siberian iris (*Iris sibirica*), bellflowers (*Campanula* spp.) and pincushion flower (*Scabiosa caucasica*).

To extend the season, add blue flowered shrubs, such as caryopteris (*Caryopteris* x *clandonensis*), and annuals, such as ageratum and lobelia. For spring

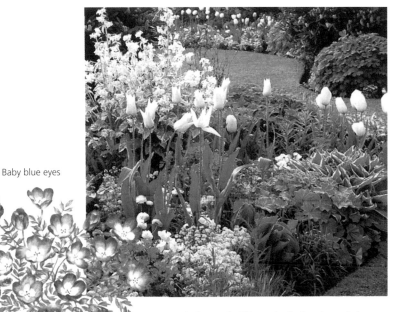

Baby blue eyes

A silver-and-white garden looks crisp and clean during the day. The light colours stand out at night, too.

colour, plant bulbs such as Spanish bluebells (*Hyacinthoides hispanica*) and Siberian squills (*Scilla siberica*). For even more choices, expand your list to include the many flowers in the blue-violet range.

Several plants offer bluish foliage; amethyst sea holly (*Eryngium amethystinum*) and blue false indigo (*Baptisia australis*) offer blue flowers as well. Many of the finest hosta cultivars – including 'Krossa Regal' and 'Hadspen Blue' – have cool blue leaves that look super in shady gardens. Rue (*Ruta graveolens*) and blue fescue (*Festuca cinerea*) produce their best blues in full sun. Also include silver foliage, which is stunning in blue borders.

Wonderful White Gardens

All-white designs are sometimes called 'moon gardens' because the flowers almost glow under the light of a full moon. This effect can also be achieved under street lights in urban gardens or at the edge of a well-lit patio. Moon gardens include many plants with silver or grey foliage; they may also

include flowers in the palest pastels, as these reflect moonlight almost as well as white. For gardens near the house, include fragrant types of white roses, and peonies, along with fragrant annuals such as sweet alyssum and flowering tobacco (*Nicotiana alata*).

Madagascar periwinkle, mealy cup sage and yellow cosmos

Pretty Pastel Plantings

Like cool-colour plantings, soft pinks, yellows and baby blues planted together tend to have a calm, soothing look. To keep the garden from looking too washed out, consider adding a little spark with some bright whites or a deeper hue of one of the colours – perhaps pure yellow marigolds or bright pink verbena (*Verbena* x *hybrida*). Pink is an easy choice for a colour theme, since so many perennials, hardy bulbs and flowering shrubs come in this colour.

Don't Forget Foliage

As you experiment with different colour combinations, remember that flowers aren't the only source of colour; leaves have lots to offer, too. They come in a surprising array of different greens, from the blue-green of California poppy (*Eschscholzia californica*) to the yellow-green of summer cypress (*Kochia scoparia*) or the deep green of geraniums. Nearly all greens go well together.

Besides the various greens, leaves can come in other colours, too. Silver-leaved plants such as dusty miller look great in almost any kind of garden. Yellowish leaves, such as those of golden feverfew or some coleus, can be pleasing with pinks and blues. You can add a bold spire of colour with the blazing red leaves of Joseph's coat (*Amaranthus tricolor*) or a subtle accent with the bronzy leaves of wax begonias.

Creating a Cottage Garden

The ultimate in informality, cottage gardens display a glorious riot of colours, textures, heights and fragrances. Cottage gardens defy many gardening 'rules': plants are packed closely together, ignoring standard spacing; colours aren't organised into large drifts; tall plants pop up in front of shorter ones; flowers are allowed to flop over and grow through

The bright flowers and ferny foliage of cosmos are excellent additions to a cottage garden. They flower in late summer.

Sweet pea

each other to create a delightful, casual mixture. While cottage gardens may appear effortless and unorganised, they need to be planned, planted and maintained just like any other garden.

The classic cottage garden is an eclectic collection of plants, including perennials, annuals, herbs and roses, allowed to ramble and intertwine. Cottage gardens usually are at least partially enclosed within walls, hedges or fences, making them a natural choice for a small suburban house or a contemporary townhouse with an enclosed garden. You might allow the plants to spread unchecked or to self-sow, letting the seedlings arise where they may. For this to work well, though, you must be willing to do some rearranging if the plants pop up where they're not wanted. Unify the scene with a permanent focal point, such as a path that marches through the garden's centre to a door, patio or bench.

Choosing a Site

Locate cottage gardens next to the house, especially by a door. A rambling rose or flowering climber draped around a door is one of the classic features of a cottage garden. If your front or side area is small, you may want to devote the whole space to the garden. In this case, a gravel, brick, stone or even cement path is essential; make it wide (at least 90 cm [3 feet]) to allow room for plants to spill out onto it, softening the edges and creating an attractive, inviting walkway. A wide path tends to make you walk more slowly.

Cottage gardens work best when they're close to the house. A mix of rounded and spiky blooms add interest. Fragrant leaves and flowers are nice too.

Picking the Plants

To create a pleasing jumble rather than a chaotic mess, combine a variety of different flower shapes and sizes. Thinking of flowers in terms of their visual impact will help you get the right balance.

'Feature' flowers are the ones that first catch your eye; they have strong shapes – like lupins and massive peonies – or bright colours.

'Filler' flowers tend to be smaller and less obvious than the feature plants. Baby's breath is a classic filler flower.

'Edgers' are low plants used in the fronts of beds or spilling over onto paths; think of thymes, edging lobelia and catmint (*Nepeta* x *faassenii*).

These categories aren't rigid: lavender and the flowers of lady's mantle (*Alchemilla mollis*) make nice fillers, but both are often used to edge paths as well. Rose campion (*Lychnis coronaria*) works as a filler, but if set among flowers with contrasting colours, its bright magenta flowers may stand out as a feature. The key is to use some flowers that serve each purpose, so you don't have all bright (and probably clashing) feature flowers, all small, modest filler flowers or all low edging plants.

As you choose plants for the garden, include some that have scented foliage or flowers; fragrance is a traditional part of the cottage garden feeling. It's also important to choose flowers that bloom at different times for a continuous display.

Perennials aren't the only plants you can grow in your cottage garden: annuals, herbs, shrubs, climbers and bulbs can all have a place in your cottage garden, too. Old-fashioned roses, either shrub types or climbers, are a classic ingredient and an important source of fragrant flowers. Climbing roses or honeysuckles look great trained over a door or archway; let clematis climb up lampposts or railings. Including unusual and unlikely plants is a long-standing cottage tradition. Accent your cottage garden with dwarf fruit trees, and tuck in some other edibles for surprise: try colourful lettuces, curly parsley, red-stemmed 'Ruby' chard and maroon-podded 'Burgundy' okra.

These great cottage garden flowers have been favourites for years. Use feature flowers for bold colours and textures, edging plants to line the front, sides and edges of paths, and filler flowers to tie the whole design together.

Feature Flowers

Alcea rosea (hollyhock)
Campanula persicifolia (peach-leaved bellflower)
Delphinium x *belladonna* (Belladonna delphinium)
Dictamnus albus (gas plant)
Iris, bearded hybrids (bearded iris)
Iris sibirica (Siberian iris)
Lilium hybrids (lilies)
Lupinus polyphyllus (garden lupin)
Paeonia lactiflora (common garden peony)
Papaver orientale (oriental poppy)
Phlox paniculata (garden phlox)
Verbascum chaixii (nettle-leaved mullein)

Edging Plants

Aubrieta deltoidea (purple rock cress)
Aurinia saxatilis (basket of gold)
Campanula portenschlagiana (Dalmatian bellflower)
Cerastium tomentosum (snow-in-summer)
Dianthus gratianpolitanus (Cheddar pinks)
Euphorbia epithymoides (cushion spurge)
Heuchera sanguinea (coral bells)
Lobelia erinus (edging lobelia)
Nepeta x *faassenii* (catmint)
Primula vulgaris (primrose)
Pulmonaria saccharata (Bethlehem sage)

Filler Flowers

Alchemilla mollis (lady's mantle)
Aquilegia x *hybrida* (hybrid columbine)
Aster novae-angliae (New England aster)
Astrantia major (masterwort)
Centaurea hypoleuca (knapweed)
Centranthus ruber (red valerian)
Chrysanthemum x *superbum* (shasta daisy)
Coreopsis verticillata (thread-leaved coreopsis)
Geranium sanguineum (blood-red cranesbill)
Gypsophila paniculata (baby's breath)
Lychnis coronaria (rose campion)

Creating a Cutting Garden

If you enjoy having armloads of flowers to bring indoors for fresh arrangements, consider adding a cutting garden to your landscape. A cutting garden is simply one or more beds where you grow flowers just for arrangements. You can collect beautiful blooms from your cutting garden without raiding your carefully planned displays in the rest of the garden.

Cutting Garden Basics

Few people have enough space to put a cutting garden truly out of sight, but the more removed it is, the less you'll worry about making it look nice. Some gardeners turn over a corner of their vegetable garden to cut flowers; others create separate cutting beds along a garage, in a sunny side area or in a sheltered corner of the back garden.

Wherever you put your cutting beds, you want them to be easy to reach and maintain. Prepare the soil well, sow seeds or set out transplants just as you would for any garden, but don't worry about grouping specific heights and colours; just plant them in rows. Mulch between the rows with a loose organic material (such as straw) to discourage weeds, keep the soil moist and prevent soil from splashing up on the flowers. Stake floppy or long-stemmed flowers – including peonies, baby's breath and delphiniums – to keep the stems upright and the flowers clean.

The daisy-like blooms of asters and orange coneflowers add bright colour and dramatic form to any arrangement.

If you don't want to set aside an area just for cut flowers, you can snip blooms from beds and borders as needed.

subtle greens and silvers to emphasise individual flowers or colours; variegated leaves make striking accents.

To add extra excitement to your arrangements, include perennials, annuals, grasses and hardy bulbs in your cutting garden. Cosmos, snapdragon, larkspur (*Consolida ambigua*) and calendula (*Calendula officinalis*) are a few of the easy-to-grow annuals that are wonderful for fresh arrangements. Ornamental grasses are great for both flowers and foliage. Spray their delicate flowers with lacquer or cheap hairspray to make them last longer.

Collecting Cut Flowers

Taking a little extra care when you collect your flowers and foliage will help them look great over a longer period. In the cool of the morning, harvest flowers that haven't fully opened using sharp clippers or a knife; immediately plunge the stems into a bucket of warm water. As you arrange the flowers: cut the stems to their final lengths under water so no air bubbles enter. Remove leaves that will be below the waterline in the finished arrangement.

After arranging your flowers, fill the vase to the top with water; refill as soon as the level drops. Add a shot of lemonade or a commercial floral preservative to keep the water fresh. Flowers will last longest in a cool room out of direct light.

Annuals for Cutting

As you decide which annuals you'll grow for cutting, keep in mind that some thrive in the heat of summer while others prefer cooler temperatures. Plan to sow some each of early-, mid- and late summer flowers to have a steady supply of blooms. Following is a list of some suitable annuals and perennials for cutting, along with their normal peak bloom season.

Annuals

Antirrhinum majus (snapdragon; midsummer)
Calendula officinalis (pot marigold; early summer)

Choosing Plants for Cutting

Choose plants that will thrive in your growing conditions; if they aren't growing well, they won't produce many flowers. Here are some other things you'll want to consider when you're deciding what plants to include:

- If space is limited, concentrate on growing plants in your favourite flower colours; if you have lots of room, plant a variety of colours to have lots of options.
- Grow plants that have different shapes to keep your arrangements from looking monotonous. Include spiky flowers and foliage for height, flat or round flowers and leaves for mass, and small, airy flowers and leaves for fillers.
- Look for flowers with long stems. Cultivars described as dwarf or compact are great for ornamental plantings, but their stems are usually too short for easy arranging, unless you have small vases.
- For extra special arrangements, include some fragrant flowers.
- Don't forget to include foliage – it adds body and filler to arrangements. Use

Callistephus chinensis (China aster; midsummer)
Celosia cristata (cockscomb; late summer)
Centaurea cyanus (cornflower; midsummer)
Consolida ambigun (rocket larkspur; midsummer)
Cosmos bipinnatus (cosmos; late summer)
Cosmos sulphureus (yellow cosmos; midsummer)
Dianthus barbatus (sweet William; early summer)
Gaillardia pulchella (blanket flower; midsummer)
Gypsophila elegans (annual baby's breath; early summer)
Helianthus annuus (common sunflower; late summer)
Iberis umbellata (annual candy tuft; early summer)
Lathyrus odoratus (sweet pea; early summer)
Matthiola incana (stock; early summer)
Rudbeckia hirta (black-eyed Susan; midsummer)
Tithonia rotundifolia (Mexican sunflower; late summer)
Viola x *wittrockiana* (pansy; early summer)
Zinnia elegans (zinnia; midsummer)

Perennials

Achillea filipendulina (fern-leaved yarrow; summer)
Alchemilla mollis (lady's mantle; early summer)
Aster novae-angliae (New England aster; late summer)
Astrantia major (masterwort; midsummer)
Baptisia australis (blue false indigo; early summer)
Boltonia asteroides (boltonia; late summer)
Chrysanthemum x *superbum* (shasta daisy; summer)
Delphinium x *belladonna* (belladonna delphinium; summer)
Dictamnus albus (gas plant; early summer)
Echinacea purpurea (purple coneflower; midsummer)
Helenium autumnale (common sneezeweed; late summer)
Heuchera sanguinea (coral bells; summer)

Iris spp. (irises; early summer)
Liatris spicata (spike gayfeather; midsummer)
Lilium hybrids (lilies; summer)
Monarda didyma (bee balm; summer)
Narcissus hybrids (daffodils; spring)
Nepeta x *faass enii* (catmint; early summer)
Phlox paniculata (garden phlox; midsummer)
Physostegia virginiana (obedient plant; late summer)
Platycodon grandiflorus (balloon flower; summer)
Rudbeckia fulgida (orange coneflower; midsummer)
Salvia x *superba* (violet sage; midsummer)
Scabiosa caucasica (pincushion flower; summer)
Thermopsis caroliniana (Carolina lupin; early summer)

Easy Everlasting Flowers

'Everlasting' annuals, which include strawflowers and statice, produce papery flowers or showy seedpods that hold their colour when they dry. They can be used in either fresh or dried arrangements, although most people grow them specifically with drying in mind.

For best results, pick flowers for drying in the morning, before they are fully open and when the dew has dried. To keep the stems straight and stiff for easy arranging, separate them into groups of six to eight stems, secure the stems with a rubber band and hang them upside down. A dark, dry place, such as a garage, shed or attic is best, as these conditions help to preserve the colours. Hang the bunches from a clothes-drying rack or from lines strung between the rafters.

Best Annuals for Drying

Ammobium alatum (winged everlasting)
Carthamus tinctorius (safflower)
Celosia cristata (cockscomb)
Gomphrena globosa (globe amaranth)
Helichrysum bracteatum (*Xerochrysum bracteatum*) (strawflower)
Helipterum mangelsii (Swan River everlasting)
Limonium sinuatum (annual statice)
Lunaria annua (honesty)
Molucella laevis (bells of Ireland)
Nigella damascena (love-in-a-mist)
Scabiosa stellata (drumstick flower)
Xeranthemum annuum (immortelle)

Gardening with Fragrance

Plants with fragrant leaves and flowers have a place in any landscape. There's nothing like the fresh scent of mint to perk you up after a long day at the office. And who could resist resting on a cosy garden bench near a patch of peonies in full, fragrant bloom? A pot or window box of basil in the kitchen not only scents

Strawflowers are great for cutting gardens, since you can use them in either fresh or dried arrangements.

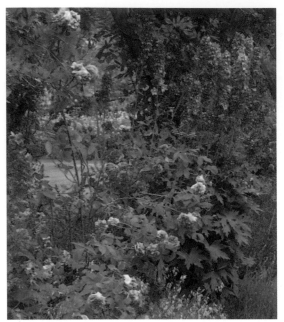

Heady-scented roses are a classic part of a fragrance garden. Combine them with perennials for extra colour.

the air, but keeps insects away as well. In beds, borders, cottage gardens, container gardens and foundation plantings, mixing in some scented plants will add an extra special touch to your garden.

Fragrance in Flowers

When you mention fragrance in the garden, most people automatically think of flowers. Peonies and lilies are probably the most well known, but many other plants have pleasing scents as well.

Traditionally, scented flowers were grown close to the house so their fragrance could be appreciated through open doors and windows. They're equally nice near outdoor eating areas, patios and porches – any place where people linger. Raised planters are great for short, fragrant flowers so you don't have to get down on your hands and knees to enjoy the scents.

Many fragrant flowers are also beautiful, so you can enjoy looking at them and sniffing them as you walk around or work in the garden. Cutting these flowers for arrangements brings this pleasure indoors.

Fragrance in Foliage

A number of plants have fragrant foliage, but you need to touch these to smell them. Plant lavender and bee balm (*Monarda didyma*) at the edge of paths where you'll brush against them as you walk by. Grow lemon balm (*Melissa officinalis*) near a garden seat or in a raised container so you can easily rub the leaves to release their delicious lemony odour. Some plants, like wormwood (*Artemisia absinthium*) and rue (*Ruta graveolens*), have leaves with a pungent scent that some people find pleasing and others find disagreeable; try sniffing these plants before you buy.

Buying and Growing Fragrant Plants

The real key to having a scented garden that you enjoy is smelling plants before you buy them. The fragrance that a friend raves about may be undetectable or even unpleasant to you. Visit nurseries or public gardens when the plants you want are flowering, and sniff the flowers or foliage to see what you think. Different cultivars of the same plant may vary widely in their scents, so smell them all before you choose.

Just as a bed of many different flower colours can look jumbled, a mixture of many strong fragrances can be distracting or even downright repulsive. As you plan your garden, try to arrange it with just one or two scented plants in bloom at any given time. That way, you can enjoy different fragrances all through the season without being overwhelmed by too many at once. Some plants release their scent only at night and they can be overpowering, particularly on hot summer nights, so try to sniff them several times at night before you decide to buy them for your garden.

Favourite Fragrant Annuals

Cheiranthus cheiri (wallflower)
Dianthus barbatus (sweet William)
Dianthus chinensis (China pink)
Heliotropium arborescens (common heliotrope)
Ipomoea alba (moonflower)
Lathyrus odoratus (sweet pea)
Lobularia maritima (sweet alyssum)
Matthiola incana (stock)
Mirabilis jalapa (four o'clock)
Nicotiana alata (flowering tobacco)
Petunia x *hybrida* (petunia)
Tagetes hybrids (marigolds)

Perennials for Fragrance

There are perennials with fragrant and unfragrant cultivars. This list includes the names of a few of the fragrant ones.
Convallaria majalis (lily of the valley): flowers
Dianthus gratianopolitanus (Cheddar pinks): flowers
Hemerocallis hybrids (daylilies): flowers of a few (mainly yellow) types
Lavandula angustifolia (lavender): leaves and flowers
Lilium hybrids (lilies): flowers of some types, including regal lilies, trumpet hybrids and oriental hybrids (such as 'Casa Blanca'), and *L. speciosum* 'Rubrum'
Narcissus hybrids (daffodils): flowers of some cultivars, including 'Geranium', 'Cragford' , 'Actaea', 'Minnow', 'Baby Moon', 'Pipit' and 'Cheerfulness'
Nepeta x *faassenii* (catmint): leaves
Paeonia lactiflora (common garden peony): flowers of some cultivars, including 'Festiva Maxima', 'Pink Parfait', 'Sarah Bernhardt', 'Edulis Superba' and 'Big Ben'

Lily of the valley

A mixture of bulbs, perennials, annuals and grasses creates a cheerful meadow garden scene with little maintenance.

Making a Meadow

Natural gardens combine the beauty of local wildflowers with an informal, often low-maintenance, design. The most popular of these are meadow gardens – informal blends of flowers and grasses growing in a sunny, open spot. They provide food and shelter for birds, beneficial insects and butterflies. They also add a casual, country touch to any garden. Best of all, established meadows require little upkeep.

If you don't have room for a whole meadow, you can create a meadow look in a smaller garden by using plenty of reliable cultivated perennials and mixing in meadow flowers and grasses among them. Common perennials that are natural choices for most meadow gardens include butterfly weed (*Asclepias tuberosa*), New England aster (*Aster novae-angliae*), purple coneflower (*Echinacea purpurea*) and bee balm (*Monarda didyma*). Look in wildflower gardening books or check with local wildflower societies to find out which plants grow best in your area.

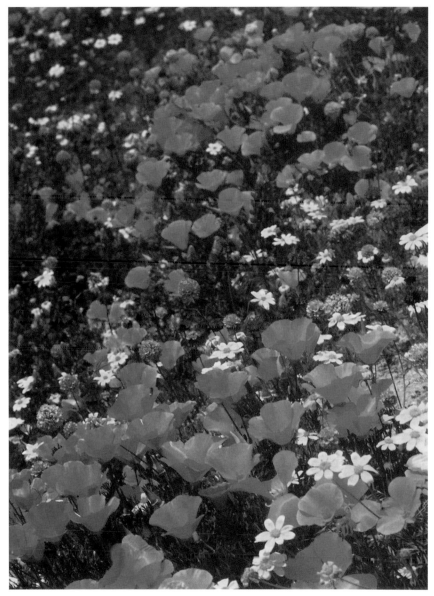

If lawn mowing is a chore you dread, consider replacing at least part of the grass with wildflowers. Once you get them established, a few hours weeding every year and an annual mowing will keep them looking good.

Steps to a Great-Looking Meadow

Once you've chosen the plants that will be in your meadow, you'll need to help them gain a roothold by preparing a good seedbed. You can't just scatter seed in a lawn or open piece of ground and expect good results.

1. Pick a site with well-drained soil and at least six hours of sun a day.
2. In spring, summer or autumn, remove existing grasses and aggressive weeds; lawn grasses can spread vigorously and smother small, new plants. Skim off slices of turf with a spade. Compost the

pieces of sod you remove or use them to fill holes in the remaining lawn.

3. Spread 2.5 to 5 cm (1 to 2 inches) of compost over the area, and dig or till it into the top 10 to 15 cm (4 to 6 inches) of soil. Use a rake to remove any rocks and smooth the soil.

4. To reduce the bank of weed seeds in the soil, water the area thoroughly to encourage surface weed seeds to sprout, then rake or hoe shallowly to kill the seedlings. Repeat the process several times before planting. Or use mulch instead of watering and hoeing; cover the area with black plastic or at least 12 layers of newspaper.

5. In autumn, set out your meadow perennials, grasses and bulbs, and mulch them well. By spring, the roots will be well established and your plants will be ready to put on great growth.

6. In spring, if you wish, rake away some mulch to sow annual wildflower seeds between the perennial meadow plants. Annuals will provide quick colour the first year while the perennials are getting established.

7. Through the first growing season, water your meadow when the top 2.5 to 5 cm (1 to 2 inches) of soil is dry to help the growing young plants get established.

Routine Meadow Maintenance

Mow your meadow once a year to keep it looking good and to keep weeds, shrubs and trees from invading. Late autumn to early winter, after plants have formed seeds, is the best time. If you want to feed the birds, leave seed heads standing until late winter or early spring; just be aware that they'll be harder to mow after winter rain and snow have beaten them down.

Cut the whole meadow to a height of about 15 cm (6 inches). Use a sickle-bar mower for large areas; a string trimmer or hand shears can handle small patches. A regular lawn mower won't work; it cuts too low. Leave trimmings in place so plants can self-sow or collect them for your compost pile.

Aside from the yearly trim, your only maintenance is to dig out tree seedlings and aggressive weeds such as couch grass, bindweed, stinging nettles and burdock as soon as they appear. Established meadows don't require water, fertiliser or mulch. As the plants get established, your meadow garden will look different each year, but it will always be beautiful.

Marvellous Meadow Perennials

The recipe for a magnificent meadow includes a blend of tough perennial flowers and non-invasive perennial grasses, with a dash of daffodils and other naturalised spring bulbs for early colour. Below you'll find some suggested flowers you can consider for your moist or dry site, along with some great meadow grasses.

Perennials for Dry Meadows

Achillea filipendulina (fern-leaved yarrow)
Asclepias tuberosa (butterfly weed)
Baptisia australis (blue false indigo)
Echirtacea purpurea (purple coneflower)
Gaillardia x *grandiflora* (blanket flower)
Helianthus x *multiflorus* (perennial sunflower)
Liatris spicata (spike gayfeather)
Oenothera tetragona (evening primrose)
Rudbeckia fulgida (orange coneflower)
Solidago rigida (stiff goldenrod)

Perennials for Moist Meadows

Aster novae-angliae (New England aster)
Chelone glabra (white turtlehead)
Eupatorium maculatum (spotted Joe Pye weed)
Eupatorium rugosum (white snakeroot)
Filipendula rubra (queen of the prairie)
Helenium autumnale (common sneezeweed)
Lobelia cardinalis (cardinal flower)

Meadow and woodland gardens are excellent options for brightening up out-of-the-way corners.

Physostegia virginiana (obedient plant)
Thermopsis caroliniana (Carolina lupin)

Great Grasses for Meadows

Andropogon virginicus (broom sedge)
Bouteloua curtipendula (side oats grama grass)
Festuca spp. (fescues)
Schizachyrium scoparium (little bluestem)
Sporobolus heterolepis (prairie dropseed)

Woodland Gardens

Take advantage of any shade to create a woodland garden. To brighten the area in early spring (before the trees come into leaf and shade the area), try early-flowering woodland wildflowers like wood anemone (*Anemone nemorosa*), wild columbine (*Aquilegia canadensis*), Virginia bluebell (*Mertensia virginica*) and common bleeding heart (*Dicentra spectabilis* syn. *Lamprocapnos spectabilis*). To extend the season of interest, add ferns and shade-tolerant perennials that retain their handsome foliage all season. These include hostas, lungwort (*Pulmonaria saccharata*), Lenten rose (*Helleborus orientalis*), Siberian bugloss (*Brunnera macrophylla*) and Solomon's seal (*Polygonatum odoratum*).

Plant your rock garden with flowers and foliage plants to add year-round interest and splashes of seasonal colour.

A bog garden is a great site for many kinds of irises. The flowers are beautiful in early summer, and the spiky leaves look great all season.

Rock Gardens

Some plants are particularly attractive grouped among rocks in a wall or rock garden. They grow best in full sun and soils that have exceptionally good drainage and low fertility. Some, such as perennial candytuft (*Iberis sempervirens*), wall rock cress (*Arabis caucasica*) and basket of gold (*Aurinia saxatilis*), cascade gracefully over the rock surface. Others, like the more petite Labrador violets (*Viola labradorica*) and primroses (*Primula* spp.), as well as a host of unusual alpine plants, nestle between the rocks. All of these plants are delightful choices for planting on rocky slopes, in raised beds or in dry stone retaining walls.

Bog Gardens

Some plants have an affinity for wet ground and will thrive at the edge of a pond or in boggy or marshy areas. Plants for low, moist areas include Japanese iris (*Iris ensma*), goat's beard (*Aruncus dioicus*), marsh marigold (*Caltha palustris*) and cardinal flower (*Lobelia cardinalis*).

If you do not have a naturally wet area but enjoy the beauty of bog plants, you can create your own bog. Dig a trench at least 30 cm (12 inches) deep and line it with a heavy plastic pond liner. Put a soaker hose on the top of the plastic and refill the trench with humus-rich soil. The open end of the hose should protrude slightly so that you can attach it to your garden hose and fill the 'bog' with water. Repeat as necessary to keep the soil moist.

Container Gardens

If you live in a high-rise apartment building where you have no ground for a garden, you can create a lush green oasis with container-grown plants on a tiny balcony or outdoor stairway. City dwellers can grow large gardens entirely in containers on building rooftops. Even if you have nothing but a wall and windows to call your own, you can fill hanging baskets with trailing plants and pack window boxes full of flowers, herbs and vegetables.

Annuals make perfect container plants. They grow quickly, flower profusely and provide a long season of good looks.

A large container can support a pleasing mixture of bushy and trailing plants.

Some also offer distinctive foliage, while others perfume the air with their sweet scents. Groups of small- and medium-sized containers create charming spots of movable colour; large planters can showcase a stunning mix of colourful flowers in a relatively small space. Window boxes and hanging baskets are other options for displaying a wide range of flowering and foliage annuals.

Wonderful Window Boxes

Nothing adds country charm to a house like lush window boxes dripping with cascades of colourful flowers and foliage. While the general principles of container planting apply here, there are a few special tips to keep in mind to plan and maintain great-looking window boxes.

Treasure flower

- Consider the site. Before you put up any window boxes, make sure you'll be able to reach them easily for watering and maintenance. Also check that the ledges or brackets that hold the window box are strong enough for the purpose. Because window boxes are so visible, it's especially important to keep them well groomed; that means regularly removing spent flowers.
- Stick with short plants. Window boxes are usually planted to be seen from the outside, but you also need to consider the view from the inside. It's generally best to stick with plants no taller than about 20 cm (8 inches); those much taller than that can block your view.
- Choose compatible colours. Look for flower and foliage colours that complement those of the house and trim. Silvers and whites look crisp and cool against warm-toned brick, for instance, while blues and purples look pretty against cream colours, and pinks and yellows add life to sombre grey cladding.

Creating Your Garden

*This is the hands-in-the-soil part of gardening, the ongoing,
regular garden maintenance that separates the
gardening dilettante from the gardener for life.
It is the essence of good gardening.*

Buying and Selecting Plants

For many people, choosing and buying plants is one of the most pleasurable aspects of creating a new garden. In the frenzy of shopping, it's easy to get carried away and go home with lots of plants you don't really need. But with a little preparation, you can take your time and get the right plant at the right price.

Begin your search in the depths of winter by browsing through the colourful and informative mail-order catalogues. Make a list of plants that appeal to you and that will suit your growing conditions. When the planting season comes, go shopping at plant sales, nurseries, garden centres and greenhouses.

There are a few common temptations to avoid. First of all, don't fall for every pretty flower. A plant blooming in the protected environment of a greenhouse may be lovely, but its beauty does not tell you whether it is prone to problems or whether it will be suited to your garden conditions. If you see a plant you love but know little about, take a 24-hour cooling-off period. Do a little research on its preferred growing conditions, seasonal appearance and potential problems. If you find it will grow well in the conditions your garden has to offer, determine if you have a place for it.

Second, use the same frame of mind to shop for plants as you would to expand your wardrobe. When you need a new shirt or skirt, you look for one that fits with the rest of your clothes. Likewise, buy only those plants that will work in your garden plans. If you like a little garden spontaneity, leave openings here and there for trial plants.

Finally, if you simply cannot resist buying or saving every plant that catches your eye, perhaps you are a candidate for a casual cottage garden rather than a more formal perennial bed or border.

Buying Healthy Plants

One of the most basic steps in preventing pest and disease problems is starting with healthy, pest-free plants. They'll become established in their new home quickly, and

When you combine plants that have similar needs, it's easy to provide the right care to keep them in top condition.

you'll avoid importing pests and plant pathogens that could spread to other plants in your garden.

Start with a Strategy

Problem prevention begins long before the growing season starts. When you're making up your list of possible plants from seed catalogues and garden books, look for plants with resistance to the pests and diseases that occur locally.

Consider the Container

Some vegetable seedlings, like courgettes and cucumbers, and herbs, like dill and parsley, don't transplant well. Look for seedlings growing in peat pots. At planting time, you can plant the whole seedling, pot and all; that way, you'll avoid disturbing the root system. Otherwise, the shock of transplanting can weaken these plants and make them more susceptible to disease and pest attack.

TOP: Gently slide a plant from its pot to check the roots before buying. Avoid plants with massed or circling roots.
BOTTOM: Good-quality plants will have healthy white roots that are still growing through the soil ball.

Inspect the Root System

Strong, healthy roots are a vital part of determining plant health. If a plant is growing in a plastic or clay container, gently remove the container and look at the roots. Roots should penetrate the soil without circling the outside of the root ball. They should be uniformly white, moist and without breaks, bumps or brown spots. Several exposed roots don't indicate stress, but avoid plants with lots of matted roots or plants that are tightly rooted to their neighbours. These plants have been sitting around for a long time in a small pot, and separating closely rooted plants can severely damage the individual root systems. It shocks the young plants and can set them back by several weeks as they grow new roots.

Check the soil, too. It should be evenly moist, or at least moist just below the surface. Plants that are allowed to dry out frequently become stressed and weakened, and their growth may be stunted.

Check Plant Colour

Healthy seedlings are usually deep green, although you can expect colour to vary among plants and cultivars. An overall pale, washed-out appearance often indicates that a nutrient is lacking. If you're not sure what a particular plant is supposed to look like, compare it with a photo from a book or catalogue. This will help you determine if those stripes, spots or colours are normal or if they indicate a deficiency of some kind.

Probe for Problems

Examine plants carefully before you buy them and reject any with signs of pests or their damage. As you inspect the foliage, make sure you turn the leaves over and check their undersides as well as the tops; lower leaf surfaces are favourite pest hideouts. Common signs of insect and other pest damage include:

- Leaves with chewed holes or edges
- Shiny slime trails
- Webs on leaves or stems
- Tiny eggs on leaves or stems
- Brown or greenish droppings
- Wilted, curled or discoloured leaves.

Don't forget to look for signs of diseases during your inspection. Also look at other plants growing in the same area – if they are showing signs of disease, another plant that looks healthy may already be infected. Common symptoms of

disease, nutrient deficiency or environmental damage include:

- Spotty, discoloured or wilted leaves
- Dead areas in leaves or stems
- Fuzzy patches of fungal spores
- Leaves, roots or stems with a soggy appearance.

How to Buy Plants

A good local nursery or garden centre – one that offers a variety of plants and takes good care of them – is a real treasure. Usually its staff members are good sources of information specific to your area, such as which plants grow well there. The nursery may even have a demonstration garden where you can see how plants look when fully grown and compare different cultivars.

Advantages and Disadvantages

One advantage of buying locally is that you can inspect plants before buying them. Also, your plants won't have to suffer through shipping. Most nurseries and garden centres offer container-grown plants, which are easiest to handle. On the down side, your selection may be limited in colour and variety, and the plants may be more expensive.

Buying Tips

When you have a choice, select small, vigorous-looking plants; they'll grow faster and soon outpace larger, already-flowering plants. While it's fun to see what flowers you're getting (and sometimes you'll want to make sure you get just the right colour), it's generally better to buy and plant perennials before they flower. That way, they can settle into the garden and establish new roots before they use their energy for flowering.

With bulbs, purchase the largest size you can afford for flower beds and borders. Smaller-sized bulbs are great for naturalising in lawns and low-maintenance areas, and you can sometimes buy quantities of 50 or 100 at a reduced price. Choose bulbs that are plump and firm with no soft spots or mouldy areas.

Buying by Post

If you want unusual plants, don't have access to a local nursery or want to get the best possible prices, mail-order sources provide limitless possibilities. Request catalogues several months before you want to plant so you'll have time to compare selections and prices. Some catalogues are

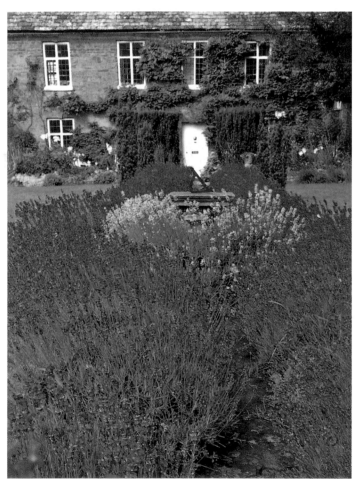

If you begin with healthy plants your garden has a better chance of being pest- and disease-resistant.

great sources of information on the virtues of specific plants and cultivars; a few even have colour photos and useful planting and growing information.

Advantages and Disadvantages

Catalogue shopping is a fun way to while away dreary winter evenings, and it's convenient, too. You can learn about exciting new plants and often find good prices when you compare several catalogues. On the down side, you don't really know what you're paying for until you get it. Shipping stress can weaken even the strongest plants. If you get bare-root perennials (with roots that are wrapped in packing material), they'll need to be planted or potted up immediately.

Buying Tips

The best approach to ordering by mail is to ask gardening friends which catalogues they've ordered from and which they would buy from again. If you don't know anyone who orders by catalogue, visit a library and get addresses and phone numbers from advertisements in recent gardening magazines.

When you order from a source for the first time, just buy a few plants and see how they look. If you're happy with the quality for the price, order more; otherwise, shop elsewhere. Remember, if an offer sounds too good to be true, it probably is!

Inspect mail-order plants as soon as they arrive. If they are damaged, you should return them; contact the source right away to find out how to do so. Mail-order perennials are often shipped when they are dormant (not actively growing) and may look dead. Plant them anyway and water them well. If they don't produce any buds or new growth in a few weeks, contact the source.

If your plants were shipped in pots, water as needed and keep them out of bright sunlight for the first few days. Mail-order plants may also arrive bare-rooted – without any pot or soil. If they're bulbs, they're happy that way; keep them cool and in the dark until you're ready to plant. Other bare-root plants need more attention; for best results, plant them within a day or two after they arrive. If you can't plant right away, keep the packing material moist – not soggy – and store the plants in a cool, shaded place. If there isn't any packing material, soak the roots in room-temperature water for an hour or two, then wrap with damp paper towels or cover with compost.

Different Ways to Buy Plants

There are several ways to buy plants – container-grown, containerised, bare-root, field-dug and root-balled. Each method has advantages and disadvantages. The planting techniques you use will depend on the way the plants were grown and sold. Whatever type you buy, keep plants protected from wind and sun when you transport them home.

Container-Grown Plants

Perennials, shrubs and climbers are most commonly sold in containers. Container-grown plants are convenient and easy to handle. Keep the pots in a well-lit location until you are ready to plant, then you can slide the root ball out and plant it in the garden. The transition will cause minimal disturbance.

However, there is a catch. Horticultural researchers are finding that roots tend to stay in the light, fluffy 'soil' of synthetic mixes, rather than branching out into the surrounding garden soil. But you can prevent this from happening by loosening the roots on the outside of the ball and spreading them out into the soil as you plant.

Container-grown plants come in different sizes, so their prices vary widely. Larger-sized pots, usually 4.5- to 9-litre (1-to 2-gallon) containers, are generally more expensive. The cost may be worthwhile if you need immediate garden impact. On the other hand, you can buy younger plants inexpensively in multi-cell packs or small pots. You'll have to wait a year or more for them to fill out and bloom, but young plants tend to become established in the garden faster than older ones, catching up to the bigger plants in a short time. Often, too, they grow into healthier, more vigorous specimens than larger transplants.

Your local garden centre will sell a wide variety of colourful plants, but mail-order sources will have even more uncommon kinds.

Bare-root Plants

You will come across many species of dormant bare-root plants for sale early in the growing season. Bare-root trees should be bought and planted from late autumn to early spring. In late summer or early autumn, you can also find bare root items such as bearded irises, common bleeding heart (*Dicentra spectabilis* syn. *Lamprocapnos spectabilis*), peonies and oriental poppies. You may choose to buy bare-root plants to save money – they are usually less expensive than large container-grown plants – or you may receive them unexpectedly. Mail-order companies often send plants bare-root to save on space and shipping. You open the box to find long spidery roots and – at best – a small tuft of foliage. These plants look more dead than alive, but fortunately, in this case looks are deceiving. If you keep the roots moist and cool and plant them quickly and properly, most plants will recover and thrive. The roots will easily adjust to your garden's soil, whereas the roots of container-grown plants have to make the transition from the nursery soil to yours.

Most deciduous trees, shrubs and climbers can be successfully grown from bare-root stock. Don't buy large trees or any evergreens bare-root; their roots can dry out easily, causing damage that's very hard to overcome.

When the plants arrive, open the box to let some air in. Your plants' roots should be wrapped in a protective medium like shredded newspaper, wood shavings or sphagnum moss. Keep this medium moist but not soggy. When it's time to plant, soak the roots in a bucket of lukewarm water for a few hours, then plant. If you can't plant right away, keep the roots moist and store them, in their original package, in a cool location for a day or two. If you need to wait longer than that to plant, pot up the roots or set them into a nursery bed until you are ready. Trees should be temporarily 'heeled in' by laying them along a shallow trench in a shady, protected area and covering their roots with soil.

Containerised Plants

Not to be confused with container-grown plants, containerised or processed-balled plants are initially dug bare-rooted. Their roots are then packed or potted in organic matter or potting medium, not field soil. As with bare-root stock, most of the roots are left behind in the field. When you buy, check inside the packing or slip the pot off and look for new roots. If all you find are a few large, cut roots but no fine, small roots, don't buy the plant. The nursery didn't hold it long enough for new roots to grow and the plant will be slow to establish.

Big or Little?

In general, the smaller the plant, the less transplant shock it will undergo. It will begin putting out new roots and leaves sooner than larger plants and may quickly catch up in size. But what if you want to establish a garden quickly? Buy the largest plants you can afford and properly handle, or, in the case of large trees and shrubs, have the nursery plant them. Many nurseries offer warranties on plants that they install.

Container-grown plants should have healthy top growth that is in proportion to the container. You can plant them anytime during the growing season.

Field-Dug Plants

You may be able to find a farmer, hobbyist plant breeder, plant collector or nursery owner who will sell you mature plants dug from the field. If you handle the root ball carefully, you can move field-dug plants much later into the summer than bare-root plants because the roots are protected by soil. To transport it, set the root ball, surrounded by soil, in a firm wooden tray or sturdy bucket. Cover it with a moist towel, damp peat moss or compost to keep the roots and soil moist. Replant it as soon as possible.

Root-Balled Plants

These are field-dug plants, usually larger trees and shrubs, with a ball of soil around the roots. The soil ball is wrapped in natural hessian or synthetic material. They are wrapped in this way either because they resent being transplanted bare-rooted, or so that you can plant them even when they are not dormant. Root-balled plants are often the most expensive, and the soil ball makes them heavier to handle. Be sure the root ball is large enough to support and anchor your plant. Properly handled root balls should be well wrapped, firm and moist. Avoid lifting root-balled plants by by the trunk, and handle them carefully or the root ball might break apart and damage the roots. Keep them in the shade, covered thickly with mulch, and water often until you plant.

Since root-balled stock comes with soil, plants have to make the transition from the nursery soil to yours. The difference in soil type can cause uneven water distribution, so water deeply and check the soil moisture regularly. There is no need to remove the hessian wrapping.

Preparing for Planting

When to Start

If you can, prepare planting areas at least a month before you plant to give soil time to settle. Ideally, start in the autumn for spring planting, or in spring for autumn planting.

Start digging when the soil is moist, but not wet. Digging moist soil is relatively easy, but dry soil requires extra effort, and working soil that's soggy can turn it into rock-like lumps. After two or three days without rain, dig up a shovelful in a couple of different spots and test for moisture by squeezing a handful of soil. If the soil oozes through your fingers or forms a sticky lump, it's too wet; wait a few days and repeat the test before digging. If the soil is dry and powdery or hard, water the area thoroughly and wait a day or two to dig.

Time your planting efforts so your new plants will start growing in a period of abundant rainfall and moderate temperatures – usually spring or autumn. Check planting instructions on the plant label and refer to the plant hardiness zone maps on pages 310–11 to find out what climate zone you live in.

Preparing the Planting Bed

Along with proper plant selection, preparing a good planting bed is critical to the success of your garden. If you do a thorough job here, you will be rewarded by quicker plant establishment and less weeding.

Making New Beds

First layout the area you want to dig, as determined in your garden plan. Use stakes and string for marking the straight sides; lay out curves with a rope or garden hose. Step back and double-check the layout from several viewpoints, including indoors.

Next, remove existing grass and weeds. Slice off manageable pieces of turf by cutting small squares, then sliding your spade just under the roots. Toss the turf into the compost pile or use it to repair bare spots in your lawn. As an alternative, you can kill the grass by covering it with black plastic. It's unattractive, but effective. However, it can take several weeks or more than a month depending on the weather – the hotter it is outside the faster the plastic works. Till in the turf when it has decayed. Pull out as many weed roots as you can. You may have to follow those like docks (*Rumex* spp.) and bindweeds (*Convolvulus* spp.) for quite some distance to get the entire root

1. To prepare a new bed, start by outlining the edge with rope or string.
2. Use a spade to strip off the turf and expose the soil.
3. If a soil test indicates the site is too acid, apply an even layer of lime to the soil.
4. Spread a layer of compost over the surface and work it into the bed.

system. If you merely snap off the top, the root will probably resprout.

Once you've cleared the beds, it's time to break up the soil. Consider your choice of tools carefully. Decades ago, gardeners turned the soil with shovels, garden spades, forks and other hand tools. In recent years, many have turned to rotary tillers. These machines can churn the top 12.5 to 15 cm (5 to 6 inches) of soil with much less effort on your part. However, tillers aren't always the best choice. Excessive tilling, or tilling when the soil is too wet or too dry, will break up the granular soil structure into tiny particles and lead to soil compaction. If you choose to use a rotary tiller, make sure you work the soil when it's evenly moist. If you're using a spade or shovel, dig down as far as your spade will reach and turn over this top layer of the soil. For even better results, double dig the bed. Double digging loosens the soil to twice the depth of single digging, providing ideal conditions for great root growth and helping to correct heavy or poorly drained soil.

Once your soil is loose, mix in fertiliser to feed the plants, and organic matter to condition the soil. Any balanced organic fertiliser will do. Scatter the fertiliser over the planting area at the application rate listed on the label.

Now spread a very thick layer of organic matter over the entire area. It should be at least 10 cm (4 inches) deep to be effective. If your soil feels as loose as a kid's sandpit (indicating drainage that's too fast) or if puddles always remain after a rain (indicating poor drainage), add even more organic matter. Use less if you want to grow yarrows, artemisias and other plants that grow best in dry, sunny sites.

Dealing with Problem Soils

Planting naturally well-adapted species is the best way to handle problem soils, particularly those with slow drainage. Building raised beds and filling them with improved soil is an option for shallow-rooted plants. But the roots of trees and many shrubs will soon outgrow the beds. If your soil is extremely sandy or clayey, save your raised beds for flowers and vegetables, and choose species of trees, shrubs and climbers that are compatible with your soil conditions.

Compost is the best source of organic matter; if you don't have enough, you may be able to buy more at your local garden centre. Leaves are excellent, too; run the lawn mower over piles to chop them first or mix them with grass clippings. Sawdust and straw are good if you also add a source of nitrogen (in the form of manure or dried blood) to help them decompose. Manure alone is fine but can contain many weed seeds. Whichever material you choose, mix it well into the top 20 cm (8 inches) of soil.

After digging in the fertiliser and organic matter, water the area thoroughly. Remember to let the soil sit for a month before planting to give the organic matter time to break down (unless you used well-decomposed compost, in which case you could plant right away). Rake just before planting to level the bed.

Double Digging for Great Plant Growth

Digging the top 20 cm (8 inches) or so of your soil will provide good growing conditions for most plants. But in many cases, digging twice as deep can give you twice the benefits. Double digging is a useful technique for breaking up compacted soil below the surface, improving drainage. It also provides twice the rooting room for deeper-rooted plants, like perennials. There's no doubt about it – double digging is a lot of work. Fortunately, the beneficial effects can last for years. And the strong, vigorous growth of your plants will more than repay the few hours of sweat you invested before planting.

Before digging, make sure the soil is at the right moisture level or you may end up

doing more harm than good. If the soil is too dry, soak the area and then wait a few days before digging. If you are preparing a new area, strip off the turf before double digging.

Start at one edge of the area by digging a 30-cm (1-foot) wide, 20- to 30-cm (8- to 12-inch) deep trench. Put the soil you are digging in a wheelbarrow. Spread a 2.5- to 5-cm (1- to 2-inch) layer of finely textured organic matter such as compost or aged manure over the newly exposed soil in the trench, then add any fertilisers or dressings the soil needs – perhaps lime or sulphur to adjust the pH, or maybe a source of phosphorus. Use a spading fork to loosen the subsoil by sticking the tines through the soil improvers and wiggling them in the soil.

Then step backwards to dig the second trench. Slide the soil from this 30-cm (1-foot) strip into the first trench, then work organic matter and amendments into the newly exposed bottom layer of soil. Repeat the process of moving a top layer and loosening the bottom layer until you get to the last strip. Cover the last bottom layer with the soil from the first trench in the wheelbarrow.

All that loosening and improving will raise the soil level a few inches. Give it a few weeks to settle before you plant, keeping it moistened in dry weather. Never walk directly on the loosened soil, or you'll undo all your hard work by compacting the soil. If you must step into the bed, lay broad boards over the bed, and walk on those instead; lift the boards when you're done.

TOP: In poor soil, double digging can help give your plants the best possible start in life.
BOTTOM: Compost bins can be attractive as well as functional – use locally available materials to make your own.

Making and Using Compost

Compost is the key to success in any kind of gardening. It is a balanced blend of recycled garden, garden and household

MAKING HOT, FAST COMPOST

1. Build your compost heap with equal amounts of high-carbon and high-nitrogen materials; add in layers or mix them up.

2. As you add new materials, sprinkle them with a watering can to keep them moist and to encourage decomposition.

3. Aerate the compost pile by turning it once every couple of days using a garden fork. This hastens the microbial activity.

wastes that have broken down into dark, crumbly organic matter. The time you spend making compost and applying it to your garden will be more than returned by improved soil and plant health.

Composting is the best way to dispose of garden and kitchen wastes, and it provides you with a free supply of organic fertiliser and soil conditioner at the same time. In addition, beneficial organisms present in finished compost may help to prevent some plant pathogens from infecting your plants in the garden.

Making compost is a lot like cooking – you mix together ingredients, stir them up and let them 'cook'. But with a compost pile, the source of heat isn't electricity or gas – it's decomposer organisms like bacteria and fungi that live in soil and break down dead plant and animal tissues. These organisms work best when given warmth, moisture, plenty of oxygen and the correct balance of carbon and nitrogen.

Composting can be fast and labour-intensive or slow and simple, depending on your needs and energy. You don't need any fancy materials to start composting-just a level, well-drained site. If you have lots of room and don't mind the appearance, you can have an uncontained heap. If you like things to be tidy, you can build a bin or pen out of wood, cement blocks or woven wire fencing, or you can buy an already-made bin. Besides keeping the compost materials in one neat pile, a container will help keep pets and wildlife out. Choose a shady, well-drained spot for your compost pile. For your convenience, put it as close to your garden as possible.

Ingredients

You can add a wide variety of materials to your compost. Vegetable scraps from the kitchen, grass clippings, fallen leaves and soft plant trimmings are all appropriate choices. If you have access to manure from animals like chickens, rabbits, cows or horses, you can add that also. There are some things you should avoid, including fats, bones and meat scraps, which can

attract scavengers to your pile. Also avoid composting manure from humans, dogs and cats – this material can carry disease organisms. Don't add infested or diseased plant material to your compost unless you are making a hot compost pile. Even then, the temperatures will not get high enough to kill some plant viruses. If you have virus-infected plants, bury them or place them in sealed containers for disposal with household rubbish.

Any kind of organic material will break down more quickly when it's already in small pieces. Use a leaf shredder or lawn mower to chop materials like leaves, hard stems, bark and twigs.

Hot, Fast Compost

Hot composting takes some work, but you'll get results quickly – sometimes as fast as two weeks. Plus, composting at high temperatures can kill pests, some plant pathogens and weed seeds that find their way into the pile.

The key to hot composting is getting a balance between high-carbon and high-nitrogen ingredients. High-nitrogen ingredients are green, sloppy materials like fresh grass clippings, kitchen scraps and manure. High-carbon ingredients include brown, woody materials like fallen leaves, straw and newspaper.

Build the pile by alternating layers of high-nitrogen materials with high-carbon materials. Use approximately equal volumes of each. If you are adding plants infested with pests or pathogens, place them in the middle where temperatures will get the hottest.

If your ingredients are fairly dry, sprinkle each layer with water as you work. The materials should be spongy moist, but not soggy. Make sure the finished pile is at least 3 feet (1 m) on each side – a smaller pile won't heat up as well and will take longer to break down.

A properly built hot compost pile will be warm to the touch in a day or two. Use a compost thermometer to monitor your pile's progress. The temperature inside the

Brew a Bucket of Compost Tea

Compost tea is a liquid fertiliser made by soaking compost in water. Put a shovelful of compost into a bag made of muslin or hessian. Tie the bag closed and suspend it in a dustbin, bucket or watering can filled with water. Keep it covered for a few days. Once it has steeped, use the liquid to drench the soil at the base of plants you want to fertilise. It's a particularly good way to fertilise container-grown plants. Or dilute the liquid with water until it is the colour of weak tea, then spray it on plant leaves. Because the nutrients are dissolved in water, the plants can take them up immediately for a quick burst of energy. (Reuse the 'tea bag' several times, then add the soaked compost to the garden.)

pile should stay near but below 71°C (160°F), since higher temperatures kill important decomposer organisms. When the pile cools off (in a few days), turning it should raise the temperature. Using a garden fork, invert the pile one forkful at a time just next to the original pile, fluffing it as you work. The more frequently you turn the pile, the more quickly it will break down. If the pile gets too hot, let it sit for a few days or add water to it.

Using this technique, you can have finished hot compost within two to six weeks. You'll know it's finished when the temperature stabilises and the individual materials are no longer recognisable.

Cold, Slow Compost

If you aren't in a hurry for finished compost, cold composting may be a good option for you. The most basic method is to simply pile together all the materials you have and let them sit for a year or more. Eventually, the pile will break down into usable compost.

For a slightly quicker version, build the pile following the directions for hot compost, then leave it for 6 to 12 months without turning.

A cold compost pile won't actually feel cold – it just won't get as warm as a hot pile. The temperatures in a cold pile won't be high enough to kill pests, pathogens or weed seeds, so don't add these materials to a cold pile.

Using Compost

Compost makes an excellent, disease-free medium for starting your own plants. Begin with compost from a hot pile, then let it rest for an additional 6 to 12 months. Shake the finished compost through 12-mm (½-inch) wire mesh to screen out large particles. Use the screened compost alone or mix it with potting ingredients like vermiculite.

In the garden, compost helps to improve soil structure and increases the soil's water-holding capacity. Spread 2.5 to 5 cm (1 to 2 inches) of finished compost over the surface of your garden each year. You can work the compost in or leave it on top as a mulch. Mixing compost into the soil distributes beneficial microorganisms that help to control soil-borne pests and diseases. As a fertiliser, homemade compost contains between 1 and 2 per cent each of nitrogen, phosphate and potash, plus small quantities of trace elements.

Enclosing Your Compost

It's not essential to enclose composting areas. You can simply heap garden leftovers up in a pile or spread them over empty garden beds to rot in place. But if you want to keep your compost neatly contained, you can enclose your pile in a bin. Commercially available barrels and bins look nice – some specially designed units may even help speed up the composting process – but they can be expensive to

buy. You can build your own three-sectioned bin with chicken wire tacked to timber framing. Make sure each section is about 90 to 120 cm (3 to 4 feet) high, wide and deep. Devote one bin to aged compost that is ready to use, another to half-cooked compost and the last to accumulating fresh scraps. Or use two or three plastic dustbins with the bottom cut out and air holes cut in the sides.

Compost Troubleshooting

If your compost pile isn't looking like it should, check the list below to see what the problem is.

- Pile doesn't heat up. Add more high-nitrogen material. If the pile is dry, add water. Try turning the pile to add more air.
- Pile smells bad. Add more high-carbon material. If the pile is too wet, turning may help to add more air.
- Finished compost is covered with seedlings. If your compost doesn't heat up enough, seeds of weeds and other plants may survive. Either avoid adding materials with seeds or put them in the centre of a hot compost pile.
- Material doesn't break down. Woody stems, prunings and dry leaves are often slow to break down; try shredding or chopping them into smaller pieces. Add more high-nitrogen ingredients to balance these high-carbon materials.

Circular woven wire bins are easy to make and use. The large stick helps direct water to the centre of the pile.

Basic Planting Techniques

Timing

For most of us, the garden year begins in the spring. A sudden spell of warm weather may have your fingers itching to dig and plant, but don't be too hasty – even cool-season crops will not grow in ice-encrusted soil. But if you wait for the right planting conditions and choose the right crops, you can start harvesting weeks before your neighbours.

How Soon Can You Plant?

There are two ways you can determine the right planting time for your area: by the temperature of the soil or by the last frost date. Monitor the soil warmth with a soil thermometer, and plant when the temperature is consistently at least 13°C (55°F) but less than 21°C (70°F). Alternatively, contact your local nursery or botanical garden to find out the average date of the last spring frost in your particular area. Then count back two to eight weeks, depending on what you're going to plant.

You can plant the hardiest of the cool-weather plants as soon as the soil is thawed and dry enough to work in spring. Less hardy plants should wait until two to four weeks before the last frost. If the weather seems exceptionally cold, wait a few days or a week to plant – most plants will grow much faster in a cool, rather than cold, soil.

Seeds or Seedlings?

Seeds are much cheaper than seedlings. A single packet of seeds can produce dozens or even hundreds of plants for a fraction of the cost of buying transplants. Sowing from seed also gives you a much greater variety of plants to choose from, since most retail sources only grow a few cultivars of the most popular plants. The disadvantage is, of course, that you have to wait for the seeds to germinate, so if you want a head start on your flowers, vegetable and herbs, it's best to buy them as seedlings.

Always use high-quality seed, packed for the current year. Buy from a reputable seed company that offers high germination rates. You can find out the rates from the percentage of viable (live) seeds listed on the package. If you have any seed left over from last year or home-collected seed, try sprouting a few before you sow a whole packet. Roll the seeds in a moist paper towel and enclose the rolled towel in a plastic bag. Keep the bag warm and watch for germination in the next several weeks. If only half of the seeds sprout, you will know you need to sow twice as much seed to get the number of plants you want.

Sowing Seeds Indoors

Sowing seeds indoors enables you to begin the new season earlier than if you plant outdoors. You'll have more control over the environment, so seeds will germinate faster and the seedlings will grow vigorously.

When to Sow

Check seed catalogue descriptions or seed packets for sowing timetables. You can sow most seeds indoors in early spring, about six to ten weeks before your last frost date, although some need to be started earlier or later.

Containers

You can sow seedlings in just about any container that has holes for drainage. Seedlings sown in their own pots won't require potting-up later. You can even purchase ready-to-use trays with cells for sowing single seeds. If you use containers such as peat pots or pellets, you can plant the pot along with the plant. They are a good choice for plants that transplant poorly, like cucumbers and rocket larkspur (Consolida ambigua).

If you're reusing last year's trays and pots, either dip them in boiling water for several minutes or rinse them in a 10 per cent bleach solution (one part household bleach to nine parts water) to kill disease organisms.

Growing Medium

New seedlings need a light, moist medium for a quick start. Fill containers with a special seedling mix of moistened vermiculite, milled sphagnum moss, perlite or sifted compost. Materials like perlite and vermiculite don't provide any

It's easy to grow annual, biennial and perennial herbs all together in one garden. Just sow the annuals and biennials from seed and use them to fill in between the longer-lived perennials.

nutrients to your seedlings. Once true leaves have developed, the young plants will require extra nutrients. Water them with a liquid organic fertiliser at half strength. Gradually increase the dose to full strength. Alternatively, you can transfer seedlings to a potting blend with extra compost, or prepare a nourishing substitute by adding 125 ml/4 fl oz (½ cup) or less of dry, organic fertiliser to each 22.5-litre (5-gallon) batch of homemade potting medium. Remember, the longer the seedlings remain in pots, the more nutrients they'll need.

Getting Ready

When you're ready to sow (or, even better, the night before), dump your seed-starting compost in a large bucket or tub and add some warm water to moisten it. Start with a few cups of water and work the mix with your hands to help it absorb the moisture. Keep adding several cups of water at a time and working it into the mix until it feels evenly moist but not soggy. (If you squeeze a handful of mix and water runs out, it's too wet; add some more dry mix to get the balance right.)

Once the compost is moist, you can fill your chosen containers. Scoop the mix into each container and level it out to about 6 mm (¼ inch) below the upper edge of the container. Don't pack down the compost; just tap the filled container once or twice on your work surface to settle the mix and eliminate air pockets.

Prepare markers for each of the plants that you plan to sow, for easy identification when transplanting.

Sowing the Seed

When you're sowing large seeds, such as four o'clocks (*Mirabilis jalapa*), use a pencil to make individual holes 12 to 25 mm (½ to 1 inch) apart. Sow more thickly if you expect poor germination. For small seeds, use a pencil to make shallow furrows, and sow as evenly as possible into the furrows. Fine seeds, such as those of petunias and begonias, can be hard to sow directly from the packet. To

Sowing Seed

1. Fill the container with a seed-raising mix.

2. Press the compost into the corners.

3. Level to 6 mm (½ inch) from the top.

4. Scatter seeds and gently press in.

5. Cover with a fine layer of compost.

6. Water them with a fine mist spray.

7. Label the container.

8. Cover with plastic, glass or damp newspaper.

distribute tiny seeds more evenly, mix them with a spoonful of dry sand, and scatter the mixture over the surface of the mix with a saltcellar. Label each row of seed as you sow.

If the seeds should be buried (as indicated on the seed packet), sprinkle the needed amount of dry mix over the seed. Fine seeds are usually not covered; just press them lightly into the surface of the compost with your fingers. Mist the surface lightly to moisten it. Seeds will rot if they are submerged in water.

Place the containers in a well-lit spot where you can check them daily for signs of the first sprouts. Keep the planting medium moist but not soggy. Cover the container with clingfilm to keep the soil evenly moist until the seeds germinate, but make sure the plastic doesn't touch the soil. Remove the covering as soon as the seedlings appear. Ventilation is important as poor ventilation encourages the development of seedling diseases.

Temperature and Light

Most annual seeds will sprout and grow well at average indoor temperatures between 16° and 24°C (60° and 75°F). Vegetable seeds germinate best at higher temperatures – between 24° and 32°C

Get a head start on spring plants by germinating your seeds indoors under lights. Or, during the heat of summer, sow seeds of cool-season plants indoors, perhaps under lights in a cool basement or garage.

(75° and 90°F). On top of a water heater or refrigerator are both good positions for these. You can even buy horticultural heating mats to keep the soil warm. Place the mats on a heatproof surface and set trays or pots on top. Once the seedlings are up and growing, they will require less warmth and will do best at 16° to 21°C (60° to 70°F) during the day, with a 5°C (10°F) drop each night.

Once your seeds have germinated, it is important that you keep them near a sunny window or under fluorescent plant lights. Garden centres and garden supply catalogues sell lights in a variety of sizes and prices. Fluorescent strip lights,

1.2-m (4-foot) long, sold in home centres also provide excellent results, and they're generally much less expensive than grow lights. The young plants will need between 10 and 16 hours of light each day. They will tolerate low-light conditions best if you keep temperatures on the low side.

Thinning and Transplanting

The first leaves to appear on the plant are actually specialised food-storage organs. These drop away quickly, and the leaves that follow are the first 'true leaves'. When seedlings develop their first set of true leaves, they'll need special attention.

If seedlings are in separate pots or cells, thin away the extra seedlings by clipping them off at soil level with sharp scissors. One healthy specimen should remain in each pot or cell. If your seedlings are crowded together in a tray, you'll need to transfer them to their own containers. Fill pots or cells with a nutrient-rich medium. Scoop one or more seedlings from the tray (a teaspoon works well), separating their root systems as gently as possible with your fingers. Poke a hole in the potting compost deep enough to accommodate the new seedling and its root system, then transfer it and firm the soil. Water as often as necessary to keep the soil moist and to prevent wilting. When you water,

STEP-BY-STEP POTTING UP
1. Place moist growing medium into new containers. Make a hole large enough to accommodate the root system of the seedling.

2. Remove one seedling at a time using a pencil or pointed stick.

3. Holding the seedling by its leaves, place it into its new container and gently firm the soil around it. Thin seedlings by clipping them off at soil level with a pair of scissors.

put the container of seedlings in a tray of water so the growing medium can soak up moisture without disrupting the seedlings. If you water from overhead, you may wash the seedlings away. Place pots away from direct light and wind for a day until the shock of transplanting is over. Feed the young plants lightly with compost tea or liquid seaweed.

Hardening Off

Hardening off allows young plants to adjust slowly to the extremes of wind, temperature and light. At least two weeks before transplanting time, begin watering less frequently and withhold fertiliser. One week before you transplant, move the plants outdoors to a spot protected from strong light and wind. Starting with one or several hours, gradually increase their time spent outdoors. Within a week, they should be outdoors permanently. They'll need more water at this time, since sun and wind quickly dry the soil. Be prepared to bring them back indoors if a cold snap or storm threatens.

Sowing Seed in the Garden

Some plants, like morning glories (*Ipomoea* spp.), beans, peas and root crops, grow better from direct-sown seed because they prefer cool outdoor temperatures or because they don't respond well to transplanting. Sowing seeds outdoors is not a good idea for seeds that are hard to germinate or for plants that need a long, warm growing season.

Before the season begins, check your seed packets or catalogue for the best time to sow outdoors. You'll need to know the expected date of the last frost for your area; ask local gardeners or contact your local nursery.

Get the soil ready for planting (see page 50) and if you're sowing in rows, as with vegetables, mark them before planting with wooden stakes at both ends. Stretch a section of lightweight string down the row and use it as a guide to keep your rows straight while you sow.

Dealing with Damping-Off

Damping-off is a disease that can strike young seedlings, killing them just before or after they emerge. Affected seedlings tend to topple over, since their stems are damaged at the soil level. Once a few seedlings are affected, the disease can quickly spread to other seedlings in the same pot or tray.

Since there's no real cure, the best way to handle damping-off is prevention. Here are some tips that might help.

- Always use fresh, 'sterile' seed-sowing compost.
- If you're reusing old pots or trays, knock out the old soil, dip the containers in a 10 per cent bleach solution (1 part household bleach to 9 parts water), and let the containers dry before using them.
- Sprinkle a thin layer of milled sphagnum moss on top of newly sown seeds.
- Improve air circulation with a small fan set to blow lightly just over the tops of the seedlings.
- If damping-off strikes outdoor-sown seeds, discard them, wait until the weather warms up (maybe two to three weeks), then try sowing again.

If you're planting annuals or perennials, sow medium-sized and large seeds individually, or scatter them evenly over the surface. Try to space them 12 to 25 mm (½ to 1 inch) apart. If you have very small seeds, mix them with a handful of dry sand and scatter over the surface.

Cover most seeds with a thin layer of fine soil or sand. After sowing, make sure the seedbed stays moist until the seedlings are visible. If rainfall is lacking, water gently with a watering can, sprinkler or fine hose spray. Covering the seedbed

Lupin seed, like others of the pea and bean family, can be sown directly into the soil in autumn.

with a layer of horticultural fleece helps to keep the soil moist and protects the seed from drying winds, heavy rain and birds. (Remove the cover once the seedlings start to emerge.)

If seedlings are crowded, you'll need to thin them out for good growth. Dig up and carefully transplant extra seedlings, or use scissors to cut off the stems of unwanted seedlings at ground level.

Planting Container-Grown Plants

If you are planting a potted plant, you can easily see how deeply to plant it. Dig deeply enough so the surface of the container soil will be at the top of the hole (adjusting accordingly for new beds).

Nursery Beds for Biennials

If you decide to grow biennial plants, such as foxgloves (*Digitalis purpurea*) and forget-me-nots (*Myosotis sylvatica*), you need a slightly different growing approach. Most biennials will sprout well when sown outdoors, so that part is easy. But if you sow them directly into the garden, their leafy, first-year growth will take up room without adding much interest to your flower display.

The easiest approach is to set aside a temporary growing area (called a nursery bed) where your biennials can grow through the summer. Prepare your nursery bed just as you would any garden area, but site it in an out-of-the-way spot. Sow the biennial seeds into the bed in spring or summer, and thin them as needed. Dig the plants and move them to their final garden spots in late summer or early autumn to flower the following year.

Forget-me-not

Fill the hole with water to moisten the soil, then let it drain away before you begin to plant. Slip the roots out of the pot. Most larger plants are root-bound enough to slide out easily. If not, you can gently squeeze the base of a plastic pot to loosen the root ball. Break up the edges of the root ball so the roots will have more contact with the surrounding soil. If the roots are wrapped around themselves, they may not break free and root into the soil. You will have to work them loose.

You can quarter the roots of fibrous-rooted perennials like chrysanthemums. Although the process may seem harsh, it will encourage new root growth. Make four deep slices, one on each side of the root ball, or make a single cut two-thirds up the centre to divide the ball in half. Mound some soil in the centre of the planting hole. Open the root quarters out from the cuts and spread them out over the mound. Cover the rest of the roots up to the crown. Don't try this technique on plants with taproots like monkshood.

After planting, firm the soil gently around the plant, water it well and mulch. Mulching your bed with organic materials like compost, straw or shredded leaves will conserve moisture and reduce weed competition. (New beds are especially weed-prone, since turning the soil exposes weed seeds.)

Planting Field-Dug Plants

Plant field-dug plants that have a large amount of soil still around the roots in a hole the same size as the root ball. If much of the soil has fallen off the roots, make the hole slightly larger so you can move the roots into the best position. Drench the hole with water and set in the plant at the same depth it was originally growing. Work any exposed roots into the surrounding soil as you refill, then firm the soil gently.

Planting Bare-Root Perennials

When you start with bare-root plants, you will have to take more time settling the plants into the ground. This process can be tricky the first few times, but be patient and don't be afraid to work with the roots. You'll soon get it right.

First, soak the roots in a bucket of lukewarm water for a few hours to prepare them for planting. When you are ready to plant, identify how deeply the plants had been growing in the nursery. The above-ground portions – green foliage tufts, leaf buds, or dormant stems – usually emerge from the root system above the former soil line. Plant so that these structures will stay slightly above the soil in your garden. (Peonies are an exception, since their shoots will emerge through the soil from about 2.5 cm [1 inch] underground.)

Next, make a hole that is deep and wide enough to set the plant crown at the

1. Dig a planting hole that is larger than the root ball of the transplant.
2. If desired, add a handful or two of compost to the hole.
3. Add water to moisten the soil before planting.
4. Gently slide the plant out of its container.
5. Use your fingers to loosen the soil mix around the roots.
6. Set the plant in the hole. Backfill with soil; firm lightly with your hands.

soil surface and stretch out the roots. Form a small mound of soil in the bottom of the hole. Set the root clump on it with the crown resting on top of the mound. Spread the roots gently in every direction and fill in around them with soil, then firm the soil gently, water and mulch. Keep the soil evenly moist for the next few weeks.

Planting Trees and Shrubs

You can plant anytime the ground isn't frozen. Plant bare-root stock when it's dormant, from late autumn to as early in spring as possible. Root-balled stock does best when planted in the cooler months of spring or autumn. You can plant container-grown stock anytime during the growing season, but if you plant during

Quartering

1. To loosen a tight root ball, use a knife to make four deep cuts.
2. Spread the quartered root ball over a mound of soil and backfill.

summer, make sure you give the plants plenty of water and watch carefully that they don't dry out.

In most cases you'll set new plants in the ground at the same depth at which they are growing presently. Replanting at the same depth keeps the crown – the point from which shoots emerge – from being buried in damp soil, where it is likely to rot. However, if you have just prepared the soil, it will settle 2.5 to 5 cm (1 to 2 inches) over the coming months. In a new bed, plant slightly deeper so the plant's roots and crown do not stick out of the soil when it has settled. Exactly how you plant depends on whether you are using bare-root, container-grown or field-dug stock.

How to Plant

Keep a firm, level area of soil in the bottom of the hole on which to set the plant and dig a few inches deeper around it so that extra water can drain away from the roots easily. Now set the plant into the hole. (If you're planting bare-root stock, build a cone of soil in the hole to support the roots. Firm the soil well and settle the plant on top of the cone, spreading the roots over it.) Stand back and make sure the plant is straight.

Now start refilling, or backfilling, with the soil you removed when you dug the hole. Backfill half the hole, then water the soil to remove large air pockets. Once the water drains away, finish backfilling and water again. With the leftover soil, build a well around the planting hole to trap and hold water over the plant's roots.

Planting in Containers

Container plants share closer quarters than garden plants, so they need some special care to stay lush and lovely. The first step to successful container growing is choosing a good container. Large pots tend to provide the best conditions for growth, since they hold more soil, nutrients and water, but they are also quite heavy if you need to move or hang them. Pots or baskets that are about 20 cm (8 inches) deep can usually hold enough soil for good growth without getting too heavy. If you don't plan to move the planter, it can be as big as you want; containers as large as half-barrels will give you ample planting space for a wide variety of plants.

Fill your container with a general potting compost from your local nursery or garden centre. Straight garden soil is generally not suitable for containers, since it will pack down with repeated watering. Add some well-rotted compost to the mix to promote root growth.

Set your plants into the container soil, firm them in and water to keep the soil moist through the season.

Planting Hanging Baskets

Most hanging basket containers look like regular pots, and you plant them in basically the same way. Baskets dry out even faster than other container plants, however, so it's a good idea to use a potting mix that holds plenty of water. Adding extra vermiculite will help. It also helps to use larger baskets – at least

To keep hanging baskets looking lush through the season, water them regularly, fertilise often and pinch off spent flowers.

30 cm (12 inches) in diameter, which will dry out more slowly. During hot summers, hanging baskets may have to be watered twice a day.

Great Balls of Flowers

If you want your hanging baskets to be a solid ball of colour, plant the sides of the containers as well as the tops. You can buy special baskets that have holes around the sides, or use wire baskets with fibre or moss liners, which allow you to cut holes for planting all round the sides.

To plant into the holes in the sides of a hanging basket, first fill the basket with potting mix to just below where the holes begin. Then remove a plant from its cell pack and wrap it loosely inside a little cylinder of newspaper. From the inside of the basket, slip the top part of the cylinder out through a hole, so the leafy top of the plant is on the outside and the roots are on the inside. Slip off the newspaper, then settle the roots in the soil. When you have all the holes filled, add more soil to within 2.5 cm (1 inch) of the rim, then set in more plants on top. Water thoroughly to allow the soil to settle around the roots.

Propagation Techniques

Depending on which propagation method you choose, you can end up with a few to a few hundred new plants, taken from a single specimen. Vegetative methods of propagation, such as division, layering and cuttings, will produce an exact clone of the parent plant in nearly every case. These are the best methods to use if you want to propagate cultivars or hybrids, which usually produce variable offspring when grown from seed.

Reproduction by Division

Many perennials flower best when they're young, and their flower production drops as they mature. To keep them flowering well, you must divide them – dig them up and split the root mass into pieces. In addition to reviving older plants, division is the easiest and fastest technique for propagating perennials. It's also a good way to keep fast-spreading perennials under control. Plus, it will give you lots of extra plants to share with family, friends and neighbours.

Division is a reliable way to propagate many clump-forming perennials, including daylilies, chrysanthemums and irises. It may not work as well with the more sensitive perennials like sea hollies (*Eryngium* spp.) and gas plant (*Dictamnus albus*).

How to Divide

Early spring and autumn are good times to divide plants, when the air temperature is low and soil moisture is usually high. Begin dividing by digging up the root system. Shake off as much loose soil as possible and remove any dead leaves and stems. You may also want to wash most of the soil off the roots and crown so you can see the roots and buds clearly.

Plants with fibrous roots, such as chrysanthemums and asters, are the easiest to dig and divide. You can pull them apart with your hands or cut them with a spade. Others, like daylilies and astilbe, can grow woody with age. You may have to pry these roots apart with a crowbar or two garden forks held back to back, or cut them with a saw or ax. Discard the woody parts, which will not reroot well.

Divide the plants into small pieces, making sure you keep several buds or growing shoots on the sections you will replant. Look for the buds growing along the length of the roots or clustered together in a central crown.

Work compost and other soil improvers into the soil before replanting. Reset divisions at the same level as they were growing originally.

Plants that send out underground rhizomes, like mint, are just as easily divided without digging up the whole plant. If you follow the underground stems that sprout new plants, you can simply lift out each new plant with a spade.

Layering

Some plants are easy to root while still attached to the mother plant, a technique called layering. Burying a section of the stem encourages roots to form at each buried leaf node (the place where a leaf joins the stem). Layering does take up some space since you need to bury the attached stem close to the parent plant. You won't get many new plants from this method (usually only one per stem), and it can take weeks or months for the stem to root. But layering is easy to do, and the resulting plants will be exact duplicates of the parent plant.

You can use this technique with plants that have flexible stems or a creeping habit and the ability to root at the leafaxils. Good candidates for layering include pinks (*Dianthus* spp.), cranesbills (*Geranium* spp.), wall rock

STEP-BY-STEP DIVISION

1. Dig around the clump.
2. Shake off as much soil as possible. Separate good shoots with roots from the parent plant.
3. Cut back ragged tops and shorten the stems.
4. Place some well-rotted compost into the planting hole and position the plant at the same depth as it was growing before.
5. Water the plant with a soluble organic fertiliser to minimise transplanting shock.

1
2
3
4
5
6

STEP-BY-STEP LAYERING
Layering is a slow but reliable method for propagating many kinds of plants, especially trees, shrubs and climbers.
1. Select a young, flexible, healthy branch about as thick as a pencil.
2. Cut off any leaves and side shoots from the section to be buried.
3. Make a slit on the underside, then insert a cocktail stick to keep it open (unnecessary with thin stems).
4. Bend the stem into the hole and anchor it with bent wire.
5. Fill the hole with enriched soil mixture and water thoroughly.
6. After a couple of months, cut off and transplant the new plant.

cress (*Arabis caucasica*), snow-in-summer (*Cerastium tomentosum*), and bellflowers (*Campanula* spp.). Layering will not work on daylilies, ornamental grasses, hostas, irises, peonies, or other bushy perennials. Spring is a good time to start a layer, although it can work anytime during the growing season.

How It Works
The first step to successful layering is finding a suitable stem. If the plant is upright, look for one or several long stems that bend easily to the ground; if the plant has a creeping habit, any stem is suitable. Leave the top three sets of leaves on the stem to nourish the plant, but remove the leaves from the stem for 5 to 17.5 cm (2 to 7 inches) below the top greenery. Strip the leaves from at least two nodes (leaf joints), carefully leaving the dormant buds undamaged. Bend the stem down

and see where the stripped area will contact the soil. Loosen the soil in that area about 10 cm (4 inches) deep and water it. Bury the stem in the loosened soil, holding it in place with a bent wire pin, and firm the soil over the stem. The stem should be buried 5 to 7.5 cm (2 to 3 inches) deep with the leafy tip still exposed. If you are layering an upright shoot, encourage the tip to return to its upright position by tying it to a small stake if necessary.

Keep the area moist and mulched while the buried stem roots. Depending on the temperature and species, it will take several weeks to several months. The easiest way to layer is to leave the plant in place until the following season. If you want faster results, check its progress by gently uncovering the stem and looking for roots, or tugging lightly to see if the shoot has become more secure in the

ground. Once the roots reach about 2.5 cm (1 inch) long you can cut the shoot free from the mother plant. Wait several weeks for more rooting, then dig and transplant the new plant.

Cuttings
Cuttings – small pieces of stem or root – are another way to propagate many plants. Cuttings take more care than other methods, like layering and division. But if you like a challenge, you can use cuttings to create many new plants from your existing perennials. Cuttings are a good way to propagate perennials that are difficult to divide and cultivars that don't come true from seed.

Stem Cuttings
Stem cuttings are effective for many kinds of plants. Try perennial flowers such as wall rock cress (*Arabis caucasica*), chrysanthemums, common sneezeweed (*Helenium autumnale*), garden phlox (*Phlox paniculata*), and pinks (*Dianthus* spp.), and herbs like scented geranium, bay, lavender, and oregano.

You should take stem cuttings when perennials are in vegetative growth: Either in spring before blooming or after flowering is finished for the season. You should select a healthy medium-soft stem – one that is not soft, new growth or hard, old growth – from the lower portion of the plant, where shoots are more likely to root quickly. Cut the stems free with a sharp, clean knife or pair of shears.

Preparing the Cuttings
Slice the stem into sections between 5 and 10 cm (2 and 4 inches) long, so that each cutting has two or three sets of leaves on the top and a couple of nodes (leaf joints) stripped of leaves on the bottom. These nodes will produce roots when you insert them into a pot of moist, sterile, peat-based growing mix. Don't be tempted to use garden soil – it's too heavy for cuttings.

Some stem cuttings, like those from blue false indigo (*Baptisia australis*), will

1

2

3

4

5

STEP-BY-STEP CUTTINGS

1. Select healthy green growth.
2. Cut the stem below the leaf node.
3. Remove the lower leaves.
4. Insert the cutting firmly into the compost.
5. Cover the cutting with a glass jar to maintain humidity. Keep out of direct sun.

root more easily if you dip their lower ends in a commercially available rooting hormone powder. However, if you find the right moisture, light and warmth levels, most plants will root without this treatment. Make a hole in the compost with a clean pencil and slide the cutting in. Firm the compost around it gently with your hands, then water with a fine spray to settle the cutting into the soil.

Caring for Cuttings

Cover the container with a clear plastic-bag tent. Prop the plastic above the plant foliage to avoid rot. Keep the cuttings in a warm place and in indirect light until they root, about two to four weeks. When they begin to grow, remove the plastic and move the plants into brighter light.

To determine if the cuttings have rooted, look to see if roots are emerging from the pot's drainage hole. You can also tug gently on the stem – if you meet resistance, the cuttings have rooted. Transplant the rooted cuttings into larger containers or a nursery bed to grow them to garden size.

Root Cuttings

Less common than stem cuttings, root cuttings are another way to produce new plants that are usually identical to the parent plant. Root cuttings are suitable for several kinds of perennials, including *Anchusa azurea*, oriental poppies (*Papaver orientale*) and garden phlox (*Phlox paniculata*).

Take root cuttings from autumn to early spring, while the parent plant is dormant. Carefully lift the plant from the garden and wash the soil from the roots. Using a sharp, clean knife, cut off a few pencil-thick roots close to the crown. Cut each root into 5- to 10-cm (2- to 4-inch) pieces, making a straight cut at the top (the end that was closest to the crown) and a slanted cut at the bottom. Insert the cuttings into a pot filled with moist, sterile potting

compost, so that the flat top of each cutting is level with or slightly below the surface of the mix. Place the cuttings in a cold frame until they root and then pot them individually. Once the plants reach the desired size, move them into the garden.

Saving Seed

Although most perennial flowers and herbs are easy to propagate vegetatively – by division, layering or cuttings – you can grow many plants from seed if you have the patience.

Annuals and biennials will seed themselves before the season ends. All that's required next season is patience while you leave the soil undisturbed to see which seedlings appear. Resist the temptation to dig or hoe in areas that were heavily seeded naturally the previous season.

When the new plants are established, dig them up while the weather is cool and move them as needed. Leave them in clumps or divide them up into individual plants as required in your garden.

To save seed for planting next spring, wait until they've matured on the plant before collecting them. Hold the seed heads over a container and gently tap to release the seeds. Alternatively, you can harvest the seed heads and then hang them upside down in paper bags to dry. The seeds should be thoroughly dried before being stored in airtight containers.

Creating the Right Environment

It is vital to prevent most cuttings from drying out while roots develop. If you have just a few cuttings, you can enclose them, pot and all, in a plastic bag; for large numbers, a cold frame may be more practical. Set your pots in a bright place out of direct sunlight or cover your cold frame with wooden lattice to shield the cuttings from the full brunt of the sun.

Propagating Garlic

Growing your own garlic is easy and rewarding. Mid-autumn is the best time for planting. The bulbs will produce roots and small shoots before the ground freezes. When the weather warms in spring, the shoots will start actively growing.

1. Harvest the bulbs as usual, allowing them to dry. Save the largest bulbs with the largest cloves for replanting and use the rest in the kitchen. There's no need to clean the bulbs you plan to replant. The more they're handled and peeled, the more likely they'll rot in storage. Store them in a dark, cool location until you're ready to plant.

2. To plant, divide the bulbs into individual cloves. Plant only the outer, large cloves; small, inner cloves will yield smaller bulbs. Keep the small cloves in the kitchen to use soon – once separated from the bulb, they won't store well.

3. Plant the individual cloves root-side down, approximately 2.5 cm (1 inch) deep and 15 cm (6 inches) apart in a deep bed with loosened soil. Work in plenty of organic material like compost, but go easy on fertiliser. Dig up when the tops die down.

WHIP AND TONGUE GRAFTING

1. Make a long sloping cut at the top of the rootstock.
2. Make a shallow cut down through the middle of the rootstock stem.
3. Prepare the scion with a matching sloping cut at the base.
4. Cut shallowly into the middle of the scion's base.
5. Slip the stock and scion together so the 'tongues' interlock.
6. Wrap the graft with tape to provide support and hold in moisture.

Grafting Trees and Shrubs

Grafting is the process of uniting two related plants using the root system of one to nourish the top of the other. An alternative to propagating by layering, cuttings or seed, grafting produces large plants quickly because the roots are already well established. The technique is used to propagate species and cultivars of flowering cherries (*Prunus* spp.) and pears (*Pyrus* spp.), dwarf conifers and Japanese maples (*Acer palmatum*) that won't come true from seed and don't root easily from cuttings or layering.

The key to grafting is to match the cambium layers – the growing green tissue under the bark – of the rooted

1. Save large, healthy garlic bulbs for replanting. Store in a dark, cool place.

2. Divide the bulbs into individual cloves; keeping the smaller ones for cooking.

3. Plant the cloves root-side down. Cover with soil rich in organic matter.

plant (called the rootstock) and the new top (called the scion). Once these two cambium layers unite, the graft grows as one plant.

Choosing a Rootstock

Grafting joins two or more pieces of different plants together to form a new plant. Compatibility between rootstock and scion is a must. Select closely related plants of the same genus or cultivars within the same species or, sometimes, species within the same family. You can grow your own rootstocks from seeds or cuttings or graft onto a mature tree. The multiflora rose (*Rosa multiflora*), for example, is a hardy, pest-resistant species that is grown easily from seed. Because of its vigour, it makes a good rootstock for a hybrid tea or an heirloom rose.

Tools and Supplies

For most home gardeners, a very sharp knife, a pair of secateurs that makes clean cuts and materials to tie and seal off the graft are all that's needed. Tying and wrapping materials hold the rootstock and scion together and keep the cambium layers from drying out. Wide rubber bands or waxed string are good for tying. Sealing materials, such as grafting wax or rubber tape, are widely available at garden centres, or you can improvise with plastic tape or petroleum jelly.

Grafting Techniques

Learning to make successful grafts requires practice. Several grafting techniques are available for you to try, including whip and tongue, side veneer and cleft grafts, and T and chip buds. Consult a propagation reference and choose the best method depending on the amount of scion wood you have, the size of the rootstock, the time of year and the effect you want to obtain. Grafting is usually done from late winter to early spring depending on the method used. Most grafts, properly done, will unite within one to two months.

Taking Tree and Shrub Cuttings

Depending on the species you're propagating and the time of year, you can take cuttings from plants with softwood, semi-hardwood or hardwood stems.

Getting Started

A sharp knife, a plastic bag, clean pots and a well-drained soilless growing medium are all you need. Be sure your knife (or secateurs) is sharp; a dull blade will crush plant tissue and invite disease. Scrub your pots – clay and plastic are both suitable – and rinse with a solution of one part bleach to nine parts water.

Use a lightweight, moisture-retentive propagation medium, free of insects, diseases and weed seeds. Garden soil is not a good choice. Use a 50-50 mix of peat moss and perlite, peat and vermiculite, or peat and sand.

Softwood Cuttings

Take softwood cuttings from the succulent new growth that occurs in the spring. Softwood stems snap easily when bent. Some plants have spurts of new growth later in the year that can also be used for softwood cuttings. Many species of shrubs and climbers, and some trees, root well from softwood cuttings, including crab apples (*Malus* spp.) and crape myrtle (*Lagerstroemia indica*).

Take softwood cuttings from late spring to early summer, when stems are soft and new leaves are fully open. Have ready a container of moist propagation medium. Snip 7.5- to 15-cm (3- to 6-inch) cuttings, including the branch tip, on a cool overcast morning, cutting just below a node (the swollen area on the stem where a leaf emerges). Remove leaves from the bottom half of the stem with secateurs. Carefully insert the cutting

Hydrangea (*Hydrangea macrophylla*) responds well to pruning and will root from softwood, semi-hardwood or hardwood cuttings.

into the compost to about one-third of its length and tamp it into place.

When the tray or pot is full, gently water the cuttings to settle the compost, then enclose the container in a plastic bag or in a cold frame. Roots will usually form in two to five weeks. If the cuttings resist when you gently tug on them, they have rooted. Harden off rooted cuttings, gradually increasing the light intensity and decreasing the humidity to adjust them to normal growing conditions. Transplant the cuttings to a nursery bed or to individual containers.

Semi-Hardwood Cuttings

Once the flush of spring growth is over, stem wood becomes firmer and leaves become fully expanded or mature. Pieces taken from this maturing wood are called semi-hardwood (or semi-ripe) cuttings. Use semi-hardwood cuttings to propagate broad-leaved evergreens, such as hollies (*Ilex* spp.) and rhododendrons (*Rhododendron* spp.), or deciduous shrubs that don't root very well from softwood cuttings, such as winged spindle tree (*Euonymus alatus*).

SEMI-HARDWOOD CUTTINGS

Semi-hardwood cuttings are a good way to propagate broad-leaved evergreen trees and shrubs, like hollies, rhododendrons and camellias. Take cuttings from partially hardened wood in later summer. Keep the finished cuttings in a humid environment to promote rooting.

1. Take cuttings from healthy, vigorous growth and remove the leaves from the bottom half.

2. Cut large leaves in half to reduce evaporation and to save space in the container.

3. Insert cuttings halfway into moist potting compost and place them in a shady position.

Take 7.5- to 15-cm (3- to 6-inch) cuttings of semi-hardwood in late summer and remove the leaves from the bottom half. Cut the foliage of broad-leaved evergreens in half to save space and to reduce water loss. Some cuttings, like hollies and rhododendrons, benefit from having a small sliver of bark sliced off the side of the base. This wounding encourages new roots to form.

Insert the cuttings into a tray or pot of moist cuttings compost, spacing them far enough apart so the leaves don't touch. Keep the air around the cuttings moist by misting them frequently, or enclose the whole container in a clear plastic bag. (Use bent wire hangers to keep the plastic from resting on the cuttings and encouraging rot.) Set the cuttings where they will get bright light but no direct sun.

Semi-hardwood cuttings usually root in one to three months. Transplant rooted cuttings into individual pots or a nursery bed until they're ready for their final position in the garden.

Hardwood Cuttings

Take hardwood cuttings from mature wood in mid- to late autumn or in winter.

Deciduous shade trees and needled evergreen shrubs, such as arbor-vitae (*Thuja* spp.), junipers (*Juniperus* spp.) and yews (*Taxus* spp.), can be propagated successfully from hardwood cuttings.

Look for mature, one-year-old wood with bark that has turned from green to (usually) brown or grey. For deciduous plants, take stem pieces 10 to 20 cm (4 to 8 inches) long starting a few inches below the terminal bud. Make a straight cut at the top of each piece just above a node or bud and a sloping cut at the base just below a node or bud. For evergreens, take 10- to 15-cm (4- to 6-inch) tip cuttings and clip off the bottom leaves.

Stick the cuttings right-side up (with the straight-cut end up) in your cuttings compost. The top bud should be about 2.5 cm (1 inch) above the soil surface. Set the pots outdoors or in a cold frame. Keep the propagation medium evenly moist, but don't worry about misting the cuttings or enclosing them in plastic; since they're not actively growing, the cuttings won't lose much water. After the ground freezes, cover your cuttings with a 15- to 20-cm (6- to 8-inch) deep layer of loose mulch, like straw. Remove the mulch in spring.

Hardwood cuttings often take several months to root. Tug gently on them to check for roots the summer or autumn after planting. Transplant rooted cuttings to individual pots or to a nursery bed for a few years. When the rooted cuttings have reached the size you need, move them to their final place in the garden.

Juniper

Caring for Your Garden

If you have chosen plants that match your site, prepared the soil thoroughly and planted carefully, you will probably find your garden demands less maintenance than your lawn. However, low maintenance isn't no maintenance. Even the toughest plants will need a little watering, fertilising, staking and weeding.

Watering

Water stress, a result of both too little or too much water, is one of the major causes of poor plant growth or even death. Selecting plants that are adapted to your site and climate is the best thing you can do to avoid problems with water stress – and to reduce watering chores. A deep layer of mulch will also help reduce water-stress problems because it helps soil retain water and controls competition from grass and weeds.

Water makes up from 85 to 95 per cent of the weight of living plants. It's not surprising that when water is lacking, a plant stops growing and wilts. After wilting comes collapse of the cell structure in the wilted leaves and stems. After that, if much of the plant is affected, comes the death of young or delicate plants! Your goal is to water before wilting occurs.

Garden plants require about the equivalent of 25 mm (1 inch) of rainfall each week under average soil and climate conditions. Gardens in hot, dry climates will lose moisture faster and may need the equivalent of up to 50 mm (2 inches) each week. In cool and wet climates, plants lose less moisture and less water evaporates from the soil, so you may not have to water at all.

To monitor rainfall, purchase a rain gauge (available at most hardware stores) and set it in or near your garden. Check it immediately after rain, before water in the gauge is lost to evaporation. If natural rainfall is inadequate, you should plan to water regularly to maintain plant health and growth. Checking your soil for moisture is also a good idea.

There are several methods of checking soil moisture. Move the surface soil or

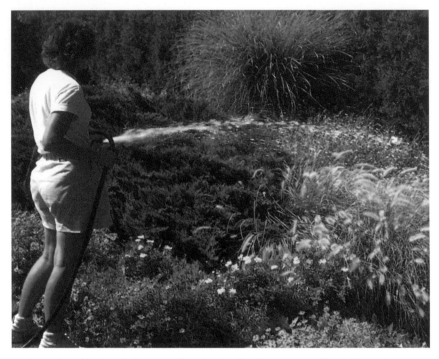

Hand-watering with a hose is fine for small gardens, but for a larger area you'll probably need soaker hoses or a drip system.

mulch and look at the soil in the root zone. Most plant roots are in the top 30 cm (12 inches) of soil. If the soil is cool and moist and there are no signs of stress – wilting – you can probably hold off on the hose. A daily check is a good idea in dry weather, particularly if it is also hot.

Or take a soil sample from the root zone and examine it. Dry, sandy soils will flow freely through your fingers but will stick together slightly with adequate moisture. Heavier clay soils will appear hard and crumbly when dry, and feel slick when adequately moist.

Water Wisely

The key to wise watering is to water slowly and deeply. You should water sufficiently to keep your plants growing, but not so much that the roots become oxygen-starved. Watering slowly ensures that all the water soaks into the soil – you don't want any water to run off or cause soil erosion. In most soils, one good

soaking is better than several shallow waterings because it encourages roots to spread deeper and wider in search of water that is farther away.

Deep watering encourages deep rooting, which makes plants more drought-tolerant. Water early or late in the day when temperatures and winds are generally lower, decreasing evaporation.

If your soil has a crust that reduces water penetration, cultivate shallowly with a trowel or hand fork. Then apply a layer of organic mulch around your plants to conserve soil moisture and to prevent future crusting.

Hand Watering

Rain-water butts, watering cans and hand-held hoses work well if you have a small garden and plenty of time. You'll know just how much water you are actually applying and where it is going. If you're tending a large garden, though, you'll probably choose overhead sprinklers or trickle irrigation.

Overhead Sprinklers

Although popular and inexpensive, overhead watering systems have two main disadvantages. First, they assume a plentiful, even extravagant, water supply. In the time it takes water to reach the soil, 30 to 50 per cent of the water used may be lost to evaporation on a hot, windy day. Secondly, sprinklers take longer to wet the soil, especially if the water must first penetrate a mulch. Fungal diseases that thrive in moist conditions spread easily and quickly when the foliage is wet. Most pathogens can remain dormant in the soil for several years, then become activated when water films form on plant surfaces. That's why you'll find more symptoms of plant disease after periods of high humidity or rainfall.

The advantage of an overhead watering system is that it requires only an inexpensive sprinkler unit and enough hosepipe to reach the garden.

While watering, monitor the rate of application by placing one or several rain gauges in your garden under the overhead sprinkler. Water for 20 to 40 minutes and check the soil again. You'll want to water until the roots receive some relief.

Hand-watering with a watering can is often a more realistic option for irrigating small gardens and potted plants and for spot-watering thirsty plants.

Water hellebores (*Helleborus* spp.) regularly for the first few years; after that, they'll tolerate dry shade.

The time required to water sufficiently will depend on your water pressure, the size of the nozzles, the distance from the tap, the diameter of your hose, your soil type, and the drying effect of wind and sun. You may need to water two or three times each week or even daily in hot, dry periods. Check the soil at root depth soon after watering to be sure you're watering enough.

Drip Systems

Drip irrigation uses less water, since it is applied directly to the soil, where plants need it. You can water more efficiently in less time since almost no water runs off or evaporates. The water stays cool and helps keep the soil temperature low, especially if you mulch. And since foliage remains dry, fungal diseases are less threatening.

The disadvantage is that drip systems, using water emitters, pressure regulators and timers, are more expensive and require installation. Once they're installed, however, you'll only need to turn on the tap to water your garden.

If you're considering purchasing a drip-irrigation system, start out small and add as you grow. Use a map of your garden to help during the planning stages. Most companies that sell drip-irrigation equipment have starter kits and will design a system to fit your needs and estimate the amount of water it will deliver.

Soaker Hoses

You can design your own much simpler drip system by using soaker hoses. Also known as dew hoses, these are much less expensive than emitter drip systems but provide many of the same benefits. Some soaker hoses release water over their entire length, while others spurt water

How to Conserve Water

- Designate separate parts of the garden for plants with low, medium or high water requirements and water them individually. Annuals will need more water than the deep-rooted, established perennials.
- Insulate the soil surface with a thick layer of organic mulch.
- Maintain your soil's organic matter by working in plenty of garden compost. Organic matter holds water in the soil like a sponge.
- Eliminate weeds as they appear.
- In dry climates, select plants that are drought-tolerant.
- If paths are included in your garden design, use gravel or pulverised bark to pave them. A living cover like grass will compete with your plants for moisture.

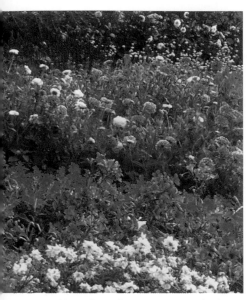

Working well-rotted compost or organic fertiliser into the soil at planting time will supply the nutrient needs of many different annuals.

through tiny holes. Make sure the holes face down into the soil when using this type of hose. A soaker-hose system needs no assembly – simply lay the hoses between plants where you need them. The hoses can be made of various kinds of plastic, rubber or canvas.

Different Plants Have Different Needs

Some plants thrive in moist soils. Others will grow weakly or rot where water is abundant. Water more often if you grow plants that need evenly moist soil. These include delphiniums, astilbes and moisture-loving bog plants like Japanese primroses (*Primula japonica*) and marsh marigolds (*Caltha palustris*).

Let the soil dry more between waterings for drought-tolerant plants, such as lavender, perennial candytuft (*Iberis sempervirens*), Cupid's dart (*Catananche caerulea*) and red hot pokers (*Kniphofia* hybrids). These plants probably need no more than 12 mm (½ inch) of water per week.

Expect to coddle new plants until their roots spread far enough to support them. If the weather is warm and dry, you may

Caring for Container Gardens

Container gardens dry out quickly, so you may need to water every day during hot weather. Very small pots, small- and medium-sized clay containers and hanging baskets dry out especially quickly; you may have to water these as often as twice a day.

If a pot or basket dries out completely, you still may be able to save the plants. Set the pot or basket in a larger container filled with water, let it sit there for an hour or two and then set the pot or basket in a shady spot for a few hours until the plants perk up again. Then move the pot or basket back to its original spot, but be extra careful to keep those container plants well watered from then on.

Besides regular watering, the other key to lush-looking containers is regular fertilising. Give them a boost by watering them with liquid fertiliser or compost tea (made by soaking a shovelful of well-rotted compost in a bucket of water for about a week, then straining out the soaked compost). Start in late spring by feeding once every two weeks, then judge the containers in midsummer. If plants look lush but aren't flowering well, change to fertilising once every three weeks. If the plants look somewhat spindly, start fertilising every week. If the plants seem to be growing and flowering well, stick with the two-week schedule.

have to water daily until a drenching rain comes. If the season is cool and rainy, you can let nature handle the irrigation.

Newly planted trees, shrubs and climbers will need special watering attention for at least the first full year of growth after planting – or better yet, two years. After that – provided you've selected plants adapted to your site, prepared the planting area properly and kept the plants well mulched – their roots should be far-reaching enough to collect adequate moisture during times of drought.

Fertilising

Supplying your plants with the nutrients they need is a critical part of keeping

them healthy and vigorous. How much fertiliser you should add to your garden will depend on how fertile the soil is and which plants you're growing. Small garden plants like vegetable and annuals need more fertiliser than large, established trees and shrubs. However, in the first few years after planting trees and shrubs, their young root system may not yet be able to reach all the necessary nutrients in the soil and they will need supplemental feeding.

How Soil Affects Fertilising

The texture and natural fertility of your soil will have a great impact on how much and how often you need to add supplemental nutrients. A sandy soil will hold fewer nutrients than a clayey soil or a soil that's high in organic matter, so you'll need to fertilise a sandy soil more frequently. If you prepared the soil thoroughly before planting and corrected nutrient shortages, you may not have to fertilise a new garden for a year or more.

Nutrient Needs Vary among Plants

Fertiliser requirements vary widely among different plants. Some are light feeders, including common sneezeweed (*Helenium autumnale*), ox-eye (*Heliopsis helianthoides*) and daisy fleabane (*Erigeron speciosus*). A light layer of compost applied once or twice a year should meet their nutrient needs. Other perennials are heavy feeders; these include delphiniums, astilbes and garden phlox (*Phlox paniculata*). They need more frequent fertilising to stay in top form.

You may want to give your plants a little fertility boost to encourage new growth or rejuvenation. Fertilise in spring

Identifying Nutrient Deficiencies

Your plants will tell you if they are suffering from nutrient imbalances or deficiencies. Look for leaves with signs of yellowing (chlorosis). An overall yellow colour may indicate severe nitrogen deficiency; yellow at the tips or edges points to a lack of potassium; yellow between the veins may result from too little magnesium, molybdenum, manganese, iron or zinc. A phosphorus deficiency may cause red or purple leaf colouration or premature autumn colour.

If your plants exhibit signs of nutrient imbalances or deficiencies, try a foliar spray of seaweed extract for fast relief. For the long-term health of your plants, have your soil tested for minor nutrient recommendations and apply the appropriate dry material, such as compost or seaweed meal, to the soil.

as plants begin growing, also after planting or dividing and after cutting back or deadheading.

Types of Fertilisers

When you fertilise, you can eliminate deficiencies by applying either liquid or dry fertiliser or both. If you decide to use a combination of fertilisers, make sure you don't apply more total nutrients than your plants need. Remember that too much fertiliser can be as bad as not enough, leading to weak stems, rampant sprawling growth and disease problems.

Liquid Fertilisers Commonly used liquid fertilisers include liquid tomato fertiliser, liquid seaweed and compost tea (*see page* 53). Use a single dose of liquid fertiliser for a quick but temporary fix of a nutrient shortage, or apply it every two weeks for a general plant boost. You can spray these materials directly on the plants, which will absorb the nutrients through their foliage.

APPLYING FERTILISER
Whichever fertilising method you use, make sure you always follow the application rates given on the package. Adding too much fertiliser can actually harm your plants.

You can punch holes in the soil and fill them with dry fertiliser.

Or sprinkle dry fertiliser around the base of the plant.

Liquid fertilisers are easy to mist onto plant leaves.

Dry Fertilisers Dry fertilisers are released to plants more slowly than liquid fertilisers. Gently fork them into the surface of the soil in a circle around the perimeter of the plant's foliage, so the nutrients are released gradually as they dissolve in soil moisture. This encourages roots to extend outwards.

Applying Fertilisers

How you physically apply the nutrients – broadcasting, drill-hole application, irrigation or foliar feeding – depends on the type of fertiliser you choose.

Broadcasting Broadcasting involves spreading the fertiliser material evenly onto the soil over the roots. Before you apply fertiliser, pull back the layer of mulch around your plants, then scatter the material over the soil and replace the mulch.

Drill-Hole Application If the soil around your plants is compacted or clayey, broadcasting may not be effective in getting the nutrients where they're needed. In this situation, use an auger or steel pipe to punch holes into the ground around

the plant. Make the holes 10 to 15 cm (4 to 6 inches) deep and fill them with fertiliser or compost. The holes help break up the compaction, get needed oxygen to the roots, and place the fertiliser directly into the root zone.

Fertilising Guidelines for Trees and Shrubs

Roots absorb nutrients from the soil when it is adequately moist and when its temperature is between 40° and 80°F (4° and 27°C). In temperate regions, apply fertilisers in spring or in mid- to late autumn. In warmer areas where plants grow year-round, apply fertilisers when plants are most actively growing.

Established Plants

Once trees, shrubs and climbers are established, your fertilising chores will be minimal. Regular applications of organic mulch are all that most of these plants need. If you have extra compost on hand, you can apply an even layer of it underneath the mulch.

New Plants

Apply an even layer of compost around the base of a new plant in a circle extending 60 to 90 cm (2 to 3 feet) past the drip line, then cover the compost with a 5- to 7.5-cm (2- to 3-inch) deep layer of mulch. Keep both the compost and the mulch a few inches away from the stem to prevent rodent damage and to allow the air to circulate freely.

Irrigation If you have a drip or soaker-hose irrigation system, you can use it to apply liquid fertiliser. Be sure to use a product such as seaweed that dissolves thoroughly to avoid clogging your emitters or pipes.

Foliar Feeding You can apply liquid fertilisers with a hand-held sprayer or mister or with a backpack sprayer. Set the

nozzle to release the finest spray possible. A surfactant such as ¼ teaspoon of mild soap per 3.8 litres (1 gallon) of spray will improve coverage, preventing the spray from beading up on the leaves. Spray in the early morning or late afternoon to avoid leaf burn. Always follow the instructions and suggested application rates for commercial foliar sprays.

Mulching

Mulching is what is known in scientific lingo as an 'elegant solution' – it's simple, but it works. All you do, in essence, is put something on top of the soil that covers up weed seeds and gets in the way of emerging weed plants. Either the seeds don't sprout at all, or the seedlings use up all of their energy and die before they reach the sunlight.

Even if it just helped to control weeds, mulch would be an important part of any garden. Happily, mulch offers many other benefits as well. It holds moisture in the soil, so you water less. It keeps soil cooler in the summer, so plant roots face less heat stress. In the winter, it keeps the ground frozen; this way, soils don't freeze and thaw repeatedly, heaving shallow-rooted plants out of the ground and leaving them on the soil surface to die. Mulch also helps reduce soil erosion, and it keeps soil from splashing upon your house or plants when rain falls. If you use a mulch that comes from a plant or animal, such as grass clippings or manure, it will also improve your soil by adding organic matter.

Unfortunately, mulch can have a few drawbacks. Slugs, cutworms, mice and some other garden pests like to hide in it. And unless you keep it a few inches away from plant stems, mulches can promote crown and stem rot. But if you select the right mulch for your conditions and manage it properly, you'll find that mulch is a valuable and easy part of your weed-control programme.

Finally, a wide ring of mulch around plants is good protection against accidental nicks and bangs from string trimmers and lawn mowers.

Bark chips are a good-looking and long-lasting mulch for permanent plants, like perennials.

Selecting a Mulch

There are two general types of mulch – organic and inorganic. Both help control weeds and hold moisture in soil, but organic mulches also add all-important organic matter to soil. Inorganic mulches don't improve soil, but they last longer than organic types. Another factor you may want to consider when choosing a mulch is its appearance. Coarse mulches like bark chunks may look fine around large trees but are overwhelming in delicate flower beds; straw is fine for the vegetable garden but too rough-looking for ornamental plantings.

Organic Mulches

Shredded leaves, grass clippings, and bark chips are all examples of organic mulches. In addition to keeping soil cool and moist, organic mulches help improve soil structure by encouraging the activity of earthworms and other soil organisms. They also add nutrients and organic matter to soil as they decompose. Good organic mulches are wood and bark chips, shredded bark, pine needles, and chopped leaves. Hay, straw, and grass clippings are also good mulches, and you can top them

Iron deficiency

Phosphorus deficiency

Magnesium deficiency

Potassium deficiency

Nitrogen deficiency

Thankfully, plants rarely show all of these nutrient deficiencies at once. If one of your plants shows any of these symptoms, try seaweed spray for a quick fix, then improve the soil with compost for a long-term solution.

Fallen leaves make an attractive, natural-looking mulch. However, they break down quickly, so must be replaced often.

with a layer of wood chips or shredded bark to improve their appearance.

The larger the particle size, the more slowly the mulch will decompose and need to be replenished. Grass clippings decompose quickly and need frequent renewal, while large bark chips will last several seasons. Flat, leathery tree leaves such as oak and sycamore will last a long time but can mat and shed water: chop these leaves in a shredder or with your lawn mower before using them as mulch.

Some organic materials are unsuitable for use as mulch because they are too attractive to weeds. Compost, aged manure or other finely shredded organic materials act like potting compost to weed seeds. In a frequently tended vegetable or flower garden, these mulches are fine. But select a less-hospitable mulch for your low-maintenance permanent plantings, or use these mulches as a base and top them with a thick layer of wood chips or other weed-resistant mulches.

You can collect materials like leaves and pine needles for mulches from your own and your friends' gardens. Wood chips and bark are widely available in bags at garden or DIY centres. Composted garden waste and wood chips are sometimes available for little or no cost from municipal composting facilities or tree-care companies.

Inorganic Mulches

Inorganic mulches include stones, marble chips and gravel, as well as black plastic and various landscape fabrics. Inorganic mulches don't decompose, so they won't need renewing like organic mulches. But they also don't improve soil as organic mulches do.

Since you won't be disturbing stone or gravel mulches with fresh applications, weeds can become a problem. You will have to hand pull weeds that sprout in these materials. These mulches are often used in combination with a weed barrier such as landscape fabric to greatly reduce the chance of weed problems.

Dark-coloured inorganic mulches heat soil, sometimes too much. A plant that prefers cool roots (such as clematis) or one that is growing in full sun may suffer stress from the heat retained by the dark stones. On the other hand, light-coloured inorganic mulches, such as marble or quartz chips, reflect sunlight and heat, which can cause leaf damage.

Mulches at a Glance

Bark Pieces Chunks, chips and shreddings of bark are attractive, long-lasting mulches. The big chunks, sometimes called nuggets, are better than bark chips and shredded bark at discouraging weeds. Weed control is best when the bark is about 15 cm (6 inches) deep. If you're using it in garden beds, however, it's better to apply it only 7.5 to 10 cm (3 to 4 inches) deep, otherwise you might also smother your desirable plants. Bark mulch is a little expensive, but you'll pay less if you can find a source that sells it unbagged.

There are a few cautions you should keep in mind when considering and using bark mulches:
- Bags labelled 'wood chips' can contain wood other than bark, including leftovers from the timber industry that might have been treated with chemicals that could harm plants.
- If you chip your own bark, let it sit outside for a few months before you use

These large bark chunks are rather coarse-looking, but they are long-lasting and useful in low-maintenance areas.

it to leach out any natural substances harmful to young plants. Turn the pile every few weeks to keep the chips from turning 'sour'.
- Cypress bark can be toxic to young, tender plants.
- Small chips and shredded bark can wash onto nearby paths and pavements when it rains, leading to more work keeping paths near mulched beds clean.

Newspaper and Cardboard Mulches of cardboard or a thick layer of newspaper aren't especially attractive, but they are effective for smothering weeds. They create a barrier that even aggressive perennial weeds have a tough time breaking, while at the same time still allowing water to pass through.

Newspaper and cardboard are inexpensive and readily available. How thick the layer is and how rainy the season is affect how long these mulches last, but you can usually count on them to last one season. It's a good idea to cover them with another mulch to make them more attractive and to anchor them; at the very least, cover the edges with soil or a few rocks to keep them from blowing away.

Leaves Leaves make a good weed-suppressing mulch. You can shred them if you want a good-looking, fine-textured mulch or use them whole to form a dense mat. Apply either shredded or whole leaves in a 10- to 15-cm (4- to 6-inch) layer. If you're using leaves as a long-term mulch around perennials, trees or shrubs, rake them off for a few weeks in the spring to let the soil warm up.

Landscape Fabric Good landscape fabric – also known as a weed barrier – can keep the areas under and around trees and shrubs nearly weed-free. For new plantings, spread these water-permeable sheets of spun or pressed plastic (now they also are made from wool!) on top of the soil, then cut holes or Xs to make room for the plants. In existing plantings, do your best to fit the fabrics around the base of the plants. Landscape fabrics can also be useful under decks, paths and walkways; lay them before you build the deck or set the paving to prevent weeds from sprouting.

The barriers do have a few drawbacks. First, they're more expensive than most organic mulches. Also, they will eventually break down, so they have to be replaced every few years; exactly how long they last varies with the brand. Some fabrics are so loosely woven that they let weeds through. And in some cases, the roots of trees and shrubs grow through the fabric, making it tough to move or remove the mulch. You'll also need to cover the fabric with a layer of other mulch to make it look more attractive and to block sunlight, which breaks it down.

Plastic Sheeting Plastic, like landscape fabric, cardboard and newspaper, is a tough barrier. Unlike those materials, however, plastic doesn't let water through. If you use it around plants, either punch little holes in it or run a soaker hose underneath so your plants will get the water they need. Or use plastic mulch where you want nothing to grow, such as under fences and along walks. When exposed to light, plastic becomes brittle and can rip; cover it with another mulch to reduce these problems.

Compost Compost is partially or completely decomposed garden waste and non-meat kitchen scraps. While it makes a great soil conditioner, it's only so-so at smothering weeds because it's usually fine-textured enough for weed seeds to grow in. And it's so rich in nutrients that weeds will thrive. For best results, apply a layer of compost under another mulch, like bark chips or shredded leaves.

Keep in mind that if you've thrown seedy plants (weeds, flowers – even rotting tomatoes) into the pile, you may end up spreading the seeds around your garden and creating a worse weed problem than before! Avoid throwing seeds into any pile, or save that compost for use as a soil conditioner instead of as a mulch.

Hay and Straw Both hay and straw are loose mulches, so you have to apply a thick layer – 15 to 25 cm (6 to 10 inches) – to get much weed control from them. Even then, tough perennial weeds that you missed before mulching can pop through, although they'll be weaker than normal. Straw is usually free of weed seeds, but hay might not be and can add to your weed problems.

Grass Clippings Grass clippings add organic matter to the soil, but you need to apply them deeply – about 15 cm (6 inches) of dry clippings or 2.5 cm (1 inch) of fresh clippings – to control annual weeds. Because clippings are lightweight and break down quickly, they aren't effective against most perennial weeds. Fresh grass clippings can mould and smell if you apply them too thickly; try mixing them with a dry mulch such as sawdust, shredded leaves or bark chips. Avoid using clippings from lawns where the grass or weeds have gone to seed and also from lawns that have been treated with pesticides or herbicides.

Straw mulches are too coarse for flower gardens, but they are great for protecting vegetable and fruit plantings.

Pine Needles Pine needles last for a long time (up to several seasons) and increase soil acidity (a real plus for acid-loving plants like blueberries, azaleas and camellias). Another advantage is their fresh piney smell. But, like grass clippings, pine needles are too loose to keep down perennial weeds. And the needles are a fire hazard during droughts. Don't collect them from the forest; leave that organic matter to fertilise the trees. Apply a 15-cm (6-inch) layer, especially around acid-loving plants.

Mulch to Deter Pests

Mulching is a routine part of conserving soil moisture and preventing weeds, but it's also effective in controlling some pests and diseases. Materials like newspaper, biodegradable paper mulch and black plastic mulch help to control thrips, leaf miners, and other pests that must reach the soil to complete their life cycle. Strips of aluminium foil repel aphids, leafhoppers and thrips on garden and greenhouse crops. (Leave the foil in place only as long as pests are a threat to avoid leaf damage from reflected heat.) Mulches also prevent raindrops from splashing soil-borne disease spores onto plant leaves.

Applying Mulch

You'll get the best results if you mulch bare soil – that means before the weeds start growing or right after you hoe, cut or pull weeds that have already come up. Also make sure the soil is moist (but not soggy) before you mulch, then spread a layer of mulch that is thick enough to discourage new weeds from sprouting. If your mulch has large particles, such as large wood or bark chips, use a 7.5- to 12.5-cm (3- to 5-inch) thick layer. Mulches with smaller-sized particles, such as grass clippings or shredded bark, allow less space for sprouting weeds, so you can apply them in a thinner layer of 5 to 7.5 cm (2 to 3 inches).

Cover the soil with a uniformly thick layer, but taper the depth of the layer near the trunks or stems of plants. Never pile mulch against your plants' trunks or stems. Mulch can hold excessive moisture around them and also reduce the amount of oxygen that reaches the crowns of the plants. To prevent this problem and to keep rodents from nesting nearby and feeding on the bark, leave about 15 to 30 cm (6 to 12 inches) between the mulch and tree and shrub trunks, and 10 to 15 cm (4 to 6 inches) between mulch and climbing plants.

Also be aware that mulch can thwart desirable seedlings as well as weed seedlings. If you're growing plants from direct-sown seed or if you're depending on self-sown seedlings from last year's plants, wait until the seedlings are about 10 to 15 cm (4 to 6 inches) tall before mulching. An added benefit of waiting is that bare soil warms up more quickly in the spring than mulched soil.

How frequently you need to renew the mulches depends on which kind you use. Long-lasting materials like wood chips may need refreshing only every two to three years. Finer materials, like compost or grass clippings, should be renewed once or twice a year. Top these materials with coarse mulches to help them last longer.

The Latest News in Mulching

To control severe weed problems, you can get extra protection by laying sheets of newspaper beneath an organic mulch. Wet the papers lightly to keep them from blowing around and overlap neighbouring sheets to cover the soil surface. Then cover the paper with several inches of an organic mulch. In a month or two, the newspaper will gradually break down with the mulch, adding extra organic matter to the soil.

Staking and Supporting Your Plants

Staking Trees and Shrubs

Staking holds trees and shrubs in place while their roots grow out from the root ball into the surrounding soil. Trees taller than 8 feet (2.4 m) or top-heavy trees with a large crown in relation to the size of the root ball benefit from the support of stakes to prevent them from falling over. Trees with straight, strong trunks that are less than 8 feet (2.4 m) tall and have small crowns usually need no staking unless they are planted in a windy location. Unstaked trees, or those staked with some slack, develop thicker, stronger trunks faster than staked trees.

If staking is necessary, use one or two stakes for small trees, two or three for large trees. Select stakes that are tall and strong enough to support your trees.

Locate the first stake facing the prevailing wind and space the others equally around the trees.

Drive the stakes several inches into firm soil on the outside of the root ball before you finish backfilling the planting hole. Attach the stakes to your trees with materials that won't cut, rub or damage the trees' bark. Plastic bands, nylon webbing and strips of manufactured fabric are good choices. Allow a few inches of slack when you attach these materials so that your trees can move slightly in the wind. This movement promotes the development of strong wood, so the tree will be able to support itself when you remove the stakes.

Unstake your trees one year after planting. By that time, a healthy tree will be well anchored into the ground with its own roots.

Staking Flowers

If you grow only short-stemmed plants, or you don't mind your flowers sprawling or leaning on each other, you won't have to worry about staking. But anyone who has seen peonies flattened by rain or has watched a perfect giant delphinium toppled in a strong wind knows that a few minutes spent placing a few stakes is time well spent.

Stake delphiniums, foxgloves and other tall perennials to keep them upright.

Weeding

Plan a Weed Control Strategy

To control your lawn and garden weeds effectively and efficiently, you need to use the right technique at the right time. This requires an essential piece of knowledge: how long do your particular weeds live? All plants have one of three life cycles – they can be annuals, biennials or perennials. Knowing the life cycles of your weeds is your key to determining how they spread and how you can stop them.

Annual Weeds Spread by Seed

Annual weeds, such as fat hen (*Chenopodium album*), live an entire life within one year; they sprout from seed, grow, flower, set seed and die.

One part of controlling annuals is never letting them set seed. If the original plants die without making more seed, they won't come back the following year.

Biennials Take Two Years

For biennial weeds, such as Queen Anne's lace (*Daucus carow* var. *carow*), the seed-to-seed cycle spreads over two years. These weeds sprout from seed in the spring or summer, then usually grow into a ground-hugging circle of leaves called a rosette. The leaves produce sugars that move down to the roots and are stored as starch. The next spring, the plant uses the stored food energy to send up a flowering stalk, which may or may not have leaves. The plant flowers, sets seed, then dies.

You have two main options for controlling biennial weeds. You could dig out the rosette – root and all – the first year. Or you could wait until the second year and cut the plant down to the ground. If you wait until the weed is just about to flower, the plant will have used up most of its stored energy and will likely not return.

Perennials Are Persistent

Wild garlic (*Allium vineale*), brambles, dandelions, stinging nettless and other perennial weeds live for three years or more. Perennials, like biennials, store carbohydrates to fuel early growth the next spring. That food energy may be stored in a taproot, in spreading underground stems called rhizomes or in spreading above-ground stems called runners or stolons. Or it may be in a tuber (like a potato) or a bulb (like an onion).

Perennials are generally the most difficult weeds to control. The stored carbohydrates give them a strong start each spring, as well as the power to grow again if their leaves are lost or damaged. Just preventing seed formation on perennials is not enough to get rid of them; you need to either dig up all of the underground structures or force them to use up their food reserves by repeatedly removing their above-ground growth.

How to Weed

The particular weeding technique you'll use depends on how many weeds you have to control, how large an area they cover and how much time you want to spend on them.

Take a Physical Approach Weed control methods that involve pulling, cutting or directly injuring weeds are called physical or mechanical controls. These methods are the most common because they are convenient and they work.

Pulling and Digging These techniques are simple and effective for getting rid of a few weeds but are pretty tiring when you're weeding large areas.

Pulling gets rid of annual weeds well, especially if the soil is damp enough that the roots come up. Just be sure not to toss weeds that reroot easily, such as purslane (*Portulaca oleracea*), on the ground. If you pull annual grasses, get as much of the roots as possible; the growing point of grasses is below the ground, and the plant might resprout if you just remove the above-ground portion.

Always try to pull annuals before they begin to flower and set seed. If they have already started flowering, collect the

When you've put time and effort into planning and planting the perfect flower garden, you don't want weeds popping up to spoil the effect.

pulled weeds in a bucket; don't leave them on the ground, since their seeds could still ripen and drop onto the soil.

Digging is a slightly better choice for perennials, assuming you get all of the buried portions. If you don't, these buried portions can produce new plants. Use hand tools to dig out small or shallow-rooted perennials. You may need a spading fork, spade or shovel for tough, deep roots, like those of dandelions.

Thorough hand-weeding before planting will help get new gardens off to a weed-free start.

Hoeing and Tilling When the weeds are too numerous to pull, a sharp hoe is a good solution. In most cases, hoes are best for young or annual weeds. But you can also deal a damaging blow to some established perennials – primarily those with thin or soft stems – by forcing them to use food reserves to replace the decapitated top growth.

If you're trying to control perennial weeds, it's most important to hoe every 7 to 14 days to cut off the top growth before it starts sending food back down to the roots.

If you have a large vegetable garden, with crops planted in rows, cultivating with a wheel hoe or rotary tiller may be more practical than with a hand-held hoe. Shallow tilling – about 2.5 cm (1 inch) deep – can uproot young weeds without bringing up too many buried seeds.

In almost all cases, it's best to avoid tilling perennial weeds with spreading roots, such as couch grass (*Agropyron repens*) and creeping thistle (*Cirsium arvense*). Even small pieces of chopped-up roots can sprout, multiplying your perennial weed problems. If you must rid an area of these weeds and can leave the spot unplanted for a growing season, you could try tilling the area shallowly every week or two until the root pieces stop sprouting new plants.

Mowing Mowing doesn't get the roots, but it can keep all but the lowest-growing weeds from setting seed. And if you mow often enough (every week or two), it can weaken perennial weeds by making them use up their food reserves to replace the top growth you removed.

Mowing works on woody shrubs and climbers as long as the stems aren't too thick for the machine. For tall, tough weeds and tree seedlings no more than 18 mm (¾ inch) in diameter, use a heavy-duty string trimmer with a blade attachment. If you must control weeds over a large area,

creeping thistle

consider renting a walk-behind tractor with a sickle bar attachment.

Try Organic Herbicides

Organic herbicides won't solve all of your weed woes, but they can be a useful alternative in certain situations. The herbicides that are acceptable to organic gardeners – basically soap, vinegar and salt – all have one thing in common: they can kill any plant they touch (assuming you get enough of the material on the plant). In gardening lingo, these are called non-selective herbicides. You must use them with caution to avoid damaging the plants you want to keep.

Soap-Based Herbicides

If you've ever used soap sprays to control insect pests, you may have noticed the warnings that these sprays can injure some plants; you may have even seen the damage yourself. Herbicidal soap sprays take this damage one step further. They are formulated to break up the protective waxy covering on the leaves, causing the weeds to slowly dry up and die.

The soap works on contact – it isn't absorbed and moved through the plant – so you need to spray the entire plant thoroughly. It takes at least a few hours for the damage to show; the plant gradually turns brown.

Herbicidal soaps work best on young weeds that haven't had time to establish a good root system. Older annuals often grow back and usually require more than one application. Perennials with well-established food reserves can grow back so many times that, unless you want to run for the herbicide every week, it's probably easier to cut off the top growth until the food stores are depleted.

Vinegar and Salt

These two controls need to be used with even more caution than herbicidal soap because they can sterilise the soil for months. The first approach is to

Whatever control you choose, use it before weeds set seed, otherwise, you'll have to deal with seedlings too.

pour vinegar in the soil, making it too acid for plants to grow. The other is to pour salt on the soil and water it in, which kills the roots. For best results in either case, cut off or pull as much of the weed as you can before applying the control.

Because both of these substances have such a drastic effect on the soil, they are only appropriate where you want nothing else to grow, such as between the cracks in paving. Otherwise, consider less-toxic controls like dousing with boiling water or pulling by hand.

When not maintained, fence lines and pathways can become an ideal site for weeds to take over.

Pests and Diseases

If pests stood up to be counted, gardeners would find pest identification and control an easier task. Unfortunately, pests often remain undetected until the harm is done. Even if you do spot damage on your plants, you may have difficulty identifying the culprit. Nutrient deficiencies or even air pollution can cause similar symptoms. But getting an accurate diagnosis is the only way to choose an appropriate and effective pest control measure.

Diagnosing Insect Damage

Fortunately, there are clues you can look for to help pin down plant problems. Follow the steps below to spot developing damage and to identify the causes.

1. Give plants a thorough inspection at least once a week. Look at both sides of the leaves, around buds and flowers, and along the stems.
2. If you find damage, jot down a few notes: the identity of the affected plant, the plant parts that are affected and the kind of damage (such as 'large holes in leaves' or 'distorted fruit').
3. Check the undersides of plant leaves, and shallowly scratch the soil or mulch, looking for likely culprits. Also search for clusters of eggs, webs or pellet- or sawdust-like insect droppings. See if neighbouring plants show similar symptoms.
4. If you actually find insects, examine them with a 10x magnifying lens (available through garden suppliers or online). Look through the photographs in insect field guides to try to identify them. Don't assume that the insects must be pests – they could just as easily be beneficials that stopped by to help.
5. If you can't find any suspects, or can't identify the ones you have, try matching the damage symptoms with those in 'Signs of Damage', opposite. This approach may help you close in on a possible cause.
6. If you still aren't sure of the cause, consider other possible sources, like

wind damage, nutrient deficiency or animal pests.
7. If all else fails, you may want to take the notes you've made, and perhaps a piece of the affected plant to your local garden nursery for help in making an accurate diagnosis.

Pyrethrum daisies are the source of pyrethrin, a potent botanical insecticide.

Diseases

What Is a Disease?

Before you can cope with diseases, you need to understand what they actually are. Unfortunately, diseases are more difficult to define than insects. After all, insects are actual organisms with specific traits and characteristics. Plant diseases, on the other hand, can be anything that interferes with normal growth functions (like water uptake and photosynthesis).

To make this definition a little more useful, it's helpful to divide plant disease into two categories. Infectious

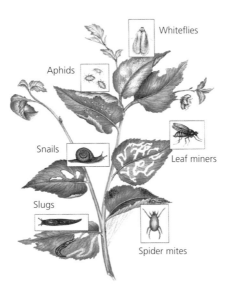

As you check for damage, inspect plants thoroughly. If you see signs of damage, look closely to check for pests.

diseases can spread from one plant to another. They're the problems we usually think of as plant diseases – like rust, fire blight, powdery mildew. Non-infectious diseases cannot be transmitted from one plant to another. Nutrient imbalances, air pollution and waterlogged soil are a few causes of non-infectious diseases.

Infectious Diseases

Infectious plant diseases are caused by microscopic living organisms called pathogens. Pathogens are commonly broken down into four groups: fungi, bacteria, viruses and nematodes.

Fungi Many kinds of moulds, mildews and mushrooms play an important part in breaking down organic matter in soil and compost. There are, however, a number of fungi that also attack living plants. These plant pathogenic fungi are the most common causes of garden diseases. Powdery mildew, damping-off, anthracnose, apple scab, club root, blight and black spot are all fungal.

Some pathogenic fungi are host-specific, but most will attack a variety of garden plants. Fungi produce spores that move with wind, soil, water and animals to plant surfaces. Given the right environmental conditions and the right host plant, spores of plant pathogenic fungi will germinate and infect plants.

Bacteria Like fungi, bacteria are specialised organisms with both beneficial and pathogenic species. Beneficial bacteria recycle soil organic matter and nutrients, and they can even help control insect pests, like caterpillars and beetles. Plant pathogenic bacteria, however, can infect plants and cause diseases like crown gall, bacterial wilt and fire blight.

Bacterial cells travel to plants the same way as fungal spores. Once they reach a susceptible plant, bacteria move into and infect plants through wounds and natural openings in leaves, stems and roots.

Viruses Viruses are the smallest disease agents. Once inside a living cell, they multiply by making their host plant produce even more virus particles, upsetting the plant's normal metabolism and causing disease symptoms. Virus particles are carried to healthy plants by pests like insects, mites and nematodes. They're also spread by taking cuttings, grafts, layers or divisions from infected plants. Compost that contains infected plants and is not properly decomposed can also spread viruses.

Viral diseases can be the most difficult to diagnose. Some common indications of viral attack include mottled or discoloured leaves. Symptoms can vary from one plant to the next; infected plants may not even show symptoms. If your plants have suffered from viral infection in the past, your best course is to become familiar with the common viruses in your neighbourhood and the symptoms they cause so that you will know when to take control measures.

Nematodes Nematodes are microscopic roundworms, which are found free-living in soil and as parasites on plants and animals. Beneficial nematodes are important members of the soil community, since they feed on decaying material and pests like cutworms and grubs. Pest nematodes damage plants by puncturing cell walls with their needle-like mouthparts and drawing out the cell contents. This causes disease-like symptoms – including yellowing, wilting, stunting and reduced yields – that are difficult to distinguish from other causes.

Plant parasitic nematodes travel to healthy plants in water and in infested soil carried on tools, boots and animals. If you suspect your plants suffer from nematode damage, you can submit root and soil samples to a diagnostic laboratory for positive identification.

Signs of Damage

Damage	Possible Causes
Leaves with large, ragged holes	Adult or larval stages of beetles like Japanese beetles, Mexican bean beetles and others; grasshoppers; moth larvae like armyworms or hornworms; slugs or snails; animal pests
Leaves curled, twisted, puckered or distorted	Aphids; leafhoppers; tarnished plant bugs; nutrient deficiency
Leaves curled, webs present	Webworms; obliquebanded leafrollers
Leaves with numerous, small holes	Adult flea beetles; plant diseases
Leaves spotted	Tarnished plant bugs; spider mites; thrips; lace bugs; plant diseases
Leaves or stems speckled or silvery	Thrips
Leaves and stems with hardened bumps, scales or cottony growths	Scales; mealybugs; plant diseases
Leaves with shallow tunnels under leaf surface	Larval leaf miners; sawflies
Leaves with shiny, slimy, frothy or sticky coating	Aphids; mealybugs; slugs and snails; scale insects; froghoppers; whiteflies; plant diseases
Fruit with tunnels throughout	Apple maggots; moth larvae like codling moths or European corn borers
Fruit distorted, twisted	European corn borers; tarnished plant bugs
Fruit spotted, sticky	Aphids; leafhoppers; froghoppers; plant diseases
Roots or bulbs with signs of feeding or dead spots	Wireworms; many kinds of beetle grubs; weevils (black vine, carrot or strawberry root weevils)
Roots or stems with galls, swellings	Gall wasps; nematodes; plant diseases
Roots or stems with excessive branching	Nematodes
Stems hollowed, with larvae inside and leaves wilted	Borers (European corn, flatheaded appletree, fruit, peachtree, roundheaded appletree and squash vine borers)
Flowers eaten	Japanese beetles; rose chafers
Flowers fall before opening	Tarnished plant bugs
Seedlings chewed off at soil level	Cutworms; animal pests

Non-Infectious Diseases

Changes in the environment and in your gardening techniques can also interfere with normal plant functions, so technically they are considered diseases. Unlike infectious diseases, though, noninfectious diseases (also called disorders) cannot be transmitted from plant to plant. Disorders can still be very serious once they occur, but they're often easy to prevent and remedy with good gardening practices, like regular soil improvement.

Symptoms of disorders vary widely, depending on the cause and the plant. You'll find more about identifying disorders under 'Disease Look-Alikes' on page 79.

Keeping your garden neat and free of debris helps remove sites for pests and disease spores.

Diagnosing Disease Problems

Like most garden problems, plant diseases are easiest to control if you catch them early. But unlike insect pests, pathogens are generally too small to see without magnification. In most cases, you won't know they've struck until your plants begin to suffer and display symptoms. Environmental and cultural problems, like frost injury, air pollution or nutrient imbalances, can also be tricky to diagnose, since the conditions that cause them are seldom visible.

Step-by-Step Disease Diagnosis

1. Identify the plant. Although it sounds obvious, this one simple step can put you surprisingly close to an accurate diagnosis in just a few minutes. Many popular garden plants are commonly attacked by easy-to-identify diseases and disorders, like black spot on roses, powdery mildew on lilacs or blossom end rot on tomatoes.

   If you're not sure what the plant is, ask a fellow gardener or seek advice at a local nursery or botanical garden. Even if identifying the plant doesn't help you diagnose the disease, it can be important later on when you are deciding on a control measure. Some plants, for instance, are sensitive to soap- or oil-based sprays, so you would want to use a different type of control on these plants to avoid causing even more damage.

2. Take a good look. Jot down anything that you notice about the affected plant. What parts seem to be most affected: the leaves, stems, flowers, or fruits? If the plant parts are spotted or discoloured, note the colour, size and general shape of the patches. If leaves are affected, is it the old or new leaves? Is the plant shorter than similar plants around it? Was it recently planted, or has it been in your landscape for many years? Anything you know or notice about the affected plant – no matter how minor – may help you in making or confirming a diagnosis of the problem.

3. Consider the environment. Extreme weather conditions, such as strong wind, hail and waterlogged or dry soils, can give plants an unhealthy appearance that resembles symptoms of plant disease. Make a note of any unusual weather conditions that you can remember. (Actually, it's a good idea to jot down weather occurrences, such as frosts, heavy rains or dry spells as they happen so you'll have those notes to refer back to when a problem strikes.) Also consider whether your plants have been exposed to pollutants like acid rain, herbicide drift or road salt.

4. Rule out insect pests. Some insects cause damage that resembles plant disease symptoms. When in doubt, use a magnifying lens to check for insect signs like webbing or droppings. Symptoms that are particularly unusual might mean that damage is the result of two or more pathogens or pests; open wounds from insects or other damage make convenient entrances for plant pathogens.

5. Do some research. Discuss the problem with neighbours who have similar plants and check reference books in your local library.

6. Consult the experts. If a particular problem has you stumped, submit samples to a disease diagnostic laboratory. Check online for possible organisations to contact and how to go about sending your plant samples by post. Local botanical gardens and arboreta may also be willing to help you identify plant problems.

Common Signs and Symptoms

Unhealthy plants have special distress signals that let you know when pathogens have attacked. Plants will respond to the stress of infection with a wide range of symptoms, from leaf spots and damaged fruit to wilting and even death. To help narrow down your diagnosis, see if any of the descriptions below match the affected parts of your plant.

Blights Leaves, flowers, stems and branches that suddenly wilt, wither and die are common indications of blight. Common garden blights include Botrytis, blight (caused by fungi) and fire blight (produced by bacteria).

Cankers Affected woody plants produce dead, and often sunken, patches in stems and branches. These cankers may ooze a sticky or foul-smelling material and can spread to kill whole trunks or shoots. The

Late blight on celery causes spots on leaves and may spread to stems.

fungal Cytospora canker is a common orchard problem; bacterial fire blight is another canker-causer.

Galls Swellings or overgrown patches of leaf or stem tissue are commonly known as galls. They may be caused by fungi (like leafy gall), bacteria (such as crown gall) or even insects (such as gall wasps).

Leaf Curl Deformed and discoloured leaves suffer from leaf curl. Peach leaf curl is caused by a fungus; viruses may also produce these symptoms.

Leaf Spots Rounded or irregular areas in various colours are common leaf symptoms. They are produced by a number of different pathogens.

Mildews Dusty white, grey or purplish patches on the surfaces or undersides of leaves are an easy clue to the fungal powdery and downy mildews.

Rots Soft or discoloured and dying plant tissue generally indicate some kind of rot. Fungi and bacteria can cause rot on fruit, stems, flowers or roots.

Rusts Orange or yellowish spots, galls or coatings are caused by rust fungi. Rusts may affect leaves, stems, flowers or fruits.

Wilts Drooping leaves and stems indicate that the plant isn't getting enough water. This may be caused by improper watering

Removing and destroying rust-infected leaves can be an effective control for this fungal disease.

or by fungi and bacteria that can clog the plant's water conducting system. Fungi cause Fusarium and Verticillium wilt; bacterial wilt is a problem in cucumbers and related crops.

Disease Look-Alikes

Although plants can adapt to many different environments, they all have certain conditions that they need to grow their best. Factors like air pollution or widely fluctuating temperatures can upset a plant's normal functions, causing symptoms that resemble plant disease. Since such problems aren't transmitted from plant to plant, they are called non-infectious diseases or plant disorders.

It's a good idea to be aware of the symptoms produced by common disorders so you can deal with them effectively when they do occur instead of mistaking them for an infectious disease.

Excessive Water Too much water means that most or all of the tiny soil pores, which normally hold some oxygen, are filled with water. When roots don't get the oxygen they need, they can't function properly and are more prone to infectious diseases, like root rot. Affected plants lack vigour and may wilt; leaves become yellow. Raised beds can help improve drainage.

Drought A shortage of soil water can stunt plant growth and slow flower and fruit production. Leaves either turn pale and wilt or develop brown, scorched areas. Shallow-rooted annual plants are often most affected. Regular deep irrigation can help mildly affected plants recover and prevent future problems. Soaker hoses are an efficient and economical way to give your plants the water they need.

Cold Stress Sudden cold snaps can kill tender buds, growing tips and other woody plant parts. Leaves turn yellow or drop, buds may drop, stems can crack and bark may split. Unseasonably low temperatures during the growing season can damage warm-weather vegetables like sweetcorn, beans and tomatoes. Protect actively growing plants with horticultural fleece or other frost shields. Avoid fertilising after midsummer; later fertilising promotes soft growth that is more frost-prone.

When the ground is frozen, dry winter winds can pull moisture out of buds and evergreen leaves, causing browning and tip dieback. Protect dormant plants with windbreaks or spray with an anti-transpirant to block moisture loss.

Heat Stress Young plants exposed to high temperatures often wilt and may die. Cold-weather vegetables like lettuce and spinach stop producing new leaves and will bolt (go to seed). Shade and water may help plants recover; shade can also help prevent damage. Water well in the early morning and again in the evening if necessary. Avoid planting cool-weather crops that will mature in midsummer. Pull out and compost plants that bolt.

Insufficient Light Plants become spindly and are more susceptible to lodging (falling over) when light is inadequate. Green leaves become pale, and variegated or coloured leaves may turn evenly green if they don't get enough light. If plants show these symptoms, try moving them to a sunnier spot.

Pruning and Training

Proper pruning can promote healthy growth on ailing plants, improve the form of poorly shaped ones, show off the natural beauty of good-looking plants and encourage the production of more or better fruits or flowers.

Why Should You Prune?

There are many reasons you may want or need to prune. Judicious pruning at planting time defines the shape of your new trees, shrubs and climbers. As your new plants grow, they will need pruning to keep them in shape. Also, they will occasionally need pruning to correct structural problems that develop, such as branches that rub or grow at tight angles. Maintenance pruning is also necessary to remove damage caused by weather, animals, people or insects and diseases. You may need to direct growth, especially of fast-growing climbers, or control the height or spread of your plants. Some climbers, especially vigorous growers like trumpet creeper (*Campsis radicans*) and wisteria (*Wisteria* spp.), need heavy pruning to keep them a manageable size and to increase the number of flowers.

When to Prune

Timing is critical to successful pruning. Adapt your pruning schedule depending on what you want to accomplish. Here are the benefits and drawbacks of pruning in each season:

- Spring pruning stimulates a flush of vigorous growth, and plants will recover fast from heavy pruning.
- Summer pruning is a good time for tidying up, but avoid heavy pruning, which can stress plants in hot weather.
- Autumn is a good time to make thinning cuts, removing branches back to a main stem. Don't prune back branch tips in autumn because the tender new growth that results can be easily damaged by freezes.
- In winter, dormant plants are particularly easy to prune to shape, since the lack of leaves makes it easy to see the plant's structure.

There are times, however, when you need to ignore the season and pick up the pruners. If damage from storms, equipment or disease occurs, you should prune immediately, removing all damaged wood.

Pruning Tools

The pruning tools you'll need depend on what you will be trimming. Hedge shears are the traditional choice for formal hedges. Secateurs are best for stems and twigs. As the diameter of the branches increases, switch to loppers, which work well on branches that are finger-sized or larger. When loppers aren't large enough, use a pruning saw.

Secateurs and loppers are available in two types. Bypass secateurs cut with a scissor action; anvil secateurs cut with a sharp blade that closes against a metal plate. Lopping shears have long handles to give you leverage and a longer reach. Test pruning tools before buying them to make sure the grip is comfortable and the mechanism is easy to work.

Pruning Techniques

Start any pruning job by removing dead wood. Dead wood is easy to spot during the growing season because it bears no leaves. It snaps easily, revealing no green under the bark.

After removing the dead wood, prune your trees and shrubs to improve their structure, making them more attractive and stronger. Remove any branches that are badly crossed or rubbing, leaving the best of the pair. Thin out or head back misplaced branches that crowd pathways or other plants.

Pruning Cuts

Pruning basically comes down to two types of cuts: thinning and heading. A thinning cut removes branches where

Thinning cuts help to retain a plant's natural branching structure and open up dense, crowded growth.

they join the stem. Be sure to cut just outside the branch collar – the raised or otherwise distinct area at the branch base. Cuts that are flush to the stem, removing the collar area, don't heal (close) well. Use thinning cuts to open the interior of a shrub or tree or to remove misplaced or crossed branches.

Heading cuts stimulate regrowth. Save them until the end of the pruning job. A non-selective heading cut slices off branch tips in midstem, bringing on a thick flush of uniform growth. Selective heading snips off the tip of a branch back to a bud or side branch. Cut slightly above a bud pointed in the direction in which you want new stems to grow. In general, prune above buds that face outwards, not inwards.

Pruning Terms

Just like any skill, pruning has its own terminology. We've tried to keep the jargon to a minimum, but there are some terms that you really need to understand to be an effective pruner. Here are definitions for some common pruning terms.

Apical dominance The condition in most plants where the tip bud grows more strongly than the buds lower on the stem. If you cut off the top bud, apical dominance is lost and the remaining buds grow more quickly.

Branch collar The zone where a branch meets a stem. The collar is usually easiest to see as a bulge at the base of a large branch, but even small branches have collars. When you make a pruning cut, always leave the collar; this is a site of rapid cell division and wound closure.

Callus The scar tissue that naturally forms around wounds, such as pruning cuts, on woody plants.

Candle The compact, expanding new growth that appears on pines, spruces and firs in the spring.

Cane A long, slender branch that originates directly from the roots.

Crotch The angle formed between two branches or between a branch and the trunk.

Deadheading The removal of spent flowers or unripe seed pods.

Lateral branch Any branch growing from a larger branch.

Leader The main, primary or tallest vertical branch originating from the trunk of a tree.

Scaffold branches The primary limbs that originate from the main trunk of a tree and form its structure.

Spur A short, often thorn-like shoot that produces flowers, fruit and leaves. Some spurs are permanent; some only live a few years. Landscape plants that have spurs include ginkgo, larch, some apples and kiwi fruit.

Stub An unsightly and soon-to-be-dead branch piece left when a cut was not made to a bud or originating branch.

Sucker shoot An upright shoot growing from a root or graft union.

Watersprout A vigorous upright branch that originates along another branch.

Pruning Large Limbs

To prune a large limb, first cut halfway through the branch from underneath, about 30cm (1 foot) out from the trunk. Move your saw a few inches in towards the trunk from the first cut and saw down from the top until the branch drops. Finish the cut by sawing just outside the

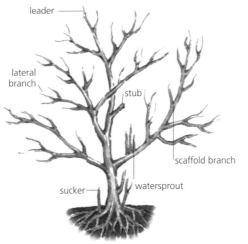

branch collar. If the crotch is too tight for easy manoeuvring, saw from the bottom up. Pruning cuts, even on large branches, need no paint or other wound dressings. They will heal fastest on their own.

Renewal Pruning

If your plants grow too large or if they contain many old or dead stems, drastic measures are often effective. Many vigorous climbing plants, including autumn clematis (*Clematis maximowicziana*) and perennial sweet pea (*Lathyrus latifolius*), can be pruned to within a few inches of the ground in late winter if they have grown much too large. In spring, the plants will regrow at a manageable size.

Multi-stemmed deciduous shrubs, such as forsythia (*Forsythia x intermedia*) and lilacs (*Syringa* spp.), which have grown old and woody with limited bloom, can also be given this drastic treatment to

stimulate new growth. However, it will take several years after such a severe pruning for the shrub to recover completely and flower again. A less-stressful renewal method for reclaiming overgrown deciduous flowering shrubs is to prune one-third of the plant each year over a period of three years. Selectively cut a few of the old stems to the ground each year until you finally have an entirely new plant with new growth, an attractive shape and a new lease of life.

When pruning, make a sloped cut just above a bud (left). Avoid cutting too close (centre) or leaving a stub (right).

Neglected young trees can develop serious flaws as they mature. Pruning a young tree carefully will give you a safe, handsome mature tree.

1. Start with a cut from underneath the branch, out from the trunk.

2. Make another cut a few inches in from the first; saw off the branch.

3. Remove the stub by carefully sawing it off just outside the branch collar.

Topping

Topping is a favourite technique of council workers and, sometimes, of desperate homeowners: large trees that interfere with wires or grow too tall for their site are simply sliced off across the top. Large branches are sawed off in mid-limb instead of being pruned at main stems.

Topping disfigures and weakens trees, stimulating undesirable water sprouts that actually accelerate the rate of top regrowth. The slow-to-heal wounds of topping are open invitations to insects and diseases, and limbs that die from these causes will soon fall in a storm, creating a danger to people and property. If your trees are so badly out of place that you would consider topping, remove them entirely and plant a better-suited species.

Pruning Hedges

How you prune your hedges depends on the effect you're looking for. If you want a natural-looking screen, a bit of selective pruning is all your hedge really needs. Prune flowering shrubs after they flower. To keep the hedge vigorous, cut two or three of the oldest stems down to the ground each year.

Many gardeners appreciate the formal look of neatly trimmed hedges. But before you decide to go this route, consider whether you'll be eager to do the frequent pruning that is necessary to maintain them. After planting, the new shoots of broad-leaved plants should be trimmed back by one-third or more each year until the plants reach the desired size. After that, shear often during the growing season to keep the hedge neat.

Pruning Climbers

Most climbing plants require little special care other than pruning to train them, limit their growth or encourage flower or fruit production. Prune away dead wood at any time during the year. To control growth or to shape a plant grown for foliage, such as Virginia creeper (*Parthenocissus quinquefolia*) or Boston ivy

A stake-and-string guide is handy to direct your cuts; this is critical for good results on formal clipped hedges.

(*P. tricuspidata*), prune in late winter or early spring. Cut back flowering plants shortly after they bloom. Trim spring-flowering plants, such as wisteria, by early summer – before the next year's flower buds develop. Summer flowerers, such as honeysuckles and climbing hydrangeas, produce flowers on new stems that grow during the spring. Prune summer-flowering plants from late autumn until late winter.

Pruning an Overgrown Climber

Every now and then you'll be faced with a long-neglected plant that's a hopeless tangle of big, woody stems. While you might be able to pick your way through the mess and remove the dead growth, the. remaining stems often end up much worse for the wear.

Fear not. One of the finer qualities of climbers is their ability to respond to rejuvenation pruning – the kind where you cut the entire overgrown mess to the ground and start again. Remember that the root system has been growing for years and – especially during the dormant season – stores much in the way of energy reserves. Take advantage of this stored energy by cutting the plant down in late

Caring for mature climbers can be a maintenance hassle. Be sure to consider how big the plant will grow before you plant it.

winter. Leave a few of the newer stems – if there are any – at the base of the plant. When growth begins in the spring and the plant sends up vigorous new shoots, remove all but the few that you'll need to train up the supports. Train them as you would any new climber.

Can Climbers and Walls Coexist?

Think very carefully before deciding to train clinging plants to the walls of your house. While the plants aren't inherently destructive, the aerial roots or adhesive discs can infiltrate already-soft mortar. If you remove a clinging vine that's been growing for many years, the exposed disintegrating mortar will be subject to further damage from wind and rain. At the very least, you'll be left with a mess of tiny rootlets stuck tight to the wall. These tenacious climbers can also damage aluminium trims, leaving a spotting pattern when you pull them off the metal.

Aggressive climbers like wisteria are notorious for taking over anything in their path. Proper pruning can help to keep these ramblers in line, but it's laborious and time-consuming work.

When planting a climber next to a wall, it's important to choose the plant carefully and, in some cases, to consider a support system that holds it away from the wall. Also be vigilant in training climbing plants away from roofs, gutters and downpipes to prevent damage.

Cutting Back and Thinning Flowering Plants

Like giving your plants a haircut, you can cut back long or straggly stems to make a plant tidier and to encourage it to produce healthy new growth. Cutting back (also known as shearing) differs from pinching out because it is done after flowering, and from deadheading because it can be more radical. Thinning involves removing whole stems, giving the remaining stems more room to expand and improving air circulation around the plant.

Cutting Back Perennials

If you have a small number of plants, use secateurs to cut back each stem to just above a leaf or bud. You should remove one-third to one-half of the stem length, encouraging a neater shape and rebranching, while deadheading at the same time. For large gardens, some landscape contractors use a string trimmer. This method is certainly fast, although it might be too rough for more delicate or disease-prone perennials like pinks (*Dianthus* spp.).

Besides making them look neater, cutting plants back can also help control insect and disease outbreaks. Simply cut back diseased or insect-infested plants to

Columbines (*Aquilegia* spp.) are beautiful in bloom but decline after flowering. Cut them back to get new leaves.

the ground and dispose of the trimmings with household rubbish. The shoots may re-emerge with clean and healthy foliage. This technique works well for controlling powdery mildew on bee balm (*Monarda didyma*), leaf miners on columbines (*Aquilegia* spp.) and galls on goldenrods (*Solidago* spp.). It is unlikely that plants will reflower during the year in which they have been subjected to this drastic treatment, but their foliage will look much more appealing for the rest of the season.

Thinning

Some mature clump-forming plants send up such a thick crop of stems that they crowd and shade each other out. As a result, they flower sparsely, and the poor circulation within the clump makes them more susceptible to diseases. Thinning – removing about half of the crowded stems – can help such mildew-prone perennials as garden phlox (*Phlox paniculata*), bee balm (*Monarda didyma*) and common sneezeweed (*Helenium autumnale*).

If your phlox has been mildewed in previous seasons, try radical thinning, leaving only four or five of the strongest stems. Prune the weaker shoots back to the ground when you can see how dense the clump will be but before it expends much energy in growth.

The remaining strong stems should be more vigorous and often are less disease-prone as a result. Dividing large clumps is another way to encourage strong new growth.

Deadheading

Deadheading – removing spent flowers – is an essential part of gardening. When you deadhead, you can enjoy a garden unmarred by brown or drooping petals. Your plants will be free from rots and other diseases that invade the decaying blossoms. And since deadheaded plants don't waste energy on seed production, they have more strength for flower production and plant growth.

When Not to Deadhead

Despite the advantages of deadheading, you may have good cause to skip it on occasion. Spare the seed pods of perennials that you want to self-sow, like wild columbines (*Aquilegia canadensis*) and foxgloves (*Digitalis* spp.). You may also want to leave attractive seedpods or cones, which can extend the beauty of certain perennials through the dormant season. Try this with the velvety black or orange-brown cones of coneflowers (*Rudbeckia* and *Echinacea* spp.), the glossy, dark seed clusters of blackberry lilies (*Belamcanda chinensis*), the dry, feathery plumes of astilbes, the russet pods of 'Autumn Joy' sedum (*Sedum* 'Autumn Joy'), and the papery 'flowers' of Lenten roses (*Helleborus* x *orientalis*). You also may want to spare the plume-like seed heads of ornamental grasses that you grow with your perennials.

Secateurs are handy for snipping off spent flowers that have thick or wiry stems.

What to Cut Back

Certain perennials are sure to benefit from cutting back. Give spring bloomers a trim after they flower to make them look neater for the rest of the season. Cut back summer bloomers after their first flush of flowers; some may bloom again later in the season. Listed below are some of the most common perennials that benefit from being cut back.

Spring bloomers: Rock cress (*Arabis caucasica*), creeping phlox (*Phlox stolonifera*), goat's beard (*Aruncus dioicus*).

Summer bloomers: Frikart's aster (*Aster x frikartii*), catmint (*Nepeta x faassenii*), Persian cornflower (*Centaurea dealbata*), common spiderwort (*Tradescantia x andersoniana*), common thrift (*Armeria maritima*), bellflowers (*Campanula* spp.), blanket flower (*Gaillardia x grandiflora*), sages (*Salvia* spp.), cotton lavender (*Santolina chamaecyparissus*), spotted lamium (*Lamium maculatum*), pincushion flower (*Scabiosa caucasica*), soapworts (*Saponaria* spp.).

Encourage evergreens to grow thicker by pinching out new growth.

flowers. For asters and chrysanthemums, you may need to pinch out twice. Make the first pinch when shoots are about 15 cm (6 inches) tall. Repeat the pinching out at 20 cm (8 inches), but not later than the end of early summer.

Pinching out

Pinching out is underrated as a pruning technique, perhaps because it requires no fancy tools – only your hands! A pinch is a heading cut, used only on very soft tissue. By removing the growing tip of the stem, you cut off the source of hormones that make that branch elongate; this frees buds lower on the stem to develop into side branches. It will make leggy plants more bushy and compact, with better branching and more (although often smaller) flowers. Perennials like common sneezeweed (*Helenium autumnale*), boltonia (*Boltonia asteroides*) or 'Autumn Joy' sedum (*Sedum* 'Autumn Joy') that otherwise need staking will be able to stand on their own if you pinch them back.

Pinch out the plant when it is young enough to develop a full shape but not so early that later growth becomes scrawny over the shapely base. Also, pinch out before flower buds develop. Otherwise, you could remove them all and lose the season's

Pruning Roses

Well-timed, careful pruning helps to keep roses healthy, vigorous and free-flowering. Although the specific recommendations for different types of roses vary, there are some basic techniques that apply to all. For instance, you'll always start pruning any rose by removing dead, damaged, diseased, thin, weak or crossing branches. Deadheading and

Pruning Tools and Power lines

When using long-handled pruners or any other extension tool, check carefully to make sure that there are no power lines running through or by the tree. Also remember that high-voltage electricity can arc over several feet outside the wires. Since you and your long-handled pruners do not want to be the ground for this electricity, stay far away from power lines. If tree limbs need to be pruned away from lines, call your electricity provider or a qualified arborist to do the work.

removing blind shoots (those with no flower buds) are also common pruning tasks on certain types of roses. Of course, you'll want to harvest some of those roses to bring into the house to scent and liven up your rooms; that's pruning, too!

Tools and Supplies

A good pair of bypass (scissor-style) secateurs and loppers are all you need to do most rose pruning. For renovation, or for large bush roses, you may also need a pruning saw. If you know that your plants are infected with a disease like canker or crown gall, plan to disinfect your tools by dipping or wiping the blades with isopropyl alcohol between cuts or at least between plants. Painting pruning cuts with wood glue can help prevent borers

The thorns on roses make pruning them difficult and sometimes painful. Long trousers, long sleeves and a sturdy pair of gloves can help.

from entering the stems. For small jobs, apply the glue right out of the bottle or tube; for large jobs, dab on the glue – from a can – with a small, cheap and disposable brush. Finally, protect your hands and arms from thorns (and from your secateurs!) with a good pair of thick gloves. Long gauntlet-style gloves are especially useful for rose pruning, since they shield both your hands and your forearms. A long-sleeved shirt and long trousers can also help prevent nicks and scratches from thorny canes.

This is the delightful rugosa rose (*Rosa rugosa*) shown with its fleshy red 'hips'. Its many thorns make it difficult to prune.

When to Prune

Good pruning starts at planting time. If you're planting a rose from bare-root stock, first look carefully at the roots. Healthy roots are normally light-coloured, firm and fibrous. Prune away any roots that are broken, dried, dead or rotten. Trim healthy roots only if you must. Try not to prune healthy roots just because they won't fit into the hole that you've dug; first consider enlarging the hole. Spread the roots out over a cone of soil in the hole, then fill the rest of the hole with soil and water well.

On container-grown stock, remove the pot and loosen any circling roots. Put the

Pruning off developing fruits can encourage your rose plant to produce more flowers.

root ball in the hole, backfill with soil and water the plant well.

Once your bare-root or container-grown rose is in the ground, remove any dead, damaged or weak twigs. Be sure to cut back into good wood and to buds pointing in directions where you want the new growth to go.

On established roses, late winter or early spring is generally the best time for major pruning. Swelling growth buds on the canes is a good sign that the time is right. During the season, remove any dead or dying stems as you see them. If you are not growing a rose for its showy fruit (hips), cut off the flowers as they fade. This kind of pruning will encourage new growth, though, so stop deadheading by late summer. Otherwise, the new growth may not have time to harden before cold weather sets in, and it may get killed or damaged by the first winter freezes.

How to Prune

Start any rose pruning session by removing any dead or diseased stems. If you need to remove a whole stem, cut it to the ground or graft union; otherwise, just trim back into good wood at least 2.5 cm (1 inch) below where any damage is evident.

If the centre, or pith, of the stem is still dark or discoloured at that point, cut the cane back farther until the pith is white. Look for and remove any weak or spindly stems that are much thinner than the others. If you see any canes that cross or rub, remove one of the two. Make each cut about 6 mm (¼ inch) above a bud, at a 45-degree angle away from the bud. In most cases, you'll want to cut to a bud that faces away from the centre of the plant to encourage outward growth and good air circulation.

Sucker Removal

Most modern roses are budded onto more vigorous species-rose rootstocks, so you'll want to control any sucker growth that you see coming from the roots. Growth from these suckers is often stronger than

the top growth (what you actually bought the rose for). If left unchecked, suckers can crowd out the more desirable growth.

To properly remove a sucker, scrape the soil away from its base and snap it off where it joins the rootstock. This technique removes any dormant buds that might be present at the point where the sucker joins the root. Don't simply cut the sucker off at ground level, because more sucker shoots will probably arise for you to deal with later.

Basic Bonsai

Bonsai is an art that attempts to replicate, in a container, the look of an old tree that has been shaped by time and the elements. The process of training beautiful bonsai requires time and patience, but the results can be stunning and gratifying.

Caring for Bonsai

Before you buy or begin a bonsai project, be aware that these plants will need some special care. Hardy bonsai normally prefer to be outdoors during the growing season. They enjoy the shelter of a lath house or some other shade-producing structure, where they will receive bright indirect light and protection from the elements. One big gust of wind can easily knock over small plants and undo months, or years, of care!

Bonsai generally grow in shallow pots, so you'll have to water them frequently – possibly as often as twice a day in hot dry weather – to keep the soil evenly damp. During the winter months, you'll need to protect bonsai from excessively cold temperatures. Many overwinter best in a cool greenhouse, where they will get a dormant, or rest, period. Without this cold period, many hardy plants will not bloom, and they'll gradually become weak and spindly. Bonsai created from houseplants such as weeping fig (*Ficus benjamina*) are somewhat easier to care for: they can adapt easily to indoor environments on sunny windowsills or under lights year-round.

Protecting Your Plants

Extending the Season

To extend the growing season of your vegetable garden, you must select the right plants for the conditions, plant them at the right time and shield them from cold spring or autumn temperatures.

Picking the Right Plants

Look for cultivars that are suited to extra-cold conditions. For late-summer and autumn crops, check out the array of winter-keeping cultivars of cabbage, lettuce and beets. 'Springtide' Chinese cabbage, corn salad, 'Easter Egg' radishes and 'Tyee' hybrid spinach are good choices for early spring. Traditional cool-season crops, like spinach, endive, escarole, broccoli, carrots, chives and kale, are natural choices for early-spring or autumn growing.

Planting at the Right Time

To start extra early in spring, prepare the soil on a well-drained site in autumn. Two weeks before you plant, heat the soil by covering it with green or black plastic. Plant thoroughly hardened-off seedlings or pre-sprouted seeds through slits or holes cut in the plastic.

To harvest in late autumn or winter, plant crops in midsummer to late summer. You can sow fast-growing crops like lettuce, spinach and radishes every two weeks, up to two weeks before your first autumn frost date if you protect the young plants. Plant beets and carrots about 65 days before the first autumn frost.

Using Frost Protectors

If cool-season crops will be growing in weather colder than about 4°C (40°F), they'll do better with some form of protection. Protective devices will also prevent frost-tender peppers, pumpkins and other long-yielding summer crops from being damaged by an early frost or two. Surround the plants with hay bales or trellising and drape hessian or horticultural fleece over them at night or during short cold spells. When Indian summer returns, these tender plants may be able to finish maturing their fruits.

Protect your tender plants from frost with a plastic cloche or cover.

Use smaller enclosures to protect young plants in early spring or late autumn. Cover them with horticultural fleece, which will help keep the air around the plants a few degrees warmer than the surrounding environment.

You also can cover plants with plastic jugs that have the bottom removed, plastic umbrellas or plastic tunnels stretched over wire hoops. These 'mini-greenhouses' can hold in too much heat during a warm sunny day, so be prepared to provide some ventilation.

Cold Frames

Use a growing frame for hardening off tender transplants and for growing cold-tolerant vegetables when garden temperatures are too low. The most simple growing structures are wooden, bottomless, boxlike frames topped with a window sash roof. They're usually called cold frames, since they're unheated.

Hot Beds

Hot beds are simply growing frames with a heat source; they are useful if you live in an area where it snows. Most gardeners rely on electric heating cables to keep their seedlings warm. First, dig a pit 30 cm (12 inches) deep to fit your frame. Follow the manufacturer's instructions for placing the cables correctly so they don't cross. Sandwich the cables at the bottom between layers of sand for drainage. Cover with a screen for protection. Top with 10 to 15 cm (4 to 6 inches) of sand. Push pots into the sand to secure them.

FOUR SEASONS IN A COLD FRAME

Spring: Harden off seedlings in your cold frame before transplanting to the garden.

Summer: Sow salad crops like spinach for autumn harvest. Lath shade keeps plants cool.

Autumn: A cold frame ensures survival of late-autumn leaf crops like lettuce after the first frost.

Winter: Use your cold frame to give spring bulbs their cold treatment before forcing.

Overwintering

Some tender perennials won't survive when exposed to cold-climate winters. Cuttings that you take in early autumn will be ready to move to the garden in spring if you nurture them indoors all winter. You can also pot up annuals and bring them indoors for winter use, or start fresh ones from seed.

Bringing Perennials Indoors

Perennials can be grown in the garden soil in summer, then potted up for winter indoors. At the beginning and end of the season, leave the plants in their pots in a shady spot outdoors for at least a week before moving them to their new home.

You can also start new plants for the winter from cuttings. You can take cuttings from established plants outdoors well into autumn, as long as there is new growth to choose from and the plants have not become dormant.

Bringing Annuals Indoors

The first frost of autumn doesn't have to signal the end of your annuals' bloom season. With just a little effort, you can enjoy their colourful flowers on your windowsills all winter.

Tender perennials that are commonly grown as annuals usually adapt best to life indoors. These include wax begonias, geraniums (both flowering and scented-leaf types), coleus, impatiens (including New Guinea types) and heliotrope (*Heliotropium arborescens*).

To overwinter annuals indoors, dig up whole plants before the first autumn frost, cut them back by about one-third and plant them in pots. Or take 7.5- to 12.5-cm (3- to 5-inch) cuttings from healthy, vigorous stems in mid- to late-summer and insert the bottom one-third of the stem in a pot of moist potting compost. Enclose the pot in a plastic bag and set it in a bright place out of direct sun. When cuttings are well rooted – usually in three to four weeks – remove the bag and move the pot to a sunny windowsill. In spring, move them outside to a shady spot to adjust.

Overwintering Outdoors

The success of overwintering your perennials outdoors in the garden depends on your climate. Hardy perennials will survive a cold winter in perfect condition, ready to grow again when temperatures rise in spring. Some of the less hardy plants may need help getting through a cold winter.

The best protection is a blanket of snow. If snowfall is minimal or absent, protect perennials from the drying effects of winter winds by covering them with evergreen boughs or surrounding them with sacking or plastic sheeting (especially bubble wrap). To overwinter small perennials, wait until the soil has frozen, then mulch heavily with straw or leaves. Remove the mulch in spring.

Putting the Garden to Bed

When all your plants have finished producing for the season – except perhaps a few late crops snuggled in a cold frame or under row covers – it's time to clean up. Spring may inspire you to clean indoors, but autumn is the best time to clean up out in the garden. Pests and diseases often linger on old plant debris or dig in near plant roots to spend the winter close to their preferred food source. When the plants go dormant, pests are trapped there, so it's the perfect opportunity for you to destroy them as you tidy up. If you get rid of old debris and weeds now, you will eliminate many pest and disease problems for the following growing season.

Dispose of Debris

Cut off old stems and put any that are disease- and seed-free in your compost pile. (Bury the rest or dispose of them with household rubbish.) You want to clear out all the brown vegetation, with a few exceptions. You can leave fallen asparagus stems (if they are not bothered by asparagus beetles) to act as a mulch. And spare the dried seed heads of companion coneflowers (*Rwlbeckia* and *Echinacea* spp.) – they can look attractive in winter and provide bird-luring seeds.

Blanket the Soil

As garden space becomes vacant in late summer and autumn, turn the soil with a spade or rotary tiller to expose hibernating pests, larvae or eggs near the soil surface. This also kills many weeds. But to be doubly thorough, pull out any roots of perennial weeds that you turn up – otherwise they could resprout. If there are several weeks before the first hard frost, plant a cover crop, such as clover or winter rye, to protect the soil from erosion and compaction. Work the crop into the soil about two weeks before planting the following spring.

If you are planting a late vegetable crop but still want a cover crop for winter, try interplanting them. Plant the vegetables as usual for autumn, and let them grow for about a month, keeping the space between plants weed-free. Then broadcast the seed of the cover crop over the growing area. By the time your late vegetables are ready for harvest, the cover crop will be large enough to walk on without damaging it.

A thick layer of mulch will provide ample protection for hardy root crops like parsnips, carrots and beets that you leave in the ground. You can also mulch some perennials once the soil freezes in late autumn. Mulch prevents the soil from heaving (shifting as it freezes and thaws), which can damage shallow-rooted perennials. Cover them with a loose, airy material such as straw or pine branches.

Planting a clover crop is a great way to protect the soil from erosion or compaction over winter.

The Ornamental Garden

A window box full of annuals on a sunny windowsill, a formal garden of neatly clipped trees and shrubs, a wild meadow in which naturalised bulbs come up year after year, a classic flower border. Whether you have lots of time, or none at all, you can have a beautiful ornamental garden.

Perennials

Aster

With so many wonderful perennials to choose from, it's hard ro resist planting one of each. But if you buy them one by one and plop them in the ground wherever there's room, your garden will look like a plant collection – interesting, perhaps, but not beautiful.

Before you dig your garden, buy plants, or start rearranging an existing planting, you need to figure out what you want to grow and where you want to grow it. Garden design is basically the process of refining your plant choices, placement and combinations to get the best effect. It's what transforms a bunch of individual plants into a pleasing composition.

Part of the fun of landscaping with perennials is creating an ever-changing display. Working with living material that changes from week to week and season to season makes designing a garden different from redecorating a room, even though it builds on the same principles of contrast, balance, texture and colour.

For a garden design to be effective, it has to match your site conditions, your style, the amount of time you have for gardening and the results you want from the garden. Ideally, it should also blend in with the topography and complement your house so everything looks like it belongs right where it is.

Why Grow Perennials?

Take a few minutes to jot down why you want to add perennials to your garden. Do you want a parade of flowers all season long or just a bit of colour to liven up a drab, shady spot? Do you want to attract butterflies, or do you want a wide selection of fresh flowers for arrangements? Do you want to plant perennials to fix an eroding hillside or camouflage the compost bin?

Identifying what you want your perennials to do will help you narrow down your planting options. If you're trying to grow perennials to solve a landscaping problem, you'll need to stick with plants that can adapt to those conditions. If you want perennials for cutting or for attracting butterflies, you'll want to choose plants that have proven themselves to be good for those purposes.

Where Can You Plant?

If you have a fairly flat site with moist but well-drained soil, you can plant a wide variety of perennials almost anywhere. But chances are good that you'll have at least one area in the garden with more challenging conditions, such as slopes or wet spots.

If you have a difficult spot, you might decide to ignore it and limit your perennial plantings to the most hospitable areas of the garden. Or you may choose to take up the challenge and plan a garden of perennials that are naturally adapted to those tough conditions. You may be pleasantly surprised to see how well-chosen perennial plantings can turn a problem site into a pleasing garden spot.

How Big Should Your Garden Be?

A key part of planning a great-looking landscape is being realistic about how much time you have to spend on it. Digging up and planting the area is the most obvious chunk of time you'll spend on the garden. But you'll also need to allow for the aftercare – the mulching, weeding, watering, fertilising, staking and pest control that your chosen plants will need to look their best.

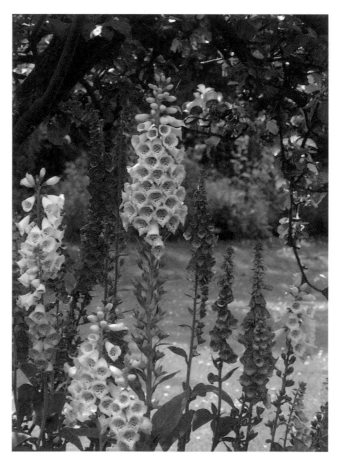

Foxgloves are one of the most popular choices for a perennial border or cottage garden.

For example, you'll probably need to spend a few hours each month to maintain an 18.6-sq-m (200-square-foot) flower garden once it's established. That doesn't include any planning or preparation time. It also assumes you keep it mulched to discourage weeds and reduce the need for watering.

Your own garden may take more or less time, depending on the plants you choose, how perfect you want them to look and how carefully you've planned it. It's always safe to start small, so plan your first garden a bit smaller than you think you want. Live with your first garden for a few years, and see how comfortable you are with the time you spend on it. As the plants become established, you'll have less watering and weeding to do, and you'll get a good idea of how much maintenance your garden really needs. Then, if you want to expand, you'll have a more realistic feel for how much garden you can actually handle.

Buying Healthy Perennials

Before you pull out your wallet to buy a new perennial, follow this checklist to help you verify the plant's quality:

1. Look to see if the plant is tagged with its botanical and cultivar name. If not, or if it's labelled only by common name or colour, chances are that it's not an improved type and you may not want it.
2. Test for root-bound plants, which may have been sitting around for a long time in a small pot. Give the plant a soft tug from the top and see if the root ball pops out of the pot readily. If the roots are packed into a solid mass or are circling around the inside of the pot, the plants are root-bound and may be slow to adapt to garden conditions.
3. Look at the roots. Firm, white roots are a sign of good health. If you can't pull the plant out of its pot to see the roots, check where the shoots emerge from the soil.

The trick to perennial gardening is finding and combining plants that will thrive in your particular conditions.

Perennials in Pots

Some perennials work very well in containers. Top choices include those with a long season of bloom, such as compact, golden orange 'Stella d'Oro' daylily. Other perennials that look especially nice in containers are those with interesting foliage, such as hostas, ornamental grasses and lady's mantle (*Alchemilla mollis*). Try using some of these plants in large containers, mixed with annual flowers to provide constant colour.

Perennials need a little more care than annuals, since you don't just pull them out at the end of the season. Because they are growing in containers, they are much more susceptible to winter damage than plants growing in the ground. In cool areas, you'll want to move container perennials to an unheated garage or cold basement to protect them from the alternate freezing and thawing cycles, which can damage or kill them. You'll need to water the pots lightly during the winter months.

Crocus and primrose

Emerging stems should not be brown, soft, blemished or wilted – these are symptoms of rots and other diseases.
4. Give the same thorough inspection to the stems and foliage. Look for signs of diseases such as brown or black leaf spots, white powdery mildew or tiny orange spots of rust. You don't want to bring these problems home with you to infect the plants in your garden.
5. Check the colour of the foliage. If it is a deep and uniform colour, the plant is most likely to be healthy and well fed.
6. Be on the lookout for weed shoots emerging through or near the crown (base) of the perennial. Although the weed leaves may have been clipped off in a pre-sale grooming, grasses and perennial weeds will re-emerge and can invade your newly planted garden.
7. Last, check for insect pests. Look beneath the leaves, along the stems, in shoot tips and on flower buds for soft-bodied aphids, cottony mealybugs and hard-shelled scale insects. Spider mites, another common pest, will make leaves stippled or turn them yellow or bronze. If pests are on one plant, they may be on every plant in that greenhouse or garden centre. Consider shopping elsewhere.

Designing Beds and Borders

Once you know what you want from your perennial landscape, you're ready to start planning the layout. Two of the most common ways to group perennial plantings are beds and borders.

Perennial borders are long planting areas that create a visual edge to a lawn or other part of the landscape. They are usually sited so they're viewed from a distance.

While they may stretch along a driveway, walkway, fence or the edge of woods, they don't really have to 'border' anything; borders may merely create the illusion of a boundary to a 'room' within the landscape.

Perennial borders are sometimes just that – only perennials. But more and more gardeners are enjoying the benefits of mixing their perennials with other plants, including shrubs, small trees, hardy bulbs, annuals and ornamental grasses. These plants complement perennials by adding extra height, texture, and colour to the border. Shrubs, trees, grasses and bulbs also add year-round interest, with early spring flowers, attractive autumn colours and showy fruits or foliage that may last well into winter.

Shapes and Sizes

Borders are often rectangular, but you can also design them with gentle curves for a more informal look. Because they're usually seen from one side, borders generally have a distinct front and back, with taller plants located to the rear.

There's no limit to how long a border can be. Long borders need a shortcut of a couple of stepping stones so you can get to the other side without having to walk around either end.

The width of the border will take some thought – 1.2 to 1.5 m (4 to 5 feet) is

Create an elegant effect by combining silvery artemisia and lamb's ear with blue-leaved pinks (*Dianthus* spp.).

Dahlias

enough room to include a good mix of plant heights. Long borders deeper than 1.5 or 1.8 m (5 or 6 feet) are a challenge to maintain because it's hard to reach more than 60 to 90 cm (2 or 3 feet) in from either side to weed, trim or dig.

If you want a border more than 90 cm (3 feet) wide in front of a hedge or wall, leave space behind it for a grassy or mulched access path so you can get to all

parts of your border. If you plan to make your border longer than about 4.5 m (15 feet), make the access path as wide as your garden trolley or wheelbarrow so you can easily haul in manure or compost and cart out trimmings.

Perennial Beds

Beds are often located closer to the house than borders, perhaps along the foundation or edging a patio. If you're going to put a bed where you'll see it all the time, choose your plants carefully for all-season interest. High-visibility beds will also need either some extra work or carefully chosen, low-maintenance plants to look their best all the time.

DIFFERENT WAYS TO BUY PERENNIALS

Container-grown perennials may cost more but give instant effect.

Field-dug plants usually adapt quickly to a new site.

Bare-root plants take a bit of care but are often less expensive.

The Shape of Beds

Perennial beds come in many shapes and sizes. Choose a shape and style (formal or informal) that matches or balances nearby features. The front can curve even if the edge against the house is straight. Keep the bed narrow enough to allow you to reach all the plants from outside the bed, or place stepping stones in it for easy access.

Island Beds

Beds surrounded by lawn are called islands; often these are oval or kidney shaped. They are a great way to add colour and height to new property while you're waiting for the trees and shrubs to mature. Island beds are also useful for replacing the grass under trees, reducing the need for trimming and making mowing easier.

Like perennial borders, island beds are usually designed to be seen from a distance. As islands are often viewed from all sides, the design needs to look attractive all around, like a table centrepiece. Since there's no 'back', put tallest plants towards the middle and surround them with lower plants.

Bed and Border Planning Pointers

Perennial borders and beds can be designed to feature one big seasonal show or to showcase long, overlapping seasons of bloom. If you have room for several different beds or borders, it can be fun to arrange each one with a different flowering season. That way you will always have at least one bed that is loaded with lovely flowers.

In small gardens or in plantings that you see every day, it's worth planning for long bloom times, attractive foliage and year-round interest. Here are some planning tips you can try.

- Include some spring-, summer- and autumn-flowering perennials in each planting area.

Persian onion (*Allium aflatunense*) and golden chain tree (*Laburnum* x *watereri*) form a splendid spring spectacle.

BELOW TOP: Healthy plants have strong, evenly coloured leaves. Check leaf undersides to make sure no pests are lurking.

BOTTOM: Before you buy, look at the leaves. Off-colour leaves may indicate nutrient deficiencies.

- Look for perennials that have great-looking foliage all season, such as hostas, artemisias, lady's mantle (*Alchemilla* spp.) and amsonias (*Amsonia* spp.).
- Pick long-flowering species and cultivars, like wild bleeding heart (*Dicentra eximia*) and 'Moonbeam' coreopsis (*Coreopsis verticillata* 'Moonbeam'); these can flower for eight weeks or longer.
- Include a few perennials with good-looking evergreen foliage for interest during the colder months. Bergenias (*Bergenia* spp.) and some coral bells (including *Heuchera americana* 'Dale's Strain' and 'Gamet') often turn a lovely red in the cool temperatures of autumn and winter.

Creating Great Plant Combinations

Great-looking gardens are basically sequences of many individual plant combinations. The best aren't just based on flower colour and season of bloom; they consider the quality, colour and texture of each plant's leaves as well. Good combinations also feature different plant heights and forms: short, medium or tall; mat-like, spiky or rounded. Equally important is overall texture – whether a plant is fine and delicate looking, like baby's breath (*Gypsophila* spp.), or coarse and dramatic, like peonies and ligularias (*Ligularia* spp.).

As you decide which plants to grow and how you want to group them, keep these different factors in mind. A little thought at the planning stage can turn a collection of different perennials into a harmonious, pleasing landscape.

Companions for Perennials

Perennials blend wonderfully with many other kinds of plants, including trees, shrubs, groundcover, climbers, annuals and ornamental grasses. Mixing these other plants with your perennials is a great way to provide excitement when the perennials aren't blooming.

To get the most out of your garden, search for plants that have multi-season interest. Many grasses, for instance, have attractive leaves in spring and summer, showy flower heads and seed heads in autumn, and golden winter foliage. Among the shrubs, consider those like shadblow serviceberry (*Amelanchier canadensis*). Its cherry-like blossoms are one of spring's earliest flowers, and the dark summer berries attract birds into your garden.

Plant spring bulbs with bushy perennials that can hide the ripening foliage and fill in when bulbs go dormant.

a landscape that is truly attractive all through the year.

All-season interest starts with flower displays that spread beyond one season. Foliage and plant form are other features you can use to keep your garden looking beautiful as flowers come and go. From spring through autumn, many perennials have leaves in attractive colours – like the maroon leaves of 'Palace Purple' heuchera (*Heuchera* 'Palace Purple') – or interesting shapes, such as the starry leaves of blood-red cranesbill (*Geranium sanguineum*). Unusual plant forms – such as the spiky leaves and flowers of yuccas, blackberry lily (*Belamcanda chinensis*) and spike gayfeather (*Liatris spicata*) – add drama, especially next to mounds such as cushion spurge (*Euphorbia epithymoides*). Use different types of foliage and forms to add contrast, or repeat similar leaves and shapes to unify a planting scheme.

You can depend on asters to produce loads of colourful blooms in late summer and autumn.

Contrasts and Complements

Well-planned gardens balance contrast and similarity. Contrasting colours, sizes or other design elements are bold and stimulating. Use contrast to draw attention to a particular location and to add a lively feel. Overusing contrast – too many different textures or too many strong colours – can give your garden a jumbled, chaotic look.

Similarity – the absence of contrasts – increases the sense of harmony. Use subtle variations of closely related colours and gradual height transitions to create soothing garden designs. Too much similarity risks being uninteresting, so add a touch of contrast – a few perennials of different height, colour or texture – for balance.

Repetition acts as a bridge between similarity and contrast. Repeating similar elements will unify even the boldest designs. Exact, evenly spaced repetitions of particular plants or combinations create a formal look. Combine different plants with similar flower colours or leaf shapes to give an informal garden a cohesive but casual look.

Orchestrating All-Season Interest

You see your garden every day of the year, so make sure it's worth looking at. A good selection of spring-, summer- and autumn-flowering perennials, plus a few plants with evergreen leaves for winter interest, will give you

Your Spring Landscape

After a long, dreary winter, few things are more welcome than colourful spring flowers. In spring, Lenten rose (*Helleborus orientalis*) and crocuses bloom before most of the garden shrugs off winter. Plant early bulbs where you'll see them from windows or as you enter the house so you can enjoy their bright colours when it's cold outside. Many wildflowers and shade-loving perennials bloom as trees leaf out, so spring is a good season to draw attention to areas that will be shady and green later on.

Supplement early-blooming perennials with the lovely early flowers of shrubs and trees such as forsythias, azaleas, magnolias, dogwoods, flowering cherries and crab apples.

A Wealth of Summer Colour

As spring turns into summer, many old-fashioned perennials – including peonies, irises and columbines (*Aquilegia* spp.) – reach their peak, making it an easy time to feature flowers. Supplement these with early summer shrubs and climbers such as rhododendrons, roses, clematis, wisteria and honeysuckle (*Lonicera* spp.).

As summer progresses, daisy-like perennials and annuals – including coreopsis and blanket flower – take centre stage. Good-looking foliage keeps up appearances where early perennials have finished blooming. Silver leaves make dramatic partners for hot- or cool-hued flowers; yellow, purple or variegated foliage also attracts attention. Flowering shrubs that are at their best in mid- to late summer include abelia (*Abelia* x *grandiflora*), butterfly bush (*Buddleja davidii*) and hydrangeas. Sourwood (*Oxydendrum arboreum*) and Japanese pagoda tree (*Sophora japonica* syn. *Styphnolobium*

japonicum) are large trees that flower prolifically in late summer, as does the large trumpet creeper vine (*Campsis* spp.).

Combinations for Autumn

Asters, boltonia and Joe Pye weeds (*Eupatorium* spp.) keep blooming after autumn frosts nip most annuals. As flowers fade, foliage brightens – and not just on trees or shrubs such as winged spindle tree (*Euonymus alatus*). Leaves of peonies and evening primrose (*Oenothera tetragona*) turn beautiful shades of red, amsonias

Campanula in raised bed

ABOVE: Plants that have variegated leaves – such as hostas (left) and some kinds of lemon balm (right) – provide all-season interest.

(*Amsonia* spp.) and balloon flower (*Platycodon grandiflorus*) leaves turn bright yellow, and many ornamental grasses bleach to gold. White baneberry (*Actaea pachypoda*) and Jack-in-the-pulpit (*Arisaema triphyllum*) are perennials with dramatic berries that may last into autumn.

Perennials for Winter Interest

After the leaves drop, attention turns to evergreen plants and those with interesting seed pods or fruits. Perennials with showy winter seed pods include blue false indigo (*Baptisia australis*), coneflowers (*Rudbeckia and Echinacea* spp.), blackberry lily (*Belamcanda chinensis*) and astilbes (*Astilbe* spp.).

Many crab apples and shrubs such as viburnums, cotoneasters and deciduous and evergreen hollies (*Ilex* spp.) display fruits well into winter. Ornamental grasses remain attractive for months; cut them to the ground when they look tattered to make way for spring's new growth.

Lenten roses (*Helleborus orientalis*) are usually sold as small plants, but they make large clumps in a few years.

Month by Month in the Perennial Garden

This calendar is based on Zone 6, where the frost-free growing season is approximately late April to mid-October. If your garden is in a different zone, it's easy to adapt this calendar to fit your region. Not sure which zone you're in? Check out the plant hardiness zone maps on pages 310–11.

In warmer climates (Zones 7 to 9), spring comes sooner, so do your March to May chores a month or two earlier (the warmer the climate, the sooner you can start); wait until frost for autumn clean-up. In Zone 10 (you lucky gardeners), ignore the autumn clean-up and mulching information; keep weeding, watering and watching for pests throughout the year.

In colder zones and at high elevations (where the frost-free season is more like late May or early June to late August or early September), this calendar will be about a month ahead of you for much of the year. Wait a month to do your March to May chores, finish the September chores in August, and start your autumn garden clean-up after the first frost.

January
- Take stock of seeds and stored summer bulbs; toss out any that aren't sound.
- Order summer bulbs and plants from mail order catalogues to avoid the rush.

February
- Inventory the garden to list clean-up chores for next month.

March
- Clean up stray leaves, winter debris and anything left undone last autumn. Cut back ornamental grasses.

Perennials That Grow Best Lean and Light

If you think more nutrients are always better, think again. Many perennials, including coreopsis (*Coreopsis* spp.), yarrows and common thrift (*Armeria maritima*), are sun-loving and drought-tolerant. They grow best where soils are not lush. If you overfeed them, they become soft and succulent – too tender to stand upright without staking. On disease-susceptible plants like garden phlox (*Phlox paniculata*), this soft, succulent tissue is more prone to mildews and other diseases. Rich soil also gives an extra boost to plants that spread by rhizomes or stolons, like bee balm (*Monarda didyma*). These creeping stems will run all over the place instead of staying in more controlled clumps. Excess fertility will also make silver- and grey-leaved perennials such as artemisias and lavenders fade to a dull green colour.

Delphiniums

- When the forsythias begin to flower, pull some of the winter mulch off of your perennial beds so the soil can warm up.
- Turn last year's compost pile so it will be ready to spread when the ground warms up.
- Take soil tests.

April
- Finish garden clean-up; pull any weeds.
- Add nutrients recommended by your soil test results.
- Start checking for pests.

- As you enjoy your spring bulbs, jot down some notes to remind you what you want to add in the autumn for next year, and where you want to put them.
- Top-dress bulb plantings with compost. Remove spent flowers, but leave the foliage until it dies back.
- Side-dress clumps of emerging perennials with compost or manure.
- Divide summer- and autumn-flowering perennials when the new shoots are about 7.5 cm (3 inches) tall.

May
- Plant bare-root perennials and container-grown plants as you get them.
- Divide and replant spring-flowering perennials and bulbs after they flower.
- Replace and replenish mulch.
- Pinch out leggy perennials.
- Pull or dig weed seedlings as soon as you spot them.
- Plant tender perennials and tender bulbs (including dahlias and gladioli) outside once danger of frost has passed.
- Plant annuals to hide dying foliage of hardy bulbs.

June
- Stake perennials that need support.
- Remove spent blossoms to prevent unwanted self-seeding.
- Watch the weather and water if rainfall is scarce. Wait until the top inch or two of soil is dry, then water thoroughly. Container plantings may need daily watering during hot spells.

July
- This is your chance to relax and enjoy the garden. Just keep watering.
- Order spring bulbs now.
- Cut flowers for indoor arrangements in the morning, before the heat of the day.
- Remove spent flowers.

August
- Keep up watering, deadheading, weeding and pest patrol.
- Cut leafy herbs for drying.

September

- Divide any perennials that have finished flowering.
- Start new beds. Plant a cover crop to protect the soil over winter. Or dig in chopped leaves and garden wastes; they will have decomposed by spring.

October

- Cover tender plants at night when frost is expected.
- Dig and store tender bulbs when their foliage withers.
- Pull annuals after frost and toss them in the compost pile.
- Rake leaves for the compost pile or till them into new beds. Chop leaves with the lawn mower for good winter mulch (but don't mulch yet).
- Plant spring bulbs.
- Water perennial beds (as well as new shrub and bulb plantings) thoroughly before they go dormant to help them survive the winter.

November

- Mow wildflower meadows.
- Drain and store hoses; shut off and drain outdoor water taps.
- Clean your gardening tools.
- After the ground freezes, add a thick layer of mulch.

December

- Make a wish list of garden supplies for holiday presents.
- Catch up on gardening reading.

Low-Maintenance Perennials and Bulbs

If you really want to avoid labour, shun tall or floppy plants – like hybrid delphinium (*Delphinium elatum*) and baby's breath (*Gypsophila paniculaw*) – that need staking. Steer clear of tender perennials, such as canna (*Canna x generalis*) and dahlia (*Dahlia* spp.), that you have to dig up and store

Sun-loving coreopsis (*Coreopsis verticillata*) is one of the brightest and most easy-care plants you can have in your garden.

Sun-Loving Perennials

The secret to an easy-care garden in the sun is to pick plants that need lots of light and aren't fussy about their soil. It's even easier if they also don't need much water or fertiliser (like the perennials listed below):

> *Armeria maritima* (thrift)
> *Coreopsis* spp. (coreopsis)
> *Echinacea purpurea* (purple coneflower)
> *Hemerocallis* spp. (daylily)
> *Rudbeckia* spp. (coneflowers)
> *Sedum spectabile* (showy stonecrop)

Shade-Loving Perennials

If your site gets some direct sun for part of the day, or light shade all day, you can still grow a variety of perennials. A few of the best and most reliable are listed below:

> *Aquilegia* spp. (columbines)
> *Astilbe* spp. (astilbes)
> *Cimicifuga* spp. (bugbanes)
> *Dicentra* spp. (bleeding hearts)
> *Hosta* spp. (hostas)
> *Pulmonaria* spp. (lungworts)

over the winter. Unless you want to cover a large area, avoid those that spread, like lamb's ears (*Stachys byzantina*) and goutweed (*Aegopodium podagraria*). Pass up those that die out after a few years, like many perennial asters (*Aster* spp.). And don't plant those that are susceptible to a serious pest in your area, unless you can get a specially resistant cultivar.

What's left? A lot, starting with dependable spring bulbs like crocuses and daffodils; irises, if iris borer isn't a severe problem in your area; daylilies (there are thousands to choose from); and hostas, for shady areas. Try short cultivars of balloon flower (*Platycodon grandiflorus*) and bellflowers (*Campanula* spp.). Choose coreopsis (*Corepsis* spp.) and other native wildflowers, especially in a natural garden. Don't forget old-time favourites like bleeding heart (*Dicentra* spp.). Ornamental grasses like fountain grass (*Pennisetum alopecuroides*) and blue fescue (*Festuca cinerea*) are great for their foliage and interesting seed heads.

The list goes on. For more ideas, look at flowers in neighbours' gardens that bloom even though no one bothers with them. Before you plant any perennial, research its growth requirements to be sure it suits your conditions.

Helenium

Annuals and Biennials

Annual flowers come in a palette of colours to suit every gardener's fancy. Some also offer handsome foliage. Others are treasured for their fragrance, their nostalgic associations or their charm as cut flowers. It's hard to imagine a garden that wouldn't benefit from the addition of a few more annuals.

Annuals for Beds and Borders

Flower beds are traditionally one of the most popular ways to display annuals. Some gardeners like to showcase their annual flowers in separate beds; others enjoy mixing annuals with bulbs, perennials, herbs, ornamental grasses and other plants. Either way, the possibilities for creating exciting plantings are virtually endless.

Annuals Alone

Setting aside separate beds for annual flowers is an easy way to go. Since you start with an empty area each year, spring soil preparation is a snap – you simply clean up any debris left in the bed, scatter some compost over the top to add nutrients and organic matter, and dig or till to loosen the top layer of soil.

When you are planning and planting annual flower beds, you need to decide if you want a formal look or an informal look. The style you choose will determine how many different annuals you'll plant and how you'll arrange them.

Formal Gardens

Formal flower beds tend to have a simple, geometric shape – such as a square, rectangle or circle – and a limited number of different plants. The simplest may contain a mass of just one annual, such as marigolds or geraniums. For a little more variety, you could combine two or three different annuals, planted in straight rows or patterns.

Sweet peas, one of the prettiest and most delightfully fragrant annuals, need rich soil, lots of sun and moisture, and a support to climb.

Many annuals, including cornflowers (*Centaurea cyanus*), will self-sow for an informal, cottage-garden look.

If you grow different annuals together, pick those with varying heights. Select one that's low and spreading – such as sweet alyssum (*Lobularia maritima*) or edging lobelia (*Lobelia erinus*) – for the outer edge. The plants for the inside of the bed should be taller, usually no more than about 60 cm (2 feet). If the bed is in a spot where you can see it from all sides, you might want to include a taller 'focal point' annual, such as castor oil plant (*Ricinus communis*) or love-lies-bleeding (*Amaranthus caudatus*), as a dramatic accent in the centre of the garden.

The key to success with a formal bed is uniformity: you want the plants to be evenly spaced and evenly developed. If you're growing a bed of just one kind of annual – all marigolds, let's say – you could sow seed over the prepared bed, thin the seedlings to an even spacing and expect fairly uniform results. In most cases, though, you'll get the best results by starting with transplants. All of the plants will be at the same stage, so they'll start blooming at the same time, and you can set them out at the proper spacing to get a nice, even look, with no bare patches.

TOP: If you like the casual look of a cottage garden, sow a mixture of plants that are adapted to your conditions.

MIDDLE: Create beautiful seasonal scenes by combining annuals with bulbs that bloom at the same time of the year.

BOTTOM: Try a colourful planting of low-growing annuals as groundcover around new tree and shrub plantings.

Informal Gardens

If you enjoy a more casual-looking garden, an informal planting may be more your style. Informal gardens can be any shape you like; they often have a flowing outline that curves around the base of shrubs or other structures. Informal plantings usually include at least three or four different annuals. As with formal plantings, the plants you choose for informal beds should have varying heights for visual interest. But you aren't limited to planting informal beds in masses or rows. You can set plants out in whatever drifts or groupings look good to you.

Starting an informal flower bed from transplants is a good idea if you have specific plant groupings in mind. Placing transplants just where you want them gives you the most control over which colours and plant heights are next to each other. If you plan to plant different annuals in separate drifts, you could also start from seed sown directly in the garden. Or, if you want a really casual, meadow-like effect, you could mix all the seeds together and scatter them over the soil.

Annuals with Other Plants

Although they look wonderful by themselves, annuals also have a lot to offer in groupings with other plants. In borders predominantly planted with perennials, bulbs and shrubs, you can use annuals as a formal or informal edging, suggesting a flowering necklace around the border. While the other plants come in and out of bloom, the annual edging adds consistent colour through most of the season. Repeating the same annual edging in different flower beds and borders is an excellent way to link the separate areas and give the garden a planned, finished look. Change the annuals every year if you like.

Of course, you can also add annuals to the inside of borders as well. While the compact, uniform annuals that are excellent for formal bedding can look stiff and awkward next to perennials, many other annuals have a looser, more graceful habit. In fact, annuals and biennials such as larkspur (*Consolida ambigua*), foxgloves (*Digitalis purpurea*) and Canterbury bells (*Campanula medium*) are so charming when mixed with perennials that they are often considered traditional parts of a perennial border. Tall annuals and biennials such as cosmos, cleome, hollyhocks and mulleins (*Verbascum* spp.) are ideal for adding height to the back of a mixed border. And shorter, airy annuals blend easily into border edgings; try plants like pot marigolds (*Calendula officinalis*), annual candytuft (*Iberis umbellata*), and annual baby's breath (*Gypsophila elegans*) with low-growing perennials and bulbs.

Besides making a great garden accent, globe amaranth (*Gomphrena globosa*) dries well for flower arrangements.

Morning glory

Annuals as Fillers

When you start any new garden, one of the hardest parts of the process is waiting for plants to fill in. This is especially true with perennial and shrub beds, since these plants can take three or four years to really get established and look like anything. New groundcover plantings can appear pretty sparse for the first few years, too. While you need to allow ample space for these plants to fill in as they mature, the bare soil in between is boring and empty, and it provides an open invitation for weeds to get established.

Planted in groups, compact zinnias make a colourful, season-long filler in flower beds and borders.

Foxgloves (*Digitalis purpurea*) will provide a temporary and very attractive 'fence' to screen your garden from the outside world.

While mulch can suppress weeds, it doesn't add much excitement to a new planting. That's where filler annuals come in handy. A few seed packets of quick-growing annuals can provide welcome colour and excitement for minimal cost. Sweet alyssum (*Lobularia maritima*), flowering tobacco (*Nicotiana alata*) and cornflower (*Centaurea cyanus*) are a few great filler annuals that can quickly cover the soil and deprive weed seeds of the light they need to grow. Many annuals may also self-sow to provide cover in succeeding years, gradually yielding space to expanding perennials.

Fillers for Flower Beds

If you're looking for annuals to fill in around new perennial plantings, choose those with a similar range of heights and colours as the perennials will have. Select a few short or trailing annuals for the front of the border, a few medium-sized plants for the middle of the border and a few tall annuals for the back. While you could sow annual seed directly into the ground around the perennials, it's often easier to start with annual transplants.

Some good filler annuals, such as cleome (*Cleome hassleriana*) and cornflower, will drop seed and come back year after year. If your annuals do reseed, thin the seedlings where they're not wanted to allow the expanding perennials room to develop.

Fillers for Groundcover

Low-growing annuals such as sweet alyssum, rose moss (*Portulaca grandiflora*) and baby blue eyes (*Nemophila menziesii*) can be excellent fillers for young groundcover planting. Stick with one kind of annual for a uniform effect. In this case, it's just as easy to scatter seed around the groundcover plants, although you could also set out annual transplants in the available spaces instead. While many low-growing annuals will self-sow, you may want to scatter some fresh annual seed over the planting for the first few springs until the groundcover fills in.

Fillers for Foundation Plantings

New foundation plantings also benefit from annuals the first few years as they develop. Shrubs and groundcover may take over their allotted space in a few years, but a carpet of annuals is most welcome in the meantime. A few market packs of your favourite annuals will be easy to plant, and the resulting flowers and foliage will provide infinitely more interest than a dull covering of bark chips.

Annuals for Screens

While the word 'annual' commonly brings to mind compact, small plants like petunias and marigolds, there are a number of fast-growing annuals that can reach amazing heights of 180 cm (6 feet) or more in a single season. There are also annual climbers, the twining stems of which quickly cover trellises for welcome shade and privacy. With these great plants to choose from, why spend another season staring at your neighbours' gardens – or your neighbours, for that matter? Screen them off with fast-growing annuals while waiting for your trees and shrubs to grow.

Hollyhocks

Tall Annuals

Grow tall annuals in your garden to block or cover unattractive features, such as dog runs, alleys or clothesline poles. Or plant a row or mass of tall annuals to create a 'neighbour-friendly' temporary fence that delineates your property line, as well as providing privacy and an attractive view. Tall annuals can also be used to separate different areas of your garden. Some

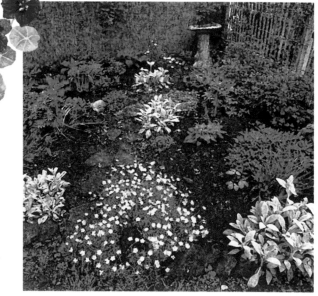

Nasturtiums

New gardens may look rather bare the first year or two. Annuals can cover the soil until perennials get established.

Black-eyed Susan climbs quickly to cover fences or trellises with bright blooms from summer into autumn.

top-notch tall annuals include castor oil plant (*Ricinus communis*), summer cypress (*Kochia scoparia*), hollyhocks (*Alcea rosea*), sunflowers (*Helianthus annuus*) and Mexican sunflower (*Tithonia rotundifolia*).

Annual Climbers

A leafy curtain of annual climbers is an ideal way to ensure privacy on a porch or patio without appearing to be unneighbourly. Flowering climbers also add a quaint, old-fashioned touch to the most ordinary support. A cloak of morning glories can convert a ho-hum garden shed into a charming and colourful garden feature, while a mass of scarlet runner beans will accent an arch or liven up a lamppost.

Most annual climbers cover territory in a hurry. You can easily train them to climb a wooden or wire trellis, chain-link fences, lattice work or even strong twine. Tall wooden or bamboo stakes also make effective supports. While annual climbers are usually lighter than woody vines (such

as wisteria or trumpet creeper), they can put on a lot of growth in one season, so supply a sturdy support. Unlike clinging plants such as ivy, annual plants climb mostly with tendrils or twining stems, so don't expect them to scamper up a bare wall without assistance.

Morning glories (*Ipomoea tricolor*) have long been loved for their heart-shaped leaves and beautiful, trumpet-shaped flowers. The closely related moonflower (*Ipomoea alba*) is another popular plant; it offers large, white, heavily fragrant flowers that open in the evening. Besides being covered with clusters of colourful blooms, scarlet runner bean (*Phaseolus coccineus*) has the added bonus of edible beans. Other popular annual vines include cup and saucer vine (*Cobaea scandens*), hyacinth bean (*Dolichos lablab*) and black-eyed Susan (*Thunbergia alata*).

Annuals for Herb Gardens

Besides adding colourful flowers and handsome foliage to your garden, some annuals can even add flavour to your food! Annual herbs are easy to grow, and they'll produce generous quantities of tasty leaves or seeds to spice up your favourite dishes.

Cosmos

As with other annuals, annual herbs are quite useful for filling the gaps around new perennial plantings. If you have a formal herb garden with traditional perennial herbs, such as sage, thyme and mint, scatter seed of annual herbs among the young plants. Or use the annual herbs throughout your garden as you would any other filler annual, and you'll have flower beds that are productive as well as beautiful. Pick herbs throughout the growing season from the outside of the clump, as evenly as you can, to keep them looking good. Pick off flower heads as they appear unless you want self-sown seeds.

Picking Annuals for Containers

As with any kind of garden, the first step to planning successful container plantings is choosing plants that have similar growth needs. If you have a shady area, impatiens, monkey flower (*Mimulus* x *hybridus*) and other shade-lovers are your

Create a colourful and practical planting by mixing herbs with annual flowers, such as pot marigold (*Calendula officinalis*).

best bets. Sunny spots can support a wider range of colourful annuals, including treasure flower (*Gazania rigens*), mealy cup sage (*Salvia farinacea*) and narrow-leaved zinnia (*Zinnia angustifolia*).

When planning a container garden – whether it is a pot, hanging basket, window box or planter – you also need to consider the ultimate height of the annuals you select. As a general guideline, try to choose annuals that are the same height or smaller than the height of the container; otherwise, the planting may look top-heavy.

Single-annual containers can be pleasing, but mixed plantings of three or four different annuals are even more exciting. While the exact plants you pick to grow together is up to you, there are some basic guidelines you can follow to create a successful container planting.

Asters, cosmos and dahlias

Shade-Loving Annuals

If your site gets some direct sun for part of the day, or light shade all day, you can still grow a variety of annuals. A few of the best are listed below:

Begonia Semperflorens Cultorum hybrid (wax begonia)
Celosia cristata (cockscomb)
Impatiens wallerana (impatiens)
Lobelia erinus (edging lobelia)
Nicotiana alata (flowering tobacco)

First, select a 'star' plant. Base your container planting around one centrepiece plant – perhaps a bushy marguerite daisy (*Chrysanthemum frutescens*), a free-flowering tuberous begonia or a bold ornamental cabbage. Then choose a 'supporting cast' to complement the star plant and fill out the container. Try one or two with bold leaves or an upright habit – such as coleus or dusty miller – and one or two that sprawl or trail – such as edging lobelia (*Lobelia erinus*) or creeping zinnia (*Sanvitalia procumbens*).

Sun-Loving Annuals

The secret to an easy-care garden in the sun is to pick plants that need lots of light and aren't fussy about their soil. Here are a few of the best easy-care annuals for sun:

Ageratum houstonianum (ageratum)

Antirrhinum majus (common snapdragon)

Calendula officinalis (pot marigold)

Centaurea cyanus (cornflower)

Helianthus annuus (common sunflower)

Lobularia maritima (sweet alyssum)

Nicotiana alata (flowering tobacco)

Verbena x *hybrida* (garden verbena)

Zinnia elegans (common zinnia)

Grow Your Own Annuals

For an 'instant' effect, you can buy and plant annuals that are already blooming. If you're not in a real hurry, however, you can grow your own plants from seed. Growing your own annuals is also a good way to save money, especially if you need a lot of plants.

Some kinds of annuals, such as marigolds, mature quickly, so you can sow them directly into outdoor pots. Other annuals that are easy from direct-sown seed include sweet alyssum (*Lobularia maritima*), nasturtiums (*Tropaeolum majus*), morning glories (*Ipomoea* spp.) and zinnias. Sweet alyssum is cold-tolerant, so you can plant the seed in early spring; for the rest, wait until after the danger of frost has passed.

Other annuals have very tiny seeds or take a little longer before they start flowering, so they are best grown indoors under lights. Check the instructions on the seed packets, and sow the seeds the recommended number of weeks before your last expected spring frost so they'll start flowering shortly after you move them outside.

Zinnias are colourful and easy to grow, but tall cultivars will need staking. Choose compact cultivars for less work.

Lovely Lilies

Lilies are the stars of the mid- to late-summer garden. True lilies (*Lilium* spp. and hybrids) grow from a bulb and have straight stems with many short leaves. Hybrid lilies are divided into several broad groups. The three main groups are the Asiatic hybrids, trumpet lilies and oriental hybrids. Asiatic hybrids are the first to bloom, flowering from late May into July in most parts of the country. They are noted for their large, beautifully coloured and shaped flowers; most are not fragrant. July and August belong to the trumpet lilies (also known as *Aurelian* hybrids). They come in a more limited colour range (mainly white, yellow, pink and apricot), but their huge, horn-shaped blooms bear a sweet perfume. Fragrance is also a feature of the oriental hybrids, which bloom from midsummer into autumn (depending on the cultivar).

Great Gladioli

Gladioli are flower-garden favourites with spikes of satin-textured blooms in an almost infinite variety of colours – from pastel pink, white and yellow to rich purple, orange and magenta. Breeders have also created many bicolour types, with various degrees of petal ruffling and feathering. If you plant at two-week intervals from mid-spring to midsummer, you can enjoy blooms throughout the growing season.

Bulbs for Autumn

The end of summer doesn't spell the end of the bulb season. The autumn show continues with holdovers from summer, such as dahlias, cannas, tuberous begonias and some oriental lilies. These are complemented by bulbs that wait until the return of cold weather to bloom, including lilies, crocus and cyclamen.

The charm of autumn-flowering bulbs is the grace and freshness they add to the late-season garden. They are wonderful companions for autumn-flowering perennials, including asters, mums and Japanese anemone (*Anemone* x *hybrida*). For extra interest, plant low-growing groundcover, such as sedums, creeping veronicas (*Veronica* spp.), creeping Jenny (*Lysimachia nummularia*) and thyme, directly over the bulbs. As the bulbs bloom, the groundcover provides a leafy backdrop that is far more pleasing than bare soil.

Bulbs for Indoor Blooms

There's nothing more heart-warming to a gardener (or anyone, for that matter) than a pot of flowering bulbs on the windowsill in the depths of winter. Happily, it's relatively easy to convince most spring bulbs to rush the season a bit. The process is called 'forcing', although there's not much force involved. You simply provide a condensed version of the winter the bulbs would otherwise get when growing in the ground outdoors.

Choosing Bulbs for Indoor Blooms

Most spring bulbs can be forced, but some perform better in pots than others. Spring-blooming crocus, Siberian squill (*Scilla siberica*), glory-of-the-snow (*Chionodoxa luciliae*) and reticulated iris (*Iris reticulata*) are very easy to chill and bring into bloom. A few tulips that perform especially well in pots include pale orange 'Apricot Beauty', plum purple 'Atilla' and some of the small, rock garden species (such as the yellow-and-white *Tulipa tarda* and the yellow or bronze-pink *T. batalinii*).

Daffodils are also gratifyingly easy to force. Although the large, yellow, trumpet daffodils are traditional favourites both in the garden and in pots, many gardeners also enjoy smaller, free-flowering cultivars such as 'Pipit', 'Hawera' and 'Tête-à-tête'. Hyacinths, too, usually perform very well in pots; a few that are especially good include pale pink 'Lady Derby', darker pink 'Pink Pearl' and deep blue 'Blue Jacket'.

Preparing Bulbs for Forcing

The best time to plant bulbs for forcing is in late autumn and early winter. Set the bulbs shoulder to shoulder in plastic or clay pots in ordinary, well-drained potting compost. This kind of crowding produces wonderful displays. The 'nose' of the bulb should just peek above the soil surface. Label the pot with the name of the bulb and the date, water it thoroughly and stash it in its winter quarters for chilling.

To get a good show, you can plant bulbs close together in the pot; it's okay if the bulbs touch.

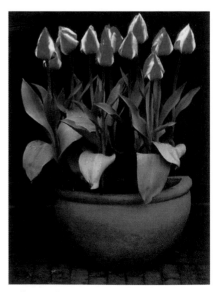

Different tulip cultivars bloom at different times, so you can enjoy them all through the spring.

Showy crocus look wonderful naturalised in grassy areas for autumn flowers.

ABOVE: Combine autumn bulbs with groundcover, such as leadwort (*Ceratostigma plumbaginoides*), to help support the blooms and keep them clean. BELOW: Belladonna lily (*Amaryllis belladonna*) and *Nerine bowdenii* ripen their leaves in spring but don't flower until autumn.

Giving Bulbs a Chance to Chill

Your bulbs need a cool, dark place while they're producing roots. The ideal temperatures for forcing bulbs are between 1° and 7°C (33° and 45°F). Protect the bulbs with a heavy layer of straw, newspaper or even old blankets to keep them from getting too cold. If you don't have another place to chill your bulbs, you can try the mound technique. Simply set the bulb pots on the ground outdoors (perhaps in a corner of the vegetable garden), cover them with several inches of perlite or potting compost, and top the whole thing with a thick insulating layer of straw or wood chips. Keep in mind, though, that this pile will provide an inviting home for local mice and other rodents, and it's a messy job to dig your bulbs out of a snow-covered pile in the middle of winter.

Bringing Bulbs into Bloom

No matter where you chill your bulbs, check on them every few weeks to see if they need more water. At the same time, look for signs of growth. Your bulbs will signal they're ready to grow in two ways: Tiny white roots will be visible in the drainage holes of the pot, and new shoots will appear at the tops of the bulbs. Crocus and reticulated iris may be ready in as little as eight weeks, while larger bulbs can take twelve weeks or more.

When the shoots are 2.5 to 5 cm (1 to 2 inches) tall, bring them inside to a cool, bright window. Fertilize lightly each time you water, and turn the pots regularly to keep the shoots from stretching unevenly towards the light. Keep pots away from radiators and other heat sources; bulbs like it cool.

Bulbs for Naturalising

Wouldn't you love to find flowers that you could plant once and enjoy forever, without lots of yearly fussing? If this is your gardening style, you'll love the idea of 'naturalised' bulbs.

Naturalising means planting bulbs in random, natural-looking drifts under trees, in woodlands or in grassy areas. It's easy to do, and the results look better and better every year as the bulbs multiply to produce even more blooms.

Deciding Where to Plant

Naturalised bulbs are often best in low-maintenance areas, where you can enjoy the flowers but not be bothered by the sight of the ripening leaves. Very early bulbs, such as spring crocus, are sometimes naturalised in lawns to provide colour. You may have to put off the first spring mowing for a week or two to let the bulb foliage turn yellow, but after that you can mow as usual. Autumn-flowering bulbs can also look good in grassy areas, but you'll have to stop mowing in late summer, as soon as you see the flower buds.

Thick grass may be too competitive for some bulbs, but a sparse lawn – especially under deciduous trees – is just the right environment to help bulbs take hold. The bulbs get plenty of spring sun and moisture before the trees leaf out, and the flowers add cheerful spring and/or autumn colour to otherwise drab areas. If you have many trees, you can combine sweeps of naturalised bulbs with shade-loving annuals, perennials and shrubs to create a charming woodland garden with four-season interest.

Create a carpet of flowers by naturalising snowdrops, winter aconite (*Eranthis hyemalis*), *Cyclamen coum* and other small spring bulbs under deciduous trees.

Best Bulbs for Naturalising

Small bulbs tend to be best for naturalising: they flower dependably, and they're easy to plant. Best of all, they're usually relatively inexpensive, so you can buy hundreds to make a good show. Daffodil bulbs tend to be large, but even they are often sold in bargain mixtures for naturalising. Listed below are some of the bulbs that adapt particularly well to naturalising.

Lily leek (*Allium moly*)
Grecian windflower (*Anemone blanda*)
Showy autumn crocus (*Colchicum speciosum*)
Crocus (*Crocus* spp.)
Common snowdrops (*Galanthus nivalis*)
Spanish bluebells (*Hyacinthoides hispanicus*)
Summer snowflake (*Leucojum aestivum*)
Grape hyacinth (*Muscari armeniacum*)
Daffodils (*Narcissus* hybrids)
Siberian squill (*Scilla siberica*)

Grape hyacinths (*Muscari* spp.) and tulips make a stunning display when mass-planted. They are both excellent cut flowers, too.

Planting Naturalised Bulbs

The key to successful naturalising is planting bulbs in random-looking arrangements rather than in straight rows or patterns. It's usually best to place them randomly over the planting area by hand until the arrangement looks right to you. Don't just toss out handfuls of bulbs from a standing position; the bulbs may get bruised or damaged as they fall and be prone to pest and disease problems. If you do want to use this super-random method, use potatoes and plant the bulbs where the potatoes fall.

Iris

Many gardeners find that a narrow trowel is the easiest tool to use for planting small bulbs. You simply insert the trowel into the ground at an angle, lift up a flap of turf, tuck the bulb into the soil and replace the flap. Or you can plant bulbs in groups by lifting up larger sections of turf, loosening the exposed soil, pressing the bulbs into the soil and replacing the turf. (This technique works best with small bulbs such as crocus.) If you have lots of bulbs to plant, you may want to try using an auger attachment that connects to a power drill to dig many holes quickly and easily. (These attachments are usually sold in garden centres.)

Buying Healthy Bulbs

A key part of growing bulbs successfully is starting with healthy plants. By being a smart shopper, you can get the best bulbs for your garden at the best possible price.

Knowing What to look For

With bulbs, as with most things, you get what you pay for. High-quality, full-sized bulbs command top dollar, based on the amount of time and labour it takes to produce them, but you can rely on them for spectacular results.

A higher price, however, doesn't always mean that one tulip or daffodil cultivar is better than another. New cultivars tend to be much more expensive than older ones that have been around

awhile. New cultivars are fun to try, but the old standbys that have proven to be good performers through the years are usually both economical and dependable.

A top-quality bulb is firm to the touch (not mushy or squishy) and free of large blemishes or scars. Some bulbs, such as tulips and hyacinths, may have a trace of blue mould on them. A few small mould spots will not harm the bulb, but a noticeable layer may indicate that the bulb was stored improperly before being offered for sale.

Look for bulbs that show little or no root or shoot growth except for a pale growth bud at the top. (Lilies are an exception, since they often have fleshy roots attached.) It's wise to shop early in the season so you can get the bulbs before they dry out from sitting in a store.

Handling Bulbs When You Get Them Home

If you can't plant right away, store your bulbs in a cool, dark and relatively dry place. Keep them in the paper or mesh bags they came in. A refrigerator can be handy for storing spring bulbs but is too cold for summer bulbs, such as gladioli or dahlias. Keep summer bulbs in a cool spot until you're ready to grow them indoors or plant them outdoors.

Planting Bulbs

The great thing about most bulbs is that they can adapt to a wide range of growing conditions. But if you really want your bulbs to thrive, it's worth putting some thought into giving them the best conditions possible. Take a little time to prepare a good growing site and plant your bulbs properly. Then you can stand back and enjoy the bounty of beautiful flowers in the years to come.

Hardy cyclamen make unusual groundcover under trees and shrubs. You'll enjoy both the leaves and the flowers.

Getting the Soil Ready

Many bulbs can grow for years in the same place, so it's worth putting some effort into preparing an ideal planting site. Bulbs tend to thrive in soil that's on the loamy or sandy side, since good drainage is critical for most bulbs. If your soil isn't naturally loamy, you can improve its drainage and fertility by adding some organic matter before you plant your bulbs. Spread a 2.5- to 7.5-cm (1- to 3-inch) layer of compost or chopped leaves over the planting area, then work it into the top 25 to 30 cm (10 to 12 inches) of soil. (When you're only planting small bulbs, such as crocus and grape hyacinths, you can get away with loosening just the top 10 to 15 cm [4 to 6 inches] of soil.) Or, if you're digging individual holes, work a handful of organic matter into the soil at the base of each hole, then add another handful to the soil you use to refill the hole. As it breaks down, the organic matter will release a steady supply of nutrients for good growth.

Planting Bulbs in Beds and Borders

Once you've loosened the soil, planting is easy – just dig the hole to the proper depth, pop in the bulb and cover it with soil. The proper depth will vary, depending on what bulbs you're growing. A general rule of thumb is that the hole should be dug to a depth that is three to four times the height of the bulb. For example, a crocus corm that measures 2.5 cm (1 inch) high should be planted 7.5 to 10 cm (3 to 4 inches) deep; a 5-cm (2-inch) high tulip bulb needs a hole 15 to 20 cm (6 to 8 inches) deep. If your soil is on the sandy side, plant the bulb or corm a bit deeper.

Set the bulb in the hole with the pointed growth bud facing upwards. If you can't tell which side should be up – as often happens with small bulbs such as Grecian windflowers (*Anemone blanda*) – set the bulb on its side or just drop it in the hole and hope for the best. Most bulbs have a strong will to grow and they'll find a way to send up their shoots.

Space the bulbs so each has ample room to grow. As a general rule, you should leave 12.5 to 15 cm (5 to 6 inches) between large bulbs and 2.5 to 7.5 cm (1 to 3 inches) between small bulbs. Once you've got the spacing the way you want it, carefully replace the soil around the

Buy generous quantities of bulbs and plant them in drifts or large clumps to create a dramatic display in the garden.

bulbs to refill the hole. Firm the soil by patting it with your hand or the back of a rake, then water thoroughly.

Caring for Bulbs

Hardy bulbs – including daffodils, crocus and other dependable favourites – are about as close to 'no work' as you can get. You just plant them once, and they come back year after year. Many will even multiply over time to produce large sweeps of blooms without any help from you. But as with any other garden plants, a little extra care can help your bulbs grow and look better.

Different bulbs need to be planted at different depths.

lily · madonna lily · tulip · squill · daffodil · hyacinth · Dutch iris · snowdrop · grape hyacinth · crocus

mulch

soil line

depth in inches

Watering for Good Growth

Watering is most important when your bulbs are actively growing. This means autumn and spring for autumn- or spring-flowering bulbs and spring through summer for summer-flowering bulbs. During these times, most bulbs can survive a moderate drought without watering, but they may not bloom well the following year.

The daisy-like blooms of Grecian windflowers are a welcome sight in spring. They will thrive in well-mulched, well-drained soil.

Mulching

Mulching your bulbs is one of the best ways to keep them healthy. Mulch will help to hold moisture in the soil and minimise rapid temperature changes, providing ideal rooting conditions. It shades the soil and helps to keep bulbs cool, protecting the shoots of bulbs from being lured out of the ground too early in spring. Mulch also benefits summer-flowering bulbs, such as lilies, which dislike hot, dry soil.

Mulch your bulbs after planting in autumn or spring. Apply a 2.5- to 5-cm (1- to 2-inch) layer of mulch over the soil. Avoid putting on more than that or your bulbs may have trouble poking their

Mulch and stake dahlias to keep them growing strong and healthy.

shoots up through the mulch. To protect hardy bulbs (such as daffodils and crocus), add more mulch each autumn to keep it at the right depth.

Fertilising

Most bulbs will get along just fine without a lot of extra fertiliser. Working compost or other organic matter into the soil at planting time and using it as a mulch will provide much of the nutrient supply that your bulbs need.

For top-notch growth, you can also sprinkle commercial organic fertiliser over the soil, following the package directions. Use a mix blended especially for bulbs, if you can; otherwise, a general garden fertiliser is acceptable. Fertilise both spring-blooming and autumn-flowering bulbs in spring. Summer-flowering bulbs usually grow best with several small applications of fertiliser in early to mid-summer.

Handling Tender Bulbs

It's easy to fall for the lure of daffodils, crocus and other cold-hardy bulbs – you just plant them once and enjoy them for years. Tender bulbs, on the other hand, tend to need more work, since you may have to dig or lift them for winter storage indoors. Exactly what counts as a tender bulb? Well, it depends on what climate, you live in, but the bulbs that usually come to mind are those that are from tropical and subtropical climates. These include dahlias, tuberous begonias, gladioli, cannas and caladiums. Some tender bulbs can take more cold than others. Cannas, for instance, may survive winters in areas as cold as Zone 7. But others, including tuberous begonias and caladiums, can survive over winter only in frost-free areas.

Lifting Tender Bulbs for Storage

Digging tender bulbs for indoor storage is just another part of routine autumn-garden clean-up. When the bulb foliage turns yellow or brown, that's a good sign that the bulb is ready for storage. If the leaves stay green or if you don't have time to dig the

bulbs when they are first ready, you can wait until just after the first frost. The cold temperatures will cause the leaves to turn black, but the bulbs are protected by the soil and should survive a light frost just fine. Don't wait any longer, though – get out and start digging, or your bulbs may be damaged by the increasingly cold temperatures.

Actually digging the bulbs is simple. First, cut any tall stems back to about 15 cm (6 inches), so you can clearly see the base of the stem. Then carefully loosen the soil all the way around the plant. Use a trowel or hand fork to work around small bulbs and those growing in pots. (You can also turn whole pots over to dump out the soil and the bulbs at the same time.) A shovel or spading fork works better for big clumps, like dahlias and cannas.

Once the soil is loose, you can lift the bulb easily. Shake off as much soil as you can from the bulbs, label them and set them on newspaper in a cool, shady place, such as a garage, potting shed or porch. Dust any cuts on the bulbs or tubers with sulphur, then leave them to dry for several days. Keep the bulbs out of the hot sun and away from areas where squirrels, mice and other animals can get at them.

Storing Tender Bulbs

Once your bulbs have dried for a few days, you can store them. Some gardeners keep their bulbs in mesh bags (like the kind onions come in) or paper bags with a few holes punched in them for better air circulation. Others prefer to store bulbs in boxes of slightly damp wood shavings or peat moss to keep the bulbs from drying out too much over winter. The storage spot should be dark to prevent the bulbs from sprouting and on the cool side – ideally about 10° to 16°C (50° to 60°F). During the storage period, check your bulbs every three to four weeks. Throw away any that are rotting. Sprinkle water on those that are starting to look shrivelled. When spring arrives, plant them as you would new bulbs.

Propagating Bulbs

Once you've had fun growing a few bulbs, it's hard to resist the urge to grow more and more.

Dividing for Multiplying

Division is the fastest and easiest way to propagate nearly all bulbs, corms, tubers, tuberous roots and rhizomes. Besides being quite simple, division has another advantage: All the new plants will be identical to the parent bulb, so you can easily increase your favourite colours and flower forms.

Dividing Bulbs and Corms Some bulbs, such as tulips and daffodils, form small 'bulblets' near their base. Gladioli and other corms produce similar offsets called 'cormels'. With good care, both bulblets and cormels can grow to full flowering size in as little as a year or two.

To divide spring bulbs, lift the clump with a spade or digging fork after the foliage has died back in late spring. To divide gladiolus corms, lift them in late summer or autumn, as the foliage turns yellow. Separate the bulblets or cormlets by gently pulling them away from the mother bulb or corm. Plant the bulblets or cormlets in a nursery bed or a corner of the vegetable garden, where they can grow undisturbed for a few years. Water and fertilise them regularly. When the bulbs reach flowering size, move them to their final spot in the garden.

Dividing Tubers and Tuberous Roots

Division is also an effective way to increase tuberous plants, such as dahlias and tuberous begonias. The best time to divide is in spring, just after you bring these tender plants out of winter storage. Use a sharp knife to cut begonia tubers into two or three pieces, each with at least one growth bud. On dahlias, cut tuberous roots apart at the stem end, so each root has at least one bud.

Plant each new piece in a pot and set it under grow lights or in a greenhouse. Keep the temperature between 18° and 24°C (65° and 75°F). Water as needed so the potting compost stays evenly moist, but not wet. (Don't fertilise newly cut bulbs – wait until they're growing in soil.) In a few weeks, you should have healthy new plants that are ready for transplanting into outdoor gardens and containers.

Dividing Rhizomes Cannas and bearded irises are the two common examples of plants that grow from rhizomes. Use a sharp knife, a spade (if the clump is really big) or your hands to pull or cut apart the rhizomes. Discard any old, woody pieces from the centre of the original clump.

Divide canna clumps into pieces about 15 cm (6 inches) square, making sure that each has at least one growth bud. The best time to divide cannas is in spring, right before you plant them in pots or outdoors in the garden. Bearded irises, on the other hand, prefer to be divided just after they flower. Separate them into pieces with at least one 'fan' of leaves on each. Trim the foliage back by at least half, and replant the irises into soil that you've enriched with compost, leaf mould or well-rotted manure.

Plant daffodils with early rhododendrons for a delightful spring display.

Growing Bulbs from Seed

If you're really patient, you can also grow your bulbs from seed. When they bloom, the seedlings may not look like the parent plant, which can be fun if you like surprises but disappointing if you wanted the exact colour of the original.

Gather seed in summer or autumn, after your bulbs flower. Check the developing seed pods every few days, then

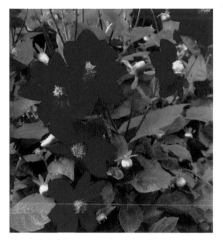
Buy new dahlia roots each year, or dig them up in autumn and store them indoors for winter.

collect the seeds as the seed pods begin to open. Sow the seed in well-drained seed compost in pots or trays. Cover it with a thin layer of compost and set the containers in a cool, shaded place outdoors. Water as needed to keep the soil evenly moist.

When seedlings appear, move the containers to a sunny place. Keep watering until the seedlings die down. (Seedlings will go dormant for part of the year, just like their garden-grown parents.) Water sparingly until new growth appears again; then keep them evenly moist. Depending on the species you're dealing with, your baby bulbs may reach flowering size in as little as one year, although they're more likely to take three to five years.

Bluebells (*Hyacinthoides* spp.) can reseed prolifically to produce large patches. Give them a site where they can spread, or mow off the seed pods to prevent reseeding.

Trees, Shrubs and Climbers

ABOVE: This magnificent white cherry, *Prunus* 'Tai Haku', is one of the finest flowering cherry trees in cultivation.

and a large tree matures at 22.5 to 30 m (75 to 100 feet) or taller. Growing conditions, climate, competition with grass and other plants, mechanical or animal damage and pollution can prevent a tree from reaching its mature height.

These versatile plants frame views, develop patterns for your landscape and unify your design. To get the most out of the trees you select, consider the following features and what they can add to your design.

Beauty Trees serve as backdrops for other plants or garden features and as focal points, like large, living sculptures. You can use them to screen unwanted views and give you privacy. Your trees establish the walls and ceilings for your outdoor rooms. You can use them to soften the architecture of your house or to call attention to it.

Climate Control By shading your house, trees keep things cool, reducing energy bills. (Don't plant evergreen trees for summer shade, though; they'll block the sun in winter, preventing passive solar heating of your house.) You can use trees as a windbreak, to intercept and buffer prevailing winds. If winter winds are your bane, needle-leaved evergreens are the best choice for a windbreak. If you live near a coastal area, choose salt-tolerant species to soften the sea winds.

Livalbility Trees absorb noise and reduce glare, and they purify the air you breathe. Patios or play areas become more usable during hot summers when shaded by trees. Many trees have edible fruits that can feed your family or attract wildlife.

Using Trees in the Landscape

The biggest investment in your landscape – in both time and money – is the selection, purchase and planting of trees. Trees dominate the landscape and have a psychological benefit, too, by making you feel rested and peaceful.

Landscaping with Trees

By horticultural definition, trees are woody plants with one main stem or trunk, although some, such as river birch (*Betula nigra*) and smoke tree (*Cotinus coggygria*), are often grown in multi-trunked clumps. Trees generally have a mature height ranging from 4.5 to 30 m (15 to 100 feet) or more. A small tree is defined as one that generally doesn't exceed 7.5 to 10.5 m (25 to 35 feet) in mature height. A medium-sized tree matures at 15 to 19.5 m (50 to 65 feet),

Consider Form and Function

When you select trees for your garden, use your landscape plan to help you decide what size and shape of tree to select and how each tree will function in the landscape. The arrangement of the branches gives each species of tree a distinctively shaped crown.

Most needle-leaved evergreens, like pines and spruces, tend to have more symmetrical or rigid shapes than deciduous trees, such as oaks or maples. Needle-leaved evergreens often display the familiar conical or pyramidal 'Christmas tree' look. Deciduous trees and broad-leaved evergreens come in many shapes, including round, vase-shaped and columnar.

Trees are often classified according to their intended use – as specimens, shade trees or street trees. Choose your landscape trees according to their function. For an upright, narrow screen, for example, you might select either a tree with a columnar shape or a pyramidal needle-leaved evergreen.

Casual plantings, with a mixture of trees, shrubs and wildflowers, can produce a charming effect.

Trees that have attractive bark, like this river birch (*Betula nigra*), can provide year-round interest.

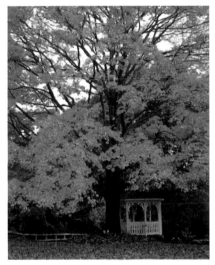

If you're looking for a large tree to add shade to your garden, consider planting a sugar maple (*Acer saccharum*). It will thrive on a sunny site with evenly moist (but not waterlogged) soil that is slightly acid.

Specimen Trees

Specimen trees are showy in some way. They may put on an eye-catching display of flowers in spring, like a flowering crab apple, or blaze with autumn colour, like the red maple 'October Glory' (*Acer rubrum* 'October Glory'). Or they may have unusually coloured leaves, such as purple smoke tree (*Cotinus coggygria*

'Royal Purple'), or bright berries, such as those on the American mountain ash (*Sorbus americana*).

Specimen trees are valuable as focal points in a winter landscape. Fruits that hang on the branches after the leaves drop, such as the fruits of crab apples, are eye-catching. Trees with attractive winter silhouettes, such as flowering dogwoods, also make good specimen trees.

Select a specimen tree that has multi-seasonal interest. A saucer magnolia (*Magnolia* x *soulangeana*) is very showy for a couple of weeks during the spring when in flower, but it fades into the background the rest of the year. A kousa dogwood (*Comus kousa*) on the other hand, bears showy flowers in spring, raspberry-like red fruits in autumn, and has attractive peeling bark in winter.

Shade Trees

Shade trees may have showy features, but it's their cooling effect that's most important. A tree with a round or vase shape is ideal for use as a shade tree. Decide the location of a new shade tree with care: make sure the shadow of the tree will shade the area you intend it to.

If you want filtered shade or want to be able to grow grass under your tree, use a tree with small, fine leaves, such as a thornless honey locust (*Gleditsia triacanthos* var. *inermis*), not one with a

dense canopy of large, overlapping leaves, such as a Norway maple (*Acer platanoides*).

Street Trees

Street trees are tough species that withstand the difficult growing conditions along the street. They're tolerant of heat and pollution, grow well in poor soils and can stand drought. Their roots must grow in very limited spaces, and their crowns must fit under overhead utility lines. Street trees have to be neat: look for trees that don't have messy fruit, falling branches or twigs, or large leaves that can block storm drains.

In spite of these demands, a number of attractive and adaptable trees are available for roadside planting. Among small trees, consider trident maple

Maple tree

Trees come in a wide range of shapes and sizes. Keep these differences in mind when planning your landscape.

Consider Growth Rates

Trees grow at different rates, ranging from less than 30 cm (1 foot) per year to about 1 m (3 feet) per year. Species with a slow-to-medium growth rate, like oaks, generally require less maintenance than fast-growing ones. Fast-growing trees, such as poplars and willows, are often short-lived, surviving only 20 to 30 years, and they also generally have weak wood, which is more susceptible to damage from wind, storms and pests.

(*Acer buergerianum*), thornless cockspur hawthorn (*Crataegus crus-galli* var. *inermis*) or golden rain tree (*Koelreuteria paniculata*). Suitable medium to large trees include thornless honey locust (*Gleditsia triacanthos* var. *inermis*), Japanese pagoda tree (*Sophora japonica* syn. *Styphnolobium japonicum*) and silver lime (*Tilia tomentosa*).

Using Shrubs in the Landscape

Shrubs are hard-working plants in any landscape. They can be used to add a touch of greenery at the foundation of the house, make a thick screen between neighbours, add seasonal colour from fruit or flowers or outline the garden's 'rooms'.

Types of Shrubs

Shrubs are woody plants with multiple stems, ranging from a few inches tall to approximately 4.5 m (15 feet) at maturity. Occasionally an individual shrub is trained to a single tree-like stem, called a standard. And large shrubs are sometimes 'limbed up', by removing the lower branches, into small trees.

Like trees, shrubs can be deciduous, evergreen or semi-evergreen. If all leaves drop each autumn, with new leaves each spring through summer, the shrub is deciduous. Deciduous shrubs, including such favourites as roses (*Rosa* spp.) and spireas (*Spiraea* spp.), often have attractive flowers. For heavy flower production, plant them in full sun. Evergreen shrubs have leaves year-round, though you will notice that each year some of the oldest leaves drop off and are replaced by new leaves. Shrubs with wide, often thick, leaves, such as rhododendrons (*Rhododendron* spp.) and camellias (*Camellia* spp.), are called broad-leaved evergreens. Shrubs with thin, narrow leaves, such as junipers (*Juniperus* spp.) and dwarf mugo pines (*Pinus mugo* var. *mugo*), are classified as needle-leaved evergreens. Semi-evergreen shrubs means

FAR LEFT: You may choose to highlight the unusual branching structure of a tree you already have. LEFT: Limes (*Tilia* spp.) can be tough, adaptable street trees. Their yellow autumn colour is a bonus.

they hold some of their leaves well into winter. Glossy abelia (*Abelia* x *grandiflora*), for example, is evergreen in warm climates, becoming semi-evergreen the farther north it is planted.

Some shrub genera include both deciduous and evergreen species. Hollies (*Ilex* spp.) are a good example. When the deciduous holly, winterberry (*I. verticillata*), drops its leaves in the autumn, large clusters of bright red berries are revealed. The berry display is generally much showier than that of many of the evergreen hollies, such as Chinese holly (*I. cornuta*) and English holly (*I. aquifolium*), whose berries are often hidden by their leaves. Other shrub genera with both deciduous and evergreen species include viburnums (*Viburnum* spp.), rhododendrons and azaleas (*Rhododendron* spp.), and barberries (*Berberis* spp.).

Hydrangea

Choosing and Using Shrubs

One of the most creative and ornamental ways to use shrubs in a landscape is in mixed plantings. Try combining deciduous and evergreen species, interplanting shrubs that bloom at different seasons, or adding flowering shrubs to a perennial border to create year-round interest.

If you need to block traffic noise year-round, plant evergreen shrubs, such as yews (*Taxus* spp.), hollies (*Ilex* spp.) or, in warm regions, camellias (*Camellia* spp.). If you want shrubs to provide privacy only

Troublesome Trees

While no tree is perfect, some species tend to be much more of a bother than others. These troublemakers may be weak-wooded (drop lots of branches that you have to pick up), produce massive quantities of annoying fruits or seeds, or just have a combination of unattractive features. Below is a list of some common nuisance trees, along with their bad habits:

Acer platanoides (Norway maple): shallow-rooted, reseeds prolifically

Ailanthus altissima (tree of heaven): reseeds prolifically, odiferous male flowers

Albizia julibrissin (mimosa): pest- and disease-prone, messy seed pods

Morus spp. (mulberries): messy fruit, pest- and disease-prone

Populus spp. (poplars): weak-wooded, invasive roots, pest- and disease-prone

Salix spp. (willows): pest- and disease-prone, weak-wooded

Ulmus pumila (Siberian elm): weak-wooded, pest-prone

for summer barbecues, deciduous shrubs would make a fine choice.

Specimens Shrubs make excellent specimen plants. Use them to call out a special feature in your garden such as the beginning of a path or the end of a border or patio. For specimens, look for shrubs

that are attractive for as many months as possible. Many viburnums, for example, have attractive spring flowers, summer fruit and good autumn colour.

Backdrops and 'Walls' You can use shrubs to mark the garden rooms or the parts of your landscape – to screen a quiet sitting area from an area designed for active play, or to wall utility areas off for rubbish or storage. You can also use shrubs as a backdrop for plantings of flowers. But if you use shrubs in this manner, look for ones that will complement but not compete with your flowers. Choose green shrubs like box or junipers, for example, and avoid those with showy blossoms of their own.

Screens and Hedges Shrubs are the perfect choice for hedges and screens, to block unattractive views or the sights and sounds of nearby neighbours and traffic. To calculate how many shrubs you need to buy for an effective hedge or screen, determine the mature spread of the species you've selected. Figure on spacing the shrubs closer together than their mature spread so that they'll form an unbroken line. For example, if a particular shrub has a mature spread of 1.5 m (5 feet), plan to space the plants 0.9 to 1.2 m (3 to 4 feet) apart, depending upon how large they are when you buy them and how quickly you want a solid screen or hedge. Divide the total hedge length by the spacing you select to determine the number of shrubs to buy.

Groundcover Shrubs are an excellent substitute for grass in areas where lawns don't grow well, where mowing is difficult or where you want less maintenance. Planted in a well-mulched bed, low-growing junipers (*Juniperus horizontalis* and *J. procumbens* 'Nana') or rock spray cotoneaster (*Cotoneaster horizontalis*) will form a low-maintenance cover on a steep hill. Where soil erosion is a problem, use shrubs

You can choose from a variety of shrub shapes.

with creeping underground stolons, such as red-osier dogwood (*Comus sericea*), or shrubs with arching stems that root when they touch the ground, such as winter jasmine (*Jasminum nudiflorum*).

Seasonal Attractions In your landscape, shrubs can be utilitarian, but they can also be a focal point. Look for shrubs with multi-seasonal interest – especially for use

BELOW TOP: A border of carefully chosen shrubs can provide an attractive, low-maintenance option to flower beds.
MIDDLE: Flowering shrubs, like this weigela, are often most attractive when allowed to grow in a natural arching form.
BOTTOM: Many flowering shrubs, such as camellias (*Camellia* spp.), can provide a dramatic show during their flowering season.

as accents or specimens. Oak-leaved hydrangea (*Hydrangea quercifolia*), for instance, has interesting oak-leaf-shaped leaves that turn purple in autumn. Its showy clusters of off-white flowers dry on the plant and persist well into the winter. The peeling bark provides additional winter interest. The fruit on shrubs such as pyracanthas (*Pyracantha* spp.) and viburnums (*Viburnum* spp.) provide food for birds, while the plants serve as protective cover. Fruiting shrubs are also excellent for attracting wildlife.

Size Up Your Selections.

If you want your shrubs to stay short, regular pruning will keep them in bounds. But a better approach is to choose shrubs that mature at the height you need. There are dwarf or miniature cultivars of many popular shrubs, including 'Bronxensis' forsythia, which matures at 60 cm (2 feet). Dwarf cultivars of many trees – especially spruces (*Picea* spp.) and arbor-vitae (*Thuja* spp.) – are also commonly used as shrubs. Look for plants with names like 'Prostrata', 'Nana', 'Compacta', 'Densa' and 'Pumila', but don't stop there. Be sure to verify mature height before you buy; compact forms of some trees and large shrubs may still be larger at maturity than you want.

Investigate Potential Pest Problems

Consider how attractive the tree or shrub may be to pests. In general, vigorous plants attract fewer pests and withstand those that do find them. But if you can choose species and cultivars that are naturally more problem-resistant, you're several steps ahead of the game. A plant's susceptibility to insects and diseases can vary depending on where you live, so check with your local nursery or garden centre to learn which pests are common in your area.

A final word about pests: planting a tree or shrub that's prone to a particular

If you like a formal look in your garden, you may choose to include tightly sheared shrubs as accents.

problem need not doom you to more work. Many insects and diseases look bad but don't really threaten the life of the plant. Lilacs, for example, often get powdery mildew, which is basically harmless and sometimes barely noticeable.

Easy-Care Foundation Plantings

That small strip of soil that surrounds the bottom of the house may be the most misunderstood area in the landscape. All too often it's relegated to a boring hodgepodge of badly pruned evergreens, but it doesn't have to be that way. The two secrets to an interesting, attractive and low-maintenance foundation planting are a simple design and well-chosen plants.

Designing a Foundation Planting

Start with a design so you can 'see' how the plants will fit together before you buy and install them. At some point, your design should be on paper, drawn to scale. You may want to draw the plan first, then try to visualise how it will look in real life. Or you may find it easier to experiment with different layouts right on the site, and then record your best effort.

To help visualise the design, lay a rope along the ground to define a possible outline for the planting. Stick in upside-down brooms or tall stakes to represent

Some shrubs, like barberries (*Berberis* spp.), offer both flowers and showy fruit for multi-season interest.

Make sure each tree and shrub has enough room to develop without crowding – you'll minimise diseases and pruning.

Foundation plantings don't have to be boring! Try a lively mixture of shrubs, trees, flowers and groundcover.

small trees; inverted baskets or buckets could stand for shrubs. As you decide where things should go, keep in mind that you'll be planting them out at least 30 cm (1 foot) beyond the drip line to protect them from rain falling off the roof. (Cover the unplanted area along the drip line with a layer of gravel or a row of flat rocks or paving blocks to prevent erosion.) When you are pleased with the broom and basket layout, translate that design to paper.

Picking the Right Plants

Once you have a pleasing design, you can select plants to fit it. The most important step to making your planting low maintenance is choosing plants that won't

get too big or too wide. That may mean selecting dwarf shrub species or cultivars that won't grow up to block your windows. It may also mean planting far enough from the house for the plants to spread out. The second most important thing is choosing plants that are well adapted to the site conditions: the soil (especially its drainage) and the amount of light (including the light and heat that bounce off the house wall).

Foundation plantings have traditionally contained mostly evergreen conifers, such as yew and juniper, or broad-leaved evergreens, like azaleas and box. Evergreens do add colour and hide the foundation all year, but deciduous shrubs have their place, too.

Many species – including dwarf fothergilla (*Fothergilla gardenii*) and Japanese kerria (*Kerria japonica*) – offer multi-season interest with flowers, autumn colour or attractive stems. Also look for dwarf or slow-growing cultivars that will stay low without regular pruning. A few interesting choices include maroon Japanese barberry (*Berberis thunbergii* f.

Large shrubs like lilacs can be 'limbed up' (by removing the lower branches) to look like small trees.

atropurpurea 'Atropurpurea Nana', white-flowered dwarf slender deutzia (*Deutzia gracilis* 'Nikko') and dwarf guelder rose (*Viburnum opulus* 'Nanum').

Though there are many wonderful plants to choose from, limit your design to a few different species – not only will it look better, but you'll have fewer types of plants to care for. If you choose interesting species, you don't have to worry that the lack of diversity will be monotonous. Look for plants with attractive textures or growth habits, or with interesting fruit, flowers or bark. And don't forget groundcover, which unifies the planting and helps link it with the house and the lawn beyond. Some also offers seasonal flowers, fruits or autumn colour.

Caring for Trees and Shrubs

One of the greatest things about trees and shrubs is that they don't need much maintenance. You need to do a few simple things to care for them while they're young and even fewer simple things once they mature.

Special Care for New Plants

Water your new plants regularly (once a week if you don't get any rain) for the first two years, until they can form enough roots to search out water on their own. To encourage a good root system, water deeply, slowly and in an area wider than the end of the branches farthest from the trunk.

Scattering fertiliser by hand is probably the best option for small areas, but it can give spotty results if you don't spread the material evenly.

Different grass species germinate at different speeds – from less than a week to as long as 30 days – so if you're planting a mixture, keep in mind that they won't all sprout at once.

Establishing Turf Install the turf as soon as it arrives, if at all possible; otherwise keep it damp and shaded until you're ready for it. Ask your supplier for instructions on handling and laying the turf strips. After installation, press the turf into the soil by tamping with the back of a rake or by rolling with a light roller, then water it thoroughly.

Planting Plugs and Sprigs Plant plugs or sprigs 15 to 30 cm (6 to 12 inches) apart in each direction in thoroughly tilled soil. (The exact spacing will vary on the type of grass you're growing; ask your supplier for the recommended spacing for the kind you purchase.) An easy method to keep the spacing right is to mark straight, shallow furrows across the lawn about 30 cm (12 inches) apart, then set the sprigs or plugs in these furrows from 15 to 20 cm (6 to 8 inches) apart. Roll the surface lightly and water it well.

After Planting Whether you have seeded the lawn, laid turf or planted plugs or sprigs, never let it dry out until the grass is

well rooted (generally after three to four weeks). If the weather is mild and not windy, a good rule of thumb is to water every two or three days for three weeks. In hot, dry weather, your new lawn may need water several times a day to keep the soil moist and allow good growth.

Don't walk on the lawn any more than necessary until the grasses are growing vigorously, and hold off on mowing until they are at least 15 to 20 cm (3 to 4 inches) tall. Set the mower about 7.5 cm (3 inches) high for the first few mowings; then reduce it to the optimum height for the grass you are growing. (This can vary between 1.5 and 10 cm [¾ and 4 inches] depending on the site.)

Renovating an Existing Lawn

Lawns often begin to look worn out as the years go by, either from neglect or because they weren't given a good start at planting time. If your lawn needs help, you must decide whether to install a completely new lawn or simply give your existing lawn a facelift. You should strongly consider starting over if:

• The ground under the lawn is so rough and bumpy that it is hard to mow.
• It has large bare spots or worn compacted areas.
• More than 50 per cent of the surface of the lawn is covered with weeds.

In such cases, the best prescription is to remove the existing turf and weeds and replant with easy-care grasses that thrive in your climate. Strip off the existing grass with a spade or a hired turf-cutting machine; pile the removed turf in an out-of-the-way spot to decompose. Then follow the instructions above for starting a new lawn.

If at least half of the area is grass, if the surface is fairly level and if the weeds aren't overpowering, improving the lawn is an easier and better alternative. The area will be less disturbed, so you'll have less dust and mud, and you can continue to use most of the lawn as you recondition the threadbare areas. Patching up a lawn is also cheaper than starting from scratch.

Begin with Spot Treatments Renovating a ragged lawn will take a little time, but it can be worth the effort. Mending the worn and torn spots is the first step in lawn renovation. If foot traffic has worn paths in the grass, build gravel, stone, brick or paved paths where you want people to walk; if necessary, plant shrubs or install low fences to discourage shortcuts. Sometimes traffic can disturb the perimeter of the lawn; repair the edges with a shovel and some new topsoil. If vigorous grasses have crept over the pavement or into the garden or street, some judicious edging may be necessary.

If you enjoy growing flowers and dislike lawn care, consider turning some of the lawn into flower beds.

In late summer or early autumn, fill in any cavities and depressions in the lawn with sifted topsoil and level off the humps. Loosen trampled, compacted areas by digging or tilling. Till or fork over any bare spots and areas of the lawn where weeds dominate (dig out the weeds by hand as thoroughly as possible first). Firm the soil with a roller, sprinkle organic lawn fertiliser over the area (following the application instructions on the bag) and rake it in lightly.

Now it's time to sow the seed. You'll find grass seed mixtures formulated especially to fill in bare spots; try to find a mix that will match the rest of your turf grass. Scatter the seed over the area and rake it into the soil, leaving it smooth.

To spruce up areas where the grass is thin, use a technique called over-seeding: rake the area thoroughly to loosen the soil surface, scatter seed over the existing grass and rake again lightly. Spread a thin layer of sifted topsoil over the seed.

Keep newly seeded lawn areas watered until the grass is established. After a few weeks, if any spots of new grass aren't growing well, sprinkle a liquid fertiliser such as liquid seaweed over them. The grasses on newly seeded plots are fragile for most of their first season, so avoid walking on them any more than necessary.

TOP: Most grasses are surprisingly problem-free. Animals such as mice and rabbits are probably the most serious pests.

BOTTOM: Upright arching grasses such as variegated Japanese silver grass (*Miscanthus sinensis*) are ideal for flower borders.

Set the mower at 7.5 cm (3 inches) for the first two or three mowings; the taller grass will be more vigorous and shade out weed seeds. After that, move the blade to the optimum height setting for the kind of grass you are mowing.

Revitalise the Whole Lawn Once you've spot-treated problem areas, let them grow for a few months until they match the rest of the lawn. The following spring is the time to give the whole lawn a thorough reconditioning.

The soil in old or worn-out lawns is often compacted and will benefit from aeration. Use an aerator over all but the newly planted areas to encourage grasses to thrive and compete better with weeds.

Worn-out lawns are likely to lack humus, too, so spread a thin layer of aged manure or compost over the entire surface. Add a nutrient boost by applying a complete organic fertiliser at the rate prescribed on the bag. If a soil test shows that the pH is too low (acidic) or too high (alkaline), wait until a rain has washed in the fertiliser, then apply lime to raise the pH or sulphur to lower it. (Your soil test results will tell you how much of either material to apply.) The little extra care and attention you spend on renovating your lawn will payoff, and the result will be lush, green and attractive.

Landscaping with Ornamental Grasses

Ornamental grasses is a loosely defined term that describes any grass-like plants that are attractive enough for planting in a landscape. This group includes bamboos, rushes and sedges; they grow in a diverse array of sizes, textures and colours. Whether you need drifts of plants in a dry, sunny border, groundcover for a shady nook, a rock garden specimen or a container plant for a roof garden, you'll find a suitable ornamental grass for the spot. These adaptable, easy-care plants serve all kinds of landscape functions, from screening unpleasant views to providing four season interest in the flower garden.

Pampas grass

Consider the Spread

Some people are wary of planting ornamental grasses, fearful that – like couch grass – they will overtake the property. 'Give them an inch, and they'll take a mile,' wary homeowners think. But that reputation is deserved only by a few particularly fast-spreading species, such as blue lyme grass (*Leymus arenarius* 'Glaucus'). Clump-forming grasses are less likely to be invasive than those that expand by rhizomes or stolons. Some, however – including pampas grass (*Cortaderia selloana*), fountain grasses (*Pennisetum* spp.) and, to a lesser extent, northern sea oats (*Chasmanthium latifolium*) – can spread by reseeding.

Before you choose a grass, always check whether it is a clump former or a runner, and whether it tends to reseed. Since some plants are rank spreaders in certain climates but well behaved in others, find out how the grass has performed for other gardeners in your area, if you're concerned about a plant's potential invasiveness. Keep fast-creeping grasses confined by paved paths, metal or plastic edging strips or other solid barriers.

Divided grass

Grasses for Challenging Sites

Ornamental grasses are great replacements for more traditional shrubs and groundcover on difficult sites. Drought-tolerant types stop erosion on steep, dry slopes. Short species line pathways nicely, serve as neat edgings in front of gardens or shrubs, or act as substitutes for lawn grasses. Many do well in wet places; some even grow in water. Salt-tolerant species – such as switch grass (*Panicum virgatum*) and dune grass (*Leymus arenarius*) – thrive at the seashore or on a roadside, where salt spray or salt-laden run-off from winter roads would destroy turf grass or evergreen shrubs.

Grasses as Screens and Hedges

Tall ornamental grasses – those that grow 1.2 m (4 feet) or more – can provide a welcome change of texture and colour from more rigid shrubs and trees. In large gardens, big grasses like pampas grass (*Cortaderia selloana*) and eulalia grasses (*Miscanthus* spp.) provide spectacular backgrounds for shorter grasses, shrubs and flowering plants.

Tall-growing grasses also make excellent quick screens to provide privacy, eliminate unpleasant views and cut down on street noise. Such screens can divide a larger area into separate 'rooms' and also protect more delicate plants from being buffeted by wind storms.

Most grasses become fully established for screening purposes within two to three years – far more quickly than a standard hedge. This makes them ideal for new gardens where you need fast-growing plants to get an almost immediate effect. Grasses can also fill space while slower-maturing shrubs are getting started. And, unlike hedges, oranamental grasses need no maintenance. Once they're planted they need little but an annual cutting back.

Begonia

Made for the Shade

Many leafy and flowering groundcover plants adapt well to life in less than ideal light. If you have a spot that gets plenty of filtered light but no direct sun, try some of the species listed below. Low-growing ferns are also naturals for shady sites.

Aegopodium podagraria 'Variegata' (variegated bishop's weed)
Ajuga reptans (ajuga)
Asarum europaeum (European wild ginger)
Astilbe chinensis var. *pumila* (dwarf Chinese astilbe)
Euonymus fortunei (winter creeper)
Galium odoratum (sweet woodruff)
Hedera helix (English ivy)
Hosta hybrids (hostas)
Lamium maculatum (spotted lamium)
Liriope spicata (creeping lily turf)
Pachysandra procumbens (Allegheny spurge)
Pachysandra terminalis (Japanese spurge)
Saxifraga stolonifera (strawberry geranium)
Tiarella cordifolia (foam flower)
Tolmiea menziesii (piggyback plant)
Vancouveria hexandra (American barrenwort)
Vinca minor (common periwinkle)
Waldsteinia fragarioides (barren strawberry)

Common periwinkle

ABOVE: Consider the sweet violet as fragrant groundcover for a cool, moist, shady spot.
BELOW: Common periwinkle provides fast-spreading groundcover that will cope very well in the shade. Its lavender-blue flowers appear in early spring.

Landscaping with Groundcover Plants

The term 'groundcover' is most often used to describe low, spreading plants- usually those that grow less than 60 cm (2 feet) tall. That still includes a wide range of plants, from spreading grasses and sedges to creeping perennials and suckering shrubs. You'll find no end to the ways you can use these versatile plants in your garden. They'll help you reduce your lawn space or even replace a lawn to save money, work and energy. In a dry, sunny climate, drought-tolerant species such as succulents are indispensable for creating a water-saving landscape; in damp areas, water-loving plants are just as handy to absorb water. Some groundcover plants attractively blanket steep banks to stop erosion and cover rough or rocky areas that are difficult to mow. Shade-lovers border woodland paths or cover low-light areas beneath trees and between buildings. Flat, creeping types fill in the gaps between paving stones and tumble attractively between the crevices in garden walls and steps. Even with the most common groundcover plants you can create pleasant, appealing plantings to beautify a garden setting or deal with a difficult site.

Choosing Groundcover Plants for Garden Challenges

Well-chosen groundcover plants are among the most versatile and easy-care garden plants you can grow. Unlike lawn grasses, groundcover plants don't need much regular maintenance: Just plant them, weed or mulch a few times for the first year or two, water them and then let the plants do the work.

Groundcover for Shady Sites Shady plantings are natural choices for woodlands and forests, but they are, of course, not limited to those spots. Sunlight is also scarce on the north side of buildings, between buildings, beneath lawn trees and behind tall hedges, fences or garden walls. It is difficult to grow many flowering plants and evergreens in these spots, but shade-loving groundcover plants are ideal there. Many of them will spread quickly and provide lush cover throughout the year. Japanese spurge (*Pachysandra terminalis*) and common periwinkle (*Vinca minor*) tolerate shade especially well, as do ferns and many less common foliage plants, and even some wildflowers.

Super Groundcover for Slopes

Fast-spreading groundcover plants are excellent choices for slopes that are too steep or rocky to mow. Set plants out a little closer than normal for quick cover and mulch between them to protect the soil until they fill in.

Achillea tomentosa (woolly yarrow)
Ajuga reptans (ajuga)
Coronilla varia (crown vetch)
Cotoneaster horizontalis (rock spray cotoneaster)
Euonymus fortunei (winter creeper)
Hedera helix (English ivy)
Hemeracallis fulva (tawny daylily)
Hypericum calycinum (rose of Sharon)
Juniperus horizontalis (creeping juniper)
Pachysandra terminalis (Japanese spurge)
Parthenocissus quinquefolia (Virginia creeper)
Potentilla fruticosa (shrubby cinquefoil)
Rosa rugosa (rugosa rose)
Stephanandra incisa (lace shrub)
Vinca minor (common periwinkle)

Groundcover to Cope with Slopes Sloping sites are another common landscaping challenge. Grassy slopes can be downright difficult, and even dangerous, to mow. Or perhaps you have an ugly, rocky slope where even grass won't grow. Besides being maintenance headaches, slopes are also prime targets for soil erosion. The run-off from heavy rains can easily carry topsoil down a bare slope, depositing the earth on paths and paving at the bottom. That makes more work for you, as you have to clean up the debris after each rain.

If your property has a troublesome slope, groundcover is a good solution.

English ivy is a dependable, easy-to-grow groundcover plant that is ideal for protecting the soil on shaded slopes.

To stabilise the soil, you need species that transplant easily and spread quickly. Drought tolerance is a plus, especially on hot, sunny sites; slopes tend to be dry, since water runs off instead of soaking in. Fortunately, there are some beautiful flowering plants – such as moss phlox (*Phlox subulata*), two-row stonecrop (*Sedum spurium*) and white evening primrose (*Oenothera speciosa*) – that are well adapted to life on dry, rocky slopes.

Lily of the valley

Groundcover for Moist Soils Wet spots can be a real landscaping hassle. They may be just moist enough that you can't get the mower in to trim until midsummer, or they're so wet that grass won't grow there at all. Instead of struggling with the site, just plant species that like 'wet feet'. Certain ferns, Japanese primroses (*Primula japonica*) and creeping Jenny (*Lysimachia nummularia*) are a few of the groundcover plants that thrive in soggy soil. Lily of the valley likes moist soil too. Combine them with moisture-loving perennials and shrubs such as turtleheads (*Chelone* spp.), blue flag (*Iris versicolor*), winterberry holly (*Ilex verticillata*) and summersweet (*Clethra alnifolia*) for interesting effects.

The Indoor Garden

Most common houseplants are truly easy to grow if you understand their basic needs for light, water and fertiliser. Even the blackest thumb can grow a drought-tolerant jade plant or pony tail palm. But why settle for the most common, easiest plants when there's a wonderful world of colourful flowers, sparkling variegated leaves, dramatic cacti and exotic orchids waiting for you to explore? Whatever time and skills you have and whatever the conditions in your home, there are dozens of beautiful houseplants you can grow!

Houseplants can be so much more than just a spot of greenery on a windowsill. Use them to fill your home with sweet scents, such as those of orange blossoms and jasmine. Brighten up the dull days of winter with the brilliant flowers of amaryllis and long-lasting orchids. Grow lush tropical plants to decorate the living room, and raise tasty herbs for the kitchen. Create a gift for a friend or a special feature for your own houseplant collection by planting a terrarium or training a fragrant rosemary plant on a circular topiary frame. With a little imagination, you'll find many wonderful ways to brighten your life with houseplants.

Buying the Best Plants

If you're out shopping and you see a houseplant you like, and the price is right, you're probably going to bring it home. It may not be the best way to get the

Agave cactus

perfect plant to match the conditions in your home, but most of the time it works out just fine.

If, on the other hand, you want a plant that will thrive in a particular location, you need to be more careful to choose just the right one. A little advance planning is especially helpful if you intend to buy a large (and therefore more expensive) plant.

Flowering houseplants generally need high light levels, so make sure you have a bright spot for them.

Estimate the Light

Your first step in buying the right plant is to consider how much light is available in the location you've chosen. Unless you're planning to place the plant directly in front of a large south, east or west window, you should avoid buying houseplants that need bright light or direct sun. Instead, stick with those that need only medium light. Flowering plants will require more light than plants grown just for their attractive foliage, so if you've bought indoor plants for their flowers, it's especially important to be sure the plant gets enough light. If you have to place a plant well away from the windows, try to select a plant that can tolerate low light levels.

Do a Little Research

Once you've estimated the light levels available in the location you've chosen, make a list of plants suitable for your chosen location. Now that you know what you're looking for, you can shop around a little. Prices can vary a lot, especially for large plants, so it's worth investigating several sources; check out the garden centres and florists in your area. Talk to the employees and find someone who can help you make a good plant selection.

When you've decided exactly which kind of plant you're going to buy and where you're going to buy it, look over all the plants of that type that the seller offers. Some plants will have a nicer overall shape than others; look for those that you find most appealing. Once you decide which plant you want, inspect it closely for any signs of insect or disease problems before you take it home.

Consider Flowering Habits

If you're buying a flowering plant for your home, there are some extra factors to consider. First of all, be aware that many flowering houseplants are grown under special controlled conditions in commercial greenhouses and are not likely to rebloom for you next year unless you have a greenhouse or can give them special care. Some, such as Persian violet (*Exacum affine*), are actually annuals that won't live more than a year or so, even with the best care.

Even though they can be relatively short-lived, flowering plants are still a good choice for brightening up indoor spaces. Live flowering plants will last at least two to three times longer than cut flowers, and some – including florist's cyclamen (*Cyclamen persicum*), orchids and African violets – will bloom non-stop

LEFT: The stunning flowers of florist's cyclamen certainly brighten dull winter days, but it can be tricky to get plants to bloom again next year. RIGHT: The flowers of potted spring bulbs and primroses will last longest if you keep them in a cool spot. Placing the pots in groups will help to keep the humidity level adequate.

Cyclamen

for many months. So go ahead and bring flowering plants home to enjoy; just don't feel like it's your fault if they don't bloom again next year. When choosing a flowering houseplant, always try to pick one that has lots of buds, with just a few already open. That way you'll get the maximum bloom time as the unopened flower buds flower over the next weeks.

Find the Right Spot

South-facing windows let in the most light, and most houseplants will flourish there. Although east and west exposures don't provide as many hours of bright light as south windows, many bright-light lovers (and all plants that need medium light) will grow well in most east- or west-facing windows. Save north-facing windows for low-light plants, especially foliage plants.

There are several things besides direction that affect the amount of light coming in a window. A very large east-facing window might actually be brighter than a small, south-facing one. Shade from trees may make a west-facing window more like a northern one.

Fortunately, most houseplants are adaptable. Your plants should do fine, as long as you do your best to match the right plant to the right window.

If you feel more comfortable with a little more precision, you can buy an inexpensive light meter, which will measure the actual amount of light at any given spot. These meters usually measure light in units known as 'foot-candles' and come with a chart that tells you how many foot-candles various plants require.

To give all of your plants ample light, you may want to rotate them so each has a chance to be near the window.

Place Plants Properly

Matching your plants to the best available windows is important, but placing each plant so it's right up near the glass is probably even more important than having the right window. The intensity of light drops off very rapidly as it enters the room, so a plant even a few feet from the window will get only half as much light as it would if it is right next to the window.

If your windowsills are too narrow to hold plants, consider adding a shelf to make the sill wider, or place a table in front of the window so you can set plants on it. Keep the windows clean and remove any sheer curtains that might cut down the light intensity.

Move Plants to Manage Light Levels

There may be times when you want to put a plant in a spot that you know doesn't provide enough light for it. For example, say you buy a spectacular flowering azalea and you really want to keep it on the dining room table where everyone can enjoy it. You can usually get away with this for a week or so, then move the plant back into brighter light in a window. Most plants won't suffer much from such a procedure. Obviously, the lower the plant's light needs, the longer it can tolerate a dim location.

Another way to keep plants thriving in low-light locations is to rotate two plants between the dark location and a bright window every few weeks or so. That way you get to enjoy a plant right where you want it all the time, and the two plants will get enough light to thrive. This is how shopping centres and offices keep

Flower production takes lots of energy, so flowering plants generally need all the light they can get.

their plants looking so good: the plants are moved back to a greenhouse periodically to recuperate, then they are returned.

By the way, placing a plant close to an incandescent light bulb doesn't help much, but there are other types of lights that work very well for growing houseplants if your window space is limited.

Is Your Plant Getting the Right Light?

If your plant isn't getting the right light, it may show symptoms that tell you it needs a new location. Sometimes, you may notice that plants growing in bright windows develop a yellow tinge or white or brown patches on the leaves that get the most sun. This may be a signal that the plant is getting too much light. This doesn't happen often with houseplants, but it could be a problem if you put a low-light plant like a Chinese evergreen (*Aglaonema* spp.) directly in a south-facing window. If these symptoms occur, move the plant slightly farther away from the window or move it to a less-bright window.

Geranium

The opposite problem – plants not getting enough light – is far more common. A plant trying to grow where there's not enough light will gradually become leggy and spindly, and its lower leaves may turn yellow and drop. Or the plant may just sit, not putting out any new growth at all. If you notice a plant is not growing, or if there's new growth but it looks weak and spindly, try moving the plant to a brighter location.

Some plants, such as weeping fig (*Ficus benjamina*), may drop a lot of their leaves when you first bring them home. This is because they were probably grown outside in very bright light. When you move them to the much dimmer interior of your home, they simply don't need as many leaves because there isn't as much light, so they drop them. Don't be alarmed by this. Keep the plant in the brightest location you have, water it moderately and wait for it to adjust to its new surroundings. It should stop dropping leaves after a few weeks.

If a plant continues to drop leaves or to grow very poorly, move it to a brighter location. Too often when houseplants grow poorly, people give them more water or fertiliser thinking that will solve the problem. Some plants do drop leaves when their soil gets too dry, but if the real cause is low light levels, extra water or fertiliser is the last thing that will help.

Watering Wisely

Next to getting the light levels right, watering is probably the most important aspect of houseplant care. You can't just water this plant once a week and that one twice a week; there are too many different factors that will affect how much water a plant needs. If you understand what those factors are and how they increase or decrease your plants' water requirements, then you'll know what to expect and be better able to give each plant the right amount of water for healthy growth.

The major factors that will affect how much water a certain plant needs include:

- The plant's particular moisture preference. Some plants need dry conditions (as succulents and cacti do) and some need constantly moist soil (as many ferns prefer). Most houseplants fall in the middle and need a steady supply of moisture with the soil surface drying out between waterings.
- The container the plant is growing in. Plants in clay pots will dry out faster than those in plastic pots. Large plants growing in small pots will also need water more frequently. (That's one of the reasons plants either need to be divided or repotted into larger pots as they grow.)
- The soil the plant is growing in. Soil containing ample compost or peat moss will absorb and hold more moisture than mixes containing lots of sand.
- The amount of light the plant gets. Plants growing in bright light will need more water than those placed in dimmer areas.
- The weather conditions. Plants will use much more water during bright, warm, summer periods when they are actively growing than in the winter, when temperatures are cooler and the daylight hours are much shorter. They also need very little water during sustained periods of cloudy weather.

Considering all these varying factors that affect how fast the soil dries, it's easy to see why it's so important to check each plant's soil before you water.

When to Water

Your first clue about when to water should be the soil surface, which usually turns a lighter colour when it's dry. If it's dark coloured and damp, do not water.

If the surface is dry, you can use your finger to check the soil an inch or two below the surface. If you still feel moisture, wait a day or two and test again. When that top layer feels dry, it's generally the right time to water.

Another way to check soil moisture is to lift the pot. You can tell immediately if the plant feels really light and thus needs water or if it feels relatively heavy, in which case you should wait a few more days before you water. This technique works especially well for small- to medium-sized plants in light plastic pots.

Some pots are just too big to lift, and the soil near the surface may dry out while there's still plenty of moisture deeper in the soil. Always check for moisture several inches deep in large pots; if you go only by whether the soil surface is dry, you could easily overwater. When in doubt, always underwater rather than risk giving too much water and thereby destroying the roots.

How to Water

Once you're sure a plant needs watering, you should water it thoroughly so that a little water runs out into the saucer under it. When you apply more water than the soil can absorb, the excess flows out the bottom into the saucer. This flow of water through the soil, similar to what happens in the garden when it rains, serves an important function in container plants. As the water runs down through the soil, it pushes out used air and allows fresh air to move into the spaces between soil particles. (Plant roots need both water and air to thrive. That's why it's so important to have a loose, well-drained potting soil and to make sure you always water thoroughly.)

By the way, always use pots with drainage holes, and always put saucers under them. Without drainage holes, it's

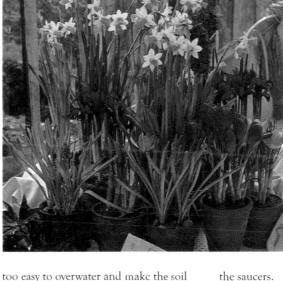

too easy to overwater and make the soil soggy. (The excess water trapped in a pot without drainage holes could cause the roots to rot and the plant to die.) And if you don't have a saucer under the plant, you'll be tempted to underwater to avoid water running out the bottom and making a mess.

Occasionally when you water, you may notice that the water seems to be running rapidly through the soil and out the bottom without being absorbed by the soil. When this happens, you've let the soil get too dry. When potting compost dries out, it shrinks away from the sides of the pot, leaving space where water can just run right through. To water a dried-out pot, you need to set the entire pot in a bowl or sink full of water up to the pot's rim and let the compost slowly absorb the water. After the soil is thoroughly rewetted, let the pot drain, then return it to its saucer.

Watering for Holidays

If you'll be away for more than a few days, there are several techniques you can use to get extra water to your plants. If you're only going to miss one of your usual watering days, you can water the plants thoroughly and add some extra water to

Clay pots tend to dry out quickly, so pay special attention to watering plants in them.

Standard fuchsia

the saucers. (While you shouldn't make a habit of leaving water standing in the saucers, it's okay to do it occasionally as a way to give plants some extra water while you're gone.)

If you're going to be away for more than just a few days, you can set your plants up to be wick-watered. To do this, use a strip of nylon stocking, a rolled-up paper towel or some other absorbent material for the wick. Insert one end of the wick into the bottom of the pot, making sure it makes good contact with the compost, then run the other end into a container of water. Recycled margarine tubs with lids work well for small plants; just cut a hole in the lid, fill the tub with water, run the wick down through the hole, then set the plant on top of the reservoir. Capillary action will draw water up along the wick and into the pot.

Humidity and Temperature

Although humidity levels and temperature levels are not as critical for good growth as light intensity or proper watering, they can have a marked effect on the health and vigour of your plants.

Handling Humidity

Almost all houseplants will grow better if you can give them higher humidity levels than those found in the average home. Indoor air is usually much drier than outdoor air, especially during the winter when heating systems drive away moisture. Summer air-conditioning also creates dry indoor air.

In general, plants with thin, delicate leaves tend to be more sensitive to low humidity, while plants like Chinese evergreen, with their thick, waxy leaves, can tolerate typical home humidity levels. There are some plants on the market, such as bird's nest fern (*Platycerium bifurcatum*), that look great at the store (because they just came from a greenhouse) but usually grow poorly in most homes unless you provide extra humidity. Always check the label and avoid buying a plant that needs extra humidity, unless you like it so much that you are willing to give it extra care.

You can buy an inexpensive humidity gauge (at hardware stores) to monitor the water vapour in the air. Most plants thrive in humidity levels very similar to those humans like – around 40 to 60 per cent humidity. It's more likely, however, that the humidity in your house is below this.

A wick-watering set-up is a handy way to water plants while you're away.

In winter, in fact, the humidity level may be as low as only 10 or 20 per cent (which is as dry as a desert!).

Symptoms of low humidity include brown leaf tips and edges, and leaf curling. Here are some ways to increase humidity levels.

Grouping Plants One way to increase humidity is to cluster your houseplants. This happens naturally when you place plants in groups near windows. As the leaves release water vapour, the extra moisture creates a more humid microclimate for the plants. Using clay pots instead of plastic also helps slightly because water vapour evaporates from the sides of the clay pots.

Misting Some people like to mist their plants directly to increase humidity, and this does help a little. However, as soon as the mist evaporates, the humidity level will drop. Misting plants so heavily that water stands on the leaves is not good, either, since that can lead to disease problems. If you decide to mist, do it during daytime hours and do it lightly.

Pebble Trays A better choice than misting is to grow your houseplants on

Signs of Overwatering and Underwatering

Overwatering is just as bad for your plants as underwatering – maybe even worse. When plants are too dry, their leaves will droop, so at least you have a clue that they need to be watered (although it's best to water just before leaves start to droop). When plants are kept too wet, you may see the same symptom – drooping leaves – but it will be because the roots are rotted and the plant can no longer get the food and water it needs from the soil. If this happens, your plant may or may not recover; your only hope is to reduce watering, and cross your fingers.

Clustering several plants together will help to raise the humidity level around the leaves.

trays containing pebbles and water. You can use any kind of saucers or shallow trays to hold the water – plastic cafeteria-type trays work well; even baking sheets are fine. Set the plants on a 2.5- to 5-cm (1- to 2-inch) layer of pebbles or gravel. Add enough water to bring the water level just below the top of the pebbles. (You don't want the bottom of the pots to be sitting in water.)

Moisture will evaporate steadily from the trays and rise to increase humidity around the plants' leaves. This is a very effective way to raise the humidity levels in a certain area, and humidity-loving plants like ferns will definitely benefit if you grow them over these water-filled trays.

Humidifiers If you happen to have a room humidifier or an automatic humidifier installed in your heating or air-conditioning system, you'll be able to raise the humidity in the whole growing area.

Combine spring bulbs with other early-flowering plants that need the same temperatures to grow.

Providing the Right Temperature

Most common houseplants prefer typical home temperatures of around 18°C (65°F) during the day and 12° to 15°C (55° to 60°F) at night. However, some do need cooler temperatures during part of the year. Certain flowering plants, such as azaleas and camellias (*Camellia japonica*), won't flower well unless you can give them a period of cooler temperatures.

Fertilising for Healthy Growth

If you want your houseplants to thrive, you have to give them food as well as water. The best organic fertilisers for houseplants are the same ones that work well outside – things like dried blood, bonemeal, and fish and seaweed products. You can also use household 'wastes' such as wood ashes and coffee grounds. But the first item on your fertiliser list should always be well-rotted compost, the organic gardener's secret for success.

Compost is especially good for container plants because it releases nutrients slowly over a long period of time, just the way plants growing in the wild receive their nutrients. Compost will never burn roots or cause major salt build-up like synthetic chemical fertilisers. Plus, compost doesn't just feed your plants – it prevents disease and improves the structure of the soil, so air and water reach the roots better. Ample compost also helps the soil retain moisture, so you won't have to water as often. If that's not enough, compost contains the major plant nutrients – nitrogen, phosphorus and potassium – plus minor nutrients and trace elements, which are not provided by chemical fertilisers.

If you aren't already making your own compost, consider starting. It's easy, and there's just nothing better for making plants grow well. And if you can't make your own compost, check with your local council – many communities are now composting garden waste and offer the compost free to anyone who wants it.

A Simple Programme for Feeding Houseplants

Use compost whenever you pot up a new plant or repot old ones, adding up to one part garden compost for every three or four parts potting compost.

Each spring thereafter, take your plants to a sink or bathtub and water them heavily with warm water until water runs steadily out the bottom for a few minutes. This leaches out any harmful salts, which can build up over time. It's a good idea to do this once a year, but you should also do it any time you notice a crusty deposit in the saucers or around the pot rims. Rinse the leaves thoroughly, too, to remove dust.

After you've completed the spring leaching treatment, add a 12- to 25-mm (½- to 1-inch) layer of fresh garden compost to all of the pots. (If there's not room in the pot, just wash away some of the soil with a hose.) Mix a small amount of a balanced organic fertiliser into the compost before you apply it to the pots. That should feed most plants well into midsummer. (Check the fertiliser packets for guidelines on how much to apply.)

Most houseplants will be getting much more light during the summer than in the winter, so a couple of months after the spring compost/fertiliser treatment, begin feeding them about once a month with a half-strength liquid fertiliser. The fertiliser should contain plenty of nitrogen, the nutrient most likely to be in short supply. Keep feeding the plants until growth slows in the autumn. Always remember that too much fertiliser can be just as bad as too little. Go easy when you fertilise plants in dim locations, and don't fertilise at all during the short days of winter unless you have a plant that continues to grow actively then.

Hibiscus

Potting and Repotting

Your houseplants will eventually need to be repotted, either because they grow too big for their pots or because they need to be moved into fresh potting compost.

Generally, you should repot your plants about once every year or two in the spring or summer, when plants are actively growing. If they get too big for their pot, they can become 'root-bound', which means they have grown so many roots that there's not enough soil left to support further growth. Most (but not all) plants shouldn't be allowed to become root-bound. You can check to see how crowded the roots are becoming by lifting the plant and tapping the pot until it slips loose. Lift out the plant to examine the root ball. If you see lots of soil with some roots, all is well. But if you see mostly roots and little soil, it's time to repot.

How to Repot a Houseplant

You have a choice when you repot – you can move the plant to a larger pot size, or you can keep the plant in the same pot. If you want the plant to grow bigger and don't mind going to a larger container, choose a new pot that's only 2.5 to 5 cm (1 to 2 inches) in diameter larger for small to medium-sized plants or 10 to 15 cm (4 to 6 inches) larger for bigger plants. (If you move a small plant into a very big

Repotting a Houseplant

Choose a new container that is slightly larger than the old one. Add a layer of potting compost.

Carefully turn the plant over onto one hand, and use the other hand to pull off the old pot.

Settle the plant at the same level in the new pot, and fill in around the sides with potting compost.

pot, you run a risk that the excess soil around the plant's roots will stay too wet and cause the roots to rot.)

When you're moving a plant to a larger pot, add some potting compost to the bottom – enough so that the soil level will be an inch or so below the pot rim when you set in the plant to allow room for watering. Then remove the plant from the pot it's growing in. Holding the base of the pot in one hand, lift the plant slightly and tap around the rim with your other hand to loosen the pot. Carefully lift the plant out and set it on the soil in the new pot, then add potting compost around the edges, using a trowel or stick to gently settle the soil around the root ball.

If you'd prefer to keep the same pot, remove the plant and shake away as much of the old soil from the roots as you can. If the plant's root ball is so dense and tangled that the soil won't shake loose, use a large knife to slice away an inch or two of the root ball on all sides and the bottom. Add fresh compost to the bottom of the pot, then set the root-trimmed plant back in and add fresh compost in the space you created around the sides. This root pruning allows you to keep the plant to a manageable size. If the plant itself can be pruned, trim it back a bit to bring the top into better balance with the reduced roots.

If you're repotting a very large plant, you may want to ask someone to help you. Removing the plant will be easier if you

lay the container on its side, then carefully pull out the plant.

Potting Compost

You can use any commercial potting compost for most houseplants, but your plants will grow much better if you add some garden compost and slow-release organic fertilisers before you plant. There are a few plants that prefer special soil mixes. Cacti and succulents, for instance, appreciate extra sand for drainage, while African violets (*Saintpaulia* spp.) thrive with extra peat moss for acidity and moisture retention. Orchids generally prefer a very loose, bark-based mix.

Trimming and Pruning

It's natural for houseplants to lose some of their older leaves as they grow. Shrubby plants such as weeping fig (*Ficus benjamina*) may also shed leaves when they're moved to a new location, sometimes leaving a tangle of bare twigs in the centre of the plant. If you spend a few minutes now and then trimming off these yellowing leaves or dead twigs, your plants will look much better.

Many houseplants don't require pruning beyond this regular trimming. If all of the leaves grow out from a single centre or crown of the plant and there are no stems or branches (as on African violets [*Saintpaulia* hybrids] and florist's cyclamen [*Cyclamen persicum*]), then you

can't (and don't need to) prune the plant. Trailing or climbing plants (such as silver inch plant [*Tradescantia zebrina*] and passion flowers [*Passiflora* spp.]), on the other hand, benefit from pruning. Pinch out or snip off unwanted leaves and stems with your fingers or scissors; use secateurs or loppers to remove woodier stems cleanly.

There are three basic reasons to prune your houseplants, as follows.

Pruning for Shape Regular trimming improves a plant's appearance by eliminating any long, awkward stems or branches that grow out of proportion to the rest of the plant. Don't hesitate about this – cutting back gangly branches will help, not harm, the plant.

Pruning to Promote New Growth Pruning is also very helpful to trailing plants, such as Swedish ivy (*Plectranthus australis*). Cutting back the growing tips causes the plant to put out more shoots and become bushier. Always make your pruning cuts right above a side branch or leaf node (the spot where a leaf joins the stem). In many cases, the plant will produce two new stems from the cut point, leading to bushier growth.

Pruning for Size Control The third way in which pruning is helpful is in keeping plants a manageable size. If a bushy plant, such as a hibiscus or a citrus tree, has become larger than you want it to be, you can prune it back really hard, cutting off as much as a third of the leaves and stems. In this why, you keep the top in balance with the roots without having to move the plant to a larger pot.

Inside Out and Outside In

Just like people, many houseplants appreciate a holiday. Moving your plants outdoors for the summer is a great way to keep them healthy and happy. When you bring them back in for the winter, you can also dig and pot up rosemary, geraniums and other flowers and herbs for indoor enjoyment. To help your plants through these transitions between house and garden, try the tips here.

Moving Indoor Plants Outside

Many indoor plants benefit from spending a summer outside. Flowering plants, which require bright light, will especially appreciate time outdoors. If your plants have aphids, scale insects or other pests, moving them outdoors can give beneficial insects a chance to attack the unwanted insects, solving your pest problems. If you have a large number of indoor plants, you may want to move the bright-light-lovers outside for the summer and shift some medium-light plants to the brighter spots vacated by the light-lovers.

Before you move plants outside, wait until the weather is warm and settled. Also, you must introduce indoor plants to outside sunlight gradually. If you don't, their leaves can show brown or white scorched spots – the plant equivalent of sunburn.

To give your houseplants time to adjust, always place them in full shade when you first move them outside. After a few weeks in the shade, you can move the kinds that enjoy brighter light out from the shade to partial or full-sun locations. Plants growing in the brighter, airier conditions of the great outdoors will grow much faster than they do indoors, so they'll need more water and fertiliser than normal. In the heat of summer they may need daily watering.

Bringing Outdoor Plants Indoors

Many plants typically grown outside can also be enjoyed inside. 'Tender perennials' will keep on growing if you protect them from freezing temperatures by moving them indoors for the winter months.

Kumquat tree

Miniature roses bloom on new wood, so they need regular trimming of the old growth to promote new flowers.

Geraniums (*Pelargonium* spp.) are a perfect example. You can enjoy their colourful flowers or pleasant scents in the garden all summer, then bring them indoors in autumn and keep them in a bright window. Other great plants for indoor growing include rosemary (*Rosmarinus officinalis*), wax begonias (*Begonia* Semperflorens Cultorum hybrids) and coleus (*Solenostemon*), just to name a few. You can even bring chilli pepper plants inside to hold them over for the next year.

To move plants indoors, you can dig them up and put them in a pot. Usually you'll want to trim them back pretty hard to bring the top growth into balance with the now much smaller root ball. After they're potted up and trimmed, keep them well watered and let them stay outside for a few weeks in part shade. This transition period will help them recover from the shock of being transplanted, so they can grow back nice and bushy. Be sure to bring any cold-tender plants inside as soon as frost is predicted.

If you'd rather have smaller plants (which fit better on windowsills), you can take root cuttings from many garden plants in summer or early autumn. Cut off 7.5- to 10-cm (3- or 4-inch) long shoot tips, then remove all but two or three of the top leaves. Insert the bottom 5 to 7.5 cm

Geraniums are dependable favourites for outdoor containers, but they also make great indoor plants.

(2 to 3 inches) of each cutting into a small pot of moist sand, vermiculite or potting compost, then cover the cuttings with a clear plastic bag to keep the humidity high. Place them in a warm, medium-bright location until they root and begin growing, then remove the bag and move them to your brightest south windows for the winter. You can move the plants back out to the garden in spring, after all danger of frost has passed.

When you bring any outdoor plants inside, there's always a chance you may bring in some pest problems as well. Once those pests are inside, they can spread to your other plants quickly, since there are no natural enemies in the house to keep them in balance.

To minimise the chance of problems, inspect your plants carefully before you bring them in. Certain garden plants are very susceptible to aphids when grown indoors. Chilli peppers are a good example. If you find that aphids keep coming back even when you have sprayed the plant several times, it may be best just to enjoy that particular plant outdoors each summer and not try to keep it indoors.

Or, if it's a plant you really love, you can order specific beneficial insects from mail-order suppliers and release them on the plants to munch on the aphids or other troublemakers.

The Productive Garden

*Home grown fruit, vegetables and herbs are not only
more delicious and nutritious than shop-bought, but there's a sense
of satisfaction unlike any other in picking your own produce.
You've planted it, watered it, nurtured it, and now you can eat it.*

The Herb Garden

There are so many wonderful herbs that it can be hard to decide which ones to grow. Some herbs, like oregano and peppermint, are used in cooking or for tea; others, like lavender and sage, are ideal for pot-pourris and other fragrant crafts. Some herbs, like bee balm, thyme and yarrow, are attractive in their own right as ornamentals, even if you never plan to harvest them for any purpose. Many herbs fall into more than one of these categories.

How you plan to use your herbs will affect how you'll grow them and how much attention they'll need from you. If you're just growing herbs to use fresh in cooking, you don't need much space for a herb garden, since one or two plants of each kind you like should be enough. You'll be most likely to use your culinary herbs if you plant them close to the house. If you're only growing one or two types, try growing them in large pots on the deck or patio. You'll need more space to grow quantities of herbs if you plan to harvest them for drying and crafting.

When planning your herb garden, don't forget to take into consideration your climate, topography and soil conditions. Ask your neighbours what grows well in their gardens – and what doesn't!

Grown in the right conditions, herbs such as chives will reward you with flowers as well as edible leaves.

Growing Your Herbs

Most herbs prefer full sun, although some (like sweet woodruff, chervil, lemon balm, and many mints) will grow in partial shade. Many herbs tolerate rocky, thin soils, but they will be more productive in average, well-drained soil. You may choose to plant your herbs in a separate garden, but they also look great mixed into flower beds and vegetable gardens.

You can grow many herbs – including such favourites as dill, sage, marjoram and basil – from seed sown directly in the garden. Other herbs are easier to grow from transplants than seeds; these include rosemary, lavender, peppermint and tarragon, among others.

Herb Garden Style

Regardless of the size, shape or location of your garden, its style is a reflection of your own tastes. At one extreme are the formal herb gardens with their angular knots and pruned hedges, and at the other are random groupings of whatever suits the season. The number of possible herb-garden styles is limited only by your imagination and creativity. You can plan one or more theme gardens to concentrate on a particular aspect.

As you choose herb plants, consider how they are going to look when grouped together.

Garden Shape

The simplest gardens to set out and manage are square or rectangular. If you must take advantage of every square inch of space, it makes sense that you will follow the general outline of your property, and land is most often sold in box-like shapes. Laying out your herb garden with square or rectangular beds not only may be the most practical way, but can give the garden a formal look that appeals to many gardeners.

Of course, squares and rectangles aren't the only shapes. You may choose to lay your garden beds following the curve of a hill, stream, fence or stone wall, or design

These diagrams show four practical approaches to designing a herb garden. Avoid circles and curves if space is limited.

them to accent the shape of a building. If you want to be especially creative, garden within unusual boundaries like circles or ovals. You can make a garden in the shape of a spiral with one continuous bed beginning in the centre and spiralling out in circles. A book or magazine on garden landscaping will offer you examples to follow in shaping your garden beds.

If you choose to garden in several small patches, position plants that need daily attention or frequent picking close to the house. If space is limited, take advantage of borders along paths and fences. At the least, you can dress your windows outdoors with boxes of luscious herbs close at hand.

Garden Design

Whatever design you choose, try it out on paper first. If you're planting in beds, keep them under 1.5 m (5 feet) wide, not more than twice the distance you are able to reach from the side. You'll want to avoid walking on beds as you work. Make garden paths 1.2 to 1.5 m (4 to 5 feet) wide. Once you've located your paths, beds or rows, begin selecting and

Working with the natural landscape, simple terracing is used to create a level herb garden on a slope.

arranging your plants. Prepare a list of the plants you want to grow, along with their growth habits, size at maturity and special soil, space or environmental requirements. Remember that single plants tend to become lost in the crowd; it's more effective to plant in clumps. It's generally best to plant the tallest herbs at the back, the shortest in the front.

Keep the following in mind when you plan the design of your herb garden:

- Use your site's limitations to your advantage. If you're confined to gardening in the shade, use the opportunity to grow as many shade-loving herbs as possible. Include angelica, chervil, lemon balm and sweet cicely. In wet areas, select from the wide assortment of plants in the mint family. You'll find herbs to fill just about every niche in your garden.

- Divide a large garden, or create several small gardens, by grouping herbs that serve particular purposes. Medicinal, dye, fragrance and culinary gardens are some examples.

- Select herbs that flower at the same time or share the same colour. Lavender and blue themes especially are easy to create with herbs. Or focus on foliage, and plant blue-green or silvery herbs mixed with darker greens for contrast.

- It's a good idea to group the perennials together since they tend to have similar requirements and this will help you avoid mistakes. If you're planning to grow invasive perennials like mint among other herbs, plant them in buried containers like clay drainage pipes or bottomless large pots that are at least 25 cm (1 foot) deep.

Ideally, the well-organised garden will include culinary herbs that are positioned as close as possible to the kitchen.

Helpful Hints for Easy Herbs

Before you decide which herbs you want to grow, check out their maintenance considerations below.

Basil: For best leaf production, pick off flower heads as they form (every few days). May also need extra water.

Chives: Easy to grow, but can reseed prolifically if you don't clip off spent flowers.

Dill: Let a few plants self-sow the first year, and you'll probably never need to replant. Pull seedlings from where they're not wanted or remove flowers, if you don't want seedlings.

Mints: Most tend to spread rapidly unless contained. Plant in bottomless pots sunk in the soil to 2.5 cm (1 inch) below the rim. Or grow as container plants.

Parsley: Seeds are slow to germinate and seedlings can get swamped by weeds. Often easiest to start from transplants.

Rosemary: In cold climates, treat as an annual and buy new plants each year.

Sage: Start from transplants; easy to grow.

Thyme: Won't compete well with weeds, so keep weeded until plants get established.

Chives are popular for their mild onion-flavoured leaves and flowers. Remove spent blooms.

Cool-Climate Herbs The following herbs are adapted to cool climates, with winter temperatures commonly dropping below –5°C (10°F). Nearly all these herbs can be grown readily in moderate climates, but in subtropical and tropical climates many of them will not thrive: angelica, anise, anise hyssop, arnica, barberry, bearberry, bee balm, betony, birch, borage, burdock, caraway, catmint, chamomile (Roman), chervil, chicory, chives, clary, comfrey, costmary, dandelion, dill, dock, elecampane, garlic, goldenrod, hop, horseradish, horsetail, hyssop, lady's bedstraw, lemon balm, lovage, marsh mallow, mugwort, mustard, nasturtium, nettle, New Jersey tea, plantain, red clover, roses, saffron, sassafras, savory (winter), soapwort, sorrel, sweet cicely, sweet woodruff, tansy, tarragon (French), valerian, vervain, wormwood, yarrow.

Borage

Moderate-Climate Herbs The following herbs prefer climates where winter temperatures do not fall below –5°C (10°F) and summers are warm and dry with cool nights: agrimony, basil, bay (sweet), calendula, cascara sagrada, coriander, eucalyptus, fennel, fenugreek, feverfew, geranium (scented), germander, horehound, lavender (English), lemon verbena, madder, marjoram, mint, oregano, orris, parsley (curled), passion flower, pennyroyal, rosemary, rue, safflower, sage, santolina, southernwood, thyme (garden), violet, witch hazel.

Warm-Climate Herbs The following herbs grow best in tropical or subtropical climates,

The key to having a beautiful and productive herb garden is using herbs that are adapted to your climate.

but some can be grown in cold climates in summer or as houseplants: aloe, cayenne pepper, coffee, ginger, lemongrass and Madagascar periwinkle.

Shade-Tolerant Herbs The following herbs will tolerate shade (although dill, fennel, rosemary and scented geraniums really prefer full sun): agrimony, angelica, bay, bergamot, betony, catmint, chamomile, chervil, comfrey, coriander, costmary, feverfew, germander, ginger, horsetail, hyssop, lemon balm, lovage, Madagascar periwinkle, mint, parsley, pennyroyal, pipsissewa, plantain, sweet cicely, sweet woodruff, tansy, tarragon, thyme, valerian, violet, wormwood.

Harvesting

One of the first rules to learn about growing herbs is to harvest them early in the morning. The best picking time is just after the morning dew has dried, but before the sun has had a chance to warm them. The reason is that essential oils, those mysterious components that give herbs their flavour and fragrance, are most intense early in the morning, and lose their quality when exposed to heat.

There's nothing wrong with morning dew, but wet leaves require a longer drying period before you can store them. For the same reason, refrain from harvesting on rainy days. A cool, dry, sunny morning is best. You need not be so fussy if you plan to use fresh herbs immediately. You may pick and use these whenever you need them.

Your herbs will produce more foliage if you pinch off the flower heads as they develop. But if you're growing the herb for seed (like dill or caraway), leave the flower head and harvest the seed after it turns brown.

The intended use of your herbs, maturity of the plant and climate all influence the time of harvesting. Cold-climate gardeners will have fewer chances to harvest; they're happy to get their herbs up and growing before the frosts return. Gardeners in warmer climates have the advantage of a longer growing season, and the chance to harvest more often.

A small herb garden can provide plenty of material for cooking, crafts or drying.

Perennials Avoid heavy harvests of perennial herbs during the first year of growth to allow them to establish themselves in their new surroundings and to encourage root growth.

You may want to trim them lightly to promote bushiness.

Once they're established, you can harvest up to two-thirds of the foliage of a hardy perennial at one time in the spring and again in summer. In colder climates, take only a third of the growth in the autumn and stop cutting 40 to 60 days before you expect the first frost. During winter, perennials will subsist mainly on foods they've stored in their roots. Plenty of foliage and lots of autumn sun will let perennials manufacture and store adequate food for winter and the following spring's new growth. If food reserves are low, they're less likely to make it through a stressful winter. In warmer climates, plants will suffer little winter stress and the plants' dormant period may be relatively short. In these areas gardeners can harvest lightly right into late autumn.

Lavender

Annuals and Biennials Since annuals are limited to one season of growth, your only concern in cold climates is harvesting as much as you can before the killing autumn frosts. The same is true if you are growing biennial herbs, like parsley, for their foliage. During the growing season, harvest annuals and biennials for foliage so that at least 10 to 12.5 cm (4 to 5 inches) of growth remains. A good general rule is to harvest no more than the top half of the plant at one cutting. Most annuals and biennials may be harvested several times each season.

Before the first frosts, you can cut annual plants to the ground or pull them for drying. If you are growing biennial plants, like caraway, for their seeds, avoid harvesting the foliage the first year. The more energy the plants can make and store, the more seeds they can set the following year.

Parsley

Coriander

How to Harvest Use sharp scissors or a garden knife when harvesting your herbs. If you're collecting leaves, cut the whole stem before stripping away the foliage. With small-leaved perennials, like rosemary and thyme, save only the leaves and discard the stems – or use them for potpourris. When harvesting herbs that spread from a central growing point, like parsley and sorrel, harvest the outer stems or leaves first. If you're collecting leaves or flowers from bushy plants, do so from the top of the plant; new growth will come from below.

Of course, you can harvest foliage and flowers from both perennials and annuals continuously if you're just snipping a few leaves and blooms here and there to collect the ingredients for a recipe.

Herbs retain their best qualities if they're left unwashed until it's time to use them. Some growers advise sprinkling the plants the day before harvesting to wash away the dust. If your plants are surrounded by a mulch that limits their contact with soil, you may not have to wash them. If they are gritty with soil, however, you can swish them through cold water and pat them dry, or hang them in shade to drip.

If you plan to dry your herbs, bunching them as you collect them saves handling

When harvesting herbs during the growing season, pick from the outside to retain their attractive shape.

time later. Collect enough stems to make a 2.5 cm (1 inch) thick bundle, then wrap a rubber band over the cut ends. When harvesting annuals in autumn, simply pull and hang the whole plant, after first cutting away the roots and soil.

Drying Herbs
Some growers claim that dried, summer-grown herbs have better flavour than herbs grown indoors in winter. If you enjoy cooking with herbs, you may want to try preserving some of the summer garden's bounty for use in winter recipes. Most herbs dry easily, and under the proper conditions they will retain their characteristic aroma and flavour.

Hanging herbs to dry in mixed bunches makes a very attractive kitchen decoration.

Where to Dry Herbs The best place for drying herbs is somewhere dry and dark, with good ventilation. Depending on what the weather is like, you may find it necessary to speed the process with fans, dehumidifiers or an air conditioner. The best weather conditions for air drying are low humidity and soft breezes.

Dried herbs store best in cool, dark places. If you like the look of the bunches, it's fine to hang some around your home for decoration. But store the herbs you plan to use for cooking in airtight jars.

Drying screens and bunches can be placed in a dry attic, around the hot-water heater, on top of the refrigerator or in a gas oven with a pilot light. Barns make excellent drying sheds as long as they are shady and well ventilated. In summer some gardeners dry their herbs on small screens placed inside the car. Cover the herbs with kitchen paper and park the car in light shade.

If the weather hasn't cooperated and the drying process seems painfully slow, you can speed the action in your oven. Just place your herbs on baking sheets and set the oven temperature at its lowest setting. Monitor progress until leaves are crispy dry.

Drying in Bunches Long-stemmed herbs like lavender, mint and yarrow are easy to dry in bunches. Select only the highest-quality foliage and blossoms, removing

Bunches of herbs hanging from a beam add a touch of summer to the kitchen.

any dead or wilted leaves. Make bunches about 2.5 cm (1 in) in diameter for quick drying; the number of stems in each bunch will naturally vary. You can tie the bunches with string, leaving a loop for hanging, but small rubber bands are easier to use.

For very simple storage, hang your herb bunches from clothes hangers. First, wrap each bunch with a rubber band. Then take one loop under the bottom of the hanger. Bring it over the wire and the top of the stems to secure the bunch.

Wire Clothes Hangers Hold the bunched stems along one side of the horizontal wire of the hanger, then pull a loop of the rubber band down and then up over the wire. Pull the band over the stems and release it. Hanging one full hanger in one spot is easier than hanging separate bunches all over the place. Each herb species or cultivar gets its own hanger, making organisation easy. You can label each bunch or each hanger. When you're ready to use the herbs, simply pull the bunch down to release it.

Hang your herbs where you have plenty of space, and where you can leave them undisturbed until they're dry. If your house has exposed ceiling rafters, arrange wooden dowels along them and hang the herbs from the dowels. Single bunches may be hung from conveniently placed hooks or nails. When the bunches are crispy dry, remove the leaves from the stems. Dried herbs will gather dust if left too long.

Dry long-stemmed herbs in paper bags. Punch a hole in the bottom of the bag, secure the stems, and hang to dry. Cut flaps in the bag to increase air circulation.
To dry seeds, place seed heads inside a paper bag, stems up. After two weeks, the seeds will collect at the bottom of the bag.

Brown Bag Method If dust is a problem, place the bunches inside paper bags, lantern style. Punch a hole in the base of the bag, pull the stems through this hole, and fasten them with string or a rubber band. Cut flaps in the side of the bag and hang in a cool, dry place. After one week, look inside a few bags to make sure the herbs are drying and free of mould. They may take up to two weeks to become crisp and crumbly. (Seeds can be dried by placing seed heads, with stems up, in an unpunched paper bag.) When the herbs are dry, remove the stems and spread the leaves on a baking sheet. Place in an oven, preheated to about 40°C (100°F), for several minutes to complete the drying.

Drying on Screens Herbs with short stems and small leaves, like thyme, are difficult to bunch. The best drying method is simply to snip off the foliage with scissors and spread it on a mesh screen in a single layer. You can dry large-leaved herbs on screens, but first strip the foliage from the stems. Hold the stems upside down in one hand while running the other hand down the stem. Loose herb blossoms and flower petals can also be dried on screens. Stir the herbs once a day on the screens for even drying.

You can construct your own screens with scrap timber and window screening, then set them on bricks or wooden blocks so that air circulates freely. If the herbs are small and fine, spread a paper towel or sheet of paper on the screen first. Your herbs should be dry in seven to ten days.

Drying in the Oven Oven-drying is the best method, since the herbs dry quickly and retain their aromatic oils. In a conventional oven, spread herbs one layer deep on kitchen paper set on baking sheets, and preheat the oven to 80° to 100°F (25 to 38°C). If you smell the herbs immediately, lower the temperature to avoid losing essential oils. Stir once every half an hour. Drying should be complete in three to six hours. Herbs with fleshy leaves will take longer than those with tiny or thin leaves, so it is wise not to mix different leaf types in one batch. Remove the herbs when they are crispy dry, and before they turn brown.

Food dehydrators are good for drying herbs, too. Follow the same instructions as for regular oven-drying.

You can also dry herbs in a microwave oven. Sandwich the herbs between sheets of microwave-safe kitchen paper. Put a cup of water in the microwave while drying the herbs. Leave the herbs in the oven for about one minute on a low setting. Remove them and check for dryness. If they're still moist, repeat the process for a few seconds. Watch the herbs carefully during drying, and stop the process if any sparks appear.

The Vegetable Garden

Anyone who has eaten really fresh produce knows that a garden that produces food is worth the effort. The trick is to be realistic about what and how much you can grow. You may require only a small vegetable garden near the kitchen that will meet your day-to-day demands for organically grown vegetables. Or you may decide to dedicate a substantial area of your garden to vegetable growing so that you'll have enough produce to freeze or store for later consumption.

The best strategy is to start small. Choose a few of the vegetables that you like best, and plant a limited quantity of each. (Maybe only one each of large plants like courgettes or cucumbers, two or three each of tomatoes and sweet peppers, and six to eight plants each of smaller crops like lettuce and beans.) In following years, adjust the amounts based on how much you used this year.

To a large extent, your climate will determine which vegetables you can grow well. Various aspects of climate, such as average high and low temperatures, frost-free periods and rainfall, can influence your choice of crops. Special areas in your garden may offer slightly different conditions than the open garden; for instance, warm, sheltered nooks can give heat-loving crops an extra boost, and lightly shaded spots can prolong the season for heat-intolerant crops. An awareness of these different microclimates will help you choose the best sites for the crops you want to grow.

Topography, exposure and soil are other factors to consider when planning your garden, Hilltops, slopes and valleys all have their unique advantages and disadvantages for gardening. The amount of sunlight a site receives will determine which vegetables you can grow there, so you'll need to keep that in mind as you choose a site for your garden. The quality of the soil is another critical factor to consider for successful garden planning. Healthy soil will yield healthy plants.

Once you've considered all of these factors, you'll want to put your new

knowledge to work in planning your best vegetable garden ever. After you know where you want to put your garden, you need to decide how big to make it, depending on the time you have to care for it and the amount of produce you plan to use. Other factors to keep in mind are the style of gardening you plan to use (such as rows or raised beds), the specific crops you want to grow and how much of each crop you're going to plant.

As you start planning your vegetable garden, you'll begin to appreciate the

value of maintaining a good system of garden records. You'll want to keep track of all the things you learn about your particular site, the decisions you make about what and how much to grow, and also the performance of your garden over each season. These sorts of garden records are invaluable reference tools for planning future gardens, and will lead you on to even greater success in growing healthy and flavourful vegetables.

Pumpkins and squash 'curing' in the sun.

This vegetable garden is sheltered by a natural windbreak. A combination of tall trees on the outside, and smaller trees and shrubs on the inside, provides a wall of protection and keeps wind damage to a minimum.

Site Selection

The first decision to make is where to locate your vegetable garden. You may want to reassign a section of your existing flower garden, or perhaps create a whole new garden devoted entirely to vegetables. Consider the site carefully, because selecting a good location now can prevent many problems later.

Let your garden site influence your selection of plants. Maybe you will have to choose vegetables that prefer shade, or species that can cope with high moisture levels for most of the year. If you have a range of possible sites, choose the one that most closely matches the requirements of your favourite crops.

Light

Most vegetable plants need six to twelve hours of sunlight each day. Pick a site well away from shade trees and buildings that cast the garden in shade for more than half the day. If you have a city garden nestled between tall buildings, you may be limited to shade-tolerant vegetables.

Gardens located to the south or west of houses or slopes will receive the most light. With such a favourable position, you can start planting as much as two weeks earlier, since the soil warms faster.

Moisture

Since most vegetables need at least 25 mm (1 inch) of water each week, be prepared to water during dry periods. Make sure you can reach the site with a garden hose or irrigation pipe, or be prepared to carry water to the site by hand. Avoid gardening in low areas that are apt to be flooded, as well as on high areas with excessive drainage.

Soil

You'll have the best success if you start with a suitable soil. Avoid heavy clays and loose sands, or improve them with plenty of organic materials (like well-rotted compost) before you start. Test the soil before you begin; adjust pH and nutrient levels the season before, if possible.

Avoid areas that have had heavy foot or vehicle traffic, because this activity compacts the soil and damages its structure. Testing your soil for pollutants is an unnecessary expense unless you suspect the presence of certain contaminants. Urban soils may be polluted by dump sites, industrial waste, motor vehicle exhaust, leaded paint and chemical insecticides. If you do plan to grow vegetables in a city garden, contact your local council to see if it tests for toxic materials, and learn how to collect the samples required for investigative testing.

Topography

Slopes and contours influence the way that you arrange your vegetable plants. Your goal is to minimise the loss of soil through erosion and maximise water retention. If you have to plant on a slope, place your rows or beds across the slope. If your rows of vegetables are arranged running up and down the slope, water will run down the slope instead of penetrating

Make sure you have paths between beds for easy access. Herbs are ideal to plant along the edges.

the soil to reach plant roots, and will also carry the precious topsoil away with it.

You'll also want to avoid gardening in low-lying areas, where poor air circulation and boggy conditions make your plants more susceptible to disease.

Obstacles and Access

Locate your garden in a place that's easily accessible, both to you and to vehicles that will deliver materials you may need later, like soil or compost. Paths should be wide enough for a wheelbarrow. As you choose a site, investigate for hidden obstacles like tree roots, shallow boulders, septic systems and utility lines, and avoid these problem areas.

Time

When planning your garden, think about how much time you will have available to spend in it. The amount of work your garden requires will depend on size and will vary with climate and seasons. Don't build a garden that is too big for you to look after. The work will be faster and easier if you have modern equipment, such as a reliable rotary tiller, than if you're using 'elbow grease', a shovel and heavy garden gloves. To save time and energy, you may want to spread the heavy work, like digging new beds or making paths, over several years.

Finances

If necessary, you can spread the cost of making your garden over several years. Although equipment such as rotary tillers can lighten the workload, it's not necessary to buy expensive equipment at the outset. Start small and enlarge your garden and your equipment collection over time. Your garden plan may include elaborate designs, but you don't need to accomplish everything in one season. If your soil is poor and dry, concentrate on the soil first, and reclaim and improve a new section each season. When vegetable production is steady and you're satisfied with the site, you can concentrate on other aspects, like planting flowers and herbs to make your vegetable garden look more attractive, or enlarging your workspace with structures like cold frames or a toolshed.

Special Requirements

Look for a site that fits your individual needs. If your mobility is limited, make sure your garden is easy to reach – for example, just outside the back door. If you're in a wheelchair, you can have a

Container gardening is an effective way of utilising space in your garden. It also has a decorative effect.

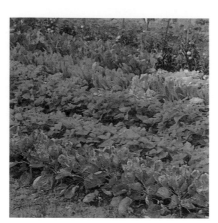

Rows are easy to plan and plant, but they may need more frequent weeding and watering due to the exposed soil.

smooth, cement path built and then sculpt a waist-high garden from a slope, or build up a terrace that you can reach easily from a chair. Chair-side gardening is easy if you grow vegetables in tall, recycled dustbins spruced up with some paint and filled with potting compost.

Picking a Planting Pattern

Once you've chosen the best site, think about how you want to arrange your plantings. Parallel rows are easy to plan and plant, but they're not necessarily easy to maintain. Since lots of soil is exposed, you'll probably need to weed and water more often, unless you mulch early and heavily, and replenish the mulch twice a year or as often as necessary.

In a small garden, planting in beds is a much more efficient use of garden space. Since plants are closer together, you'll do less weeding and get higher yields from small areas. The beds do take some time to make the first year, but in following years, you can concentrate your soil-improvement efforts there instead of working on the whole garden area.

Garden Records

Once you have chosen a site, style and size for your garden, it's a good idea to draw your plan on paper before you go out and start digging.

Use graph paper marked to the appropriate scale (900 sq cm [1 square foot] per square works well). Mark the outline of your garden first, then add permanent features like trees and paths.

Next, make a list of vegetables you want to grow and then arrange them on your graph paper in rows or beds. Keep in mind their planting and harvest dates, size at maturity and any special growth requirements they might have.

As the season progresses, keep track of planting dates, pest problems, fertiliser rates and harvests. Some gardeners make notes in a diary or on a calendar. You can create your own tables of garden data using column headings like planting date, harvest date, yield and quality. As well as monitoring your vegetable garden's day-to-day progress, your garden records will also help you plan for greater success with the next harvest. For example, by keeping a note of planting dates and harvest, you can record how well different cultivars perform in your garden, or when space will become available for replanting. Update your map and other records with each new gardening season.

Choosing Your Crops

Deciding what you'll grow is one of the most fun parts of garden planning. The best way to start is to list the vegetables you like to eat already. Then, if lack of time or garden space must limit what you grow, you will have to make some choices. If you just can't live without fresh sweetcorn, for instance, you may decide to devote all your available time and space for one short but glorious harvest. If you'd rather grow a variety of vegetables but still have a minimum of work, concentrate on crops that will bear over a long season. Climbing beans, sweet peppers, carrots, cucumbers, summer squash and tomatoes can yield produce over a period of weeks or months from a single planting. As a bonus, these all produce slowly but steadily, so you won't have to be out harvesting every day, and you won't be swamped by an excess of produce at one time.

A well-organised vegetable garden can be an attractive and functional part of even the smallest garden.

Before selecting cultivars, you need to think about how much you want your plants to yield, which cultivars will be best suited to your garden, how much time you're prepared to spend dealing with pests and what qualities are important to you in your vegetables.

When you go to buy your vegetable seeds and plants, you'll often have a choice between several different cultivars of the same crop. Cultivars can vary widely in characteristics like heat tolerance, size and disease resistance. If your garden is in a particularly cool or hot area, it's smart to select cultivars adapted to those extremes. Check for frost resistance, hardiness and the number of days to maturity. Pick one or several cultivars that fit your planting schedule,

Herbs are excellent companions for vegetables. Cabbage pests are repelled by mint, while chives repel aphids.

especially if you plan to make successive sowings or use season extenders. Whenever possible, use cultivars that have a good local reputation. Check at your local nursery and ask your vegetable-growing neighbours. If a cultivar of runner bean has done well for your neighbour's family over several years, chances are it will do just as well for you.

Bean seeds require warm soil to germinate and are an ideal crop for a warm-weather garden. Climbing beans take more time to mature than bush beans but bear their crops for longer.

Yield If you have a large family to feed, you might prefer a cultivar that has a high yield. You might choose a less productive cultivar if some other factor, like flavour or pest tolerance, has greater priority.

Pest Resistance Choose insect- and disease-resistant cultivars whenever possible. These are plants that have been bred specifically for their pest resistance,: Older cultivars that were selected before the widespread use of synthetic pesticides may also offer some pest resistance.

Other Considerations Most gardeners want high yields, but there are also other factors that you'll want to keep in mind when selecting which vegetables and cultivars you want to grow. Flavour, for example, is a top priority with many growers. If you're going to the trouble of growing your own vegetables, you want

them to taste better than their shop-bought cousins. Heirloom cultivars in particular are known for their 'true' flavours, although many new cultivars also offer good flavour.

Another thing you might want to consider is the ease of harvest. Harvesting can quickly turn from a pleasure to a chore if your crops are difficult to pick. Vegetables like French beans are easier to pick if the pods are clustered at the top of the plant, instead of at the bottom. If you have sensitive skin, prickly vines and leaves may cause a rash, so look for 'hairless' or 'spineless' cultivars of squash, okra and other vegetables. If you have trouble bending over, you may want to choose climbing cultivars that you can train up a fence or wall, putting the harvest within arm's reach.

Keep in mind that the ripening and harvesting period for each vegetable varies. Commercial growers find it easier to harvest cultivars that ripen all at once, but a home gardener may prefer to spread out the harvest with a cultivar that ripens over a period of several weeks. You'll also want to consider how much time you are willing to contribute to harvesting. Some crops, like sweetcorn and French beans, require daily harvesting to get produce at the peak of quality, so unless you have time to do this, avoid these plants. Others,

Before planting a high-yield garden, take into account how much produce you will actually use, to avoid waste.

raspberries, so the weight won't damage fruit on the bottom of the container. You can gather dropped fruit from the ground if it's not bruised, but use it immediately.

As you pick, make sure you keep your safety in mind. Get a sturdy, no-tip ladder if you need to climb up into fruit or nut trees. Or, better yet, check garden-supply catalogues for a long-handled fruit picker – basically a small wire basket with curved 'fingers' that pull off the fruit and let it drop into the basket. The long handle lets you pick from the safety of the ground.

Wear leather gloves when harvesting from thorny-stemmed plants, such as raspberries.

Apples get sweeter as they mature on the tree, so you can spread out your harvest over a few weeks.

Storing Your Bounty

Most fruit, nut and berry plants will produce more fruit than you'll be able to eat right away. If you store the produce properly, you can enjoy it over a long period without letting any go to waste.

If you grow grapefruit or persimmons, you can leave them on the plant for weeks

Clues to Fruit Ripeness

It's important to know how to tell when fruit is ripe, so you can harvest it at its prime. Most fruit is ready when the skin changes to its ripe colour and the fruit becomes soft, sweet and easy to pluck from the plant. There are a few exceptions, however, listed below.

- Apples: Pick when the fruit is firm but fully coloured and the seeds are brown. Take one apple and try it for flavour and seed colour before picking them all. Leave the stem on for storage.
- Blueberries: Let the berries turn blue, then wait a few days – or for rabbit-eye blueberries, a week or two – until the fruit is sweet and comes off easily.
- Cherries: Harvest cherries when they're fully coloured. Sweet cherries should taste sweet and juicy. Pick sour cherries when they're still firm for cooking, or let them soften on the tree to eat fresh. If rain threatens when cherries are nearly ripe, pick them all to prevent cracking.
- Citrus: No matter what the skin colour is, evaluate fruit flavour and harvest when it's sweet enough to your taste.
- Gooseberries: Berries will remain firm even when ripe, so go by the colour to judge picking time.
- Grapes: Pick when the fruit turns to its ripe colour and is flavourful but still firm.
- Nuts: Collect nuts once they've fallen to the ground.
- Pears: Pick European pears slightly underripe, when the pores on the fruit surface change from white to brown. The pear will be rounded with waxy skin and brown seeds. Let it finish ripening at room temperature. Allow Asian pears to ripen on the tree until they are sweet but still crisp.

in cool weather, harvesting as you need them. Most other fruits require cold storage. The ideal is 0°C (32°F) and 90 per cent relative humidity. Under these conditions, late apples and pears will store for months, especially if you wrap them in

oiled paper or newspaper or nestle them in shredded paper.

You can make a special fruit storage area in a cold, damp root cellar. Or keep fruit in a second refrigerator with the temperature set low and an open bowl of water in it to raise the humidity.

Perishable berries and soft fruit (such as peaches, cherries and plums) will only last for a few days in cold storage. An ordinary refrigerator is fine for keeping them. Eat them up as soon as possible and freeze, can or make preserves out of the extra. Wash berries just before use, not before refrigeration.

After harvesting nuts, keep them dry and cool. Stamp on or thrash the nuts to remove the hulls, husks or burs. Dry all nuts except chestnuts until the shells are crackling dry. Pop chestnuts and any other hulled nuts into the freezer. Store dry nuts at about 70 per cent humidity and 2° to 4°C (35° to 40°F); in warmer temperatures they are likely to become rancid.

Fruits for Small Gardens

Fruiting plants can pack a lot of pizzazz into small gardens, letting you make the most of limited space. But you'll need to choose pint-sized plants that won't overwhelm your garden or require extensive pruning to stay small. Fortunately, you can choose from a wide array of compact edibles that let you grow two or three plants in the space you'd otherwise devote to one full-sized tree. Adding a few more fruit crops in containers will further expand your planting options.

Fruit-bearing bushes and groundcover are natural choices for spots where space is limited. Fruit trees are also an option, since they come in an assortment of sizes.

Victoria plums

Super-Easy Alpine Strawberriess

Alpine strawberries (*Fragaria vesco*) are an excellent choice for low-maintenance gardens. Even if these tidy little plants never produced fruit, they'd be worth growing for their tiny white flowers, lush green leaves and compact habit. But as a bonus, you get tiny and flavour-packed berries all season long. These plants don't produce runners, so they are great as edgings for flower or vegetable gardens, and they will produce for several years. Look for alpine strawberry plants at your local garden centre or grow your own plants from seed.

Currants grow on bushy plants that are useful for hedges and shrub borders. The fruit is beautiful too.

The smallest are normal trees grafted on dwarfing rootstocks or natural dwarfs growing on their own roots.

Grafted Dwarf Trees When fruit trees are grafted, the top of the graft is called the scion, and the bottom part of the graft is called the rootstock. The scion grows into the trunk and branches and produces the fruit. The rootstock forms the base of the tree and the roots.

Fruit trees are sometimes grafted onto particular rootstocks to take advantage of the rootstocks' special characteristics, such as dwarfing. Dwarfing rootstocks can keep a normally full-sized tree from growing out of your reach, which is convenient when tending the tree and nearly essential in a small garden. Although the plant is dwarf, the fruit is full-sized. Compared with full-sized trees of the same cultivar, dwarfs bear fewer fruit per tree, but you can plant more dwarf trees in a given space and end up with a larger harvest.

Pears

Many dwarfing rootstocks have been developed for apples. These different rootstocks are best for different soil conditions and climates; some are even resistant to common soil-borne diseases. If none of the dozens of dwarfing apple rootstocks is perfect for your situation, you can buy a tree grafted on more vigorous roots with a dwarfing interstem (a short piece of trunk from a compact tree) that will keep its height down.

Dwarfing rootstocks are not as well developed for other fruit trees. Most pears can be dwarfed with reasonable success by grafting them onto quince rootstocks. Cherries will grow a little smaller if grafted on roots of *Prunus mahaleb*. Plums can grow on over 50 other species of plant roots, including some good dwarfing forms. Peaches and nectarines also have a wide variety of root compatibility. To date, there are no truly dwarfing rootstocks for apricots, sweet cherries or nut trees. But work is continuing on dwarfing rootstocks, so keep an eye on the nursery catalogues for new developments.

While dwarfing rootstocks are very useful, they are not without drawbacks. They do, for instance, tend to shorten the lifespan of peach and nectarine trees. Most dwarfing apple roots are brittle, so you'll need to stake dwarf apple trees to keep them from falling over when laden with fruit or tossed in a strong wind. 'Bartlett' pears tend to bond weakly with quince roots, so the resulting trees may break off at the graft. And 'Anjou' pears grafted onto *Pyrus betulifolia* roots will develop dark, corky spots inside the fruit. Differences caused by rootstocks are less common in cherry, peach and nut trees than in apple, pear and plum types.

When growers mix up tree parts in an attempt to build a better plant, they can end up with some unexpected results. The same rootstock, for instance, can produce very different-sized trees when grafted to scions of different cultivars. Reputable nurseries should be able to tell you what characteristics to expect from the different grafts they sell.

Apple tree

Genetic Dwarf Trees You can avoid rootstocks entirely by planting genetic dwarfs, which grow on their own roots. These plants naturally stay small and bushy, and they grow well in containers. Unfortunately, genetic dwarfs often lack good fruit flavour and disease resistance.

But now that they have the size down, fruit breeders are working on developing great flavour, so keep an eye out for improved types in new nursery catalogues.

Use dwarf and semi-dwarf fruit trees in place of small falowering trees for seasonal interest.

Great Fruits and Nuts for Small Gardens

Even if your growing space is limited, your choices aren't! Here are some suggestions for compact fruiting plants that can enhance any small garden.
- **Trees:** Dwarf and spur forms of apples, dwarf peaches and nectarines, dwarf pears, dwarf plums, sour cherries, Nanking cherries, compact citrus, dwarf almonds and dwarf figs
- **Shrubs:** Blueberries, elderberries, blackberries, raspberries, currants and gooseberries
- **Perennials:** Strawberries

Peaches

Nut-Bearing Plants

Nut trees are attractive and productive additions to any landscape. You'll enjoy the beautiful pink flowers on almonds and the creamy-coloured flower clusters on chestnuts. For great autumn foliage colour, try hazelnuts, which change to burgundy before the leaves drop. As a bonus, you'll get a crop of tasty nuts from any of these easy-care plants.

As with any crop, the key to success with nut growing depends on choosing the right plants for your site and needs. First, decide what role you want the plant to play in your landscape. For a tall, regal shade tree, consider plants such as chestnuts, hickories, oaks, pecans and walnuts. If space is limited, smaller plants are probably more in line with your needs. Almonds make good small ornamental trees, while bushy hazelnuts look great in shrub borders or as informal hedges. Once you have an idea of the kind of plant you want, take a look at your growing conditions – especially the soil.

Almonds

Hazelnuts

- Pecans and shell-bark hickories grow in rich, moist bottomlands. Pecans tend to grow in hotter climates, while shell-bark hickories are naturally more common in cooler climates.
- Shag-bark hickories thrive on slightly higher land that's better drained.
- Black and English walnuts grow in deep, rich but well-drained soil. They will thrive on slight slopes or in sandy soil along rivers.
- Chestnuts are native to sandy mountain sides with acidic soil; good drainage is critical.

It's also important to choose a spot with good air circulation and lots of sunlight. Before finalising your choice, make sure you have enough room for the plants to reach their mature size. Pecans, for instance, can reach 45 m (150 feet) tall and 15 m (50 feet) across.

You'll actually need twice this space, however, since pecans and most other nut-bearing plants require a second compatible tree for pollination. Also keep in mind that big trees can drop their nuts quickly, so keep them away from patios, walkways, children's playing areas and other places where the falling nuts could be a problem. Most nut trees have long taproots, which make them hard to handle in the nursery and hard to get going when planted out. It's best to start with a young field-grown plant that's been specially handled several times to develop a bushy set of roots.

Put the young plant in a broad, deep hole with loose soil, then keep the planting site moist until the tree begins growing strongly.

Walnuts have deep roots, so it's easy to plant under them. However, they also release a substance that is harmful to some plants.

Strawberries are super for containers. Try them in pots or hanging baskets, or grow them in special 'strawberry planters'.

Easy Edibles for Containers

Containers are a great way to grow fruit crops without putting a lot of work into a full-scale garden. You can have a steady supply of fresh produce right outside your door, within easy reach for a finishing touch to any meal. Mix some flowers in with your edibles, and you can have a container garden that's pretty as well as productive.

Choose Compact Crops

Standard selections of some fruits can get too big for successful container culture. Fortunately, plant breeders have worked with many crops to develop compact cultivars specifically suited for container growing. Read the descriptions in your favourite seed and nursery catalogues to find cultivars that are recommended for container growing.

Consider the Container

You'll get better yields if you use a good-sized container – one that can hold at least 9 litres (2 gallons) of potting compost. If you're more interested in production than how beautiful your containers are, 23-litre (5-gallon) plastic buckets make excellent inexpensive and effective

containers. (You may be able to find some used buckets you can recycle from a restaurant or delicatessen. Be sure to drill plenty of drainage holes in the bottom.)

Fruits for Containers

Strawberries You can buy strawberry plants from your local garden centre in the spring and pop them into pots and planters for luscious, full-sized fruit. Or you might want to try the super-flavourful alpine types like 'Mignonette', which can be grown from seed. Their great taste more than makes up for the smaller size of the berries. Strawberries look good in almost any container or hanging basket. There are even special pots called strawberry planters, with holes all around the sides so you can cover the planter with berry plants.

Blueberries Another top container choice is blueberries. They're small shrubs that grow only a few feet high, so they don't need a lot of pruning. Even if you have room for them in the garden, you may choose to grow your blueberries in containers; it's easier to meet the plants' need for acid soil by blending a special container growing compost. Use a soil mix that's at least one-quarter to one-half acidic peat moss and never add any lime, and you'll have blueberries before you know it.

Mixed berries

Citrus How about your very own lemons, limes and oranges? Citrus trees can't tolerate frost, but they grow nicely in containers, especially if you buy plants that have been grafted onto a special dwarfing rootstock to keep them small.

Containers allow you to grow fruit in areas that you normally can't plant, such as patios and sunny decks.

The plants need plenty of sun and fertiliser in the summer. Bring them inside in the winter (except in very mild climates, where they can stay outside year-round), and place them next to a very bright south-facing window. Not only will they give you fruit but the flowers are also wonderfully fragrant.

Dwarf Fruit Trees You can enjoy harvesting full-sized apples, peaches and cherries from container-sized dwarf fruit trees. Provide rooting room by choosing a container at least 75 cm (30 inches) wide and deep. In cold climates (Zone 5 or colder), move the pots to an unheated garage during the coldest part of the winter. In warmer zones, potted fruit trees can stay outside through the winter. Some fruits – including apples and peaches – need a certain amount of cold to set fruit properly, so if you live in Zone 8 or warmer, make sure you buy 'low-chill' cultivars, developed especially to grow well in your climate.

Trees in containers can be heavy; the containers will be easier to move if you set them on a wheeled platform.

Encyclopedia of Popular Garden Plants

Plants are arranged alphabetically by their botanical names, with their most often-used common name displayed prominently. Each plant is illustrated with a colour photograph to make identification easy. Here you'll find plant descriptions, cultivation tips and a guide to the right climate zone.

Acanthus mollis
ACANTHACEAE

BEAR'S BREECHES

Bear's breeches is a robust plant with lustrous evergreen leaves, 30–60 cm (1–2 feet) long and edged with jagged teeth. It grows from a stout crown with thick, fleshy roots.

Flower colour Unusual 2.5-cm (1-inch) flowers with three white petals and overarching purple hoods carried in tall spikes.
Flowering time Late spring or summer; flowers open sequentially up the spike.
Height and spread 75–120 cm (2½–4 feet) tall; 90 cm (3 feet) wide. Spreads to form broad clumps.
Temperature requirements Zones 8–10. Sensitive to winter frost and humidity.
Position Evenly moist, humus-rich soil. Full sun to partial shade.
Cultivation Mulch after the ground freezes in winter and remove mulch gradually in spring to protect plants from heaving. Keep moist; dry soil will reduce the size of the leaves.
Propagation Divide plants in spring when they first emerge or take root cuttings in spring or late autumn. Roots left in the ground when plants are divided will form new shoots.
Pest and disease prevention Bait slugs with dishes of beer set flush with the surface of the soil.
Landscape use Use bear's breeches as foundation plantings or as bold accents in formal and informal gardens.

Achillea filipendulina
COMPOSITAE

FERN-LEAVED YARROW

Fern-leaved yarrow bears flat-topped heads of tiny flowers on dozens of tall, leafy stems. This aromatic herb grows from fibrous roots and has deeply incised, ferny, olive-green leaves.

Flower colour Dozens of tightly packed golden yellow flowers cluster in heads 10–12.5 cm (4–5 inches) across.
Flowering time Summer. Flowers last for several weeks; rebloom if deadheaded.
Height and spread 90–120 cm (3–4 feet) tall; 90 cm (3 feet) wide.
Temperature requirements Zones 3–9. Thrives in moderate summer humidity.
Position Average, dry to moist, well-drained soil. Full sun to light shade.
Cultivation Plants spread rapidly and need frequent division. Lift and divide clumps every three years to keep vigorous.
Propagation Take tip cuttings in spring or early summer. Divide in early spring or autumn. Replant healthy divisions into soil enriched with organic matter.
Pest and disease prevention Plants develop powdery mildew, a cottony white coating on the leaves, especially in areas with warm humid nights. Rot causes stems to blacken and topple over. Remove and destroy all affected parts and dust plants with sulphur.
Landscape use Plant at the front or middle of formal perennial borders or with grasses in wildflower meadows. Use them in cutting gardens or on dry, sunny banks.

Alstroemeria aurantiaca
ALSTROEMERIACEAE

PERUVIAN LILY

Peruvian lilies have tall, leafy stems crowned by open clusters of flaring, saucer-shaped flowers. The grey-green leaves are narrow and pointed. Plants grow from thick, fibrous roots.

Flower colour Showy orange or yellow flowers with brownish purple flares on the upper petals.
Flowering time Throughout summer.
Height and spread 60–90 cm (2–3 feet) tall; 60 cm (2 feet) wide.
Temperature requirements Zones 7–10.
Position Evenly moist but well-drained, humus-rich soil. Full sun to partial shade; protect from strong winds.
Cultivation Plant dormant roots in early spring or autumn. Growth begins early in the season, and plants may be damaged by late frost. Mulch with organic matter in autumn to avoid frost heaving. Achieves best performance after the third year.
Propagation Divide clumps in early spring or autumn. Take care not to damage the brittle roots. Sow fresh seed indoors after 4–6 weeks of cold (4°–5°C [35°–40°F]), moist stratification. To stratify, mix seed with damp peat moss or seed-growing medium in a plastic bag and close with a twist-tie. Place the bag in the refrigerator for the appropriate time period, then sow the mixture as you would other seed.
Pest and disease prevention No serious pests or diseases.
Landscape use Plant in beds and borders.

Anemone x hybrida
RANUNCULACEAE

JAPANESE ANEMONE

Japanese anemones produce clouds of flowers on slender stems. The deeply divided, hairy leaves are mostly basal. Stem leaves have fewer dissections. Plants grow from thick, tuberous roots.

Flower colour Ranges from white to pink and rose; single or double blooms.
Flowering time Late summer and autumn.
Height and spread 90–150 cm (3–5 feet) tall; 60–90 cm (2–3 feet) wide.
Temperature requirements Zones 5–8.
Position Humus-rich, evenly moist soil. Full sun to light shade. Protect from hot afternoon sun in warmer zones.
Cultivation Spreads by creeping underground stems to form broad clumps once established. Thin overgrown clumps in spring if flowering wanes. Replant into soil that has been enriched with organic matter. Mulch plants in colder zones.
Propagation Take root cuttings after plants become dormant in autumn. Sow fresh seed outdoors in summer or autumn. Divide in early spring.
Pest and disease prevention No serious pests or diseases.
Landscape use Group with other late-season perennials and ornamental grasses. Combine with shrubs or ferns in moist, open shade.
Cultivars 'Honorine Jobert' bears pure white single blooms. 'Margarete' has deep pink semi-double flowers. 'Max Vogel' has large pink single flowers.

Aquilegia x hybrida
RANUNCULACEAE

HYBRID COLUMBINE

Hybrid columbines are graceful plants with curious nodding flowers. Each flower has five spurred petals surrounded by five petal-like sepals. Plants grow from a thick taproot.

Flower colour Single- or bi-coloured variable flowers. Yellow, red, blue, purple, pink and white are common. The spurs may be 12–100 mm (½–4 inches) long.
Flowering time Spring and early summer.
Height and spread 60–90 cm (2–3 feet) tall; 30–60 cm (1–2 feet) wide.
Temperature requirements Zones 3–9. Tolerate heat and cold.
Position Light, average to humus-rich, well-drained soil. Full sun to partial shade.
Cultivation They generally live two to four years, rewarding the gardener with a month or more of flowers. Self-sowing.
Propagation Sow seed outdoors in spring or summer. Sow indoors in winter after dry storing them in a refrigerator for four to six weeks.
Pest and disease prevention Leaf miners create pale tunnels and blotches in the leaves. Remove and destroy damaged foliage. In severe cases spray weekly with insecticidal soap. Borers cause the plant to collapse dramatically. Remove and destroy all portions of affected plants.
Landscape use They look best in groups or drifts. Plant with spring and early-summer perennials, tulips and daffodils. Combine with wildflowers in light shade.

Armeria maritima
PLUMBAGINACEAE

THRIFT

Thrift forms dense tufts of grass-like, grey-green evergreen leaves. The taller flower stalks arise from the centres of the tightly packed rosettes.

Other common names Sea pink.
Flower colour Small pink flowers crowded into rounded 2.5-cm (1-inch) heads.
Flowering time Late spring and summer.
Height and spread 25–35 cm (10–14 inches) tall; 20–25 cm (8–10 inches) wide.
Temperature requirements Zones 4–8.
Position Average to humus-rich, moist but well-drained soil. Full sun. Prefers cool nights and low humidity.
Cultivation Drought-tolerant once established; will grow in rock crevices where water is scarce. Tolerates air- and soil-borne salt; perfect for seaside gardens.
Propagation Divide clumps in early spring or autumn. Sow seed indoors in winter on a warm (21°C [70°F]) seedbed.
Pest and disease prevention No serious pests or diseases.
Landscape use Plant in rock and wall gardens or along paths.
Cultivars 'Alba' has white flowers on 12.5-cm (5-inch) stems. 'Düsseldorf Pride' has wine red flowers on 15–20-cm (6–8-inch) stems. 'Robusta' has 7.5-cm (3-inch) pink flower heads on 30–37.5-cm (12–15-inch) stems. 'Vindictive' is only 15 cm (6 inches) tall with bright rose pink flowers.

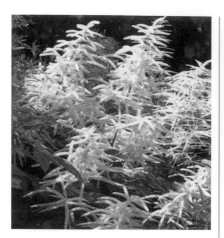

Aruncus dioicus
ROSACEAE

GOAT'S BEARD

Goat's beards are showy shrub-like perennials with large three-lobed leaves and airy plumes of flowers. Male and female flowers are borne on separate plants.

Flower colour Creamy white flowers with small petals.
Flowering time Late spring and early summer.
Height and spread 90–180 cm (3–6 feet) tall; 90–150 cm (3–5 feet) wide.
Temperature requirements Zones 3–7; avoid areas with hot nights.
Position Moist, humus-rich soil. Full sun (in cooler zones) to partial shade.
Cultivation Plant 1.2–1.5 m (4–5 feet) apart to allow for the plants' impressive mature size. The tough rootstocks are difficult to move once established. Divide plants only if necessary to revitalise the clumps. Lift in early spring and replant strong, healthy divisions into soil that has been enriched with organic matter.
Propagation Sow seed in summer outdoors or inside on a warm (21°C [70°F]) seedbed.
Pest and disease prevention No serious pests or diseases.
Landscape use Use with ferns, wildflowers and hostas in a lightly shaded woodland garden or as an accent with flowering shrubs. Combines well with other perennials in beds and borders.

Aster nouae-angliae
COMPOSITAE

NEW ENGLAND ASTER

New England asters are tall, stately plants with hairy stems and clasping, lance-shaped leaves. Most work best at the back of the perennial border.

Flower colour Lavender to purple 3.5–5-cm (1½–2-inch) flowers with bright yellow centres. Flowers may vary in colour from white to pink and rose.
Flowering time Late summer to autumn.
Height and spread 90–180 cm (3–6 feet) tall; 90 cm (3 feet) wide. Matures into broad clumps.
Temperature requirements Zones 3–8.
Position Moist, humus-rich soil. Full sun to light shade.
Cultivation Clumps become quite large with age. Divide every three to four years in spring. Plants may need staking.
Propagation Take l0–15-cm (4–6-inch) stem cuttings in late spring or early summer. Divide in early spring or autumn.
Pest and disease prevention Powdery mildew turns leaves dull grey. Thin stems to promote air circulation. Dust affected plants with sulphur.
Landscape use Plant with autumn perennials like sunflowers (*Helianthus* spp.), Japanese anemone (*Anemone* x *hybrida*) and ornamental grasses.
Cultivars 'Alma Potschke' has dark salmon-pink flowers on 60–120-cm (2–4-foot) plants. 'Purple Dome' is a dwarf selection with royal purple flowers.

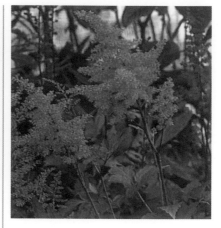

Astilbe x arendsii
SAXIFRAGACEAE

ASTILBE

Astilbes have showy flower clusters and ferny, dissected leaves with shiny broad leaflets. The emerging spring shoots are often tinged with red.

Flower colour Upright, often-plumed flower clusters bear tightly packed, fuzzy blooms in shades of red, pink, rose, lilac, cream, and white.
Flowering time Spring and early summer.
Height and spread 60–120 cm (2–4 feet) tall; 60–90 cm (2–3 feet) wide. Leafy clumps spread steadily outwards.
Temperature requirements Zones 3–9.
Position Moist, slightly acid, humus-rich soil. Full to partial shade; tolerates more sun in cool-summer areas.
Cultivation Benefits from an annual application of balanced organic fertiliser. Top-dress with compost or lift and replant the clumps if crowns rise above the soil. Divide clumps every three to four years and replant into soil enriched with organic matter. Keep plants well watered.
Propagation Propagate the true species by sowing fresh seed outdoors in summer or early autumn. Propagate cultivars by spring or autumn division only.
Pest and disease prevention Spider mites may be a problem in warm areas. Spray with insecticidal soap as necessary. Control root rot with good drainage and good air circulation.
Landscape use Plant at stream- or pondside and in borders.

Aurinia saxatilis
CRUCIFERAE

BASKET OF GOLD

Basket of gold produces mounds of 15-cm (6-inch) oblong grey-green leaves from a thick crown. Hairy leaves and deep roots help the plant endure dry soil and warm temperatures.

Flower colour Brilliant yellow flowers have four rounded petals and are carried in upright, branched clusters.
Flowering time Early spring.
Height and spread 25–30 cm (10–12 inches) tall; 30 cm (12 inches) wide.
Temperature requirements Zones 3–7. Tolerates hot, dry conditions.
Position Average, well-drained, loamy or sandy soil. Full sun. Avoid excessively hot and humid climates.
Cultivation Clumps spread by creeping stems and may flop after flowering. Cut stems back by two-thirds after flowering to encourage compact growth.
Propagation Divide in autumn. Take stem cuttings in spring or autumn. Sow seed in autumn.
Pest and disease prevention Heavy moist soils and high humidity will encourage root rot. Plant in well-drained soils only.
Landscape use Basket of gold lends colour to rock walls, rock gardens and walkways. Combine with rock cresses (*Aubrieta* spp.) and pinks (*Dianthus* spp.).
Cultivars 'Citrina' has clear lemon yellow flowers. 'Compactum' forms tight clumps only 20 cm (8 inches) tall. 'Sunny Border Apricot' has peach-coloured flowers.

Boltonia asteroides
COMPOSITAE

BOLTONIA

Boltonias are tall, late-season perennials with masses of flowers smothering the grey-green willow-like foliage. The mounded plants are lovely in foliage; the flowers are a bonus.

Flower colour A profusion of 2.5-cm (1-inch) white daisies with bright yellow centres is carried in open clusters.
Flowering time Late summer to autumn.
Height and spread 1.2–1.8 m (4–6 feet) tall; 1.2 m (4 feet) wide.
Temperature requirements Zones 3–9.
Position Moist, humus-rich soil. Full sun to light shade. Dry soil produces much smaller plants.
Cultivation These easy-to-grow plants form sturdy, dense stems that will seldom need staking.
Propagation Divide oversized clumps in spring. Take cuttings in early summer. Seed collected from cultivars will produce seedlings unlike the parent plants and in most cases inferior to them.
Pest and disease prevention No serious pests or diseases.
Landscape use Combine with autumn-flowering perennials like asters, Japanese anemones (*Anemone* x *hybrida*), goldenrods (*Solidago* spp.), Joe Pye weeds (*Eupatorium* spp.) and ornamental grasses.
Cultivars 'Pink Beauty' sports soft-pink flowers in open clusters. Cool summers produce brighter colours. 'Snowbank' is a compact selection with white flowers.

Campanula carpatica
CAMPANULACEAE

CARPATHIAN HAREBELL

Adaptable Carpathian harebell spreads to form tidy mounds of dark green leaves topped with cup-shaped, blue-purple flowers. Mulch to keep the roots cool in warm climates.

Flower colour Clumps of lively blue-purple or white flowers.
Flowering time Early summer.
Height and spread 22.5 cm (9 inches); slightly wider spread.
Temperature requirements Zones 3–8.
Position Well-drained, moist, fertile soil. Full sun; light shade in hotter sites.
Cultivation Mulch with compost during summer. Water in drought.
Propagation Short-lived unless you divide and renew every couple of years. Deadhead for an extended flowering period or leave a few flowers on so the plant can self-sow.
Pest and disease prevention Trap slugs and snails in saucers of beer set shallowly in the ground near the plants.
Landscape use Set in clumps or rows in front of a flower or shrub border. Or use plants individually in a rock garden or beside a stone patio.
Cultivars 'Alba' has pure white flowers.

Catananche caerulea
COMPOSITAE

CUPID'S DART

Cupid's dart produces tufts of narrow, woolly leaves from a fibrous rootstock. The straw-like flowers look great in the summer garden and dry easily for flower arrangements.

Flower colour Blue 5-cm (2-inch) flowers resemble asters but lack the bold yellow centre. Carried singly on wiry stems.
Flowering time Summer.
Height and spread 45–60 cm (18–24 inches) tall; 25–30 cm (10–12 inches) wide.
Temperature requirements Zones 4–9. Heat tolerant.
Position Light, well-drained, humus-rich soil. Full sun. Good drainage is imperative for healthy growth.
Cultivation Plants may be short-lived, especially in heavy soil. Divide plants every year to promote longevity.
Propagation Divide in autumn. Take 5–7.5-cm (2–3-inch) root cuttings in autumn or winter. Sow seed indoors in early spring. Plants will flower the first year.
Pest and disease prevention No serious pests or diseases.
Landscape use Use in mass plantings in rock gardens or at the front of a dry, sunny perennial garden. Combine with yarrows and evening primrose (*Oenothera* spp.).
Cultivars 'Blue Giant' is a stout cultivar with dark blue flowers. 'Major' has lavender-blue flowers on 90-cm (3-foot) stems.

Chrysanthemum x *superbum* (*Leucanthemum* x *superbum*
COMPOSITAE

SHASTA DAISY

Shasta daisies are showy, summer-flowering plants with dense clusters of shiny 25-cm (10-inch), deep green, toothed leaves and short, creeping, fibrous-rooted stems.

Flower colour Bright white 7.5-cm (3-inch) daisies with large, bright yellow centres are carried on stout, leafy stems.
Flowering time Throughout summer.
Height and spread 30–90 cm (1–3 feet) tall; 60 cm (2 feet) wide.
Temperature requirements Zones 3–10. Extremely cold and heat tolerant. Exact zones vary by cultivar.
Position Average to rich, well-drained soil. Full sun. Tolerates seaside conditions but not waterlogged soil.
Cultivation Shasta daisies are easy-care perennials. Deadhead plants to promote continued flowering. Plants grow quickly but may be short-lived especially in warmer zones. Divide and replant clumps in organically enriched soil every three to four years to keep them vigorous.
Propagation Remove offsets from the main clump or divide in spring.
Pest and disease prevention No serious pests or diseases.
Landscape use Combine with summer-flowering perennials like daylilies, irises and poppies. In a seaside garden, plant them with blanket flowers (*Gaillardia* spp.) and coreopsis.

Coreopsis verticillata
COMPOSITAE

THREAD-LEAVED COREOPSIS

Thread-leaved coreopsis is an airy, rounded plant with thread-like, three-lobed leaves and masses of bright yellow summer flowers. Plants grow from a fibrous-rooted crown.

Flower colour The 2.5–5-cm (1–2-inch) starry flowers are butter to golden yellow.
Flowering time Throughout summer.
Height and spread 30–90 cm (1–3 feet) tall; 60–90 cm (2–3 feet) wide.
Temperature requirements Zones 3–9.
Position Average to rich, moist but well-drained soil. Full sun or light shade; drought-tolerant once established.
Cultivation Thread-leaved coreopsis is an easy-care perennial that demands little attention once established. Plants eventually die out at the centre. Divide old clumps and replant in enriched soil.
Propagation Divide in spring or autumn. Take stem cuttings in early summer.
Pest and disease prevention No serious pests or diseases.
Landscape use Perfect for the front of the border with cranesbills (*Geranium* spp.), yarrows, daylilies and cone flowers (*Rudbeckia* and *Echinacea* spp.). Combine them with ornamental grasses or use a mass planting with shrubs.
Cultivars 'Golden Showers' grows 60 cm (2 feet) tall with golden yellow flowers. 'Moonbeam' is a spreading plant with pale yellow flowers. 'Zagreb' is a compact selection similar to 'Golden Showers'.

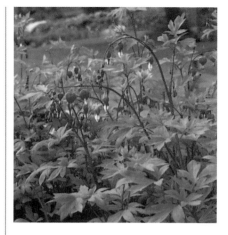

Delphinium elatum hybrids
RANUNCULACEAE

HYBRID DELPHINIUM

Hybrid delphiniums are stately border plants with dense flower clusters atop tall stems with deeply cut, palmately lobed leaves. Plants grow from stout crowns with thick, fleshy roots.

Flower colour White through all shades of true blue to lavender and purple.
Flowering time Late spring through summer. Plants may rebloom in autumn.
Height and spread 1.35–1.8 m (4½–6 feet) tall; 60–90 cm (2–3 feet) wide.
Temperature requirements Zones 4–7.
Position Evenly moist but well-drained, fertile, humus-rich soil. Full sun.
Cultivation Often short-lived in warm climates. Delphiniums benefit from an annual spring top-dressing of organic fertiliser. Set out new plants in spring, thin the clumps to three to five stems as they emerge. To encourage plants to rebloom, cut off old flowering stems above the foliage below the flower spike. Divide overgrown plants.
Propagation Divide in spring. Sow fresh seed in summer or autumn. Take cuttings in spring from the new shoots; use the stems removed from thinning for propagation.
Pest and disease prevention Powdery mildew may cause white blotches on the leaves. Dust affected parts with sulphur.
Landscape use Plant at the rear of borders where their showy spires will tower over other summer-flowering perennials.

Dianthus plumarius
CARYOPHYLLACEAE

COTTAGE PINKS

Cottage pinks are popular, sweet-scented plants for the garden or for cutting. The broad, mounded plants produce dense clusters of 7.5 cm (3-inch), blue-green, grass-like leaves.

Flower colour Fragrant white or pink flowers are borne in clusters on wiry stems.
Flowering time Early to mid-summer.
Height and spread 45–60 cm (1½–2 feet) tall; 30 cm (1 foot) wide.
Temperature requirements Zones 3–9. Tolerates extreme heat and cold.
Position Average, well-drained, sandy or loamy soil. Full sun. The soil should be neutral or only slightly acid for best growth. Plants tolerate alkaline soil.
Cultivation Plants may be short-lived, especially in warmer zones. Divide clumps every two to three years.
Propagation Layer or take stem cuttings from the foliage rosettes in summer. Strip leaves from the lower third of a 5–7.5-cm (2–3-inch) cutting. Place cutting in a medium of one part vermiculite and two parts sand or perlite to allow excellent drainage and air circulation.
Pest and disease prevention Rust causes yellow blotches on the upper surface of the leaves and raised orange spots on the lower surface. To discourage rust, thin clumps for better air circulation and dust with sulphur.
Landscape use Plant at the front of borders or use them as an edging along paths. Grow them in sunny rock gardens.

Dicentra spectabilis (Lamprocapnos spectabilis)
PAPAVERACEAE

COMMON BLEEDING HEART

Common bleeding hearts are beloved, old-fashioned perennials with strings of hearts held above deeply divided blue-green foliage. Plants grow from thick, fleshy roots.

Flower colour Bright pink heart-shaped flowers consist of two reflexed lobes with a central column that resembles a dangling drop of blood.
Flowering time Early spring to early summer.
Height and spread 30–75 cm (1–2½ feet) tall; 60–90 cm (2–3 feet) wide.
Temperature requirements Zones 2–9. Extremely tolerant of heat and cold. Mulch in winter in colder zones.
Position Evenly moist, humus-rich soil. Partial shade; full sun in cooler zones.
Cultivation They will bloom for four to six weeks in spring. In warm climates or if soil is dry, plants will become dormant after flowering. Top-dress with well-rotted manure in early spring to maintain soil fertility. If plants lose vigour, lift and divide.
Propagation Divide clumps in autumn. Sow fresh seed in summer. Take root cuttings in late summer.
Pest and disease prevention No serious pests or diseases.
Landscape use Plant common bleeding hearts with spring bulbs, primroses and wildflowers for a striking spring display. In warm zones combine them with hostas to fill the void left by the declining foliage.

Digitalis x mertonensis
PLANTAGINACEAE

STRAWBERRY FOXGLOVE

The popular strawberry foxglove has fuzzy, broad, lance-shaped leaves. Rosettes of foliage form at the base of the flowering stems and persist over winter.

Flower colour The 5–7.5-cm (2–3-inch) tubular flowers are flushed with pink, rose, or purple on the outside and heavily spotted with dark purple or brown on the inside. Some selections are pure white.
Flowering time Plants flower throughout summer and often rebloom.
Height and spread 90–120 cm (3–4 feet) tall; 30 cm (1 foot) wide.
Temperature requirements Zones 3–8.
Position Moist but well-drained, humus-rich soil. Full sun to partial shade.
Cultivation Strawberry foxgloves are easy-care perennials that flower tirelessly with little care. Divide overgrown clumps and replant into soil that has been enriched with organic matter. Remove spent flower stalks to promote rebloom. Leave one stalk to self-sow.
Propagation Divide in spring or autumn. Sow fresh seed outdoors in autumn. Seedlings emerge the next spring and will flower the second year.
Pest and disease prevention No serious pests or diseases.
Landscape use Plant at the middle or rear of perennial gardens. In informal and cottage gardens combine them with ferns and ornamental grasses. Use mass plantings along a wall or fence.

Doronicum orientale
COMPOSITAE

LEOPARD'S BANE

Leopard's bane is a brightly coloured spring daisy with deep green, triangular leaves in open clusters from a fibrous-rooted crown.

Flower colour Dozens of 2.5–5-cm (1–2-inch) bright yellow single daisies are borne on slender, leafless stems.
Flowering time Spring and early summer.
Height and spread 30–60 cm (1–2 feet) tall; 30 cm (1 foot) wide.
Temperature requirements Zones 3–8.
Position Moist, humus-rich soil. Full sun to shade.
Cultivation Leopard's bane emerges early in spring and may be damaged by late frosts. Plants become dormant after flowering in warmer zones. In colder zones, the foliage remains all season, so moist soil is imperative. Mulch will help keep the soil cool. Divide clumps every two to three years to keep them vigorous.
Propagation Divide in spring or autumn. Sow seed indoors in late winter or early spring.
Pest and disease prevention No serious pests or diseases.
Landscape use Combine with clustered bellflower (*Campanula glomerata*), Virginia bluebells (*Mertensia virginica*), spring bulbs and wildflowers. Plant foliage plants such as hostas to fill the voids when plants become dormant.
Cultivars 'Magnificum' has showy 5-cm (2-inch) flowers.

Echinacea purpurea
COMPOSITAE

PURPLE CONEFLOWER

Purple coneflowers are showy summer daisies with sparse, 15-cm (6-inch) oval or broadly lance-shaped leaves on stout, hairy stems. Plants grow from thick, deep taproots.

Flower colour Red-violet to rose pink flowers have broad, drooping rays (petal-like structures) surrounding raised, bristly cones.
Flowering time Mid- to late summer.
Height and spread 60–120 cm (2–4 feet) tall; 30–60 cm (1–2 feet) wide.
Temperature requirements Zones 3–8. Extremely heat tolerant.
Position Average to humus-rich, moist but well-drained soil. Full sun. Drought tolerant once established.
Cultivation Plants increase from basal buds to form broad, long-lived clumps. Division is seldom necessary and is not recommended,
Propagation Sow seed outdoors in autumn or indoors after stratification. To stratify, mix seed with moist peat moss or seed-growing medium in a plastic bag. Close the bag with a twist-tie and place it in the refrigerator for four to six weeks. Sow the mixture as you would normal seed. Take root cuttings in autumn.
Pest and disease prevention No serious pests or diseases.
Landscape use Plant in formal perennial gardens or meadow and prairie gardens.

Erigeron speciosus
COMPOSITAE

DAISY FLEABANE

Daisy fleabane forms leafy clumps of hairy, 15-cm (6-inch) lance-shaped leaves that spring from fibrous-rooted crowns. The colourful flowers bloom in summer.

Flower colour The pretty 3.5-cm (1½-inch) aster-like flowers have white, pink, rose or purple rays which surround bright yellow centres.

Flowering time Early to mid-summer; occasional rebloom.

Height and spread 45-75 cm (1½-2½ feet) tall; 30-60 cm (1-2 feet) wide.

Temperature requirements Zones 2-9. Tolerant of heat and cold.

Position Moist but well-drained, average to humus-rich soil. Full sun to light shade.

Cultivation Fleabanes are long-lived perennials that benefit from division every two to three years.

Propagation Divide in autumn. Take cuttings in spring before the flower buds form. Sow seed outdoors in autumn or indoors in spring.

Pest and disease prevention No serious pests or diseases.

Landscape use Plant at the front of beds and borders with summer-flowering perennials like cranesbills (*Geranium* spp.), cinquefoils (*Potentilla* spp.), evening primroses (*Oenothera* spp.) and phlox. Daisy fleabanes make long-lasting and delightful cut flowers.

Filipendula rubra
ROSACEAE

QUEEN OF THE PRAIRIE

Queen of the prairie is a towering perennial with huge flower heads on stout, leafy stalks. The showy 30-cm (1-foot) leaves are deeply lobed and star-like. Plants grow from creeping stems.

Flower colour Small five-petalled pink flowers are crowded into large heads that resemble candyfloss.

Flowering time Late spring and early summer.

Height and spread 1.2-1.8 cm (4-6 feet) tall; 60-120 cm (2-4 feet) wide.

Temperature requirements Zones 3-9.

Position Evenly moist, humus-rich soil. Full sun to light shade. Plants will not tolerate prolonged dryness.

Cultivation Established clumps make an arresting display when in bloom. If leaves become tattered after flowering, cut plants to the ground; new leaves will emerge. Plants spread quickly in moist soil. Divide every three to four years to keep them from overtaking their neighbours.

Propagation Division is the best method. Lift clumps in spring or autumn, or dig crowns from the edge of the clump. Sow seed indoors in spring.

Pest and disease prevention No serious pests or diseases.

Landscape use Plant queen of the prairie at the rear of borders with shrub roses, irises, daylilies and phlox. Use them at the side of ponds with ferns and ornamental grasses.

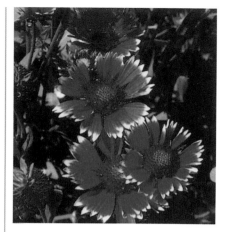

Gaillardia x *grandiflora*
COMPOSITAE

BLANKET FLOWER

The showy hybrid blanket flower flowers throughout the summer on loose stems with hairy, lobed leaves. Plants grow from fibrous-rooted crowns and may be short-lived.

Flower colour Ragged yellow-and-orange daisy-like flowers have single or double rows of toothed petal-like rays surrounding a raised yellow centre.

Flowering time Throughout summer.

Height and spread 60-90 cm (2-3 feet) tall; 60 cm (2 feet) wide.

Temperature requirements Zones 4-9.

Position Average to poor, well-drained soil. Full sun. Rich, moist soil causes plants to overgrow and flop.

Cultivation Blanket flowers are drought tolerant and thrive in seaside conditions. Divide every two to three years.

Propagation Divide in early spring. Sow seed outdoors in autumn or indoors in spring after stratification. To stratify, mix seed with moist peat moss or seed-growing medium in a plastic bag. Close the bag with a twist-tie and place it in the refrigerator for four to six weeks. Sow the mixture as you would normal seed. Seedlings often flower the first year.

Pest and disease prevention No serious pests or diseases.

Landscape use Choose blanket flowers for rock gardens, seaside gardens or borders.

Gaura lindheimeri
ONAGRACEAE

WHITE GAURA

White gaura is a shrubby perennial with airy flower clusters on wiry stems and small, hairy leaves. This dependable, long-flowering plant grows from a thick, deep taproot.

Flower colour Unusual white flowers are tinged with pink. They have four triangular petals, long curled stamens (male reproductive structures) and dance in slender spikes above the foliage.
Flowering time Throughout summer.
Height and spread 90–120 cm (3–4 feet) tall; 90 cm (3 feet) wide.
Temperature requirements Zones 5–9. Extremely heat-tolerant.
Position Moist, well-drained, average to rich soil. Full sun.
Cultivation White gaura is an easy-care perennial that thrives for years with little attention. Plants flower non-stop all summer despite high heat and humidity. Remove old flower stalks to make way for the new ones.
Propagation Sow seed outdoors in spring or autumn. Self-sown seedlings are likely.
Pest and disease prevention No serious pests or diseases.
Landscape use White gaura is a lovely addition to formal and informal gardens alike. The flower clusters look like a swirl of dancing butterflies. Combine them with low-mounding perennials like verbenas (*Verbena* spp.), cranesbills (*Geranium* spp.) and sedums.

Helenium autumnale
COMPOSITAE

COMMON SNEEZEWEED

Common sneezeweed is a showy, late-season perennial with tall, leafy stems that spring from a fibrous-rooted crown. The hairy, lance-shaped leaves are edged with a few large teeth.

Other common names Autumn Helen flower.
Flower colour The 5-cm (2-inch), golden yellow daisy-like flowers have broad, petal-like rays.
Flowering time Late summer and autumn.
Height and spread 90–150 cm (3–5 feet) tall; 60–90 cm (2–3 feet) wide.
Temperature requirements Zones 3–8.
Position Evenly moist, humus-rich soil. Full sun or light shade. Tolerates wet soil.
Cultivation Either stake it or pinch out the stem tips in early summer to promote compact growth. Divide the clumps every three to four years to keep them vigorous.
Propagation Divide in spring or autumn. Take stem cuttings in early summer. Sow seed outdoors in spring or autumn.
Pest and disease prevention No serious pests or diseases.
Landscape use Common sneezeweeds offer late-season colour. Combine them with asters, goldenrods (*Solidago* spp.) and garden phlox (*Phlox paniculata*).
Cultivars 'Butterpat' has bright yellow flowers on 90–120-cm (3–4-foot) stems. 'Crimson Beauty' has mahogany flowers. 'Riverton Beauty' has golden yellow flowers with bronze-red centres.

Hemerocallis hybrids
HEMEROCALLIDACEAE

DAYLILY

Daylily hybrids are among the most popular perennials. Although each flower lasts only one day, a profusion of new buds keeps the plants in bloom for a month or more.

Flower colour Daylily flowers vary in colour and form. The majority of the wild species are orange or yellow with wide petals and narrow, petal-like sepals. Modern hybrids come in many colours.
Flowering time Spring through summer.
Height and spread 30–150 cm (1–5 feet) tall; 60–90 cm (2–3 feet) wide.
Temperature requirements Zones 3–9.
Position Evenly moist, average to humus-rich soil. Full sun to light shade.
Cultivation Plant container-grown or bare-root plants in spring or autumn. Place the crowns just below the soil surface. Plants take a year to become established and then spread quickly to form dense clumps.
Propagation Divide hybrids in autumn or spring. Seed-grown plants will be variable and often inferior to the parent plant.
Pest and disease prevention Aphids and thrips may attack the foliage and flower buds. Wash off aphids with a stream of water or spray them with insecticidal soap. Thrips make small white lines in the foliage and may deform flower buds if damage is severe. Spray with insecticidal soap or a botanical insecticide.
Landscape use Perfect for mass plantings in beds and borders.

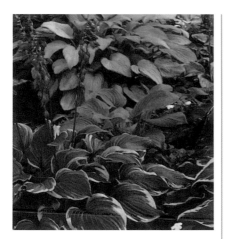

Hosta hybrids
ASPARAGACEAE

HOSTA

Hostas are indispensable foliage plants for shaded gardens. Their thick, pleated or puckered leaves grow from stout crowns with thick fleshy roots.

Flower colour Lavender, purple or white flowers are carried in slender spikes.
Flowering time Summer or autumn depending on hybrid and origin.
Height and spread 15–90 cm (6 inches–3 feet) tall; 15–150 cm (6 inches–5 feet) wide.
Temperature requirements Zones 3–8. Some selections are hardy to Zone 2.
Position Evenly moist, humus-rich soil. Light to full shade. Adaptable to both dry and wet soil conditions. Filtered sun encourages the best leaf colour in the gold- and blue-leaved forms. All hostas need protection from hot afternoon sun, especially in warm zones.
Cultivation Hostas take several years to reach mature form and size; allow ample room when planting. New shoots are slow to emerge in spring, so take care not to damage them during the spring clean-up.
Propagation Divide in late summer.
Pest and disease prevention Set shallow dishes of beer flush with the soil surface to drown slugs and snails.
Landscape use Use the smaller cultivars to edge beds or as groundcover under shrubs and trees. Choose giants for creating drama in a mixed planting or alone as an accent.

Iris sibirica
IRIDICEAE

SIBERIAN IRIS

Siberian irises produce graceful early-summer flowers in a wide range of colours. Plants form tight fans of narrow sword-like leaves from slow-creeping rhizomes.

Flower colour Flowers range in colour from pure white, cream and yellow to all shades of blue, violet and purple. Some cultivars come close to true red.
Flowering time Early summer; some cultivars rebloom.
Height and spread 30–90 cm (1–3 feet) tall; 30–60 cm (1–2 feet) wide.
Temperature requirements Zones 3–9. Heat and cold tolerant.
Position Evenly moist, humus-rich soil. Full sun to partial shade. Plant bare-root iris in autumn and container-grown plants in spring, summer and autumn.
Cultivation Siberian irises thrive for many years without division. If flowering begins to wane, divide and replant.
Propagation Divide plants in late summer. Seed collected from cultivars will be variable and often inferior to the parent plant. Sow fresh seed of the species outdoors in summer or autumn.
Pest and disease prevention Susceptible to iris borer. Smash the grubs between your fingers while they are in the leaves. Dig up affected plants and cut off affected portions of the rhizome.
Landscape use Plant with perennials, ornamental grasses and ferns.

Lobelia cardinalis
CAMPANULACEAE

CARDINAL FLOWER

Cardinal flowers have fiery-coloured flower spikes on leafy stems and grow from a fibrous-rooted crown. The lance-shaped leaves may be fresh green or red-bronze.

Flower colour Brilliant scarlet tubular flowers have three lower and two upper petals that look like delicate birds in flight.
Flowering time Late summer to autumn.
Height and spread 60–120 cm (2–4 feet) tall; 30–60 cm (1–2 feet) wide.
Temperature requirements Zones 2–9.
Position Evenly moist, humus-rich soil. Full sun to partial shade.
Cultivation Cardinal flowers are shallow-rooted and subject to frost heaving. Where winters are cold, mulch plants to protect the crowns. In warmer zones winter mulch may rot the crowns. Replant in spring if frost has lifted them. Plants may be short-lived, but self-sown seedlings are numerous.
Propagation Divide in late autumn or spring. Sow seed uncovered outdoors in autumn or spring, or indoors in late winter. Seedlings grow quickly and will flower the first year from seed.
Pest and disease prevention No serious pests or diseases.
Landscape use Cardinal flowers need even moisture so they are commonly used around pools, along streams or in informal plantings. Combine them with irises, hostas, ligularias (*Ligularia* spp.) and ferns.

Lupinus polyphyllus
LEGUMINOSAE

WASHINGTON LUPIN

Washington lupins have conical flower spikes on stout stems with large palmately divided leaves. Plants grow from thick roots. Lupins add a dramatic vertical accent to borders.

Flower colour The 18-mm (¼-inch), blue-purple or yellow pea-like flowers are crowded into 30–60 cm (1–2-foot) spikes.
Flowering time Spring and summer.
Height and spread 90–150 cm (3–5 feet) tall; 60–90 cm (2–3 feet) wide.
Temperature requirements Zones 3–7. Sensitive to high summer temperatures.
Position Moist but well-drained, acid, humus-rich soil. Full sun to light shade.
Cultivation They are heavy feeders. Top-dress in spring with organic fertiliser. Protect plants from hot, dry winds.
Propagation Remove sideshoots from around the clump in autumn. Sow seed outdoors in autumn or inside in winter. Before sowing indoors, soak seed overnight and then stratify. To stratify, mix seed with moist peat moss or seed-growing medium in a plastic bag. Close the bag with a twist-tie and place it in the refrigerator for four to six weeks. Sow the mixture as you would normal seed.
Pest and disease prevention No serious pests or diseases.
Landscape use Plant with border perennials like columbines (*Aquilegia* spp.), cranesbills (*Geranium* spp.), bellflowers (*Campanula* spp.), irises and peonies.

Lychnis chalcedonica
CARYOPHYLLACEAE

MALTESE CROSS

Maltese cross is an old-fashioned perennial with brilliant flower clusters atop tall stems with. opposite, oval leaves. Plants grow from fibrous-rooted crowns.

Flower colour Brilliant scarlet flowers are held in compact, domed, terminal clusters.
Flowering time Midsummer.
Height and spread 60–90 cm (2–3 feet) tall; 30–45 cm (1–1½ feet) wide.
Temperature requirements Zones 4–8.
Position Average to humus-rich, moist but well-drained soil. Needs full sun to light shade.
Cultivation Maltese cross spreads quickly to form tight clumps. Divide every two to three years to keep it strong and healthy.
Propagation Divide in spring or autumn. Sow seed outdoors in autumn.
Pest and disease prevention No serious pests or diseases.
Landscape use Use the strong-coloured flowers of Maltese cross to create excitement in a subdued scheme of blues and pale yellows. Perfect for hot-colour combinations with cone flowers (*Rudbeckia* spp.), blanket flowers (*Gaillardia* spp.) and evening primrose (*Oenothera* spp.).

Monarda didyma
LABIATAE

BEE BALM

Bee balm is a lovely perennial with bright flowers on sturdy stems that grow from fast-creeping runners. The pointed oval leaves give Earl Grey tea its distinctive aroma and flavour.

Other common names Bergamot, oswego tea.
Flower colour Tight heads of tubular red flowers are surrounded by a whorl of coloured leafy bracts (modified leaves).
Flowering time Summer.
Height and spread 60–120 cm (2–4 feet) tall; 60–90 cm (2–3 feet) wide.
Temperature requirements Zones 4–8.
Position Evenly moist, humus-rich soil. Full sun to partial shade. If plants dry out, the lower foliage will be shed.
Cultivation Plants spread quickly; divide every two to three years.
Propagation Divide in spring or autumn. Sow seed indoors or outdoors in spring.
Pest and disease prevention Powdery mildew causes white blotches on the foliage and may cover the entire plant. Thin the stems for good air circulation. Cut affected plants to the ground.
Landscape use Plant in formal or informal gardens. Bee balm's lovely flowers add brilliant colour to the summer garden and are favoured by bees and butterflies.
Cultivars 'Blue Stocking' has violet flowers. 'Cambridge Scarlet' has brilliant scarlet flowers. 'Croftway Pink' is soft pink. 'Mahogany' has ruby red flowers.

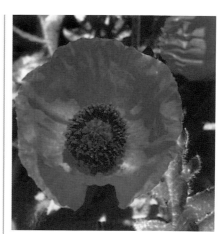

Oenothera macrocarpa
ONAGRACEAE

OZARK SUNDROPS

Ozark sundrops are showy perennials with yellow flowers and narrow pale green leaves on sprawling stems. Plants grow from a deep taproot and spread by creeping stems.

Flower colour Bright lemon yellow flowers are saucer-shaped and 7.5–10 cm (3–4 inches) wide.
Flowering time Late spring and early summer, sporadically through the season.
Height and spread 15–30 cm (6–12 inches) tall; 30 90 cm (12–36 inches) wide.
Temperature requirements Zones 4–8.
Position Average to humus-rich, well-drained soil. Full sun. Established plants are extremely drought and heat tolerant.
Cultivation Plants form large clumps with age so space at least 75 cm (30 inches) apart. Stems root as they spread.
Propagation Divide rosettes in early spring. Take stem cuttings in early summer. Sow seed outdoors in autumn or indoors in early spring.
Pest and disease prevention No serious pests or diseases.
Cultivars 'Greencourt Lemon' has 5-cm (2-inch) soft, sulphur yellow flowers.
Landscape use Use ozark sundrops at the front of borders with phlox, cranesbills (*Geranium* spp.), catmints (*Nepeta* spp.), yarrows and other early-season perennials. Performs well in rock gardens and looks lovely in meadow plantings.

Paeonia lactiflora
PAEONIACEAE

COMMON GARDEN PEONY

Common garden peonies are shrub-like, with sturdy stalks clothed in compound, shiny green leaves. Plants grow from thick, fleshy roots and may live 100 years or more.

Flower colour Ranges in colour from white, cream and yellow to pink, rose, burgundy and scarlet. Flowers may be single, semi-double or double.
Flowering time Common garden peonies are classified by their flowering time; early May (April in hot climates) flowering; mid-May flowering; and late May (early June in cooler climates) flowering.
Height and spread 45–90 cm (1½–3 feet) tall; 90–120 cm (3–4 feet) wide.
Temperature requirements Zones 2–8.
Position Moist, humus-rich soil. Full sun to light shade. Good drainage is important.
Cultivation Plant container-grown peonies in spring or autumn. Plant bare-root plants in September and October. Mulch new plants to protect from frost heaving. Taller selections and those with double flowers may need staking to keep their faces out of the mud. Lift plants in autumn, divide the roots leaving at least one eye (bud) per division and replant.
Propagation Divide in autumn.
Pest and disease prevention Spray or dust foliage with an organically acceptable fungicide to discourage Botrytis.
Landscape use Combine with early spring bulbs like snowdrops and squills.

Papaver orientale
PAPAVERACEAE

ORIENTAL POPPY

Oriental poppies are prized for their colourful, crepe-paper-like flowers. Plants produce rosettes of coarse, hairy, lobed foliage from a thick taproot. They often become dormant after flowering.

Flower colour The 7.5-10-cm (3–4-inch) flowers have crinkled scarlet-red petals with black spots at their base. They surround the seed pod.
Flowering time Early summer.
Height and spread 60–90 cm (2–3 feet) tall; 60–90 cm (2–3 feet) wide.
Temperature requirements Zones 2–7.
Position Average to rich, well-drained, humus-rich soil. Full sun to light shade. Established plants are long-lived.
Cultivation In warm zones plants become dormant after flowering, leaving a bare spot. In autumn new foliage rosettes emerge. Divide overgrown plants at this time.
Propagation Divide in autumn. Take root cuttings in late summer, autumn or winter.
Pest and disease prevention No serious pests or diseases.
Landscape use Plant showy oriental poppies with border perennials and ornamental grasses. Combine them with bushy plants like catmints (*Nepeta* spp.) or asters, which will fill the gap left by the declining foliage.
Cultivars 'Bonfire' has brilliant red flowers. 'Helen Elizabeth' has pale salmon-pink flowers without spots. 'Snow Queen' is pure white with large black spots.

Penstemon barbatus
PLANTAGINACEAE

BEARDED PENSTEMON

Bearded penstemon is a showy plant with erect flower spikes clothed in shiny, broadly lance-shaped leaves. Flowering stems and basal foliage rosettes grow from fibrous-rooted crowns.

Flower colour The 2.5–3.5 cm (1–1½-inch) irregular tubular pink flowers have two upper and three lower lips.
Flowering time Late spring to early summer.
Height and spread 45–90 cm (1½–3 feet) tall; 30–60 cm (1–2 feet) wide.
Temperature requirements Zones 3–8.
Position Average to humus-rich, well-drained soil. Full sun to light shade. Good drainage is essential for success.
Cultivation Plants form dense clumps with maturity and benefit from division every four to six years. More frequent division is required in rich soil.
Propagation Divide in spring. Sow seed outdoors in autumn or indoors in winter after stratification. To stratify, mix seed with moist peat moss or seed-growing medium in a plastic bag. Close the bag with a twist-tie and place it in the refrigerator for four to six weeks. Sow the mixture as you would normal seed. Seedlings may flower the first year.
Pest and disease prevention No serious pests or diseases.
Landscape use Plant in formal borders, informal gardens and rock gardens.

Phlox paniculata
POLEMONIACEAE

GARDEN PHLOX

Garden phlox is a popular summer-flowering perennial with domed clusters of fragrant, richly coloured flowers atop stiff, leafy stems. Plants grow from fibrous-rooted crowns.

Flower colour Varies from magenta to pink and white. Hybrids have a wide colour range, including purples, reds, and oranges. There are also bicoloured and 'eyed' forms.
Flowering time Mid- to late summer.
Height and spread 90–120 cm (3–4 feet) tall; 60–120 cm (2–4 feet) wide.
Temperature requirements Zones 3–8. Cold hardiness varies with cultivars.
Position Moist but well-drained, humus-rich soil. Full sun to light shade.
Cultivation Divide clumps every three to four years to keep them vigorous.
Propagation Divide in spring. Take stem cuttings in late spring or early summer. Take root cuttings in the autumn.
Pest and disease prevention Powdery mildew causes white patches on the leaves or, in bad cases, turns entire leaves white. To avoid problems, thin the stems before plants flower to increase air circulation. Select resistant cultivars, especially hybrids with *P. maculata*.
Landscape use Garden phlox are beautiful and versatile garden perennials. Combine with summer daisies, bee balm (*Monarda* spp.), daylilies, asters, goldenrods (*Solidago* spp.) and ornamental grasses.

Platycodon grandiflorus
CAMPANULACEAE

BALLOON FLOWER

Balloon flowers are showy summer-flowering plants with saucer-shaped flowers on succulent stems clothed in toothed, triangular leaves. Plants grow from thick, fleshy roots.

Flower colour The rich blue flowers have five-pointed petals that open from inflated buds that resemble balloons.
Flowering time Summer.
Height and spread 60–90 cm (2–3 feet) tall; 30–60 cm (1–2 feet) wide.
Temperature requirements Zones 3–8.
Position Well-drained, average to humus-rich soil. Full sun to light shade. Established plants are drought tolerant.
Cultivation New shoots are slow to emerge in spring. Take care not to damage them by mistake. Remove spent flowers to encourage more flowering. Established clumps seldom need division.
Propagation Lift and divide clumps in spring or early autumn; dig deeply to avoid root damage. Take basal cuttings of non-flowering shoots in summer, ideally with a piece of root attached. Sow seed outdoors in autumn. Self-sown seedlings occur.
Pest and disease prevention No serious pests or diseases.
Landscape use Plant balloon flower with summer perennials like yellow yarrows (*Achillea* spp.), sages (*Salvia* spp.), bee balm (*Monarda* spp.) and phlox.

Primula x *polyantha*
PRIMULACEAE

POLYANTHUS PRIMROSE

Polyanthus primroses are hybrids with large, showy flowers in a rainbow of colours. The broad, crinkled leaves rise directly from stout crowns with thick, fibrous roots.

Flower colour Flat, five-petalled flowers vary in colour from white, cream and yellow to pink, rose, red and purple. Many bicoloured and 'eyed' forms are available.
Flowering time Spring and early summer.
Height and spread 20–30 cm (8–12 inches) tall; 30 cm (12 inches) wide.
Temperature requirements Zones 3–8.
Position Evenly moist, humus-rich soil. Light to partial shade. Plants can tolerate dryness in the summer if they are dormant.
Cultivation In cooler zones mulch plants to avoid frost heaving and crown damage. Divide overgrown clumps after flowering and replant into soil that has been enriched with organic matter.
Propagation Divide in autumn to increase stock. Easy to grow from fresh seed sown outdoors or indoors in early spring.
Pest and disease prevention No serious pests or diseases.
Landscape use Plant drifts of primroses with spring bulbs like daffodils, tulips and Spanish bluebells (*Hyacinthoides hispanicus*). Combine them with early-flowering perennials like hellebores (*Helleborus* spp.), lungwort (*Pulmonaria* spp.), forget-me-nots (*Myosotis* spp.) and cranesbills (*Geranium* spp.).

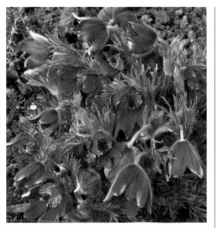

Pulsatilla vulgaris
RANUNCULACEAE

PASQUE FLOWER

Pasque flowers are early-flowering perennials with cupped flowers over rosettes of deeply incised, lobed leaves clothed in soft hairs. Plants grow from deep, fibrous roots.

Flower colour The purple flowers have five starry petals surrounding a central ring of fuzzy orange-yellow stamens (male reproductive structures). The flowers are followed by clusters of fuzzy seeds.
Flowering time Early to mid- spring.
Height and spread 15–30 cm (6–12 inches) tall; 25–30 cm (10–12 inches) wide.
Temperature requirements Zones 3–8.
Position Average to humus-rich, well-drained soil. Full sun to light shade. Does not tolerate soggy soil.
Cultivation Pasque flowers begin flowering in spring and continue for several weeks. After seed is set, plants become dormant unless conditions are cool. Seldom needs division.
Propagation Divide clumps after flowering or in autumn. Sow seed outdoors in autumn or spring. Self-sown seedlings appear.
Pest and disease prevention No serious pests or diseases.
Landscape use Perfect for rock gardens with bulbs, rock cresses (*Arabis* spp.), basket of gold (*Aurinia saxatilis*), perennial candytuft (*Iberis sempervirens*) and columbines (*Aquilegia* spp.).

Rodgersia pinnata
SAXIFRAGACEAE

RODGERSIA

Rodgersias are bold perennials with pinkish red flowers and large, pinnately compound leaves. These moisture-loving plants grow from stout, fibrous-rooted crowns.

Other common names Rodger's flower.
Flower colour The small rose red flowers are carried in 30–60-cm (1–2-foot) plume-like clusters.
Flowering time Late spring and early summer.
Height and spread 90–120 cm (3–4 feet) tall; 1.2 m (4 feet) wide.
Temperature requirements Zones 4–7.
Position Constantly moist, humus-rich soil. Partial to full shade. Protect from hot afternoon sun in warm zones.
Cultivation Rodgersias form huge clumps from large crowns that can remain in place for years. Be sure to provide at least 90–120 cm (3–4 feet) for each plant.
Propagation Divide plants in autumn or spring. Sow seed outdoors in autumn or indoors in spring.
Pest and disease prevention No serious pests or diseases.
Landscape use Plant rodgersias in bog and water gardens or along streams. Combine them with hostas, irises, astilbes, ferns, ligularias (*Ligularia* spp.) and primroses.

Rudbeckia fulgida
COMPOSITAE

ORANGE CONEFLOWER

Orange coneflowers are summer daisies with oval to broadly lance-shaped, rough, hairy foliage on stiff stems. Plants grow from fibrous-rooted crowns.

Other common names Black-eyed Susan.
Flower colour The daisy-like flowers have yellow-orange rays (petal-like structures) and raised dark brown centres.
Flowering time Mid- to late summer.
Height and spread 45–90 cm (1½–3 feet) tall; 60–120 cm (2–4 feet) wide.
Temperature requirements Zones 3–9. Extremely heat-tolerant.
Position Average, moist but well-drained soil. Full sun to light shade. Good drainage is important.
Cultivation Orange coneflowers are tough, long-lived perennials. They spread outwards to form large clumps. The edges of the clumps are the most vigorous. Divide every two to four years and replant into soil enriched with organic matter.
Propagation Divide in spring or autumn. Sow seed outdoors in autumn or spring, or indoors in late winter.
Pest and disease prevention No serious pests or diseases.
Landscape use Plant orange cone flowers with other daisies, sedums, phlox, bee balm (*Monarda* spp.), chrysanthemums and ornamental grasses.

Salvia x *superba*
LABIATAE

VIOLET SAGE

Violet sage is covered with colourful flower spikes in summer. The bushy, well-branched plants have aromatic triangular leaves. They grow from a fibrous-rooted crown.

Flower colour The violet-blue flowers are carried in narrow spikes. Below each flower is a leaf-like bract.
Flowering time Early to mid- summer. Plants often rebloom.
Height and spread 45–105 cm (1½–3½ feet) tall; 60–90 cm (2–3 feet) wide.
Temperature requirements Zones 4–7.
Position Average to humus-rich, moist but well-drained soil. Full sun to light shade. Drought tolerant once established.
Cultivation After flowering wanes, shear back flowering stems to promote fresh growth and renewed bloom. Plants seldom need division.
Propagation Divide in spring or autumn. Take cuttings in late spring or early summer; remove the flower buds.
Pest and disease prevention No serious pests or diseases.
Landscape use Plant violet sages in borders or rock gardens with early summer perennials such as yarrow, lamb's ears (*Stachys byzantina*), daylilies, coreopsis (*Coreopsis* spp.) and ornamental grasses.

Sanguinaria canadensis
PAPAVERACEAE

BLOODROOT

Bloodroot is a bright, spring wildflower with a single, deeply cut, seven-lobed leaf that emerges wrapped around the single flower bud. Plants grow from a thick, creeping rhizome.

Flower colour The snow-white flowers have 8–11 narrow petals surrounding a cluster of yellow-orange stamens (male reproductive structures). Flowers last only a few days.
Flowering time Early to mid- spring.
Height and spread 10–15 cm (4–6 inches) tall; 15–20 cm (6–8 inches) wide.
Temperature requirements Zones 3–9.
Position Moist, humus-rich soil. Light to full shade. Spring sun is important but summer shade is necessary. During prolonged dry spells, plants become dormant with no ill effect.
Cultivation Bloodroot foliage remains attractive all summer when ample moisture is available. Plants form dense clumps that can be divided.
Propagation Divide in late summer. Sow fresh seed outdoors in summer. Self-sown seedlings often appear.
Pest and disease prevention No serious pests or diseases.
Landscape use Plant bloodroot in woodland gardens with spring bulbs, wildflowers, hostas and ferns. Use them as groundcover under shrubs.

Sedum spectabile
CRASSULACEAE

SHOWY STONECROP

Showy stonecrops are late summer perennials with clusters of pink flowers atop thick stems clothed in broad grey-green leaves. Plants grow from fibrous-rooted crowns.

Flower colour Small bright pink flowers are borne in 10–15-cm (4–6-inch) domed clusters. The pale green buds are attractive in summer and the brown seed heads hold their shape all winter.
Flowering time Mid- to late summer.
Height and spread 30–60 cm (1–2 feet) tall; 60 cm (2 feet) wide.
Temperature requirements Zones 3–9. Plants are heat tolerant.
Position Average to humus-rich, well-drained soil. Full sun. Extremely drought-tolerant.
Cultivation Clumps get quite full with age and may fall open. To counteract this, divide overgrown plants.
Propagation Divide anytime from spring to midsummer. Take cuttings of non-flowering shoots in summer. Sow seed in spring or autumn.
Pest and disease prevention No serious pests or diseases.
Landscape use Plant in formal borders, informal gardens and rock gardens. Combine with yarrow, purple coneflowers (*Echinacea* spp.), cranesbill (*Geranium* spp.), coreopsis (*Coreopsis* spp.) and ornamental grasses.

Stokesia laeois
COMPOSITAE

STOKE'S ASTER

Stoke's aster is attractive in foliage and flower. The broad, lance-shaped leaves are deep green with a white mid-vein. The leaves form a rosette from a crown with thick, fibrous roots.

Flower colour The 5–7.5-cm (2–3-inch) daisy-like flowers have ragged blue rays and fuzzy white centres.
Flowering time Summer.
Height and spread 30–60 cm (1–2 feet) tall; 60 cm (2 feet) wide.
Temperature requirements Zones 5–9.
Position Average to humus-rich, moist but well-drained soil. Full sun to light shade. Established plants tolerate dry soil.
Cultivation Plants can grow undisturbed for many years. Divide in spring or autumn.
Propagation Divide in early spring. Sow seed outdoors in autumn or indoors in winter after stratification. To stratify, mix seed with moist peat moss or seed-growing medium in a plastic bag. Close the bag with a twist-tie and place it in the refrigerator for four to six weeks. Sow the mixture as you would normal seed.
Pest and disease prevention No serious pests or diseases.
Landscape use Combine with verbenas (*Verbena* spp.), phlox, goldenrod (*Solidago* spp.), columbines (*Aquilegia* spp.) and ornamental grasses.
Cultivars 'Alba' has white flowers. 'Blue Danube' has lavender-blue flowers. 'Klaus Jelitto' has deep blue flowers.

Thalictrum aquilegiifolium
RANUNCULACEAE

COLUMBINE MEADOW RUE

Columbine meadow rue has billowy plumes crowning erect stalks clothed in intricately divided leaves that resemble those of columbines. Plants grow from fibrous-rooted crowns.

Flower colour The 1 cm (½-inch) lavender or white flowers consist of many fuzzy stamens (male reproductive structures) in dense, branched clusters.
Flowering time Late spring and early summer.
Height and spread 60–90 cm (2–3 feet) tall; 30–60 cm (1–2 feet) wide.
Temperature requirements Zones 5–8.
Position Evenly moist, humus-rich soil. Full sun or partial shade. Plants tolerate wet soil.
Cultivation Clumps spread slowly and seldom outgrow their position. Can be divided if necessary.
Propagation Divide in spring or autumn. Sow seed outdoors in autumn or indoors in early spring.
Pest and disease prevention No serious pests or diseases.
Landscape use Plant columbine meadow rue in formal or informal gardens. It performs well at pondsides or along streams with irises, hostas, hibiscus (*Hibiscus* spp.), daylilies and ferns.
Cultivars 'Album' has white flowers. 'Atropurpureum' has violet flowers. 'Thundercloud' has deep purple flowers.

Alcea rosea
MALVACEAE

HOLLYHOCK

Hollyhocks are perennials usually grown as annuals or biennials. Cut down the flower stalks after the blooms fade, or leave a few to set seed and self-sow.

Description Hollyhocks form large clumps of rounded leaves and thick flower stalks. Plump flower buds produce bowl-shaped, single or double blooms up to 12.5 cm (5 inches) wide from midsummer until autumn in white or shades of red, pink and yellow.
Height and spread Height 90–180 cm (3–6 feet); spread about 60 cm (2 feet).
Best site Needs full sun; average, well-drained soil.
Growing guidelines For flowers the same year, sow seed indoors eight weeks before your last frost date. Sow 6 mm (¼ inch) deep in individual pots. After risk of frost has passed, set plants out 45–60 cm (18–24 inches) apart. For earlier flowers the following year, sow outdoors in large pots or in a nursery bed in spring or early summer. Move the young plants to their garden position in autumn. Stake hollyhocks growing in exposed sites to keep stems upright. Hollyhocks are prone to rust, a fungal disease that produces orange spots on leaves. If rust shows up in your garden, pull plants out after flowering.
Landscape use Use the tall spires of hollyhocks as accents in a flower border, with shrubs, or along a wall or fence.

Antirrhinum majus
PLANTAGINACEAE

SNAPDRAGON

A mass planting of snapdragons makes an eye-catching landscape accent. Pinch out the stem tips of dwarf types once after transplanting to promote branching and bushiness.

Description These tender perennials are usually grown as hardy or half-hardy annuals. The plants may be low and mound-forming or tall and spiky. The slender stems carry narrow, bright green leaves and are topped with spikes of tubular flowers. The velvety flowers bloom through summer in nearly every colour but true blue; some have two colours in one flower.
Height and spread Height ranges from 30 cm (1 foot) to 1.2 m (4 feet). Spread ranges from 20–45 cm (8–18 inches).
Best site Full sun to light shade; average, well-drained soil with compost added.
Growing guidelines Buy transplants in spring, or grow your own by planting seed indoors six to eight weeks before your last frost date. Sow seed directly into prepared garden soil after the last frost date. Water during dry spells. Snapdragons are prone to rust, a fungal disease that shows up as brownish spots on leaves. The best prevention is to grow them as annuals.
Landscape use Use the low-growing cultivars in masses or as edging plants for annual beds. Tall-stemmed snapdragons are a must in the cutting garden for fresh arrangements, and in cottage gardens.

Begonia Semperflorens Cultorum hybrid
BEGONIACEAE

WAX BEGONIA

Wax begonias require little or no care during the season. Pull them out after frost, or cut them back by one-third after frost and pot them up for indoor flowers in winter.

Description These tender perennials are grown as tender annuals. The succulent stems bear shiny, rounded, green or reddish brown leaves. The mounded plants are covered with single or double, 3.5-cm (1½-inch) flowers in red, pink or white from June until frost.
Height and spread Height and spread 15–20 cm (6–8 inches).
Best site Partial shade to sun; evenly moist soil with added organic matter. Morning sun and afternoon shade is ideal in hot-summer areas. Brown-leaved types tend to be more sun and heat tolerant.
Growing guidelines Wax begonias are easiest to grow from purchased transplants in spring. If you want to try raising them yourself, sow the dust-like seed at least 12 weeks before your last frost date. Don't cover the seed; just press it lightly into the soil and place the pot in a plastic bag until seedlings appear. Plant transplants 15–20 cm (6–8 inches) apart after the last frost date, when temperatures stay above 10°C (50°F) at night.
Landscape use Wax begonias are ideal as edging plants for flower beds. They also look great in pots, window boxes and hanging baskets.

Brachyscome iberidifolia
COMPOSITAE

SWAN RIVER DAISY

If Swan River daisy plants get floppy after the first flush of flowers, shear them back by half and water well to promote compact growth and more flowers until frost arrives.

Description This half-hardy annual forms bushy mounds of thin stems and lacy, finely cut leaves. From midsummer until frost, plants bear many 2.5-cm (1-inch), rounded, daisy-like flowers in shades of blue, purple, pink and white. The delicately scented blooms may have a black or yellow centre.
Height and spread Height to 30 cm (12 inches); spread to 45 cm (18 inches).
Best site Full sun; average, well-drained soil with added organic matter.
Growing guidelines For earliest flowers, buy flowering plants and plant them out after your last frost date. You can also grow Swan River daisy from seed planted indoors or outdoors. Sow indoors six to eight weeks before your last frost date. Scatter the seed over the surface, lightly press it into the soil, then enclose the pot in a plastic bag until seedlings appear. Plant out the last frost date, or sow directly into the garden in late spring. Space plants 15–20 cm (6–8 inches) apart to form a solid, even carpet of flowers.
Landscape use Swan River daisy makes an unusual edging for beds and borders. Its trailing habit is ideal for window boxes and hanging baskets.

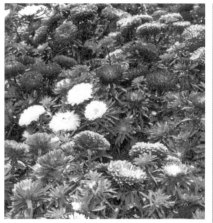

Callistephus chinensis
COMPOSITAE

CHINA ASTER

China asters flower from late summer to frost in white, cream, pink, red, purple or blue. To minimise disease problems, plant them in a different spot each year.

Description This tender annual is grown for its showy flowers. The stems carry toothed, green leaves and are topped with daisy-like or puffy, single or double flowers up to 12.5 cm (5 inches) wide.
Height and spread Height 30–60 cm (12–24 inches); spread 30–45 cm (12–18 inches).
Best site Full sun; average, well-drained soil with added organic matter.
Growing guidelines For late-summer flowers, buy transplants in spring or sow seed indoors, 3 mm (⅛ inch) deep, six weeks before your last frost date. Plant out 12 weeks after the last frost date, when the weather is warm. For autumn flowers, sow seed directly into the garden after the last frost date. Pinch out stem tips once in early summer to promote branching. Stake tall cultivars. Control aphids with soap sprays to prevent the spread of aster yellows, which causes yellowed, stunted growth; destroy infected plants. Aster wilt is a soil-borne disease that causes plants to droop; destroy infected plants.
Landscape use Grow in masses or mix with other plants in beds, borders and planters for late-season colour. Grow a few in the cutting garden, too.

Catharanthus roseus
APOCYNACEAE

MADAGASCAR PERIWINKLE

In most areas, Madagascar periwinkle flowers from early summer until frost; it can flower nearly any time of the year in frost-free climates. Try it in pots and planters.

Other common names Rosy periwinkle, vinca.
Description A tender perennial commonly grown as a tender annual, Madagascar periwinkle forms compact, bushy clumps of glossy, dark green leaves with white central veins. Stems are topped with flat, five-petalled, white, rose or pink flowers up to 5 cm (2 inches) wide.
Height and spread Height and spread usually 30–45 cm (12–18 inches); larger in frost-free areas.
Best site Full sun; average, well-drained soil. Tolerates heat, pollution and drought.
Growing guidelines For best results, buy transplants in spring; it grows slowly from seed. If you want to try raising your own, sow seed 6 mm (¼ inch) deep indoors 10–12 weeks before your last frost date. Keep pots in an especially warm place (24–27°C [75–80°F]) until seedlings appear, then move pots to regular room temperature. Set transplants out 12 weeks after the last frost date, when the soil is warm. Pinch off stem tips in early summer for compact growth and more flowers.
Landscape use This is a beautiful, easy-care annual for edging flower beds, borders and walkways.

Centaurea cyanus
COMPOSITAE

CORNFLOWER

Push twiggy prunings into the ground around young cornflower plants to support the stems as they grow. Pinching off spent flowers can prolong flowering.

Other common names Bachelor's buttons.

Description This is a dependable, easy-care, hardy annual. The bushy plants have narrow, lance-shaped, silvery green leaves and thin stems topped with fluffy flower heads. The 2.5–5-cm (1–2-inch) flowers bloom through the summer in white or shades of blue, purple, pink or red.

Height and spread Height 30–75 cm (12–30 inches); spread to 30 cm (12 inches).

Best site Full sun, but tolerates partial shade; average, well-drained soil.

Growing guidelines Grows easily from seed sown directly into the garden in early autumn (in mild-winter areas) or early spring. Plant seed 3 mm (⅛ inch) deep. To extend the flowering season from an early-spring planting, sow again every two to four weeks until midsummer. Other ways to establish cornflowers include buying transplants in spring or starting the seed indoors about eight weeks before your last frost date. Plant outdoors about two weeks before the last frost date. Cornflowers will self-sow if you leave a few flowers to set seed.

Landscape use Cornflowers are charming in meadow gardens and flower beds. They are also excellent cut flowers.

Cheiranthus cheiri (Erysimum cheiri)
CRUCIFERAE

WALLFLOWER

The fragrant flowers of wallflowers are normally orange or yellow, but they also bloom in shades of red, pink or creamy white. The flowers are ideal for spring arrangements.

Description This perennial is commonly grown as a half-hardy annual or biennial. The bushy clumps of slender green leaves are topped with clusters of 2.5-cm (1-inch) wide four-petalled flowers from mid-spring to early summer.

Height and spread Height 30–60 cm (12–24 inches); spread to 30 cm (12 inches).

Best site Full sun to partial shade; average to moist, well-drained soil, ideally with a neutral to slightly alkaline pH.

Growing guidelines Sow outdoors in early spring or indoors about eight weeks before your last frost date. Plant seed 6 mm (¼ inch) deep. Plant out 20–30 cm (8–12 inches) apart around the last frost date. In frost-free areas, grow wallflowers as biennials. Sow seed in pots or in a nursery bed in early summer; move plants to their flowering position in early autumn. Water during dry spells to keep the soil evenly moist. Compost plants when they have finished flowering.

Landscape use Grow in masses or in flower beds for spots of early colour. One classic combination is orange wallflowers underplanted with blue forget-me-nots (*Myosotis sylvatica*). Wallflowers also combine beautifully with tulips.

Cleome hassleriana
CLEOMACEAE

CLEOME

Cleome is a must for butterfly-attracting gardens; it's also popular with bees. Plant it in large groupings to show off the spidery white, pink or rosy lavender flowers.

Other common names Spider flower.

Description Cleome is a fast-growing half-hardy annual. Its tall, sturdy stems and palm-like leaves are slightly sticky and have a musky odour. Small spines form on the stems and on the undersides of the leaves. From midsummer until mid-autumn, the stems are topped with globes of four-petalled flowers. Long stamens protrude from the flowers, giving them a spidery look. The blooms are followed by long, narrow seed pods.

Height and spread Height 90–120 cm (3–4 feet); spread 45 cm (18 inches).

Best site Full sun to light shade; average, well-drained soil with added compost.

Growing guidelines Easy to grow from seed sown directly in the garden in mid- to late spring. For earlier flowers, buy transplants or start your own by sowing seed indoors about four weeks before your last frost date. Lightly press the seed into the surface, then enclose the pot in a plastic bag until seedlings appear. Plant out around the last frost date.

Landscape use Try cleome in the back of flower beds and borders. Its pretty, delicate blooms look particularly nice in cottage gardens.

Coleus x *hybridus (Solenostemon)*
LABIATAE

COLEUS

Keep favourite coleus plants from year to year by taking cuttings in summer; they'll root quickly in water. Pot up the cuttings for winter, then put them outdoors in spring.

Description These tender perennials are grown as bushy, tender annuals. Their sturdy, square stems carry showy, patterned leaves with scalloped or ruffled edges. Each leaf can have several different colours, with zones, edges or splashes in shades of red pink, orange, yellow and cream.
Height and spread Height 15–60 cm (6–24 inches); spread 20–30 cm (8–12 inches).
Best site Partial shade; average to moist, well-drained soil with added well-rotted organic matter.
Growing guidelines Buy transplants in spring, or grow your own by sowing seed indoors eight to ten weeks before your last frost date. Don't cover the seed; just press it lightly into the soil and enclose the pot in a plastic bag until seedlings appear. Plant out 20–30 cm (8–12 inches) apart after the last frost. Water during dry spells. Pinch out the spikes of the pale blue flowers to promote more leafy growth.
Landscape use Coleus are great for adding all-season colour to beds, borders and container plantings. Groups of mixed leaf patterns can look too busy when combined with flowering plants, so grow them alone in masses.

Coreopsis tinctoria
COMPOSITAE

CALLIOPSIS

Calliopsis grows easily from direct-sown seed and needs little fussing. Shearing the plants back by one-third in mid- to late summer can prolong the flowering season.

Description Calliopsis is a colourful, fast-growing, hardy annual. Its wiry stems carry narrow, green leaves and 2.5–5-cm (1–2-inch)-wide, single or double, daisy-like flowers. The flowers are usually golden yellow with maroon centres but may also be all yellow or all orange. Plants can flower from midsummer until frost.
Height and spread Height 30–90 cm (24–36 inches), depending on the cultivar; spread to 30 cm (12 inches).
Best site Full sun; average, well-drained soil. Adapts well to poor soil.
Growing guidelines Grows quickly from seed sown directly into the garden in early to mid-spring. You can also sow seed 3 mm (⅛ inch) deep indoors about six weeks before your last frost date. Plant out around the last frost date. Space transplants or thin seedlings to stand about 20 cm (8 inches) apart. Push twiggy brush into the soil around young plants of tall-growing cultivars to support the stems as they grow.
Landscape use Depend on calliopsis for adding fast, easy-care colour to beds and borders. It also looks wonderful in meadow gardens. Grow some in the cutting garden for fresh arrangements.

Cosmos bipinnatus
COMPOSITAE

COSMOS

Use fast-growing cosmos to fill spaces left by early-flowering annuals and perennials. Remove spent flowers to encourage more flowering; leave a few to self-sow.

Description These popular half-hardy annuals are grown for their colourful flowers. The bushy plants bear many finely cut, green leaves. In late summer and autumn, the stems are topped with white, pink or rosy red flowers. The single of semi-double daisy-like blooms can grow up to 10 cm (4 inches) across.
Height and spread Height 90–120 cm (3–4 feet); spread to 45 cm (18 inches).
Best site Full sun is best, although plants can take partial shade; average to moist, well-drained soil.
Growing guidelines For earliest flowers, buy transplants in spring or start seed indoors three to four weeks before your last frost date. Plant seed 6 mm (¼ inch) deep. Plant out 12 weeks after the last frost date. You can also sow seed directly into the garden around the last frost date. Pinch out stem tips in early summer to promote branching and more flowers. Stake individual stems as needed, or let plants sprawl and send up more flowering stems.
Landscape use Cosmos adds height and colour to flower beds, borders and meadows. They look great in cottage gardens. Grow a few in the cutting garden for arrangements.

Dianthus barbatus
CARYOPHYLLACEAE

SWEET WILLIAM

Sweet Williams may rebloom the following year if you shear them back after flowering, but you'll generally get a better show by growing new plants each year.

Description This short-lived perennial is grown as a hardy biennial or annual. It forms clumps of narrow, lance-shaped, green leaves and the stems are topped with dense, slightly rounded clusters of five-petalled flowers in early to mid- summer. Each fragrant bloom is 6–12 mm (¼–½-inch) wide. Red, pink and white are the most common colours; some flowers have eyes, or zones of contrasting colours.
Height and spread Height 30–45 cm (12–18 inches); spread 20–30 cm (8–12 inches).
Best site Full sun to partial shade; average, well-drained soil.
Growing guidelines For earliest flowers, grow as a biennial. Sow seed outdoors in pots or in a nursery bed in summer, then move plants to their garden position in autumn. For flowers the same year, sow seed indoors (just barely cover it) about eight weeks before your last frost date. Plant out two to three weeks before the last frost date. Space transplants 20–25 cm (8–10 inches) apart. Sweet William will self-sow if you leave a few flowers to form seeds.
Landscape use Sweet William looks super as an early-summer filler for beds and borders. It is ideal for fresh arrangements.

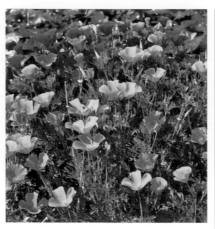

Eschscholzia californica
PAPAVERACEAE

CALIFORNIA POPPY

The cup-shaped flowers of California poppy open during sunny days but close in cloudy weather and at night. Pinch off developing seed pods to prolong the flowering season.

Description This tender perennial is usually grown as a hardy annual. Plants form loose clumps of deeply cut, blue-green leaves. The thin stems are topped with pointed buds that unfurl into single, semi-double or double flowers up to 7.5 cm (3 inches) across in early summer through early autumn. The silky-looking petals are usually orange or yellow, but they can also flower in white, pink or red.
Height and spread Height 30–45 cm (12–18 inches); spread 15–30 cm (6–12 inches).
Best site Full sun; average to sandy, well-drained soil.
Growing guidelines They transplant poorly, so it's usually not worth growing seed indoors. Plants will grow quickly from seed sown directly into the garden in very early spring (or even in autumn in frost-free areas). Scatter the seed over the soil surface and rake it in lightly. Thin seedlings to 15 cm (6 inches) apart. If blooms are sparse by midsummer, cut plants back by about one-third to encourage a new flush of flowers. Plants usually self-sow in mild-winter areas.
Landscape use Grow as fillers for flower beds and borders and in meadow gardens.

Gypsophila elegans
CARYOPHYLLACEAE

ANNUAL BABY'S BREATH

Sowing seed of annual baby's breath every two to three weeks from early to late spring can extend the flowering season well into summer. Pull out plants that have finished flowering.

Description This hardy annual is grown for its airy sprays of dainty flowers. Plants form loose clumps of slender stems with pairs of narrow, grey-green leaves. Loose clusters of many five-petalled flowers bloom atop the stems for up to two months in spring and early summer. The 6–12-mm (¼–½-inch) wide flowers are usually white or light pink; some cultivars have deeper pink flowers.
Height and spread Height 45–60 cm (18–24 inches); spread 15–30 cm (6–12 inches).
Best site Full sun (afternoon shade in hot areas); average, well-drained soil.
Growing guidelines Plant seed directly into the. garden where you want plants to grow; cover it with 3 mm (⅛ inch) of soil. Sow seed in early spring (or in autumn in mild winter areas). Thin seedlings to 15 cm (6 inches) apart. Push twiggy brush into the soil around young plants to support the stems as they grow.
Landscape use Makes a nice filler for flower beds and borders. It looks especially charming in masses with other cool-loving annuals, such as rocket larkspur (*Consolida ambigua*) and sweet peas (*Lathyrus odoratus*).

Helianthus annuus
COMPOSITAE

COMMON SUNFLOWER

Common sunflowers are much-loved hardy annuals grown for their large, showy blooms (and often for their tasty seeds as well). Tall cultivars will usually need staking.

Description This easy-to-grow plant produces large, sturdy stalks with coarse, heart-shaped leaves. From midsummer through mid-autumn, the stems are topped with flat, daisy-like flower heads to 30 cm (12 inches) wide or more. The flower heads normally have a purple-brown centre, with bright yellow, bronze, mahogany red or orange petals.
Height and spread Height 60–240 cm (2–8 feet) or more; spread 30–45 cm (12–18 inches).
Best site Thrives in full sun; needs average, well-drained soil.
Growing guidelines Common sunflowers grow so quickly that it's easiest to sow seed directly into the garden after your last frost date. Plant seed 12 mm (½ inch) deep. Thin seedlings to 30 cm (12 inches) apart. Unless you're growing plants for the edible seeds, remove spent flowers to prolong the flowering season.
Landscape use Sunflowers tend to drop their leaves along the bottom half of their stem, so place them in the middle or back of the border where other plants will hide their bare ankles. Small-flowered types are excellent as cut flowers. Plant seed-producing types in the vegetable garden.

Helichrysum bracteatum (Xerochrysum bracteatum)
COMPOSITAE

STRAWFLOWER

Cutting strawflowers for fresh arrangements or drying will promote branching and prolong the flowering season. The flowers dry quickly when hung upside down in a dark, airy place.

Description This half-hardy annual is grown for its colourful, long-lasting blooms. The bushy plants have long, narrow, green leaves and daisy-like flower heads with stiff, papery, petal-like bracts. The flower heads bloom from midsummer until frost in white, pink, rose, red, orange or yellow. Fully open flower heads are 2.5–5 cm (1–2 inches) wide and have yellow centres.
Height and spread Height 60–120 cm (24–48 inches); spread to 30 cm (12 inches).
Best site Needs full sun; average, well-drained soil.
Growing guidelines For earliest flowers, buy transplants or grow your own by sowing seed indoors six to eight weeks before your last frost date. Just press the seed lightly into the surface and enclose the pot in a plastic bag until seedlings appear. Plant out two weeks after the last frost date, or sow seed directly into the garden after the last frost date.
Landscape use Strawflowers add long-lasting colour to flower beds and borders. Grow an ample supply in the cutting garden for drying, as well. Harvest flowers when they are about one-quarter open; they'll open more as they dry.

Iberis umbellata
CRUCIFERAE

ANNUAL CANDYTUFT

Annual candytuft needs little care and tends to self-sow. In hot-summer areas, pull out plants after flowering and replace them with summer- to autumn-flowering annuals.

Other common names Globe candytuft.
Description This dependable, hardy annual forms mounds of narrow, green leaves on many-branched stems. The mounds are covered with dense, slightly rounded flower clusters approximately 5 cm (2 inches) across from late spring through midsummer. Each cluster contains many 6–12-mm (¼–½-inch) wide, four-petalled blooms. Flowers may be white, pink, pinkish purple, rose or red.
Height and spread Height 20–30 cm (8–12 inches); spread 20–25 cm (8–10 inches).
Best site Full sun to partial shade; average, well-drained soil.
Growing guidelines For the earliest flowers, sow seed indoors six to eight weeks before your last frost date. Plant seed 6 mm (¼ inch) deep. Plant out around the last frost date. Annual candytuft also grows easily from seed sown directly into the garden. Make the first sowing in early to mid- spring, sowing again every three to four weeks. Thin seedlings or space plants to 15–20 cm (6–8 inches) apart.
Landscape use Annual candytuft makes a colourful edging or filler for flower beds and borders.

Impatiens walleriana
BALSAMINACEAE

IMPATIENS

A mixed planting of impatiens makes a colourful annual groundcover under trees and shrubs. For good growth, they need moist soil; mulch them and water during dry spells.

Other common names Busy Lizzie, patient Lucy, patience, sultana.

Description Plants form neat, shrubby mounds of well-branched, succulent stems; the lance-shaped, green or bronze-brown leaves have slightly scalloped edges. The plants are covered with flat, spurred flowers up to 5 cm (2 inches) wide from late spring until frost. The single or double blooms may be white, pink, red, orange or lavender; some have an eye, or swirls of contrasting colours.

Height and spread Height 15–60 cm (6–24 inches); similar spread.

Best site Shade; average to moist, well-drained soil with added organic matter.

Growing guidelines Buy transplants in spring or sow seed indoors eight to ten weeks before your last frost date. Don't cover the seed; just press it lightly into the soil surface. Enclose the pot in a plastic bag and keep it in a warm place until seedlings appear. Young seedlings tend to grow slowly. Plant out about two weeks after your last frost date.

Landscape use Impatiens are the stars of shady gardens. Mix them with other annuals and perennials in beds and borders, or grow them alone in masses under trees.

Lathyrus odoratus
LEGUMINOSAE

SWEET PEA

Dozens of sweet pea cultivars are available in a range of heights and colours. Many modern cultivars aren't very fragrant; check catalogue descriptions to find scented types.

Description These old-fashioned hardy annuals are grown for their charming flowers. Plants produce leafy stems that climb by tendrils. Dainty, pea-like flowers to 5 cm (2 inches) long bloom on long, slender flower stems from mid-spring into summer. Flower colours are usually white or bright or pastel shades of pink, red or purple. The flowers often have crimped or ruffled petals.

Height and spread Height usually 1.2–1.8 m (4–6 feet); spread 15–30 cm (6–12 inches).

Best site Full sun (or afternoon shade in hot-summer areas); loose, evenly moist soil enriched with organic matter.

Growing guidelines Before planting, set up some sort of string or netting trellis for the plants to climb. Start seed indoors six to eight weeks before your last frost date. Soak seed in warm water overnight, then plant 12 mm (½ inch) deep in peat pots. Plant out in mid-spring, after danger of frost, or sow seed directly into the garden in early spring.

Landscape use Train sweet peas to climb a tripod of stakes as an early-season accent for beds, borders and cottage gardens. Include them in the cutting garden.

Limonium sinuatum
PLUMBAGI NACEAE

ANNUAL STATICE

Annual statice is a natural for fresh or dried arrangements. To dry it, pick stems when the clusters are about three-quarters open; hang them in a dark, airy place.

Description This biennial or tender perennial is usually grown as a half-hardy annual. Plants form low rosettes of wavy-edged, green leaves that send up sturdy, winged stems in summer. The loosely branched stems are topped with flattened clusters of 6-mm (¼-inch) wide, white flowers, each surrounded by a papery, tubular calyx – the colourful part of the flower head. Annual statice comes in many colours, including white, pink, peach, red, orange, yellow, purple and blue.

Height and spread Height 30–60 cm (12–24 inches); spread to 30 cm (12 inches).

Best site Needs full sun; average, well-drained soil.

Growing guidelines Buy transplants in spring, or sow seed indoors six to eight weeks before your last frost date. Plant the seed 3 mm (¼ inch) deep. Move seedlings to individual pots when they have two or three sets of leaves. Plant them in the garden around the last frost date, or sow seed directly into the garden after the last frost date. Space transplants or thin seedlings to 20–25 cm (8–10 inches) apart. Established plants need little care.

Landscape use An attractive filler for flower beds and borders.

Lobelia erinus
CAMPANULACEAE

EDGING LOBELIA

If you grow edging lobelia from seed or buy seedlings in trays, transplant them in clumps (rather than separating them into individual plants) to avoid damaging the stems.

Description This tender perennial is usually grown as a half-hardy annual. Plants form trailing or mounding clumps of slender stems with small, narrow, green leaves. Plants are covered with 12–18-mm (½–¼-inch) wide flowers from late spring until frost. The five-petalled flowers bloom in white and shades of blue, purple and pinkish red.
Height and spread Height 15–20 cm (6–8 inches); spread 15–25 cm (6–10 inches).
Best site Full sun to partial shade (especially in hot-summer areas); average, well drained soil with added compost.
Growing guidelines Buy transplants in spring, or grow your own by sowing seed indoors eight to ten weeks before your last frost date. Don't cover the seed; just press it lightly into the soil and enclose the pot in a plastic bag until seedlings appear. Plant out 15–20 cm (6–8 inches) apart after the last frost date. Water during dry spells. Shear plants back by half after each flush of flowers and fertilise for rebloom.
Landscape use Looks great along the front of beds and borders or as a filler among taller plants. Cascading types make attractive fillers for container gardens.

Lobularia maritima
CRUCIFERAE

SWEET ALYSSUM

Sweet alyssum may stop flowering during summer heat but will start again when cool weather returns. Shear off spent flowers and water thoroughly to promote new growth.

Description Sweet alyssum is a tender perennial grown as a hardy annual. Plants form low mounds of many-branched stems and narrow, green leaves. Domed clusters of many 6-mm (¼-inch) flowers cover plants in summer and autumn. The sweetly scented, four-petalled flowers bloom in white and shades of pink and purple. Sweet alyssum is also listed in seed catalogues as *Alyssum maritimum*.
Height and spread Height 10–20 cm (4–8 inches); spread 25–30 cm (10–12 inches).
Best site Full sun to partial shade (especially in hot-summer areas); average, well-drained soil.
Growing guidelines Buy transplants in spring, or sow seed indoors six to eight weeks before your last frost date. Just barely cover the seed with soil. Plant out around the last frost date. It also grows easily from seed sown directly into the garden in mid- to late spring. Space transplants or thin seedlings to stand 15 cm (6 inches) apart.
Landscape use Grow as an edging or filler in flower beds and borders or as groundcover under roses and shrubs. It also grows well in container gardens.

Malcomia maritima
CRUCIFERAE

VIRGINIA STOCK

Virginia stock can flower in as little as four weeks from seed sown directly into the garden. Sow every three to four weeks through midsummer to have flowers from summer until first frost.

Description The upright, branching stems of this fast-growing hardy annual carry small, pointed, greyish green leaves. Flat, four-petalled, lightly fragrant flowers bloom in loose clusters atop the stems. The purple, pink or white flowers are 6–12 mm (¼–½ inch) wide.
Height and spread Height 10–20 cm (6–8 inches); spread to 10 cm (4 inches).
Best site Full sun to partial shade (in hot-summer areas); average, well-drained soil.
Growing guidelines Grows best from seed sown directly in the garden. For the longest flowering season, sow at three to four week intervals from early spring through midsummer. (In mild-winter areas, you can sow in autumn for even earlier spring flowering.) Rake the seedbed to cover the seed lightly, then keep the soil moist until seedlings appear. Thin seedlings to 7.5–10 cm (3–4 inches) apart. Plants will often self-sow freely.
Landscape use Virginia stock makes a nice filler or edging annual for flower beds and borders. The flowers are very popular with bees.

Matthiola incana
CRUCIFERAE

COMMON STOCK

The fragrant, single or double flowers of common stock bloom in white and shades of pink, red, yellow and purple. They are wonderful in the garden or in arrangements.

Description This biennial or short-lived perennial is usually grown as a hardy annual. The fast-growing, bushy plants have upright stems and lance-shaped, greyish leaves. The stems are topped with spikes of four-petalled, 2.5-cm (1-inch) wide flowers in summer.
Height and spread Height 30–60 cm (12–24 inches); spread to 30 cm (12 inches).
Best site Full sun; average, well-drained soil with added organic matter.
Growing guidelines Grows easily from seed sown directly into the garden. Make the first sowing about one month before your last frost date. To extend the flowering season, make another sowing in late spring or early summer. (In mild-winter areas, you can also sow in late summer for winter and early-spring flowers.) Scatter seed on the soil surface, then rake lightly to just cover the seed. Keep the seedbed moist until seedlings appear. Thin seedlings to 15–20 cm (6–8 inches) apart. Mulch plants to keep the roots cool and moist. Water during dry spells.
Landscape use Use as a filler in beds and borders near your house or outdoor sitting areas, where you can enjoy the sweet fragrance.

Myosotis sylvatica
BORAGINACEAE

FORGET-ME-NOT

Forget-me-not blooms are often sky blue with white or yellow centres, but they can also be pink or white. They are ideal companions for spring bulbs and other early annuals.

Description These short-lived perennials are usually grown as hardy biennials or annuals. Plants form dense clumps of narrow, lance-shaped, hairy leaves. Sprays of many 8-mm (⅓-inch) wide flowers bloom over the leaves from mid-spring through early summer.
Height and spread Height usually 30–45 cm (12–18 inches); spread 20–25 cm (8–10 inches).
Best site Partial shade; average to moist, well-drained soil with added compost.
Growing guidelines To grow forget-me-nots as biennials, sow seed outdoors in pots or in a nursery bed in spring or summer. Plant seed 3 mm (⅛ inch) deep. Move plants to the garden in early autumn. For flowers the same year, buy plants in early spring, or grow seed indoors four to six weeks before your last frost date. Plant out 12 weeks before the last frost date. Space plants or thin seedlings to 15 cm (6 inches) apart. Water during dry spells. Shearing off spent flowers often promotes rebloom. Plants often self-sow freely.
Landscape use Forget-me-nots are invaluable for spring colour in shady gardens. Try them as early-season groundcover under shrubs.

Nemesia strumosa
SCROPHULARIACEAE

NEMESIA

Nemesia usually stops flowering in warm weather, but plants may recover and rebloom if you cut them back by half, water thoroughly and give them a dose of fertiliser.

Description Nemesia is a tender, cool-weather annual grown for its beautiful flowers. Plants form clumps of branched stems with pairs of narrow, slightly toothed, green leaves. Clusters of trumpet-shaped, lipped flowers bloom atop the stems in summer. The 2.5-cm (1-inch) wide flowers bloom in a range of colours, including white, pink, red, orange, yellow, lilac and even light blue.
Height and spread Height 30–60 cm (12–24 inches); spread 15–20 cm (6–8 inches).
Best site Full sun to partial shade; evenly moist, well-drained soil with added organic matter. Nemesia needs a long, cool growing season; it does not tolerate heat or humidity.
Growing guidelines Grow seed indoors six to eight weeks before your last frost date. (In mild-winter areas, you can also sow in autumn for winter flowers.) Sow seed 3 mm (⅛ inch) deep. Plant out 10–15 cm (4–6 inches) apart after the last frost date.
Landscape use Nemesia makes an attractive edging for flower beds and borders. It is also showy when planted in masses for early-summer colour. Try a few in containers and window boxes.

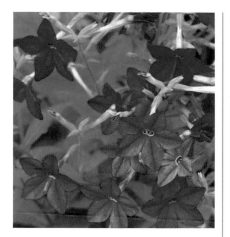

Nicotiana alata
SOLANACEAE

FLOWERING TOBACCO

Hybrids and red-flowered types of flowering tobacco often have little or no scent, but old-fashioned, white-flowered types tend to be quite fragrant, especially at night.

Description This tender perennial is usually grown as a half-hardy annual. Plants form lush rosettes of broad, oval to pointed, green leaves and many-branched stems; both the stems and leaves are sticky and hairy. Trumpet-shaped flowers to 5 cm (2 inches) across bloom atop the stems from midsummer until frost. Flowers come in a range of colours, including white, pink, purple and red.
Height and spread Height 45–90 cm (18–36 inches); spread to 30 cm (12 inches).
Best site Full sun to partial shade; average to moist, well-drained soil with added organic matter.
Growing guidelines Buy transplants in spring, or grow seed indoors six to eight weeks before your last frost date. Don't cover the fine seed; just press it into the soil and enclose the pot in a plastic bag until seedlings appear. Plant out 25–30 cm (10–12 inches) apart after the last frost date. Water during dry spells. Cut out spent stems to prolong the flowering season. Plants may self-sow.
Landscape use Excellent as a filler or accent in beds and borders. Grow some in the cutting garden and plant fragrant types around outdoor sitting areas.

Nigella damascena
RANUNCULACEAE

LOVE-IN-A-MIST

Sowing every three to four weeks from early spring to early summer can extend the flowering season of love-in-a-mist through the summer and possibly into autumn.

Other common names Fennel flower, devil-in-the-bush.
Description A fast-growing, hardy annual that forms bushy mounds of slender stems and thread-like, bright green leaves. Single or double, 2.5–5-cm (1–2-inch) wide flowers are nestled into the leaves at the tops of the stems. The blue, pink or white flowers are followed by swollen, striped seed pods with short, pointed horns.
Height and spread Height 45–60 cm (18–24 inches); spread 15–20 cm (6–8 inches).
Best site Full sun to partial shade; average, well-drained soil.
Growing guidelines For the earliest flowers, grow seed indoors six to eight weeks before your last frost date. Sow seed (just barely cover it with soil) in peat pots. Move plants to the garden after the last frost date. In most cases, though, you'll get better results by sowing directly into the garden, starting in early spring. Space transplants or thin seedlings to 15 cm (6 inches) apart. Established plants are care-free. Plants may self-sow.
Landscape use Grow as a filler in beds, borders and cottage gardens. It's also a natural for the cutting garden. Leave some plants to mature into the puffy seed pods.

Papaver nudicaule
PAPAVERACEAE

ICELAND POPPY

Removing spent flower stems can prolong Iceland poppy's flowering season. As summer approaches and new growth slows, leave a few flowers to mature so plants can self-sow.

Description This short-lived perennial is usually grown as a hardy biennial or annual. Plants form compact rosettes of hairy, deeply cut, grey-green leaves. Long, slender, leafless stems are topped with plump, hairy, nodding buds that open to bowl-shaped, four-petalled flowers. The 5–10-cm (2–4-inch) wide, lightly fragrant flowers have crinkled petals. They flower mainly in early to mid-summer in a range of vibrant colours, including white, pink, red, orange and yellow.
Height and spread Height 30–45 cm (12–18 inches); spread 10–15 cm (4–6 inches).
Best site Full sun; average, well-drained to dry soil. Grows poorly in hot weather.
Growing guidelines Easiest to grow from seed sown directly into the garden. Plant in late autumn or very early spring for summer flowers. (In hot-summer areas, sow this cool-loving plant in late summer to early autumn for spring flowers.) Scatter the fine seed over the soil and rake it in lightly. Thin seedlings to about 15 cm (6 inches) apart.
Landscape use Plant Iceland poppies for early colour in beds and borders; follow them with summer-flowering annuals. Grow some in the cutting garden, too, for fresh cut flowers.

Pelargonium x hortorum
GERANIACEAE

ZONAL GERANIUM

Colourful and dependable, zonal geraniums are a mainstay of summer flower gardens. You can also bring them indoors in the autumn and enjoy their flowers through the winter.

Description The sturdy, branched stems carry hairy, rounded, bright to dark green leaves with scalloped margins. The pungent leaves are often marked with dark green or brown, curved bands (zones). Plants produce thin but sturdy stems topped with rounded clusters of many 5-cm (2-inch) wide flowers. The single or double flowers bloom from late spring until frost in white or shades of pink, red, salmon and bicolours.
Height and spread Height 30–60 cm (12–24 inches); spread 30–45 cm (12–18 inches).
Best site Full sun to partial shade; average, well-drained soil.
Growing guidelines If you just need a few geraniums or if you want special kinds (such as those with double flowers or fancy leaves), start with a few purchased plants in spring. During the summer, pinch out spent flower stems to promote rebloom. To save special plants for next year, dig them up in autumn, move them into pots and grow them on a sunny windowsill. Take 10-cm (4-inch) long cuttings from the shoot tips in spring.
Landscape use Grow them alone in masses, or tuck them into beds and borders.

Petunia x hybrida
SOLANACEAE

PETUNIA

Petunias are tender perennials usually grown as half-hardy annuals. They may self-sow, but the seedlings seldom resemble the parent plants.

Description Plants form clumps of upright or trailing stems with oval, green leaves. Funnel-shaped, single or double flowers bloom from early summer until frost in nearly every colour of the rainbow; some have stripes, streaks or bands of contrasting colours.
Height and spread Height 15–25 cm (6–10 inches); spread to 30 cm (12 inches).
Best site Full sun (can take light shade); average to moist, well-drained soil.
Growing guidelines Petunias are among the most popular annuals, and many types are sold as transplants each spring. You can also grow your own from seed, although the fine, dust-like seed can be hard to handle. If you want to try, sow the seed indoors eight to ten weeks before your last frost date. Don't cover the seed; just press it lightly into the soil and enclose the pot in a plastic bag until seedlings appear. Move plants to the garden 12 weeks after the last frost date; space them 20–30 cm (8–12 inches) apart. Water during dry spells.
Landscape use Petunias – especially the multiflora and floribunda types – are favourites for flower beds and borders, planted alone in masses or mixed with other plants. They are particularly good for filling in gaps in the garden.

Phlox drummondii
POLEMONIACEAE

ANNUAL PHLOX

Annual phlox is a hardy annual grown for its colourful flowers. If plants stop blooming, cut them back by half and water thoroughly; they should resprout and rebloom in autumn.

Description Plants form bushy clumps of narrow, lance-shaped, green leaves. From midsummer to autumn, the leafy stems are topped with clusters of flat, five-petalled flowers, each 12–25 mm (½–1 inch) across. The flowers bloom in a wide range of colours, including white, pink, red, pale yellow, blue and purple; some have a contrasting eye.
Height and spread Height 15–45 cm (6–18 inches), depending on the cultivar; spread 15–20 cm (6–8 inches).
Best site Needs full sun; average, well-drained soil.
Growing guidelines For the earliest flowers, buy transplants in spring, or grow seed indoors six to eight weeks before the last frost date. Sow seed 3 mm (⅛ inch) deep in individual pots. Plant out around the last frost date. You can also sow seed directly into the garden around the last frost date. Set plants or thin seedlings to stand 15 cm (6 inches) apart. Pinching off spent flowers and watering during dry spells can prolong the flowering season.
Landscape use An excellent filler for flower beds and borders. Try the compact cultivars in container gardens. Tall cultivars are excellent cut flowers.

Portulaca grandiflora
PORTULACACEAE

ROSE MOSS

Rose moss comes in many vibrant colours, including white, pink, red, orange, yellow and magenta. The flowers tend to close by afternoon and stay closed on cloudy days.

Description A low-growing, tender annual, rose moss forms creeping mats of fleshy, many-branched stems with small, thick, almost needle-like leaves. Single or double, 2.5-cm (1-inch) wide flowers bloom from early summer through autumn.
Height and spread Height to 15 cm (6 inches); spread 15–20 cm (6–8 inches).
Best site Full sun; average, well-drained to dry soil.
Growing guidelines For earliest flowers, buy transplants in spring, or sow seed indoors six to eight weeks before your last frost date. For easy transplanting later, sow the seed in cell packs or small pots. Do not cover the seed; just press it lightly into the soil and enclose the containers in a plastic bag until seedlings appear. Plant out 12 weeks after the last frost date, when the soil is warm; space them about 15 cm (6 inches) apart. You can also sow the fine seed directly into the garden after the last frost date; keep the soil moist until seedlings appear. Thin seedlings only if they're crowded. Plants may self-sow.
Landscape use Makes great groundcover for dry, rocky slopes. It also looks charming as an edging for sunny beds and borders.

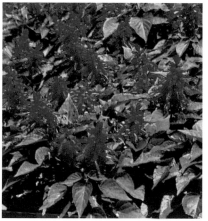

Salvia splendens
LABIATAE

SCARLET SAGE

Compact cultivars of scarlet sage tend to flower mostly in summer; taller types generally start flowering in midsummer and last until frost. Pinch off faded spikes.

Description This tender perennial is grown as a half-hardy annual. Plants form clumps of upright stems with oval, deep green leaves that have pointed tips and slightly toothed edges. The stems are topped with thick, showy spikes of colourful, petal-like bracts and 3.5-cm (1½-inch) long tubular flowers. The flowers are most often red, but they are also available in white, pink, salmon and purple.
Height and spread Height 30–60 cm (12–24 inches); spread to 30 cm (12 inches).
Best site Needs full sun; average, well drained soil.
Growing guidelines Widely sold as transplants in spring. If you really want to grow your own, sow indoors eight to ten weeks before your last frost date. Don't cover the seed; just press it lightly into the soil and enclose the pot in a plastic bag until seedlings appear. Plant out after the last frost date; space them 20–30 cm (8–12 inches) apart. Fertilise several times during the summer.
Landscape use If you enjoy mixing bright colours, grow scarlet sage as an edging or filler for flower beds and borders. For a somewhat more restrained effect, surround scarlet sage with leafy green herbs.

Senecio cineraria
COMPOSITAE

DUSTY MILLER

Dusty miller can live through mild winters, but second-year plants tend to be more open Where uniformity is important (as in an edging), start with new plants each year.

Description This tender perennial is usually grown as a half-hardy annual. Plants form shrubby mounds of deeply lobed leaves that are covered with matted, white hairs. The plants may produce clusters of daisy-like yellow flowers in summer, but these are usually removed so they won't detract from the silvery foliage. Dusty miller is also listed in seed catalogues as *Cineraria maritima*.
Height and spread Height 20–60 cm (8–24 inches); spread to 30 cm (12 inches).
Best site Needs full sun; average, well-drained soil.
Growing guidelines Buy transplants in spring. They grow slowly from seed, but if you want to raise your own, sow seed indoors eight to ten weeks before your last frost date. Don't cover the seed; just press it lightly into the soil and enclose the pot in a plastic bag until seedlings appear. Plant out after the last frost date; space them 20 cm (8 inches) apart. Pinch out stem tips in early summer for bushy growth.
Landscape use Dusty miller's silvery foliage is invaluable as an edging or accent for flower beds, borders and all kinds of container plantings. The silvery leaves and stems also dry well.

Tagetes hybrids
COMPOSITAE

MARIGOLDS

Marigolds can add bright colour to any sunny spot. Mix them with other annuals and perennials, or grow them alone in masses. Tall-stemmed types may need staking.

Description These popular half-hardy annuals are grown for their bright, 5–10-cm (2–4-inch) wide summer flowers and bushy mounds of lacy, green leaves. African or American marigolds (*T. erecta*) tend to be large plants, with 45–90-cm (18–36-inch) stems and large, usually double, yellow or orange flowers. French marigolds (*T. patula*) tend to be much daintier, with many smaller, single or double flowers in yellow, orange or red on 30-cm (12-inch) tall plants.

Height and spread Height 15–90 cm (6–36 inches); spread 15–45 cm (6–18 inches).

Best site Full sun; average, well-drained soil. Light afternoon shade can help prolong flowering in hot-summer areas, especially for creamy-flowered cultivars.

Growing guidelines For earliest flowers (especially for tall-growing types), sow seed indoors four to six weeks before your last frost date. Plant seed 3–6 mm (⅛–¼ inch) deep. Plant out after your last frost date. You can also sow seed of small, early-flowering types directly into the garden after the last frost date.

Landscape use Grow as summer fillers or edgings for flower beds and borders.

Tithonia rotundifolia
COMPOSITAE

MEXICAN SUNFLOWER

Mexican sunflowers are popular with bees and butterflies, and they make good cut flowers. Pinch off spent blooms to extend the flowering season.

Other common names Torch flower.

Description Mexican sunflower is a half-hardy annual with colourful blooms. Plants produce tall, sturdy, hairy stems with velvety, lobed or broadly oval, pointed, dark green leaves. During summer, the shrubby clumps are accented with many 7.5-cm (3-inch) wide, glowing orange, daisy-like flowers.

Height and spread Height 1.2–1.8 m (4–6 feet); spread 45–60 cm (18–24 inches).

Best site Full sun; average, well-drained soil with added organic matter.

Growing guidelines For earliest flowers; sow seed indoors six to eight weeks before your last frost date. Sow seed 6 mm (¼ inch) deep in individual pots (two or three seeds per pot); thin to leave one seedling per pot. Plant out after the last frost date. Mexican sunflowers also grow quickly and easily from seed sown directly into the garden about two weeks after the last frost date. Plant or thin seedlings to 45 cm (18 inches) apart. Water during dry spells. Plants growing in exposed sites may need staking.

Landscape use Makes an attractive flowering screen or hedge. It also looks great as a tall accent or background plant.

Torenia fournieri
LINDERNIACEAE

WISHBONE FLOWER

Wishbone flowers are usually purplish blue with a yellow throat; they may also be white or pink. The mouth of each flower has two short, curved stamens that resemble a wishbone.

Other common names Bluewings.

Description This tender, shade-loving annual forms clumps of upright, many-branched stems with oval, pointed to narrow, toothed, green leaves that take on reddish purple tints in autumn. The stems are topped with trumpet-shaped, lipped blooms to 2.5 cm (1 inch) long from early summer through autumn.

Height and spread Height to 30 cm (12 inches); spread 15–20 cm (6–8 inches).

Best site Partial shade; moist, well-drained soil. Plants can take more sun in cool-climate gardens.

Growing guidelines Sow seed indoors eight to ten weeks before your last frost date. Don't cover the seed; just press it lightly into the soil. Enclose the pot in a plastic bag, and set it in a warm, dark place. When seedlings appear (in about one week), remove the bag and set the pot in a bright place. Plant out after the last frost date; space them 15 cm (6 inches) apart. Water during dry spells. If plants start to flop, shear them back by about half to promote branching.

Landscape use Use as an edging or filler for shady beds and borders. It also looks good in containers and window boxes.

Tropaeolum majus
TROPAEOLACEAE

GARDEN NASTURTIUM

Garden nasturtiums are half-hardy annuals with brightly coloured flowers. Bushy types are great as edgings or fillers for beds and borders. Nasturtiums may self-sow.

Description Plants grow either as a climbing or trailing vine or as a bushy mound. The plants bear showy, fragrant, five-petalled blooms to 5 cm (2 inches) wide from early summer through autumn. Garden nasturtiums bloom in a range of colours, including cream, rose, red, orange and yellow.

Height and spread Height of climbing types to about 2.4 m (8 feet), bush types to about 30 cm (12 inches); spread 15–30 cm (6–12 inches).

Best site Full sun; average, well-drained to dry soil.

Growing guidelines If you're growing climbing types, put up some kind of support before planting. For an extra-early start, sow seed indoors four to six weeks before your last frost date. Soak the seed overnight before planting, then sow it 6–12 mm (¼–½ inch) deep in peat pots. Plant out after the last frost date. They will also grow easily from seed sown directly into the garden 12 weeks before your last frost date. Watch for aphids; use a strong spray of water to wash them off.

Landscape use Use climbing types to quickly cover trellises; grow the compact types in containers or as edgings or fillers.

Viola x wittrockiana
VIOLACEAE

PANSY

To keep pansies happy, mulch the soil around them and water during dry spells to keep the roots moist. Pinching off spent flowers can prolong flowering; leave a few to self-sow.

Description These short-lived perennials are usually grown as hardy annuals or biennials. Plants form tidy clumps of oval to narrow, green leaves with rounded teeth. Flat, five-petalled flowers bloom just above the clumps, mainly in spring but also sometimes in autumn. The 5–12.5-cm (2–5-inch) wide flowers bloom in a range of colours, including white, pink, red, orange, yellow, purple, blue and near black; many have contrasting faces.

Height and spread Height 15–20 cm (6–8 inches); spread 20–30 cm (8–12 inches).

Best site Full sun to partial shade; moist, well-drained soil.

Growing guidelines For flowers the same year, buy plants in early spring or sow seed indoors eight to ten weeks before your last frost date. Sow seed 3 mm (⅛ inch) deep. Set the pot in a refrigerator for 12 weeks, then move it to a bright place. Plant seedlings out 12 weeks before your last frost date. To grow pansies as biennials for earlier spring flowers, sow the seed outdoors in a nursery bed in late spring; move plants to the garden in mid-autumn.

Landscape use Use them as fillers or as an edging. They are also cute in containers.

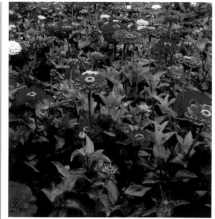

Zinnia elegans
COMPOSITAE

COMMON ZINNIA

Common zinnias are excellent for replacing early-flowering annuals and filling in gaps left by dormant spring-flowering bulbs and perennials. They are also great cut flowers.

Description Plants produce stiff, sturdy stems with pairs of oval to pointed, green leaves. The stems are topped with blooms from midsummer until frost in nearly every colour of the rainbow (except true blue). Common zinnias come in a range of flower forms, from 2.5–15 cm (1–6 inches) across. The petals of the single or double flowers may be quilled (curled), ruffled or flat.

Height and spread Height 15–90 cm (6–36 inches), depending on the cultivar; spread usually 30–60 cm (12–24 inches).

Best site Full sun; average, well-drained soil with added organic matter.

Growing guidelines Buy transplants in spring, or sow seed indoors three to four weeks before your last frost date. Plant seed 6–12 mm (¼–½ inch) deep in peat pots (two or three seeds per pot). Thin seedlings to one per pot. Plant out after the last frost date. Common zinnias also grow quickly from seed sown directly into the garden one to two weeks after the last frost date, when the soil is warm. Mulch plants to keep the roots moist. Tall cultivars may need staking.

Landscape use Grow them alone in masses, or mix them with other plants in flower beds, borders and cottage gardens.

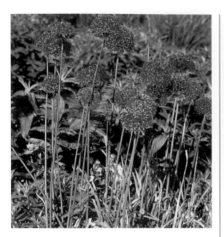

Allium giganteum
ALLIACEAE

GIANT ONION

The large bulbs of giant onion produce showy flower heads in early summer. Plant perennials or summer-flowering annuals at the base to fill in when the bulbs become dormant.

Description Wide, flat, sprawling, blue-green leaves emerge in mid- to late spring; they have an oniony odour when bruised. A tall, slender stem rises from the centre of the leaves in late spring. By early to mid-summer, the stem is topped with a 15-cm (6-inch) globe that's densely packed with many small, reddish purple flowers. The leaves will turn yellow and die back to the ground by midsummer.
Height and spread Height of leaves usually 15–30 cm (6–12 inches); flower stems grow to 1.5 m (5 feet). Spread to about 30 cm (12 inches).
Best site and climate Full sun, but tolerates light shade; average, well-drained soil. Zones 5–8.
Growing guidelines Plant bulbs in early to mid-autumn or in early spring. Set them in individual holes or larger planting areas dug 20 cm (8 inches) deep. In Zones 5 and 6, protect bulbs over winter with a loose mulch; remove in spring. Cut down spent flower stems, unless you want to collect seed or use the dried seed head for arrangements. Leave established bulbs undisturbed in the garden.
Landscape use A show-stopping accent for the back of flower beds and borders.

Anemone blanda
RANUNCULACEAE

GRECIAN WINDFLOWER

Grecian windflowers bloom in mid- to late spring in most areas; in warm-climate gardens, they may appear in late winter or early spring. They thrive in sun or light shade.

Description Grecian windflowers grow from knobbly tubers to produce carpets of deeply lobed, toothed, green leaves. Daisy-like blue, pink, or white spring flowers to 5 cm (2 inches) across bloom just above the ferny leaves.
Height and spread Height of leaves and flowers to 15 cm (6 inches); spread 10–15 cm (4–6 inches).
Best site and climate Full sun to partial shade (ideally under deciduous trees and shrubs); average to moist, well-drained soil. Zones 5–8.
Growing guidelines Buy and plant the tubers in late spring through early autumn. Soak them overnight before planting, then set them in individual holes or larger planting areas dug about 5 cm (2 inches) deep. It can be hard to tell which side is up. If you can see a shallow depression on one side, plant with that side up; otherwise, plant the tubers on their sides or just drop them into the hole. Space the tubers 10–15 cm (4–6 inches) apart. Grecian windflowers propagate themselves by spreading and self-sowing.
Landscape use Naturalise masses of them under trees for sheets of spring colour. They combine well with daffodils.

Begonia x *tuberhybrida*
BEGONIACEAE

HYBRID TUBEROUS BEGONIA

Hybrid tuberous begonias flower in a wide range of colours, except for blues and purples; many are edged or shaded with other colours. Pinch off spent flowers to keep plants tidy.

Description Hybrid tuberous begonias grow from flattened, circular, light brown tubers. These tubers produce fleshy, upright or trailing stems with pointed oval to heart-shaped, hairy, toothed, green leaves. The bushy plants produce an abundance of gorgeous single or double flowers up to 10 cm (4 inches) across from summer through autumn.
Height and spread Height to 45 cm (18 inches); spread 30–45 cm (12–18 inches).
Best site and climate Partial shade; evenly moist but well-drained soil with added organic matter. Hardy in Zone 10; elsewhere, grow as annuals or store indoors in winter.
Growing guidelines Buy thick tubers that are 3.5–5 cm (1½–2 inches) across. Start them growing indoors about four weeks before your last frost date. Give developing plants plenty of bright light, and keep the soil evenly moist. Plant out when night temperatures stay above 10°C (50°F). Water and mulch to keep the soil evenly moist. Fertilise several times during the season.
Landscape use Plants are beautiful in shaded beds and borders and in containers and hanging baskets.

Caladium x *hortulanum*
ARACEAE

CALADIUM

Caladiums are grown for their showy leaves; pinch out any of the small, hooded flowers that appear in summer. These shade-loving plants thrive in heat and humidity.

Description Caladiums grow from tubers. They produce bushy clumps of long-stalked and usually heart-shaped leaves from late spring until first frost. The lush leaves are shaded and veined with combinations of green, white, pink and red.
Height and spread Height 30–60 cm (12–24 inches); spread to 30 cm (24 inches).
Best site and climate Partial shade; moist but well-drained soil with added organic matter. Hardy in Zone 10; elsewhere, grow as annuals or store indoors for winter.
Growing guidelines Grow the tubers indoors in early spring. Pot them with the knobby side up in pots of moist potting compost, and cover them with 5 cm (2 inches) more soil. Keep them in a warm, bright spot and keep the soil evenly moist. Move plants out to the garden when night temperatures stay above 16°C (60°F); space them about 30 cm (12 inches) apart. Mulch and water as needed to keep the soil moist until late summer. When the leaves die, dig up the tubers and store them in a warm place.
Landscape use Caladiums provide summer colour in shady beds and borders, especially in warm- and hot-summer areas.

Camassia quamash
ASPARAGACEAE

COMMON CAMASSIA

In full sun, steady soil moisture is critical for success with common camassia; in lightly shaded spots, the bulbs can withstand drier conditions.

Other common names Quamash, wild hyacinth.
Description In spring, common camassia produces grassy clumps of long, narrow, grey-green leaves. By late spring, these clumps send up leafless stems topped with dense, spiky flower clusters. These spikes are made up of many 2.5–5-cm (1–2-inch) wide, starry flowers in white, or pale to deep blue. The leaves die in mid- to late summer. Common camassia is also sold as *C. esculenta*.
Height and spread Height 60–75 cm (24–30 inches); spread to 30 cm (12 inches).
Best site and climate Full sun to partial shade; moist but not waterlogged soil. Zones 4–8.
Growing guidelines The bulbs usually aren't available for sale at garden centres, so you'll probably have to buy them from a mail-order source. Plant the bulbs as soon as they arrive in autumn. Set them in individual holes or in larger planting areas about 10 cm (4 inches) deep. Space the bulbs 20–25 cm (8–10 inches) apart. Cut down faded flower stems after flowering.
Landscape use A natural choice for planting in low spots or along streams and ponds. It also grows well with moisture-loving shrubs and perennials.

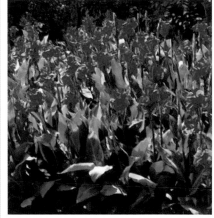

Canna x *generalis*
CANNACEAE

CANNA

Cannas are drought tolerant, but they grow even better with mulch and watering during dry spells. Pinch off spent flowers to prolong flowering.

Description Cannas grow from thick rhizomes. They produce tall, sturdy stems with large, oval, green or reddish purple leaves from spring until first frost. The stems are topped with showy clusters of broad petalled flowers up to 12.5 cm (5 inches) across from mid- to late summer. The flowers bloom in shades of pink, red, orange and yellow, as well as bicolours.
Height and spread Height 60–180 cm (2–6 feet) or more; spread 30–60 cm (12–24 inches).
Best site and climate Full sun to partial shade; average to moist, well-drained soil with added organic matter. Usually hardy in Zones 7–10; elsewhere, grow as annuals or store indoors in winter.
Growing guidelines For the earliest flowers, start rhizomes indoors in pots about one month before your last frost date. Set out started plants two to three weeks after the last frost date. Or plant rhizomes directly into the garden around that time, planting them 7.5–10 cm (3–4 inches) deep and 30–45 cm (12–18 inches) apart.
Landscape use Grow them alone in masses, or plant them with annuals and perennials in beds and borders. Cannas also grow well in containers.

Colchicum speciosum
COLCHICACEAE

SHOWY AUTUMN CROCUS

Showy autumn crocus grows from large, plump corms. Once established, each corm will produce showy clumps of rosy pink flowers in late summer to early autumn.

Description Wide, flat, glossy green leaves emerge in late autumn or early spring, elongate through spring, then turn yellow and die to the ground in early summer. Rosy pink, 10-cm (4-inch) wide, goblet-shaped, stemless flowers rise directly from the ground in late summer to early autumn.
Height and spread Height of leaves to about 20 cm (8 inches); flowers 10–15 cm (4–6 inches) tall. Spread to about 15 cm (6 inches).
Best site and climate Full sun to partial shade; average, well-drained soil. Zones 4–9.
Growing guidelines Plant corms in mid- to late summer, as soon as they are available; they may begin to bloom even before you plant them if you delay. Plant the corms in individual holes or in larger planting areas dug about 10 cm (4 inches) deep. Space bulbs 15 cm (6 inches) apart. Divide just after the leaves die down only if needed for propagation.
Landscape use Showy autumn crocus is beautiful but a little tricky to site effectively. It's usually best coming up through low groundcover or under shrubs, where the coarse spring leaves won't detract from or smother other flowers.

Crocus vernus
IRIDACEAE

DUTCH CROCUS

Dutch crocus is one of the earliest spring flowers, a welcome sight after a long, cold winter. After flowering, the leaves continue to elongate until they ripen and die back to the ground in early summer.

Description Dutch crocus grow from small corms. They appear in late winter to early spring, with leaves and flowers at the same time. The grass-like leaves are thin and green with a white centre stripe. Goblet-shaped, stemless flowers up to 7.5 cm (3 inches) across bloom just above the leaves. The flowers are white, lavender, purple or yellow; they may be striped with contrasting colours.
Height and spread Height of leaves to 20 cm (8 inches); flowers usually to 10 cm (4 inches) tall. Spread 2.5–7.5 cm (1–3 inches).
Best site and climate Full sun to partial shade (under deciduous trees and shrubs); average, well-drained soil. Zones 3–8.
Growing guidelines Plant the corms in autumn. Set them pointed side up in individual holes or larger planting areas dug 5–10 cm (2–4 inches) deep. Space the corms 5 cm (2 inches) apart. Dutch crocus usually return year after year and spread to form showy clumps. Interplanting crocus corms with daffodil bulbs (which are toxic if eaten) may help discourage mice.
Landscape use Include them in beds and borders for early colour. Grow them in containers for outdoor spring flowers.

Cyclamen hederifolium
PRIMULACEAE

HARDY CYCLAMEN

Hardy cyclamen grow well under shrubs and trees – even in dry summer shade – and are attractive through most of the year. Top-dress with a thin layer of compost in late summer.

Description Hardy cyclamen grow from smooth tubers. They flower in early autumn, with leafless flower stalks topped with pink or white flowers. The 2.5-cm (1-inch) long, nodding flowers have upward-pointing petals. Handsome, heart-shaped, silver-marked, green leaves emerge shortly after the flowering finishes. The leaves die back by midsummer but return again by mid-autumn.
Height and spread Height and spread of flowers and foliage 10–15 cm (4–6 inches).
Best site and climate Partial shade; average, well-drained soil. Zones 5–9.
Growing guidelines Many commercial cyclamen sources sell wild-collected tubers. Avoid supporting this irresponsible practice. Buy nursery-propagated tubers or grow your own from seed. Soak the seed overnight, then sow it 6 mm (½ inch) deep in a pot. Enclose the pot in a plastic bag, then put it in a dark place. Plant out in the garden in spring or summer. Or plant dormant tubers shallowly in summer, making sure the smooth, unmarked side is at the bottom.
Landscape use Hardy cyclamen look good in shady spots with ferns and hellebores (*Helleborus* spp.).

Dahlia hybrids
COMPOSITAE

DAHLIAS

Pinch out stem tips in early summer to promote bushy growth and more (but smaller) flowers. Or, to get the largest flowers, pinch out sideshoots to leave one or two main stems.

Description Some types, known as bedding dahlias, form compact, bushy plants; others produce the tall, large-flowered border favourites. Both types have upright stems with divided, green (or sometimes purple-tinted) leaves. Dahlias flower from midsummer to autumn, with flowers 2.5–20 cm (1–8 inches) across. They come in almost every colour but true blue – even in near black and bicolours.
Height and spread Height varies from 30 cm (1 foot) for bedding types to 1.5 m (5 feet) for border types. Spread to 30 cm (1 foot) for bedding types and 1.2 m (4 feet) for border types.
Best site and climate Full sun; average, well-drained soil. Hardy in Zones 9 and 10; elsewhere, grow as annuals.
Growing guidelines Grow bedding types from seed sown indoors six to eight weeks before your last frost date. In cooler climates, plant tuberous roots indoors two to three weeks before your last frost date, then plant out one to two weeks after the last frost date. Elsewhere, plant the roots directly into the garden around the last frost date.
Landscape use Plant in beds and borders and in the cutting garden.

Fritillaria imperalis
LILIACEAE

CROWN IMPERIAL

Crown imperials may take a few seasons to get established and flower well; mature clumps can live for many years. All parts of the plant have a musky odour.

Description Crown imperial grows from a large, fleshy bulb. Sturdy shoots of green stems and glossy green leaves emerge in early spring and elongate for several weeks. By mid- to late spring, the tall stems are topped with a tuft of green leaves and hanging, bell-shaped, yellow, orange or red flowers about 5 cm (2 inches) long. Soon after flowering, the leaves and stems turn yellow; they die back to the ground by midsummer.
Height and spread Height 60–120 cm (24–48 inches); spread to 30 cm (12 inches).
Best site and climate Full spring sun; average to sandy, well-drained soil. Zones 5–9.
Growing guidelines Plant the bulbs in late summer or early autumn. Dig a large hole for each bulb or prepare a large planting area; make either about 20 cm (8 inches) deep. Loosen the soil at the base of the hole to promote good drainage. When you put the bulb in the hole, tilt it slightly to one side to discourage water from collecting in the depression at the top of the bulb.
Landscape use Crown imperials make striking spring accents for beds and borders.

Fritillaria meleagris
LILIACEAE

CHEQUERED LILY

The pretty nodding flowers of chequered lilies add a charming touch to spring gardens. Naturalise them in wild areas, or plant them in clumps in beds and borders.

Other common names Guinea-hen flower, snake's head lily.
Description Chequered lily grows from small bulbs. Slender, arching stems with narrow, grey-green leaves rise in early spring. By mid-spring, broad, nodding, bell-like blooms dangle from the ends of the nodding stems. The 2.5–5-cm (1–2-inch) long flowers range in colour from white to deep purple; many are marked with a chequered pattern. Chequered lilies die back to the ground by midsummer.
Height and spread Height to 30 cm (12 inches); spread 5–10 cm (2–4 inches).
Best site and climate Partial shade; average, well-drained soil. Zones 3–8.
Growing guidelines Plant in early autumn. Dig the holes or planting areas 5–7.5 cm (2–3 inches) deep. Space bulbs 10–15 cm (4–6 inches) apart. Leave established clumps undisturbed to form large sweeps of spring colour.
Landscape use Chequered lilies look lovely when naturalised in masses in woodland or meadow gardens. Or grow them in beds and borders under deciduous trees; these small bulbs combine beautifully with ferns and hellebores (*Helleborus* spp.).

Galanthus nivalis
AMARYLLIDACEAE

COMMON SNOWDROP

Common snowdrops are among the earliest flowers to bloom in the spring garden. Established bulbs are trouble-free; they will spread and reseed freely.

Description Common snowdrops grow from small bulbs. Each bulb produces two or three flat, narrow, green leaves and an upright to arching green flower stem in midwinter through early spring. Dainty, nodding flowers to 2.5 cm (1 inch) long bloom at the tips of the stems in late winter or early spring. The single or double flowers are white; each of the shorter, inner petals has a green tip. Plants die back to the ground by early summer.

Height and spread Height of flowers and foliage to 15 cm (6 inches); spread 5–7.5 cm (2–3 inches).

Best site and climate Full sun to partial shade; average to moist, well-drained soil with added organic matter. Zones 3–9.

Growing guidelines Plant bulbs in autumn. Set them in individual holes or larger planting areas dug 7.5–10 cm (3–4 inches) deep. Space each bulb 7.5–10 cm (3–4 inches) apart.

Landscape use Grow clumps of common snowdrops in the garden with other early flowers, such as snow crocus and Christmas rose (*Helleborus niger*). Or naturalise them in lawns, as groundcover and in low-maintenance areas or under deciduous trees and shrubs. (In lawns, you'll have to wait until the leaves have died before mowing.)

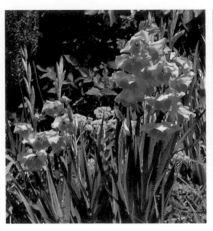

Gladiolus x *hortulanus*
IRIDACEAE

GLADIOLUS

Gladioli flower in nearly every colour but true blue; many have spots or splashes of contrasting colors. For cut flowers, pick them just as the bottom bud begins to open.

Description Gladioli grow from flattened corms. They produce tall fans of flat, sword-shaped, green leaves. A slender flower stem rises from the centre of each fan in summer to early autumn (depending on the planting time). The flower stem is topped with a many-budded spike that flowers from the bottom up. The buds produce open, funnel-shaped flowers up to 10 cm (4 inches) across. The leaves usually turn yellow several weeks after flowering.

Height and spread Height 60–150 cm (2–5 feet); spread 15–30 cm (6–12 inches).

Best site and climate Full sun; average, well-drained soil. Usually hardy in Zones 8–10; elsewhere, grow as annuals.

Growing guidelines Start planting the corms outdoors after the last frost date in spring. Plant in individual holes or larger planting areas dug 10–25 cm (4–6 inches) deep. To extend the flowering season, plant more corms every two weeks until midsummer. Tall-flowering types benefit from staking. In cold areas, dig up the corms before or just after the first frost and store them indoors in a frost-free area.

Landscape use Plant in the middle and back of beds and borders.

Hyacinthoides hispanica
ASPARAGACEAE

SPANISH BLUEBELLS

Established patches of Spanish bluebells increase quickly, often to the point of becoming invasive. Removing spent flower stalks will minimise reseeding; mow unwanted plants.

Description Spanish bluebells grow from small bulbs. In spring, the plants form clumps of sprawling, strap-shaped, green leaves. Upright, leafless flower stems topped with spikes of many bell-shaped flowers appear in late spring. The 18-mm (¾-inch) wide flowers bloom in white, pink or shades of purple-blue. Plants are dormant by midsummer. Spanish bluebells are still sold under a variety of former names, including *Scilla campanulata*, *Scilla hispanica* and *Endymion hispanicus*.

Height and spread Height of flowers 30–45 cm (12–18 inches); leaves usually to 20 cm (8 inches) tall. Spread 10–15 cm (4–6 inches).

Best site and climate Full sun to partial shade; average, well-drained soil with added organic matter. Zones 4–8.

Growing guidelines Plant the bulbs in autumn. Set them in individual holes or larger planting areas dug 7.5–10 cm (3–4 inches) deep. Space each bulb 10–25 cm (4–6 inches) apart.

Landscape use Include clumps in beds and borders, combine them with groundcover or naturalise them in woodlands and low-maintenance areas.

Hyacinthus orientalis
ASPARAGACEAE

HYACINTH

After the first year, hyacinth flower spikes tend to become smaller; in some cases, they may not flower at all. Plant new bulbs every year or two to ensure a good display.

Description Hyacinths grow from plump bulbs. Sturdy shoots with wide, strap-shaped, green leaves and upright flower stalks emerge in early spring. By mid-spring, each stalk is topped with a dense spike of starry, 2.5-cm (1-inch) wide, powerfully fragrant flowers. The single or double flowers bloom in a wide range of colours, including white, pink, red, orange, yellow, blue and purple. Hyacinths become dormant in early summer.
Height and spread Height 20–30 cm (8–12 inches); spread to 10 cm (4 inches).
Best site and climate Full sun; average, well-drained soil with added organic matter. Zones 4–8.
Growing guidelines Plant bulbs in mid-autumn. Set them in individual holes or larger planting areas dug 12.5–15 cm (5–6 inches) deep. Space the bulbs 15–20 cm (6–10 inches) apart. Double-flowered types may need staking. Remove spent flower stalks. Dig up and divide crowded clumps as the leaves yellow.
Landscape use Hyacinths contribute cheerful spring colour to flower beds and borders. Combine them with primroses and pansies for extra excitement. They also grow well in containers.

Iris reticulata
IRIDACEAE

RETICULATED IRIS

Reticulated irises return year after year to grace your garden with their delicate spring flowers. Tuck them into beds, borders and rock gardens; they look great in pots, too.

Description Reticulated irises grow from small bulbs. The dainty blue, purple or white early-spring flowers have three upright petals (known as standards) and three outward-arching petals (known as falls). The falls have gold and/or white markings. The grass-like, dark green leaves are short at flowering time but elongate after the flowers fade; they ripen and die back to the ground by early summer.
Height and spread Height of flowers 10–15 cm (4–6 inches); leaves to 30 cm (12 inches). Spread to 5 cm (2 inches).
Best site and climate Full sun; average, well-drained soil. Zones 5–9.
Growing guidelines Plant the bulbs in autumn. Set them in individual holes or larger planting areas dug 7.5–10 cm (3–4 inches) deep. For propagation, lift and divide clumps after the leaves turn yellow.
Landscape use The delicate, lightly fragrant flowers are beautiful in spring beds and borders. For extra colour, combine them with Grecian windflowers (*Anemone blanda*) and early crocus. Reticulated irises also grow well in pots for spring flowering outdoors or winter forcing indoors.

Leucojum aestivum
AMARYLLIDACEAE

SUMMER SNOWFLAKE

Despite their name, summer snowflakes actually flower in spring. Plant the small bulbs in groups; over time, they'll form large clumps.

Other common names Giant snowflake.
Description Clumps of strap-shaped, green leaves emerge in early spring. In mid- to late spring, plants produce slender, green flowering stems tipped with loose clusters of nodding, bell-shaped, 18-mm (¾-inch) wide flowers. The white flowers have a green spot near the tip of each petal. After bloom, the leaves turn yellow and die back to the ground by midsummer.
Height and spread Height of foliage and flowers to 45 cm (18 inches); spread to 15 cm (6 inches).
Best site and climate Full sun to partial shade; moist but well-drained soil with added organic matter. Zones 4–9.
Growing guidelines In early autumn, set bulbs in individual holes or larger planting areas dug 10 cm (4 inches) deep. Space them about 15 cm (6 inches) apart. For propagation, divide in early autumn.
Landscape use Grow summer snowflakes with tulips and daffodils in flower beds and borders. Interplant with summer- and autumn-flowering annuals that will fill in when the bulbs are dormant. They also look great naturalised in moist meadows and woodlands.

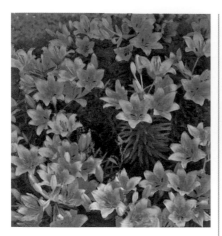

Lilium hybrids
LILIACEAE

LILIES

Lilies are excellent as cut flowers; pick them when the first one or two buds open. You may want to remove the orange anthers to stop pollen dropping.

Description Lilies grow from scaly bulbs. They produce upright, unbranched stems with narrow to lance-shaped, green leaves in spring to early summer. By early to late summer (depending on the hybrid), the long, plump flower buds open to showy, flat or funnel-shaped flowers. After flowering, the leaves and stems usually stay green until late summer or early autumn.

Height and spread Height 60–150 cm (2–5 feet), depending on the hybrid; spread usually 15–30 cm (6–12 inches).

Best site and climate Full sun to partial shade; average, well-drained soil. Usually Zones 4–8.

Growing guidelines Plant bulbs in autumn or early spring. Dig individual holes or larger planting areas 15–20 cm (6–8 inches) deep. Pinch off spent flowers where they join the stem. Cut stems to the ground when the leaves turn yellow; divide clumps at the same time if needed for propagation.

Landscape use Lilies add height and colour to any flower bed or border. They're also elegant mixed into foundation plantings, grouped with shrubs or naturalised in woodlands. Combine them with mounding annuals, perennials or groundcover that can shade the soil.

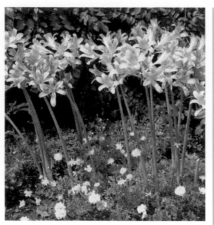

Lycoris squamigera
AMARYLLIDACEAE

MAGIC LILY

Magic lily bulbs produce leaves in spring and leafless flower stalks in late summer. Some gardeners like to combine them with bushy plants to hide the bare stems.

Description Slender, greenish brown, leafless stems rise from the ground in late summer to early autumn. They are topped with loose clusters of funnel-shaped, rosy pink flowers up to 10 cm (4 inches) long. The broad, strap-shaped, green leaves usually begin to emerge several weeks after the flowers fade. The foliage elongates in spring and dies back to the ground in summer, one to two months before new flowers appear.

Height and spread Height of flowers to 60 cm (24 inches); leaves to 30 cm (12 inches). Spread to 15 cm (6 inches).

Best site and climate Full sun to partial shade; average, well-drained soil that's dry in summer. Zones 5–9.

Growing guidelines Plant bulbs in midsummer. Set them in individual holes or larger planting areas dug 10–12.5 cm (4–5 inches) deep. Space bulbs about 20 cm (8 inches) apart. Water during dry spells in autumn and spring. Protect the leaves over winter with a loose mulch, such as evergreen branches, pine needles or straw.

Landscape use They grow best when naturalised on slopes, among groundcover, or in low-maintenance areas.

Muscari armeniacum
ASPARAGACEAE

GRAPE HYACINTH

Once planted, grape hyacinths are trouble-free. They naturalise well under trees and shrubs, and they look attractive combined with groundcover.

Description Grape hyacinths grow from small bulbs. The narrow, grass-like, green leaves appear in autumn and elongate through the spring. The clumps are accented by short, leafless stems topped with dense spikes of grape-like blooms in early spring. The individual purple-blue, white-rimmed flowers are only 6 mm (¼ inch) wide. The leaves turn yellow and die back to the ground by early summer.

Height and spread Height of flowers and foliage 15–20 cm (6–8 inches); spread 7.5–10 cm (3–4 inches).

Best site and climate Full sun to partial shade (under deciduous trees and shrubs); average, well-drained soil. Zones 4–8.

Growing guidelines Plant bulbs in early to mid- autumn, as soon as available. Set them in individual holes or larger planting areas dug 5–7.5 cm (2–3 inches) deep. Space the bulbs about 10 cm (4 inches) apart. For propagation, divide just after the leaves die back in early summer. Otherwise, leave the bulbs undisturbed to form sweeps of spring colour.

Landscape use Scatter the bulbs liberally throughout flower beds and borders. Mix them with primroses, pansies, daffodils and tulips for an unforgettable spring show.

Narcissus hybrids
AMARYLLIDACEAE

DAFFODILS

It's hard to imagine a garden without at least a few daffodils for spring colour. Grow them in borders, plant them under trees or naturalise them in low-maintenance areas.

Description Daffodils grow from large, pointed bulbs. Clumps of flat, strap-shaped, green leaves emerge in early spring, along with leafless flower stalks. The sometimes-fragrant flowers appear in early, mid- or late spring. Each flower has a cup or trumpet (technically known as a corona) and an outer ring of petals (known as the perianth). The single or double flowers are most commonly white or yellow but may also have pink, green, or orange markings.
Height and spread Height of foliage and flowers 15–50 cm (6–20 inches), spread usually 10–20 cm (4–8 inches).
Best site and climate Full sun to partial shade; average, well-drained soil with added organic matter. Zones 4–8.
Growing guidelines Plant the bulbs in early to mid- autumn. Set them in individual holes or larger planting areas dug 10–20 cm (4–8 inches) deep. Allow the leaves to turn yellow before cutting them back or pulling them out.
Landscape use Create unforgettable combinations by grouping daffodils with other early bloomers, including pansies, crocus, Siberian squill (*Scilla sibirica*), grape hyacinths (*Muscari* spp.) and Grecian windflower (*Anemone blanda*).

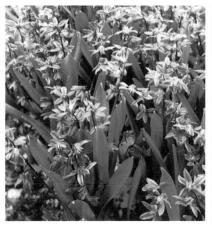

Scilla siberica
ASPARAGACEAE

SIBERIAN SQUILL

The deep blue flowers of Siberian squill look marvellous in masses. They also combine beautifully with many other spring-flowering bulbs, annuals and perennials.

Description Siberian squills grow from small bulbs. They produce narrow, strap-shaped, green leaves and leafless flower stems starting in late winter. By early to mid- spring, the flower stems are topped with clusters of nodding, starry or bell-shaped blue flowers to 12 mm (½ inch) across. By early summer, the leaves gradually turn yellow and die back.
Height and spread Height of flowers and foliage to 15 cm (6 inches). Spread 5–7.5 cm (2–3 inches).
Best site and climate Full sun to partial shade; average, well-drained soil. Zones 3–8.
Growing guidelines Plant bulbs in early to mid- autumn, as soon as available. Set them in individual holes or larger planting areas dug 7.5–10 cm (3–4 inches) deep. Established bulbs are trouble-free. For propagation, divide bulbs after the leaves turn yellow; otherwise, leave them undisturbed to spread into large clumps.
Landscape use Tuck them into beds and borders with pansies, primroses and daffodils. They are also excellent for naturalising in lawns and low-maintenance areas and under trees and shrubs; wait until the bulb leaves have turned yellow to mow.

Tulipa hybrids
LILIACEAE

TULIPS

Hybrid tulips often flower poorly after the first year. For a great show each year, pull them out after flowering and replace them with summer annuals; plant new tulips in autumn.

Description Tulips grow from plump, pointed bulbsThe bulbs produce broad, dusty-green leaves that are sometimes striped with maroon in early to mid-spring. The slender, upright, usually unbranched flower stems are topped with showy single or double flowers up to 10 cm (4 inches) across. By midsummer, leaves gradually turn yellow and die back to the ground.
Height and spread Height from 15–90 cm (6–30 inches), depending on the cultivar; spread 15–25 cm (6–10 inches).
Best site and climate Full sun to partial shade; average, well-drained soil that's dry in summer. Usually best in Zones 3–8; in Zones 9, and 10, treat hybrid tulips as annuals and plant pre-cooled bulbs each year in late autumn or early winter.
Growing guidelines Plant bulbs in mid- to late autumn. Set them in individual holes or larger planting areas dug 10–15 cm (4–6 inches) deep. Pinch off the developing seed pods after flowering, and allow the leaves to yellow before removing them. Or pull them out after bloom.
Landscape use Tulips are an indispensable part of the spring garden. They are also charming as cut flowers.

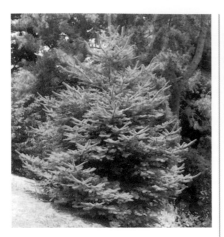

Abies homolepis
PINACEAE

NIKKO FIR

Like all firs, Nikko fir is a coniferous evergreen tree that grows best in cool, moist climates. It has a columnar habit and glossy needle-like leaves held in whorls on the branches.

Flower colour and season Insignificant green or yellowish flowers in spring, followed by upright tannish cones in summer to winter.
Height and spread To 30 m (100 feet) tall and 9 m (30 feet) wide.
Best climate and site Zones 4–7. Deep, moist, well-drained soil. Full sun to light shade.
Cultivation Best transplanted in spring or winter, as root-balled plants. Pruning not necessary.
Propagation Sow seed in autumn. Take cuttings in winter. Graft in late winter and early spring.
Pest and disease prevention Heat- and water-stressed plants are more attractive to pests and susceptible to diseases. Mulch regularly with organic matter to keep soil moist. Avoid planting in hot, dry areas.
Common problems Intolerant of city pollution.
Landscape use Specimen tree; screens.
Other species *A. concolor*, white or Colorado fir, has curving, claw-shaped needles that are grey-green or blue-grey. It grows to 30 m (100 feet) tall and 12 m (40 feet) wide. 'Conica' is a dwarf pyramidal form.

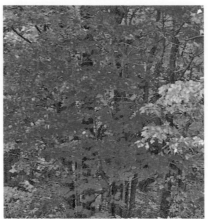

Acer spp.
SAPINDACEAE

MAPLE

A. saccharum, sugar maple, is a handsome shade tree for a large garden. Prized in the landscape for its outstanding autumn colour, it is also the chief source of maple syrup and sugar.

Flower colour and season *A. griseum*: yellow-green flowers; *A. palmatum*: purple flowers; *A. platanoides*: yellow flowers; *A. rubrum*: red flowers; *A. saccharum*: greenish yellow flowers. All flower in early spring.
Height and spread Height varies from 3.6 m (12 feet) to 30 m (100 feet); spread from 4.5 m (15 feet) to 21 m (70 feet).
Best climate and site Depending on species, Zones 3–9. Partial shade for *A. palmatum*; other species prefer full sun.
Cultivation Transplant bare-root, container-grown or root-balled plants in spring. Prune in winter only to initially shape the young tree.
Propagation Sow seed in autumn or spring. Take cuttings in late spring or winter. Graft in late winter or early spring.
Pest and disease prevention Avoid damaging the bark with gardening tools such as lawnmowers. Wounds are entry points for pests and diseases.
Common problems Many maple species have shallow, spreading roots that make growing other plants under them difficult.
Landscape use Specimen plant; shade trees. *A. platanoides* and *A. rubrum* make excellent street trees.

Betula papyrifera
BETULACEAE

CANOE BIRCH

Native to northeastern North America, canoe birch is a tall deciduous tree that grows best in cool climates. Its mature trunks and branches are white with distinct black markings.

Flower colour and season Tannish green flowers in catkins in early to mid- spring.
Height and spread To 18 m (60 feet) tall and 9 m (30 feet) wide.
Best climate and site Zones 2–6. Moist, well-drained, deep soil. Full sun to partial shade.
Cultivation Plant in spring. Prune only in late summer or autumn, as pruning at other times can cause excessive 'bleeding'. Pruning is only necessary initially to shape the tree.
Propagation Sow seed in autumn. Graft in late winter and early spring.
Pest and disease prevention Drought stress can weaken trees, making them more susceptible to pests and diseases. Plant in evenly moist soil and water during extended drought periods.
Common problems Can be short-lived, especially in hot, dry areas.
Landscape use Specimen tree; group plantings.
Other species *B. nigra*, river birch, is a pyramidal tree with reddish brown exfoliating bark. It is tolerant of swampy conditions. Zones 4–8. *B. pendula*, silver birch, has silvery white bark marked with black. Zones 2–6.

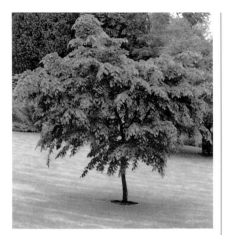

Carpinus betulus
BETULACEAE

COMMON HORNBEAM

Common hornbeam is a slow-growing deciduous tree with an upright oval form and serrated green leaves. This easy-care tree tolerates heavy pruning and is often used for hedges.

Flower colour and season Yellowish green flowers in catkins in early to mid- spring.
Height and spread To 18 m (60 feet) tall and 9 m (30 feet) wide.
Best climate and site Zones 5–9. Moist, well-drained soil. Full sun to partial shade.
Cultivation Plant in spring. Prune in winter for hedges.
Propagation Sow seed in autumn. Graft in late winter or early spring.
Pest and disease prevention May be subject to scale infestation. Prune and destroy affected parts. Plants in fertile soil with adequate moisture tolerate attacks better than plants that are water-stressed, nutrient-deficient and overcrowded.
Common problems Common hornbeam is difficult to transplant; plant young container-grown plants.
Landscape use Specimen tree; group plantings; hedges.
Other species *C. caroliniana*, American hornbeam, is a small bushy tree that provides excellent red autumn foliage. 'Pyramidalis' grows to a pyramidal shape. Zones 2–7.

Cercidiphyllum japonicum
CERCIDIPHYLLACEAE

KATSURA TREE

Katsura tree is a deciduous tree from China and Japan. Its leaves are heart-shaped and mostly opposite; they turn yellow, orange or red in autumn and become sweetly fragrant.

Flower colour and season Small reddish flowers without petals in mid- to late spring.
Height and spread To 18 m (60 feet) tall and 0.9–15 m (3–50 feet) wide.
Best climate and site Zones 4–8. Very moist, well-drained soil. Full sun to light shade.
Cultivation Transplant container-grown or root-balled plants in early spring. Prune only to shape when young.
Propagation Sow fresh seed as soon as available. Take cuttings in winter.
Pest and disease prevention Water during prolonged periods of drought to maintain vigour. Healthy plants are less susceptible to pest and diseases.
Common problems Usually trouble-free.
Landscape use Specimen tree; street trees, screens. If it grows to a single trunk, the form is markedly columnar; if multiple trunks form, the result is a wide-spreading tree.

Cercis canadensis
LEGUMINOSAE

EASTERN REDBUD

Eastern redbud is a flat-topped, broadly spreading deciduous tree native to eastern North America. It produces masses of pink flowers in spring; the foliage may turn yellow in autumn.

Flower colour and season Pink flowers in mid- to late spring before leaves appear. Flowers are produced profusely at the joints of old wood (even along the trunk).
Height and spread To 9 m (30 feet) tall and 6 m (20 feet) wide.
Best climate and site Zones 4–9. Tolerant of a variety of soil conditions. Full sun to light shade.
Cultivation Difficult to transplant; best moved in winter when young.
Propagation Sow seed immediately upon ripening in late summer or autumn.
Pest and disease prevention Keep vigorous by regular watering and feeding. Healthy plants are less susceptible to pests and diseases.
Common problems Sometimes subject to canker and verticillium wilt.
Landscape use Excellent small specimen tree; use alone or in combination with *Cornus florida* as a shade tree.
Other species *C. siliquastrum*, Judas tree, is very similar but is native to the eastern Mediterranean and Asia Minor. It produces purplish rose flowers and yellow autumn foliage. Zones 6–9.

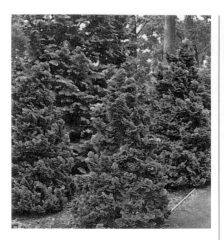

Chamaecyparis obtusa
CUPRESSACEAE

HINOKI FALSE CYPRSS

Hinoki false cypress is a slow-growing coniferous evergreen tree with flat sprays of waxy, dark green scale-like foliage. It grows in a broadly pyramidal form.

Flower colour and season Inconspicuous flowers in spring, followed by brown cones in autumn.
Height and spread To 30 m (100 feet) tall and 12 m (40 feet) wide.
Best climate and site Zones 5–8. Deep, loamy, moisture-retentive soil. Full sun.
Cultivation Transplant container-grown or root-balled plants in spring. Prune plants to shape in spring.
Propagation Take cuttings in autumn.
Pest and disease prevention Avoid damaging the trunk with lawnmowers or sharp gardening tools; these wounds are common entry points for pests and diseases.
Common problems Plants may be subject to a fungal disease that attacks roots. Dig out and destroy diseased plants. Plant in moist but well-drained soil to help prevent injury.
Landscape use Specimen tree; background trees.
Other species *C. lawsoniana*, Lawson's false cypress, is a slender to broadly pyramidal tree with horizontal branches. The scale-like leaves differ widely in colour. 'Allumii' is a conical spreading form with blue foliage. 'Aurea' has golden leaves.

Chionanthus virginicus
OLEACEAE

WHITE FRINGE TREE

White fringe tree is a deciduous small tree or large shrub with medium green leaves that turn yellow in autumn. The loose clusters of white flowers bloom from late spring into summer.

Flower colour and season Slightly fragrant white flowers borne in loose clusters from late spring to early summer, followed by blue grape-like fruit on female plants.
Height and spread To 9 m (30 feet) tall and as wide.
Best climate and site Zones 5–8. Humus-rich, moisture retentive, well-drained soil. Full sun.
Cultivation Transplant root-balled or container-grown plants in spring. Prune after flowering only if shaping is required.
Propagation Sow seed in autumn; may take two years to germinate. Take semi-hardwood cuttings in late summer.
Pest and disease prevention No serious pests or diseases.
Common problems Slow-growing.
Landscape use Specimen tree or shrub.
Other species *C. retusus*, Chinese fringe tree, is native to China, Korea and Japan. It has smaller leaves and grows to 6 m (20 feet) tall with a rounded bushy form.

Cladrastis lutea
LEGUMINOSAE

AMERICAN YELLOWWOOD

Native to the southeastern United States, American yellowwood is a deciduous tree growing to a wide-spreading rounded form. The bark is pale grey and glossy; the leaves are compound.

Flower colour and season Bell-shaped slightly fragrant white flowers, marked with yellow, borne in 30-cm (1-foot) long terminal clusters from late spring to early summer; flowers attractive to bees.
Height and spread To 12 m (40 feet) tall and slightly wider.
Best climate and site Zones 3–8. Tolerates a wide range of soil conditions but needs good drainage. Full sun to light shade.
Cultivation Transplant young root-balled or container-grown plants in autumn or spring. No pruning necessary unless shaping is desired.
Propagation Sow seed in autumn. Take root cuttings in winter.
Pest and disease prevention No serious pests or diseases.
Common problems Bleeds profusely if pruned in winter or spring. Prune only in late summer or autumn.
Landscape use Specimen tree; woodland plantings.
Cultivars 'Rosea' has light pink flowers.

Cornus spp.
CORNACEAE

DOGWOOD

Cornus florida, flowering dogwood, is often considered to be one of the finest flowering trees. It produces showy white blooms in spring and red berries in autumn.

Flower colour and season C. *alternifolia*: small white or yellow flowers late winter to early spring; C. *florida*: inconspicuous yellow flowers with four broad, rounded white bracts in mid- to late spring; C. *kousa*: similar flowers to C. *florida* from late spring to early summer, but bracts are pointed at the tips; C. *mas*: profuse yellow flowers from late winter to early spring.
Height and spread Height varies from 6 m (20 feet) to 12 m (40 feet); spread from 3.6 m (12 feet) to 12 m (40 feet).
Best climate and site Depending on species, Zones 3–9. Moisture-retentive, humus-rich, well-drained soil. Full sun to partial shade.
Cultivation Young plants transplant best during early spring. Prune trees only if necessary to shape.
Propagation Remove seed from its fleshy covering and sow in autumn. Take cuttings in late spring. Graft in early spring.
Pest and disease prevention Plant in evenly moist soil.
Common problems Anthracnose has become a severe problem for North American species, particularly C. *florida*.
Landscape use Excellent specimen or lawn tree, used singly or in groups.

Fagus sylvatica
FAGACEAE

COMMON BEECH

Common beech is a magnificent long lived deciduous tree with smooth grey bark. It varies considerably in growth habit and in the form and colour of its large leaves.

Flower colour and season Inconspicuous greenish flowers in mid-spring, followed by small triangular nuts.
Height and spread To 30 m (100 feet) tall; spread varies with cultivar.
Best climate and site Zones 4–8. Deep, loamy, moist, humus-rich, well-drained soil.
Cultivation Transplant root-balled plants in spring. Prune in summer only when young enough to establish a straight, upright trunk.
Propagation Graft in late winter and early spring. Sow seed in autumn.
Pest and disease prevention Avoid overfeeding, which results in succulent growth that is attractive to aphids. Protect the shallow roots from compaction and other forms of soil disturbance.
Common problems Intolerant of poor drainage. The shallow roots and dense shade make it difficult to grow other plants under these trees.
Landscape use Specimen tree; shade trees; hedges.
Cultivars 'Laciniata' has ferny and deeply incised leaves. 'Pendula' has a weeping habit.

Gleditsia triacanthos
LEGUMINOSAE

HONEY LOCUST

Honey locust is a deciduous tree with compound leaves, and trunks and branches armed with sharp thorns. 'Sunburst' is a thornless cultivar with golden yellow young leaves.

Flower colour and season Greenish flowers borne in clusters in late spring. The female flowers are followed by long scimitar-shaped brown pods.
Height and spread To 30 m (100 feet) tall and 18 m (60 feet) wide.
Best climate and site Zones 4–8. Moist, loamy, well-drained soil. Full sun.
Cultivation Plant in winter or spring. Prune in autumn if necessary.
Propagation Graft in late winter or spring. Sow seed in spring.
Pest and disease prevention Honey locusts are prone to many pests and diseases. Healthy plants are more resistant to pest invasion. Mulch to keep the soil evenly moist. Look for resistant cultivars.
Common problems The thick, sharp thorns can be hazardous; choose thornless cultivars. Self-sown seedlings can be a nuisance; plant male cultivars.
Landscape use Specimen tree; shade trees.
Other species 'Moraine' is a thornless male cultivar that is somewhat resistant to webworm.

Halesia carolina
STYRACACEAE

CAROLINA SILVERBELL

Native to the southeastern United States, Carolina silverbell is a deciduous tree or shrub with elliptical leaves. The delicate bell-shaped white flowers bloom in spring.

Other common names Snowdrop tree.
Flower colour and season Bell-shaped white flowers in clusters of three to five from mid- to late spring.
Height and spread To 9 m (30 feet) tall and as wide.
Best climate and site Zones 5–8. Moisture-retentive, humus-rich, well-drained soil. Full sun to light shade; shelter from strong winds.
Cultivation Transplant root-balled or container-grown plants in spring. Rarely needs pruning.
Propagation Sow seed in autumn; may take two years to germinate.
Pest and disease prevention No serious pests or diseases. Keep soil moist with organic mulch.
Common problems Loses leaves very early in the season.
Landscape use Specimen tree, most effective against an evergreen background; woodland planting.
Cultivars 'Rosea' has light pink flowers.

Koelreuteria paniculata
SAPINDACEAE

GOLDEN RAIN TREE

Golden rain tree is a deciduous tree with compound leaves that turn bright yellow in autumn. Its showy yellow summer flowers come at a time when few other trees are flowering.

Flower colour and season Rich yellow flowers borne in dense, terminal racemes in midsummer, followed by bladder-like greenish pods.
Height and spread To 15 m (50 feet) tall and 12 m (40 feet) wide.
Best climate and site Zones 5–9. Adapts to a variety of soil conditions; tolerant of heat, drought and air pollution. Full sun.
Cultivation Transplant container-grown or root-balled plants in autumn and spring. Pruning is unnecessary except to shape the tree, then prune in winter.
Propagation Sow seed in autumn. Take root cuttings in winter.
Pest and disease prevention No serious pests or diseases.
Common problems Will flower poorly, or not at all, in shade.
Landscape use Good specimen tree for midsummer colour.
Cultivars 'Apiculata' has finely divided leaves. 'Fastigiata' has a narrow columnar habit. 'September' is late-flowering with exceptionally large flower clusters.
Other species *K. bipinnata* is a similar but late-flowering species. Zones 8–10.

Laburnum x watered
LEGUMINOSAE

GOLDEN CHAIN TREE

Golden chain tree is a deciduous tree with trifoliate leaves. L. x watereri 'Vossii', a cultivar of this hybrid, has a denser habit and exceptionally long flower clusters.

Flower colour and season Golden yellow flowers borne in long, pendulous clusters in late spring, followed by 5–7.5 cm (2–3 inch) pods.
Height and spread To 9 m (30 feet) tall and 5.4 m (18 feet) wide.
Best climate and site Zones 5–9. Virtually any well-drained soil. Full sun.
Cultivation Transplant container-grown or root-balled plants in spring. Prune after flowering only as necessary to remove unwanted or crowded shoots.
Propagation Sow seed in autumn. Graft in spring.
Pest and disease prevention No serious pests or diseases.
Common problems Tends to be short-lived. Remove whatever seed pods you can to counteract this. Seeds are poisonous when ingested.
Landscape use Particularly effective grouped against a background of evergreens; shrub borders.
Other species *L. anagyroides* is a wide-spreading tree with branches close to the ground. It grows to 6 m (20 feet) tall. 'Aureum' has golden yellow leaves. 'Involutum' has curled leaves. 'Pendulum' is a form with weeping branchlets.

Lagerstroemia indica
LYTHRACEAE

CRAPE MYRTLE

Crape myrtle is a summer-flowering deciduous tree with grey peeling bark and privet-like leaves that are bronze in spring, deep green in summer, and yellow, orange and red in autumn.

Flower colour and season Curiously crinkled white, pink, red, lavender or purple flowers in terminal 15–23-cm (6–9-inch) clusters in mid- to late summer.
Height and spread To 6 m (20 feet) tall and 3.6 m (12 feet) wide.
Best climate and site Zones 7–10. Moist, deep, well-drained soil. Full sun.
Cultivation Transplant container-grown or root-balled plants in spring. Prune in early spring, shortening the previous year's shoots to half or one-third of their length.
Propagation Take cuttings in late spring or early summer.
Pest and disease prevention Allow sufficient air circulation between plants to deter mildew.
Common problems Stems may die back to the ground in particularly cold winters; new flowering shoots will grow up from the roots.
Landscape use Specimen tree; shrub borders; screens. Plants often have multiple trunks.
Cultivars 'Catawba' has dark purple flowers and is mildew-resistant. 'Natchez' has white flowers and is mildew-resistant.

Liquidambar styraciflua
HAMAMELIDACEAE

SWEET GUM

Native to the eastern United States, sweet gum is a deciduous tree growing to pyramidal form. It has star-shaped leaves that turn shades of purple, crimson and orange in autumn.

Flower colour and season Insignificant yellow-green flowers in downy spikes in late spring, followed by ball-shaped fruit.
Height and spread To 30 m (100 feet) tall and 15 m (50 feet) wide.
Best climate and site Zones 3–8. Moist well-drained soil. Full sun to light shade.
Cultivation Transplant root-balled or container-grown plants in spring. Prune in early winter only if necessary to shape young trees or to remove dead wood.
Propagation Sow seed in autumn. Take cuttings from semi-hardwood in summer.
Pest and disease prevention No serious pests or diseases.
Common problems Difficult to transplant and slow to become established. The persistent spiny fruit can be a nuisance.
Landscape use Specimen tree; woodland plantings.
Cultivars 'Pendula' has pendulous branches. 'Variegata' has leaves marked with yellow.

Magnolia spp.
MAGNOLIACEAE

MAGNOLIA

Magnolias are deciduous or evergreen trees and shrubs with simple leaves. M. stellata, star magnolia, is a bushy shrub or small tree with starry white spring flowers.

Flower colour and season M. *grandiflora*: fragrant, waxy, creamy white flowers from late spring to midsummer; M. *kobus*: white, six-petalled flowers in mid-spring; M. x *soulangeana*; saucer-shaped white or rosy purple flowers in early spring; M. *stellata*: white flowers with strap-shaped petals in early spring; M. *virginiana*: fragrant creamy white flowers from late spring to early autumn.
Height and spread Height varies from 1.5 m (15 feet) to 27 m (90 feet); spread from 4.5 m (15 feet) to 16.5 m (55 feet).
Best climate and site Depending on species, Zones 5–10. Moist, humus-rich, well-drained soil. Partial shade.
Cultivation Transplant root-balled or container-grown plants in spring. No need to prune.
Propagation Layer in spring. Remove seed from its covering and sow in autumn. Take cuttings in mid- to late summer. Graft in winter.
Pest and disease prevention If scale insects attack, causing yellow leaves, prune out badly infested growth and spray the remaining stems with horticultural oil.
Common problems Late frosts can spoil early-flowering plants.

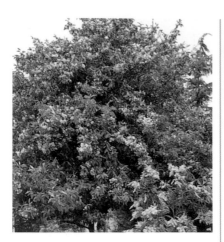

Malus floribunda
ROSACEAE

CRAB APPLE

Japanese flowering crab apple is a round-headed deciduous tree. It is prized for its profuse display of pink spring flowers, followed by showy yellow-red fruit in autumn.

Flower colour and season Deep pink flowers in spring, followed by red or yellow fruit.
Height and spread To 6 m (20 feet) tall and slightly wider.
Best climate and site Zones 4–8. Deep, humus-rich, moist, slightly alkaline soil. Full sun.
Cultivation Plant early in spring. Prune soon after flowering.
Propagation Graft in spring. Take softwood cuttings in late spring.
Pest and disease prevention Avoid overfeeding, which results in succulent growth attractive to aphids and other insects. To reduce possibility of rust, keep at least 150 m (500 feet) from eastern red cedar (*Juniperus virginiana*). Prune to keep the centre of the plant open to light and air to reduce disease problems. Choose disease-resistant cultivars.
Common problems Many cultivars flower heavily only in alternate years.
Landscape use Specimen tree; shade trees for small gardens.

Nyssa sylvatica
NYSSACEAE

BLACK TUPELO

Black tupelo is a deciduous tree of pyramidal form. The branches are somewhat pendulous; the leaves are leathery and glossy dark green, turning brilliant orange or scarlet in autumn.

Other common names Black gum, pepperidge.
Flower colour and season Greenish white flowers in late spring, followed in midsummer by small blue fruits on the female trees.
Height and spread To 27 m (90 feet) tall and 13.5 m (45 feet) wide.
Best climate and site Zones 4–8. Moist, humus-rich, well-drained sail. Full sun.
Cultivation Transplant small root-balled or container-grown plants in early spring.
Propagation Sow seed when ripe in autumn.
Pest and disease prevention Few serious pests or diseases. Mulch with organic matter to keep soil moist and to provide a home for beneficial insects.
Common problems Black tupelo is intolerant of alkaline soil.
Landscape use Specimen tree; woodland plantings; chiefly valued for its autumn colour.

Ostrya virginiana
BETULACEAE

AMERICAN HOP HORNBEAM

American hop hornbeam is a slow-growing deciduous tree with alternate simple leaves and graceful horizontal or drooping branches. It ultimately forms a round-headed tree.

Other common names Ironwood.
Flower colour and season Inconspicuous greenish catkins in early spring.
Height and spread To 12 m (40 feet) tall and 9 m (30 feet) wide.
Best climate and site Zones 4–9. Tolerant af a variety of well-drained soils. Full sun to partial shade.
Cultivation Transplant root-balled or container-grown plants to permanent position in spring.
Propagation Sow seed when ripe in autumn.
Pest and disease prevention No serious pests or diseases.
Common problems Difficult to. transplant and slow to establish.
Landscape use Specimen or street tree; chiefly valued where other trees will not grow.

Oxydendrum arboreum
ERICACEAE

SOURWOOD

Native to the eastern United States, sourwood is a slow-growing deciduous tree or shrub with oval leaves that turn vivid scarlet in autumn. The tree usually grows in pyramidal form.

Other common names Sorrel tree.
Flower colour and season White flowers borne in pendulous clusters in midsummer.
Height and spread To 15 m (50 feet) tall and 6 m (20 feet) wide.
Best climate and site Zones 5–9. Moist, well-drained, humus-rich, acid soil. Full sun.
Cultivation Transplant root-balled or container-grown plants in late winter or early spring. Plant in permanent position as established plants are difficult to move. Sourwood rarely needs pruning.
Propagation Sow seed indoors in spring. Take cuttings in midsummer. Cuttings should be 5–7.5 cm (2–3 inches) long and made of short sideshoots with a thin heel of old wood. Bottom heat promotes rooting.
Pest and disease prevention No serious pests or diseases.
Common problems Flowering and autumn colour are less dramatic in shade.
Landscape use Specimen tree.

Parrotia persica
HAMAMELIDACEAE

PERSIAN PARROTIA

A wide-spreading, round-headed deciduous tree, Persian parrotia is often multi-trunked with horizontal branching. Leaves turn orange, yellow and scarlet in autumn.

Flower colour and season
Inconspicuous, petal-less flowers with protruding red stamens from late winter to early spring.
Height and spread To 12 m (40 feet) tall and 13.5 m (45 feet) wide.
Best climate and site Zones 5–10. Tolerant of a variety of well-drained soils. Full sun for best leaf colour.
Cultivation Transplant root-balled or container-grown plants in early spring.
Propagation Sow seed in autumn. Graft in late winter or early spring on witch hazel (*Hamamelis* spp.). Take cuttings in midsummer.
Pest and disease prevention No serious pests or diseases.
Common problems Large trees are difficult to transplant, so they are best moved when small.
Landscape use Specimen tree; of interest for its autumn foliage colour and for its mottled bark.

Platanus occidentalis
PLATANACEAE

AMERICAN PLANE

American plane is native to eastern North America. This moisture-loving tree has coarse dark green leaves and mottled white bark.

Other common names Plane, buttonwood, American sycamore.
Flower colour and season Inconspicuous cream flowers in spring, followed by ball-shaped fruit.
Height and spread To 27 m (90 feet) tall and 19.5 m (65 feet) wide.
Best climate and site Zones 4–8. Adaptable to most well-drained soils, but grows to greatest size in rich, moist soil. Full sun. Tolerates air pollution.
Cultivation Prune in winter if necessary.
Propagation Take hardwood cuttings in winter. Sow seed in spring.
Pest and disease prevention Avoid damaging the bark with sharp gardening tools; such wounds are prime entry sites for diseases. Clean up dropped leaves and twigs to remove overwintering sites for disease spores.
Common problems Drops leaves, twigs and fruit, which may become unsightly.
Landscape use Specimen tree; street trees. Plant in borders of large properties.
Other species *P.* x *acerifolia*, London plane, has palmately lobed leaves to 25 cm (10 inches) wide and grows in wide-spreading form. 'Bloodgood' and 'Liberty' are very disease-resistant.

Populus deltoides
SALICACEAE

EASTERN COTTONWOOD

Eastern cottonwood is a fast-growing deciduous tree with large leaves. It is planted primarily for its rapid growth and ability to survive where few other trees can.

Flower colour and season Inconspicuous greenish catkins from mid- to late spring.
Height and spread To 27 m (90 feet) tall and 21 m (70 feet) wide.
Best climate and site Zones 2–8. Tolerant of a variety of soil conditions, even poor, dry ones, but prefers deep, moist, well-drained soil.
Cultivation Plant in autumn or spring. Prune in summer or autumn; bleeds if pruned at other times.
Propagation Sow seed in summer.
Pest and disease prevention Keep soil evenly moist with organic mulch. Healthy plants will resist pests and diseases far better than stressed plants.
Common problems Weak-wooded and short-lived. Questing roots can spread into and clog drains and sewers.
Landscape use Screens and mass plantings.
Other species *P. alba*, white poplar, has whitish bark and white undersides to the leaves. 'Richardii' has yellow upper leaf surfaces. *P. nigra* 'Italica', Lombardy poplar, is a narrow columnar grower to 27 m (90 feet) tall.

Prunus serrulata
ROSACEAE

FLOWERING CHERRY

Japanese flowering cherry is a rounded deciduous tree with an eye-catching display of spring flowers. The new leaves are often reddish brown; they mature to deep green.

Flower colour and season Clustered white or pink flowers, single, semi-double or double in form, in mid-spring.
Height and spread To 7.5 m (25 feet) tall and nearly as wide.
Best climate and site Zones 5–8. Deep, humus-rich, well-drained, moist soil. Full sun.
Cultivation Transplant container-grown or root-balled plants in spring. Prune after flowering.
Propagation Sow seed in autumn. Take cuttings in summer or autumn. Graft in late winter and early spring.
Pest and disease prevention Avoid overfeeding, which can stimulate succulent growth that is susceptible to pests and diseases. Also avoid planting in poorly drained soil.
Common problems Plants tend to be short-lived.
Landscape use Specimen tree; mass plantings.
Cultivars 'Kwanzan' ('Sekiyama') has bronze foliage and double deep pink flowers. 'Shirotae' ('Mt. Fuji') has semi-double white flowers. 'Ukon' has bronze new foliage and unusual pale yellow flowers.

Pyrus calleryana
ROSACEAE

CALLERY PEAR

Callery pear is a pyramidal to round-headed deciduous tree grown primarily for its spring flower display. Its rounded glossy dark green leaves turn purplish or reddish in autumn.

Flower colour and season White flowers from early to mid-spring, followed by roundish green fruit.
Height and spread To 9 m (30 feet) tall and 5.4 m (18 feet) wide.
Best climate and site Zones 5–9. Deep, moist, humus-rich, well-drained soil. Full sun.
Cultivation Transplant container-grown or root-balled plants in late winter while they are still dormant. Prune in winter or early spring.
Propagation Sow seed in autumn. Graft in late winter and early spring.
Pest and disease prevention Avoid injury with sharp gardening tools; these wounds provide easy access for pests and diseases. Try to buy disease-resistant cultivars for best results.
Common problems Callery pear tends to form narrow branch angles that are prone to splitting.
Landscape use Specimen tree.
Cultivars 'Aristocrat' has darker foliage and better autumn colour. 'Bradford' is more vigorous and bigger than the species, growing to 15 m (50 feet) tall and 9 m (30 feet) wide.

Quercus spp.
FAGACEAE

OAK

Q. rubra, red oak, is an adaptable, fast-growing tree with dark green leaves that may turn red in autumn. Unlike some other species, red oak is not too difficult to transplant.

Flower colour and season Inconspicuous greenish catkins in mid-spring, followed by roundish fruit (acorns).

Height and spread Height from 13.5 m (45 feet) to 30 m (100 feet); spread from 10.5 m (35 feet) to 30 m (100 feet).

Best climate and site Depending on species, Zones 4–9. Tolerant of a variety of soil conditions but thrives in moist, humus-rich, well-drained soil. Full sun.

Cultivation Transplant young root-balled plants in autumn and spring. Prune in winter only as necessary to shape the tree.

Propagation Graft in late winter and early spring. Sow seed in autumn.

Pest and disease prevention Tie hessian bands around main trunks to trap gypsy moth larvae; remove and destroy the caterpillars as they accumulate. Build up soil organic matter content with mulch and correct nutrient imbalances to ensure healthy plants with greater vigour to fight pest invasions.

Common problems Many species difficult to transplant.

Landscape use Specimen tree; shade trees for large properties. *Q. palustris* is an excellent street tree.

Robinia pseudoacacia
LEGUMI NOSAE

BLACK LOCUST

A thorny deciduous tree, black locust has an open, upright habit and pinnately compound leaves. The cultivar 'Frisia' has bright yellow foliage all season long.

Flower colour and season White or pink pea-like flowers borne in long pendulous clusters in early summer, followed by long brown pods.

Height and spread To 22.5 m (75 feet) tall and 13.5 m (45 feet) wide.

Best climate and site Zones 3–8. Tolerant of a variety of soil conditions but prefers slightly alkaline soil. Full sun to partial shade.

Cultivation Plant in winter or early spring. Prune in late summer or autumn only if necessary to shape the tree; bleeds if pruned in winter or spring.

Propagation Graft in spring. Sow seed when ripe in autumn. Remove rooted suckers from the parent plant in winter.

Pest and disease prevention Mulch with organic matter to keep the soil evenly moist. Healthy, vigorous plants are most resistant to borers and other pests.

Common problems Tends to produce many new shoots (suckers) at the base. Thorns can be hazardous and plant parts may be toxic.

Landscape use Mass plantings for difficult sites, especially where other trees won't thrive.

Sopnora japonica (Styphnolobium japonicum)
LEGUMINOSAE

JAPANESE PAGODA TREE

Japanese pagoda tree is a deciduous tree from the Orient. It grows to a round-headed form and has alternate, compound leaves. It is one of the last of the large trees to flower.

Flower colour and season Profuse creamy white mildly fragrant flowers in large 30- by 30-cm (12- by 12-inch) pendant terminal clusters in late summer and early autumn, followed by brown pods that persist most of the winter.

Height and spread To 19.5 m (65 feet) tall and 12 m (40 feet) wide.

Best climate and site Zones 4–8. Prefers moist, well-drained soil. Full sun to light shade. Widely tolerant of city conditions, heat and drought.

Cultivation Transplant young root-balled or container-grown plants in autumn or early spring. Prune in autumn only if necessary to shape the tree.

Propagation Sow seed when ripe in autumn.

Pest and disease prevention No serious pests or diseases.

Common problems Species tends to grow in a rather loose, open form.

Landscape use Specimen tree; street trees.

Cultivars 'Fastigiata' is an upright grower. 'Pendula' is a densely rounded tree with pendulous branches. 'Regent' is a fast grower with an upright habit and deeper leaf colour.

Sorbus aucuparia
ROSACEAE

COMMON MOUNTAIN ASH

Common mountain ash is a deciduous tree with compound leaves that turn red in autumn. The white spring flowers are followed by clusters of showy orange-red fruit.

Other common names Rowan tree.
Flower colour and season Clustered small white flowers in late spring, followed by bright orange-red fruit.
Height and spread To 10.5 m (35 feet) tall and nearly as wide.
Best climate and site Zones 2–7. Tolerant of a variety of well-drained soil conditions. Full sun to partial shade. Grows best in cooler climates.
Cultivation Transplant root-balled or container-grown plants in autumn or spring.
Propagation Graft in late winter and early spring. Sow seed in spring.
Pest and disease prevention Avoid overfeeding, which can stimulate young succulent growth that is susceptible to rusts and fire blight. Keep soil moist with organic mulch.
Common problems Short-lived in alkaline or dry soil.
Landscape use Specimen tree; shade trees.
Cultivars 'Edulis' bears large fruit, often used for preserves. 'Fastigiata' is a very upright, columnar form. 'Pendula' has pendulous branches. 'Xanthocarpa' has yellow fruit.

Styrax japonicus
STYRACACEAE

JAPANESE SNOWBELL

Japanese snowbell is a showy deciduous tree with a horizontal branching structure. The bell-shaped white flowers bloom profusely on the undersides of the branches.

Flower colour and season Pendulous white flowers bloom from late spring to early summer.
Height and spread To 9 m (30 feet) tall and nearly as wide.
Best climate and site Zones 5–9. Moist, humus-rich, well-drained, acid soil. Full sun to light shade. Tolerates city conditions; shelter from strong winds.
Cultivation Transplant container-grown or root-balled plants in early spring. Prune in summer only if necessary to shape the plant.
Propagation Take cuttings in summer. Sow seed in summer; may take two years to germinate.
Pest and disease prevention No serious pests or diseases. Keep soil moist by mulching with organic matter.
Common problems Plants grow poorly in dry or alkaline soil.
Landscape use Handsome small trees, ideal as a specimen near a patio; excellent shade trees.
Other species *S. obassia*, fragrant snowbell, bears its flowers in long clusters. It grows to 6 m (20 feet) tall and 4.5 m (15 feet) wide. Zones 6–9.

Thuja occidentalis
CUPRESSACEAE

AMERICAN ARBORVITAE

American arbor-vitae is a large upright pyramidal evergreen tree with scale-like dark green or golden green leaves borne in flattened fans. The leaves are aromatic when crushed.

Flower colour and season Inconspicuous reddish male and yellowish brown female flowers in mid-spring, followed by small dried capsules.
Height and spread To 18 m (60 feet) tall and 6 m (20 feet) wide.
Best climate and site Zones 2–7. Best where atmospheric moisture is high. Tolerant of a variety of soil conditions but prefers deep, loamy, humus-rich soil. Full sun.
Cultivation Transplant root-balled plants preferably in spring. Prune in early spring if necessary.
Propagation Sow seed in autumn or spring. Take cuttings in late summer.
Pest and disease prevention Mulch to keep the: soil evenly moist. Bagworms may attack, producing soft cone-like cocoons; use a knife to carefully cut the cocoons from the branches.
Common problems Subject to sun scorch when exposed to bright afternoon winter sun and wind.
Landscape use Screens; hedges; foundation plantings; accent plants.

Tilia x *europaea*
MALVACEAE

COMMON LIME

Common lime is a tall, fast-growing deciduous tree with heart-shaped leaves. The creamy white summer flowers are exceptionally fragrant and attractive to bees.

Flower colour and season Fragrant creamy white flowers in drooping clusters in early summer.
Height and spread To 30 m (100 feet) tall and 18 m (60 feet) wide.
Best climate and site Zones 3–7. Tolerant of a wide variety of soil conditions but thrives in deep, moist humus-rich, well-drained soil. Full sun. Adaptable to city conditions.
Cultivation Plant in winter or early spring. Thin out branches in late summer when overcrowded.
Propagation Graft in late winter and early spring. Sow seed in autumn.
Pest and disease prevention Mulch with organic matter to keep soil evenly moist. Healthy plants are more resistant to pests and diseases. Clean up dropped leaves to remove overwintering sites for pests and diseases.
Common problems Leaves can turn brown and become unsightly during summer droughts.
Landscape use Specimen tree; street trees; hedges.

Ulmus parvifolia
ULMACEAE

CHINESE ELM

Chinese elm is a round-topped usually deciduous tree that is semi-evergreen in the warmer portions of its range. Its bark peels off in irregular contrasting patches, giving the trunk an interesting look.

Flower colour and season Inconspicuous reddish flowers in autumn.
Height and spread To 15 m (50 feet) tall and 12 m (40 feet) wide.
Best climate and site Zones 5–9. Moist, humus-rich, well-drained soil. Full sun.
Cultivation Plant in winter or early spring. Prune in autumn.
Propagation Sow seed when ripe. Graft in spring.
Pest and disease prevention Keep soil moist with organic mulch. Maintain vigour by feeding and watering copiously. Vigorous trees are less susceptible to pests and diseases.
Common problems Usually trouble-free.
Landscape use Specimen tree; shade trees; street trees.
Cultivars 'Drake' has more upright branches than the species. 'Sempervirens' has broadly arching or weeping branches with smaller leaves than the species. 'True Green' has small glossy leaves and is usually more evergreen and less hardy than the species.

Zelkova serrato
ULMACEAE

JAPANESE ZELKOVA

Japanese zelkova is a deciduous tree from Japan, closely related to the elms. Its habit is rounded with numerous ascending branches; the leaves turn yellow or russet in autumn.

Flower colour and season Inconspicuous greenish flowers in early spring.
Height and spread To 27 m (90 feet) tall and nearly as wide.
Best climate and site Zones 5–8. Tolerant of a variety of soil conditions and air pollution. Full sun to light shade.
Cultivation Transplant root-balled or container-grown plants in autumn or spring. No pruning is necessary except to shape the trees by thinning crowded branches in late summer.
Propagation Sow seed in autumn. Take cuttings in summer.
Pest and disease prevention No serious pests or diseases.
Common problems Young plants are subject to frost injury.
Landscape use Specimen tree; street trees; screens.
Cultivars 'Village Green' is a fast-growing, vigorous form that is hardier than the species; its leaves turn a reddish colour in autumn.

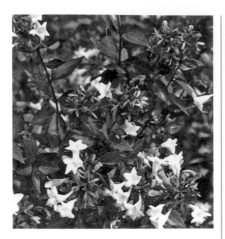

Abelia x *grandiflora*
CAPRIFOLIACEAE

GLOSSY ABELLA

Glossy abelia is a dense, semi-evergreen shrub with dark green opposite leaves that turn bronze or purple in autumn. The flowers are lightly fragrant.

Flower colour and season Pinkish purple or white tubular flowers borne in loose, terminal clusters in late spring to early summer.
Height and spread To 1.8 m (6 feet) tall and as wide.
Best climate and site Zones 6–10. Deep moist, well-drained, humus-rich soil. Full sun.
Cultivation Plant in spring or winter. Grow in a protected site in the colder portion of its range. Prune in late winter or early spring to remove winter-damaged wood.
Propagation Take softwood cuttings in early summer, hardwood cuttings in autumn.
Pest and disease prevention No serious pests or diseases.
Common problems Usually trouble-free.
Landscape use A good specimen tree; or use in informal hedges, foundation plantings or shrub borders.
Cultivars 'Sherwood' is a compact form only 90 cm (3 feet) tall.

Aesculus parviflora
HIPPOCASTANACEAE

BOTTLEBRUSH BUCKEYE

Bottlebrush buckeye is a deciduous shrub, occasionally growing as a single-trunked small tree. Its compound leaves consist of five to seven leaflets.

Flower colour and season Upright panicles of white flowers with pink stamens and red anthers in midsummer; followed by spiny fruit.
Height and spread 3–3.6 m (10–12 feet) tall and nearly as wide.
Best climate and site Zones 4–8. Deep, moist, humus-rich soil. Full sun to light shade.
Cultivation Transplant container-grown or root-balled plants in early spring.
Propagation Sow seed in autumn. Layer established plants in spring.
Pest and disease prevention Provide good air circulation to avoid fungal diseases such as leaf blotch and canker. Healthy plants are better able to resist pests and diseases.
Common problems Spreads freely by suckers. Japanese beetles may attack leaves. To control, knock beetles into a bucket of soapy water.
Landscape use Specimen shrubs; shrub borders. Especially valued as a midsummer source of colour.
Cultivars 'Rogers' is a late-blooming form with very long inflorescences.
Varieties *A. parviflora* var. *serotina* is a late-flowering form with larger flowers.

Aronia arbutifolia
ROSACEAE

RED CHOKEBERRY

Red chokeberry is a vigorous deciduous shrub planted for its spectacular display of brilliant red fruit in autumn and winter.

Flower colour and season White flowers, sometimes tinged with pink, borne in loose clusters in late spring, followed by conspicuous red fruit.
Height and spread To 2.4 m (8 feet) tall and as wide.
Best climate and site Zones 4–8. Average, well-drained soil. Full sun to light shade. Adapts well to both dry or wet conditions.
Cultivation Plant in spring. Best fruit production in full sun. Red chokeberry seldom requires pruning.
Propagation Take cuttings in early summer. Divide in early spring or autumn. Remove seed from its fleshy coating and sow in autumn.
Pest and disease prevention Choose a site with good air circulation. Clean up all dropped leaves to remove overwintering sites for disease spores. Prune off canes damaged by borers and seal ends with paraffin wax.
Common problems Plants tend to become leggy. Prune after flowering if necessary to promote a bushier habit. Also produces suckers.
Landscape use Valued for its autumn fruit colour. Most effective in mass plantings.

Aucuba japonica
GARRYACEAE

JAPANESE LAUREL

Japanese laurel is a shade-loving evergreen shrub with opposite glossy green leaves. The variegated cultivars are often grown as houseplants.

Flower colour and season Small purple flowers in terminal clusters in late winter to early spring, followed by bright scarlet fruit on female plants.
Height and spread To 3 m (10 feet) tall and as wide.
Best climate and site Zones 6–10. Deep, moist, well-drained soil. Tolerates dense shade, air pollution and competition from tree roots.
Cultivation Plant in winter or spring. Male and female flowers are borne on separate plants. You'll need to buy at least one male plant if you want fruit on the females. Seldom need pruning.
Propagation Take semi-hardwood cuttings in late spring.
Pest and disease prevention No serious pests or diseases.
Common problems In colder areas subject to leaf browning when exposed to wind or afternoon winter sun.
Landscape use Shrub borders; under trees; foundation plantings; containers.
Cultivars 'Crassifolia' is male with large green leathery leaves. 'Crotonifolia' may be either male or female with large leaves speckled with yellow. 'Variegata' is female with leaves blotched creamy yellow.

Berberis thunbergii
BERBERIDACEAE

JAPANESE BARBERRY

Japanese barberry is a dense, very thorny shrub with small leaves that, while deciduous, often turn red or purple and remain on the plant into winter.

Flower colour and season Small yellow flowers in late spring, followed by bright red persistent fruit.
Height and spread To 2.4 m (8 feet) tall and 4.5 m (15 feet) wide.
Best climate and site Zones 4–10. Deep, moist, well-drained soil. Full sun to almost full shade.
Cultivation Plant in spring. Prune if necessary to remove overcrowded shoots after flowering or in winter after fruiting.
Propagation Take cuttings in late spring. Remove seed from its fleshy coating and sow in autumn.
Pest and disease prevention No serious pests or diseases.
Common problems Does poorly in excessively wet soils. Spiny stems often trap leaves and other debris within the plant, giving it an untidy appearance.
Landscape use Informal hedges; foundation plantings; shrub border. Readily lends itself to pruning as a formal hedge.
Cultivars 'Aurea' has yellow leaves. *B. thunbergii* f. *atropurpurea* 'Atropurpurea Nana' is a dwarf form with red-purple foliage. 'Rose Glow' has purple leaves.

Buddleja davidii
SCROPHULARIACEAE

BUTTERFLY BUSH

Butterfly bush is a deciduous shrub, native to China, with long, narrow, opposite leaves. It dies back to the roots in cold areas.

Flower colour and season White, pink, red, purple, violet or pale purple flowers borne in upright, terminal spikes in midsummer to early autumn.
Height and spread To 4.5 m (15 feet) tall and as wide.
Best climate and site Zones 5–10. Deep, moist, well-drained, humus-rich soil. Full sun.
Cultivation Plant in spring. Cut back severely in late winter or early spring.
Propagation Take cuttings in early summer or early autumn. Sow seed in spring or autumn.
Pest and disease prevention No serious pests or diseases.
Common problems In the northern portion of its range, treat *B. davidii* and its cultivars as herbaceous perennials by cutting the stems to the ground and covering them with mulch.
Landscape use Best used towards the back of flower borders. Also great for shrub borders and informal hedges. Highly attractive to butterflies.
Cultivars 'Black Knight' has deep purple flowers. 'Charming' bears light lavender pink flowers. 'Nanho Purple' has red-purple flowers and dwarf, spreading habit. 'Royal Red' bears wine-red flowers.

Buxus sempervirens
BUXACEAE

COMMON BOX

Common boxw is a spreading shrub with small, glossy dark green leaves. Its dense branching structure make it popular for use in hedges.

Flower colour and season Inconspicuous pale green flowers in early spring.
Height and spread To 6 m (20 feet) tall and slightly wider.
Best climate and site Zones 6–10. Deep, moist, well-drained soil. Full sun to partial shade.
Cultivation Transplant root-balled or container-grown plants in spring. Use a compost or bark mulch around the base of the plants. This will help keep the shallow roots cool and moist and reduce the need for cultivation.
Propagation Take cuttings in summer.
Pest and disease prevention Leaf miner larvae can burrow inside leaves and produce tan patches. Remove and destroy affected leaves to prevent adult flies from multiplying.
Common problems Leaves often turn brown if exposed to cold, dry winter winds. Spray foliage with an anti-dessicant in autumn to prevent this from occurring. Prune out damaged stems.
Landscape use Informal hedges; foundation planting; screen planting; topiary. Lends itself well to pruning.
Cultivars 'Argentea' has leaves bordered with white. 'Aureo-variegata' has leaves variegated with yellow.

Calycanthus floridus
CALYCANTHACEAE

CAROLINA ALLSPICE

Deciduous Caralina allspice bears reddish or yellow flowers and glossy green leaves that turn bronze or purple in autumn.

Other common names Carolina sweet shrub, common sweet shrub, pineapple shrub, strawberry shrub.
Flower colour and season Very fragrant, strap-shaped reddish purple petals, tinged with brown, in early summer.
Height and spread 1.8–2.4 m (6–8 feet) tall and nearly as wide.
Best climate and site Zones 4–9. Humus-rich, well-drained but moisture-retentive soil. Full sun to light shade. Tends to be much shorter when grown in full sun.
Cultivation Plant in spring. Prune after flowering is finished.
Propagation Take cuttings in early summer. Layer in autumn. Sow seed in autumn. Remove rooted suckers in spring.
Pest and disease prevention No serious pests or diseases.
Common problems Fragrance varies among plants; smell before you buy.
Landscape use shrub borders; plant near outdoor living areas for fragrance.
Cultivars 'Athens' is yellow-flowered.

Camellia japonica
THEACEAE

COMMON CAMELLIA

Common camellia is an evergreen shrub or tree with deep green glossy leaves. It is commonly planted in warm climates for its colourful flowers.

Flower colour and season Single, semi-double or fully double flowers in shades of white, pink or red in late winter to early spring.
Height and spread 6–7.5 m (20–25 feet) tall and nearly as wide.
Best climate and site Zones 7–10 or in slightly colder areas if protected from winter sun and winds. Peaty, lime-free, humus-rich soil. Partial shade.
Cultivation Transplant container-grown or root-balled plants in winter or early spring. Apply adequate water to keep soil evenly moist during summer and winter. Mulch to keep roots cool and moist and to prevent weed problems.
Propagation Take cuttings of current season's growth in late summer.
Pest and disease prevention Flower blight can cause brown spots on petals. Avoid problems by buying only bare-root plants; also pick off and destroy any flower buds before planting. If the disease strikes, remove and destroy all infected buds and flowers, then apply a fresh layer of mulch around the base of the plant.
Common problems Flower buds can be damaged by untimely frosts.
Landscape use Specimen shrub; shrub borders; informal hedges.

Caryopteris x *clandonensis*
LAMIACEAE

BLUEBEARD

Bluebeard is a deciduous subshrub of hybrid origin with blue flowers and dull green leaves. In cold areas it dies back to the roots each winter.

Flower colour and season Blue flowers borne in dense spikes in mid- to late summer.
Height and spread To 1.2 m (4 feet) tall and as wide.
Best climate and site Zones 5–9. Moist, well-drained, loamy soil. Full sun and a sheltered position, such as near a sunny wall, in colder zones.
Cultivation Plant in late winter or spring. Cut back nearly to the ground in late winter since the flowers grow on new wood.
Propagation Take cuttings in early summer. Divide in spring.
Pest and disease prevention No serious pests or diseases.
Common problems Usually trouble-free.
Landscape use Informal hedges; shrub borders; perennial borders.
Cultivars 'Dark Knight' is a compact grower with darker foliage and deep blue flowers. 'Ferndown' has dark blue flowers. 'Heavenly Blue' has light blue flowers.

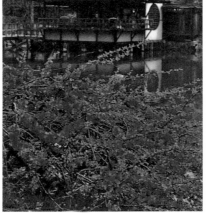

Chaenomeles speciosa
ROSACEAE

JAPANESE QUINCE

Native to China, Japanese quince is a spreading deciduous shrub with spiny branches. Its oval, alternate leaves are deep green above, paler below.

Flower colour and season Clusters of showy red flowers, followed by pear-shaped yellow-green fruit. Flowers bloom in late winter (in warm or protected areas) or in late spring to early summer. Sometimes will rebloom lightly in autumn.
Height and spread To 3 m (10 feet) tall and 6 m (20 feet) wide.
Best climate and site Zones 4–10. Deep, moist, humus-rich, well-drained soil. Full sun.
Cultivation Plant in autumn or spring. Regular renewal pruning will promote more lavish bloom.
Propagation Take cuttings in late summer. Layer in spring.
Pest and disease prevention Subject to scale insects and aphids. Avoid overfeeding, which causes succulent growth that attracts pests. To control scale insects, prune and destroy infested parts; spray remaining stems with horticultural oil. Control aphids by spraying with insecticidal soap.
Common problems Leaves can turn yellow when plants are grown in an alkaline soil.
Landscape use Shrub borders; specimen shrubs; informal hedges.

Clethra alnifolia
CLETHRACEAE

SUMMERSWEET

Native to the southeastern United States, summersweet is a deciduous shrub valued primarily for its fragrant flower spikes.

Flower colour and season White, very fragrant flowers borne in long, narrow upright clusters in mid- to late summer. The leaves turn bright yellow or orange in autumn.
Height and spread 1.5–2.4 m (5–8 feet) tall and as wide.
Best climate and site Zones 5–9. Well-drained, loamy soil. Full sun.
Cultivation Plant in spring. Prune in late winter.
Propagation Take cuttings in midsummer. Sow seed in late autumn.
Pest and disease prevention No serious pests or diseases.
Common problems Sometimes slow to become established.
Landscape use Hedges; shrub borders.
Cultivars 'Rosea' has deep pink buds opening to soft-pink flowers.
Other species *C. acuminaw*, cinnamon clethra, has nodding flower clusters and cinnamon brown bark. Zones 5–9.

Corylopsis spicata
HAMAMELIDACEAE

Spike winter hazel

Spike winter hazel is a compact deciduous shrub of particular interest for its early flowering period. Fragrant yellow flowers bloom before leaves emerge.

Flower colour and season Drooping clusters of fragrant yellow flowers in late winter to early spring.
Height and spread To 1.8 m (6 feet) tall and slightly wider.
Best climate and site Zones 5–9. Moist, well-drained, slightly acid soil. Full sun to partial shade.
Cultivation Transplant container-grown or root-balled plants in autumn or spring.
Propagation Take softwood cuttings in summer. Leave the cuttings undisturbed until growth begins the following spring, then transplant to a nursery bed or individual containers. Layer in autumn.
Pest and disease prevention No serious pests or diseases.
Common problems Flower buds can be injured by late spring frosts.
Landscape use Woodland plantings; shrub borders. Best displayed against a background of evergreens.
Other species *C. glabrescens*, fragrant winter hazel, blooms in early to mid-spring. It grows to 4.5 m (15 feet) tall and 3 m (10 feet) wide. Zones 5–9.

Cotoneaster horizontalis
ROSACEAE

Rock spray cotoneaster

Rock spray cotoneaster is a spreading deciduous shrub with bright red fruit and dark green leaves that turn red in autumn and persist well into winter.

Flower colour and season Pink flowers in mid- to late spring, followed by bright coral red fruit.
Height and spread To 90 cm (3 feet) tall and 1.8 m (6 feet) wide.
Best climate and site Zones 4–9. Moist, deep, well-drained soil. Full sun.
Cultivation Transplant container-grown plants in autumn or early spring.
Propagation Take cuttings in early summer. Sow seed in spring. Layer in autumn.
Pest and disease prevention Take care not to damage the plant with sharp garden tools; these wounds are common entry points for pests and diseases such as fire blight and borers. Lace bugs and spider mites can cause yellow or white speckling on leaves. Spray leaves, especially the undersides, with insecticidal soap.
Common problems Because of rather sparse root systems, plants are often slow to establish. Mulch with organic matter to keep the soil evenly moist, especially while the shrubs are young.
Landscape use Mostly used in rock gardens or as groundcover.
Cultivars 'Little Gem' is a dwarf, mound-shaped form. 'Variegatus' has leaves edged with white, turning pink in autumn.

Daphne cneorum
THYMELEACEAE

Rose daphne

Rose daphne is a low-growing evergreen shrub with narrow, strap-shaped leaves and exceptionally fragrant spring flowers.

Flower colour and season Dense terminal heads of fragrant pink flowers in late spring, sometimes repeating in autumn.
Height and spread To 30 cm (1 foot) tall and 90 cm (3 feet) wide.
Best climate and site Zones 4–9. Moist, well-drained, neutral or slightly alkaline soil. Full sun with protection from winter winds.
Cultivation Transplant container-grown plants in early autumn or early spring.
Propagation Layer in autumn. Take cuttings in late summer.
Pest and disease prevention Few serious pests or diseases. Rose daphne does not like strong fertilisers. A leafy mulch applied in early spring will supply adequate nutrients.
Common problems Plants are often slow to establish.
Landscape use Foundation shrubs; front of shrub borders.
Cultivars 'Alba' has white flowers. 'Eximia' is larger in leaf and flower.
Other species *D. adora*, winter daphne, has purple-and-white flowers and dark green oval leaves. 'Alba' has white flowers. 'Aureomarginata' is hardier than the species, with yellow-edged leaves. Zones 7–10.

Deutzia gracilis
HYDRANGEACEAE

SLENDER DEUTZIA

Slender deutzia is a deciduous shrub with long, lance-shaped leaves and clusters of white blooms in spring. Deutzias look lovely in shrub borders.

Flower colour and season Clusters of white flowers in late spring.
Height and spread To 1.8 m (6 feet) tall and nearly as wide.
Best climate and site Zones 4–9. Deep, moist, well-drained soil. Full sun.
Cultivation Plant in spring. After flowering, thin out drastically by cutting away weak and old wood, but leave the young shoots alone as these will bear the best flowers.
Propagation Sow seed in autumn. Take softwood cuttings in summer.
Pest and disease prevention Few serious pests or diseases.
Common problems Lack of pruning will result in few flowers.
Landscape use Specimen shrub; flowering shrub borders.
Cultivars 'Aurea' has yellow leaves. The leaves of, Marmorata are spotted with yellow.
Other species *D. scabra*, fuzzy deutzia, has oval or heart-shaped leaves and brown peeling bark. Its white early-summer flowers are often tinged with pink. 'Candidissima' bears double white flowers. Zones 5–9.

Enkianthus campanulatus
ERICACEAE

REDVEIN ENKIANTHUS

Native to Japan, redvein enkianthus is a tall deciduous shrub with oval, whorled leaves clustered at the ends of the branchlets.

Flower colour and season Drooping clusters of creamy yellow flowers, lightly tinged with red, in late spring. Leaves turn brilliant scarlet in autumn.
Height and spread To 3.6 m (12 feet) tall and not as wide.
Best climate and site Zones 4–8. Deep, moist humus-rich, well-drained, acid soil. Full sun to dense shade.
Cultivation Plant in spring. Expose to western sun for best autumn colour. No pruning is necessary.
Propagation Take cuttings in late spring. Sow seed in early spring. Layer in autumn.
Pest and disease prevention No serious pests or diseases.
Common problems Will not flourish in dry or alkaline soils. Mulch with compost to keep the soil evenly moist.
Landscape use Foundation plantings; shrub borders; woodland plantings.
Cultivars 'Albiflorus' has pure white flowers; 'Red Bells' has red flowers.

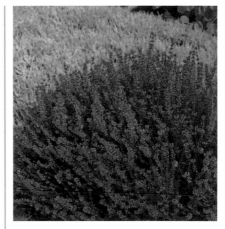

Erica cineria
ERICACEAE

BELL HEATHER

Bell heather is an evergreen shrub with small bell-shaped flowers and tiny needle-like leaves on stiff, much-divided branches.

Flower colour and season White, pinkish red, or purplish flowers in early to late summer.
Height and spread To 45 cm (18 inches) tall and 1.2 m (4 feet) wide.
Best climate and site Zones 5–7. Acid, moist, peaty soil, preferably low in fertility. Full sun to light shade. Best where nights are cool and moist.
Cultivation Plant in autumn or spring. Prune lightly after flowering. Do not fertilise. Shelter plant from sweeping winds, and keep watered during dry periods.
Propagation Sow seed or take cuttings in spring. Layer in summer.
Pest and disease prevention No serious pests or diseases.
Common problems Will not flourish where summers are extremely hot and winters extremely cold. Intolerant of drought; mulch to keep the soil evenly moist. High soil fertility can cause loose, open growth.
Landscape use Looks at its best used in masses as groundcover.
Other species *E. carnea*, spring heather, has white, pinkish red or purplish flowers in winter to mid-spring.

Euonymus alatus
CELASTRACEAE

WINGED SPINDLE TREE

Native to China and Japan, winged spindle is a deciduous shrub with dark green leaves that turn rich rosy scarlet in autumn.

Other common names Burning bush.
Flower colour and season Inconspicuous green white flowers in mid- to late spring; followed by purplish fruit.
Height and spread 3–4.5 m (10–15 feet) tall and nearly as wide.
Best climate and site Zones 3–9. Virtually any well-drained soil. Full sun to partial shade.
Cultivation Transplant root-balled or container-grown plants in autumn or spring. Prune in winter if you want to shape the plant, otherwise it seldom requires pruning.
Propagation Take cuttings during the growing season. Remove seed from its fleshy coating and sow in autumn.
Pest and disease prevention Prune and destroy parts infested by scale insects, which cause leaves to yellow and drop.
Common problems Not tolerant of very wet or very dry soil.
Landscape use Specimen shrub; shrub borders; informal hedges.
Cultivars 'Compacta' is a low-growing, dense plant.

Forsythia x intermedia
OLEACEAE

BORDER FORSYTHIA

Border forsythia is a deciduous shrub with clusters of yellow flowers that flower in spring before the leaves emerge. The foliage may turn purple in autumn.

Flower colour and season Bright yellow flowers in early to mid- spring.
Height and spread To 2.4 m (8 feet) tall and nearly as wide.
Best climate and site Zones 5–9. Deep, moist, well-drained soil; tolerates lime and air pollution. Full sun.
Cultivation Plant in spring. Remove older weak-growing or dead wood after flowering.
Propagation Take softwood cuttings in summer or hardwood cuttings in late autumn. Layer in autumn. Remove suckers in autumn.
Pest and disease prevention No serious pests or diseases.
Common problems In severe climates, late frosts can damage flowers.
Landscape use Specimen shrub; informal hedges. Plant in masses against an evergreen background.
Cultivars 'Lynwood' has yellow flowers as long entire stems. 'Spring Glory' bears pale yellow flowers.
Other species *F. suspensa*, weeping forsythia, is a rambling shrub with yellow spring flowers, arching branches and three-lobed leaves. It grows to 3 m (10 feet) tall. Zones 5–9.

Fothergilla gardenii
HAMAMELIDACEAE

DWARF FOTHERGLLLA

Dwarf forthergilla is a low-growing deciduous shrub with fragrant white flowers in spring and dramatic yellow or orange autumn colour.

Flower colour and season Fragrant white flowers borne in spikes in mid- to late spring.
Height and spread To 90 cm (3 feet) tall and as wide.
Best climate and site Zones 5–9. Deep, moist, humus-rich, well-drained soil. Full sun to partial shade.
Cultivation Transplant container-grown or root-balled plants in late winter or early spring.
Propagation Sow seed in summer. Take cuttings in summer and leave rooted cuttings undisturbed until the following year. Layer in autumn.
Pest and disease prevention No serious pests or diseases.
Common problems Will not thrive in wet or alkaline soils.
Landscape use Useful in shrub borders or as woodland plantings.
Cultivars 'Blue Mist' has frosty blue foliage that turns yellow and red in autumn.
Other species *F. major* is a larger pyramidal or rounded plant, growing to 2.7 m (9 feet) tall and as wide. Zones 5–9.

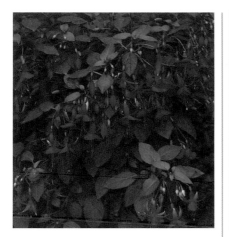

Fuchsia x *hybrida*
ONAGRACEAE

COMMON FUCHSIA

Largely derived from South American species, common fuchsias are alternate-leaved deciduous shrubs of upright or spreading habit.

Flower colour and season Pendant flowers, usually with contrasting corollas, in combinations too numerous to name. Possible colours include white, yellow, pink, red, and purple. Flower in early summer to autumn. Leaves are often tinged with purple.
Height and spread To 1.8 m (6 feet) tall and as wide.
Best climate and site Zones 9-10. Deep, moist, humus-rich, well-drained soil. Partial shade.
Cultivation Plant in winter or spring. Prune in early spring. Do not allow to dry out, particularly when grown in baskets.
Propagation Take cuttings in autumn and early winter.
Pest and disease prevention Sprinkle foliage with water during hot, dry weather to discourage spider mites. If they become a problem, spray the undersides of the leaves with insecticidal soap.
Common problems May die to the ground in winter, but will flower on new wood produced in spring.
Landscape use Where hardy, shrub borders and informal hedges. Upright types can be trained to standard form. Widely used as hanging basket plants.

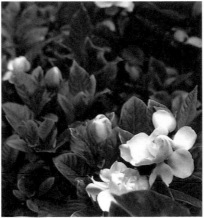

Gardenia jasminoides
RUBIACEAE

COMMON GARDENIA

Native to China, common gardenia is an evergreen shrub with very glossy leathery leaves. Its creamy white, waxy summer flowers are intensely fragrant.

Other common names Cape jasmine.
Flower colour and season Very fragrant single, semi-double or double white flowers in early to mid-summer.
Height and spread To 1.8 m (6 feet) tall and as wide.
Best climate and site Zones 8-10. Peaty, humus-rich, moisture-retentive, acid soil. Partial shade; protect from hot afternoon sun.
Cultivation Transplant in spring. Cut untidy plants well back in early spring.
Propagation Take cuttings in summer.
Pest and disease prevention Avoid damaging plants with gardening tools; these wounds are common entry points for pests and diseases such as mealybugs and stem canker. If affected by mealybugs, aphids or whiteflies, spray with insecticidal soap.
Common problems Sensitive to dry soil; mulch to help retain moisture.
Landscape use Where hardy, foundation shrubs or specimen plants; elsewhere, a greenhouse plant. Gardenias also grow well in containers.
Cultivars 'Mystery' is a bushy plant with large, double flowers. 'Radicans' is low-growing and has small flowers.

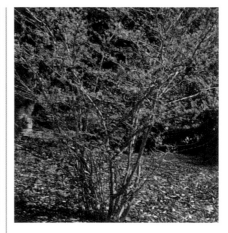

Hamamelis mollis
HAMAMELIDACEAE

CHINESE WITCH HAZEL

Chinese witch hazel is a deciduous shrub or tree with heart-shaped leaves and zigzag branches that are downy when young.

Flower colour and season Fragrant yellow flowers with strap-shaped petals in winter.
Height and spread To 7.5 m (25 feet) tall and nearly as wide.
Best climate and site Zones 5-9. Light, moist, well-drained, humus-rich soil. Full sun.
Cultivation Transplant container-grown or root-balled plants in autumn or spring. For best habit train to single stem by removing low-growing side branches.
Propagation Layer in late summer. Graft in spring. Sow seed outdoors in summer; may take up to two years to germinate.
Pest and disease prevention No serious pests or diseases.
Common problems Intolerant of dry soil.
Landscape use Specimen plant; shrub borders; woodland plantings; city gardens.
Other species *H.* x *intermedia* is of hybrid origin and has variously coloured fragrant spring flowers. 'Arnold Promise' is free-flowering, with yellow flowers and good reddish autumn colour. 'Feuerzauber' has copper red flowers. Zones 5-9. *H. virginiana*, Virginian witch hazel, is an autumn-flowering shrub to 3 m (10 feet) tall. Zones 5-9.

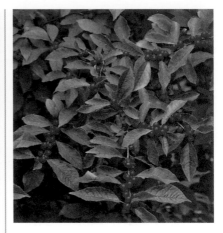

Hibiscus syriacus
MALVACEAE

ROSE MALLOW

Rose mallow is a late-flowering deciduous shrub with upright branches and a bush habit. It has showy hibiscus-like single or double flowers.

Flower colour and season 6–10-cm (2½–4-inch) trumpet-shaped flowers in white, pink, red, lavender or purple in late summer to early autumn.
Height and spread To 4.5 m (15 feet) tall and 3 m (10 feet) wide.
Best climate and site Zones 5–9. Deep, moist, well-drained soil. Full sun.
Cultivation Plant in spring or autumn. Prune in winter by removing at least two-thirds of the previous season's growth.
Propagation Take cuttings during summer. Layer in spring. Graft in late winter and early spring.
Pest and disease prevention If aphids or whiteflies attack leaves, spray with insecticidal soap. Control Japanese beetles by knocking them into a bucket of soapy water.
Common problems Lack of pruning will result in small flowers. Young, vigorous plants can be winter-killed. Protect from wind and do not fertilise after midsummer. Self-sown seedlings can be a problem; choose cultivars such as 'Diana' and 'Helene' that set little if any seed.
Landscape use Use as a specimen plant or in shrub borders.
Cultivars 'Blue Bird' has blue flowers. 'Diana' has pure white flowers.

Hydrangea spp.
HYDRANGEACEAE

HYDRANGEA

Hydrangeas are deciduous shrubs with opposite, broad leaves and showy summer flowers which are blue or pink, depending on soil pH.

Flower colour and season *H. macrophylla* has blue or pink flowers (blue in acid soils, pink in alkaline) borne in large, flat clusters up to 25 cm (10 inches) across in midsummer. *H. paniculata* has white flowers in immense pyramidal clusters in midsummer to early autumn. *H. quercifolia* has white flowers borne in erect, pyramidal clusters in early to late summer. Flower clusters contain both fertile and sterile flowers; the latter are more showy.
Height and spread Height varies according to cultivar to 6 m (20 feet); spread to 3 m (10 feet).
Best climate and site Zones 4–9, depending on cultivar. Deep, moist, well-drained soil. Partial shade; protect from hot afternoon sun.
Cultivation Plant in autumn or spring. Keep well watered in summer. Prune after flowering for more compact growth.
Propagation Propagate by cuttings, layering or seed, depending on cultivar.
Pest and disease prevention No serious pests or diseases. Mulch with organic matter to keep the soil evenly moist.
Common problems Buds or stems may be damaged in cold-winter areas.
Landscape use Best as a specimen shrub, or use in shrub borders.

Ilex spp.
AQUIFOLIACEAE

HOLLY

The brilliant red berries of I. verticillata, winterberry, are a natural choice for brightening up the winter garden. This deciduous holly loves moist, acid soil.

Flower colour and season Inconspicuous white flowers in late spring to early summer, followed by red or occasionally yellow fruit on female plants.
Height and spread Height varies according to cultivar to 18 m (60 feet) with a similar spread.
Best climate and site Zones 5–8. Deep, moist well-drained soil. Full sun to light shade.
Cultivation Transplant container-grown or root-balled plants in autumn or spring. Hollies are dioecious, which means that the male and female flowers are borne on separate plants. You'll need at least one male for every five female plants of the same species to get berries on the females. Prune in late spring if necessary. Mulch to keep soil moist.
Propagation Layer in summer. Take cuttings of evergreen types anytime, deciduous types in midsummer. Remove seed from fleshy covering and sow in autumn; may take 18 months to germinate.
Pest and disease prevention Leaf miners are a major problem. Remove and destroy affected leaves.
Common problems Leaves may turn yellow due to lack of nitrogen; fertilise regularly to keep plants green.

Itea virginica
ITEACEAE

VIRGINIA SWEET SPIRE

A summer-flowering deciduous shrub native to the eastern United States. Its alternate leaves are narrowly oval, turning brilliant red in autumn.

Flower colour and season Creamy white fragrant flowers borne in dense, narrow terminal clusters in early summer.
Height and spread To 1.5 m (5 feet) tall but not as wide.
Best climate and site Zones 5–9. Deep, humus-rich, constantly moist soil. Full sun to partial shade.
Cultivation Plant in spring. Rarely requires pruning.
Propagation Take cuttings in early summer. Divide or remove rooted suckers in spring.
Pest and disease prevention No serious pests or diseases. Avoid growing in dry, alkaline soil.
Common problems Does not do well in dry soil.
Landscape use Woodland plantings; shrub borders. Valued for its fragrance and autumn colour.
Cultivars 'Henry's Garnet' has reddish purple autumn colour and long flower clusters.

Juniperus spp.
CUPRESSACEAE

JUNIPER

Junipers are evergreen shrubs or trees. Their leaves are needle-like when young, becoming flat and scale-like when mature.

Flower colour and season Inconspicuous spring flowers, yellow on the male, greenish on the female, followed by small blue fruit on the female.
Height and spread Height varies according to cultivar to 18 m (60 feet); spread to 3 m (10 feet).
Best climate and site Zones 3–8, depending on cultivar. Widely tolerant of different soil conditions – even dry. Full sun to light shade.
Cultivation Transplant container-grown or root-balled plants in late winter or spring. No pruning is necessary.
Propagation Take cuttings in late summer, autumn or winter. Layer low-growing types in summer. Remove seed from its fleshy covering and sow in autumn.
Pest and disease prevention Hand-pick and destroy bagworms, which spin silken bags that are studded with needles and resemble pine cones. Plant as groundcover to encourage predators of mites, or spray leaves with insecticidal soap. Prune and destroy infected parts.
Common problems Several species are alternate hosts to cedar-apple rust. Avoid planting junipers near apple trees.
Landscape use Specimen shrub; foundation plants; groundcover.

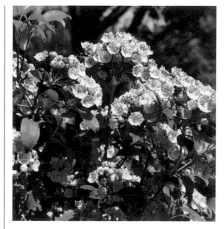

Kalmia latifolia
ERICACEAE

MOUNTAIN LAUREL

Native to the eastern United States, mountain laurel is a robust evergreen shrub with alternate glossy green leaves.

Flower colour and season White, pink, or rose flowers in terminal clusters in late spring to early summer.
Height and spread To 6 m (20 feet) tall and as wide.
Best climate and site Zones 4–7. Moisture-retentive, humus-rich, peaty soil. Full sun to partial shade.
Cultivation Transplant container-grown or root-balled plants in spring or autumn. Mulch to keep shallow roots cool and to control weeds. No pruning.
Propagation Layer in autumn. Sow seed in early spring. Cuttings in late summer.
Pest and disease prevention Avoid damaging plants with sharp gardening tools; these wounds are common entry points for pests such as borers. Lace bugs can cause yellow speckling on leaves; spray foliage (especially the undersides of the leaves) with insecticidal soap.
Common problems Grows poorly in dry or alkaline soil.
Landscape use Foundation shrubs; shrub borders; woodland plantings.
Cultivars 'Bullseye' bears white flowers banded with red. 'Elf' is a very dwarf form with pink buds that open to near white flowers. 'Ostbo Red' has red buds that open to light pink flowers.

Kerria japonica
ROSACEAE

JAPANESE KERRIA

Japanese kerria is a bushy deciduous shrub with slender green branches that hold their colour year-round. Yellow spring flowers.

Flower colour and season Golden yellow five-petalled flowers in mid- to late spring.
Height and spread To 1.8 m (6 feet) tall and as wide.
Best climate and site Zones 4–8. Deep, moist, humus-rich, well-drained soil. Full sun to partial shade.
Cultivation Plant in early spring. Thin out old stems after flowering. Mulch with compost or aged manure after pruning.
Propagation Take cuttings in summer or autumn. Divide clumps in autumn.
Pest and disease prevention No serious pests or diseases.
Common problems Slow to establish.
Landscape use Use as a specimen shrub or in shrub borders.
Cultivars 'Pleniflora' has ball-shaped double flowers. 'Variegata' has single flowers with leaves that are deeply margined in white.

Lavandula angustifolia
LABIATAE

LAVENDER

Lavender is a rounded shrub beloved for its herbal and ornamental qualities. It has fragrant grey-green leaves with spikes of purple-blue flowers.

Flower colour and season The 1-cm (½-inch) purple-blue flowers are carried in tight, narrow clusters in summer.
Height and spread 60–90 cm (2–3 feet) tall; similar spread.
Best climate and site Zones 5–8. A verage to humus-rich, well-drained soil. Full sun to light shade. Neutral or slightly alkaline soil is best. Lavender is extremely drought-tolerant.
Cultivation Prune out any dead wood and reshape the shrubs in spring. Shear plants every few years to encourage fresh new growth and to promote flowering.
Propagation Layer or take tip cuttings in summer. Place cuttings in a well-drained medium; transplant them as soon as they root to avoid rot.
Pest and disease prevention No serious pests or diseases.
Common problems Shoots may be partially killed in winter.
Landscape use Plant lavender in ornamental and herb gardens. Use as an edging plant or to configure knot gardens. In borders combine them with other plants that need excellent drainage such as yarrow and evening primrose (*Oenothera* spp.).

Mahonia aquifolium
BERBERIDACEAE

OREGON GRAPE

Oregon grape is a broad-leaved evergreen shrub with prominent yellow flower clusters that give way to showy blue fruit that resembles grapes.

Other common names Holly grape.
Flower colour and season Clustered bright yellow flowers in late spring to early summer, followed by grape-like blue fruit.
Height and spread To 90 cm (3 feet) tall and as wide.
Best climate and site Zones 5–9. Deep, moist, well-drained soil. Full sun to light shade.
Cultivation Transplant container-grown or root-balled plants in spring. After flowering cut a few of the oldest stems to the ground each year for more compact growth.
Propagation Take cuttings in late winter. Sow seed in late spring. Divide in autumn.
Pest and disease prevention Alternate host to black stem rust; avoid planting where what is a major commercial crop.
Common problems In colder zones the leaves may be damaged if exposed to winter winds and afternoon sun.
Landscape use Specimen shrub; foundation plantings; shrub borders.
Other species *M. bealei*, leather-leaved mahonia, has leathery blue-green leaves and very fragrant flowers. It grows to 1.8 m (6 feet) tall and as wide. Zones 6–9.

Myrica pensylvanica
MYRICACEAE

BAYBERRY

Bayberry is a deciduous or semi-evergreen shrub with fragrant leaves. The wax-coated fruits are sometimes used in candle making.

Flower colour and season Insignificant greenish catkins in late spring, followed by clustered waxy white fruit.

Height and spread To 2.7 m (9 feet) tall and as wide.

Best climate and site Zones 2–7. Adapts to a wide range of soil conditions. Good tolerance to seaside conditions. Full sun to partial shade.

Cultivation Transplant container-grown or root-balled plants in spring. Prune lightly anytime to encourage compact growth; rejuvenate older plants by pruning heavily every couple of years.

Propagation Take cuttings in late spring. Layer in autumn. Soak seed in hot water or rub it against a rough surface to remove the waxy coating, sow in autumn.

Pest and disease prevention No serious pests or diseases.

Common problems Leaves can become chlorotic (turn yellow) when grown in alkaline soils.

Landscape use Shrub borders; hedges; woodland plantings.

Other species *M. cerifera*, wax myrtle, is an evergreen native to the southeastern United States and grows as a tall shrub or tree. Zones 6–9.

Nandina domestica
BERBERIDACEAE

HEAVENLY BAMBOO

Heavenly bamboo is an evergreen shrub with glossy green alternate, compound leaves that turn rich red in autumn. Young foliage is often tinged with pink.

Flower colour and season White flowers are borne in large clusters in midsummer, followed by clustered red fruit that persists nearly all winter.

Height and spread To 3 m (10 feet) tall and 1.8 m (6 feet) wide.

Best climate and site Zones 6–10. Deep, moisture-retentive, well-drained soil. Full sun to dense shade.

Cultivation Transplant container-grown or root-balled plants in late winter or spring. Cut a few of the oldest stems to the ground each spring to encourage new growth.

Propagation Take cuttings in summer. Remove seed from its fleshy covering and sow in autumn.

Pest and disease prevention No serious pests or diseases.

Common problems Plants may be damaged by low winter temperatures, especially in the colder areas.

Landscape use Use as foundation plantings or hedges.

Cultivars 'Alba' is white-fruited. 'Compacta' is a dwarf form. 'Harbour Dwarf' is a dwarf form with foliage that is tipped pink or bronze in spring and that turns orange or bronzy red in winter. 'Royal Princess' has delicate foliage.

Nerium oleander
APOCYNACEAE

OLEANDER

Native to the Mediterranean coast, oleander is a vigorous evergreen shrub with narrow, leathery dark green leaves.

Flower colour and season Single or double flowers in various shades of white, yellow, pink, red and purple, sometimes measuring up to 7.5 cm (3 inches) across, in mid-spring to late summer.

Height and spread To 6 m (20 feet) tall and 3 m (10 feet) wide.

Best climate and site Zones 7–10. Widely tolerant of heat, drought and seaside conditions. Full sun.

Cultivation Plant in spring. Prune lightly after flowering to maintain thick bushy growth. Prune by half to rejuvenate old plants in winter.

Propagation Take cuttings anytime in growing season.

Pest and disease prevention Subject to scale insects, which turn plants yellow. Prune off infested plant parts.

Common problems All parts of the plant are toxic if eaten.

Landscape use Informal hedges; screen plantings; shrub borders; street plantings; container plantings.

Cultivars 'Calypso' bears single cherry red flowers. 'Isle of Capri' has single light yellow flowers. 'Mrs. Reoding' has double salmon-pink flowers. 'Sister Agnes' has single white flowers.

Osmanthus fragrans
OLEACEAE

FRAGRANT OLIVE

Native to Asia, fragrant olive is an evergreen shrub with holly-like dark green opposite leaves. Clusters of sweetly scented white flowers start in spring.

Other common names Sweet olive.
Flower colour and season Very fragrant, small white tubular flowers in drooping clusters in early spring to early summer, followed by blue-black berries.
Height and spread To 6 m (20 feet) tall and as wide.
Best climate and site Zones 8–10. Deep, moist, well-drained soil. Full sun to light shade.
Cultivation Plant in winter, autumn or spring. Cut back after flowering to maintain desired height and form.
Propagation Take cuttings in late summer. Layer in spring or summer.
Pest and disease prevention No serious pests or diseases.
Common problems Very frost-sensitive.
Landscape use Informal hedges; foundation plantings; shrub borders; container plantings.
Forms *O. fragrans* f. *aurantiacus* has orange flowers.

Paeonia suffruticosa
PAEONIACEAE

TREE PEONY

Unlike the more familiar garden peony, tree peonies do not die back to the roots each winter. Instead, they form a magnificent dense, deciduous shrub.

Flower colour and season Very large single or double flowers in white, pink, red, lavender or yellow in mid- to late spring.
Height and spread To 1.5 m (5 feet) tall and slightly wider.
Best climate and site Zones 5–8. Deep, moist, humus-rich, well-drained soil. Full sun to partial shade.
Cultivation Plant in spring or autumn. Keep soil evenly moist in summer. Benefits from organic mulch. Do not cut back when foliage dies in winter, as you would an herbaceous peony. Just prune off any winter-damaged wood in spring.
Propagation Layer in spring. Graft onto the roots of herbaceous peonies in late summer.
Pest and disease prevention No serious pests or diseases.
Common problems Leaves and flowers can be damaged by late spring frosts.
Landscape use A magnificent specimen shrub – truly a garden gem.
Cultivars 'Age of Gold' bears golden yellow double flowers. 'Godaishu' has pure white semi-double flowers. 'Hana Kisoi' has deep shell pink semi-double flowers. 'Kamada Nishiki' has raspberry red double flowers.

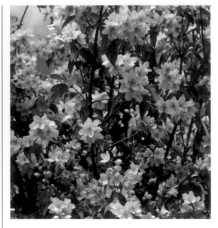

Philadelphus coronarius
HYDRANGEACEAE

SWEET MOCK ORANGE

Native to southern Europe, sweet mock orange is a deciduous shrub with opposite leaves. The single or double white flowers are usually very fragrant.

Flower colour and season Single or occasionally double white flowers, usually highly fragrant, in late spring.
Height and spread To 2.4 m (8 feet) tall but not as wide.
Best climate and site Zones 4–9. Tolerant of many soil conditions, even dry soil. Full sun to partial shade.
Cultivation Plant in spring. Prune leggy plants immediately after flowering. Cut back by one-third and cut out old canes.
Propagation Take cuttings in summer. Remove a few rooted stems in spring or autumn.
Pest and disease prevention No serious pests or diseases.
Common problems Provides little interest when not in flower.
Landscape use Shrub borders.
Cultivars 'Belle Etoile' bears single flowers over 5 cm (2 inches) in diameter. 'Boule d' Argent' has double flowers that are 5 cm (2 inches) in diameter. 'Minnesota Snowflake' has double flowers that are 5 cm (2 inches) in diameter; it is exceptionally vigorous and winter-hardy. 'Virginal' bears double flowers that are 5 cm (2 inches) in diameter.

Pieris japonica
ERICACEAE

JAPANESE PIERIS

Japanese pieris is an evergreen shrub with dark green leaves that are often bronze or reddish when young. Flower buds are conspicuous all winter.

Flower colour and season Fragrant white flowers in mid-spring.
Height and spread To 2.4 m (8 feet) tall and as wide.
Best climate and site Zones 4–9. Moist, humus-rich, well-drained, acid soil. Full sun to light shade.
Cultivation Transplant container-grown or root-balled plants in spring. Prune after flowering.
Propagation Layer in spring or summer. Take cuttings in summer. Sow seed in autumn or early spring.
Pest and disease prevention Lace bugs frequently attack, causing yellow leaves. To control, spray leaves (especially the undersides) with insecticidal soap.
Common problems Cannot tolerate poorly drained soil.
Landscape use Specimen shrub; shrub borders; foundation plantings.
Cultivars 'Dorothy Wycoff' is a compact grower with deep red buds that open to pink. 'Red Mill' is exceptionally hardy. 'Valley Valentine' bears very long-lasting deep pink flowers. 'Variegata' has white-edged leaves. 'White Cascade' has pure white flowers.

Potentilla fruticosa
ROSACEAE

SHRUBBY CINQUEFOIL

Shrubby cinquefoil is a compact deciduous shrub. The flowers are usually yellow, but also come in red, pink, orange or white.

Flower colour and season Yellow five-petalled flowers in early summer to early autumn.
Height and spread To 1.2 m (4 feet) tall and as wide.
Best climate and site Zones 2–8. Tolerant of many soil conditions including alkaline soil. Full sun to very light shade.
Cultivation Transplant in spring. Prune during winter for a thicker habit. Cut all stems back by one-third or remove a few of the oldest stems at ground level.
Propagation Take cuttings in summer. Sow seed in autumn.
Pest and disease prevention No serious pests or diseases.
Common problems Will not thrive in dense shade.
Landscape use Informal hedges; shrub borders; edgings.
Cultivars 'Coronation Triumph' is a vigorous form with soft green foliage and many bright yellow flowers. 'Katherine Dykes' has pale yellow flowers and silvery green foliage. 'Mount Everest' has large white flowers. 'Tangerine' has orange flowers (when grown in light shade).

Pyracantha coccinea
ROSACEAE

SCARLET FIRETHORN

Scarlet firethorn is grown for its masses of orange-red berries that last through autumn. Evergreen in warm areas, deciduous in colder regions.

Flower colour and season White flowers in flat clusters from late spring to early summer, followed by persistent fruit that is typically red but occasionally orange or even yellow.
Height and spread To 4.5 m (15 feet) tall and as wide.
Best climate and site Zones 6–9. Deep, moist, humus-rich, well-drained soil. Full sun to light shade.
Cultivation Transplant container-grown or root-balled plants in spring. Prune anytime to remove suckers or excessively long shoots.
Propagation Take cuttings in summer. Sow seed in autumn or late winter.
Pest and disease prevention Avoid over-fertilising, which can promote succulent growth that is subject to fire blight. Plant disease-resistant cultivars.
Common problems Leaves may be damaged by cold winter temperatures.
Landscape use Specimen shrub; foundation plantings; espalier; hedges.
Cultivars 'Aurea' has yellow fruit. 'Lalandei', somewhat hardier than the species, is an upright grower to 3.6 m (12 feet) tall with orange-red fruit; it is resistant to scab and fire blight.

Rhododendron spp. and hybrids
ERICACEAE

RHODODENDRON

The genus Rhododendron is generally divided into smaller-leaved, deciduous types called azaleas, and larger-leaved evergreen rhododendrons.

Other common names Azalea.
Flower colour and season White, pink, red, lavender, orange, rosy purple or yellow flowers in early spring to midsummer, varying with cultivar.
Height and spread Height varies according to cultivar to 6 m (20 feet); similar spread.
Best climate and site Zones 4–9, varying with cultivar. Moist, acid soil. Light shade.
Cultivation Transplant container-grown or root-balled plants in spring. Prune after flowering to control size.
Propagation Take cuttings in midsummer. Layer in summer. Sow seed indoors in late winter.
Pest and disease prevention Avoid planting in poorly drained soil. Mulch with compost or aged manure to keep the shallow roots cool and moist.
Common problems Very sensitive to salinity and high pH.
Landscape use Foundation plantings; specimen shrub; massed plantings; container plantings.
Species *R. arborescens*, sweet azalea; *R. calendulaceum*, flame azalea; *R. carolinianum*, Carolina rhododendron; *R. catawbiense*, Catawba rhododendron.

Rosa hybrids
ROSACEAE

ROSE

Floribunda roses, such as the red-flowered 'Europeana', bear large clusters of flowers on vigorous plants.

Flower colour and season White, pink, orange, yellow, red, lavender or multicoloured single or double flowers, often fragrant, from late spring to late summer, depending on cultivar.
Height and spread Depends on type and cultivar.
Best climate and site Zones 4–10, varying with cultivar. Deep, moist, well-drained, humus-rich soil. Full sun.
Cultivation Transplant bare-root plants in autumn or winter or container-grown plants in autumn or spring. Fertilise regularly in spring and again in summer to ensure many blooms. Prune hybrid tea and floribunda roses in early spring, and climbers and species roses after flowering.
Propagation Take softwood cuttings in summer, hardwood cuttings in winter. Layer in spring or autumn. Remove seed from its fleshy covering and sow in spring or autumn. Bud-graft hybrids in spring.
Pest and disease prevention Choose a site with full sun and good air circulation. Plant disease-resistant species and cultivars. Avoid wetting foliage.
Common problems Hardiness varies greatly among species and cultivars. Some plants may be damaged or killed by cold winter temperatures.

Spiraea thunbergii
ROSACEAE

THUNBERG SPIREA

Thunberg spirea is a small twiggy deciduous shrub that produces masses of small white flowers in spring before the leaves appear.

Flower colour and season Clusters of small white flowers in mid-spring.
Height and spread To 1.5 m (5 feet) tall and as wide or slightly wider.
Best climate and site Zones 4–8. Tolerates a wide range of soil conditions. Full sun to partial shade.
Cultivation Plant in spring. Prune back after flowering.
Propagation Sow fresh seed in summer. Take cuttings in midsummer. Divide in spring or autumn.
Pest and disease prevention Avoid overfeeding, which promotes succulent growth that is attractive to aphids. If these pests become a problem, spray with insecticidal soap.
Common problems Will not thrive in poorly drained soils.
Landscape use Informal low hedges; shrub borders; specimen shrub.
Other species *S. japonica*, Japanese spirea, produces small pink flowers in flat clusters in late spring to early summer. 'Atro-sanguinea' has deep red flowers. 'Ruberrima' has deep pink flowers. 'Shirobana' has white, pink and red flowers borne simultaneously. Zones 5–9.

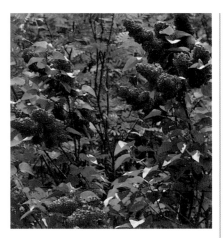

Syringa vulgaris
OLEACEAE

COMMON LILAC

Common lilac is a deciduous shrub with heart-shaped leaves. The species bears lavender-purple spring flowers.

Flower colour and season Very fragrant lavender flowers in long clusters in mid-to late spring.
Height and spread To 6 m (20 feet) tall and 3.6 m (12 feet) wide.
Best climate and site Zones 3–7. Neutral or alkaline, humus-rich, well-drained soil. Full sun to light shade.
Cultivation Plant in autumn or spring. Prune after flowering to prevent seed formation. Cut some of the oldest stems to the ground each year.
Propagation Take cuttings in autumn. Layer in spring or summer.
Pest and disease prevention Thoroughly clean up dropped leaves to remove overwintering sites for disease spores. Select sites with good air circulation.
Common problems Lilacs are sometimes grafted onto privet (*Ligustrum* spp.) rootstocks, which produce suckers. Prune off suckers as they appear.
Landscape use Specimen shrub; shrub borders; screens or hedges.
Cultivars 'Lavender Lady' bears lavender flowers and blooms reliably in areas too warm for other lilacs. 'Miss Ellen Willmott' bears double white flowers. 'President Lincoln' has single blue flowers. 'Sensation' has wine-red flowers.

Viburnum carlesii
ADOXACEAE

FRAGRANT VIBURNUM

Fragrant viburnum is a deciduous shrub with dark green leaves that turn purplish-red in autumn. The pink flower buds open to scented white flowers.

Flower colour and season Very fragrant white flowers tinged with pink in mid-spring, followed by blue-black fruit.
Height and spread To 1.5 m (5 feet) tall and nearly as wide.
Best climate and site Zones 4–9. Virtually any well-drained soil. Full sun to light shade.
Cultivation Plant in autumn or spring. If necessary, prune after flowering to shape the plant.
Propagation Take cuttings in summer. Sow seed when ripe. Layer in autumn.
Pest and disease prevention Avoid overfeeding, which encourages succulent growth attractive to aphids. If aphids attack, spray with insecticidal soap. Clean up dropped leaves to remove overwintering sites for mildew spores.
Common problems Avoid poorly drained soils.
Landscape use Specimen shrub; shrub borders; screens or hedges.
Other species *V. opulus*, guelder rose, has clusters of white flowers in mid-spring, yellowish to purplish red autumn colour, and red fruit that persists into winter. Zones 3–8.

Weigela florida
CAPRIFOLIACEAE

WEIGELA

Weigela is an opposite-leaved free-flowering deciduous shrub native to Korea and northern China. It has pink spring flowers.

Flower colour and season Funnel-shaped, rosy pink flowers in late spring.
Height and spread To 2.4 m (8 feet) tall and nearly as wide.
Best climate and site Zones 4–8. Cool, deep, moist, humus-rich, well-drained soil. Full sun to light shade.
Cultivation Transplant bare-root or container-grown plants in spring or autumn. Prune back severely after flowering.
Propagation Take cuttings in summer.
Pest and disease prevention No serious pests or diseases.
Common problems Old canes produce few flowers.
Landscape use Use in shrub borders and mass plantings.
Cultivars 'Bristol Ruby' has ruby red flowers. 'Bristol Snowflake' has white flowers tinged with pink. 'Candida' has pure white flowers. 'Eva Supreme' is very dwarf with deep red flowers. 'Foliis Purpureis' is a dwarf form with purplish foliage. 'Variegata' has leaves edged with page yellow.
Varieties The variety *venusta*, with its purplish pink flowers, is hardier than the species.

Actinidia kolomikta
ACTINIDIACEAE

HARDY KIWI

Hardy kiwi is a twining deciduous plant with heart-shaped leaves. The foliage is purple at first and later becomes variegated with pink and white, especially on male plants.

Other common names Cape gooseberry, kolomikta.

Flower colour and season Fragrant white or green flowers in late spring and early summer, followed by edible green fruit on female plants.

Height and spread To 6 m (20 feet) with support.

Best climate and site Zones 4–10. Moist, well-drained soil. Full sun to partial shade. Alkaline soil produces best leaf and flower colour.

Cultivation Plant in early spring. Prune in winter if necessary. Male and female flowers are borne on separate plants. You'll need to buy one male for every three to four female plants to get fruit on the females.

Propagation Layer in spring. Take cuttings in midsummer.

Pest and disease prevention Keep soil moist in hot weather. No serious pests or diseases.

Common problems Will not survive severe drought.

Landscape use Excellent foliage plants to use on wire supports.

Ampelopsis brevipedunculata
VITACEAE

PORCELAIN AMPELOPSIS

A deciduous climber native to Asia, porcelain ampelopsis bears three or occasionally five-lobed leaves and distinctly hairy young shoots. It is a vigorous grower, climbing by tendrils.

Flower colour and season Clusters of small white flowers in late spring; followed by clustered fruits of amethyst-blue in autumn.

Height and spread To 6 m (20 feet) with support.

Best climate and site Zones 4–9. Humus-rich, moist, well-drained soil. Full sun to partial shade.

Cultivation Plant in winter or spring. Grows quickly. Cut to ground in late winter to produce new fruiting growth.

Propagation Take cuttings in midsummer.

Pest and disease prevention Avoid planting in poorly drained soil.

Common problems Japanese beetles may attack and skeletonise the leaves. Shake. beetles from plants into a bucket of soapy water in early morning. Deter with an organically acceptable insecticide.

Landscape use Chiefly valued for its striking fruit. Grow on fences, arbours or trellises.

Cultivars 'Elegans' has foliage handsomely variegated with white and pink. Less hardy than the species. Zones 5–9.

Aristolochia elegans
ARISTOLOCHIACEAE

CALICO DUTCHMAN'S PIPE

Calico Dutchman's pipe is a twining evergreen plant with heart-shaped alternate leaves. The speckled flowers are curiously twisted and resemble a curved smoking pipe.

Flower colour and season 7.5-cm (3-inch) purple-and-yellow scentless flowers in late spring and early summer.

Height and spread 3–4.5 m (10–15 feet) with support.

Best climate and site Zones 9–11. Rich moisture-retentive but well-drained soil. Full sun to partial shade.

Cultivation Transplant container-grown plants in spring. Cut back in winter to control size.

Propagation Take stem cuttings in early summer or root cuttings in late winter. Sow seed in spring.

Pest and disease prevention Avoid poorly drained soil.

Common problems Occasionally susceptible to spider mites, which cause yellow curled leaves with fine webs on undersides. Deter with an organically acceptable insecticide, such as insecticidal soap.

Landscape use Grow on fences or trellises; excellent for screening.

Bougainvillea glabra
NYCTAGI NACEAE

LESSER BOUGAINVILLEA

Native to Brazil, lesser bougainvillea is a spiny alternate-leaved vine that occasionally grows into a loose shrub. The small summer flowers are surrounded by showy bracts.

Other common names Paper flower.
Flower colour and season Inconspicuous flowers surrounded by brilliantly coloured bracts of red, yellow, purple, white, or magenta all summer.
Height and spread 6–9 m (20–30 feet) with support.
Best climate and site Zone 10. Well-drained, humus-rich soil. Full sun.
Cultivation Plant in spring. Cut back severely after flowering to maintain desired shape and size. Mulch freely in spring with aged cow manure or compost.
Propagation Take cuttings during active growth.
Pest and disease prevention Avoid damaging with pruning tools; these wounds are common entry points for pests and diseases.
Common problems Vigorously growing plants often produce ferocious thorns; avoid planting in areas where children play or where passers-by will come in contact with the thorns.
Landscape use Where hardy, excellent to cover trellises and porches or to hang over walls and banks. Elsewhere, a lovely hanging basket plant.

Campsis radicans
BIGNONIACEAE

TRUMPET VINE

Trumpet vine is a summer-flowering deciduous climber that supports itself by means of root-like holdfasts. Its leaves are pinnately compound, with 7–11 leaflets.

Flower colour and season Orange or red flowers, borne in pendulous, terminal clusters of 5-cm (2-inch) wide, trumpet-shaped flowers in early to late summer.
Height and spread 9–12 m (30–40 feet) with support.
Best climate and site Zones 4–9. Virtually any well-drained soil. Full sun.
Cultivation Plant in early spring. Prune in spring to restrain growth. Often needs additional support because of its weight.
Propagation Take cuttings in spring to summer; layer in autumn to spring; sow seed in spring.
Pest and disease prevention Enrich soil with organic matter to promote healthy growth. No serious pests or diseases.
Common problems C. *radicans* can become invasive as it tends to spread by underground runners. Remove unwanted shoots at soil level.
Landscape use Excellent flowering plants for fences, walls and trellises or to climb up trees.
Cultivars 'Fiava' bears yellow flowers.
Other species C. *grandiflora*, Chinese trumpet creeper, native to China, is somewhat less rampant. Its leaves consist of seven to nine leaflets. Zones 7–11.

Clematis spp. and hybrids
RANUNCULACEAE

CLEMATIS

Clematis are usually deciduous plants with opposite, compound leaves that climb by twining. C. montana 'Rubens ' has fragrant lavender-pink flowers in early summer.

Flower colour and season White, pink, red, blue, lavender or purple blooms, in early summer to mid-autumn – varying according to cultivar.
Height and spread 2.4–7.2 m (8–24 feet) with support, varying with species or cultivar.
Best climate and site Zones 5–9. Moisture-retentive, humus-rich soil. Full sun at the tops, partial shade at the roots.
Cultivation Plant in spring or autumn. Prune after flowering to remove dead wood and to shape the plant. Many clematis tend to die back during winter in the colder parts of their range. Mulch around the root of the climber to keep it cool. Water regularly during hot weather.
Propagation Take cuttings in spring or early summer. Layer in spring.
Pest and disease prevention When planting, set the crown 5–7.5 cm (2–3 inches) below the soil surface to encourage strong, healthy growth.
Common problems Clematis borer may be a problem. Prune off damaged canes and seal ends with paraffin.
Landscape use Outstanding flowering plants to grow on arbours, trellises or even to intertwine with climbing roses.

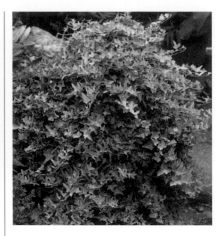

Clerodendrum thomsoniae
LAMIACEAE

BLEEDING GLORY BOWER

Native to West Africa, bleeding glory bower is a twining evergreen climber with opposite 12.5-cm (5-inch) leaves. The showy red-and-white flowers bloom from summer into autumn.

Other common names Bag flower, bleeding heart vine, glory tree, tropical bleeding heart.
Flower colour and season Clusters of flowers with red petals, striking white calyces and long, curving, protruding stamens in summer and autumn.
Height and spread To 3 m (10 feet) with support.
Best climate and site Zones 9–10. Rich, loamy, moisture-retentive soil. Partial shade.
Cultivation Plant in spring. Prune lightly after flowering if needed to control growth. Never allow to dry out.
Propagation Sow seed in spring. Take cuttings in spring and summer.
Pest and disease prevention Avoid overwatering during winter when plant is not growing as quickly. Mulch with organic matter to keep soil evenly moist during spring and summer.
Common problems Drought-sensitive.
Landscape use Where hardy, grow on a fence or trellis. Elsewhere, a fine hanging-basket plant.

Gelsemium sempervirens
GELSEMICEAE

YELLOW JESSAMINE

Native to the southeastern United States, yellow jessamine is a twining climber with glossy opposite leaves; it is evergreen in the warmer portions of its range.

Other common names Carolina jasmine, evening trumpet flower, woodbine.
Flower colour and season Funnel-shaped, fragrant yellow flowers borne in axillary clusters in early to mid- spring.
Height and spread To 6 m (20 feet) with support.
Best climate and site Zones 7–10. Virtually any well-drained soil. Full sun to light shade.
Cultivation Transplant container-grown plants. in spring. If necessary, prune after flowering to control growth.
Propagation Take cuttings in summer. Sow seed in spring.
Pest and disease prevention Avoid waterlogged sites. No serious pests or disease problems.
Common problems Flowers, leaves and roots are poisonous when eaten. Keep children and animals away from plants.
Landscape use Excellent flowering climber for woodland plantings or as groundcover for banks. Plant on a fence, trellis or arch as a screen.
Cultivars 'Price of Augusta' ('Plena') is a vigorous and free-flowering double form.

Hedera helix
ARALIACEAE

ENGLISH IVY

English ivy is a vigorous evergreen vine native throughout Europe. It climbs by means of root-like holdfasts. Leaves are lobed, except on mature, fruiting stems.

Flower colour and season Cream-coloured flowers on mature plants in autumn, followed by inconspicuous black fruit.
Height and spread 9–12 m (30–40 feet) with support.
Best climate and site Zones 5–10. Virtually any well-drained soil. Full sun to partial shade.
Cultivation Plant in spring or autumn. In colder zones shield from winter sun. Cut back in late winter to promote growth.
Propagation Take cuttings or layer in spring or summer.
Pest and disease prevention Choose a site with good air circulation and thoroughly clean up all dropped leaves to remove attractive overwintering sites for disease spores.
Common problems In colder areas leaves tend to turn brown if exposed to winter afternoon sun. Subject to attack by scale insects, mealybugs and red spider mites; deter with organically acceptable insecticides. Bacterial leaf spot may also be a problem; destroy infected plants.
Landscape use Excellent foliage plants to climb walls and trees or to use as groundcover.

Humulus lupulus
CANNABACEAE

HOP

Hops are hardy, deciduous twining plants with large, three- to five-lobed leaves. The female plants are the source of hops used in the commercial brewing industry.

Flower colour and season Insignificant greenish flowers in late spring, followed, on female plants, by green cone-like pods.
Height and spread To 9 m (30 feet) with support.
Best climate and site Zones 3–8. Virtually any well-drained soil. Full sun to light shade. Best where nights are cool and moist.
Cultivation Plant in spring. Prune to the ground after frost.
Propagation Take cuttings in spring.
Pest and disease prevention No serious pests or diseases.
Common problems Can be invasive.
Landscape use A fast-growing cover or screen plant for a trellis, arch or pergola.
Cultivars 'Aureus' has attractive golden yellow leaves.

Hydrangea anomala subsp. petiolaris
HYDRANGEACEAE

CLIMBING HYDRANGEA

Climbing hydrangea is a deciduous plant with rounded, glossy dark green leaves, white summer flowers and peeling brown bark. It climbs by means of root-like holdfasts.

Flower colour and season White flattened clusters with large, sterile flowers on the outside of the clusters and small fertile ones in the centre; flowers in early summer.
Height and spread To 18 m (60 feet) with support.
Best climate and site Zones 4–9. Virtually any moisture-retentive soil. Full sun to nearly full shade.
Cultivation Transplant container-grown plants in spring. Prune only if necessary to maintain shape.
Propagation Cuttings will root if taken in early summer.
Pest and disease prevention Mulch with organic matter to keep the soil evenly moist. No serious pests or diseases.
Common problems Often very slow to grow until established.
Landscape use A superb flowering plant for walls or to climb on trees or over boulders.

Ipomoea purpurea
CONVOLVULACEAE

COMMON MORNING GLORY

Common morning glory is a twining plant grown in many gardens for its colourful flowers. Although perennial in the warmest zones, it is most commonly used as an annual.

Flower colour and season White, pink, red, blue or variegated, according to species and cultivar; summer to early autumn.
Height and spread To 5 m (15 feet) with support.
Best climate and site Zone 10; grow it as an annual in colder regions. Rather dry, moderately fertile soil. Full sun.
Cultivation Plant in spring. Water freely during spring and summer and less at other times. Thin out or cut back congested growth of perennials in spring.
Propagation Sow seed in spring. Take cuttings in summer.
Pest and disease prevention Avoid overfeeding, which promotes succulent growth that is attractive to pests.
Common problems Seedlings slow to develop. Excessive fertility and moisture can promote vegetative growth at the expense of flowers.
Landscape use Use on a trellis or fence or grow in containers.
Other species *I. alba*, moonflower, is also sold as *Calonyction aculeatum*. It bears oval or three-lobed leaves and fragrant white flowers that open at night. *I. nil* bears large flowers in a range of colours.

Jasminum officinale
OLEACEAE

COMMON WHITE JASMINE

Native to the Near East and China, common white jasmine is a vigorous semi-evergreen climber or loose shrub with compound leaves. The white flowers are delightfully fragrant.

Other common names Poet's jessamine.
Flower colour and season Very fragrant white flowers which bloom in late spring to late summer.
Height and spread 9 m (30 feet) with support.
Best climate and site Zones 8–10. Moist, humus-rich, well-drained soil. Full sun to light shade.
Cultivation Plant during spring. Prune after flowering to keep vigorous growth under control.
Propagation Take cuttings during active growth in spring or autumn.
Pest and disease prevention Keep soil evenly moist in summer to avoid stressing the plant. No serious pests or diseases.
Common problems Needs protection, such as a warm wall, in all but the warmest zones.
Landscape use Where hardy, excellent for growing on trellises or arbours.
Varieties *J. officinale* var. *grandiflorum* bears larger flowers, up to 4.3 cm (1¾ inches) across.

Lonicera periclymenum
CAPRIFOLIACEAE

WOODBINE HONEYSUCKLE

Woodbine honeysuckle is a scrambling shrub or climber with oval, deciduous leaves. The fragrant late-spring to late-summer flowers are followed by small red berries.

Flower colour and season Fragrant flowers in varying proportions of yellow, white and red that bloom in late spring to late summer.
Height and spread To 9 m (30 feet) with support.
Best climate and site Zones 4–9. Moist, humus-rich, well-drained soil. Full sun to partial shade.
Cultivation Plant in spring. Prune back after flowering to keep vigorous growth under control.
Propagation Cuttings will root if taken in early spring.
Pest and disease prevention Mulch with organic matter to keep soil moist.
Common problems Subject to scale insects that suck the plant sap, weakening plants and causing them to turn yellow. Prune and destroy infested parts; spray remaining stems with organically acceptable insecticide such as horticultural oil.
Landscape use Well suited for clambering over bushes and fences.

Mandevilla laxa (M. suaveolens)
APOCYNACEAE

CHILEAN JASMINE

Chilean jasmine is a fast-growing, twining semi-evergreen vine with narrow heart-shaped leaves. Clusters of fragrant white flowers grace the plant in summer.

Flower colour and season Very fragrant white to pinkish trumpet-shaped flowers borne in clusters in late spring to midsummer.
Height and spread To 6 m (20 feet) with support.
Best climate and site Zones 9–10. Any well-drained, humus-rich soil. Full sun to light shade.
Cultivation Plant in spring. Water freely when in full growth; sparingly at other times. Thin out and cut back in early spring.
Propagation Take cuttings or sow seed in spring.
Pest and disease prevention No serious pests or diseases when grown outdoors. As a greenhouse plant, whiteflies and spider mites may cause trouble. Spray with insecticidal soap to deter pests.
Common problems Sensitive to frost.
Landscape use Where hardy, an excellent plant for growing on a pillar. Elsewhere, a lovely greenhouse or hanging-basket plant.

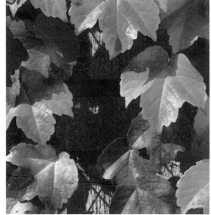

Mina lobata (Ipomoea lobata)
CONVOLVULACEAE

SPANISH FLAG

Spanish flag is a vigorous, twining herbaceous plant with alternate three-lobed leaves. Clusters of reddish flower buds fade to orange and yellow as the flowers open.

Flower colour and season Long-stalked clusters of fiery scarlet buds and creamy yellow-and-orange flowers all summer.
Height To 6 m (20 feet) with support.
Best climate and site Zones 8–10; in colder regions, treat as an annual. Light, well-drained soil. Full sun to light shade.
Cultivation Plant in spring. Mulch with organic matter to keep soil evenly moist.
Propagation Start seed indoors in pots about five weeks before planting outside.
Pest and disease prevention No significant pest or disease problems.
Common problems Will not thrive in poorly drained soil or in dense shade.
Landscape use Use on a trellis or fence.

Parthenocissus quinquefolia
VITACEAE

VIRGINIA CREEPER

Virginia creeper is a native plant that grows as either a clinging vine or groundcover. The deciduous leaves turn bright red before dropping in autumn.

Other common names Woodbine.
Flower colour and season Shiny, green leaves with five leaflets turn shades of brilliant scarlet and red in autumn. Birds enjoy the black fruits that come in clusters, like grapes.
Height To 18 m (60 feet) with support.
Best climate and site Zones 3–9. Most soil types; salt-tolerant. Sun to partial shade.
Cultivation Plant 60–180 cm (2–6 feet) apart in spring or autumn. Prune anytime to control growth.
Propagation Take hardwood cuttings in early spring, or layer stems anytime.
Pest and disease prevention No significant pest or disease problems.
Common problems Plantings easily become invasive. Grow where the spread isn't a problem, or cut back heavily in late autumn if necessary.
Landscape use Use to cover a wall, fence, tree trunk or pergola.
Cultivars 'Engelmannii' has smaller leaflets than the species and a more compact growth habit.

Parthenocissus tricuspidata
VITACEAE

BOSTON IVY

Boston ivy is a deciduous plant that climbs by means of root-like holdfasts. The large, maple-like, three-lobed leaves turn from lustrous green to brilliant scarlet in autumn.

Other common names Japanese ivy.
Flower colour and season Inconspicuous creamy white flowers in late spring; followed by purple fruit.
Height and spread To 18 m (60 feet) with support.
Best climate and site Zones 4–10. Humus-rich, well-drained soil. Full sun to light shade.
Cultivation Transplant container-grown plants in early spring.
Propagation Take softwood cuttings in late summer; hardwood cuttings in early spring.
Pest and disease prevention Avoid overfeeding, which provides succulent growth that is attractive to pests.
Common problems Sometimes slow to become established. Japanese beetles, which skeletonise leaves, may be a major problem. Shake beetles into a bucket of soapy water. Scale insects, mildew and leaf spot may also appear. Prune and destroy infested parts.
Landscape use The premier foliage plant to mask a wall.
Cultivars 'Lowii' has small leaves that are sometimes purple when young. 'Veitchii' bears small purple leaves.

Passiflora caerulea
PASSIFLORACEAE

BLUE PASSION FLOWER

Blue passion flower is a deciduous summer-flowering plant that climbs by means of tendrils. It dies back to the roots each winter in the colder portions of its range.

Flower colour and season Blue or (rarely) white flowers in summer, followed by conspicuous orange fruit.

Height and spread To 3.6 m (12 feet) with support.

Best climate and site Zones 7–10. Well-drained, humus-rich soil. Full sun to light shade.

Cultivation Plant in spring near a warm wall for winter protection.

Propagation Sow seed in spring. Take cuttings in summer.

Pest and disease prevention Mulch with organic matter to keep soil evenly moist. No serious pests or diseases.

Common problems Dies back to the ground annually in all but the warmest portions of its range.

Landscape use Grow on a trellis for the flowers and fo liage.

Cultivars 'Constance Elliott' is a white-flowered form.

Other species *P. incarnata*, wild passion flower or maypop, is native to the southeastern United States and has three-lobed leaves. It bears white flowers with blue stamens in summer, followed by edible fruit.

Stephanotis floribunda
ASCLEPIADACEAE

MADAGASCAR JASMINE

Madagascar jasmine is a twining opposite-leaved climber with rather large round to oval glossy green leaves. Its beautiful waxy white summer flowers are highly fragrant.

Flower colour and season Narrowly tubular waxy white flowers borne in clusters in mid-spring to autumn.

Height and spread To 3.6 m (12 feet) with support.

Best climate and site Zone 10. Humus-rich, moisture-retentive soil. Full sun to light shade.

Cultivation Plant in spring. Cut back long or crowded stems in autumn.

Propagation Take cuttings in summer.

Pest and disease prevention Keep soil moist with organic mulch. Avoid dry or poorly drained soil. Ensure adequate air circulation.

Common problems Subject to scale insects and mealybugs when grown as a greenhouse plant. Treat plants with insecticidal soap.

Landscape use Where hardy, a compact plant to grow on a trellis. Elsewhere a beautiful greenhouse plant. Also grown for its cut flowers, which are used in bridal bouquets and leis.

Thunbergia alata
ACANTHACEAE

BLACK-EYED SUSAN

Black-eyed Susan is a perennial climber that is commonly grown as an annual. The triangular bright green leaves are accented by the colourful summer flowers.

Other common names Clock vine.

Flower colour and season White, yellow or orange blooms, often with purple-black centres, in midsummer.

Height and spread To 1.8 m (6 feet) with support.

Best climate and site Zone 10; in colder regions, treat as an annual. Moist, humus-rich, well-drained soil. Full sun to partial shade.

Cultivation Plant in spring. Thin crowded stems in early spring. Water during periods of drought.

Propagation Sow seed in spring. Take cuttings in summer.

Pest and disease prevention Avoid dry or poorly drained soil. No serious pests or diseases.

Common problems Very sensitive to frost. Protect with mulch.

Landscape use Use on trellises or fences. Also a good hanging-basket plant.

Cultivars The 'Susie' series has white, yellow or orange flowers, with or without black eyes.

Trachelospermum jasminoides
APOCYNACEAE

STAR JASMINE

Star jasmine is a rapidly growing, evergreen twining plant with glossy green leaves up to 10 cm (4 inches) long. Its fragrant white flowers bloom in late spring to summer.

Other common names Chinese jasmine, confederate jasmine.
Flower colour and season Very fragrant 2.5-cm (1-inch) white flowers borne in clusters in late spring to early summer.
Height and spread To 6 m (20 feet) with support.
Best climate and site Zones 8–10. Moisture-retentive, humus-rich soil. Sun to partial shade.
Cultivation Plant in spring. Mulch to keep roots cool. Prune after flowering to control vigorous growth.
Propagation Take cuttings in late summer or autumn. Sow seed in spring. Layer in summer.
Pest and disease prevention Take care not to damage plant when pruning; these wounds are common entry points for pests and diseases.
Common problems Tends to grow beyond desired bounds. Prune back annually to control.
Landscape use Excellent for screening or for growing on a trellis, up trees or as groundcover.

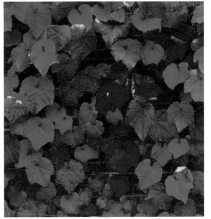

Vitis coignetiae
VITACEAE

CRIMSON GLORY

Crimson glory climbs by means of tendrils. It is an extremely rapid grower, capable of covering up to 300 sq. m (1,000 square feet) of trellis in one year. It displays red autumn colour.

Flower colour and season Clusters of small inconspicuous cream flowers in late spring, followed by black fruit in autumn.
Height and spread To 30 m (100 feet) with support.
Best climate and site Zones 5–9. Well-drained soil of low nutrient content. Full sun.
Cultivation Plant in winter or spring. Prune to desired dimensions in winter. Provide stout wire or trellis support on which to climb.
Propagation Layer in autumn. Take cuttings in autumn; graft in late winter or early spring. Sow seed in spring.
Pest and disease prevention Take care not to damage plant when pruning. These wounds are common entry points for pests and diseases.
Common problems *V. coignetiae*, as a result of its enormous growth rate, can easily exceed its desired limits. Choose a site carefully to avoid problems. Japanese beetles may skeletonise leaves; shake or brush beetles into a bucket of soapy water.
Landscape use Especially valued for its autumn foliage colour. An excellent cover for trellises or arbours.

Wisteria floribunda
LEGUMINOSAE

JAPANESE WISTERIA

Japanese wisteria is a deciduous, vigorous twining climber with alternately compound leaves. The plants are covered with long hanging flower clusters in late spring.

Flower colour and season Long clusters of slightly fragrant white, pink, lavender or violet flowers in late spring.
Height and spread To 15 m (50 feet) with support.
Best climate and site Zones 4–10. Moist, well-drained soil preferably with low nitrogen content. Lighter, infertile soil reduces vegetative growth and increases flowering. Grows best in full sun to light shade.
Cultivation Plant in spring. Prune back after flowering.
Propagation Take cuttings in late winter and spring. Layer in autumn. Graft in late winter or early spring. Sow seed in autumn or spring.
Pest and disease prevention Avoid poorly drained soil. Stress makes plants more prone to pests and diseases.
Common problems Requires stout hardwood or wire support. Plants produced from seed may be slow to flower. Subject to leaf beetles, scale insects, crown gall, leaf spot and mildew. Treat with organically acceptable controls.
Landscape use Fine plant to climb on stout supports like arches or pergolas. May be trained to standard form.

Ajuga reptans
LABIATAE

AJUGA

The short, spinach-like leaves of this excellent, low-growing groundcover spread rapidly to form a solid carpet. There are many colourful cultivars of ajuga to choose from.

Best climate and site Zones 3–8. Thrives in well-drained garden soil. Full sun to partial shade (shade is especially important in hot climates).
Height and spread Height of foliage to 7.5 cm (3 inches); spread unlimited. Flower height to about 15 cm (6 inches).
Description The leaves are usually dark green; cultivars are available with purple, bronze or variegated foliage. Ajuga is evergreen in warm areas but tends to turn brown by midwinter in cold climates. Spikes of 6-mm (¼-inch) blue or purple flowers bloom in spring or early summer.
Growing guidelines Plant 30–37.5 cm (12–15 inches) apart during the growing season. They need little maintenance. Don't give them fertiliser, otherwise the lush growth will be prone to fungal disease. Propagate by division any time during the growing season.
Landscape use Plant ajuga as flowering groundcover under trees and shrubs and on slopes. It will easily invade lawns, creating a maintenance headache; use an edging strip to avoid the problem. Ajuga can also overwhelm less vigorous plants, so it's not a good choice for edging flower beds or borders.

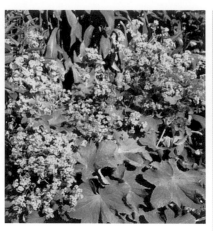

Alchemilla mollis
ROSACEAE

LADY'S MANTLE

Lady's mantle is superb as a carpet beneath trees. It also looks great in borders and rock gardens, but there you'll want to snip off the spent flowers to prevent reseeding.

Best climate and site Zones 3–8. Grows well in light-textured, well-drained, humus-rich, fertile soil. Likes partial shade; tolerates full sun in cooler climates.
Height and spread Height of foliage 22.5–30 cm (9–12 inches); spread to 60 cm (2 feet). Flower height to 37.5 cm (15 inches).
Description Grow lady's mantle for its attractive mounds of soft, silvery grey, deeply lobed, rounded foliage. The large leaves can grow up to 15 cm (6 inches) wide. Small, greenish yellow, petal-less flowers bloom in airy clusters in late spring and early summer.
Growing guidelines Plant 50 cm (20 inches) apart in spring. If leaves look tattered by midsummer, cut plants to the ground to get a flush of new growth. Plants self-sow easily and can become weedy; cut off the spent flowers to prevent seed formation or grow the plants where reseeding isn't a problem. Propagate by division in spring or autumn, or by seed in summer.
Landscape use Plant alone or combined with other vigorous perennials in flower borders. They also make an excellent, long-lasting cut flower.

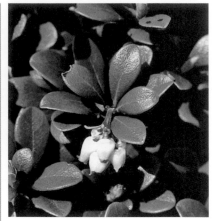

Arctostaphylos uva-ursi
ERICACEAE

BEARBERRY

Bearberry, also called kinnikinnick, is a native American evergreen with spring flowers and red autumn berries. It is one of the best groundcover plants for hot, sandy areas.

Best climate and site Zones 2–7, but varies with cultivars. Sandy, dry, acid, poor soil. Full sun.
Height and spread Height 15–30 cm (6–12 inches); spread to 3.6 m (12 feet).
Description Bearberry forms creeping mats of woody stems clothed in shiny green leaves that turn bronze in winter. The stems are tipped with tiny, waxy, bell-shaped, white to light pink flowers in spring and bright red berries in autumn.
Growing guidelines Plant out about 30 cm (1 foot) apart. They can be slow to establish, so be prepared to weed between plants until they fill in. They're difficult to propagate, but you could try layering (covering parts of the creeping stems with soil until roots form); it's best to use nursery-grown transplants.
Landscape use Bearberry is ideal for erosion control on well-drained slopes; it looks particularly nice with rocks. It is also excellent in seaside gardens; it thrives in sandy soil.

Asarum europaeum
ARISTOLOCHIACEAE

EUROPEAN WILD GINGER

European wild ginger is one of the best evergreen groundcover plantss for partial shade. The glossy, leathery leaves and thick, creeping roots are aromatic when you walk on them.

Best climate and site Zones 4–8. Moisture-retentive, humus-rich, somewhat acid soil. Partial shade.
Height and spread Height 12.5–17.5 cm (5–7 inches); spread to 30 cm (1 foot).
Description European wild ginger forms spreading colonies of kidney-shaped, evergreen leaves that are up to 7.5 cm (3 inches) wide. In late spring, small, purplish brown flowers bloom beneath the foliage.
Growing guidelines Plant 20–30 cm (8–12 inches) apart in early spring. Don't plant too deep; set the crowns (where the leaves meet the roots) just at the soil surface. Keep them evenly moist the first season after planting; water established plantings in dry weather. Fertilise lightly in early spring with a light top-dressing of compost or leaf mould. To propagate, divide in spring.
Landscape use European wild ginger grows quickly into a weed-suppressing clump. Combine it with ferns and shade-loving perennials, such as hostas and crested iris (*Iris cristata*).

Bergenia cordifolia
SAXIFRAGACEAE

HEART-LEAVED BERGENIA

Sometimes called elephant's ears or heart-leaf, this evergreen native of Siberia is grown for its thick, handsome leaves. The flower buds may be killed by very cold winters.

Best climate and site Zones 3–8. Humus-rich, well-drained, moist, slightly alkaline soil; but will grow anywhere if kept watered. Partial shade.
Height and spread Height of foliage to 30 cm (1 foot); spread to 60 cm (2 feet). Flower stems to 45 cm (18 inches) tall.
Description The heart-shaped, evergreen foliage turns shades of red-bronze in autumn and holds the colour well into winter. Clusters of tiny, rose-pink flowers hang on stems that emerge from the base of the plant in mid- to late spring.
Growing guidelines Set plants 60 cm (2 feet) apart in spring or autumn. It's best to choose a location sheltered from wind so the leaves won't get tattered. Mulch lightly before winter, especially in the coldest parts of its range. Use a loose mulch like coarse leaves, and remove it in early spring so the flower stems can emerge. Cut off old, damaged leaves as needed. Trap slugs under cabbage leaves (remove pests daily). Propagate by division in spring, or sow fresh seed in late summer.
Landscape use Dramatic along paths, under shrubs or trees, in large rock gardens, near ponds and in containers.

Campanula portenschlagiana
CAMPANULACEAE

DALMATIAN BELLFLOWER

The trailing stems of Dalmatian bellflower creep over the ground or sprawl over stone walls. This pretty plant is also attractive along the front of flower borders or in pots.

Best climate and site Zones 4–8. Well-drained, sandy soil. Full sun; light shade in hot climates.
Height and spread Height 15–20 cm (6–8 inches); spread to 60 cm (2 feet).
Description This low-growing campanula has heart-shaped, toothed leaves. It is covered with large numbers of bell-shaped, lavender-blue, 2.5-cm (1-inch) flowers from late spring to midsummer.
Growing guidelines Plant 30–45 cm (12–18 inches) apart in spring. Plants are easy to grow and need no special care. Propagate by division in early spring.
Landscape use Dalmatian bellflower is ideal as groundcover in rock gardens, on rocky slopes and in nooks and crannies in stone walls.
Cultivars 'Resholt' has deep violet flowers that are larger than the species. It thrives in partial shade as well as in sunny conditions.

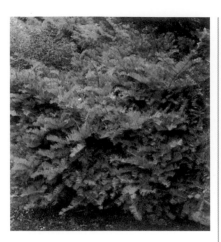

Cephalotaxus harringtonia
'Prostrata' CEPHALOTAXACEAE

JAPANESE PLUM YEW

Try Japanese plum yew where you need a large, shrubby groundcover plant. It's one of the few needle-leaved evergreens that grows very well in shady spots.

Best climate and site Zones 6–9. Average, well-drained soil. Partial shade.
Height and spread Height to 90 cm (3 feet); spread to 3.6 m (12 feet) or sometimes more.
Description This shrubby, shade-tolerant evergreen resembles true yews (*Taxus* spp.) but has larger, flat needles. The dark green colour is best in shade – too much sun may cause the needles to turn yellowish. The insignificant flowers bear only the male parts, so the plant does not set seed. Japanese plum yew seems to be deer-resistant.
Growing guidelines Plant 90 cm (3 feet) or more apart in spring. Japanese plum yew needs practically no maintenance to thrive. Propagate by layering branches (covering them with soil where they touch the ground to encourage rooting).
Landscape use Japanese plum yew is excellent evergreen groundcover for shady sites. It's a good substitute for yews where deer are a problem.

Cerastium tomentosum
CARYOPHYLLACEAE

SNOW-IN-SUMMER

Snow-in-summer carpets the ground with mats of woolly grey leaves. It can become invasive in spots it likes, so plant it where it can spread, or surround it with a barrier strip.

Best climate and site Zones 2–10. Dry, well-drained, poor soil – even sand. Needs full sun.
Height and spread Height 15–25 cm (6–10 inches); spread to 90 cm (3 feet) or sometimes more.
Description This fast-growing evergreen with light grey, woolly foliage forms large mats with its creeping stems. Its abundant white flowers with star-shaped petals cover the foliage for several weeks in late spring.
Growing guidelines Plant 30–45 cm (12–18 inches) apart in spring. Once they are established, cut the stems back after flowering to prevent seeding. Snow-in-summer can become invasive; divide plants every few years as they get out of bounds, or cut them back hard in early spring to control the spread. Propagate by division or seed in spring or autumn, or take cuttings in early summer.
Landscape use Snow-in-summer forms good groundcover for dry, sunny spots, especially in difficult spots like dry, rocky slopes. Plant it where the spread won't be a problem, or surround the planting with an edging strip.

Clematis integrifolia
RANUNCULACEAE

SOLITARY CLEMATIS

Unlike most other clematis, which grow as climbers, solitary clematis forms a sprawling mound that makes an unusual and attractive lavender-blue-flowering groundcover plant.

Best climate and site Zones 4–9. Light, loamy, alkaline soil. Full sun.
Height and spread Height 60–90 cm (2–3 feet); similar spread.
Description Solitary clematis forms bushy mounds of egg-shaped, deciduous leaves. Bell-shaped, lavender-blue flowers bloom over a long period in midsummer, followed by charming silvery seed heads.
Growing guidelines Set plants out 60–90 cm (2–3 feet) apart in spring or autumn. Maintain an organic mulch (such as compost or shredded leaves) to keep the soil cool and moist; otherwise, plants need no special care. Propagate by seed in late summer or cuttings in late spring.
Landscape use Solitary clematis is not especially showy, but the flowers and seed heads can provide several months of subtle interest. It looks best combined with other plants, as part of a perennial border or as an accent with other low-growing groundcover plants.
Cultivars 'Rosea' has pink flowers.

Convallaria majalis
ASPARAGACEAE

LILY OF THE VALLEY

Established clumps of lily of the valley compete well with weeds and can thrive in the same spot for decades with little or no care. They spread quickly by creeping roots.

Best climate and site Zones 2–8. Moist, well-drained, fertile soil enriched with organic matter. Partial to full shade.
Height and spread Height of foliage 15–20 cm (6–8 inches); spread unlimited. Flower height 20–25 cm (8–10 inches).
Description Lily of the valley is beloved for its fragrant, bell-shaped, waxy, white flowers. Each crown (known as a pip) produces two large, oblong, green leaves and one upright flower spike in late spring. The flowers may be followed by glossy, orange-red berries in summer.
Growing guidelines Plant 10–15 cm (4–6 inches) apart in late autumn or very early spring. The deciduous leaves turn brown in mid- to late summer, so place them where the unsightly appearance isn't a problem. If desired, you can cut down the brown leaves to tidy up the planting. Lily-of-the-valley benefits from an application of compost or leaf mould each autumn if the area isn't fertile. Thin out crowded plantings if they stop blooming well. Propagate by division after flowering or in autumn.
Landscape use Clumps of lily of the valley are ideal groundcover in shady borders and foundation plantings.

Delosperma cooperi
AIZOACEAE

HARDY ICEPLANT

Long-blooming hardy iceplant offers a colourful show of purple flowers from summer to first frost. It looks wonderful cascading down slopes and over stones in rock gardens.

Best climate and site Zones 7–9. Rich, well-drained, dry soil. Full sun.
Height and spread Height 10 cm (4 inches); spread to 30 cm (12 inches).
Description This low-growing South African succulent is becoming increasingly popular for its small, rosy purple, daisy-like flowers, which bloom from summer until frost over mats of narrow, curving leaves.
Growing guidelines Plant 30 cm (12 inches) apart in spring. They like dry soil in winter and do best when temperatures don't go below 10°C (50°F). In warm climates, the plants flower all year but grow mostly in the summer. Established plants need little care. Propagate by seed or cuttings in spring or summer.
Landscape use Hardy iceplant is a tough, beautiful, long-blooming groundcover for rock gardens, driveways or sunny banks.
Other species *D. nubigenum* grows to 5 cm (2 inches) tall and 20–25 cm (8–10 inches) wide. This fast-growing, tough plant has bright yellow flowers in late spring and yellow-green leaves that turn red in winter. Zones 5–9.

Epimedium x versicolor
BERBERIDACEAE

PERSIAN EPIMEDIUM

Persian epimedium is a good plant for growing along the edge of woods. Established clumps compete well with tree and shrub roots to get the moisture and nutrients they need.

Best climate and site Zones 5–8. Humus-rich, moist, somewhat acid soil. Light to heavy shade; plants tolerate some sun if they receive enough moisture.
Height and spread Height to 30 cm (1 foot); spread 22.5–30 cm (9–12 inches).
Description Striking, heart-shaped, leathery leaves on wiry stems are purple-red or mottled in early spring and later become green. Clusters of distinctive, hooded, waxy, red-and-yellow flowers that resemble columbines bloom on wiry stems in early to mid- spring. Persian epimedium is evergreen in hot climates; leaves in cooler climates turn brown by midwinter.
Growing guidelines Plant about 30 cm (12 inches) apart in spring. In early spring, cut all of the leaves to the ground to tidy the planting and to make it easier to see the delicate flowers. To propagate, divide after flowering.
Landscape use Use Persian epimedium in shady rock gardens and woodland gardens and as an edging along paths. It is also an excellent foundation plant for the north side of a building.

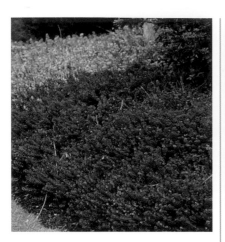

Erica carnea
ERICACEAE

SPRING HEATHER

Spring heather grows in low, spreading clumps with evergreen, needle-like leaves and bell-shaped spring flowers. It prefers a sunny site with moist but well-drained, acid soil.

Best climate and site Zones 5–7. Well-drained, sandy, acid soil with plenty of moisture. Full sun.
Height and spread Height to 45 cm (18 inches); spread to 90 cm (3 feet).
Description This small, evergreen shrub forms clumps or woody stems with narrow, needle-like, dark green foliage. Clusters of bell-shaped, red flowers bloom along shoot tips over a long period in early spring.
Growing guidelines Plant 90 cm (3 feet) or more apart in spring or early autumn. Keep the soil mulched, and water as necessary to keep it evenly moist. Clip plants back after flowering to promote compact growth. Propagate by softwood cuttings in early summer, by division in early spring or layering (covering parts of low-growing stems with soil to promote rooting) anytime.
Landscape use Spring heather forms an excellent and long-flowering cover for slopes and rock gardens.
Cultivars 'Springwood Pink' has clear pink flowers and bronze foliage in spring. 'Springwood White' has pretty creamy white flowers.

Euonymus fortunei
CELASTRACEAE

WINTER CREEPER

This evergreen produces long stems that take root as they travel over the earth. The clinging stems will also climb up trees, walls and buildings. It prefers sun, but will grow in shade.

Best climate and site Zones 5–9. Well-drained, slightly acid, fertile, humus-rich soil. Sun to partial shade.
Height and spread Height 30–60 cm (1–2 feet); stems spread to about 9 m (30 feet).
Description The oval, waxy, green, 5-cm (2-inch) leaves become deep red in autumn when grown in full sun. Inconspicuous white flowers bloom on mature stems in summer, followed by pink fruits in autumn.
Growing guidelines Plant 30 cm (1 foot) or more apart in spring or autumn. Trim and shape established plants as needed in early spring. Plants may be susceptible to euonymus scale, especially in warm areas. Spray with organic insecticide such as insecticidal soap, if necessary. Propagate by cuttings in early summer or by layering anytime.
Landscape use Winter creeper is useful as a low-growing evergreen for erosion control on banks. It grows relatively slowly in shade, but it is one of the best groundcover plants for dry, shady spots.

Galium odoratum
RUBIACEAE

SWEET WOODRUFF

Delicate-looking sweet woodruff is a fast-spreading groundcover plant for shady gardens. It can crowd out less vigorous plants but combines well with shrubs and trees.

Best climate and site Zones 3–8. Well-drained, moist, humus-rich, somewhat acid soil. Partial to full shade.
Height and spread Height 15–30 cm (6–12 inches); spread to 60 cm (2 feet).
Description Sweet woodruff forms carpets of deciduous, 2.5-cm (1-inch) leaves in whorls on square stems. The leaves have a sweet fragrance when dried. In early spring, loose clusters of small, star-shaped, white flowers appear just above the leaves. Sweet woodruff is also commonly called bedstraw and was formerly known as *Asperula odorata*.
Growing guidelines Set plants 20 cm (8 inches) apart in spring. Trim back established plants in spring to prevent leggy growth, but always leave the foliage closest to the ground intact. Propagate by division in spring or autumn.
Landscape use Sweet woodruff is charming groundcover for woodland gardens. It is also useful under shrubs, such as rhododendrons. The dried leaves are used in sachets.

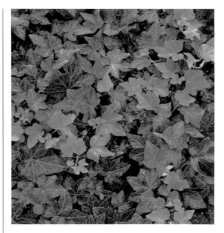

Gaultheria procumbens
ERICACEAE

WINTERGREEN

Wintergreen spreads slowly to form handsome carpets of glossy evergreen leaves in spots with moist, humus-rich, acid soil. The leaves are accented by bright red autumn fruit.

Best climate and site Zones 3–8. Acid, humus-rich, evenly moist soil. Plant in light shade or in sunny spots that get midday shade.
Height and spread Height 7.5–10 cm (3–4 inches); spread to 30 cm (1 foot).
Description This evergreen native of eastern North America has shiny, oval, 5-cm (2-inch) leathery leaves that become reddish in autumn. The leaves are fragrant when crushed. Small, solitary, nodding, urn-shaped, white flowers dangle under the leaves in early summer, and edible, bright red fruits appear in autumn. Wintergreen spreads slowly by creeping underground roots.
Growing guidelines Set plants about 30 cm (1 foot) apart in spring. A thick mulch is beneficial in hot climates to keep the roots cool and moist. Propagate by division in spring or autumn or by cuttings in summer.
Landscape use Wintergreen makes a nice year-round cover in naturalised woodland plantings, under trees and in shady rock gardens.

Geranium macrorrhizum
GERANIACEAE

BIG-ROOT CRANESBLLL

Big-root cranesbill grows in spreading clumps to form lush mats of aromatic, lobed, green leaves. The foliage turns reddish in autumn and may hold its colour into early winter.

Best climate and site Zones 3–8. Well-drained, fairly rich, moist soil; tolerates dry soil once established. Sun or light shade. (Plants prefer not to be in hot sunlight all day, particularly in southern regions.)
Height and spread Height 30–45 cm (12–18 inches); spread 60–90 cm (2–3 feet).
Description This slow-spreading, mound-forming perennial is one of many delightful and versatile species of hardy geranium (*Geranium* spp.) – not to be confused with *Pelargonium* spp., the common houseplant geranium. Big-root cranesbill bears 2.5-cm (1-inch) pink or reddish purple flowers in early summer. The spreading clumps of aromatic, lobed, green leaves stay attractive throughout the season and turn reddish in autumn.
Growing guidelines Set plants about 60 cm (2 feet) apart in early spring. They need little maintenance, but divide them whenever they become too large and stop flowering well. Propagate by division in spring or autumn.
Landscape use Grow big-root cranesbill in border plantings, rock gardens and wild gardens and on slopes. It can even take dry shade.

Hedera helix
ARALIACEAE

ENGLISH IVY

English ivy is available in a range of leaf colours and patterns. The plain green ivies tend to be most cold-tolerant, but many of the variegated ones are surprisingly hardy.

Best climate and site Zones 5–9. Prefers moist, well-drained, rich soil; tolerates poor, dry soil. Partial to full shade.
Height and spread Height to 15 cm (6 inches); forms a mat that spreads limitlessly.
Description This handsome evergreen vine has lobed, green leaves that are 5–12.5 cm (2–5 inches) long on woody stems. The stems creep over the ground, sending down roots as they travel. When they meet an upright surface, they climb with clinging rootlets. These upright stems mature to produce unlobed leaves, green flowers and black berries.
Growing guidelines Plant about 60 cm (2 feet) apart in spring or autumn. Prune as needed to control and direct the growth. Propagate by cuttings in early spring to early summer and by layering (covering parts of the creeping stems to promote rooting) anytime.
Landscape use English ivy is dependable, fast-spreading groundcover. Use it on slopes for erosion control. It's also attractive as groundcover beneath deciduous trees. English ivy can quickly become invasive in spots it enjoys, creating a maintenance nightmare.

Helianthemum nummularium
CISTACEAE

SUN ROSE

Sun rose, also called rock rose, is a low-growing shrub with small green or grey-green leaves. It blooms for many weeks, although each flower only lasts for one day.

Best climate and site Zones 6–8. Well-drained, sandy, neutral to slightly alkaline soil. Full sun.
Height and spread Height 20–45 cm (8–18 inches); spread to 90 cm (3 feet).
Description This low-growing woody shrub forms spreading mounds of narrow, hairy, evergreen leaves. Clusters of yellow, pink or white flowers that resemble single roses begin blooming just above the foliage in late spring or early summer.
Growing guidelines Plant 60 cm (2 feet) apart in spring or autumn. This shrub needs little or no care. Prune back by one-third to one-half after flowering stops if you wish to stimulate a second flush. Protect plants with a light winter mulch in the coldest parts of their range; you may also need to trim them back in early spring to remove winter-damaged tips. Propagate by cuttings in summer.
Landscape use Sun rose is a good choice as drought-tolerant cover for dry, hot, troublesome areas. It is also a fine addition to rock gardens and borders.

Houttuynia cordata
SAURURACEAE

VARIEGATED HOUTTUYNIA

Variegated houttuynia is a fast-spreading groundcover plant that thrives in moist soil. The showy green, red and yellow leaves are accented by white flowers in summer.

Best climate and site Zones 5–9. Damp, rich soil; will grow in standing water. Partial to full shade.
Height and spread Height 37.5–45 cm (15–18 inches); spread 45 cm (18 inches).
Description Variegated houttuynia forms creeping clumps of 5–7.5-cm (2–3-inch) long, green leaves variegated with reds and yellows; the leaves turn purplish in autumn. Some people describe the crushed leaves as citrus-scented; others call them foul-smelling. Small white flowers surrounded with white, petal-like bracts in summer resemble tiny dogwood blossoms. Plants are deciduous in cold climates and evergreen in warm areas. The species was named after Dutch horticulturist Martin Houttuyn; the name is pronounced 'how-tyne-nia'.
Growing guidelines Plant 30 cm (12 inches) apart in spring. In ideal (boggy) areas, houttuynia can become invasive. Propagate by division in spring or autumn or take cuttings in summer.
Landscape use Variegated houttuynia is useful for stabilising banks along ponds and streams. Or try it as groundcover for moist woodlands. Just make sure you're prepared to deal with the spread.

Juniperus horizontalis
CUPRESSACEAE

CREEPING JUNIPER

Plant creeping junipers for erosion control on slopes or for an evergreen accent in rock gardens and foundation plantings. They prefer full sun and well-drained soil.

Best climate and site Zones 3–9. Prefers well-drained, sandy soil, but tolerates any soil, even clay. Full sun.
Height and spread Height varies with cultivar, from 15–45 cm (6–18 inches); spread also variable to 2.4 m (8 feet).
Description Creeping junipers are low-growing, evergreen shrubs with spreading branches carrying scaly or needle-like, blue-green leaves. Dark-coloured fruits form on short stems in late summer.
Growing guidelines Spacing varies according to size; check the ultimate spread in the catalogue description. Plant out bare-root plants in spring and potted or root-balled plants any time during the growing season. Prune in summer only to control size. Don't just shear off shoot tips; cut unwanted stems back to another stem or to the ground. Phomopsis twig blight may be a problem in wet springs, causing browned shoot tips; remove and destroy diseased branches. Propagate by cuttings or seed in summer.
Landscape use Junipers are ideal for covering slopes, including steep slopes where other plants won't thrive.

Lamium maculatum
LABIATAE

SPOTTED LAMIUM

Spotted lamium, also known as spotted dead nettle, is a vigorous groundcover plant for shady gardens. It is a good choice for growing under trees and shrubs.

Best climate and site Zones 3–8. Prefers moist, rich soil; tolerates dry shade. Partial to deep shade.

Height and spread Height 30–35.5 cm (12–14 inches); spread to 60 cm (2 feet) or sometimes more.

Description This vigorous plant grows quickly to form a dense cover of dark green, oval or heart-shaped leaves with a distinctive silvery white mid-rib. Lavender-pink, hooded, 2.5-cm (1-inch) flowers bloom in clusters throughout the summer. Spotted lamium is less invasive than its relative, yellow archangel (*Lamiastrum galeobdolon*), but it is still a fast grower.

Growing guidelines Plant 30–35 cm (12–14 inches) apart in spring or autumn. Cut plants back by about half in midsummer to promote a new flush of leaves. Plants often self-sow. Propagate by division in spring or autumn or by cuttings in summer.

Landscape use Spotted lamium is handsome in wild areas, woodland gardens and shady rock gardens.

Cultivars 'Alba', white lamium, has white flowers and green leaves with silver centres. 'Aureum' has yellow leaves with a creamy white stripe and pink flowers.

Lysimachia nummularia
PRIMULACEAE

CREEPING JENNY

Creeping Jenny is an attractive groundcover plant for moist-soil areas where its spread isn't a problem. The yellow-leaved cultivar 'Aurea' is less invasive than the species.

Best climate and site Zones 3–8. Moist, fertile soil. Full sun (in cool climates) to full shade (in warm climates).

Height and spread Height 10–20 cm (4–8 inches); spread to 90 cm (3 feet).

Description This creeping perennial, also known as moneywort, has shiny, round, 18-mm (¾-inch) leaves that resemble coins. The trailing stems bear bright, 2.5-cm (1-inch), yellow flowers throughout the summer. The stems root rapidly as they creep over the soil.

Growing guidelines Plant 20 cm (8 inches) apart in spring or autumn. Creeping Jenny can be very invasive, and it rapidly becomes a weed problem when it spreads into lawn areas. Propagate by division in spring or autumn.

Landscape use Creeping Jenny is a particularly good groundcover plant around ponds and streams.

Cultivars 'Aurea', golden creeping Jenny, grows 5 cm (2 inches) tall with golden yellow spring foliage that turns lime green in summer. It is a vigorous mat-forming creeper but not as invasive as the species. Zones 4–8.

Mazus reptans
PHRYMACEAE

MAZUS

Mazus forms ground-hugging mats of small leaves topped with tubular, lipped flowers in spring and early summer. It thrives in moist soil in sun or partial shade.

Best climate and site Zones 5–8. Well-drained, moist, rich soil. Full sun to partial shade.

Height and spread Height 2.5–5 cm (1–2 inches); spread 37.5–45 cm (15–18 inches).

Description This creeping plant from the Himalayas sends out roots along its stems to form a carpet of bronzy green, toothed, 2.5-cm (1-inch) leaves. Light blue-violet, 18-mm (¾-inch) flowers have a lower lip spotted in white, greenish yellow and purple in spring and early summer. Plants are evergreen only in warm climates.

Growing guidelines Plant 30 cm (12 inches) apart in spring. They can be invasive; surround plantings with edging strips if the spread is a problem. Propagate by division in spring or autumn or by cuttings in summer.

Landscape use Plant mazus in crevices between flagstones on pathways; it mingles happily with creeping thyme and similar low-growing plants. Grow it in rock gardens as a carpet for small bulbs, like crocuses. Mazus competes with grass and will invade lawns.

Cultivars 'Alba' has white flowers.

Oenothera speciosa
ONAGRACEAE

WHITE EVENING PRIMROSE

White evening primrose spreads quickly by underground runners. They bloom in early summer during the day, unlike the many night-blooming species of the Oenothera genus.

Best climate and site Zones 3–8. Well-drained, average soil. Full sun to very light shade.
Height and spread Height to 45 cm (18 inches); spread to 60 cm (2 feet) or more.
Description White evening primrose produces wiry stems clothed in toothed, green leaves and topped with 5-cm (2-inch), cup-shaped, white flowers that fade to soft pink and turn towards the sun.
Growing guidelines Plant about 60 cm (2 feet) apart in spring or autumn. White evening primroses can be invasive, especially in moist, fertile soil; plant where the spread isn't a problem, or surround the planting with an edging strip that extends a few inches below the ground. Propagate by division or seed in spring or autumn.
Landscape use Plants look wonderful massed in low-maintenance areas, such as dry, sunny slopes.
Cultivars 'Rosea' grows to 37.5 cm (15 inches) with clear pink, 7.5-cm (3-inch) flowers.

Ophiopogon japonicus
ASPARAGACEAE

MONDO GRASS

Mondo grass is an excellent, mound-forming, grass-like perennial from the Orient. It is sometimes confused with lily turf (Muscari spp.), which it closely resembles.

Best climate and site Zones 7–9. Light-textured, well-drained, humus-rich, fertile soil with a pH of 5–7. Full sun to shade; does not tolerate midday sun in hot climates.
Height and spread Height to 20 cm (8 inches); spread unlimited.
Description The dark green, coarse-textured leaves are 37.5 cm (15 inches) long and 3 mm (⅛ inch) wide. Lavender to white, 6-mm (¼-inch) flowers bloom in summer in short, loose clusters that are often hidden by the leaves. The flowers are followed by blue, pea-sized fruits. Mondo grass spreads by rhizomes (underground runners).
Growing guidelines Plant about 30 cm (1 foot) apart in spring. If the foliage has deteriorated over the winter, you can cut it down in spring. Slugs can be a problem; trap them under cabbage leaves (remove pests daily) or in saucers of beer set flush with the soil surface. Propagate mondo grass by division in spring or early autumn.
Landscape use Mondo grass is excellent groundcover under trees in warm climates. It is also a fine choice for seaside planting, and a good edging for borders.

Pachysandra terminalis
BUXACEAE

JAPANESE SPURGE

Japanese spurge is one of the most common evergreen groundcover plants for shady spots, especially in cooler climates. Established plantings need very little in the way of maintenance.

Best climate and site Zones 4–8. Fertile, moist, neutral to slightly acid soil. Partial to deep shade.
Height and spread Height 20–25 cm (8–10 inches); spread unlimited.
Description Attractive, shiny, dark green, oval leaves, 3.7–10 cm (1½–4 inches) in diameter, grow at the top of upright stems. The leaves are toothed near the ends. In spring, clusters of fragrant, creamy white flowers bloom at the stem tips. On mature plants, the flowers are sometimes followed by white berries in the autumn. Japanese spurge spreads rapidly by rhizomes (underground runners) but it can be controlled.
Growing guidelines Plant 20–30 cm (8–12 inches) apart in spring. Top-dress plantings yearly with compost or organic fertiliser. Prune back or mow every few years in spring. Euonymus scale can be a problem; cut down and destroy infested plants that have pear-shaped, white-and-grey scales on the leaves. Propagate by division in spring or by cuttings in summer.
Landscape use Plant under deciduous or evergreen trees or in any shady area. It forms a good covering for slopes or banks.

Phlox stolonifera
POLEMONIACEAE

CREEPING PHLOX

Creeping phlox is available in many colours, making it a versatile plant for mixing with small bulbs and perennials that flower at the same time.

Best climate and site Zones 2–8. Moist, light, fertile, slightly acid soil. Prefers partial to full shade; will grow in sun.
Height and spread Height of foliage 7.5–12.5 cm (3–5 inches); spread to 45 cm (18 inches). Flower height 15–30 cm (6–12 inches).
Description Creeping phlox is grown for its masses of delicate lavender, pink, blue or white, 2.5-cm (1-inch) wide flowers that bloom in late spring. Long, creeping, strawberry-like runners clad in small, oval, evergreen leaves root as they touch the earth to form solid mats. This shade-loving groundcover plant is native to eastern North America.
Growing guidelines Set plants 30–60 cm (1–2 feet) apart in spring. For more compact growth, trim back flowering shoots after blooming. Propagate by division after flowering or by cuttings in late spring to early summer.
Landscape use Creeping phlox is ideal groundcover for moist woodland plantings, beneath deciduous trees, in front of shady borders or along the north and east sides of buildings. For a pretty colour combination, try purple cultivars with bright yellow primroses or pink fringed bleeding heart (*Dicentra eximia*).

Potentilla tridentata (Sibbaldiopsis tridenta)
ROSACEAE

THREE-TOOTHED CINQUEFOIL

Three-toothed cinquefoil is evergreen, mat-forming groundcover with glossy green leaves. It prefers sunny, well-drained sites in cool climates.

Best climate and site Zones 3–7. Well-drained, sandy, slightly acid soil. Full sun.
Height and spread Height to 30 cm (1 foot); spread to 60 cm (2 feet).
Description Each leaf is divided into three leaflets that are three- to five-toothed at their tips. The leaves turn wine red in autumn, giving the plant another common name: wine-leaved cinquefoil. Clusters of tiny, 6-mm (¼-inch) white flowers bloom in early summer and intermittently the rest of the season.
Growing guidelines Plant 30–60 cm (1–2 feet) apart in early spring. Three-toothed cinquefoil spreads fairly rapidly and needs little care. Propagate by removing rooted suckers in early spring or by cuttings in early summer.
Landscape use Three-toothed cinquefoil is a natural choice for covering dry, rocky slopes.
Cultivars 'Minima' is low-growing, reaching only to 7.5 cm (3 inches) tall.
Other species *P. tabernaemontani*, spring cinquefoil, has five-toothed, evergreen, green leaves and 12-mm (½-inch) bright yellow flowers in late spring. Height to 10 cm (4 inches); spread to 60 cm (2 feet). Zones 4–7.

Pulmonaria saccharata
BORAGINACEAE

BETHLEHEM SAGE

The early-spring flowers of Bethlehem sage combine nicely with daffodils and other bulbs. The foliage looks wonderful with hostas, which enjoy the same growing conditions.

Best climate and site Zones 3–8. Moist, well-drained, humus-rich soil. Partial to full shade; tolerates some sun if the soil is kept moist.
Height and spread Height 20–37.5 cm (8–15 inches); spread 45 cm (18 inches) or more.
Description These easy-to-grow plants form broad clumps of white-mottled, slightly fuzzy leaves. In early spring, cheery, small, tubular flowers bloom in profusion over mounds of foliage. The pink buds open to pink flowers that age to blue.
Growing guidelines Plant 60 cm (2 feet) apart in spring or autumn. Plants may wilt if the soil becomes dry, but they revive quickly when watered; mulch helps to keep the roots moist. Propagate by division after flowering or in autumn.
Landscape use The clumps of mottled foliage look nice all summer at the front of the border, under trees or in a shady rock garden.
Cultivars 'Mrs Moon' has silver-spotted leaves and pink flowers that mature to blue. 'Sissinghurst White' has pure white flowers and silvery mottled foliage.

Sagina subulata
CARYOPHYLLACEAE

PEARLWORT

Pearlwort, also known as Irish moss, is a dainty little evergreen for partial shade. It can withstand some foot traffic and looks great growing between stepping stones.

Best climate and site Zones 5–7. Prefers well-drained, moist, fertile soil; tolerates dry, sandy soil. Partial shade.
Height and spread Height of foliage 2.5–5 cm (1–2 inches); spread to 30 cm (1 foot). Flower height to 12.5 cm (5 inches).
Description This moss-like, perennial, evergreen groundcover plant forms dense mounds of tiny, 6-mm (¼-inch) leaves. Numerous small, translucent white flowers bloom in midsummer.
Growing guidelines Plant 30 cm (1 foot) apart in spring. Slugs and snails can be problems; trap them under cabbage leaves (remove pests daily) or in shallow dishes of beer set flush with the soil surface. Propagate by division in spring.
Landscape use Grow pearlwort in lightly shaded rock gardens and between flagstones since it tolerates foot traffic.
Cultivars 'Aurea', commonly called Scotch moss, has yellow-green foliage.

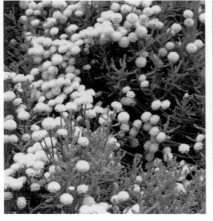

Santolina chamaecyparissus
COMPOSITAE

COTTON LAVENDER

Cotton lavender is a shrubby, aromatic evergreen that's native to areas of the Mediterranean. The dried leaves and stems were once used indoors to repel moths.

Best climate and site Zones 5–9. Dry, poor, well-drained soil, including sand and gravel. Full sun.
Height and spread Height 45–60 cm (18–24 inches); spread to 90 cm (3 feet).
Description Cotton lavender forms bushy clumps of many branches with fine, needle-like, aromatic, silvery grey leaves. Bright gold, 18-mm (⅛ inch) flowers bloom in profusion in midsummer. Cotton lavender can tolerate both heat and drought.
Growing guidelines Plant 60–90 cm (2–3 feet) apart in spring. Cut stems back by half after flowering each year (or before flowering, if you don't like the flowers) to encourage compact growth., Propagate by cuttings in early summer or by division in early spring.
Landscape use Cotton lavender is ideal for a low-growing hedge or edging and for shrub borders. The grey shade combines well with lavender and low-growing ornamental grasses.
Cultivars 'Nana' is a dwarf form. 'Plumosus' has lacy, silvery grey foliage.

Saponaria ocymoides
CARYOPHYLLACEAE

ROCK SOAPWORT

Rock soapwort produces many bright pink flowers in summer. Cut the stems back by half after flowering to keep plants compact and to promote possible rebloom.

Best climate and site Zones 4–10. Light-textured, average, well-drained soil. Full sun.
Height and spread Height 12.5–20 cm (5–8 inches); spread to 60 cm (2 feet).
Description Rock soapwort is a trailing, mat-forming plant with semi-evergreen leaves less than 2.5 cm (1 inch) long. Its star feature is the clusters of phlox-like, bright pink, five-petalled, 12-mm (½-inch) flowers in early to mid-summer.
Growing guidelines Set plants about 50 cm (20 inches) apart in spring. Propagate by seed in spring, by division in spring or autumn, or by cuttings at the beginning of summer.
Landscape use Rock soapwort trails beautifully over walls, raised beds and terraces. It also makes a good groundcover plant for sunny slopes.
Cultivars 'Alba' has white flowers that are somewhat smaller than the species. 'Rubra Compacta' forms compact mounds of deep pink to red flowers. 'Splendens' has rose-pink flowers.

Saxifraga stolonifera
SAXIFRAGACEAE

STRAWBERRY GERANIUM

Strawberry geranium is commonly sold as a houseplant, but its rounded, silver-marked, green leaves also make a handsome groundcover plant in warm-climate gardens.

Best climate and site Zones 6–9. Moist, well-drained, slightly acid soil. Partial shade; thrives in morning sun and afternoon shade.

Height and spread Height of foliage to 15 cm (6 inches); spread to 45 cm (18 inches). Flower stalks to 30 cm (1 foot).

Description Strawberry geranium is excellent evergreen groundcover for warm climates. It is also called strawberry begonia and mother of thousands, as it spreads by runners (like strawberries). The hairy, rounded, dark green leaves are 10 cm (4 inches) wide, have scalloped edges and are beautifully veined with silver. White flowers bloom on spikes in early summer.
This species is also listed as *S. sarmentosa*.

Growing guidelines Plant 30–45 cm (12–18 inches) apart in early spring. To propagate, dig up the small plantlets that form on runners and transplant in spring.

Landscape use Strawberry geranium is a handsome and unusual groundcover plant for shady rock gardens or borders. Grow it under trees and shrubs as well.

Sedum spurium
CRASSULACEAE

TWO-ROW STONECROP

Two-row stonecrop is a tough, durable spreader for dry soil. Its mats of fleshy green leaves are topped with clusters of pink flowers in midsummer.

Best climate and site Zones 3–8. Well-drained, sandy, average to poor soil. Light to partial shade.

Height and spread Height of foliage to 15 cm (6 inches); spread to 60 cm (2 feet). Flower height to 25 cm (10 inches).

Description This semi-evergreen, creeping succulent quickly forms carpeting groundcover with dark green, 2.5-cm (1-inch) long leaves that turn reddish in late autumn. Flat, 5-cm (2-inch) clusters of pink flowers appear in midsummer. Stems stay reddish throughout the winter.

Growing guidelines Set plants 25 cm (10 inches) apart in spring. After flowering, cut off the spent flowers with shears or a string trimmer. Although it spreads quickly, two-row stonecrop is easy to control because it has shallow roots. Propagate by seed or division in early spring or by cuttings in early summer.

Landscape use Try two-row stonecrop as groundcover on dry, lightly shaded, rocky slopes, alone or mixed with other *Sedum* species.

Stachys byzantina
LABIATAE

LAMB'S EARS

Lamb's ears has fuzzy leaves that may rot in humid conditions. Plants usually recover and produce new growth when cool weather returns; in the meantime, remove damaged leaves.

Best climate and site Zones 4–8; thrives in Zone 3 with snow cover. Average, well-drained soil; plants tolerate drought once established. Prefers full, hot sun; tolerates light shade.

Height and spread Height of foliage to 20 cm (8 inches); spread to 90 cm (3 feet). Flower stems to 45 cm (18 inches).

Description This charming groundcover plant is grown mostly for its woolly, soft, silvery white, 10-cm (4-inch) leaves. Fuzzy, square flowering stems bearing lavender flowers bloom in early to mid- summer. This species is also listed as *S. lanata* or *S. olympica*.

Growing guidelines Plant 30–40 cm (12–16 inches) apart in spring. Cut back any damaged leaves in spring. Remove flower stems before they bloom, if desired, to keep plantings tidy. Propagate by division any time during the growing season or by seed in spring.

Landscape use The grey foliage of lamb's ears is an excellent foil for brightly coloured flowers in beds and borders. The leafy clumps form an attractive edging for garden paths.

Tellima grandiflora
SAXIFRAGACEAE

FRINGE CUPS

Fringe cups are ideal for lightly shaded gardens. Their clumps spread slowly but steadily, and they may self-sow in ideal growing conditions.

Best climate and site Zones 5–8. Fertile, well-drained, slightly acid, cool soil. Light shade.

Height and spread Height of foliage to 30 cm (1 foot); spread to 50 cm (20 inches). Flower stems grow to 60 cm (2 feet) tall.

Description Fringe cups form tidy clumps of heart-shaped, scalloped, hairy, cupped leaves that are 10 cm (4 inches) wide. The green leaves turn reddish in autumn. Loose clusters of small, bell-shaped, nodding flowers with fringed petals are greenish white when they open in spring and turn reddish. Fringe cups are evergreen in warm climates and deciduous in cool zones.

Growing guidelines Plant 45–60 cm (18–24 inches) apart in spring. Divide when plants become crowded. Propagate by division in spring.

Landscape use This slow spreader makes an attractive, dense cover for the rock garden or woodland garden.

Cultivars 'Rubra' has maroon leaves.

Tiarella cordifolia
SAXIFRAGACEAE

FOAM FLOWER

Foam flower tolerates deep shade and dry conditions once established. It looks great as groundcover beneath deciduous and evergreen trees and as an edging plant.

Best climate and site Zones 3–8. Well-drained, moist, fertile, slightly acid soil. Light shade.

Height and spread Height of foliage to 15 cm (6 inches); spread to 60 cm (2 feet). Flower stems 22.5–30 cm (9–12 inches) tall.

Description This evergreen native of eastern North American forests forms clumps of heart-shaped, lobed and toothed green leaves. The leaves are up to 10 cm (4 inches) wide and turn bronze to burgundy in autumn; they are evergreen in warm climates. Feathery bottlebrush-like spikes of tiny white flowers bloom in mid-spring.

Growing guidelines Plant 60 cm (2 feet) apart in spring. Removing spent flower spikes may extend the flowering season. Propagate by division in spring or autumn or sow seed in spring.

Landscape use Foam flowers are ideal for massed woodland plantings, shady rock gardens, borders and edgings.

Cultivars 'George Shenk Pink' has foamy, pink flowers in spring. 'Oakleaf' has deeply lobed leaves and airy, deep pink blooms that last for several weeks.

Vancouveria hexandra
BERBERIDACEAE

AMERICAN BARRENWORT

American barrenwort may look delicate, but it's a tough, vigorous perennial that spreads by underground stems. It prefers moist soil but can adapt to dry conditions.

Best climate and site Zones 5–8. Moist, well-drained, fertile soil, rich in leaf mould. Prefers partial shade but will tolerate full shade.

Height and spread Height to 30 cm (1 foot); spread to 60 cm (2 feet) or more.

Description Spreading clumps of wiry stems are topped with thin, heart-shaped, three-lobed, deciduous, green leaves to 3.7 cm (1½ inches) wide. In late spring or early summer, tiny, 12-mm (½-inch) white flowers bloom in drooping clusters just above the leaves.

Growing guidelines Plant 45–60 cm (18–24 inches) apart in spring. They may be slow getting started but will begin to spread by the second growing season. Mulch to keep plants moist and cool in summer. If the soil is sandy, feed plants once a year with compost or leaf mould. To propagate, divide in spring.

Landscape use American barrenwort makes attractive groundcover beneath trees, in shady rock gardens and in wild gardens. It's also a nice edging for shady beds of hostas.

Veronica prostrata
PLANTAGINACEAE

ROCK SPEEDWELL

The spreading foliage mats of rock speedwell are accented by spikes of blue flowers in late spring. This plant is a perfect choice for sunny slopes and rock gardens.

Best climate and site Zones 4–8. Well-drained, moist, average garden soil. Prefers full sun; tolerates partial shade.
Height and spread Height 20–25 cm (8–10 inches); spread to 45 cm (18 inches) or more.
Description Spikes of deep blue flowers bloom on upright stems in late spring above creeping mats of 3.7-cm (1½-inch) green leaves. Rock speedwell is also known as Hungarian speedwell or harebell speedwell.
Growing guidelines Plant at least 60 cm (2 feet) apart in spring or autumn. If needed, surround plantings with an edging strip to keep them in bounds. Propagate by division in spring or autumn, by stem cuttings in summer or by seed in spring.
Landscape use Rock speedwell is a charming groundcover plant in rock gardens and on rocky slopes.
Cultivars 'Alba' has white flowers that bloom over a long season. 'Mrs Holt' has rose-pink flowers.

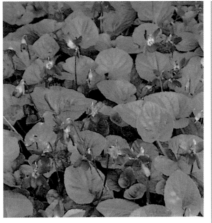

Viola odorata
VIOLACEAE

SWEET VIOLET

Sweet violet, also called English violet, is the common violet used by florists. It spreads by runners that take root and produce new plants.

Best climate and site Zones 6–8. Well-drained, moist, fertile, cool soil. Full sun to partial shade; tolerates full shade in hot climates.
Height and spread Height 12.5–20 cm (5–8 inches); spread to 60 cm (2 feet).
Description Fragrant, five-petalled, deep violet blooms come up in early spring from clumps of heart-shaped leaves that are 7.5 cm (3 inches) long.
Growing guidelines Plant 30 cm (12 inches) apart in spring. Start a new patch when older plants become overgrown and weak. Spider mites may be a problem, causing yellowed or browned leaves; spray cold water over the plants or use a slurry made from buttermilk, wheat flour and water.
Landscape use Sweet violet makes fragrant groundcover in wild gardens and rock gardens and under trees and shrubs.
Cultivars 'Royal Robe' has purple flowers with a white eye on long, 20-cm (8-inch) stems. 'White Czar' has white flowers veined with deep purple on 15-cm (6-inch) stems. Other cultivars come in shades of blue, pink, purple and white.

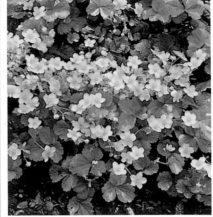

Waldsteinia fragarioides
ROSACEAE

BARREN STRAWBERRY

Barren strawberry has shiny, evergreen leaves that take on a purplish colour in cold weather. It grows well in partial shade but will take sun if the soil is kept moist.

Best climate and site Zones 5–8. Well-drained, fertile soil. Prefers partial shade, but will tolerate sunny spots if kept moist.
Height and spread Height to 15 cm (6 inches); spread unlimited.
Description This evergreen plant is native to eastern North America. It spreads by creeping roots to form a thick, flat carpet of shiny, strawberry-like foliage that turns purplish in autumn. Clusters of five-petalled, 12-mm (½-inch) wide, yellow flowers appear on 15–20-cm (6–8-inch) stems in late spring, followed by inedible, dry, hairy fruits.
Growing guidelines Plant about 60 cm (2 feet) apart in spring. Keep watered in dry periods and divide when overcrowded. Propagate by division in early spring or autumn; by seed in spring.
Landscape use Grow barren strawberry in rock gardens, on banks and rocky ledges or cascading over walls.
Other species *W. temata* grows 15–20 cm (6–8 inches) tall with glossy, green, evergreen leaves and clusters of yellow, strawberry-like flowers in spring. Zones 4–9.

Agrostis tenuis
GRAMINEAE

BENT GRASS, COLONIAL

Think carefully before sowing bent grass in a home lawn. Pure bent grass turf demands lots of maintenance to look respectable, and it's prone to drought and diseases.

Best climate and site Zones 3–8. Light-textured, well-drained soil that contains an average amount of humus and nutrients and has a pH of 6–7. Can tolerate acid soil. Full sun, but tolerates light shade.
Characteristics This creeping grass has fine leaves and a pale green colour. Bent grass has good salt tolerance and withstands close mowing, but it can't stand heavy foot traffic. It needs regular watering and fertilising, and it is prone to many pests and diseases. When mixed with other species, bent grass can crowd them out, leading to patchy turf. For this reason, bent grass is sometimes considered a weed in home lawns.
Getting started If you are willing to put the time and effort into putting-green-quality turf, sow bent grass seed in the spring at the rate of 900 g per 93 sq m (2 pounds per 1,000 square feet). Seed germinates in 12–26 days.
Mowing height 6–25 mm (½–1 inch).
Special maintenance Needs close mowing as often as twice a week and preferably with a reel-type mower. Frequent watering and frequent light applications of fertiliser are necessary.

Festuca arundinacea
GRAMINEAE

FESCUE, TALL

Thanks to its deep roots, tall fescue is heat-tolerant and among the most drought-resistant of all cool-season grasses. It is also an excellent choice for erosion control.

Best climate and site Zones 2–7. Grows well in most soil types. Can take both full sun or light shade.
Characteristics Sometimes called meadow fescue, tall fescue is a wide-bladed, sharp-edged, clump-forming grass that takes a great deal of wear and tear. It grows so strong that it can crowd out weeds as well as less vigorous, fine-textured lawn grasses. Tall fescue is a good choice for play areas, roadsides and low-maintenance areas. The only place you'd probably want to avoid it is in a highly manicured lawn, where its broader blades and clumping habit would give the turf a coarse look.
Getting started Plant in either spring or autumn, sowing 3.2 kg per 93 sq m (8 pounds per 1,000 square feet). Seed germinates in 12–22 days.
Mowing height 5–7.5 cm (2–3 inches).
Special maintenance Tall fescue doesn't need much special care. You may need to overseed bare spots in spring or autumn. Mow fairly high so the grass stays vigorous and looks more even.

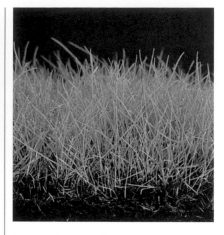

Festuca rubra var. *rubra*
GRAMINEAE

FESCUE, CREEPING RED

The soft, fine-textured blades of creeping red fescue are pleasant to walk on, but they can't take heavy wear. This grass isn't a good choice for play areas.

Best climate and site Zones 2–8. Adapts to most soil types, even dry soil. Full sun or light shade.
Characteristics Creeping red fescue spreads slowly by rhizomes, survives in difficult locations and looks nice when cut high. Its thin, fine blades are deep green, but the base of the plant is red. Creeping red fescue is not rugged enough for heavy foot traffic, but it is one of the best grasses for shady spots in cool climates. It is often mixed with perennial ryegrass to overseed warm-season grasses when they become dormant in autumn.
Getting started For an all-fescue lawn, sow at the rate of 1.8 kg per 93 sq m (4 pounds per 1,000 square feet) in spring or early autumn. You may also find creeping red fescue mixed with blue grass or perennial ryegrass; apply according to the rate suggested on the packet. Seed germinates in 12–22 days.
Mowing height 5 cm (2 inches).
Special maintenance Fertilise only when growth is poor; creeping red fescue is actually less competitive when it gets lots of fertiliser. It is quite drought-tolerant. Overwatering may encourage fungal diseases, which are also prevalent in hot, humid seasons.

Lolium multiflorum
GRAMINEAE

RYEGRASS, ANNUAL

Annual ryegrass is used mainly for quick cover while perennial grasses are getting established. It grows rapidly, so it needs frequent mowing.

Best climate and site Zones 3–7. Grows on a wide range of soil types. Full sun or light shade.

Characteristics Annual ryegrass is a rather coarse grass with light green leaves. It is rugged enough to stand moderate use, it holds its colour well and it is drought-resistant. It will set seed and die after one season, so it is not meant for permanent lawns. It is used primarily in mixes with perennial grasses as a quick cover to hold the soil until the higher-quality grasses sprout and take hold. However, beware of cheap lawn mixes that are more than 20 per cent annual rye. Straight annual rye can be used to overseed warm-season lawns to provide green during winter.

Getting started Sow annual rye in the spring in cool climates at the rate of 0.9–1.35 kg per 93 sq m (2–3 pounds per 1,000 square feet) for an all-rye lawn. If sowing a mix, follow the rate suggested on the packet. In warm climates, overseed existing warm-season lawns in autumn at 1.35–2.25 kg per 93 sq m (3–5 pounds per 1,000 square feet). Seed germinates in 7–12 days.

Mowing height 5 cm (2 inches).

Special maintenance Annual rye is disease- and insect-resistant.

Lolium perenne
GRAMINEAE

RYEGRASS, PERENNIAL

Perennial ryegrass is one of the most popular cool-season lawn grasses. It looks great alone or mixed with blue grass, and it's relatively pest- and disease-resistant.

Best climate and site Zones 3–7. Grows on a wide range of soil types. Full sun but tolerates light shade.

Characteristics Perennial ryegrass sprouts quickly for a fast lawn effect. It is tolerant of foot traffic and is more insect- and disease-resistant than other lawn grasses, especially when it's enhanced with endophytes (fungi that live within the grass plants and discourage insect pest feeding). Perennial ryegrass is one of the most popular choices for home lawns.

Getting started Plant either in spring or late summer in cool climates. For an all-perennial-ryegrass lawn, sow 0.9–1.35 kg per 93 sq m (2–3 pounds per 1,000 per square feet). For a finer-quality lawn, choose a perennial ryegrass/blue grass mix; seed at the rate suggested on the packet. If oversowing an existing warm-season lawn, sow in autumn at 1.35–2.25 kg per 93 sq m (3–5 pounds per 1,000 square feet). Perennial rye grass seed germinates in 7–12 days.

Mowing height Cut at 7.5 cm (3 inches) for the first three mowings of the season and 5 cm (2 inches) for later mowings.

Special maintenance Perennial ryegrass needs little fertiliser once it's established.

Poa pratensis
GRAMINEAE

BLUE GRASS

Fine-bladed blue grass forms a beautiful smooth turf in full sun. To keep it in peak condition, you need to fertilise it every year and water it regularly in dry weather.

Best climate and site Zones 4–7. Light-textured, well-drained soil that contains an average amount of organic matter and nutrients and has a pH of 6.5–7. Full sun.

Characteristics Blue grass is one of the highest-quality, fine-bladed grasses for cool-season lawns that receive plenty of sunlight and moisture. Its narrow, upright-growing, blue-green blades have a smooth look when mown. Blue grass can't tolerate a lot of traffic, so don't plant it alone for a heavily used lawn.

Getting started Sow blends of several compatible blue grass cultivars at 675–900 g per 93 sq m (1½–2 pounds per 1,000 square feet). Seed germinates in 12–30 days. For a more rugged lawn, use a mix of blue grass, perennial rye and fescues, especially those that are endophyte-enhanced. Blue grass is one of the most popular grasses grown on turf farms; blue grass turf is often available in blends and mixtures.

Mowing height Mow species at 5–6 cm (2–2½ inches). Some cultivars tolerate lower mowing.

Special maintenance Frequent watering during dry periods and an annual light feeding in late summer or early autumn.

Andropogon glomeratus
GRAMINEAE

BUSHY BLUESTEM

Grow bushy bluestem for its showy flower plumes and purplish autumn colour. Steady soil moisture is important for the best growth, especially in hot, sunny sites.

Type of plant Warm-season, clumping perennial grass.
Best climate and site Zones 5–10. Moist, fertile soil. Prefers full sun; tolerates light shade.
Height and spread Height 30–60 cm (1–2 feet); similar spread. Flowering stems grow 60–90 cm (2–3 feet) tall.
Description Bushy bluestem is grown for its dense clusters of fluffy, cotton-like flowers above clumps of attractive green foliage in late summer. In late autumn the seed heads become orange, and the leaves turn purplish.
Growing guidelines Plant 60–75 cm (24–30 inches) apart in spring. Cut them back to about 15 cm (6 inches) by late winter. Propagate by seed or division in spring.
Landscape use Bushy bluestem grows best near streams and in wetlands. It will grow in containers if you keep the soil moist. It looks equally wonderful as a specimen plant or in masses. Use the flowers or seed heads in arrangements. Be aware that bushy bluestem reseeds readily in moist areas and can become invasive under those conditions.

Briza media
GRAMINEAE

QUAKING GRASS

The flowers of quaking grass tremble in the slightest breeze, adding movement to flower borders and rock gardens. Cut plants back in midsummer to promote new leaves.

Type of plant Cool-season, clumping perennial grass.
Best climate and site Zones 4–10. Grows well in a wide range of soil types, but prefers moist, humus-rich soil. Full sun; tolerates light shade.
Height and spread Height 30–60 cm (1–2 feet); clumps to about 30 cm (1 foot) wide. Flowers bloom on 60–90-cm (2–3-foot) tall stems.
Description Quaking grass is an easy-to-grow plant. The tiny, showy, heart-shaped, bright green florets shake in the breeze in late spring, giving the grass its name. They turn purple, then golden yellow in summer. The leaves are green in spring but turn straw-coloured by summer.
Growing guidelines Plant 30–60 cm (1–2 feet) apart in spring or autumn. Don't fertilise. Cut back the old flower heads and unsightly old foliage to a few inches above the crown in midsummer to encourage fresh leaves to grow from the base. Cut back again in late autumn. Propagate by division in spring or autumn, or sow seed in spring.
Landscape use Quaking grass is good for edgings, rock gardens and flower borders, or as groundcover.

Calamagrostis x *acutiflora* 'Stricta'
GRAMINEAE

FEATHER REED GRASS

One of the most spectacular grasses, feather reed grass has an upright habit and stiff, narrow leaves that are evergreen in warm climates and deciduous in cold regions.

Type of plant Cool-season, clumping perennial grass.
Best climate and site Zones 5–9. May not flower well in hot climates. Tolerates most soil types, but prefers it moist and humus-rich. Full sun or light shade.
Height and spread Height 45–60 cm (18–24 inches); spread to about 60 cm (2 feet). Flowering stems may rise to 1.8 m (6 feet) tall.
Description Flowers appear in late spring or early summer on tall, erect spikes and consist of 30-cm (1-foot) long, pinkish green clusters that later become beige. Seed clusters form in July and last well into winter.
Growing guidelines Plant 60–90 cm (2–3 feet) apart in spring or autumn (spring is best in cool areas). Cut back by late winter. Divide plants in spring in cool climates and in spring or autumn in warmer ones.
Landscape use Feather reed grass is an excellent tall accent plant. Its rich, golden, late-summer colours make spectacular screens or masses in backgrounds. Its flowering stems sway in the slightest breeze, adding movement to the garden.

Cortaderia selloana
GRAMINEAE

PAMPAS GRASS

Pampas grass is one of the showiest and most popular ornamental grasses where it is hardy. Wear long sleeves, long trousers and gloves when working around the sharp leaves.

Type of plant Warm-season, clumping perennial grass.

Best climate and site Zones 8–10. Fertile, well-drained soil. Prefers full sun; takes light shade.

Height and spread Height 1.5–3.6 m (5–12 feet); spread to 3.6 m (12 feet). Flowering stems may be 2.4–4.5 m (8–15 feet) tall.

Description Plants form neat clumps of sharp-edged leaves that are usually deciduous in autumn. Spectacular, plume-like, 30–90-cm (1–3-foot) flower heads, either white or pink, rise on tall spikes in midsummer and last until late autumn.

Growing guidelines Plant 1.5–2.4 m (5–8 feet) apart in spring in a spot where each can reach its huge, full beauty without being crowded. They tolerate dry soil but do better with adequate moisture. Cut back the foliage every year or two in early spring. Propagate plants by division in spring. Look for cultivars of *C. selloana*, or buy the species from a reputable nursery to be sure you're getting the right plant.

Landscape use Dramatic tall screens or backgrounds and elegant specimens. The plumes are wonderful as cut flowers.

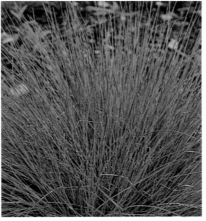

Festuca cinerea
GRAMINEAE

BLUE FESCUE

The leaf colour of blue fescue can range from dark green to bright blue, depending on the cultivar. Most plants will produce spiky clumps of blue-grey foliage.

Type of plant Cool-season, clumping perennial grass.

Best climate and site Zones 4–9. Moist, well-drained soil. Full sun; light shade in hot climates. Plants are drought-resistant but grow poorly in hot, humid conditions.

Height and spread Height 20–30 cm (8–12 inches); clumps spread to 60 cm (2 feet).

Description Blue fescue is noted for its rounded mounds of beautiful silver-blue, spiky, evergreen foliage. The grey-green flowers are not especially noteworthy. Blue fescue is also sold as *F. glauca*, *F. avina* and *F. avina* 'Glauca'.

Growing guidelines Plant 30–60 cm (1–2 feet) apart in spring or autumn. Cut back in early spring or autumn to promote tidy, new growth. Individual plants are short-lived; divide and replant every two to three years. Blue fescue may self-sow readily, and the seedlings may range in colour from blue to green; clipping off the flower spikes can prevent reseeding. Grow species plants from seed or division and cultivars by division in early spring.

Landscape use Accent plants for borders and rock gardens. Also container plants, groundcover and seaside plants.

Hakonechloa macra 'Aureola'
GRAMINEAE

VARIEGATED HAKONE GRASS

Variegated hakone grass forms slow spreading clumps of elegant, bamboo-like leaves. The yellow-striped foliage takes on pink or reddish tints in autumn.

Type of plant Warm-season, slow-spreading perennial grass.

Best climate and site Zones 6–9. Moist, well-drained, fertile soil. Light shade.

Height and spread Height 45–60 cm (18–24 inches); spread to 60 cm (2 feet), sometimes more.

Description Variegated hakone grass is a well-behaved, low-growing, arching, deciduous grass. Its star feature is its soft, bright yellow, bamboo-like leaves that are striped with green in summer and reddish in autumn. Clumps get larger with age but are not invasive. Inconspicuous flowers bloom in late summer.

Growing guidelines Set plant 60 cm (2 feet) or more apart in spring or early autumn. Keep them out of full sun, and water during dry spells to keep the soil evenly moist at all times. Propagate by division in spring.

Landscape use This handsome grass is lovely either as a single specimen plant or massed in a shady spot. It is good for edgings, in containers and as groundcover under trees. It is a favourite for oriental gardens because of its bamboo-like appearance.

Imperata cylindrica 'Red Baron'
GRAMINEAE

'RED BARON' BLOOD GRASS

If possible, site 'Red Baron' blood grass where the morning or late afternoon sun can shine through it; backlighting can really make the red colour glow.

Type of plant Warm-season, slow-spreading perennial grass.

Best climate and site Zones 6–9. Fertile, moist, well-drained soil. Full sun; partial shade in hot climates.

Height and spread Height 30–45 cm (12–18 inches); spread to 60 cm (2 feet).

Description This Japanese grass has spectacular foliage, especially in spring and autumn. It starts green with red tips in spring but gradually becomes more red; by summer's end, it is deep blood red. The leaves turn copper in late autumn, and the colour endures throughout winter. Unlike the species, the cultivar 'Red Baron' does not flower, so it does not set seed and is not invasive.

Growing guidelines Plant 30–60 cm (1–2 feet) apart in spring or early autumn. Red colour is best in full sun, except in hot climates, where plants need partial shade during the heat of the day. Blood grass tolerates drought, but watering in dry spells will prevent leaf tips from turning brown. Propagate in spring by division.

Landscape use Blood grass is dramatic as a mass planting. It also adds a colourful touch to flower borders or containers. Blood grass makes a unique background for a low border.

Koeleria glauca
GRAMINEAE

LARGE BLUE HAIR GRASS

Large blue hairgrass is a short-lived perennial that tends to die out in the centre as it ages. Divide and replant clumps every two or three years to keep them vigorous.

Type of plant Cool-season, clumping perennial grass.

Best climate and site Zones 6–9; can survive in colder areas with dependable winter snow cover. Well-drained, somewhat alkaline soil with average fertility. Full sun.

Height and spread Height 15–30 cm (6–12 inches) for leaves; similar spread. Flowering stems to 45 cm (18 inches) tall.

Description The narrow, flat, blue-green leaves grow upright in tight clumps. Striking blue-green flower clusters rise above the foliage in late spring; they later change to a buff colour.

Growing guidelines Plant 30 cm (1 foot) apart in spring or early autumn. Cut back leaves and flower stems in midsummer to encourage new growth. Propagate by seed in spring or division in spring or autumn.

Landscape use Single specimens are good accent plants in the front of borders. In groups they make effective edgings and good companion plants for low-growing evergreens. Large blue hair grass is also an interesting pot plant for a terrace or deck. The cut flowers look beautiful and dramatic in arrangements.

Miscanthus sinensis
GRAMINEAE

JAPANESE SILVER GRASS

Japanese silver grass, also cammonly called eulalia grass, is one of the best large ornamental grasses. It is especially attractive near streams and ponds.

Type of plant Warm-season, clumping perennial grass.

Best climate and site Zones 5–9. Light, moist, humus-rich soil. Full sun.

Height and spread Height 90–150 cm (3–5 feet) for foliage; spread to 90 cm (3 feet) or more. Flowering stems can grow 1.8–3 m (6–10 feet) tall.

Description Large clumps of long, pointed, sharp-edged leaves show a silvery colour in early summer; later they turn beautiful autumn reds, yellows, rusts and browns. Tall, decorative flower plumes in hues from silver to reddish purple bloom above the foliage from midsummer through early autumn.

Growing guidelines Plant 60–120 cm (2–4 feet) apart in spring. Provide light shade and extra water in hot climates. Stake the tall, floppy kinds if necessary, and divide in spring when the plant clumps begin to die in the centre. Most cultivars are pest-resistant, but some are susceptible to mealybugs and rust. Propagate the species by seed or division, and cultivars by spring division only.

Landscape use Large cultivars are excellent for screens, hedges and background plantings; choose compact **Cultivars** for flower beds and borders.

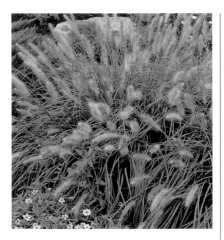

Pennisetum alopecuroides
GRAMINEAE

FOUNTAIN GRASS

Fountain grass is one of the most beautiful and adaptable of all ornamental grasses. The showy seed heads cascade, like a fountain, over mounds of glossy green leaves.

Type of plant Warm-season, clumping perennial grass.
Best climate and site Zones 5–9. Prefers fertile, moist, well-drained soil but adapts well to other soil types. Full sun; tolerates light shade.
Height and spread Height of foliage to 90 cm (3 feet); similar spread. Flowering stems grow to 1.2 m (4 feet) tall.
Description Fountain grass blooms in midsummer, with creamy white to pinkish flowers in 10–25-cm (4–10-inch) long clusters shaped like little foxtails. The seed heads later turn reddish brown and remain until autumn.
Growing guidelines Plant 60–90 cm (2–3 feet) apart in spring. Keep them watered in dry weather for best growth. Cut off seed heads in autumn to keep them from spreading their seeds throughout the garden. Cut back dead leaves by early spring. Propagate the species by division or seed and propagate cultivars by spring division only.
Landscape use Fountain grasses are excellent single accent plants in borders or grow them in drifts as groundcover. They are a good choice for coastal plantings, too, since they tolerate wind.

Schizachyrium scoparium
GRAMINEAE

LITTLE BLUESTEM

Little bluestem is a good groundcover plant for large areas, for erosion control on dry slopes and for naturalising in meadows – wherever its reseeding habit isn't a problem.

Type of plant Warm-season, clumping perennial grass.
Best climate and site Zones 3–10. Any soil that is not soggy. Full sun.
Height and spread Height of foliage to about 30 cm (1 foot); spread to about 30 cm (1 foot). Flowering stems grow to 90 cm (3 feet) tall.
Description This common North American native has light green, somewhat hairy, deciduous leaves. The plant is not especially showy in summer, but the cool temperatures of autumn transform its green leaves into shades of copper and bright orange. Spiky flowers in midsummer become attractive seed clusters in autumn.
Growing guidelines Plant about 60 cm (2 feet) apart in spring. Cut back dead leaves and stems by early spring. Propagate by seed or divide the clumps in spring.
Landscape use Little bluestem can make a fine accent plant in the border if you remove the seed heads by late summer to prevent reseeding. The cut flowers and foliage are handsome and dramatic in arrangements.

Stipa gigantea
GRAMINEAE

GIANT FEATHER GRASS

Giant feather grass, also known as golden oats, is especially stunning where its handsome flower plumes are backlit by the morning or late afternoon sun. The seed heads remain showy until autumn.

Type of plant Cool-season, clumping perennial grass.
Best climate and site Zones 7–9. Well-drained, fertile soil. Established plants are somewhat drought-tolerant; must have excellent drainage wherever rainfall is heavy. Full sun.
Height and spread Height of foliage to 60 cm (2 feet); clumps spread to 60 cm (2 feet) or more. Flowering stems grow to 1.5 m (5 feet).
Description Giant feather grass forms dramatic clumps of arching, rolled, evergreen leaves. Golden flowers hang from tall stems that rise 60–90 cm (2–3 feet) above the grey-green foliage in late spring.
Growing guidelines Plant 60–90 cm (2–3 feet) apart in spring or autumn. If needed, cut back the foliage to about 15 cm (6 inches) by early spring. Propagate by early-spring or autumn division, which can be difficult with the tight-growing clumps, or by seed, which may take three months or more to germinate.
Landscape use Looks great in masses as a screen or singly as a dramatic, tall specimen. The cut flowers are captivating in fresh or dried arrangements.

Allium sativum
ALLIACEAE

GARLIC

Garlic is one of the most familiar herbs, used to flavour dishes from almost every ethnic group. It is easy to grow from shop-bought bulbs.

Best climate and site Zones 5–10. Full sun to partial shade.
Ideal soil conditions Humus-rich, deep, well-drained soil.
Growing guidelines Separate individual cloves from the bulb immediately before planting, then plant in October for harvesting the following summer; space 15 cm (6 inches) apart and 5 cm (2 inches) deep. For largest bulbs, prune away flowering stems that shoot up in early summer; side-dress with compost in early spring; avoid planting after heavy applications of fresh manure.
Growing habit Biennial or perennial; height to 60 cm (2 feet); foliage narrowly strap-shaped.
Flowering time Early summer; small, white to pinkish blooms atop a tall, central stalk.
Pest and disease prevention Avoid wet soil to prevent bulb diseases.
Harvesting and storing Dig bulbs after tops have died down, and before bulb skins begin to decay underground; place in a single layer in a shaded spot to dry, then cut away tops leaving a 5-cm (2-inch) stem; or plait together the tops of freshly dug plants. Hang plaits from the ceiling in a cool, humid, dark place.

Allium schoenoprasum
ALLIACEAE

CHIVES

The graceful leaves and blossoms have a mild onion flavour, especially when used fresh. Use the leaves in cooking and toss the flowers in salads.

Best climate and site Zones 3–9. Full sun.
Ideal soil conditions Well-drained soil high in organic matter.
Growing guidelines Sow seed indoors in late winter, covering seed lightly and keeping the soil moist; transplant in clumps in early spring; space 12–20 cm (5–8 inches) apart. Sow outside in spring. Divide older clumps in early spring every three years, and freshen with compost or rotted manure.
Growing habit Height 15–30 cm (6–12 inches); perennial bulb with green, tubular leaves.
Flowering time June; pink or lavender to purple globular flower heads.
Pest and disease prevention Avoid wet, boggy areas that encourage stem and bulb diseases.
Harvesting and storing Use fresh leaf tips all summer once plants are 15 cm (6 inches) tall; leave at least 5 cm (2 inches) remaining. Best used fresh; or chop and dry. Freezes poorly.
Special tips Chives are recommended companion plants for carrots, grapes, roses and tomatoes.

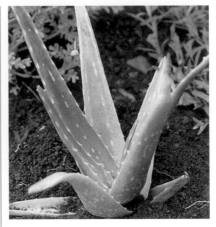

Aloe barbadensis [A. vera]
ASPHODELACEAE

ALOE

For colour and textural contrast, grow several of the more than 300 perennial species of succulent aloe. They contain a medicinal as well as cosmetic gel.

Other common names First-aid herb, healing herb, medicine plant.
Best climate and site Zones 9–10. Prefers full sun but tolerates light shade.
Ideal soil conditions Well-drained soil low in organic matter.
Growing guidelines Separate new shoots from established plants. In cool climates, plant in pots and move them indoors in winter. Aloes thrive with little attention. Indoors, avoid overwatering and mix coarse sand with potting compost to facilitate good drainage.
Growing habit Variable height; stemless rosette of spiny, tapered leaves.
Flowering time Rarely flowers in cool climates; drooping, tubular, yellow flowers atop a stalk up to 90 cm (3 feet) tall.
Pest and disease prevention Spray with insecticidal soap to control mealybugs, or purchase biological controls. Control insect pests before bringing indoors.
Harvesting and storing Cut leaves for gel as needed; remove outer leaves first.
Special tips Grow on sunny windowsills in the kitchen and bathroom.
Precautions Unsafe to use internally.

Anethum graveolens
UMBELLIFERAE

DILL

*Select dill varieties for either seed or foliage (called
'dill weed') production. Dill's tall, graceful habit
makes it an attractive background in flower beds.*

Best climate and site Zones 2–9.
Full sun.
Ideal soil conditions Well-drained soil
rich in organic matter.
Growing guidelines Sow seed shallowly
in rows or in 12-cm (5-inch) bands
outdoors in early spring after danger of
frost; thin to 20–25 cm (8–10 inches);
transplants poorly. Keep seedlings moist;
weed diligently until plants shade the soil.
Growing habit Height 60–90 cm
(2–3 feet); dill is a hardy annual,
resembling fennel.
Flowering time Summer to autumn;
yellowish flowers in umbels.
Pest and disease prevention Usually
free from pests and diseases.
Harvesting and storing Clip fresh leaves
at the stem as needed. Freeze whole
leaves, or chop first; or dry foliage on
non-metallic screens. Collect flower heads
before the seeds mature and fall; hang in
paper bags or dry on paper. Store dried
foliage and seeds in an airtight container.
Fresh leaves can be refrigerated for up to
one week.
Special tips Sow seeds at two- or
three-week intervals for a continuous
leaf harvest through autumn.

Anthriscus cerefolium
UMBELLIFERAE

CHERVIL

*Chervil grows best when temperatures are cool in
spring and autumn. Grow this lacy, delicate-looking
plant for medicinal, culinary and craft uses.*

Other common names Garden chervil.
Best climate and site Zones 3–7.
Partial shade.
Ideal soil conditions Moist, but
well-drained humus-rich garden soil.
Growing guidelines Sow fresh seed
shallowly outdoors in early spring or
autumn; thin to 22.5–30 cm
(9–12 inches); keep seedlings moist. Sow
again at two-week intervals until mid-July
for continuous harvest. Transplants
poorly. Mulch to protect autumn-sown
seeds. Chervil can seed itself each year if
flowers are left to mature in the garden.
Growing habit Annual; height 30–60 cm
(1–2 feet); fern-like leaves.
Flowering time Summer; small, white
umbrella-like clusters.
Pest and disease prevention Usually
free from pests and diseases.
Harvesting and storing Snip leaves
continuously after six to eight weeks; best
used fresh.
Special tips Loses flavour quickly when
heated, so add to recipes at the end.

Armoracia rusticana
CRUCIFERAE

HORSERADISH

*Horseradish is the white perennial root of a woody
herb. Folklore claims that horseradish should be
planted near potatoes to protect them from disease.*

Best climate and site Zones 5–8.
Full sun.
Ideal soil conditions Fertile, moist but
well-drained soil.
Growing guidelines Plant straight, young
roots 20–22.5 cm (8–9 inches) long and
1 cm (½ inch) wide so that crown or
growing point is 7.5–12.5 cm (3–5 inches)
below the soil surface, and plants are
30–45 cm (12–18 inches) apart. Plant at
an angle to the horizontal.
Growing habit Second-year plants grow
60–90 cm (2–3 feet) tall; leaves are
stalked and oblong.
Flowering time Midsummer; small, white
blossoms do not produce viable seed.
Pest and disease prevention Usually
free from pests and diseases.
Harvesting and storing Harvest roots in
late October or November, and scrub
them before storing in the refrigerator, or
pack in dry sand in the cellar for spring
planting. Or leave roots in the soil and
harvest as required.
Special tips Harvest early for the most
tender roots.

Artemisia dracunculus var. *sativa*
COMPOSITAE

TARRAGON, FRENCH

Tarragon's heavy liquorice flavour holds well in cooking, making it an extremely useful herb in the kitchen. It's traditionally served with chicken dishes.

Best climate and site Zones 4–8. Full sun to partial shade.
Ideal soil conditions Well-drained garden soil.
Growing guidelines Cannot be grown from seed. Take cuttings from new growth in autumn, overwintering the young plants indoors until the following spring. Or divide older plants in spring every three years; space 30–60 cm (12–24 inches) apart. Prune away flower stems each year for most vigorous growth and best flavour. To grow indoors in winter, pot young plants in summer, cutting foliage to just above the soil. Seal pot in a plastic bag and refrigerate to mimic winter. In autumn, unwrap and place in a sunny window for winter harvests.
Growing habit Height 60–120 cm (2–4 feet); hardy perennial with long, branched green stems.
Flowering time Remove inconspicuous yellow-green flowers to encourage growth of foliage.
Pest and disease prevention Generally free from pests and diseases.
Harvesting and storing Clip foliage as needed all summer. Fresh foliage lasts several weeks in the refrigerator wrapped in kitchen paper inside a plastic bag.

Borago officinalis
BORAGINACEAE

BORAGE

This green, robust and bristly plant contrasts nicely with dark greens in the garden. The drooping clusters of blossoms attract honeybees.

Best climate and site Zones 3–9. Prefers full sun but tolerates partial shade.
Ideal soil conditions Fairly rich, moist soil with good drainage.
Growing guidelines Sow seed 1 cm (½ inch) deep outdoors after danger of hard frost. Indoors, plant in pots to avoid disturbing the sensitive taproot when transplanting. Control weeds to reduce competition for moisture. To promote blooming, go easy on the nitrogen. Self-sows well. Tall plants may need support.
Growing habit Annual; height 45–60 cm (1½–2 feet), width up to 45 cm (18 inches) with broad, hairy leaves arising from a central stalk.
Flowering time Continuously from midsummer until first frost; star-shaped circles of pink, purple, lavender or blue, with black centres.
Pest and disease prevention Mulch with light materials like straw to keep foliage off soil and prevent rotting.
Harvesting and storing Harvest foliage anytime and use raw or cooked. Snip blossoms just after they open and candy or toss fresh in a salad.
Precautions Borage may be toxic if eaten in large quantities over a long period of time.

Carum carvi
UMBELLIFERAE

CARAWAY

The seeds of this annual or biennial have been used for 5,000 years for flavouring and for their corminative effect.

Best climate and site Zones 3–7. Full sun to light shade.
Ideal soil conditions Prefers fertile, light garden soil.
Growing guidelines Sow seed shallowly outdoors as early as the soil can be worked, or indoors in pots; thin to 15–30 cm (6–12 inches). Sow seed outdoors for early spring plants. Don't allow seedlings to dry out. A long taproot makes transplanting difficult.
Growing habit Height 30–60 cm (1–2 feet); glossy, fine dissected foliage resembling the carrot plant.
Flowering time Spring and early summer of the second year; white or pink flowers in umbels on stalks.
Pest and disease prevention Watch for pests in dried, stored seeds.
Harvesting and storing Snip tender leaves in spring and use fresh in salads, soups and stews. After flowering, cut plants when seeds are brown and almost loose, then hang them upside down in paper bags to dry. Collect seeds and dry a few more days in the sun; store in a tightly sealed container.
Special tips Excessive pruning during the first year weakens the plant.

Chamaemelum nobile
COMPOSITAE

CHAMOMILE, ROMAN

Herb gardens of yesterday often included a lush lawn of chamomile that released a sweet, apple-like scent when walked upon. The tea is relaxing after a stressful day.

Other common names Garden chamomile, ground apple, Russian chamomile.
Best climate and site Zones 3–8. Full sun to partial shade.
Ideal soil conditions Light, moist but well-drained garden soil.
Growing guidelines Sow seed indoors or outdoors; thin to 15 cm (6 inches). Once established, it can self-sow. Divide older plants in early spring. In the first year, clip to prevent flowering and encourage vegetative growth while it becomes established. Chamomile is a poor competitor, so weed often. Established lawns can be mowed like grass.
Growing habit Height 15–22.5 cm (6–9 inches); low-growing perennial with aromatic lacy foliage.
Flowering time Summer; white daisy-like flowers with yellow centres.
Pest and disease prevention Usually free from pests and diseases.
Harvesting and storing Collect flowers at full bloom and dry on mesh screens or paper. Store in tightly sealed containers.

Coriandum sativum
UMBELLIFERAE

CORIANDER

In seed catalogues, select types grown for either seed or foliage production. The seeds become more fragrant with age, and are popular ingredients in the kitchen and in pot-pourri.

Other common names Chinese parsley, cilantro.
Best climate and site Zones 2–9. Full sun to partial shade.
Ideal soil conditions Moderately rich, well-drained soil.
Growing guidelines Sow seed 1 cm (½ inch) deep outdoors after danger of frost, or in autumn; thin to 10 cm (4 inches). Can self-sow. Weed diligently to prevent delicate seedlings from being overcome by more vigorous weeds. To prevent sprawling, avoid feeding with heavy applications of nitrogen.
Growing habit Annual; height 30–90 cm (1–3 feet); graceful, glossy, finely dissected foliage, which resembles Queen Anne's lace.
Flowering time Early to late summer, depending on when sown; tiny white flowers in umbels.
Pest and disease prevention Usually free from pests and diseases.
Harvesting and storing Harvest foliage before seeds form and use fresh. Harvest ripe seeds before they shatter, dry them and store them in airtight containers in the refrigerator.

Cymbopogon citratus
GRAMINEAE

LEMONGRASS

Grassy foliage provides contrast with broad-leaved garden herbs. Use the dried foliage for teas or add it to pot-pourri. Only the lower part of the stem is used in cooking.

Other common names Fevergrass, West Indian lemon.
Best climate and site Zones 9–10. Full sun to partial shade.
Ideal soil conditions Well-drained garden soil enriched with organic matter.
Growing guidelines Propagate by division of older plants. Trim the leaves to several inches before dividing.
Growing habit Tender perennial; height to 1.8 m (6 feet); forms dense clumps of typical grass leaves.
Flowering time Seldom flowers.
Pest and disease prevention Usually free from pests and diseases.
Harvesting and storing Snip fresh foliage as needed. Harvest foliage anytime in summer; dry quickly for best flavour. Use the base of fresh stems, crushed or sliced, in stir-fries and other Asian dishes.

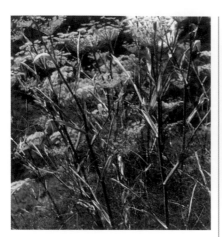

Foeniculum vulgare
UMBELLIFERAE

FENNEL

Grow liquorice-scented fennel as a tall ornamental in the flower garden, and for its culinary properties in the kitchen. Both leaves and seeds are used.

Best climate and site Zones 6–9. Full sun.
Ideal soil conditions Humus-rich, well-drained soil.
Growing guidelines Sow seed shallowly outdoors in spring or autumn and keep moist; thin to 15 cm (6 inches); fennel transplants poorly.
Growing habit Semi-hardy perennial usually grown as an annual; height to 1.2 m (4 feet); leaves are feathery, and a blue-green colour.
Flowering time July to October; small yellow flowers in umbels.
Pest and disease prevention Usually free from pests and diseases.
Harvesting and storing Snip leaves before flowers bloom for fresh use; leaves can also be frozen. Collect seeds when dry but before they shatter, and dry them on paper.
Special tips Fennel's delicate flavour is destroyed by heat, so add at the end of the recipe. Try the bronze-coloured variety for foliage contrast outdoors, and on the dinner plate as a garnish.

Laurus nobilis
LAURACEAE

BAY, SWEET

Bay leaf garlands represent victory and accomplishment. Use leaves for flavour in stews and soups, and as an aromatic addition to pot-pourri.

Best climate and site Zones 8–9, but needs a sheltered site in colder areas. Full sun to partial shade.
Ideal soil conditions Well-drained soil, rich in organic matter.
Growing guidelines Take cuttings from fresh green shoots in autumn and keep the soil in which you plant them moist, since rooting may take three to nine months. In warm climates, sow seed outdoors; germination may require 6–12 months. Survives light frost in the garden. Grows well in cool climates in pots if moved indoors for the winter; trim away roots from large, pot-bound plants and add fresh compost to stimulate new growth.
Growing habit Evergreen tree; height up to 18 m (60 feet) but easily kept to any desired size with pruning.
Flowering time Spring; but not very conspicuous, yellowish flowers; rarely flowers in pots.
Pest and disease prevention Watch for signs of scale insects and wipe them away with alcohol swabs. Dried leaves sprinkled throughout kitchen cupboards are said to repel storage pests.
Harvesting and storing Collect and dry the leaves as needed; store in jars.

Levisticum officinale
UMBELLIFERAE

LOVAGE

If you are unsuccessful growing celery, try this easy and flavourful substitute. The leaves, stems and seeds are all edible.

Best climate and site Zones 5–8. Prefers full sun but tolerates partial shade.
Ideal soil conditions Fertile, moist, but well-drained soil.
Growing guidelines Sow ripe seed shallowly in late summer or early autumn; thin to 60–90 cm (2–3 feet) apart. Prune flowers to encourage vegetative growth. Each spring, mulch with compost or well-rotted manure. Replace plants every four to five years.
Growing habit Perennial; height to 1.8 m (6 feet) or more; hollow, ribbed stems; glossy, dark green leaves.
Flowering time June to July; tiny greenish yellow flowers in umbels.
Pest and disease prevention Mainly trouble-free.
Harvesting and storing Once established, harvest leaves as needed for fresh use. In autumn, bunch foliage and stems and hang to dry. Or blanch small bunches before freezing for winter use. Seeds are ripe and ready to harvest when the fruits begin to split open. Dig roots in late autumn, wash and slice into 1-cm (½-inch) pieces, and dry before storing.

Melissa officinalis
LABIATAE

LEMON BALM

Lemon balm has a fragrance much like lemon-flavoured sweets. Both foliage and flowers are attractive in flower beds.

Other common names Sweet balm, bee balm.
Best climate and site Zones 4–9. Full sun to partial shade.
Ideal soil conditions Any sandy, well-drained soil.
Growing guidelines Sow shallowly in spring, thinning to 45–60 cm (18–24 inches); readily self-sows. Take cuttings or divide older plants in spring or autumn. Each autumn, cut away old stalks.
Growing habit Perennial; height 30–60 cm (1–2 feet); stems square, branching, with oval, fragrant leaves.
Flowering time June to October; small white tubular blossoms in bunches in the upper leaf axils.
Pest and disease prevention Thin dense plantings for best air circulation to prevent powdery mildew. Rarely bothered by insects.
Harvesting and storing Collect leaves in late summer and dry quickly to prevent them from turning black. Cut the entire plant, leaving about 5 cm (2 inches) of stem. Use leaves fresh in salads and for cooking, or dry them for making tea.

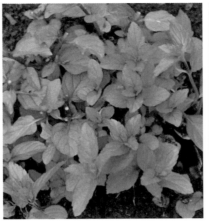

Mentha spp.
LABIATAE

MINT

The mints are herbaceous perennials that thrive in moist locations. Fresh and dried foliage provide flavouring for both sweet and savoury dishes.

Best climate and site Zones 5–9. Full sun or partial shade.
Ideal soil conditions Prefers moist, well-drained soil.
Growing guidelines Propagate from new plants that spring up along roots, or by cuttings in spring or autumn. Allow 30–45 cm (12–18 inches) between plants. Mint is a rampant spreader. To control, plant in bottomless containers 25 cm (10 inches) deep, or in large pots. Top-dress with compost or manure in autumn.
Growing habit Height up to 75 cm (30 inches) or more; square stems with smooth lance-like leaves.
Flowering time July to August; tiny purple or pink blossoms in whorled spikes.
Pest and disease prevention Thin crowded clumps for good air circulation to prevent root and foliage diseases. Watch for aphids, which stipple leaves; control them with a strong spray of water.
Harvesting and storing Harvest fresh leaves as needed. Just before blooming, cut the stalks and hang in bunches to dry; store in airtight containers.
Special tips Mints do well when planted where water drips, such as near outdoor taps that are used often in summer.

Ocimum basilicum
LABIATAE

BASIL, SWEET

Sweet basil is one of the most popular herbs in home gardens, mainly due to its strong flavour (with hints of liquorice and pepper).

Best climate and site Zones 4–10. Thrives on heat and full sun.
Ideal soil conditions Accepts a wide range of soil textures; likes rich, moist, well-drained soil.
Growing guidelines Sow seed outdoors, after all danger of frost, to a depth of 3 mm (⅛ inch), then thin to 15 cm (6 inches). Or sow indoors in seed trays in warmth, six weeks before last frost, then transplant to small pots before setting outdoors. Mulch with compost to retain soil moisture. Side-dress with compost in mid-season to enhance production. Basil is easily damaged by cold temperatures. In autumn, cover with plastic to prolong the season and protect from the earliest frosts.
Growing habit Annual; height 30–60 cm (1–2 feet), width 45 cm (18 inches).
Flowering time Continuous, beginning in midsummer; white blooms, carried in leafy terminal spikes.
Pest and disease prevention Plant away from mint to prevent damage from plant bugs.
Harvesting and storing Harvest leaves every week, pinching terminal buds first to encourage branching. Leaves can be used fresh or dried.

Origanum majorana
LABIATAE

MARJORAM, SWEET

Some herb growers find this bushy aromatic plant with lush foliage an easy-to-grow substitute for oregano.

Other common names Annual marjoram, knotted marjoram.
Best climate and site Zones 9–10. Full sun.
Ideal soil conditions Prefers light, well-drained soil.
Growing guidelines Sow seed shallowly indoors in spring; germinates slowly. Set plants out after danger of frost, spacing clumps of several plants 15–30 cm (6–12 inches) apart. Cut back by half just before flowering to maintain vegetative growth. In autumn, divide roots and bring indoors in pots to a cool location, replanting outdoors in early spring.
Growing habit Height to 60 cm (2 feet); bushy, tender perennial.
Flowering time August to September; white or pink blossoms.
Pest and disease prevention Usually free from pests and diseases.
Harvesting and storing Cut fresh leaves as needed for cooking; hang small bunches in an airy location to dry, then store in airtight containers.

Origanum vulgare
LABIATAE

OREGANO

Experiment with several types to find the flavour you like most. Sprigs with small, rounded leaves and miniature blossoms make an attracive garnish.

Other common names Wild marjoram, pot marjoram.
Best climate and site Zones 6–9. Full sun.
Ideal soil conditions Well-drained, average garden soil.
Growing guidelines Sow seed shallowly indoors in winter for best germination; sow outdoors if soil temperature is above 7°C (45°F). Plant in clumps 30 cm (1 foot) apart. Prune regularly for best shape. Since seedlings will not always produce the same flavour as the original plants, take cuttings or divide roots in spring or early autumn for best results. Lightly mulch each spring with compost or well-rotted manure.
Growing habit Perennial; height 30–75 cm (12–30 inches); herbaceous and shrubby.
Flowering time July to September; tubular, rose to white blossoms in broad terminal clusters.
Pest and disease prevention Provide good drainage to prevent root diseases. Wash away mites and aphids with water.
Harvesting and storing Snip fresh sprigs as needed all summer; cut whole plant in June and again in late August; hang foliage in bunches to dry.

Pelargonium spp.
GERANIACEAE

GERANIUM, SCENTED

Apple-scented geranium has an intense scent and, like the rose-scented geranium, is a source of geranium oil.

Best climate and site Perennial in Zone 10, annual in cooler zones. Full sun.
Ideal soil conditions Rich, loamy, well-drained soil.
Growing guidelines Cuttings root quickly and easily from new growth in spring or late summer. Grows well in pots near a sunny window. Apply a liquid plant food, like liquid seaweed or compost tea, but hold back on the nitrogen for the best fragrance. Plants more than one year old tend to get over-large; take new cuttings and discard the old plants. Remove dead foliage regularly.
Growing habit Height up to 90 cm (3 feet), foliage and growth habit vary with species or cultivar; leaves frilly, variegated, ruffled, velvety or smooth.
Flowering time Three to six months from rooting; sometimes inconspicuous.
Pest and disease prevention Vacuum whiteflies from foliage, or control with weekly sprays of insecticidal soap or a botanical insecticide. Avoid overwatering.
Harvesting and storing Pick leaves throughout the summer and dry them, storing in an airtight container, to use in winter pot-pourris. Use fresh leaves in jellies and tea, or as an aromatic garnish.

Petroselinum crispum var. *crispum*
UMBELLIFERAE

PARSLEY, CURLED

Kitchen gardens always include parsley, since it is required in so many recipes. The delicate, dark green foliage makes it an excellent plant for borders or growing on windowsills.

Best climate and site Zones 5–9. Full sun to partial shade.
Ideal soil conditions Moderately rich, well-drained soil.
Growing guidelines Sow seed shallowly outdoors in early spring when soil reaches 10°C (50°F), thinning to 20 cm (8 inches) apart; germinates slowly. Or soak seeds overnight in warm water before sowing in peat pots indoors in early spring. Remove all flower stalks that form, and prune away dead leaves. For productive plants, side-dress with compost in mid-season. Usually survives the winter, but quickly goes to flower in spring. Plants may be grown in pots to bring indoors for winter harvests.
Growing habit Biennial grown as an annual; height 20–30 cm (8–12 inches); leaves are finely divided, on a long stalk.
Flowering time Early spring of second year; tiny, greenish yellow umbels.
Pest and disease prevention Usually free from pests and diseases.
Harvesting and storing Cut leaf stalks at the base for fresh foliage all summer. Hang in bunches to dry in shade, or freeze whole or chopped.

Pimpinella anisum
UMBELLIFERAE

ANISE

Use these liquorice-scented leaves and seeds in salads, especially when combined with apples. The crushed, aromatic seeds enhance the fragrance of homemade pot-pourris.

Best climate and site Zones 4–9. Full sun.
Ideal soil conditions Poor, light, well-drained soil.
Growing guidelines Sow seed outdoors in spring where plants will stand, then thin to 30 cm (1 foot) apart. Or sow several seeds in pots several months before the last frost in a warm (21°C [70°F]) room. Transplants poorly. Stake or grow in clumps to prevent plants from sprawling.
Growing habit Annual; height up to 60 cm (2 feet); lacy foliage.
Flowering time Summer; dainty white blossoms in umbels.
Pest and disease prevention Anise oil is said to have insect-repellent properties; few pests bother this plant.
Harvesting and storing Seeds are ready to harvest when they fall easily from the head. Dry seeds on paper for several sunny days outdoors, then pasteurise in an oven at 38°C (100°F) for 15 minutes and store in airtight containers. Snip foliage as needed.
Special tips Enhances the growth of coriander. Anise was once used as a bait in mousetraps.

Rosmarinus officinalis
LABIATAE

ROSEMARY

Rosemary is a highly scented herb used to season meat, poultry and fish (particularly when roasted), bread and desserts. Use both the flowers and leaves for cooking and garnishing.

Best climate and site Zones 7–9. Grown outdoors where temperatures remain above -12°C (10°F). Full sun to partial shade.
Ideal soil conditions Prefers light, well-drained soil.
Growing guidelines Sow seed shallowly indoors in early spring, then transplant to pots outdoors; plant out in the garden for the second season, spacing 90 cm (3 feet) apart. Or take cuttings from new growth in autumn, or layer the stems in spring. Larger plants may overwinter better outdoors than smaller ones. Potted plants may be brought into a sunny greenhouse for the winter; or keep them at 7°C (45°F) in a sunny garage or enclosed porch, watering infrequently.
Growing habit Height 60–180 cm (2–6 feet); tender perennial with scaly bark and aromatic, needle-like leaves.
Flowering time Spring and summer. Small pale blue to pink tubular flowers in axillary clusters.
Pest and disease prevention Indoors, wipe scale pests from foliage with cotton soaked with rubbing alcohol.
Harvesting and storing Snip fresh foliage as needed all year.

Rumex spp.
POLYGONACEAE

SORREL

In the spring, use sorrel's tender new leaves to make a delicate soup or add them to salads. The older the leaves, the more bitter the taste.

Best climate and site Zones 5–9. Full sun.

Ideal soil conditions Moderately fertile, moist garden soil.

Growing guidelines Sow seed shallowly outdoors in late spring, thinning to 45 cm (18 inches). Or divide older plants in early spring or autumn.

Growing habit Hardy perennial; height 75–90 cm (30–36 inches); wavy, green leaves.

Flowering time Midsummer; greenish yellow to red flowers.

Pest and disease prevention Hand-pick snails from new spring leaves.

Harvesting and storing Harvest the outside leaves regularly to promote new growth. Sorrel leaves are best eaten fresh, but may also be blanched and frozen.

Species French sorrel (*R. scutatus*): lower-growing perennial; best-tasting flavour. Garden sorrel (*R. acetosa*): also called sour dock; has a very bitter flavour.

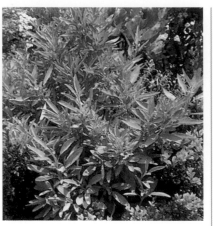

Salvia officinalis
LABIATAE

SAGE

Sage is an easy-to-grow, shrubby perennial with aromatic foliage used most often with poultry. A tea of sage is said to settle the stomach.

Best climate and site Zones 4–8. Full sun to partial shade.

Ideal soil conditions Well-drained garden soil.

Growing guidelines Sow seed shallowly outdoors in late spring or indoors in late winter; plant at 50–60-cm (20–24-inch) intervals. Take cuttings or divide older plants in spring or autumn. Remove flowering spikes when young. Grows easily for several years, then begins to decline.

Growing habit Height 30–60 cm (1–2 feet); woody stems have wrinkled grey-green foliage.

Flowering time Spring; tubular purple flowers in whorled spikes.

Pest and disease prevention Plant in a sandy location at the proper spacing (or best drainage and air circulation necessary for preventing disease and slug problems. Rarely bothered by other pests.

Harvesting and storing Snip fresh leaves as needed, or bunch them and hang to dry for use during winter months. Refrain from harvesting the first year.

Satureja montana
LABIATAE

SAVORY, WINTER

This aromatic bushy, hardy perennial has a peppery flavour and has been used in cooking for 2,000 years.

Best climate and site Zones 6–9. Full sun.

Ideal soil conditions Prefers poor, well-drained soil.

Growing guidelines Sow seed shallowly outdoors in late spring, thinning to 30 cm (1 foot). Germinates slowly. Take cuttings, or divide older plants in spring or autumn.

Growing habit Height 15–30 cm (6–12 inches); branched, woody stems, oblong, needle-like leaves.

Flowering time June; pale purple blossoms in terminal spikes.

Pest and disease prevention Usually free from pests and diseases.

Harvesting and storing Harvest fresh as needed, or cut and dry the foliage just before flowering. Use as a flavouring in a variety of dishes, teas, herb butters and vinegars.

Other species Summer savory (*S. hortensis*): annual; prefers light, well-fertilised soil; transplants poorly; height 30–45 cm (12–18 inches); linear, downy leaves; pale lavender or white blossoms; used as an anti-flatulent.

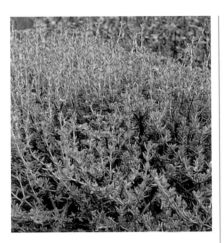

Thymus vulgaris
LABIATAE

THYME, GARDEN

Thyme is a favourite of cooks and gardeners, as it grows easily and there is at least one variety to suit every taste and location.

Best climate and site Zones 5–9. Full sun to partial shade.

Ideal soil conditions Prefers sandy, well-drained soil.

Growing guidelines Sow seed shallowly in late winter indoors, keeping the soil at 21°C (70°F) for best germination. Plant outdoors in late spring in clumps, 30 cm (1 foot) apart. You can divide older plants in spring or take cuttings in late summer or autumn. In winter, mulch with a light material like straw. Replace plants every three to four years to control woody growth.

Growing habit Height 15–38 cm (6–15 inches); hardy perennial; woody stems; tiny grey-green, aromatic leaves.

Flowering time Midsummer; tubular lilac to pink blossoms in clusters.

Pest and disease prevention Plant in well-drained soil to prevent root and stem diseases.

Harvesting and storing Snip foliage as needed during the summer, or harvest entirely twice per season, leaving at least 7.5 cm (3 inches) of growth. Bunch together and hang to dry, or first strip the leaves and dry on a fine mesh screen. Foliage freezes well in airtight containers or bags.

Trigonella foenum-graecum
LEGUMINOSAE

FENUGREEK

Fenugreek is a member of the same family as beans and clover. The seeds are used as a substitute for maple flavouring in baked goods.

Other common names Bird's foot, Greek hayseed.

Best climate and site Zones 6–10. Full sun.

Ideal soil conditions Rich soil.

Growing guidelines When springtime soil temperatures reach 15°C (60°F), sow a thick band of seed outdoors, covering shallowly. Avoid growing in cold, wet soils since seeds are likely to rot before they germinate.

Growing habit Annual; height 30–60 cm (1–2 feet); clover-like stems and leaves.

Flowering time Summer; white flowers that resemble garden pea blossoms.

Pest and disease prevention Hand-pick snails from new growth.

Harvesting and storing Harvest pods when ripe but before they fall, like garden beans; leave seeds in the sun to dry, then store in an airtight container.

Zingiber officinale
ZINGIBERACEAE

GINGER

Fresh ginger has a zing that the powdered spice lacks. Grow your own in pots placed outdoors during the warm season.

Best climate and site Zones 9–10. Partial shade.

Ideal soil conditions Fertile, moist, well-drained garden soil.

Growing guidelines Plant rhizomes in pots in a mix containing peat, sand and compost; keep indoors or in a greenhouse in winter, moving the pots outdoors in warm summers.

Growing habit Tender perennial; height 60–120 cm (2–4 feet); leaves strap-shaped, 15–30 cm (6–12 inches) long.

Flowering time Rarely flowers under cultivation; in the wild, dense cone-like spikes on a stalk have yellow-green and purple flowers.

Pest and disease prevention Usually free from pests and diseases. For healthy growth, water well during the hot, summer months.

Harvesting and storing Dig plant after one year and remove the leaf stems, cutting away as much root as you need; replant the remaining root. Refrigerate harvested roots wrapped in kitchen paper inside a plastic bag for up to one month. Or dry shaved bits of root and store in an airtight container.

Abelmoschus esculentus
MALVACEAE

OKRA (CUMBO)

The essential ingredient in gumbo, okra is also admired for its lovely, hollyhock-like flowers. It loves hot weather.

Best climate and site Zones 5 and warmer. Full sun.
Ideal soil conditions Fertile and well-drained soil; pH 6.5-7.5.
Growing guidelines Sow when frost danger is past and the soil is warm. Pre-warming the soil with black plastic mulch will speed germination. In cooler areas, start indoors in individual pots two to four weeks before last frost and set out when the weather is settled. Set out or thin to stand 30-38 cm (12-15 inches) apart. Grows quickly in warm weather and needs both food and water; irrigate in dry spells and give it compost tea or liquid fertilizer once a month.
Pest and disease prevention Little troubled by pests. Aphids are a sign of water stress.
Common problems In cooler areas, okra will not bear as prolifically as in warm climates. Red-podded cultivars, such as 'Burgundy', are often better producers.
Days to maturity 50-60 frost-free days.
Harvesting and storing Clip or pinch off young pods when they are 2.5-10 cm (1-4 inches) long and still soft. Larger pods will be woody. Harvest daily in warm weather. Freezes well.
Special tips Blossoms are edible.

Allium ampeloprasm, Porrum group

LEEK

Leeks are grown for their stout, flavourful white stem. These onion relatives hold well in the ground for late harvest.

Best climate and site Zones 3 and warmer; grow as a winter vegetable in mild areas. Full sun.
Ideal soil conditions Loose, very rich, well-drained soil; pH 6.0-7.5.
Growing guidelines Sow indoors up to 12 weeks before last spring frost. Transplant from seed trays to small, individual pots when large enough to handle. Set out after frost, 15 cm (6 inches) apart, in a 15-cm (6-inch) deep trench, covering all but 2-3 cm (1 inch or so) of leaves. Keep well weeded. As leeks grow, fill in the trench gradually or, if planted on level soil, 'hill' them by drawing soil up around the stems. This produces a longer white stem. Keep the soil moist, especially early in the season.
Pest and disease prevention To avoid root maggot damage, do not plant where other onion family members have grown the previous year.
Common problems Short, tough stems indicate lack of moisture or fertility or inadequate hilling.
Days to maturity 70-105 days in garden. Young plants take light frost; mature ones, severe frost.
Harvesting and storing Dig or pull when large enough for use.

Allium cepa, Aggregatum group
ALLIACEAE

SHALLOT

An onion relative, shallots produce small, firm bulbs that keep like garlic but are much milder in flavour. They are excellent in sauces.

Best climate and site All Zones; may be autumn-planted in Zones 6 and warmer. Full sun.
Ideal soil conditions Humus-rich, well-drained soil. Will tolerate all but the most acid soil.
Growing guidelines Shallots do not grow from seed but from bulblets or 'sets'. Plant two to four weeks before last spring frost, 2.5 cm (1 inch) deep and 10-15 cm (4-6 inches) apart. Keep cultivated or mulch and water regularly to encourage strong early growth. Each set will produce eight to ten shallots.
Pest and disease prevention To avoid root maggots, do not plant where shallots or their relatives, such as onions or leeks, have grown the previous year.
Common problems Dry conditions or poor soil produces scrawny shallots. Work in plenty of compost or well-rotted manure and water regularly.
Days to maturity 120-150 days; or pull earlier to eat as spring onios. Will withstand moderate frost.
Harvesting and storing When the tops are nearly dry, pull plants and dry the bulbs in a well-ventilated, sunny area. Store by hanging in a cool, dry place, or clip stems and store bulbs in mesh bags.

Allium spp.
ALLIACEAE

ONION

A staple since before the pharaohs, the bulb of the versatile onion provides plenty of good eating in little garden space.

Best climate and site All Zones for spring onions or 'green onions'; Zones 3 and warmer for bulb onions, choosing cultivars suited to day length. Full sun.
Ideal soil conditions Humus-rich, well-drained soil; pH 6.0–7.5.
Growing guidelines For summer harvest, sow indoors three to four months before last spring frost and set out 8–10 cm (3–4 inches) apart a month before last frost. Sow autumn storage onions a month before last frost; thin to 8–10 cm (3–4 inches) apart. For quicker crops or in colder areas, grow onions from small bulbs called 'sets'. Irrigate and fertilise with liquid fertiliser or compost tea to encourage good early growth.
Pest and disease prevention Rotate plantings of onions and their relatives, such as garlic and leeks.
Common problems Failure to form bulbs usually indicates an unsuitable cultivar.
Days to maturity 60–115 days from transplanting. Spring onions from sets may be harvested in as few as 35 days.
Harvesting and storing Pull spring onions and onions for fresh use as needed. For storage onions, wait until tops have fallen over; pull the onions two days later, then let them dry in a cool, dry place.

Apium graveolens var. *dulce*
UMBELLIFERAE

CELERY

It requires care and attention to thrive, but if you're willing to supply its needs, celery will do beautifully in the veg plot.

Best climate and site Zones 5 and warmer, except where early summer temperatures fall below 13°C (55°F). Autumn and winter crop in mild areas. Full sun.
Ideal soil conditions Moisture-retentive, rich soil, with adequate calcium and plenty of well-rotted manure or compost worked in; pH 5.5–7.5.
Growing guidelines Sow indoors four to six weeks before last spring frost. Germination and seedling growth are slow. Keep seedlings watered and do not expose to temperatures below 13°C (55°F), which can cause plants to bolt (go to seed). Plant out when the weather is well settled, 25–30 cm (10–12 inches) apart. Do not allow the soil to dry out; feed plants with liquid fertiliser or compost tea at least once a month.
Pest and disease prevention Rotate plantings to avoid blight problems. Hand-pick parsleyworms or celeryworms.
Common problems Excessive heat, inadequate moisture or lack of fertility will result in tough or stringy celery.
Days to maturity 80–105 days.
Harvesting and storing Cut celery for immediate use just below soil level.

Apium greolens var. *rapaceum*
UMBELLIFERAE

CELERIAC

In salads, soups, and stews, or as a cooked vegetable, the root of celeriac has all the flavour of celery.

Other common names Celery root.
Best climate and site Zones 5 and warmer. Use as an autumn and winter crop in mild areas. Full sun.
Ideal soil conditions Rich, moisture-retentive soil with adequate calcium and plenty of well-rotted manure or compost worked in; pH 5.5–7.5.
Growing guidelines Start indoors six to eight weeks before last spring frost and set out 25–30 cm (10–12 inches) apart when the frost threat is past. Keep bed well weeded and watered. Apply compost tea or liquid fertiliser at least monthly.
Pest and disease prevention Rotate plantings of celeriac and celery to avoid blights to which they are both vulnerable. Hand-pick celeryworms or parsleyworms.
Common problems Inadequate moisture and fertility produce small, tough, or fibrous celeriac.
Days to maturity 110–120 days; can withstand increasingly severe frost for the last 30–45 days.
Harvesting and storing Harvest the turnip-like root when large enough for your needs. Harvest all plants before the ground freezes; cut stems close to the roots and store like turnips in damp sawdust or sand in a cool place.

Asparagus officinalis
ASPARAGACEAE

ASPARAGUS

This classic spring vegetable requires well-prepared soil with high fertility. A well-maintained patch may yield for decades.

Best climate and site Zones 3 and warmer, but asparagus grows best in areas where soil freezes in winter. Avoid low-lying areas subject to heavy dew and morning fogs to reduce the possibility of rust. Prefers full sun, but will tolerate some shade.
Ideal soil conditions Fertile, well-drained soil; will tolerate slightly alkaline pH (6.5–6.8) and saline soils.
Growing guidelines Grow from seed sown indoors or in an outdoor seedbed; or hasten the first harvest by using year-old crowns. Follow directions on the seed packet or from your supplier for planting and cultivation.
Pest and disease prevention Asparagus rust can be a serious problem in damp locations; use rust-resistant cultivars. Burn or hot-compost old asparagus foliage and cultivate the asparagus patch shallowly before applying autumn mulch to reduce damage from asparagus beetles.
Common problems Be sure the area is free of perennial weeds before planting.
Days to maturity New hybrid cultivars may be picked sparingly for one to two weeks in the second year.
Harvesting and storing Harvest while tips of spears are still tightly closed.

Beta vulgaris
AMARANTHACEAE

BEETROOT

Start harvesting beetroot when it is 2.5 cm (1 inch) in diameter. You can eat both the leaves and roots.

Best climate and site Beetroot thrives in almost any climate, but where summers are hot (Zones 8 and warmer), grow them as an autumn, late winter and early spring crop. Full sun.
Ideal soil conditions Well-drained, rich, neutral soil, free of stones; pH 6.0–7.5.
Growing guidelines Soak the seeds in tepid water for several hours to encourage germination. Plant 2.5 cm (1 inch) deep and 5–10 cm (2–4 inches) apart, about one month before last spring frost. Firm the seedbed well. Thin the young plants when they are 5–8 cm (2–3 inches) tall. Beets need regular watering to keep them tender and to prevent interior discolouring that results from uneven soil moisture.
Pest and disease prevention Horticultural fleece will thwart flea beetles and leaf miners. Discourage the disease leaf spot by not growing beetroot where it or its relatives, such as spinach and chard, has been grown the previous year.
Common problems Beetroot does poorly in hot weather and dry soil.
Days to maturity 55–70 days.
Harvesting and storing Harvest greens as soon as they are large enough for use. When removing tops, leave 2.5 cm (1 inch) of stem to prevent bleeding.

Beta vulgaris var. *cicla*
AMARANTHACEAE

SWISS CHARD

Vigorous and easy to grow, a single planting of Swiss chard can provide a full season of fresh greens. Use it like spinach.

Other common names Silverbeet.
Best climate and site Zones 3 and warmer; grow as a winter vegetable in mild areas. Full sun or, in warm areas, partial shade.
Ideal soil conditions Not fussy, but prefers rich, well-drained soil; pH 6.0–6.8.
Growing guidelines Sow one to two weeks before last spring frost. Plant 12 mm (½ inch) deep and firm the soil with the back of a hoe. Thin to 20–30 cm (8–12 inches) apart, using thinnings in salads or transplanting them to new beds. Cultivate and water regularly to keep plants growing strongly.
Pest and disease prevention Little troubled by pests. Horticultural fleece will deter flea beetles.
Common problems Fairly tolerant, but water stress causes tough stems.
Days to maturity 50–60 days; thinnings may be harvested sooner.
Harvesting and storing Pick large outer leaves by pulling stems from the base with a slight twist. Leave the centre to sprout new leaves. Leaves are usually cooked separately from the wide inner rib, which is often steamed and eaten like asparagus. You can freeze leaves in the same way as you would spinach.

Brassica napus, Napobrassica group
CRUCIFERAE

SWEDE

A favourite in Scandinavian countries, swede is a rugged garden vegetable that shrugs off cold and adverse conditions.

Other common names Rutabaga, yellow turnip.

Best climate and site Zones 3 and warmer; grow as a winter vegetable in mild areas. Full sun.

Ideal soil conditions Fertile, well-drained soil. Will tolerate heavy soil better than most other root vegetables; pH 5.5–6.8.

Growing guidelines Sow 12–14 weeks before first autumn frost and thin to stand 10–15 cm (4–6 inches) apart. Cultivate early; the plant's large leaves will quickly grow to shade out weeds.

Pest and disease prevention Rotate swede and other root crops to avoid root maggots. Protect young plants from flea beetles with horticultural fleece; larger plants may suffer cosmetic damage that will not affect yield.

Common problems Swede that matures in hot weather may be tough.

Days to maturity 90–110 days. Will withstand severe frost.

Harvesting and storing Pull swede when it is large enough for use. The greens also are edible. Harvest all roots before hard frosts and store in damp sand or sawdust in a cool place.

Brassica oleracea, Botrytis group
CRUCIFERAE

BROCCOLI

Virtually unknown in American gardens 50 years ago, broccoli is now a cool-weather favourite. It can be eaten raw or cooked.

Best climate and site Zones 3 and warmer; grow as a winter crop in mild-climate areas. Where springs are cool, grow as a spring and autumn crop; otherwise does best in autumn. Full sun.

Ideal soil conditions Well-drained soil with plenty of calcium; pH 6.7–7.2.

Growing guidelines Grow spring seedlings indoors, about two months before the last spring frost. Set out hardened-off transplants in the garden a month before the last frost. Sow autumn crops directly about 90 days before the first autumn frost, or transplant about 60 days before frosts. Cultivate or mulch and keep the soil evenly moist.

Pest and disease prevention Use metal 'collars' or cardboard to deter cutworms. Horticultural fleece will thwart flea beetles, caterpillars and root maggots.

Common problems In some areas, spring broccoli bolts (goes to seed prematurely) at the onset of hot weather. Choose quick-maturing cultivars and expect spring-grown broccoli heads to be smaller than those grown in autumn.

Days to maturity 70–95 days.

Harvesting and storing Harvest broccoli heads when they have reached maximum size but before flower buds turn yellow.

Brassica oleracea, Botrytis group
CRUCIFERAE

CAULIFLOWER

Cauliflowers are heavy feeders that require plenty of water. Blanching is necessary to keep the heads white. Purple cauliflowers are also available.

Best climate and site Zones 3 and warmer. Use as spring and autumn crops in cool-spring areas, and as a winter vegetable in mild climates. Full sun.

Ideal soil conditions Rich, well-drained soil with plenty of calcium, and ample amounts of well-rotted manure or compost worked in; pH 6.0–7.0

Growing guidelines Sow spring crops indoors and do not plant out too early; severe frost may cause the plant to form a 'button' instead of a full-sized head. Sow autumn crops 90–120 days before autumn frosts; set out when seedlings are four to five weeks old. Keep cauliflower growing steadily with plenty of water and one or more applications of liquid fertiliser or compost tea. When heads appear, use a clothespeg to clip several large leaves together over the head to shade it and keep it white, or remove a large lower leaf and lay it over the developing head.

Pest and disease prevention Control caterpillars with horticultural fleece or a spray or dust of BT.

Common problems In humid areas, heads may discolour during blanching.

Days to maturity 50–72 days.

Harvesting and storing Cut heads before curds begin to coarsen and separate.

Brassica oleracea, Capitata group
CRUCIFERAE

CABBAGE

Valued for thousands of years because of its hardiness and storage life, cabbage can be grown almost anywhere.

Best climate and site Zones 3 and warmer, with soil-cooling mulch in hotter climates. Use as a winter vegetable in mild areas. Full sun.

Ideal soil conditions Any soil texture, provided it is well drained and fertile; pH 6.0–6.8.

Growing guidelines Grow as a spring and autumn crop in most areas, or as a winter crop where temperatures rarely drop below freezing. Avoid plantings that will mature in hot, dry weather. Grow spring crops in a cool place indoors six to eight weeks before last spring frosts and set out four weeks before the last frost. Give seedlings plenty of light. Cabbage prefers rich soil; add compost or rotted manure before planting and apply liquid fertiliser or compost tea a month after planting.

Pest and disease prevention Use BT or horticultural fleece to control caterpillars.

Common problems Use a shovel to sever roots on one side of the plant when the head is fully formed. This slows maturity and prevents the cabbage from splitting.

Days to maturity 60–110 days.

Harvesting and storing Harvest early cultivars as needed; harvest storage-type cabbage before hard frosts and store, roots and all, in dry leaves in a cold cellar.

Brassica oleracea, Gemmifera group
CRUCIFERAE

BRUSSELS SPROUTS

Individual Brussels sprouts resemble tiny cabbages. They are a late-season treat, when frost has sweetened their flavour.

Best climate and site Zones 4–7, and Zone 8 as a winter vegetable. Generally unsuited to warmer climates. Full sun.

Ideal soil conditions Well-drained and fertile soil, with adequate calcium levels; pH 6.0–6.8.

Growing guidelines Require a long growing season and are best when matured in cool weather. Short-season vegetable gardeners may plant out transplants when they sow other spring crops; in other areas, wait until late spring. Space plants about 60 cm (24 inches) apart and keep weeded or mulched. Pinch out top leaves to encourage side growth.

Pest and disease prevention Rotate with non-cabbage-family crops to avoid soil-borne fungal and viral diseases. Use horticultural fleece to deter flea beetles, caterpillars and root maggots, or BT for caterpillars. Keep well watered and grow in fertile soil to reduce vulnerability to aphids.

Days to maturity 90–120 days. Mature plants withstand heavy frost.

Harvesting and storing Harvest lower sprouts first, anytime until early winter. Complete harvest before the ground freezes. Harvested sprouts freeze well.

Brassica rapa, Rapifera group
CRUCIFERAE

TURNIP

Grown both for its tender leaves and for its crisp root, turnip is at its best in cool weather. Baby turnips are especially tender.

Best climate and site All Zones; grow as a winter vegetable in mild climates. Full sun.

Ideal soil conditions Loose, deep, humus-rich soil; pH 5.5–6.8.

Growing guidelines Sow 12 mm (½ inch) deep four to six weeks before last spring frost. Thin to 7.5 cm (3 inches) apart; use thinnings as fresh or cooked greens. Water regularly for fast growth in spring, since turnip bolts in hot weather. Sow autumn crop eight to ten weeks before first autumn frosts.

Pest and disease prevention Use horticultural fleece to protect from flea beetles. Reduce root maggot damage, especially in spring crops, by not planting where other root crops have grown the previous year.

Common problems Turnips that mature in hot weather may be fibrous or strong-flavoured. For spring crops, choose quick-maturing cultivars.

Days to maturity 35–60 days. Turnips will withstand light frost.

Harvesting and storing Pull turnips as needed, as 2.5-cm (1-inch) wide 'babies' up to 8–10-cm (3–4-inch) roots. Larger turnips may be woody. Turnips are more tender than other root vegetables and are damaged by hard frost.

Capsicum annuum
SOLANACEAE

SWEET PEPPER

Sweet peppers are crisp and juicy when green, but sweeter when allowed to ripen to red, yellow or orange, depending on cultivar.

Best climate and site Zones 4 and warmer. Full sun.

Ideal soil conditions Light, well-drained soil, not overly rich; pH 6.0–7.0.

Growing guidelines Sow indoors six to eight weeks before last spring frosts. Do not overwater pepper seedlings. Set out 25–38 cm (10–15 inches) apart when the soil has warmed. Cultivate shallowly; do not mulch until the soil is thoroughly warm. Magnesium is critical; in magnesium-poor soils, scatter 1 teaspoon of Epsom salts around the base of each plant. Irrigate in dry spells.

Pest and disease prevention Do not plant where peppers or other nightshade family members, such as tomato and aubergine, have grown for two years. Protect young plants from cutworms with cardboard or foil collars.

Common problems Sun-scald can cause dry, sunken patches on the fruit.

Days to maturity 55–80 days from transplanting for green peppers; 15–20 days more for mature peppers.

Harvesting and storing Pick green peppers when large enough for use. Pick mature peppers when 50–75 per cent coloured; they will finish ripening in one to two days at room temperature.

Cichorium endiva
COMPOSITAE

ENDIVE AND ESCAROLE

In warm areas grow escarole in between tomatoes, where it will appreciate the shade and save space. The leaves of endive and escarole are slightly tangy.

Best climate and site Zones 4 and warmer; grow as a winter vegetable in mild areas. Full sun or partial shade in warm areas.

Ideal soil conditions Fertile, welldrained and well-limed soil; pH 5.5–7.0.

Growing guidelines In cool-spring areas, sow indoors eight weeks before last frost and set out a month before last frost, 25–30 cm (10–12 inches) apart. Cover plants if hard frost threatens. In warmer areas, they're best as autumn crops, sown in midsummer and planted out two months before first autumn frost, or even later in mildest areas. May be blanched by inverting a pot or box over the plant, or by tying outer leaves together at the top. In humid areas, blanching by tying may cause inside leaves to rot.

Pest and disease prevention Provide good air circulation to avoid moulds. Control slugs with shallow dishes of beer set into the soil.

Common problems Water well and provide shade in hot spells to prevent brown, crisp ends on endive leaves.

Days to maturity 80–100 days.

Harvesting and storing Cut the entire head at its base in the morning. Rinse; wrap in kitchen paper and then in plastic.

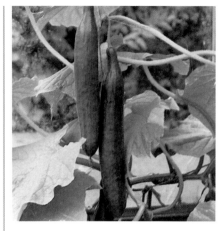

Cucumis sativus
CUCURBITACEAE

CUCUMBER

Prized in salads and pickles, cucumbers are heat-loving plants that can be grown on a trellis or fence to save garden space.

Best climate and site Zones 4 and warmer. Full sun, in a site with good air circulation.

Ideal soil conditions Light soil with well-rotted manure or compost worked in; pH 6.0–7.0.

Growing guidelines Cucumbers dislike cold soil, so wait for three to four weeks after the last frost to direct-sow or transplant them into the garden. Mulch, or keep cultivated until plants begin to vine. Cucumbers need ample food and water; irrigate in dry spells and give them liquid fertiliser or compost tea once a month. Plant successive crops six weeks apart, where the growing season permits. Grow on a trellis or fence to save space.

Pest and disease prevention Use horticultural fleece to protect young plants from cucumber beetles, but remove when plants flower. Trellising will improve air circulation and reduce mildew.

Common problems Sudden collapse of cucumber plants indicates wilt disease, which is spread by cucumber beetles. Straw mulch may help deter beetles.

Days to maturity 48–70 frost-free days.

Harvesting and storing Pick often, especially during hot spells, to encourage continued fruiting. Pickle excess crop.

Cucurbita pepo var. melopepo
CUCURBITACEAE

SQUASH, SUMMER

Courgettes are best picked when less than 20 cm (8 inches) long. The flowers are also edible, but must be used soon after they're picked.

Best climate and site Zones 3 and warmer. Full sun in a site with good air circulation.

Ideal soil conditions Humus-rich, well-drained, soil; pH 6.0–6.5.

Growing guidelines Sow when all danger of frost is past, or start indoors in individual pots two to three weeks before last frost and transplant carefully to avoid breaking roots. Squash needs ample moisture to keep the fruit coming, and it benefits from compost or manure.

Pest and disease prevention Use row covers to protect young squash plants from cucumber beetles and squash borers; remove covers when the plants bloom. If plants are attacked by mildew, spray foliage thoroughly with a mild baking soda solution (1 teaspoon per litre [quart] of water).

Common problems Fruit that turns black and rots before reaching picking size has not been pollinated. This often happens early, before male blossoms appear, or in cool spells, when pollinating insects are less active.

Days to maturity 42–65 frost-free days.

Harvesting and storing Pick squash small for best flavour. Pick blossoms in early morning, before pollination.

Cucurbita pepo var. pepo
CUCURBITACEAE

PUMPKIN

As familiar a sight in autumn as falling leaves, pumpkin makes fine pies and baked dishes, as well as jack-o'-lanterns.

Best climate and site Zones 4 and warmer. Full sun.

Ideal soil conditions Not fussy about texture, but likes a fertile soil; pH 6.0–7.0.

Growing guidelines Sow after last spring frost, two or three seeds to a hill, in hills 1.2–1.5 m (4–5 feet) apart. In short-season areas, sow seeds indoors in individual pots two to three weeks before last frost. Plant out carefully to avoid disturbing the roots. A good shovelful of compost or well-rotted manure in each hill will boost growth. Mulch or cultivate until the plants begin to vine. Pumpkin's broad leaves will shade out most weeds.

Pest and disease prevention Fleece will deter cucumber beetles and squash borers, but remove when plants flower to allow pollination. Straw mulch also helps deter cucumber beetles. Prevent mildew by providing good air circulation.

Common problems Plants that collapse before setting fruit are probably victims of the squash borer. Those that collapse before fruit ripens may be infected with a wilt disease spread by cucumber beetles.

Days to maturity 100–115 frost-free days.

Harvesting and storing Harvest when they are fully coloured and their skins are hard. Store in a dry, cool area.

Cynara scolymus
COMPOSITAE

ARTICHOKE, GLOBE

This plant is grown chiefly for its large, edible flower heads, but suckers also may be blanched and eaten like asparagus.

Best climate and site Mild coastal climates, Zones 8–9; can be grown in Zones 5–7 with special winter care. Full sun and protected exposure.

Ideal soil conditions Rich, well-drained soil; near-neutral pH.

Growing guidelines Sow seed indoors in late winter and transplant in late spring, when soil has warmed thoroughly. Can reach 1.5 m (5 feet) or more in height; space seedlings 60 cm (24 inches) apart in the row and allow 90 cm (3 feet) or more between rows. Be generous with compost or manure. Water deeply; mulch well between rows.

Pest and disease prevention Susceptible to crown rot. Well-drained soil is essential. Do not allow mulch to smother the crown.

Common problems In Zones 7 and colder, winter-kill is the chief problem. Cut the plant back in late autumn and protect over winter by inverting a basket or box over the crown and mulching deeply.

Days to maturity May produce edible buds the first year but more likely will not yield a harvest until the second year.

Harvesting Cut buds before the scales have begun to open, with 2.5 cm (1 inch) of stem attached.

Daucus carota var. *sativus*
UMBELLIFERAE

CARROT

Carrots were well known to the ancient Greeks, who used their delicate foliage in corsages and floral decorations.

Best climate and site Zones 3 and warmer. Plant quick-maturing carrot **Cultivars** in colder areas. Full sun.
Ideal soil conditions Deep, light soil. Improve clayey soil with organic matter; pH 5.5–6.8.
Growing guidelines Sow the first crop in early spring, after severe frost threats are past. Seed is very small; mix half-and-half with fine sand to help avoid overseeding. Plant a scant 12 mm (½ inch) deep and firm the seedbed gently with the back of a hoe. Keep the soil evenly moist until the carrots are up. Thin to 5–8 cm (2–3 inches) apart. Plant successive crops every few weeks until three months before autumn frost. Do not overwater as a continually wet soil can cause root rot.
Pest and disease prevention Use row covers to deter carrot flies. Rotate plantings to avoid bacterial diseases.
Common problems Do not use high-nitrogen fertiliser or fresh manure on carrot beds. Splitting may occur when heavy rain follows a dry period.
Days to maturity 50–70 days.
Harvesting and storing Ready to eat as soon as they have developed full colour. Pull when the ground is moist to avoid breaking roots, or dig with a garden fork.

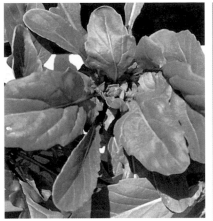

Eruca uesicaria subsp. *sativa*
CRUCIFERAE

ROCKET

The tender leaves of this European garden favourite add a nutty, peppery bite to salads and sandwiches. It is also known as arugula.

Best climate and site All Zones. Full sun as well as half-day sun or partial shade. Avoid hot, dry positions. In mild climates, grow as a winter vegetable.
Ideal soil conditions Not fussy, but prefers fertile, moist soil; pH 6.0–7.0.
Growing guidelines Direct-sow as early as possible in spring. Light frost will not harm the seedlings. Thin to 20 cm (8 inches) apart, using thinnings in salads.
Pest and disease prevention Use horticultural fleece to deter flea beetles.
Common problems Sown too late, spring-planted rocket will bolt (go prematurely to seed) in warm weather before reaching harvestable size. In cold climates, sow seed indoors and plant out as soon as ground can be worked. An autumn crop, direct-sown or planted out as seedlings one to two months before the first autumn frost, will stand longer without bolting. Extend the harvest with successive plantings a week apart.
Days to maturity 40 days, although thinnings may be harvested earlier.
Harvesting and storing Pick large leaves from the bottom of plant. New leaves will sprout from centre crown. Weekly picking should yield 8–12 large leaves per plant. Use fresh; do not freeze.

Foeniculum vulgare var. *azoricum*
UMBELLIFERAE

FENNEL, FLORENCE

Florence fennel is grown chiefly for its enlarged leaf bases, which have the flavour of liquorice. The feathery leaves are used as a herb.

Best climate and site Zones 4 and warmer; grow as a winter vegetable in mild areas. Full sun.
Ideal soil conditions Fertile and well-drained soil; pH 6.5–7.0.
Growing guidelines In cool-spring areas, direct-sow spring crop two to four weeks before last frost and thin to 20–25 cm (8–10 inches) apart. Transplants poorly, but may need a head start in warmer areas since it bolts quickly in hot weather. Start seedlings in individual pots or peat pots a month before last frost; do not let roots outgrow the pots before planting out. Sow small, successive crops where the season permits; avoid plantings that will mature in hot, dry weather. Autumn crops are easier to transplant; plant out two months before first frost. Keep well weeded or mulch; water in dry spells.
Pest and disease prevention Hand-pick celeryworms or parsleyworms (green caterpillars with black and yellow stripes).
Common problems Florence fennel becomes woody when over-mature. Plant small, successive crops to prolong harvest.
Days to maturity 65–90 days.
Harvesting and storing Cut the entire plant below the base of the bulb.

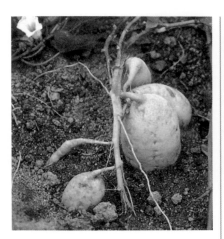

Ipomoea batatas
CONVOLVULACEAE

SWEET POTATO

Sweet potatoes are a warm-weather crop that produces tasty and nutritious tuberous roots. Sweet potatoes are often erroneously called yams.

Best climate and site Zones 5 and warmer. Full sun.
Ideal soil conditions Loose, well-drained soil that is not too rich; pH 5.5-6.5.
Growing guidelines Plant from growing shoots or 'slips', which are available by mail order. Plant after frost danger is well past. With a rake, make a ridge of soil 15-25 cm (6-10 inches) high and 15-20 cm (6-8 inches) wide. Plant slips into the ridge about 30 cm (12 inches) apart. Mound soil onto the ridge at least once before the vining plants make further cultivation impossible. Keep newly set slips watered until they begin to grow. After that, irrigate sweet potatoes only in extended dry spells.
Pest and disease prevention Use disease-free slips. Rotate plantings and keep soil organic matter high to reduce nematode damage.
Common problems Deer love the tender leaves and shoots; if they are a problem in your area, you may need to fence off your sweet potatoes.
Days to maturity 90-120 frost-free days.
Harvesting and storing Dig sweet potatoes before frost or as soon as the vines have been killed by a light frost.

Lactuca sativa
COMPOSITAE

LETTUCE

Leaf lettuce is the quickest and easiest-to-grow member of the lettuce clan. It can double as an ornamental garden edging.

Best climate and site All Zones; grow as a winter vegetable in mild areas. Full sun in cool weather, partial shade in warm weather.
Ideal soil conditions Fertile, well-drained soil; pH 6.0-6.8.
Growing guidelines Direct-sow leafy types a month before last frost. Barely cover the seeds and firm the soil with the back of a hoe. Sow head-forming types indoors six to eight weeks before last frost and plant out 20-25 cm (8-10 inches) apart, one to two weeks before last frost. Leave leaf lettuces unthinned for 'baby' salad leaves or thin to encourage large-leaved plants. Water frequently.
Pest and disease prevention Rotate crops to avoid soil-borne diseases. Control slugs by trapping them in shallow dishes of beer set flush with the soil surface.
Common problems Bitter leaves suggest heat and water stress, or simply over-mature lettuce. Plant small crops at frequent intervals.
Days to maturity 40-90 days.
Harvesting and storing Harvest as needed for fresh use. Cut unthinned leaf lettuce with scissors 2.5 cm (1 inch) above roots, leaving the plants to resprout for a second harvest.

Lycopersicon esculentum
SOLANACEAE

TOMATO

To minimise the build-up of soil-borne pests and diseases, avoid planting tomatoes where related plants grew the previous year.

Best climate and site Zones 3 and warmer. Full sun.
Ideal soil conditions Fertile, deep, well-drained soil; pH 6.0-7.0.
Growing guidelines In long-season areas, tomatoes may be direct-sown, but they are usually started indoors five to six weeks before last spring frost. Plant out 60-90 cm (24-36 inches) apart if plants are to be allowed to sprawl, or as close as 38 cm (15 inches) if they are to be staked or caged. Water tomatoes regularly but do not fertilise until the plant is well established and in full blossom. Then give weak compost tea or liquid fertiliser.
Pest and disease prevention Protect young plants from cutworms with cardboard or metal collars. Hand-pick tomato horn worms or use BT.
Common problems Blossom end rot indicates that the plant is not taking up enough calcium from the soil. Dark brown, circular spots on tomato leaves suggest fungal disease or blight. Provide good air circulation and do not disturb plants when they are wet.
Days to maturity 52-90 frost-free days.
Harvesting and storing Pick the fruit when it is evenly coloured but still firm. Can, freeze or dry excess tomatoes.

Nasturtium officinale
CRUCIFERAE

WATERCRESS

At its best in autumn and early spring, watercress is a tasty and healthful addition to salads, soups and sandwiches.

Best climate and site Zones 3 and warmer; grow as a winter vegetable in warmer areas or indoors in pots almost anywhere. Full sun or partial shade.
Ideal soil conditions Wet, humus-rich, well-limed soil, preferably at the edge of a stream or stream-fed pond; pH 6.0–7.0.
Growing guidelines Sow indoors four to eight weeks before the last spring frost, or sprinkle seeds as thinly as possible where they are to grow, about a month before the last frost, pressing them into the soil. Watercress can be grown in pots, indoors or out. Set pots in dishes of water and change the water daily.
Pest and disease prevention Little troubled by pests and diseases.
Days to maturity 120–150 days. In short-season areas, a newly established watercress bed may not produce a harvest the first year.
Harvesting and storing Harvest leaves as needed, mid-autumn through early spring, including winter where climate permits. Flavour deteriorates during flowering.

Phaseolus vulgaris
LEGUMI NOSAE

FRENCH BEAN

Climbing beans are the perfect vegetable for a small garden. They crop over a long period and may be grown on a trellis or fence.

Best climate and site Zones 3 and warmer; cold climates may require a quick-maturing cultivar. Full sun.
Ideal soil conditions Likes humus-rich but not excessively fertile soil; pH 6.0–7.5.
Growing guidelines Sow seed after frost danger is past. Sow bush French beans about 2.5 cm (1 inch) deep and 7.5 cm (3 inches) apart in single or double rows. Keep well weeded, or mulch. Thorough watering is critical when beans are in flower. Bush French beans crop heavily but only for a few weeks. To ensure a steady supply, make several small plantings three to four weeks apart, ending two months before the first autumn frost date.
Pest and disease prevention Mexican bean beetles can be serious pests from midseason onwards; horticultural fleece helps exclude these pests.
Common problems Sown too early in cold, wet soil, bean seeds may rot before germinating. A small planting for early harvest may be worth the risk, but larger plantings for freezing or canning should be delayed until the weather is settled.
Days to maturity 42–55 frost-free days.
Harvesting and storing Pick at any size, but before seeds have begun to swell.

Pisum sativum var. *sativum*
LEGUMINOSAE

PEA

Tall-growing peas will need some type of trellis to support their climbing stems. They look attractive at the back of a flower garden.

Best climate and site Zones 2 and warmer; grow as a spring and autumn crop in most Zones, and as a winter vegetable in frost-free climates. Full sun on a site with good air circulation.
Ideal soil conditions Loose, well-drained soil; pH 6.0–7.0.
Growing guidelines Peas do poorly in hot weather, so plant spring crops early to beat the heat unless your springs are long and cool. In Zones 7 and warmer, seed planted in late autumn often overwinters and germinates in early spring. In colder Zones, plant four to eight weeks before last spring frost. Sow autumn crops 10–12 weeks before first autumn frost. Peas do not need supplementary fertiliser, but make sure you provide adequate moisture when they are in flower.
Pest and disease prevention Rarely troubled by insects.
Common problems Autumn plantings in humid areas, even of resistant cultivars, are often plagued by powdery mildew. Spray foliage thoroughly with a baking soda solution (1 teaspoon per litre [quart] of water).
Days to maturity 55–80 days.
Harvesting and storing Pick shelling-type peas when pods are full and plump.

Rapnanus sativus
CRUCIFERAE

RADISH

Fast-growing radishes add a crisp, colourful touch to spring salads. Harvest them while they are young and tender.

Best climate and site All Zones; grow as a winter vegetable in mild areas.

Ideal soil conditions Loose, moisture-retentive soil; pH 5.5–6.8.

Growing guidelines Sow spring radishes three to five weeks before last spring frost, 12 mm (½ inch) deep in double or triple rows. Make the rows short and sow small successive crops every two weeks until a month after frost. Sow autumn crops starting eight weeks before autumn frost and continuing until frost. Keep radishes moist to avoid strong flavour and toughness. Mulch between rows to keep soil moist in hot weather.

Pest and disease prevention Rotate radishes and other root crops to reduce damage from root maggots. Spring crops are more vulnerable than autumn crops.

Common problems Spring radishes, especially slender French breakfast types, become woody when over-mature.

Days to maturity 21–35 days for spring radishes; 50–60 days for winter radishes. Will withstand moderate frost.

Harvesting and storing Pull spring and autumn crops when large enough for use. Pull winter radishes as needed when they reach eating size; harvest all roots before hard frosts. Store in damp sand.

Solanum melongena var. *esculentum*
SOLANACEAE

AUBERGINE

Aubergines thrive in hot weather. They need ample amounts of water and fertiliser to produce fruit. Also known as eggplant.

Best climate and site Zones 5 and warmer. Full sun.

Ideal soil conditions Light, rich, well-drained, warm soil; pH 5.5–6.8.

Growing guidelines Aubergines like hot weather, so it does not pay to start the plants too soon or plant them out too early. Start eight weeks before the time when night temperatures can be counted on to stay above 10°C (50°F). Night covers may be needed in colder climates. Space the plants 45–60 cm (18–24 inches) apart. Aubergines need plenty of water and food to produce well. Use liquid fertiliser or compost tea at least once a month.

Pest and disease prevention Use fleece to deter flea beetles. Hand-pick Colorado potato beetles; a light dusting of ground limestone often repels this pest.

Common problems Provide adequate soil moisture and calcium to prevent blossom-end rot, which shows up as a soft, brown spot at the blossom end of the fruit.

Days to maturity 50–75 frost-free days.

Harvesting and storing Clip the fruit with some stem attached; harvest often to encourage further fruiting. Standard aubergine cultivars, such as 'Black Beauty', will bear four to ten full-sized fruits, or more if picked small.

Solanum tuberosum
SOLANACEAE

POTATO

Red potatoes are delicious simply boiled or baked in their jackets. They have moist, white flesh. Salad potatoes are waxy, ideal in salads.

Best climate and site Zones 3 and warmer. Full sun.

Ideal soil conditions Loose, well-drained, slightly acid soil with plenty of potash; ideal pH 5.2–5.7, but will also do well at pH 5.8–6.5.

Growing guidelines Potatoes are planted from pieces of tuber called 'seed potatoes'. Each piece should be about the size of an egg and contain one or more 'eyes', or dormant buds. Cut seed potatoes to size and let the pieces dry for one day to prevent rotting in the ground. Plant two to four weeks before last spring frost, about 30 cm (1 foot) apart in a 8–10-cm (3–4-inch) deep trench. Water regularly.

Pest and disease prevention Covering plants with fleece or dusting them with ground limestone helps deter flea beetles and Colorado potato beetles.

Common problems Exposed to light, potato tubers develop green patches that contain the toxic alkaloid solanine. Earth up or mulch deeply to prevent sunlight from reaching the tubers.

Days to maturity 55–80 days.

Harvesting and storing When foliage dies back, potatoes are mature; dig as needed. Store in well-ventilated boxes.

Spinacia oleracea
CHENOPODIACEAE

SPINACH

Delicious and healthy fresh or cooked, spinach needs cool weather and plenty of water to make abundant crisp leaves.

Best climate and site All Zones. Full sun or partial shade.
Ideal soil conditions Moist, fertile, well-limed soil; pH 6.0–7.0.
Growing guidelines Sow 12 mm (½ inch) deep, four to six weeks before last spring frost. In very short-season areas, or where hot weather sets in abruptly, sow spinach indoors. Plant out or thin to 10–15 cm (4–6 inches) apart. Keep weed-free and water regularly. Sow autumn crops four to six weeks before first frost, or later for overwintering. Seed autumn crops heavily, as spinach germinates poorly in warm soil.
Pest and disease prevention Use horticultural fleece to protect from leaf miners and chewing insects.
Common problems Hot weather and lengthening days can cause plants to bolt (go to seed). Use heat-resistant cultivars and sow spring crops early.
Days to maturity 40–53 days, although thinnings may be harvested sooner. Spinach will withstand moderate frost.
Harvesting and storing Pick larger outside leaves or harvest whole plant at its base. Spinach freezes well for use as a cooked vegetable.

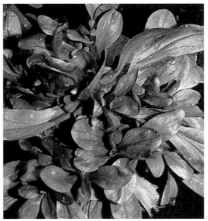

Valerianella locusta
VALERIANACEAE

CORN SALAD

Small, tender, green corn salad can be planted in autumn to grace spring's earliest salads. It's expensive to buy, but easy to grow.

Other common names Fetticus, lamb's lettuce, mache.
Best climate and site Zones 2 and warmer. Overwinters in Zones 5 and warmer; grow as a winter vegetable in mild areas. Full sun or partial shade.
Ideal soil conditions Not fussy, but prefers humus-rich soil; pH 6.0–7.0.
Growing guidelines Sow in early spring, two to four weeks before last frost; cover with fine soil and firm with the back of a hoe. Plant thickly in rows or more thinly in wide.beds; keep moist. Thin to 5 cm (2 inches) apart; use thinnings in salads. Avoid plantings that will mature in hot weather. Plant in autumn near first frost date; mulch lightly after hard frosts. Remove mulch in early spring.
Pest and disease prevention Little troubled by pests or diseases.
Common problems In colder areas, mulch more heavily to avoid heaving of plants over winter.
Days to maturity 45–60 days from spring seeding; thinnings can be harvested earlier. Will withstand light frost.
Harvesting and storing Harvest entire rosettes by pinching out at ground level. Some cultivars remain sweet even when in flower; taste to check.

Zea mays var. rugosa
GRAMINEAE

SWEETCORN

Tender and succulent, fresh sweetcorn is a classic summer treat from the garden. Shop-bought corn cobs can't compare with its taste.

Best climate and site Zones 3 and warmer. Use only short-season cultivars in coldest areas. Full sun. Avoid high-wind areas.
Ideal soil conditions Accepts many soil textures; prefers deep, well-manured soil with high organic content; pH 6.0–6.8.
Growing guidelines Sow after last spring frost, or one to two weeks earlier if soil has first been warmed by covering with black plastic for a week or more in sunny ;weather. Corn seed germinates poorly in cold, wet soil and may rot. Sweetcorn grows rapidly and needs adequate fertility and water. Apply liquid fertiliser or compost tea after one month and again when the tassels appear. Water is most critical when sweetcorn is in tassel.
Pest and disease prevention Help control earworms by dropping mineral oil into the immature ears as soon as you see the pest's sticky frass on the silks (the hair-like fibres).
Common problems Patchy spots on kernels, or ears that are not filled to the tip, indicate inadequate pollination.
Days to maturity 54–94 frost-free days.
Harvesting and storing Harvest when the silks have turned brown and dry and the ear feels full.

Actinidia chinensis
ACTINIDIACEAE

KIWI

Kiwi plants make excellent covering for trellises and arbours. You can enjoy the shade and reach up to pick the fruit easily.

Best climate and site Zones 7–9. Plant in full sun to light shade in average to poor, well-drained soil.
Height and spread Height 1.2–1.8 m (4–6 feet); spread 4.5 m (15 feet).
Growing guidelines With the exception of a few self-fertile cultivars such as 'Issai' and 'Blake', kiwi plants have either male or female flowers. For pollination, plant a male plant within about 12 m (40 feet) of the females – closer if possible. One male will pollinate up to eight female plants. Keep the soil moist up to harvest time, but water less as winter approaches. Mulch well, but fertilise lightly, if at all.
Pruning Before planting, install a sturdy post-and-wire trellis (as you would for grapes). Insert a stake next to the plant at planting time, and cut out all but one stem. Remove any sideshoots from the remaining stem and train it up the stake.
Propagation Cuttings or grafting.
Pest and disease control Surround young plants with a circle of wire mesh fencing to prevent cats from chewing or rolling on the leaves and stems.
Harvesting and storage Pick kiwi fruit in autumn, when the seeds are black and most of the fruit is still firm. Peel before eating.

Carya pecan
JUGLANDACEAE

PECAN

Established pecans seldom need much pruning; just trim out dead or damaged branches as you spot them. Call an arborist to remove large limbs.

Best climate and site Zones 6–9. Plant in full sun in average to rich, well-drained soil.
Height and spread Height 15–45 m (50–150 feet); spread 10.5–15 m (35–50 feet).
Growing guidelines The male (pollen-providing) and female (nut-producing) flowers on pecan trees usually don't open at the same time. For this reason, you usually need to plant another tree that can provide pollen when the main crop tree is ready. Space trees 10.5–15 m (35–50 feet) apart. Mulch with compost and irrigate during drought.
Pruning Pecans naturally take on a central-leader shape. Prune as needed to remove branches that are competing with the main trunk.
Propagation Propagate by grafting.
Pest and disease control Diseases such as scab can be a problem in humid areas. Pecan weevils lay their eggs in almost-mature nuts. Rake up and destroy damaged nuts.
Harvesting and storage Grafted trees will begin bearing nuts in four to seven years. Tap limbs with a padded stick or pick up fallen nuts. Remove the husks and dry the nuts for several weeks.

Castanea spp.
FAGACEAE

CHESTNUT

American chestnuts (Castanea dentata) have been destroyed by chestnut blight disease. But you can still grow blight-resistant Chinese chestnuts.

Best climate and site Zones 5–9. Plant in full sun in average to rich, well-drained acid soil.
Height and spread Height 12 m (40 feet) or more; spread 6–12 m (20–40 feet).
Growing guidelines Chestnuts produce more reliable crops if cross-pollinated with another tree. They can be spaced up to 30 m (100 feet) apart, but for best nut production, plant them 12–14 m (40–80 feet) apart. Mulch to eliminate weeds; apply compost or balanced fertiliser in late spring after the danger of frost has passed.
Pruning Train chestnut trees to a central-leader system. Remove dead or damaged limbs as you spot them, along with any low-hanging branches.
Propagation Propagate by seed.
Pest and disease control Grow resistant chestnut species and cultivars to avoid the deadly chestnut blight disease. Chestnut weevil larvae may feed inside nuts and then enter the soil when nuts fall to the ground.
Harvesting and storage Chestnuts bear in three to five years. In autumn, the nuts mature and drop to the ground. Pick them up promptly.

Chaenomeles spp.
ROSACEAE

QUINCE, FLOWERING

Flowering quince fruits are yellowish green. Even when ripe, they are rock hard and astringent, but they make good jellies and jams.

Best climate and site Zones 5–8. Full sun, slightly acid soil. Tolerates dry soil.
Height and spread Height 90–300 cm (3–10 feet); similar spread.
Growing guidelines Plant container-grown shrubs any time the ground isn't frozen, or plant out bare-root plants in spring or autumn, while they are dormant. Space plants 90–300 cm (3–10 feet) apart. Flowering quince is self-fruitful, so you need only one plant to get fruit.
Pruning Prune in winter, periodically cutting away the oldest stems at ground level to make room for young stems. For drastic renovation, just lop the whole plant almost to the ground. Flowering quince can also withstand being sheared as a hedge, although you'll lose some of the flowers and fruit.
Propagation Seed germinates readily following two to three months of cool, moist conditions. Propagate cultivars by softwood cuttings, layering or division.
Pest and disease control Minimise leaf spot problems by planting in full sunlight in a breezy location, and pruning for good air circulation.
Harvesting and storage Fruits ripen late in the season, changing colour slightly. Store in the refrigerator.

Citrus spp.
RUTACEAE

CITRUS

Citrus trees seldom need much pruning; just trim out crossing branches and head back long shoots in late winter.

Best climate and site Zones 8–10. Frost will damage the fruit of any citrus plants and sometimes the rest of the tree. Plant in full sun to light shade in average to rich, well-drained soil.
Height and spread Height 3–9 m (10–30 feet); similar spread.
Growing guidelines Citrus trees are nearly all self-fertile, so you need to plant only one to get a good harvest. Space large citrus trees at least 7.5 m (25 feet) apart and dwarf trees 3 m (10 feet) apart. Paint the trunk with white latex paint (diluted with an equal amount of water) to prevent sunburn. Keep the soil moist to prevent early fruit drop. Mulch well, and fertilise as needed.
Pruning Remove damaged or diseased branches and upright-growing shoots that emerge from the roots. Trim back long branches to shape the plant.
Propagation Propagate by bud grafting.
Pest and disease control Keep an eye out for scale insects, whiteflies, thrips and mites. Use beneficial insects, traps and insecticidal soap for prevention.
Harvesting and storage Most citrus trees produce fruit three or four years after planting. The only way to know if fruit is ripe is to taste it.

Ficus carica
MORACEAE

FIG

Figs are productive and generally easy to grow. They are seldom troubled by pests, except for birds. Net the tree to discourage them.

Best climate and site Zones 8–10. Plant in full sun in average well-drained soil. In cool climates figs can be planted in large containers and moved inside for winter.
Height and spread Height 3–7.5 m (10–25 feet); similar spread.
Growing guidelines Select self-pollinating cultivars. Space large cultivars up to 7.5 m (25 feet) apart; smaller trees can go as close as 1.5 m (5 feet) apart. Mulch with compost as needed.
Pruning Thin out excess growth as needed to control plant size and allow for good light penetrations into the centre of the plant. You can also train figs as espaliers to grow on walls.
Propagation Propagate by cutting rooted suckers off the roots or taking hardwood cuttings.
Pest and disease control Place netting over trees to discourage birds, or grow green-fruited cultivars, which are less appealing to birds.
Harvesting and storage Fig trees produce their first crop a year after planting. Ripe figs are soft, with a slightly flexible 'neck'; sometimes the skin splits. You can keep figs for a few days in the refrigerator or cut them into sections and dry them.

Fortunella spp.
RUTACEAE

KUMQUAT

Kumquat fruit looks like a miniature orange – about the size of a cherry and either round or elongated. The skin is edible and sweet.

Best climate and site Zones 9–10. Plant in full sun and well-drained, slightly acid soil. Kumquat tolerates winter weather as cold as -7.7°C (18°F), but without sufficient heat in summer, the fruits are few and of poor quality.

Height and spread Height 2.4–4.5 m (8–15 feet); spread 1.8–3.6 m (6–12 feet).

Growing guidelines Plant container-grown stock anytime, or plant out bare-root plants in spring or autumn, while they are dormant. Space plants 1.8–3.6 m (6–12 feet) apart. Kumquats make beautiful potted plants that also fruit reliably. Provide a cool, sunny room in winter and repot every year.

Pruning No pruning other than to shape the plant and thin out crowded branches.

Propagation Kumquats are usually grafted onto trifoliate orange (*Poncirus trifoliata*), which also dwarfs the tree, or onto sour orange (*Citrus aurantium*) or grapefru it rootstock.

Pest and disease control Few problems, but keep an eye out for scale insects, mealybugs, mites and whiteflies.

Harvesting and storage Harvest fruits when they are fully coloured. They keep well in the refrigerator.

Fragaria spp.
ROSACEAE

STRAWBERRY

You'll avoid most problems by starting with certified disease-free plants of disease-resistant cultivars. Strawberries are self-fruitful.

Best climate and site Zones 3–10. Plant in full sun in average to rich, well-drained soil.

Height and spread Height 25 cm (10 inches); spread 30–60 cm (12–24 inches).

Growing guidelines Add extra organic matter to the soil before planting to make it rich and moist. Space plants 30–60 cm (1–2 feet) apart and keep the soil moist until the berries are almost ripe.

Pruning Weed, pinch out unwanted runners and mow along the edge of the beds as needed to keep walkways clear.

Propagation Propagate by transplanting rooted runners.

Pest and disease control Pick ripe fruit frequently to keep grey mould (Botrytis blight) at bay. Remove and destroy damaged flowers and fruits as you spot them. If plants wilt, dig them up and destroy them.

Harvesting and storage Pick the berries when they are fully coloured, tender and sweet. Leave the stem on for better storage. Eat the fruit fresh, refrigerate it for a few days or can or freeze as soon as possible after picking.

Comments For the longest harvest, grow some of each type (June-cropping, perpetual-fruiting and day-neutrals).

Fragaria vesca
ROSACEAE

ALPINE STRAWBERRY

The fruits of alpine strawberries may be small, but they offer a big taste. The compact, runnerless plants make a tidy garden edging.

Best climate and site Zones 3–10. Plant in full sun or partial shade, with well-drained, humus-rich soil.

Height and spread Height to 15 cm (6 inches); spread 15–30 cm (6–12 inches).

Growing guidelines Set out container-grown plants anytime the ground isn't frozen, or plant bare-root stock in spring or autumn, while the plants are dormant. Set plants 15–30 cm (6–12 inches) apart, planting so that the ground level is just below the lowest leaves on the crown. Alpine strawberries are self-fruitful, so you can get a harvest from just one plant.

Pruning None.

Propagation To divide old plants, dig them up and cut off young crown pieces (with attached roots) from the outside of the clump. Throw away the old centre part and replant the divisions. To grow from seed, scatter the fine seed on the surface of potting compost in a container. Transplant the seedlings when they are large enough to handle.

Pest and disease control Keep birds at bay with netting, or grow white-fruited cultivars, which birds leave alone.

Harvesting and storage Harvest the fruits when they are soft and aromatic. Eat them fresh; they do not store well.

Malus pumila
ROSACEAE

APPLE

To get high yields from your apples, you'll need to grow at least two compatible cultivars so they can cross-pollinate.

Best climate and site Zones 3–9, but pick a cultivar that's suited to your area. Plant in full sun and well-drained soil.
Height and spread Height 2.4–9 m (8–30 feet); similar spread.
Growing guidelines Plant full-sized apple trees 7.5–9 m (25–30 feet) apart, semi-dwarfs 3.6–4.5 m (12–15 feet) apart, and dwarfs 1.8–2.4 m (6–8 feet) apart. Provide plenty of moisture and nutrients to keep young trees growing quickly. Mulch with compost in spring, and make sure the soil is moist around mature trees when they're in flower.
Pruning Apple trees grow best when trained into a pyramidal, central leader form, with one trunk and several sets of branches emerging off it. Start pruning young trees just after spring planting (or in the spring following autumn planting). Continue thinning and pruning each year until the trees mature.
Propagation Propagate by grafting.
Pest and disease control Some problems that might occur are apple maggots, codling moths, plum curculios, rust, scab, mildew and fire blight.
Harvesting and storage Apples will start producing fruit in two to five years, depending on the rootstock.

Malus spp.
ROSACEAE

CRAB APPLE

Some crab apples taste delicious out of hand, while others taste good only when cooked with sweetener into jellies. You can eat the whole fruit.

Best climate and site Zones 3–9. Plant in full sun and well-drained soil.
Height and spread Height 2.4–7.5 m (8–25 feet); similar spread.
Growing guidelines Plant container-grown stock anytime the ground isn't frozen, or plant out bare-root plants in spring or autumn, while they are dormant. Space plants 2.4–7.5 m (8–25 feet) apart. The plants need cross-pollination, but the pollinator can be an apple or a crab apple.
Pruning Train young plants to a sturdy framework of wide-angled, well-spaced main limbs. Mature plants need little pruning beyond removing watershoots and thinning congested growth.
Propagation Graft or bud cultivars onto seedling apple or crab apple rootstocks. Seed, for seedling rootstocks, germinates readily once it has been kept cool and moist for two to three months.
Pest and disease control Crab apples can have the same pest and disease problems as apples but are usually less troubled by them.
Harvesting and storage Pick fruits when they are fully coloured and come off the plant easily. Store in the refrigerator in a plastic bag with a few holes in it.

Morus spp.
MORACEAE

MULBERRY

Mulberry trees produce black, red or white blackberry-shaped fruits. Flavour ranges from sweet with a refreshing tang to purely sweet.

Best climate and site Zones 5–10. Plant in full sun and average, well-drained soil.
Height and spread Height 4.5–9 m (15–30 feet); spread 3–6 m (10–20 feet).
Growing guidelines Plant container-grown stock anytime the ground isn't frozen, or plant out bare-root plants in spring or autumn, while they are dormant. Space plants 3–9 m (10–30 feet) apart. Do not plant mulberries where falling fruits will cause problems with staining. Cultivars selected for fruit production generally do not need cross-pollination.
Pruning No regular pruning is necessary.
Propagation Russian mulberry (M. alba 'Tartarica') makes a good rootstock for most other mulberries. Softwood or hardwood cuttings of most species usually root readily. With hardwood cuttings, either split the lower end or take a small 'heel' of two-year-old wood along with the one-year-old wood used for the cutting.
Pest and disease control Control scale insects with dormant oil, and handle die back by cutting off infected portions.
Harvesting and storage To harvest in quantity, spread a clean sheet under the tree and shake the branches. Ripe fruits do not keep well fresh but can be dried.

Prunus amygdalus
ROSACEAE

ALMOND

Most almonds need cross-pollinotion to set their crop; check catalogue descriptions to make sure you get the right companions.

Best climate and site Zones 6–9. Grow in full sun in average to fertile, well-drained soil.

Height and spread Height 4.5–9 m (15–30 feet); similar spread.

Growing guidelines Most almonds require another tree to pollinate them. Plant trees 7.5 m (25 feet) apart and mulch with compost each spring. Water plants regularly when the weather is hot.

Pruning Train almonds into an open-centre form, but as you prune each year, do more heading and less thinning than you would for trees such as peaches, to develop a thick network of branches and, consequently, to get more nuts.

Propagation Propagate by grafting.

Pest and disease control Unfortunately, disease resistance is minimal in almonds so they're seldom grown outside a dry climate. Keep mulch away from the trunk to discourage rodent activity. Pick up all fallen nuts and destroy the bad ones to reduce problems with navel orangeworm – white, brown-headed caterpillars that feed on the nut meat.

Harvesting and storage Most almond trees begin to produce nuts in three to four years. Use a padded stick to knock the nuts from the tree.

Prunus avium
ROSACEAE

CHERRY

Sweet cherries tend to need a compatible partner for cross-pollination. Sour cherries are self-fertile, so you can get a harvest from just one tree.

Best climate and site Zones 4–9. Plant in full sun in average to poor, well-drained soil. Cherries prefer arid climates.

Height and spread Height 4.5–9 m (15–30 feet);similar spread.

Growing guidelines Space standard sweet cherry trees 6–9m (20–30 feet) apart, sour cherries 6 m (20 feet) apart, and dwarf cherries 3 m (10 feet) apart. Mulch with compost in early spring. In cooler climates, plant with a northern exposure away from valleys to protect cherry flowers from frost.

Pruning Train naturally spreading cherry trees to an open-centre form; for more upright growing trees, prune to a central leader form. See your nursery for more specific information.

Propagation Propagate by grafting.

Pest and disease control The major problem with cherry trees is birds. Be prepared to net the trees once the fruit starts to ripen to keep the birds away. Try to grow the cultivars that are resistant to the diseases most prevalent in your area.

Harvesting and storage Cherries begin to produce fruit three to seven years after planting. If the weather is dry, let cherries ripen on the trees for best flavour. They should be fairly soft and very sweet.

Prunus armeniaca
ROSACEAE

APRICOT

Ripe apricots are so soft that they don't ship well. The way to enjoy them at their peak is to grow your own.

Best climate and site Zones 5–9. Plant in full sun in average to poor, well-drained soil. Early opening flowers should be sheltered from frost.

Height and spread Height 2.4–7.2 m (8–24 feet); spread 4.8–7.2 m (16–24 feet).

Growing guidelines Many apricots are self-fertile and will produce some fruit if planted alone. But most will produce more abundant yields with a second cultivar for cross-pollination. Plant full-sized trees 7.5 m (25 feet) apart and dwarf trees 3.6–4.5 m (12–15 feet) apart. Mulch with compost in spring and fertilise as needed.

Pruning Some cultivars will fruit only every other year unless the fruits are thinned out to leave them 5 cm (2 inches) apart. Apricot trees should be pruned using the open-centre system where the leader branch is removed and the tree is pruned to an open vase shape.

Propagation Propagate by bud grafting.

Pest and disease control Susceptible to Eutypa dieback, a disease that attacks through pruning cuts. Treat scale insect, mite and aphid infestations with oil sprays.

Harvesting and storage Pluck the fruits when they're soft and sweet.

Prunus persica
ROSAECEAE

PEACH AND NECTARINE

Both peaches and nectarines are attractive as fan-shaped espaliers. Growing them on a wall provides extra warmth.

Best climate and site Zones 5–9.
Plant in full sun in average to poor, well-drained soil.
Height and spread Height 2.4–4.5 m (8–15 feet); spread 3–6 m (10–20 feet).
Growing guidelines Most peaches and nectarines are self-pollinating, so you can get a full crop from just one tree. Fertilise with compost in early spring and again with a balanced organic fertiliser when the fruit first forms. Spray the leaves with liquid seaweed every three to four weeks during the growing season.
Pruning Train peach trees to an open-centre form. Thin young trees lightly in summer to remove unneeded branches. When the tree is mature, cut half the older branches back by about half of their total length during the dormant season so they'll resprout productive new wood.
Propagation Propagate by bud grafting.
Pest and disease control If you live in an area that's prone to peach tree diseases, start with disease-resistant cultivars. Otherwise you may have to spray to control diseases.
Harvesting and storage Peach and nectarine trees begin producing fruit two to four years after planting. Harvest when the fruit is well coloured and sweet.

Pyrus communis
ROSACEAE

PEAR

Most pears require cross-pollination to set fruit, so you'll need to plant at least one compatible companion to get a good crop.

Best climate and site Zones 4–9.
Plant in full sun in average to poor, well-drained soil.
Height and spread Height 2.4–6 m (8–20 feet); similar spread.
Growing guidelines Space full-sized trees 4.5–6 m (15–20 feet) apart and dwarfs 2.4–3.6 m (8–12 feet) apart. Water and mulch as necessary to keep the soil moist and prevent damage to foliage and fruit. Mulch with compost in spring.
Pruning Use the central leader system to shape upright-growing European pears. Heavy-bearing trees will need some fruit thinning. In June, remove the smaller fruit, leaving one or two of the best fruit per cluster.
Propagation Propagate by grafting.
Pest and disease control Keep an eye out for pear psyllas, tiny insects that suck sap from tender shoot tips and fruit, and spread diseases. During the growing season, use insecticidal soap or horticultural oil sprays to control psyllas. Select pear cultivars that are resistant to fire blight.
Harvesting and storage Pear trees generally begin to produce fruit three to five years after planting. Pick European pears when they are mature but not ripe.

Prunus domestica
ROSACEAE

PLUM

'Santa Rosa' is a Japanese plum (p. salicina) with large, high-quality fruit. It yields best when planted with other Japanese plums.

Best climate and site Zones 4–10. Plant in full sun in average to rich soil.
Height and spread Height 2.4–6 m (8–20 feet); similar spread.
Growing guidelines Many European plums and damson plums will self-pollinate, so one tree is enough. But if you plant two compatible cultivars they may set more fruit. Space full-sized plum trees 6–7.5 m (20–25 feet) apart and dwarf trees 2.4–3.6 m (8–12 feet) apart. Mulch with compost in spring and keep the soil moist through the growing season. Apply a complete fertiliser when the petals fall.
Pruning Train upright-growing cultivars to a central leader. Open-centre training works better for more spreading plums, including most Japanese types. Thin the fruit on trees that are overburdened.
Propagation Propagate by bud grafting.
Pest and disease control Plums are susceptible to black knot, a fungus that causes dark swellings on tree limbs. If black knot was a problem the previous year, spray with lime-sulphur when the buds swell, then reapply a week later.
Harvesting and storage Plum trees generally begin to crop three to four years after planting. Pick when soft and sweet.

Ribes spp.
GROSSULARIACEAE

CURRANT AND GOOSEBERRY

The tart berries of currants are excellent for jams or juice. Plant two or more cultivars if possible; cross-pollination will increase yields.

Best climate and site Zones 3–7. Plant in full sun to light shade in average soil.
Height and spread Height 0.9–2.1 m (3–7 feet); similar spread.
Growing guidelines Most currants and gooseberries are self-pollinating, however, if interplanted with two or three other culivars they'll produce higher yields. Space the plants 1.8 m (6 feet) apart and mulch well. Add compost and a potassium-rich fertiliser in early spring. Water regularly in dry weather.
Pruning At planting time, select one branch to be the main trunk and remove all others. Each winter, remove all shoots that are over three years old (or over two years old on black currants)j then remove all but six of the remaining shoots.
Propagation By hardwood cuttings.
Pest and disease control Powdery mildew can devastate gooseberries, and sulphur sprays are not always an effective treatment. Buy mildew-resistant cultivars. Mildew resistance is also available in many currant cultivars.
Harvesting and storage For cooking or making jelly, pick currants and gooseberries when they are not quite ripe. For fresh eating, let them ripen on the bush until they taste right to you.

Rubus idaeus
ROSACEAE

RASPBERRY

If birds are beating you to your berries, cover the plants with netting. Roll back the cover as needed to harvest.

Best climate and site Zones 3–9. Plant in full sun in average to poor soil.
Height and spread Height 1.2–1.8 m (4–6 feet); spread 0.6–1.2 m (2–4 feet).
Growing guidelines Buy bare-root plants if possible and plant them 60 cm (2 feet) apart in a row. They'll fill in within a year or two. Apply compost and a little balanced organic fertiliser in late winter, if needed, for good growth. Mulch to discourage weeds and keep the soil evenly moistj water during dry spells.
Pruning Cut off all the old canes at ground level when they have finished fruiting. Leave the new current-season canes to produce berries next year.
Propagation Propagate by division or layering, but only if you are sure your plants are healthy.
Pest and disease control Buy only certified disease-free plants. Several fungal diseases may attack raspberries: powdery mildew, anthracnose and cane blight. If these diseases were a problem the previous year, spray with lime-sulphur when the buds begin to turn green. Remove and destroy any plant that is affected with any other diseases.
Harvesting and storage Harvest berries when they're sweet and ripe.

Rubus spp.
ROSACEAE

BLACKBERRY

Blackerrries are at their best flavour when the fruits turn dark and lose some of their glossiness. Many thornless blackberry cultivars need support.

Best climate and site Zones 5–9. Plant in full sun in average to rich soil.
Height and spread Height 1.2–2.1 m (4–7 feet); spread 0.9–1.8 m (3–6 feet).
Growing guidelines Buy blackberries as bare-root plants, or as tissue-cultured plantlets. They need plenty of space and good air circulation. Plant thorny cultivars 90–120 cm (3–4 feet) apart and thornless cultivars 1.2–1.8 m (4–6 feet) apart. Make paths between the rows for good sun exposure and adequate air circulation. Keep the soil evenly moist and mulch with compost in early spring.
Pruning Cut fruit-bearing canes to the ground right after harvest. In early spring, thin to leave seven strong canes per plant. Shorten side branches to about 30 cm (1 foot) long. For maximum yields, train blackberries to a trellis.
Propagation By division or layering.
Pest and disease control Watch for distorted growth, sterile canes or orange-spotted leaves that drop early. These are all symptoms of incurable viral or orange rust diseases. Remove infected plants.
Harvesting and storage Blackberries are ready when they turn entirely black and get a little dull, soft and sweet. Eat them right away or freeze them.

Vaccinium spp.
ERICACEAE

BLUEBERRY

Some blueberries need cross-pollination, so make sure you check catalogue descriptions to get the appropriate partners.

Best climate and site Zones 3–9. Plant in full sun in average to rich, well-drained soil.
Height and spread Height 0.6–4.9 m (2–15 feet); spread 0.9–3 m (3–10 feet).
Growing guidelines Depending on whether you're growing low-bush, high-bush, mid-high or rabbit-eye blueberries, plant them from 0.6–2.5 m (2–8 feet) apart. Apply a thick layer of mulch to keep the soil evenly moist. Add compost each spring.
Pruning Pinch off all the flowers on a young blueberry bush the first year after planting so the bush will grow strong. The next year you'll have to remove only dead or damaged wood. Let plenty of sun and air penetrate the entire plant.
Propagation Propagate by hardwood or softwood cuttings, or by division, depending on cultivar.
Pest and disease control If stems begin to die back or show unusual cankers or cracks, cut them back to healthy tissues. Use sticky red balls (such as apple maggot traps) to catch blueberry maggots before they can tunnel into ripening berries.
Harvesting and storage Harvest after the berries turn blue. Don't pick underripe berries; they won't ripen.

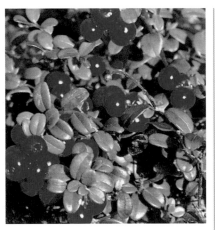

Vaccinium macrocarpon
ERICACEAE

CRANBERRY

Cranberries grow as low, creeping bushes. Their white flowers are followed by hard, red berries, each about the size of a thumbnail.

Best climate and site Zones 2–6. Cranberries thrive in sun and moist, well-drained, humus-rich soil with a very acid pH (4.0–5.5). The plants do not tolerate dry soil, but they can withstand flooding in cold weather.
Height and spread Height to 30 cm (1 foot); spread unlimited.
Growing guidelines Plant in spring or autumn where winters are mild or in spring where winters are severe. Space plants 30 to 60 cm (1 to 2 feet) apart. Mix plenty of acid peat into the soil before planting. Mulch with sawdust or sand; renew the mulch periodically.
Pruning Cut away some of the sprawling stems and some of the upright fruiting stems when they become overcrowded.
Propagation Summer stem cuttings root readily. Where winters are mild, set rooted cuttings outdoors in autumn; otherwise, set them out as early as possible in spring.
Pest and disease control No problems.
Harvesting and storage Pick berries in autumn, after they are fully coloured. Cranberries will keep for two to four months at high humidity and temperatures just above freezing.

Vitis spp.
VITACEAE

GRAPE

Growing clusters tend to ripen unevenly; prevent this by thinning in early summer, when fruits are small and hard.

Best climate and site Zones 4–10. Plant in full sun in average to rich soil.
Height and spread Height 1.2–1.8 m (4–6 feet); spread 2.4–4.5 m (8–15 feet).
Growing guidelines Start with one-year-old plants that are virus-indexed and certified disease-free. Before planting, set up a support system for the vines to cling to. After planting, let the grapevine grow untrained for a year to develop a strong set of roots. Pinch off grape flowers during that year. Keep the soil moist and mulch well. Feed with compost in spring.
Pruning Train the vines over wire strung between posts. In late winter, cut the vine back to a stump with two buds. When the buds start growing, leave the stronger shoot and remove the other one.
Propagation Propagate by cuttings, grafting or, for some varieties, layering.
Pest and disease control Black rot causes reddish brown leaf spots and hard, shrivelled fruit. Botrytis bunch rot causes a fluffy grey-brown coating on the fruit. Anthracnose infection produces sunken, dark-ringed spots on leaves and fruit. Remove and destroy all infected fruit and leaves.
Harvesting and storage Harvest the clusters by clipping them off the vine.

Anthurium spp.
ARACEAE

FLAMINGO FLOWERS

The lacquered-looking, puckered blooms of flamingo flowers often fool people into thinking they must be artificial. Each flower can last two to three months.

Description This upright, many-stemmed plant can grow to 50 cm (20 inches) tall, with long, graceful, leathery, green leaves. The flowers can be 7.5–15 cm (3–6 inches) long and range in colour from deep red to pink, salmon, white and speckled. Miniature types are available.
Light needs Medium indirect light.
Best temperatures Warm year-round. Ideal conditions are 29°C (85°F) days and 18°C (65°F) nights. To encourage plants to bloom, reduce the nighttime temperature to 16°C (60°F) for six weeks.
Water and humidity needs Provide constant moisture and high humidity while plants are actively growing. Let the soil dry out a bit between waterings in winter, but never allow it to get bone dry.
Growing guidelines Grow in a mix of equal parts potting compost and sphagnum moss. Repot plants in spring if needed. Fertilise with an all-purpose, organic fertiliser twice a month from early spring to early autumn; do not fertilise in winter.
Common problems Flamingo flower does not appreciate cold temperatures or hard water. Keep the temperature at least 16°C (60°F).
Propagation Divide in spring or summer, or grow new plants from seed.

Begonia spp.
BEGONIACEAE

FLOWERING BEGONIAS

The thousands of begonia hybrids and species provide a wealth of houseplant choices. Those grown for flowers often have beautiful foliage too.

Other common names Angelwing (cane), Reiger and wax begonias.
Description Angelwing begonias can grow to 1.8 m (6 feet) tall, with showy flower clusters and relatively narrow, pointed leaves. Reiger begonias offer outstanding huge flowers and medium to dark green leaves on 30–45-cm (12–18-inch) stems. Wax begonias are compact, 15–30-cm (6–12-inch) plants with succulent stems and thick, waxy leaves. The white, pink or red single or double flowers form in small clusters.
Light needs Medium; protect from hot summer sun.
Best temperatures Average room temperature; prefers at least 16°C (60°F).
Water and humidity needs Let dry slightly between waterings.
Growing guidelines Grow in humus-rich, soil-less compost. Repot in spring as needed. Fertilise lightly twice a month from spring to autumn. Pinch out the stem tips every month or so to encourage branching. To reflower, Reiger begonias need a three-month, cool, dry rest period after flowering.
Common problems Lower leaves may drop if plants get too little or too much water; overwatering can also lead to rot.
Propagation By tip cuttings or seed.

Chrysanthemum spp.
COMPOSITAE

CHRYSANTHEMUMS

Potted chrysanthemums provide a magnificent, if brief, show. Plant spring-flowering kinds outdoors for another set of flowers before frost.

Other common names Florist's chrysanthemum.
Description These 37.5-cm (15-inch) tall, bushy plants come in a wide array of flower colours and shapes – often daisy-like, button or pompon – and may bloom for two to three weeks.
Light needs Medium, indirect light.
Best temperatures Flowers last longest in cool 13°C (55°F) temperatures.
Water and humidity needs Water frequently to keep the soil evenly moist.
Growing guidelines Grow in well-drained, all-purpose potting compost. Discard the autumn-flowering potted mums after bloom. To get a late-season garden display from spring bloomers, cut them back by one-half to two-thirds after flowering and plant them in the ground. Pinch out the shoot tips every two weeks until mid-July, then stop pinching out to allow flower buds to form. Plants may or may not live through the winter.
Common problems Aphids may feed on leaves, shoots and buds, causing distorted growth. Knock them off with a strong spray of water, or spray with insecticidal soap, superior oil or neem.
Propagation Take tip cuttings in spring.

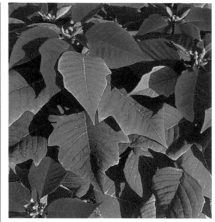

Clivia miniata
AMARYLLIDACEAE

CLIVIA

Clusters of spectacular, trumpet-shaped blooms and handsome, glossy leaves make this flowering houseplant a favourite of many indoor gardeners. Clivias may take several years to flower.

Description The strap-like, leathery, green leaves of clivia emerge from a bulbous base. Mature plants can reach 60 cm (2 feet) tall and 90 cm (3 feet) wide. Clusters of winter blooms are usually orange-red with yellow interiors.
Light needs Medium to high indirect light is best.
Best temperatures Average room temperature in spring and summer; much cooler in autumn and winter.
Water and humidity needs Keep the soil evenly moist in spring and summer; allow it to dry a bit between waterings in autumn and winter.
Growing guidelines Start clivias in small clay pots. Use a blend of three parts all-purpose potting compost and one part sand, with a handful or two of bonemeal. Clivias seem to grow best when crowded, so leave them in their pot for about three years before repotting them in late winter. Feed with liquid fertiliser twice a month during spring and summer.
Common problems Mealybugs produce cottony white clusters on leaves. Knock them off with a strong spray of water.
Propagation Divide when you repot them, or remove offsets in late winter.

Cyclamen persicum
PRIMULACEAE

FLORIST'S CYCLAMEN

The butterfly-like blooms of florist's cyclamen flutter gracefully over beautiful silver-marked leaves. The flowers come in pink, red, lavender and white.

Description Florist's cyclamen forms compact, 30-cm (12-inch) tall clumps of heart-shaped leaves that grow from an underground tuber. The single-stemmed flowers emerge from October to April.
Light needs High indirect light while in bloom; medium light after bloom.
Best temperatures During the day, florist's cyclamen prefers 16°–22°C (60°–72°F); at night, keep temperatures at 4.5°–16°C (40°–60°F).
Water and humidity needs Keep the soil evenly moist while plant is flowering.
Growing guidelines Grow in all-purpose, soil-based compost. Repot crowded plants to a slightly larger container only when nights are above 13°C (55°F). Fertilise twice a month from autumn to early spring. Plants need a cool, dry rest period in the summer to rebloom. Put them outdoors in the shade and turn the pots on their side; water occasionally to keep them barely moist until new leaves begin to appear.
Common problems Spider mites and cyclamen mites can cause distorted growth. Discard infested plants.
Propagation Sow seed in September and keep it dark until seedlings appear. Put seedlings in a cool, bright spot for the winter; repot them in May.

Euphorbia pulcherrima
EUPHORBIACEAE

POINSETTIA

This Mexican native now reigns as the quintessential winter holiday plant. Its showy blooms last for months, with petal-like bracts in red, pink, yellow or cream.

Description These shrubby plants usually grow to about 60 cm (2 feet) tall in containers. The sturdy stems carry broad, green leaves up to 17.5 cm (7 inches) long. In winter, the stems are tipped with tiny flowers surrounded by leafy bracts.
Light needs High light.
Best temperatures Cool conditions, with days not over 21°C (70°F) and nights around 13°C (55°F).
Water and humidity needs Allow to dry between waterings.
Growing guidelines Grow in well-drained, all-purpose compost. If you want it to bloom again, repot it and cut the stems back to 15 cm (6 inches). Water as needed and fertilise weekly from September to the end of November. Give the plant 14 hours of total darkness at night for eight weeks beginning in mid-September, with temperatures of 24°C (75°F) during the day and 16°C (60°F) at night. Don't fertilise while the plant is flowering.
Common problems Leaves will drop due to low light, draughts or overwatering.
Propagation Take tip cuttings in late spring and early summer; allow to dry overnight before rooting in moist sand.

Hippeastrum hybrids
AMARYL LIDACEAE

AMARYLLIS

Spectacular and astonishingly easy to bring into bloom, amaryllis makes a perfect winter gift plant. Keep the plant cool when it is in bloom so the flowers last longer.

Description The large bulb of amaryllis sends up a 60-cm (2-foot) tall flower stalk, along with, or slightly before, the long strap-like leaves. One to ten trumpet-shaped, single or double flowers bloom atop the stalk for up to a month.
Light needs Medium light when planted; increase to half a day of sun when the flower stalk is 15 cm (6 inches) tall.
Best temperatures Warm days – 21°C (70°F) – and 16°C (60°F) nights.
Water and humidity needs Moisten the soil thoroughly at planting time, then wait until growth starts before watering again. Keep the soil evenly moist while the plant is actively growing.
Growing guidelines Position the bulb in well-drained potting compost so the top quarter is sticking out of the soil. Choose a pot that is 2.5 cm (1 inch) wider than the bulb. Feed monthly while the plant is growing; stop fertilising and watering when the leaves turn yellow. Allow the bulb to rest for a month, then repot or replace the top inch of potting soil with fresh compost and 1 teaspoon of bonemeal.
Common problems Lots of leaves but no flowers usually means the pot is too large.
Propagation Remove and replant offsets.

Hoya carnosa
APOCYNACEAE

WAX PLANT

Wax plant's long stems can climb up trellises or trail around window frames. This milkweed relative produces clusters of very fragrant, starry blooms from May to September.

Other common names Honey plant, porcelain flower.
Description Wax plant has succulent, 7.5-cm (3-inch), silvery green leaves atop trailing vines that climb to 6 m (20 feet). Clusters of small, pinkish, red-centred flowers dangle from the stems in summer.
Light needs High light; avoid direct, midday sun.
Best temperatures Intermediate to warm conditions not below 10°C (50°F).
Water and humidity needs Let the soil dry between waterings. In winter, reduce water drastically, just enough to prevent shrivelling. Do not use cold water.
Growing guidelines Grow in a peat-moss-based compost in a pot, or in a hanging basket lined with sphagnum moss. Provide potted plants with a trellis or wire hoop; wind the stems anticlockwise around the support. Fertilise once in spring with an all-purpose fertiliser. Once buds form, avoid moving the vine. Wax vines must be 90 cm (3 feet) long to flower, so avoid pruning.
Common problems White, cottony growths are signs of mealybugs. Wash them off with a strong spray of water.
Propagation Take cuttings in spring.

Kalanchoe blossfeldiana
CRASSULACEAE

KALANCHOE

This Madagascar native has beautiful glossy foliage and huge clusters of winter flowers held high above the leaves. Remove the stalks when the flowers fade.

Other common names Flaming Katy.
Description Kalanchoe forms clumps of succulent, 7.5-cm (3-inch), deep green leaves. Plants flower for two to three months with clusters of red, pink, yellow, orange or white flowers on 30-cm (12-inch) stems.
Light needs High, indirect light.
Best temperatures Provide cool conditions (10°–16°C [50°–60°F]) in autumn while buds are forming, then move to average room temperature.
Water and humidity needs Let the soil dry between waterings. Do not overwater.
Growing guidelines Grow kalanchoe in all-purpose potting compost with added sand. Fertilise with liquid fertiliser once a month from when flowering ends until late summer. Put the plant outdoors for the summer, then give it a cool, drier rest period in autumn to encourage bud formation.
Common problems Aphids and mealybugs may feed on leaves and stems. Knock the pests off with a strong spray of water, or spray the plant with insecticidal soap or neem.
Propagation Take stem cuttings in summer, or grow plants from seed.

Various genera
ORCHIDACEAE

ORCHIDS

Some 25,000 species and 100,000 hybrids make this the largest flowering plant group on Earth, with something for every grower.

Description Most orchids are tropical epiphytes (plants that grow on the sides of trees instead of in the ground). Indoor orchids usually flower in winter.
Light needs Low to high light, depending on the type of orchid.
Best temperatures Cool to warm conditions, depending on the type of orchid. A 6–9°C (10°–15°F) temperature drop at night is essential, especially in autumn, to set buds.
Water and humidity needs Allow pots to dry between waterings; overwatering is deadly. Extra humidity results in better growth and flowering.
Growing guidelines Grow in small pots in a well-drained epiphytic mix of three-quarters fir bark chips to one-quarter perlite. Repot after flowering with fresh mix to maintain good drainage. Fertilise twice a month with a weak solution of liquid fertiliser, compost tea or all-purpose fertiliser.
Common problems Aphids, mealybugs and scale insects may feed on orchid plants; treat infected parts with insecticidal soap, superior oil or neem.
Propagation Divide sympodial types, leaving three stems on each. Remove rooted offshoots from monopodia types.

Saintpaulia hybrids
GESNERIACEAE

AFRICAN VIOLETS

The colourful flowers and compact habit of African violets make them the most popular of all flowering houseplants. Grow them on windowsills or under fluorescent lights.

Description African violets have velvety, green or variegated, fleshy leaves. Single or double flowers to 5 cm (2 inches) wide appear just above the leaves on and off year-round. The flowers can be blue, purple, pink, red, white or green; some are multicoloured or marked with a white edge or star.
Light needs Medium to high indirect light is best.
Best temperatures Warm conditions, with a temperature around 18°C (65°F).
Water and humidity needs Allow the soil to dry slightly between waterings. Try to avoid wetting the leaves.
Growing guidelines Grow in soil-based African violet potting compost in shallow pots, repotting yearly. Fertilise every two weeks in spring and summer with quarter-strength African violet-type fertiliser.
Common problems Wash off aphids and mealybugs with tepid water, or dab them with a cotton swab soaked in witch hazel. A lack of flowers may be caused by not enough light, the temperature being too high or the soil too dry. Cold water can cause spots on leaves.
Propagation Take leaf cuttings and replant with the stem in a moist medium.

Schlumbergera bridgesii
CACTACEAE

CHRISTMAS CACTUS

The showy flowers and distinctive, segmented, trailing stems make Christmas cactus an attractive choice for hanging baskets. Put plants outdoors for the summer.

Description This shrubby, 30-cm (12-inch) cactus has arching, flat-jointed, thornless green leaves and stems. It flowers abundantly in winter with starry, 7.5-cm (3-inch) flowers. Red is a traditional favourite, although you can also find pink, white or yellow flowers.
Light needs Medium to high, indirect light suits the plant best.
Best temperatures Average room temperature for most of the year; provide 13°C (55°F) nights in autumn to set buds.
Water and humidity needs Keep the soil evenly moist most of the year, but reduce watering in autumn until buds form.
Growing guidelines Grow in small pots with a well-drained mixture of soil, sand, peat moss and compost. Repot with fresh mix in spring. Bring indoors before frost in autumn, and set in a cool dark room to promote bud formation.
Common problems Control aphids by knocking them off with a strong spray of water or insecticidal soap. Too much or too little water, or water that is too cold can cause leaves to drop. Leaves may turn yellow if the light is too bright.
Propagation Take tip cuttings at any time of the year.

Sinningia hybrids
GESNERIACEAE

GLOXINIAS

Gloxinias' velvety leaves make a beautiful background for the showy blooms. The plants grow from firm, rounded tubers and thrive in the same conditions as African violets.

Description The trumpet-shaped, wavy-edged flowers range from reds, pinks and white to purples and blues. They flower primarily in summer but may flower year-round.
Light needs Medium to high, diffused light. Gloxinias also grow well under fluorescent light.
Best temperatures Warm conditions, around 18°–21°C (65°–70°F); cooler dormancy after flowering.
Water and humidity needs Keep the soil evenly moist and use tepid water. Provide high humidity.
Growing guidelines Pot in African violet potting compost, positioning tubers with the cupped side up. Repot each year when new growth begins. Fertilise during growth with African violet-type fertiliser. If the leaves start to die down after flowering, give plants a rest period; cut down on watering and reduce temperatures to 10°–16°C (50°–60°F).
Common problems Cold water can stain leaves. If the leaf edges curl under, the plant isn't getting enough light.
Propagation Take leaf cuttings and replant the leaf with its stem in a moist but loose medium.

Streptocarpus
GESNERIACEAE

CAPE PRIMROSE

These African violet relatives boast a long period of colourful bloom; try them in a north window or under fluorescent lights. Pinch off faded flowers before the seed pods form.

Description The compact, hairy-leaved rosettes of cape primrose grow up to 30 cm (12 inches) tall. They freely produce 5-cm (2-inch) wide trumpets of red, pink, blue or purple flowers atop 15-cm (6-inch) stalks nearly all year.
Light needs Medium, indirect light.
Best temperatures Average indoor conditions, with a slight drop at night.
Water and humidity needs Keep the soil moist but not soggy. After flowering, allow it to dry somewhat between waterings.
Growing guidelines Grow in shallow pots in African violet potting compost, repotting only when absolutely necessary. Fertilise twice a month with African violet fertiliser, or add bonemeal or aged manure to the compost when you repot. Provide a drier rest period after bloom.
Common problems Limp stems and leaves indicate too little light; wilted, yellowed leaves indicate root rot from overwatering; plants may recover if you let the soil dry out between waterings.
Propagation Take leaf cuttings by slicing a leaf into three or four parts crossways and replanting them upright in a moist growing medium. You can also divide plants in spring.

Aglaonema spp.
ARACEAE

CHINESE EVERGREENS

Chinese evergreen offers gorgeous foliage marked with a mixture of green, pewter, silver, cream and white; some kinds may even show a bit of pink. Few houseplants adapt as well to a dark corner.

Description These shrubby, many-stemmed plants can reach 90 cm (3 feet) tall. They are notable for their patterned, elliptic foliage, which grows up to 30 cm (12 inches) long and 10 cm (4 inches) wide.
Light needs Low (even dark).
Best temperatures Warm, 18°C (65°F) nights to 29°C (85°F) days.
Water and humidity needs Keep just moist. Use unchlorinated water, allowing tap water to stand overnight before use for best results.
Growing guidelines Pot in a peat-based potting compost, repotting when the plant looks tired. Fertilise three times a year, or less if in low light. Putting the plant out in the rain will clean leaves.
Common problems Brown leaf edges indicate dry air, bad drainage or too many minerals or salts from tap water. Leaf variegation fades in too much light. Mealybugs hide at leaf bases. Wash off with a sharp stream of water or drench with insecticidal soap or horticultural oil or neem.
Propagation Take stem cuttings, divide the stalks or air layer at any time.

Aphelandra squarrosa
ACANTHACEAE

ZEBRA PLANT

For dramatic foliage, it's hard to beat the highly striped leaves of zebra plant. It can also produce bright yellow flowers in late summer and autumn.

Other common names Saffron spike.
Description Zebra plant produces oval, glossy, green leaves with cream-coloured veins. Individual leaves can reach 30 cm (1 foot) long. The shrubby plants grow to 90 cm (3 feet) tall, although compact cultivars are more popular.
Light needs High, indirect light.
Best temperatures Warm conditions, at least 18°C (65°F).
Water and humidity needs Provide abundant water from spring to autumn; allow to dry somewhat during winter rest. Provide high humidity.
Growing guidelines Grow zebra plant in all-purpose potting compost, and fertilise twice a month from spring to autumn. After flowering, cut the stem back drastically to just above the lowest node (where the lowest pair of leaves join the stem). Pinch out the tips of new growth when it reaches 15 cm (6 inches).
Common problems Spider mites can cause stippling on leaves; raise the humidity and spray the plant with superior oil. Knock mealybugs off with a strong spray of water. It is normal for leaves to fall after the plant flowers.
Propagation Take tip cuttings in late winter to early summer.

Araucaria heterophylla
ARAUCARIACEAE

NORFOLK ISLAND PINE

Norfolk Island pine's graceful habit makes it a winning houseplant. Purchase full, dense plants, since sparse-looking specimens will stay that way when you get them home.

Description This pyramidal, tiered tree has bright green, soft needles. It can grow up to 60 m (200 feet) tall in nature. Fortunately for indoor gardeners, it usually only reaches about 2.1 m (7 feet) tall as a houseplant. The branches have resinous sap.
Light needs High light, with full sun, is best, but plants can live with less.
Best temperatures Ideal conditions are 21 °C (70°F) during the day and 10°–13°C (50°–55°F) at night (particularly in winter). Norfolk Island pine can, however, adapt to a range of temperatures from 7°–29°C (45°–85°F).
Water and humidity needs Keep evenly moist at all times.
Growing guidelines Grow Norfolk Island pine in African violet compost. Repot every three years. Fertilise four times a year.
Common problems Needles drop if the air is too hot and dry; move the plant to a cooler spot and increase the humidity. Lower branches fall as the plant ages.
Propagation Buy new plants or grow them from seed. Taking cuttings will ruin the shape of your plant.
Comments Use Norfolk Island pine as a small Christmas tree.

Asparagus densiflorus
ASPARAGACEAE

ASPARAGUS FERN

Show off asparagus fern's arching stems by displaying the plant in a hanging basket. The needle-like leaves are actually flattened stems; they are soft when young.

Other common names Emerald fern.
Description This plant has delicate, feathery, arching, green plumes on distinctive spiny stems to 90 cm (3 feet) long. It has tiny, pink flowers, followed by small berries that turn successively from white to green to red to black.
Light needs High, indirect light.
Best temperatures Average to cool conditions (13°–21°C [55°–70°F]).
Water and humidity needs Keep the soil just moist.
Growing guidelines Grow asparagus fern in a humus-rich compost. Fertilise four times a year. Repot whenever the fast-growing roots start creeping out of the pot.
Common problems Yellowed foliage means too much light or a lack of nitrogen; reduce the light slightly and fertilise with liquid fertiliser. Brittle stems and dropping leaves usually indicate that the plant has outgrown its pot; move the plant to a larger pot with fresh compost.
Propagation Divide large plants by cutting all the stems down to the soil, then slicing the root ball into 10-cm (4-inch) wide wedges; plant the wedges in individual pots. You can also grow asparagus ferns from seed.

Aspidistra elatior
ASPARAGACEAE

CAST-IRON PLANT

Known since the Victorian age, this Chinese native is renowned for its 'cast-iron' constitution. It's suitable for even the most black-thumbed gardener.

Other common names Bar room plant.
Description Usually between 45 and 60 cm (18 and 24 inches) tall, cast-iron plant has an upright growth habit. Its leaves grow to 75 cm (30 inches) long and 10 cm (4 inches) wide. The foliage is generally dark green, although you can occasionally find variegated forms. Small, bell-shaped, purple flowers may form at the base of the plant.
Light needs Tolerates low light, even very dim corners.
Best temperatures Average room temperature during the day; around 10°C (50°F) at night.
Water and humidity needs Keep evenly moist at all times.
Growing guidelines Repot in all-purpose potting compost only every five years. Fertilise once in spring (and again in autumn if the plant gets medium light).
Common problems Spider mites occasionally attack the foliage. Control these pests by washing the leaves monthly with plain water or with a solution of insecticidal soap.
Propagation Divide the roots in early spring and replant in fresh compost; plant two or three pieces together in each pot.

Beaucarnea recurvata
AGAVACEAE

PONY TAIL PALM

Native to the deserts of Mexico, pony tail palm has a thick, swollen base that can store up to a year's supply of water. It's a good choice if you tend to forget to water regularly!

Other common names Elephant foot palm.
Description When young, pony tail palm is just a grassy clump of narrow leaves growing from a swollen, enlarged base. As it ages, the base expands, and the plant develops a greenish brown trunk topped with a tuft of thin, leathery, strap-like, green leaves. Mature plants can reach 90 cm (3 feet) tall.
Light needs High or medium light.
Best temperatures Average room temperature but cooler than 24°C (75°F) in winter.
Water and humidity needs Water thoroughly, then allow the soil to dry before you water again.
Growing guidelines Grow pony tail palm in a well-drained cactus compost. Wait several years between repottings. Fertilise annually in early spring.
Common problems Too little sun causes limp, pale leaves; move the plant to a brighter location. Otherwise, pony tail palm is generally easy.
Propagation Separate and repot offsets.
Comments Pony tail palm produces only one flush of growth a year in spring.

Begonia spp.
BEGON IACEAE

FOLIAGE BEGONIAS

Who needs flowers when you can have leaves like these? Actually, some foliage begonias do produce flowers, but the blooms tend to be inconspicuous.

Other common names Painted begonia.
Description Foliage begonias mostly grow from rhizomes (creeping underground stems) to a height of about 40 cm (16 inches). The leaves are often hairy and heart-shaped, with bold or subtle markings in the form of marbling, mottling, spots or zones. Leaf colours range from green to silver, bronze, purple, red, pink and black.
Light needs Medium to high, indirect light; protect from direct sun. They also grow. well under fluorescent lights.
Best temperatures Warm – 24°C (75°F) during the day and at least 16°C (60°F) at night – for most of the year; slightly cooler in winter.
Water and humidity needs Allow the soil to dry between waterings, especially in winter. Provide extra humidity.
Growing guidelines Grow in all-purpose potting compost in shallow pots. Repot only when the plant outgrows its container. Fertilise monthly from spring to autumn, allowing a slight dormancy in winter.
Common problems Leaf drop in winter is normal. If leaf colours fade, move the plant to a brighter spot.
Propagation Take stem or leaf cuttings at any time. Divide rhizomes in spring.

Various genera
BROMELIACEAE

BROMELIADS

Bromeliads include a variety of striking, slow-growing tropical plants. They may take several years to flower; in the meantime, enjoy their colourful, beautifully marked leaves.

Other common names Air plants, living vase plants.
Description Bromeliads produce rosettes of stiff leaves that range in height from 2.5 cm (1 inch) to 90 cm (3 feet) tall. Flowers may arise from the centre of a rosette, with showy spikes of red, yellow, pink and green.
Light needs High light with some direct sun; protect from midday sun.
Best temperatures At least 16°C (60°F) or warmer.
Water and humidity needs Keep the centre cups of vase-shaped types filled with rainwater; refill the cups every week or two. Other types can dry between waterings. Provide extra humidity.
Growing guidelines Plant in clay pots and an epiphytic wood chip mix. Provide liquid fertiliser twice a month in spring and summer and once a month during the rest of the year. Put plants outdoors for the summer.
Common problems Too much light can burn leaves; if you notice white stains (salt or lime build-up) on leaves, flush the cups weekly with rainwater.
Propagation Remove and pot up offsets, or grow plants from seed.

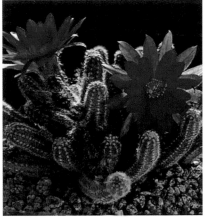

Various genera
CACTACEAE

CACTI

Cacti are generally rugged enough for even black-thumbed gardeners. Their brilliant flowers are often surprisingly large compared to the size of the plant.

Description Cacti have no leaves to speak of, just thickened, water-storing, spiny stems. They come in a wide variety of shapes and sizes.
Light needs High light, with direct sun.
Best temperatures Average room temperature for most of the year; cool conditions – approximately 18°C (65°F) days and 4.5°C (40°F) nights – in winter.
Water and humidity needs In late March and April, water thoroughly and wait until the soil surface feels dry before watering again. Begin decreasing water steadily from May to December; give almost no water in winter.
Growing guidelines Keep cacti potbound in well-drained clay pots of all-purpose compost with added sand. Fertilise once a year in early spring. Put plants outdoors for the summer. Provide a cool, dry winter rest.
Common problems Plants that do not get a winter rest period may produce weak, spindly growth. Overwatering can lead to wilting and root rot.
Propagation Take stem or leaf cuttings, remove and repot offsets, or grow new plants from seed. Any cactus can be grafted to another by placing the cut bottom of one atop a cut tip of another and tying them firmly until they unite.

Chlorophytum comosum
ASPARAGACEAE

SPIDER PLANT

One of the most common plants for a hanging basket, spider plant is beloved for its graceful habit. It produces baby plants at the ends of its long, arching stems.

Other common names Ribbon plant, spider ivy.
Description Spider plant grows from rhizomes (creeping underground stems) to produce arching, narrow, 30–45-cm (12-18-inch) long, green leaves. It also sends out long, pale yellow stems, with small white flowers along their length.
Light needs Medium light; avoid strong, direct sun.
Best temperatures Average room temperature during the day; approximately 10°C (50°F) at night.
Water and humidity needs Allow the soil surface to dry between waterings. Plants can take dry conditions but prefer extra humidity and rainwater.
Growing guidelines Use all-purpose potting compost in small hanging baskets, leaving 2.5 cm (1 inch) between the rim of the pot and the top of the soil. Fertilise twice a month in spring and summer.
Common problems High temperatures and over-drying can cause brown leaves.
Propagation Divide the parent plant or grow new plants from seed. You can also remove plantlets and set the base of the plantlet in water until roots begin to form, then move it to a pot.

Cissus spp.
VITACEAE

GRAPE IVY

Grape ivies make splendid foliage climbers, adapting to low light and dry air without too much fuss. Provide some kind of trellis so plants can climb.

Other common names Kangaroo vine.
Description These tendril-climbing plants can grow to 3 m (10 feet). The fleshy, green leaves grow to 10 cm (4 inches) long; they are sometimes fuzzy underneath. Grape ivy (*C. rhombifolia*), from tropical America, has large, metallic green, lobed leaves and is very easy to grow. Kangaroo vine (*C. antarctica*) is a vigorous grower with shiny, leathery leaves; it hails from Australia. Dwarf grape ivy (*C. striata*), from Chile, is a compact climber with small, five-lobed leaves.
Light needs Medium to high light, but keep the plant out of direct sun.
Best temperatures Warm conditions but cooler than 24°C (75°F).
Water and humidity needs Keep evenly moist, but don't let the plant sit in water. Tolerates low humidity.
Growing guidelines Provide all-purpose compost in very well-drained baskets. Repot as needed. Fertilise twice a month in spring and summer. Pinch sideshoots back frequently to encourage dense growth.
Common problems Grape ivies are generally problem-free.
Propagation Take stem cuttings at any time, or grow new plants from seed.

Dieffenbachia amoena
ARACEAE

DUMB CANE

Bold, fancy leaves are the trademark of this popular plant. It gets the name dumb cane from its irritating sap, which causes swelling and pain of the tongue if eaten.

Other common names Mother-in-law's tongue.
Description The upright stems of dumb cane grow to 1.8 m (6 feet) tall, with elliptical leaves. The green foliage is marked and spotted in various shades of green, cream and yellow.
Light needs High, indirect light is best, although the plant can adapt to less.
Best temperatures Warm conditions (at least 16°C [60°F]). Keep out of draughts.
Water and humidity needs Allow the soil to dry a bit between waterings. Provide extra humidity.
Growing guidelines Grow dumb cane in all-purpose potting compost, and keep it potbound. Fertilise lightly with liquid fertiliser twice a month in warm seasons. Rinse dust off the leaves several times a year.
Common problems Overwatering and lack of light can produce thin stems and widely spaced leaves. To rejuvenate the plant, cut the stem to about 15 cm (6 inches) tall. Control spider mites by raising the humidity and spraying with superior oil. Knock mealybugs off the plant with a strong spray of water.
Propagation Air layer the stems, or take tip or stem cuttings.

Dizygotheca elegantissima
ARALIACEAE

FALSE ARALIA

False aralia sports upright stems clad in lacy leaves. This South Pacific native is a good choice for warm, shaded, humid spots with low to medium light.

Description This elegant, shrubby tree grows to 1.8 m (6 feet) tall, with serrated, fern-like, palmate leaves. The young foliage is coppery bronze, sometimes mottled with cream; the leaves change to dark greenish black as they age.
Light needs Low to medium, indirect light suits the plant best.
Best temperatures Warm conditions; at least 16°C (60°F) in winter.
Water and humidity needs Allow the soil surface to dry between waterings. Provide extra humidity.
Growing guidelines Grow in all-purpose potting compost. Repot every few years as needed. Fertilise twice a month in spring and summer.
Common problems If spider mites cause light-coloured stippling on leaves, control the pests by raising the humidity and spraying the plant with superior oil. Leaves may drop as the plant ages or if it is overwatered or moved from place to place. Age, cold and lack of humidity can cause the plant to get scraggly; take cuttings in spring and summer to make new plants and keep them in a warm, humid location.
Propagation Take stem cuttings in spring and summer.

Dracaena spp.
AGAVACEAE

DRACAENA

Dracaenas are tough, adaptable plants that are easy to find and easy to grow. With age, they produce a thick trunk and lose their bottom leaves.

Description Dracaenas are tree-like plants that can grow anywhere from 45 cm (18 inches) to 2.4 m (8 feet) tall. They are noted for their distinctively marked, bold, often sword-like foliage.
Light needs High, indirect light is best, but dracaena tolerates less.
Best temperatures Warm conditions (18°–21°C [65°–70°F]).
Water and humidity needs Keep evenly moist most of the year; allow it to dry somewhat between waterings in winter. Provide extra humidity.
Growing guidelines Grow dracaenas in all-purpose potting compost. Fertilise twice a month in warm seasons.
Common problems Low light causes thin stems and faded leaves. Browned leaf edges indicate the plant is overdry or that there's a salt build-up.
Propagation Take tip or stem cuttings, or air layer the trunk.

Various genera
POLYPODIACEAE

FERNS

Beloved for their gracefully arching, often feathery fronds, ferns are a mainstay for houseplant growers. These flowerless plants grow from rhizomes and reproduce via spores.

Description Ferns are a broad group of plants that includes many different genera including Boston fern, maidenhair ferns and rabbit's foot fern.
Light needs Medium to high, indirect light suits ferns best.
Best temperatures Average conditions, with day temperatures up to 24°C (75°F) and nights between 13° and 18°C (55° and 65°F).
Water and humidity needs Keep evenly moist; water daily if necessary. Extra humidity is a plus.
Growing guidelines Grow ferns in small pots in light, well-drained, all-purpose compost with added peat moss and perlite. Repot in spring as needed. Fertilise twice a year – in early spring and early summer – with liquid fertiliser.
Common problems Scale insects may produce small, irregularly spaced spots on the fronds; scrape them off with your fingernail or with a cotton swab.
Propagation Divide clump-forming ferns, grow new plants from spores or pin the runners to the soil and repot them when they are rooted.

Ficus spp.
MORACEAE

FIGS

This large group of tropical plants has produced some of our best -known and easiest-to-grow houseplants. All these plants produce a harmless milky sap when cut.

Other common names Ficus, rubber plant.
Description Figs can be trees, shrubs or woody vines, usually with thick leaves.
Light needs Medium to high light.
Best temperatures Average room temperature; avoid moving plants from high to low light.
Water and humidity needs Allow the soil to dry somewhat between waterings. Keep creeping types evenly damp.
Growing guidelines Grow figs in all-purpose compost that's been enriched with garden compost. Keep them potbound to prevent overwatering; repot only every three to four years. Feed twice a year, occasionally providing a very dilute vinegar solution. Wipe large-leaved types periodically with a damp sponge. Fresh air is beneficial.
Common problems Spider mites and scale insects can attack if the air is hot and dry. Treat by spraying with superior oil. Lower leaves may drop due to temperature or light changes, draughts or too much or too little water.
Propagation Air layer the stems of upright types. Root creeping types from tip cuttings or divide the rooting stems.

Maranta leuconeura
MARANTACEAE

PRAYER PLANT

This showy foliage houseplant has two special features: the unique markings that look as though a rabbit left tracks down the leaves and the way the leaves fold upwards at night.

Other common names Rabbit tracks.
Description Prayer plant's branching stems form clumps to 30 cm (12 inches) tall, with 12.5-cm (5-inch) long, oval leaves. The bright green, satiny foliage is very distinctively marked with brownish purple 'rabbit tracks' on either side of the midrib. Each leaf has large, rosy pink veins and a red-purple underside.
Light needs Medium, indirect or artificial light.
Best temperatures Warm conditions, between 16° and 21°C (60° and 70°F).
Water and humidity needs Keep the soil evenly moist through most of the year and somewhat drier in winter. Mist often.
Growing guidelines Grow prayer plant in soil-less potting compost. Repot into fresh compost each year in early spring. Fertilise twice a month from spring to autumn; do not fertilise in winter.
Common problems Prayer plant likes fresh air, but cold draughts can lead to poor growth and a gradual decline in health.
Propagation Divide in spring.
Cultivars The variety *kerchoveana* is deep green and chocolate without rosy veins; 'Variegata' indicates it has yellow and pink spots.

Various genera
PALMAE

PALMS

Palms appreciate a summer holiday outdoors; just make sure they're sheltered from direct sun. If you notice the leaf tips have turned brown, you can trim them off with scissors.

Description Indoor palms range in size from 0.9–4.5 m (3–15 feet) tall, with stiff trunks and fan-like or feathery, compound leaves. Popular species include parlour palm, Chamaedoreas palms and kentia palm.
Light needs Medium, indirect light.
Best temperatures Average room temperature, not below 13°C (55°F).
Water and humidity needs Water abundantly while the plant is in active growth; allow the soil surface to dry just slightly between waterings.
Growing guidelines Grow in a mixture of equal parts all-purpose potting compost and sandy, organic topsoil. Provide liquid fertiliser from late spring to early autumn. Repot as needed in spring or summer. Put plants outdoors for the summer. Wash foliage frequently with a hose or do it in the shower.
Common problems If spider mites attack, raise the humidity and spray with superior oil.
Propagation Grow new palms from seed.

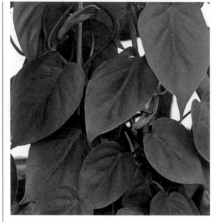

Philodendron spp.
ARACEAE

PHILODENDRON

If you're nervous about growing houseplants, start with philodendrons – they're durable plants that don't take much fussing to stay looking good.

Description Philodendrons produce climbing or bushy growth that can eventually reach 2.7 m (9 feet) tall. Their stems carry thin aerial roots and usually lobed green leaves that can be marked with gold, red or white. The young leaves are often not as distinctively shaped or coloured as the older ones.
Light needs Medium to high, indirect light; bushy types tolerate lower light.
Best temperatures Warm conditions, with nights around 18°–21°C (65°–70°F).
Water and humidity needs Keep the soil just moist.
Growing guidelines Philodendron grows fine in almost any potting compost; it will even root and grow in water! Repot at any time. Fertilise every three months.
Common problems Direct sun can produce tan patches of sunburn on leaves; move the plant out of the sun to prevent further damage.
Propagation Take tip or stem cuttings from climbing types at any time. Grow self-heading (bushy) types from seed, or separate and pot up the offsets.

Rhaphidophora aurea
ARACEAE

POTHOS

Pothos is a trailing or climbing houseplant that's often confused with philodendron. It's a real survivor that can take some neglect.

Other common names Devil's ivy.
Description This climbing plant produces long stems that can climb to 12 m (40 feet) if left unpruned. The stems will trail out of a hanging basket or climb a support, clinging with aerial roots. The leathery, heart-shaped leaves grow to 10 cm (4 inches) long. The foliage and stems are bright green and richly splashed with yellow and/or white.
Light needs High, indirect light is best, although the plant adapts to less.
Best temperatures Average room temperature suits very well.
Water and humidity needs Let the soil dry somewhat between waterings, especially for plants growing in low light. Make sure the soil is not very wet or dry.
Growing guidelines Grow pothos in a soil-based potting mix in hanging baskets or trained on wire wreath forms. Fertilise twice a year, while the plant is producing new growth. Cut the stems back if they get leggy. Wash the leaves occasionally.
Common problems Pothos is generally pest-free. If you notice the leaf and stem markings are fading, move the plant to a brighter spot.
Propagation Take tip cuttings at any time of the year.

Sansevieria trifasciata
AGAVACEAE

SNAKE PLANT

Extraordinarily striped, stiff leaf swords have made snake plants very popular. They often look dreadful when neglected but are very handsome if you give them just a little care.

Description Snake plant's tall, upright, stemless, spear-like leaves can grow to 1.2 m (4 feet) tall. The green foliage is cross-banded in darker green, yellow, white and/or black. Plants sometimes produce tall sprays of green-white, fragrant flowers.
Light needs High light is best, although plants can tolerate almost any light level.
Best temperatures Average conditions, with 18°C (65°F) nights.
Water and humidity needs Allow the soil surface to dry between waterings in spring to autumn. In winter, water only enough to prevent shrivelling. Snake plant endures drought well.
Growing guidelines Grow snake plant in cactus or all-purpose potting compost in a well-drained pot. This slow-growing plant can wait three to four years between repottings. Fertilise infrequently.
Common problems Cold temperatures can cause leaf edges to turn brown.
Propagation Divide plants at any time, or separate and pot up offsets. Propagate green-leaved types by leaf cuttings. (Leaf cuttings from yellow-edged types will root, but the plants they produce will be all green.)

Spathiphyllum hybrids
ARACEAE

PEACE LILY

Peace lily is popular for its graceful, shiny, green leaves, as well as its curious, hooded flower spikes. This tolerant plant adjusts to many conditions and is generally problem-free.

Other common names Spathe flower.
Description Peace lily grows to 60 cm (2 feet) tall, with sword-like, long leaves. The many-stemmed plant blooms occasionally throughout the year, first in white, then turning green. The flowers can last for six weeks.
Light needs Low to medium, indirect light best suits the plant.
Best temperatures Warm to average conditions (around 18°–21°C [65°–70°F]).
Water and humidity needs Keep the soil evenly moist.
Growing guidelines This easy grower thrives in all-purpose potting compost enriched with garden compost or other organic material. Fertilise twice a month. Repot in early spring as needed. Provide monthly showers to keep the leaves clean.
Common problems Too much light actually inhibits flowering. If you want flowers but none are appearing, try moving your plant to a slightly darker spot. Too much fertiliser or too little water can cause brown leaf tips.
Propagation Remove and repot offsets, or divide the clumps in spring.

USDA Plant Hardiness Zone Map

These maps of the United States, Canada and Europe are divided into ten zones. Each zone is based on a 5.6°C (10°F) difference in average annual minimum temperature. Some areas are considered too high in elevation for plant cultivation and so are not assigned to any zone. There are also island zones that are warmer or cooler than surrounding areas because of differences in elevation; they have been given a zone different from the surrounding areas. Many large urban areas, for example, are in a warmer zone than the surrounding land. Plants grow best within an optimum range of temperatures. The range may be wide for some species and narrow for others. Planes also differ in their ability to survive frost and in their sun or shade requirements.

The zone ratings indicate conditions where designated plants will grow well and not merely survive. Many plants may survive in zones warmer or colder than their recommended zone range. Remember that other factors, including wind, soil type, soil moisture, humidity, snow and winter sunshine, may have a great effect on growth .

Some nursery plants have been grown in greenhouses and they might not survive in your garden, so it's a waste of money, and a cause of heartache, to buy plants that aren't right for your climate zone.

Canada

United States of Amerca

Pacific Ocean

Atlantic Ocean

Average annual minimum temperature °C (°F)

Zone 1		Below -45°C (Below -50°F)
Zone 2		-45° to -40°C (-50° to -40°F)
Zone 3		-40° to -34°C (-40° to -30°F)
Zone 4		-34° to -29°C (-30° to -20°F)
Zone 5		-29° to -23°C (-20° to -10°F)
Zone 6		-23° to -18°C (-10° to 0°F)
Zone 7		-18° to -12°C (0° to 10°F)
Zone 8		-12° to -7°C (10° to 20°F)
Zone 9		-7° to -1°C (20° to 30°F)
Zone 10		-1° to 4°C (30° to 40°F)

Index

Page references in *italics* indicate photos and illustrations

Credits and Acknowledgments

l=left, r=rightl c=center, t=top, b=bottom, fp=full page

Addington Turf & Horticultural Consultants 263l (Kenneth R. Smith).

Heather Angel 269r, 277r.

Ardea 4lcr (Francois Gohier), 292r (John Mason), 277c (A. P. Patterson).

Allan Armitage 174c, 178c.

Auscape 44/45fp (Jerry Harpur).

A-Z Botanical 299c (The Picture Store), 253r, 271c, 275c, 288l, 290r (Malcolm Richards), 163c.

Gillian Beckett 86tc, 188c, 193c, 204r, 250l, 251l, 253l, 255c, 258l, 258c, 258r, 265l, 265c, 265r, 301r, 302c, 303l, 303r, 304r, 306l, 306r, 308l, 308r, 309r.

Geoffrey Burnie 44fp.

John Callahan 6lall, 59all, 63tr all, 65all, 71d, 83all, 116c, l20d, 123r, 172l, 173c, 174r, 175l, 177c, 179l, 180l, 183r, 184l, 187r, 216l, 219c, 233c, 235l, 237l, 237r, 239l, 245r.

Leigh Clapp 2fp, 4fp, 6c, 92fp, 140fp.

Bruce Coleman 81tr (Jane Burton), 117c (Jules Cowan), 237c, 261l (Eric Crichton), 91b (Geoff Dore), 276l (Halle F1ygare), 260l (Michael Freeman), 297c (Charlie Ott), 103t, 133tr (Hans Reinhard), 210c (John Shaw), 264l (Sullivan & Rogers), 270r (Michael Viard), 12br (R. Wanscheidt), 118l (Carl Wallace) 75tr.

Michael Dirr 185r, 211l, 214l, 216r, 217c, 218r, 222r, 224c, 233l, 234l, 234c, 242l.

Thomas Eltzroth 17tr, 2i bc, 90t, 102br,

107b, 129b, 130t, 153c, 155r, 158c, 169l, 172c, 172rr, 173l, 173r, 176c, 176r, 178r, 179r, 180c, 181l, 181c, 181r, 182r, 183l, 184c, 187c, 188l, 188r, 189c, 190l, 191c, 191r, 192l, 192c, 192r, 193l, 194l, 195l, 195c, 196l, 196r, 197r, 198l, 198r, 199l, 199c, 200r, 201l, 201r, 202r, 203r, 204l, 205r, 207r, 213r, 214l, 215l, 215r, 220l, 221c, 222c, 223l, 228c, 230c, 233r, 238c, 240l, 240c, 241l, 243r, 244c, 244r, 245l, 249r, 250c, 250r, 251l, 252l, 252c, 252r, 254l, 254c, 254r, 256r, 257r, 25gc, 260c, 260r, 261c, 261r, 262l, 262c, 262r, 263c, 263r, 264r, 267l, 278r, 279r, 291r, 292l, 293r, 295l, 295r, 298l, 298c, 299l, 302r, 305c, 306c, 309l.

Derek Fell 14c, 33tr, 39b, 41cl, 50all, 66t, 104bl, 106tl, 109t, 117l, 120cr, 121bl, 127t, 129c, 133c, 142l, 158r, 159r, 175c, 177l, 178l, 183c, 189r, 208c, 213l, 214c, 223c, 224r, 247l, 264c, 267c, 281l, 295e.

Garden Picture Library 1r, 38c, 103c, 128r, 133d, 194r (Lynne Brotehie), 120bl (Linda Burgess), 12bl, 53tr, 120cl, 143l, 145l, 146c, 259r (Brian Carter), 84tr (Dennis Davis), 30bl, 68t, 78cl, 87t, 103b, li Sc, 164l, 168l, 197c (John Glover), 11, 163r, 165bl, 165c, 294r (Neil Holmes) 139c (Michael Howes), 82t, 134d (Lamontagne), 135c, 162r, 166l, 291e (Mayer/Le Scanff), 146l (Clive Nichols), 31b, 105b (Jerry Pavia), 126l (Joanne Pavia) 104br (Gary Rogers), 113r (J .S. Sira), 1c, 124b, 152c, 162l (Brigitte Thomas), 21bl, 21br, 98c, 112r, 128t (Steven Wooster), 25tr, 89t, 147l, 162c, 195r, 198c, 200c, 202l, 203l, 203c, 289l.

Holt Studios International 246c, 253c, 290c, 293l, 294l, 294c, 302l, 307r, 301l, 30lc (Nigel Catdin), 299r, 299r.

Andrew Larson 46tc, 89b, 99el, 102bl, 106br, 164r.

Robert E. Lyons 212c, 228r.

Stirling Macoboy 211r, 238r, 271l, 210l, 236e.

Cheryl Maddocks 280l, 284l, 284r.

S & O Mathews 15er, 19d, 26l, 36b, 73b, 84tc, 94b, 108br, l 11d, 113l, 11 5br, 132c, 189l, 191l, 194c, 199r, 200l, 202c, 204c, 206r, 209l, 293e.

Clive Nichols 14t, 15br, 16er, 20bc, 34c, 34b, 35tr, 38t, 40t, 43eb, 47b, 67t, 74er, 86er, 96t, 97t, 98br, 99cr, 99bc, 109c, 110br, 11 l bl, l 11tr, 112l, 114bl, 114d, 115tr, 124t, 125b, 130b, 139r, 160c, 190c, 205c, 206l, 207c, 208r, 108bl.

Jerry Pavia 18el, 36t, 43ct, 121c, 165d, 169r, 190r, 193r, 197l, 201c, 205l, 207l, 208l, 209r, 305l.

Joanna Pavia 152l, 108t.

Photos Horticultural 16br, 17c, 19tr, 20bl, 20br, 21tl, 21 tr, 23fp, 29bl, 29br, 31tl, 3ltr, 33tl, 34t, 43tl, 46cr, 5lcl, 51tl, 64t, 71tr, 72t, 74br, 75br, 85bl, 88t, 95t, 101t, 104tr, 20r, 110tr, 117r, 118c, 121d, 126r, 13lt, 136c, 137t, 145b, 153r, 154r, 157r, 167l, 168r, 174l, 176l, 177r, 179c, 185l, 185c, 186l, 186c, 187l, 196c, 210r, 210r, 211c, 212r, 215c, 216c, 217l, 217r, 221r, 222c, 225l, 226c, 226r, 227l, 227r, 228l, 230r, 231l, 235r, 236l, 238l, 239c, 240r, 24 lc, 24lr, 242c, 243l, 243c, 244l, 245c, 247c, 255r, 279l, 283r, 290l, 292c, 296c, 296r, 297l, 297r, 303e.

Lee Reich 291l.

G. R. Dick Robert's 10fp, 170fp.

Rodale Stock Images 54b, 142r, 149l, 156l, 268l, 278l, 282c, 285r.

Tony Rodd 218c, 222l, 223 r, 224l, 229c, 229r, 231r, 232c, 232r, 234r, 235c, 236r, 239r, 242r, 246l, 268c, 270c, 272l, 272c.

Lorna Rose 143r, 1 82c.

Susan Roth 220c, 221l, 225c, 225r, 226l, 227c.

Anita Sabarese 229l.

Harry Smith Collection 79tc, 121tr, 153tl, 175r, 230l, 232l, 246r, 247r, 249l, 249c, 251c, 255l, 256l, 256c, 257l, 257c, 259l, 267r, 272r, 296l, 298r, 304l, 304c, 305r, 307l, 307c, 308c, 309e.

John J. Smith 186r, 219r.

David Wallace 46br, 54all, 55all, 57all, 58all, 60el, 60cr & b, 62et, 62el, 62bl, 62br, 62d, 63ball, 85br, 97c, 97b, 146r, 150r, 151r, 153bl, 156c, 158l, 159c, 180r, 184r, 212l, 213c, 218l, 219l, 23 Ic, 268r, 269l, 269c, 270l, 271c, 271r, 271l, 271r, 273l, 273c, 273r, 275l, 275r, 276c, 276r, 277l, 278c, 27gc, 280c, 280r, 281c, 281r, 282l, 282r, 283l, 283c, 284c, 285l, 285c, 286l, 286c, 286r, 287l, 287c, 287r, 288c, 288r, 289c, 289r.

Mel Watson 70t.

Weldon Russell 148c (Carlo Cantini), 154c (David Wallace), 182l.

Weldon Trannies 79tl.

Ron West 8l tc.

All illustrations by Barbara Rodanska except the following.
Tony Britt-Lewis, 113, 129, 138; Mike Gorman, 129, 130; Stuart McVicar 310, 311; Edwina Riddell, 12, 14, 32, 69, 73, 83, 87, 90, 96; Jan Smith, 73, 83, 136; Kathie Smith, 90, 143, 147.

With special thanks to Geoff Burnie, horticultural consultant; Sarah Anderson, editorial support; Claire Craig and Janet Healey, proofreading; Sally Beach, Lisa Boehm, Peta Gorman and Michael Hann, scanning; Caroline Colton & Associates, indexing.